THE CANADIAN

INTERNATI

20

ANNUAIRE

DE DROIT IN

The Canadian Yearbook of International Law

VOLUME XLII   2004   TOME XLII

Annuaire canadien de Droit international

Published under the auspices of
THE CANADIAN BRANCH, INTERNATIONAL LAW ASSOCIATION
AND
THE CANADIAN COUNCIL ON INTERNATIONAL LAW

Publié sous les auspices de
LA SECTION CANADIENNE DE L'ASSOCIATION DE DROIT INTERNATIONAL
ET
LE CONSEIL CANADIEN DE DROIT INTERNATIONAL

UBC Press
VANCOUVER / TORONTO

Printed in Canada on acid-free paper ∞

ISBN 0-7748-1232-X
ISSN 0069-0058

Canadian Cataloguing in Publication Data

The National Library of Canada has catalogued this publication as
follows:

*The Canadian yearbook of international law — Annuaire canadien de
droit international*

> Annual.
> Text in English and French.
> "Published under the auspices of the Canadian Branch,
> International Law Association and the Canadian Council on
> International Law."
> ISSN 0069-0058

> 1. International Law — Periodicals.
> I. International Law Association. Canadian Branch.
> II. Title: Annuaire canadien de droit international.
> JC 21.C3   341'.05   C75-34558-6E

Données de catalogage avant publication (Canada)

*Annuaire canadien de droit international — The Canadian yearbook of
international law*

> Annuel.
> Textes en anglais et en français.
> "Publié sous les auspices de la Branche canadienne de
> l'Association de droit international et le Conseil canadien de
> droit international."
> ISSN 0069-0058

> 1. Droit international — Périodiques.
> I. Association de droit international. Section canadienne.
> II. Conseil canadien de droit international.
> III. Titre: The Canadian yearbook of international law.
> JC 21.C3   341'.05   C75-34558-6E

UBC Press
University of British Columbia
2029 West Mall
Vancouver, BC v6t 1z2
(604) 822-3259
www.ubcpress.ca

Contents / Matière

Book Reviews / Recensions de Livres

THE CANADIAN YEARBOOK OF INTERNATIONAL LAW

2004

ANNUAIRE CANADIEN DE DROIT INTERNATIONAL

The Legality and Legitimacy of Unilateral Armed Intervention in an Age of Terror, Neo-Imperialism, and Massive Violations of Human Rights: Is International Law Evolving in the Right Direction?

J.-G. CASTEL

INTRODUCTION

When the United Nations was created in 1945, its main purpose was to deal with threats to international peace and security in order to prevent states from waging aggressive wars. Today, especially since 9/11, terrorism, the spread of weapons of mass destruction, and internal conflicts involving massive violations of human rights are some of the new challenges confronting this organization. The Security Council, which is charged with the maintenance of international peace and security, has not been very consistent and quick in addressing these issues. As a result, when it has failed to authorize collective action, some states have resorted to unilateral military action to respond to real state and human security needs. Such action has prompted the international community to reconsider the international law rules applicable to these new challenges. This article considers whether a state or a coalition of states without UN authorization may or must take military action against another state sponsoring terrorism or depriving its nationals of their internationally recognized human rights.

WEAKNESS OF INTERNATIONAL LAW WHEN CONFRONTED WITH AN IMPERIAL POWER

International law is a body of rules, processes, and institutions derived from international agreements and customary practice developed over the centuries governing international society. By

J.-G. Castel, O.C., Q.C., O.O., F.R.S.C., L.S.M., S.J.D., L.L.D., Chevalier de la Légion d'honneur, Distinguished Research Professor Emeritus, Osgoode Hall Law School. This article is a revised version of a public lecture given at York University on 7 February 2005. The author is grateful to Matthew Castel for his excellent research assistance.

3

restraining the conduct of states and adjusting their respective jurisdictions, it insures systemic international stability and the coexistence of equal independent sovereign states with different values, concepts, and beliefs. International law also promotes cooperation in various domains of human activities in order to achieve certain fundamental common goals — for instance, the protection of human rights — and providing a moral dimension. Today, international law is evolving in such a way that solidarity and cooperation have become more important than coexistence.

However, although world solidarity and cooperation have increased considerably, especially since the end of the Cold War, and most states consider that they belong to a true international community, sharing a common destiny that creates obligations that cannot be ignored, state sovereignty is still alive and well. As a result, states, especially powerful ones, do not bear well outside constraints and often resort to unilateral action that may not be in conformity with the dictates of international law. This is particularly true with respect to the type of neo-imperialism practised by the United States.

After the Cold War ended, the international community hoped that a new world order would emerge that would emphasize greater political, social, and economic cooperation based on international law and international institutions. Unfortunately, the threat of terrorism has forced some states and especially the United States[1] to pursue their national security interests with vigour. To counter this threat, the United States has embarked upon a full-scale transformation of the international order, by force if necessary, sometimes in disregard of the long-term interests and expectations of the international community.

Throughout the history of the United States, Americans have at times been isolationists and at times interventionists. Today, interventionist tendencies prevail, as there is no security in isolationism. It is evident that the United States has an exceptional role to play in human rights crises by virtue of its founding principles, its moral ideals, and its status as sole remaining superpower. However, it must be able transcend its national interest in favour of these universal moral ideals, just as power must be combined with principle. This is not easily achieved as realism is the central tenet of the national interest and there always exists a state of tension between this interest and moral obligations.

---

[1] S. Talbott and N. Chandra, eds., *The Age of Terror* (2001).

Whereas during the Cold War, US policy was defensive, now it is largely offensive in order to maintain American political, economic, and cultural hegemony on a global scale. As President Bill Clinton's secretary of state, Madeleine Albright, stated,[2] the United States is the indispensable nation endowed with unique responsibilities and obligations. The United States wants to shape a new global order in its own image that will preserve and expend its *imperium*. This new form of imperialism does not seek territorial gains but to create an open and integrated international order based on the principles of democratic capitalism guaranteed and enforced by the United States.[3] Current American reliance on military power to set things right has reached a new height as the US defensive perimeter now encompasses the whole world. The war on terrorism, which began on 9/11, is really a war to preserve and advance the strategy of openness, free trade, and globalization, thereby ensuring US hegemony.

President George W. Bush has not changed the goals set by his predecessors. After his re-election, he declared that in the future he is still prepared to act unilaterally and to use military power if necessary, as in Afghanistan and Iraq in order to ensure American security and continued prosperity. On 1 December 2004, in a keynote speech delivered in Halifax, he declared: "There is only one way to deal with enemies who plot in secret and set out to murder the innocent and the unsuspecting. We must take the fight to them. We must be relentless and we must be steadfast in our duty to protect our people."[4] These goals comprise the promotion of peace, freedom, and democracy as well as the protection of human rights around the world on the ground that liberal democracies do not wage war against one another. The United States will achieve them by persuasion or by force even if it involves the removal of dictators and non-democratic regimes that stand in the way. It will also maintain the right to resort to anticipatory or preventive self-defence if it finds itself threatened in any way, especially by terrorism.

Many states and individuals are opposed to this approach on the ground that it is contrary to international law in so far as intervention constitutes an unjustified interference in the internal and external affairs of states that is prohibited by the Charter of the United

---

[2] "If we have to use force, it is because we are America. We are the indispensable nation," quoted by A.J. Bacevich, *American Empire* (2003) at x.

[3] *Ibid.* at 3.

[4] *Globe and Mail,* 2 December 2004, at A11.

Nations (UN Charter).[5] Only with the approval of the Security Council, pursuant to Chapter VII of this UN Charter, could intervention be justified or when it takes place within the strict confines of self-defence. Thus, unilateral armed intervention motivated by the non-democratic form of government of the target state is not an exception to the principle of non-intervention.

The dilemma faced by the United States is to reconcile a concern for moral principles and international law with the imperatives of national and international power to pursue the national interest. What is good for General Motors may not be good for the whole world! International law is foremost an instrument of international politics, which it serves in order to create a modicum of stability and predictability in international relations either directly or through international organizations. Thus, when a state believes that a rule of international law is contrary to its national or international interests, its natural tendency is not to reject it but to re-interpret it in a way that supports such interests or to deny its application to the situation at hand. In the absence of a superior authority whose decision is binding, and although all states are deemed to be equal, the temptation to do so is much greater when the state is a powerful one and the other members of the international community are weak or dependants. This is particularly true today in light of American neo-imperialism.[6] As George Orwell[7] wrote in the book *Animal Farm: A Fairy Story,* all animals are equal but some are more equal than others! This attitude on the part of powerful states is a persistent factor that weakens international law. A democracy without values turns into open or thinly disguised totalitarianism.

Another weakness of the present system is that there can be no objective determination of the conduct of a state. As the Permanent Court of International Justice stated in the the *Steamship Lotus* case,[8] "[i]nternational law governs relations between independent states. The rules of law binding upon states therefore emanate *from*

---

[5] Charter of the United Nations, 26 June 1945, Can. T.S. 1945 No. 7 (amended in 1965, 1968, and 1973) [UN Charter].

[6] Noam Chomsky, *Hegemony or Survival: America's Quest for Global Dominance* (2003); T. Roszac, *La menace américaine* (2004). On American national interest, see Condoleezza Rice, "Campaign 2000: Promoting the National Interest" (Jan./Feb. 2000) 79 Foreign Affairs 47.

[7] George Orwell, *Animal Farm: A Fairy Story* (1945) at 90 and Ch. X.

[8] *The Steamship Lotus,* [1927] P.C.I.J. Series A, No. 10, p. 18.

their own free will." Being the creators of the norms, it is for them to interpret these norms according to their national and international interests. They decide for themselves if their actions are in conformity with international law. This determination is essentially subjective since they are judge and party.[9]

A further difficulty arises from the emergence of new categories of superior norms of international law such as *jus cogens,* which comprises rules that are peremptory, permitting no derogation, and the breach of which constitutes an international crime,[10] for instance, the principle of the UN Charter prohibiting the use of force[11] and genocide[12] and obligations *omnium erga omnes* incurred by all states towards the international community in general, for instance, in the field of human rights.[13] How and by whom are their existence and scope to be determined?

The consequences of the violations of international law norms and rules are also uncertain as each state is free to decide what should be done if its rights have been infringed. In doing so, political considerations are paramount, which explains why some states escape sanctions for violating international law. With the emergence of a single superpower, resort to armed unilateral action without the approval of the United Nations when the national or international interests of that power are at stake raises the question of its legality and legitimacy under international law. The legality and legitimacy of the 2003 unilateral armed intervention in Iraq by the the United States and its allies, without the approval of the United

---

[9] The International Court of Justice (ICJ) deals with legal disputes only with the consent of the parties or in an advisory manner at the request of the United Nations. See Statute of the International Court of Justice, available at <http://www.icj-cij.org/icjwww/ibasicdocuments/ibasictext/ibasicstatute.htm> at Articles 36, 38, and 65.

[10] See Vienna Convention on the Law of Treaties, 1969, 1155 U.N.T.S. 331 1969 (in force 1980) at Article 53.

[11] UN Charter, *supra* note 5 at Article 2(4). Note that other principles found in the Charter cannot be contradicted by customary international law rules unless such rules are *jus cogens.*

[12] Convention on the Prevention and Punishment of Genocide, 1948, 78 U.N.T.S. 277 (1951) [Convention on Genocide].

[13] *Barcelona Traction, Light and Power Co. (Second Phase) (Belgium v. Spain),* [1970] I.C.J. Rep. 3, paras. 33–34. Self determination is a right *erga omnes,* Advisory opinion on *The Legal Consequences of the Construction of a Wall in the Occupied Palestinian Territory,* available at <http://www.icj-cij.org/> at para. 88, citing *East Timor (Portugal v. Australia),* [1993] I.C.J. Rep. 90, para. 29 and advisory opinion on *The Legality of the Threat or Use of Nuclear Weapons,* [1996] I.C.J. Rep. 226, para. 79.

Nations, illustrates the dilemma that the international community faces today since the reasons given for such intervention were both self-defence and the violation of human rights. Does such armed intervention constitute a desirable evolution of international law or has international law been eroded by it?

NON-INTERVENTION: THE BASIC RULES AND PRINCIPLES

Intervention consists of any act by one state or a group of states that attempts to interfere or interferes by force or by other means in the internal or external affairs of another state. The basic rules and principles of international law governing intervention are enshrined primarily in the UN Charter, which codifies the principle of non-intervention based on the sovereign equality of states.[14] Article 2(4) of the Charter declares that "[a]ll members shall refrain in their international relations from the threat or use of force against the territorial integrity or political independence of any state, or in any other manner inconsistent with the purposes of the United Nations." Paragraph (7) of the same article states that "[n]othing contained in the present Charter shall authorize the United Nations to intervene in matters which are essentially within the domestic jurisdiction of any state or shall require the Members to submit such matters to settlement under the present Charter; but this principle shall not prejudice the application of enforcement measures under Chapter VII." This principle, which applies to the United Nations as an organization, extends *a fortiori* to all member states in their relations with other states. The exception to the prohibition enables the Security Council to take military action against a state to maintain or restore international peace and security provided the Security Council has first determined that there exists a threat to the peace, a breach of the peace, or an act of aggression.[15] In principle, the Security Council can only intervene in matters related to international peace and security.

Unilateral armed intervention, which is prohibited by Article 2(4) and (7) of the UN Charter, except in very limited circumstances (for instance, by the lawful exercise of the right of self-defence

---

14 UN Charter, *supra* note 5 at Chapter 1 "Purposes and Principles" and Chapter VII "Action with Respect to Threats to the Peace, Breaches of the Peace, and Acts of Aggression." See also G.M. Lyons and M. Mastanduno, eds., *Beyond Westphalia? State Sovereignty and International Intervention* (1995).

15 UN Charter, *supra* note 5 at Article 39. Article VIII of the Convention on Genocide, *supra* note 12, may be an exception to this requirement.

pursuant to Article 51)[16] and by customary international law, pre-supposes effective institutions and the proper implementation of Chapter VII. When the system of collective security fails, states may be inclined to resort to unilateral armed intervention on their own initiative. Other international documents such as the 1965 UN Declaration on the Inadmissibility of Intervention in the Domestic Affairs of States and the Protection of Their Independence and Sovereignty,[17] the 1970 UN Declaration on Principles of International Law Concerning Friendly Relations and Co-operation among States in Accordance with the Charter of the United Nations (Declaration on Friendly Relations),[18] and the 1975 Final Act of the Helsinki Conference on Security and Cooperation in Europe[19] reiterate the same principles.[20]

INTERVENTION IN IRAQ

DESERT STORM 1990–91: STATE VERSUS STATE-ARMED AGGRESSION

When, on 1 August 1990, Saddam Hussein's army entered Kuwait, Iraq clearly violated Article 2(4) of the UN Charter. The next day, the Security Council condemned Iraq's invasion and demanded the immediate and unconditional withdrawal of its forces.[21] Iraq did not comply and, on 8 August, announced the annexation of Kuwait. This action was immediately declared illegal, null, and void by the Security Council.[22] On 29 November 1990, the Security Council

---

[16] UN Charter, *supra* note 5 at Article 51: "Nothing in the present Charter shall impair the inherent right of individual or collective self defence if an armed attack occurs against a Member of the United Nations, until the Security Council has taken measures necessary to maintain international peace and security."

[17] UN Declaration on the Inadmissibility of Intervention in the Domestic Affairs of States and the Protection of Their Independence and Sovereignty, Res. 2131, UN Doc. A/RES/213 (XX)/Rev. 1, reprinted in (1966) 60 Am. J. Int. L. 662.

[18] UN Declaration on Principles of International Law Concerning Friendly Relations and Co-operation among States in Accordance with the Charter of the United Nations, 1971, UNGA Res. 2625 (XXV), UNGAOR, 25th Sess., Supp. No. 28 at 121, UN Doc. A/8028/ [Declaration on Friendly Relations].

[19] Final Act of the Helsinki Conference on Security and Cooperation in Europe, 1 August 1975, reprinted in (1975) 14 I.L.M. 1292.

[20] The charters of a number of regional organizations contain similar rules. See, for example, Charter of Organization of American States, 1948, as amended, Can. T.S. No. 23, 1990, at Article 18.

[21] Resolution 660, UN Doc. S/RES/ 660 (2 August 1990).

[22] Resolution 662, UN Doc. S/RES/ 662 (9 August 1990).

authorized the use of force in order to reverse the invasion unless Iraq evacuated Kuwait before 15 January 1991.[23] Since Iraq failed to comply with this resolution by the appointed time, Operation Desert Storm began on 17 January 1991. The UN military operation was led by the United States. Kuwait was liberated and victory was declared on 27 February 1991. As a member of the United Nations, the United States had to support the action taken against Iraq. The intervention did not violate international law since the United States was acting in compliance with the resolutions of the Security Council pursuant to Chapter VII of the UN Charter.

SECOND GULF WAR: 2002–3: THE IMPACT OF THE AGE OF TERROR

Pre-emptive, Anticipatory, or Preventive?

In the fall of 2002 and in the winter of 2003, the United States argued before the Security Council that there was evidence that Iraq had not complied with UN Security Council Resolutions 687[24] and 1441,[25] ordering it to destroy the weapons of mass destruction (WMD) that it was supposed to possess, and that there was a danger that some of these weapons would be supplied to Al-Qaida and other terrorist groups to be used against a number of states, especially the United States. Thus, military action was necessary to force compliance. The Security Council did not believe the Americans and was not prepared to authorize the use of force, which was possible pursuant to Resolution 1441, paragraph 13, which states "that the Council has repeatedly warned Iraq that it will face serious consequences as a result of its continued violations of its obligations." The Security Council relied on the opinion of Hans Blix, the UN chief weapons inspector who reported that the inspection, which had resumed after an interruption of four years ordered by Saddam Hussein, was now proceeding smoothly, and although no WMD had yet been found, more time was necessary before concluding that Iraq was in breach of its obligations.

As a result of this lack of support by the Security Council, the United States withdrew its proposed resolution authorizing the use of force to secure compliance and, acting outside the United Nations, organized the Coalition of the Willing, which included the

---

[23] Resolution 678, UN Doc. S/RES/678 (29 November 1990).

[24] Resolution 687, UN Doc. S/RES/687 (3 April 1991).

[25] Resolution 1441, UN Doc. S/RES/1441 (8 November 2002).

United Kingdom, Spain, Italy, Australia, and others. The 2003 campaign to depose Saddam Hussein was short and successful.

Legality

When a state sponsors terrorist acts or aids terrorist groups in any way to further its or their goals against other states or their nationals, this action constitutes a violation of Article 2(4) of the UN Charter and the 1970 Declaration on Friendly Relations.[26] It is also an act of aggression according to the 1974 definition of aggression.[27]

If attacked by a terrorist act perpetrated or sponsored by a state, a victim state can respond in self-defence[28] until the Security Council becomes seized of the matter, pursuant to Article 39 of the UN Charter and authorizes collective enforcement action.[29] Collective security is the basis upon which the Security Council has the right to deal effectively with acts of international terrorism. Should a state be threatened by a terrorist act, the customary international law right of individual or collective self-defence also comes into play.

In order to establish the legality of unilateral intervention without UN approval and in the absence of an actual armed attack by Iraq on the United States, the United States and its allies relied on a variation of the customary international law right of pre-emptive self-defence against a threat of imminent attack. The doctrine of pre-emptive self-defence has its origin in the *United Kingdom v. United States* case (*Caroline* case).[30] It also finds support in *Military and Paramilitary Activities in and against Nicaragua (Merits)*,[31] where the

---

[26] Declaration on Friendly Relations, *supra* note 18.

[27] GA Resolution 3314, 14 December 1974, reprinted in (1974) 13 I.L.M. 710 at Article 3(g). "The sending by or on behalf of a state of armed bands, irregulars, or mercenaries, which carry out acts of armed force against another state of such gravity as to amount to acts listed above or its substantial involvement therein."

[28] UN Charter, *supra* note 5 at Article 51.

[29] SC Resolution 748, UN Doc. S/RES/748 (31 March 1992), with respect to Libya.

[30] *United Kingdom v. United States* (1837), 2 Moore 409 [*Caroline* case].

[31] *Military and Paramilitary Activities in and against Nicaragua (Nicaragua v. United States of America) (Merits)*, [1986] I.C.J. Rep. 14, at paras. 187–93 [*Military Activities in Nicaragua*]. See also UN SC Resolution 1368, UN Doc.S/RES/1368 (12 September 2001), and SC Resolution 1373, UN Doc. S/RES/1373 (28 September 2001), which reaffirm the inherent right of individual or collective self-defence. Note that the latter resolution recognizes that acts of terrorism constitute

International Court of Justice expressed the view that customary international law on the use of force exists independently of Article 2(4) of the UN Charter. Therefore, pre-emptive self-defence exists outside Article 51 of the UN Charter, which only deals with self-defence against an actual armed attack until the Security Council takes action. The customary international law right of pre-emptive self-defence is the inherent and natural right of a state to act for self-preservation in the face of a serious and imminent or proximate threat to its national security and territorial integrity (for instance, troops of a hostile country are massed at the borders ready to attack). As opposed to Article 51 of the UN Charter, no actual armed attack need to have taken place before pre-emptive self-defence can be used. However, fundamental to the exercise of the right of pre-emptive self-defence, the intervention must be born out of necessity and the level of force must be proportional to the harm it seeks to redress. In other words, the response must not be unreasonable or excessive.[32]

The variation added by the United States to the customary international law of pre-emptive self-defence is *anticipatory* or *preventive* self-defence against states sponsoring terrorism. As one aspect of the so-called Bush doctrine,[33] it purports to allow a state, without

---

a threat to international peace and security without ascribing these acts to a particular state. This is a new approach to the concept of self-defence. Does it mean that where a state without sponsoring terrorism fails to take appropriate measures on its territory to prevent the occurrence of terrorist acts in another state, the latter state would be able to intervene to make up for this deficiency? Per Justice Kooijmans in a separate opinion to the advisory opinion on *The Legal Consequences of the Construction of a Wall in the Occupied Palestinian Territory*, 9 July 2004, I.C.J. No. 131, at paras. 35–36, available at <http://www.icj-cij.org/>. The court held that a state has no right to use force in self-defence against terrorist attacks that are not imputable to a foreign state. See also SC Resolution 1566, UN Doc. S/RES/1556 (8 October 2004), at para. 1: "acts of terrorism ... by whomsoever committed."

32 *Military Activities in Nicaragua*, *supra* note 31 at para. 176; and advisory opinion on *The Legality of the Threat or Use of Nuclear Weapons*, [1996] I.C.J. Rep. 226, paras. 37–50.

33 Speech by George W. Bush, White House, 17 September 2002, available at <http://www.whitehouse.gov/nsc/print/nssall.html> at 1. The new policy was fully delineated on that day in a National Security Council text entitled *The National Security Strategy of the United States of America*, available at <http://www.whitehouse.gov/nsc/print/nssall.html> at chs. III and V. See also J. Record, "The Bush Doctrine and War with Iraq" (Spring 2003) Parameters: U.S. Army War College Quarterly 4–21.

prior approval of the Security Council, to act in anticipatory self-defence, not just pre-emptively against an imminent or proximate threat but preventively against a non-imminent or non-proximate but still real threat. Its rationale rests on a definition of the threat to a state based on a combination of "radicalism and technology," that is, political and religious extremism joined by the availability of WMD. Thus, the second Iraqi war became part of the war on terrorism. In light of the lack of action by the Security Council, the United States, as the intended victim of terrorism, was free to decide for itself that security problems justified armed intervention.

Having experienced 9/11, the United States and its allies argued that Saddam Hussein was now an evil *terrorist* since, allegedly, there was proof that he was prepared to supply Osama bin Laden and other Al-Qaida terrorists with WMD to be used against America on its territory. President Bush maintained that the nexus between terrorist organizations of global reach, states sponsoring terrorism, and WMD makes small or impoverished states and even small groups of individuals dangerous adversaries. A good example is Al-Qaida, a non-governmental terrorist organization, which is not subject to international law since it is not a state. Therefore, the Cold War concepts of deterrence and containment are irrelevant against such organizations.

Since the attacks by terrorists in the United States and elsewhere before the intervention by the Coalition of the Willing, as a result of a message by Al-Qaida aired on Al Jazeera, were perceived as potential and even imminent, they required an urgent response. Thus, the United States and its allies had to resort to anticipatory or preventive self-defence against Iraq and its chief villain Saddam Hussein even though he had not attacked the United States and was not planning to do so directly in the future. The concept of imminent threat relevant to pre-emptive self-defense had to be adapted to the capabilities and objectives of today's adversaries. The United States maintained that it must be able to reach potential threats to its security at their source before they could cause harm to the homeland or to the country's interests in the world. To defend itself, the United States and its allies had to eliminate Saddam Hussein to prevent him from supplying terrorists with WMD to be used presently or in the immediate future against the United States. In this way, the United States could overcome the legal limitations imposed by international law on pre-emptive self-defence since there was a lack of convincing evidence of imminent direct attack by Iraq against the United States.

The Bush doctrine, which states that in the case of an imminent or anticipated attack by a terrorist group such as Al-Qaida, acting as the agent, surrogate, or proxy of Saddam Hussein, a state unilaterally can resort to pre-emptive or anticipatory-preventive self-defence and intervene by force against the state that supplied the weapons to the terrorist group, is not yet sanctioned by international law.

Legitimacy

The use of military force by the Coalition of the Willing must be not only legal but also legitimate. Precautionary principles of legitimacy must be met before intervening. Although the threatened harm to the intervening states may have justified *prima facie* the use of military force, it is not clear that its primary purpose was to thwart the threat of terrorism. Securing Iraqi oil resources may have been more important. In addition, not all non-military options for meeting the threat in question had been explored before resorting to military action as a last resort since Iraq was willing to cooperate with the UN inspectors on the destruction of WMD. In response to this willingness, the Coalition of the Willing stated that based on past experience such inspections would not be effective. Finally, although the military action was proportional to the threat and was successful in meeting it, the consequences of the intervention seem to be worse today than the consequences of inaction.

Although Saddam Hussein's WMD ambitions were a potential and probably an inevitable threat rather than an imminent one, potential threats must be addressed by the international community. When they materialize, as in North Korea or Iran today, the crisis that is caused is much more dangerous than the crisis looming. The difficulty is how to deal with the latter. By allegedly waging war by proxy against the United States, Iraq should not have been able to avoid being the target of anticipatory-preventive self-defence.

In its 2 December 2004 report entitled *A More Secure World: Our Shared Responsibility*, the UN High-Level Panel on Threats, Challenges and Change recognizes that "if there are good arguments for preventive military action with good evidence to support them, they should be put to the Security Council, which can authorize action if it chooses to ... [I]n a world full of perceived potential threats, the risk to the global order and the norm of non intervention on which it continues to be based is simply too great for the legality of unilateral preventive action, as distinct from collectively endorsed action, to be accepted. Allowing one to so act is to allow all."[34] The panel rejects unilateral action in favour of collective action authorized by the Security Council in cases of perceived potential threats. For this reason, it is against rewriting or reinterpreting Article 51 of the UN Charter. In light of the present state of international law, one cannot escape the conclusion that the intervention by the Coalition of the Willing was illegal and illegitimate unless anticipatory-preventive self-defence is considered to be a logical evolution of the customary international law of pre-emptive self-defence.

UNILATERAL HUMAN RIGHTS INTERVENTION

The United States and its allies also argued that military intervention is legitimate and morally justified when a state treats its people in such a substandard way that they are denied their fundamental human rights, including democratic rights, and the protection of these rights can only be assured from the outside. In the case of Iraq, it was clear that Saddam Hussein was a dictator who had a long record of massive human rights abuses and that any move against him could be morally justified. Human rights considerations outweighed the reasons against intervention.[35] Armed intervention to force a state to respect human rights has now become the primary official justification by the Coalition of the Willing since, so far, no WMD or links with Al-Qaida have been found. However, it is a doctrine that is not yet well established under international law except when non-military humanitarian assistance is requested by a state as a result of physical calamities such as earthquakes, floods, famine, and epidemics.

Legality and Legitimacy

When a state exercises its jurisdiction, it must be not only in the interest of its people but also in the interest of the international

---

[34] UN High-Level Panel on Threats, Challenges and Change, *A More Secure World: Our Shared Responsibility*, UNGA Doc. A/59/565, at paras. 190–92 [*More Secure World*]. See also Kofi A. Annan, Speech to the UN General Assembly, 23 September 2003, available at <http://.unausa.org/aboutus/annan092303.asp>.

[35] The concern is with the violation of human rights, for instance, the violation of rights found in the International Covenant on Civil and Political Rights, (1966), 999 U.N.T.S. 171, and not with the violations of international humanitarian law in the case of armed conflict as in the 1949 Geneva Convention IV (civilians) (1950), 75 U.N.T.S. 287, or in cases of humanitarian assistance in the case of natural disasters or epidemics.

community as a whole. A state has the responsibility to protect its people. State sovereignty must yield to international obligations; it is not absolute and unconditional. In this context, human rights intervention is the threat to use force or its use by a state, a group of states, or an international organization for the purpose of protecting the nationals of the targeted state from widespread deprivation of internationally recognized human rights by that state and without its consent.

Is the threat or use of force for the purpose of protecting and enforcing human rights lawful under international law as an exception to Article 2(4) and (7) of the UN Charter whether the intervening states are acting with or without the express authorization of the United Nations? Although a modern doctrine of human rights intervention is slowly emerging,[36] the right to intervene forcibly and unilaterally for human rights reasons without obtaining the consent of the targeted state or that of the Security Council or collectively with the approval of the Security Council is still a very controversial subject. The UN Charter does not expressly recognize the right to use force to protect the people of a state from their own government or in the event of an overall breakdown in governmental authority, even in the face of genocide.[37]

The first legal objection to such a type of intervention is based on Article 2(4) of the UN Charter, which, as already noted, prohibits any type of intervention except as provided for in Chapter VII of the Charter. In other words, even when a state has abused its sovereign powers by violating the basic human rights of the people within its borders, it should not be liable to any type of intervention by another state or group of states. If we consider forcible collective human rights intervention by the United Nations under Chapter VII as an exception permitted by the UN Charter, the Security

---

36 See in general P. Malanczuk, *Humanitarian Intervention and the Legitimacy of the Use of Force* (1993); K. Tomasevsky, *Responding to Human Rights Violations 1946–1999* (2000); S. Hoffmann, *The Ethics and Politics of Humanitarian Intervention* (1996); Don Hubert and Rob McRae, *Human Security and the New Diplomacy* (2002); S.D. Murphy, *Humanitarian Intervention* (1996); M.S. Klimow, *Moral Versus Practical: The Future of US Armed Intervention* (1996); O. Corten and P. Klein, *Droit d'ingérance ou obligation de réaction?* (1992); C. Scott, "Interpreting Intervention" (2001) 39 Can. Y.B. Int. L. 333; P. Garigue, "Intervention-Sanction and 'droit d'ingérence' in International Humanitarian Law" (1993) 48 Int. J. 668; and M. Toufayan, "Deployment of Troops to Prevent Impending Genocide: A Contemporary Assessment of the UN Security Council's Powers" (2002) 40 Can. Y.B. Int. L. 195.

37 However, see Convention on Genocide, *supra* note 12 at Article VIII.

Council must still determine authoritatively whether in the particular situation the human rights violations constitute a "threat to the peace or breach of the peace or act of aggression."[38] Recent events in various parts of the world, for instance, in Iraq, Liberia, Somalia, Bosnia-Herzegovina, Kosovo, Afghanistan, Rwanda, East Timor, and Darfur, have clearly indicated that the consideration of human rights tragedies that could trigger Chapter VII is an important element in the maintenance of peace and security. At the time of drafting Chapter VII, human rights intervention was not envisaged. Its purpose was to deal with classic interstate conflicts and international security. However, in some cases, human rights abuses can become a threat to, or a breach of, the peace without a transnational nexus justifying the measures under Chapter VII. Unlike Article 33 of Chapter VI,[39] Article 39 in its opening words does not speak of "international" peace and security but simply of a "threat to the peace, breach of the peace," although its closing words refer to "measures to maintain or restore international peace." Thus, Chapter VII could also be used to address internal violence and unrest that threaten the peace within a state as well as genocide.[40] Article 2(4) aims to protect the territorial sovereignty and political independence of a state, which is not the case with respect to human rights intervention since the intervening state does not seek to deprive the targeted state of its territorial or political attributes.

A second legal objection to human rights intervention is based on Article 2(7) of the UN Charter, which prohibits intervention in the domestic affairs of a state. Although the early practice of the United Nations was to interpret broadly the words "within the domestic jurisdiction" so as to include human rights within such jurisdiction, thus preventing the Security Council from taking action against a member of the UN for violating human rights recognized by the UN Charter,[41] this is no longer the case. The United Nations has since admitted that, in some instances, individuals may become subjects of international law and has adopted numerous international covenants, charters, and declarations dealing with human

---

[38] UN Charter, *supra* note 5 at Article 39.

[39] *Ibid.* at Chapter VI, which deals with the pacific settlement of disputes.

[40] Convention on Genocide, *supra* note 12 at Article VIII, which does not refer to international peace and security.

[41] UN Charter, *supra* note 5 at Articles 55.c (respect and observance of human rights by members) and 56 (cooperation of members with the United Nations for the achievement of the purposes of Art. 55.c).

rights. How can violations of human rights be considered a domestic matter when such rights create obligations *erga omnes* and some of them such as genocide are *jus cogens*?[42] To overcome the prohibition of Article 2(7), it is sufficient to show that human rights crises do not fall "essentially within the domestic jurisdiction of any state." They are the concern of the international community as a whole. Of course, for each state, the scope of the reserved domain of non-intervention is variable. It depends upon the international human rights obligations it has accepted unless they are *jus cogens*. Today, Article 2, paragraphs (4) and (7), can no longer be considered to be obstacles to UN intervention for the protection of human rights. National sovereignty cannot be invoked to immunize a state or a dictator such as Saddam Hussein and others from international sanctions.

International law has evolved in the right direction by enabling the Security Council to resort to enforcement measures under Chapter VII. It took such action in 1991 to protect the Kurds and the Shiite Moslems in Iraq,[43] although no direct collective armed intervention took place. At that time, most members of the Security Council were of the opinion that the Kurds' situation was a threat to international peace and security.[44] As then, Secretary General Javier Perez de Cuellar wrote in his annual report on the work of the United Nations, which was presented to the General Assembly in September 1991, Article 2(7) can no longer be regarded as a protective barrier behind which human rights can be massively or systematically violated with impunity: "What is involved is not the right of intervention but the collective obligation of states to bring relief and redress in human rights emergencies. It seems beyond question that violations of human rights imperil peace."[45] However, he added that international action for protecting human rights must be based on a decision taken in accordance with the UN Charter. It must not be a unilateral act. Therefore, if one accepts this view, the Coalition of the Willing was in breach of international law.

[42] See notes 10–13 in this article.

[43] SC Resolution 688, UN Doc. S/RES/688 (5 April 1991), (1991) 30 I.L.M. 858.

[44] See also East Timor, SC Resolution 1264, UN Doc. S/RES/1264 (15 September 1999); Somalia, SC Resolution 794, UN Doc. S/INF/48 (3 December 1992) (partial armed intervention).

[45] *Annual Report on the Work of the United Nations*, Doc. A/46/1, GADR 46th Sess., Suppl. No.1, ST/JPDI/1168. See also Kofi A. Annan, "Two Concepts of Sovereignty," *The Economist*, 18 September 1999.

Another question left unanswered is whether intervention to re-store or establish democracy is part of human rights intervention?[46] Trying to change the political situation directly is dangerous since human rights intervention lacks the mandate to alter the funda-mental causes of inhumane conditions. Yet, why should the root causes of human rights intervention, for instance, Saddam Hussein, be left in place? Is it wrong to support or establish a democratic system of government in another state against an illegitimate re-gime? At the present international law does not support this type of intervention.[47]

Although the principle of non-intervention should not be lightly cast aside, it appears that Chapter VII provides a good legal justifi-cation for forcible collective intervention by the Security Council when there are serious questions concerning the violation of hu-man rights and humanitarian law, the need for humanitarian assis-tance, and perhaps a lack of democracy. The protection of human rights abolishes the distinction between the domestic and interna-tional jurisdiction of states. A state derives legitimacy in part from its citizens. If it denies them their fundamental rights, the constraint against external intervention no longer applies.

If the Security Council is incapable or unwilling to deal with the issue of gross violations of human rights, for instance due to a veto, the UN General Assembly could act pursuant to the Uniting for Peace Resolution precedent.[48] Regional and sub-regional organi-zations could also take action pursuant to Chapter VIII of the UN Charter. These international bodies would add legitimacy to the intervention as they would be less suspect of serving any particular national agenda.

HUMAN RIGHTS INTERVENTION AS AN INDEPENDENT DOCTRINE OF CUSTOMARY INTERNATIONAL LAW

Where action by the United Nations or a regional or sub-regional organization has been solicited and rejected, may a state or a group

---

[46] This was one of the reasons given for the US intervention in Panama in 1989. See also Article 21 of the Universal Declaration of Human Rights (free elec-tions), UN Doc. A/810 (1948). However, see Declaration on Friendly Relations (freedom to choose political system), *supra* note 18; and *Military Activities in Nicaragua. supra* note 31 at paras. 206 and 209.

[47] See, for example, *Military Activities in Nicaragua, supra* note 31 at paras. 202–9.

[48] Uniting for Peace Resolution, 1951, GA Res. 377 (V) UN GAOR, 5th Sess., Supp. No. 20, UN Doc. A/1775 at 10. The resolution does not authorize intervention

of states, such as the Coalition of the Willing, unilaterally intervene in another state to protect human rights? In other words, is there a customary international law right to intervene by force for human rights reasons whether or not collective security fails to function? Since Article 2(4) of the UN Charter imposes a virtually all-embracing ban on the use of force with the exception of self-defence in Article 51, it would seem that resort to human rights intervention without UN approval pursuant to Chapter VII is not possible. However, as already mentioned, the International Court of Justice (ICJ) in the *Nicaragua* case[49] was of the opinion that there exists a customary law on the use of force independent of Article 2(4). Thus, it is arguable that there is also a customary international law right of intervention in the case of massive and systemic violations of human rights by a state, which is independent of Article 2(4) and (7) of the UN Charter. The right coexists with Article 2(4) and (7), just as the customary right of pre-emptive self-defence coexists with Article 51. Therefore, customary human rights intervention is not linked with collective security under Chapter VII.[50]

Human rights intervention as an independent doctrine of customary international law and as an adjunct to Chapter VII could perform a function that this chapter does not cover, for instance, in the case of intra-state massive human rights abuses that do not involve threats to international peace and security. In most cases, however, it is likely that customary intervention would only take place in the absence of UN intervention pursuant to Chapter VII. The costs of the intervention would be borne by the intervening states and not by the United Nations. As for the nature of the intervention, it would have to comply with the criteria of the *Caroline* case.[51]

When comparing both mechanisms, one cannot fail to notice that the fact that Chapter VII provides a legal basis for the Security Council to intervene does not guarantee that the intervention is legal as there is a lack of substantive standards as to what constitutes a threat

---

itself but only recommends action to the General Assembly. See also UN Charter, *supra* note 5 at Article 11 (maintenance of international peace and security); Article 13 (assisting in the realization of human rights and fundamental freedoms); and Article 14 (measures for the peaceful adjustment of any situation).

[49] *Military Activities in Nicaragua, supra* note 31.

[50] Note that unilateral human rights intervention has taken place on a few occasions, for instance, India in East Pakistan (1971), Vietnam in Cambodia (1978), and Tanzania in Uganda (1979).

[51] *Caroline* case, *supra* note 30.

to international peace and security. It is also subject to the veto[52] that makes intervention selective and uneven. Financial constraints may also prevent intervention except in the most shocking cases. Even if the Security Council were the exclusive authority to approve armed human rights intervention, it would not be able to manage the crisis without the economic and military support of a few major powers, which raises serious questions about the legitimacy of the whole process. On the other hand, armed intervention pursuant to a customary international law right of human rights intervention, coexisting with Article 2(4) and (7) of the UN Charter and not linked with collective security, would not be subject to the veto, and its legality and justification could be challenged before the ICJ, which is not the case with respect to Security Council resolutions. Judicial review of the decisions of the Security Council is a controversial matter. The principle is that the ICJ is not generally empowered to overrule or undercut decisions made by the Security Council under Articles 39, 41, and 42 of the UN Charter to determine the existence of any threat to the peace, breach of peace, or act of aggression and to decide upon responsive measures to be taken to maintain or restore international peace and security. In the 1998 preliminary objections to the *Case Concerning Questions of Interpretation and Application of the 1971 Montreal Convention Arising from the Aerial Incident at Lockerbie (Libyan Arab Jamahiriya v. United Kingdom and Libyan Arab Jamhiriya v. United States of America)*,[53] the majority of the court side-stepped the judicial review issue. However, on previous occasions, the court had stated that it does not possess powers of judicial review or appeal in respect of the decisions taken by the Security Council.[54]

By developing an independent doctrine of human rights intervention under customary international law that is not linked to international peace and security, international law would recognize the intrinsic value of human rights and be free of the shackles of Chapter VII, which must not be the sole legal basis for such type of

---

[52] See the incapacity of the Security Council to act with respect to Kosovo because of the potential use of the veto by China and the Russian Federation as a result of which the North Atlantic Treaty Organization (NATO) intervened.

[53] *Case Concerning Questions of Interpretation and Application of the 1971 Montreal Convention Arising from the Aerial Incident at Lockerbie (Libyan Arab Jamahiriya v. United Kingdom and Libyan Arab Jamhiriya v. United States of America)* (preliminary objections), (1998), 37 I.L.M. 587 at paras. 46–50.

[54] *Advisory Opinion with Respect to Namibia*, [1971] I.C.J. Rep. 16, at 45.

intervention irrespective of whether or not collective security mechanisms are functioning effectively. Thus, it would be a progressive step if the international community were to adopt a doctrine of customary intervention and restrict Chapter VII to interstate conflicts, as it was intended originally, since you cannot extend the mandate of the Security Council to deal with every human rights issue as one of international peace and security.

New Developments and Suggestions for the Future

The existence of, or the need for, a customary right of human rights intervention is not addressed by the International Commission on Intervention and State Sovereignty, which concentrated on the UN Charter and the role of the Security Council in this area of protection and enforcement of human rights. In its 2001 report entitled *The Responsibility to Protect*, the commission dealt with the question of "when, if ever, it is appropriate for states to take coercive — and in particular — military action, against another state for the purpose of protecting people at risk in that other state."[55] The report is intended to provide precise guidance for states faced with human rights protection claims in other states. It acknowledges that the primary responsibility rests on each state to protect its population from harm and that the secondary responsibility rests on the international community to act where that state is unable or unwilling to protect its people or is the perpetrator of the harm in question. The report goes on to state that, "[w]here a population is suffering serious harm as a result of internal war, insurgency, repression or state failure, and the state in question is unwilling or unable to halt or avert it, the principle of non-intervention yields to the international responsibility to protect."[56]

Such responsibility embraces three different expectations:

1. *The responsibility to prevent,* by addressing both the root causes and the direct causes of internal conflict and other man-made crises putting populations at risk. Prevention is the most important dimension of the responsibility to protect before any intervention is contemplated.

---

[55] International Development Research Centre, *The Responsibility to Protect,* December 2001, available at <http://www.idrc.ca> at foreword [*Responsibility to Protect*].

[56] *Ibid.* at synopsis (1) Basic Principles B.

2. *The responsibility to react*, with appropriate measures that may include coercive measures such as sanctions, international prosecution, and, in extreme cases, military intervention. Such types of intervention are only warranted when there is serious and irreparable harm occurring to human beings or that is imminently likely to occur, such as a large-scale loss of life that may amount to genocide or a large-scale "ethnic cleansing."
3. *The responsibility to rebuild* after military intervention.

When military intervention takes place, it must meet several precautionary principles:

1. *Right intention.* The purpose of the intervention must be to halt or avert human suffering, no matter what other motives intervening states may have.
2. *Last resort.* Military intervention can only be justified when every non-military option for the prevention or peaceful resolution of the crisis has been explored.
3. *Proportional means.* The scale, duration, and intensity of the planned military intervention (as in the case of self-defence) should be the minimum necessary to secure the defined human protection objective.
4. *Reasonable prospect of success.* There must be a reasonable prospect of success in halting or averting the suffering that has justified the intervention, with the consequences of the action not likely to be worse than the consequences of inaction.

With respect to authorization of any military operation, the report states that the United Nations is the only organization with the universally acceptable authority to validate such operations.[57] Within the United Nations, only the Security Council can authorize military intervention for the protection of vulnerable populations. The task is not to find alternatives to the Security Council as a source of authority but rather to make the Security Council work much better than it has in the past. In order to validate any human rights intervention by a state or coalition of states, the authorization of the Security Council must be sought before any military action is carried out. The Security Council must deal promptly with any request, and its permanent members must agree not to apply

---

[57] *Ibid.* at para. 6.12; and UN Charter, *supra* note 5 at Article 24 (responsibility of the Security Council for the maintenance of peace and security).

their veto power in matters where their vital interests are not involved. Should the Security Council reject a proposal or fail to deal with it in a reasonable amount of time, the report suggests that the matter be referred to the UN General Assembly meeting in an emergency special session under the Uniting for Peace Resolution[58] or to the relevant regional or sub-regional organization under Chapter VIII of the UN Charter, subject to their seeking subsequent authorization from the Security Council.[59]

What if these international bodies fail to discharge their responsibilities? It is doubtful and unrealistic to expect that when they fail to act, a state or a coalition of states, such as the Coalition of the Willing, will not take unauthorized action and undertake military operations in conscience-shocking situations that cry for immediate intervention. The report raises this issue, but it is not clear whether military action outside the United Nations is legal as a last resort. It merely recognizes that this possibility should prompt the Security Council to act in order not to damage the credibility of the international organization.[60]

Although, undoubtedly, the primary responsibility to deal with human rights crises rests with the United Nations, one should not rule out unilateral armed action based on a customary right of intervention to meet the gravity and urgency of the situation, provided the intervening states fully observe the necessary precautionary principles governing military intervention. It would seem that the intervention by the Coalition of the Willing in Iraq observed some of these principles, although the principles of last resort and of reasonable prospect of success were not fully met.

Unilateral armed intervention could be justified even in the absence of UN or regional or sub-regional approval in cases of urgency when the reasons for withholding approval are not weighty and there is ample evidence that the cause and the motives of those who would intervene are morally justified. However, who will determine whether the cause is just and whether the intervener has no other motive than the enforcement of what is right? This decision could be made by an impartial body, such as the ICJ, which would make it on an expedited basis. The violation of human rights must cause irreparable injury, and the intervention

---

[58] Uniting for Peace Resolution, *supra* note 48.

[59] For example, Liberia in 1992, Sierra Leone in 1997, and NATO in Kosovo in 1999. Note that NATO is not a regional organization.

[60] *Responsibility to Protect, supra* note 55 at para. 6.36.

must cause less damage to the targeted society than would inaction. The goal is to stop the wrongdoing and protect the victims, not attack the whole nation. Therefore, the methods used to achieve these goals must be subject to the principle of proportionality as in the case of self-defence.

It is suggested that armed human rights intervention by a state or group of states primarily for the purpose of protecting the nationals of the targeted state from widespread deprivation of their internationally recognized human rights should be possible without the authorization of the targeted state or the international community in very urgent situations. Critics maintain, however, that powerful states are often tempted to use a dubious general customary international law right to intervene forcibly to fight terrorism or to protect human rights as an excuse for meddling in the affairs of less powerful states. Only the United Nations, they say, should be able to authorize action on behalf of the entire international community instead of a select few, since such action might not be conducted for the right reasons or the right commitment to the necessary precautionary principles that are applicable. Unfortunately, unilateral action is generally motivated by a narrow set of economic or other interests and ideological goals. It does not provide a degree of predictability, which is most important in international relations. For instance, although American security concerns and human rights abuses were the two official legal and moral justifications for intervening in Iraq for the second time, the real reason for intervening probably was to secure the supply of oil for the American economy. In the first Gulf war, the United States wanted to protect the oil resources of Kuwait and Saudi Arabia. In the second Gulf war, it was Iraqi oil resources that had to be secured. In both instances, the national interest of the United States dictated its course of action.

In the report *A More Secure World: Our Shared Responsibility*, the UN High-Level Panel on Threats, Challenges and Change endorsed "the emerging norm that there is a collective international responsibility to protect, exercisable by the Security Council, authorizing military intervention as a last resort, in the event of genocide and other large scale killing, ethnic cleansing or serious violations of international humanitarian law which sovereign Governments have proved powerless or unwilling to prevent."[61] The panel remarked that the effectiveness of the global collective security system depends ultimately not only on the legality of the decisions made but also on

---

[61] *More Secure World, supra* note 34 at para. 203.

the common perception of their legitimacy.[62] Agreed guidelines should be adopted, which go "directly not to whether force can legally be used but whether, as a matter of good conscience and good sense, it should be."[63] Thus, in deciding whether to authorize or endorse the use of military force, the Security Council should consider at least the following five basic criteria of legitimacy: the seriousness of the threat; the proper purpose of the military action; last resort; proportional means; and the balance of consequences. The panel believed that taking these into account would minimize the possibility of individual member states by-passing the Security Council.[64]

WHAT SHOULD BE THE POSITION OF CANADA?

The difficulty with the "war on terror" is that the enemy is invisible and its tentacles reach across national boundaries. Terrorism does not involve interstate conflicts unless it is state sponsored. Similarly, violations of human rights rarely involve interstate conflicts. However, the absence of interstate conflicts does not mean that terrorism and massive violations of human rights do not endanger the peace and security of mankind. New strategies and tactics are needed. Is Canada prepared to contribute to their formulation and implementation? Canada should not restrict itself to the role of peacemaker or peacekeeper. Canada must collaborate with the United States and other states in the pursuit of common interests. It must continue to support the war against terrorism and be prepared to take an active part in the worldwide protection and enforcement of human rights. Canada must understand that the United States is often interested in quick results, whether or not they can be achieved with UN support. It is to the credit of the United States that in the Security Council its representatives argued at length before intervening in Iraq. Cheap knee-jerk anti-Americanism is not the answer in view of the importance of good

---

[62] *Ibid.* at para. 204.

[63] *Ibid.* at para. 205.

[64] *Ibid.* at paras. 205–7. See also Scott, *supra* note 36 at 366–67, who favours the adoption by the UN General Assembly of a declaration as to when and how legitimate humanitarian intervention should take place with or without Security Council backing and the creation of a special committee of the General Assembly meeting in informal sessions to deal with humanitarian crises that are on an alert list so as to pass judgment should the Security Council fail to act in accordance with the criteria set out in the declaration.

Canada-United States relations.[65] In a unipolar world, it is better to exercise influence on the United States through a close friendly relationship than to adopt a confrontational attitude. The interests of Canada in the world are best served by such a close relationship, as it is not productive to chart a foreign policy course that conflicts with the one adopted by Washington. This position does not mean that Canadian foreign policy must be in step with American foreign policy. We can disagree when our views are different but let us do it in a civilized manner. Our relationship with the United States must be based on mutual respect, common values, and the pursuit of common interests.

Canada must promote human security and protect individuals from violence and repression wherever they are, and it should even resort to military intervention *if absolutely necessary*. However, as a general rule, UN authorization should be sought first since this body can confer greater legitimacy to intervention than a coalition of states acting outside of it. When it is not possible, Canada should be willing to act unilaterally or as part of a coalition of states to uphold the principle of protection provided precautionary principles are followed. Canada must be uncompromising about human rights on the international stage as it was in Kosovo in 1999 as part of the North Atlantic Treaty Organization and as it has been recently in the Darfur region of Sudan.

Precautionary principles that are relevant to military operations in the case of human rights intervention are equally relevant when dealing with international terrorists and those who harbour them. In both situations, action should always be exercised in a principled way that, as noted previously, embraces the principles of right intention, last resort, proportional means, and reasonable prospects of success. Before resorting to unilateral armed intervention, noncoercive measures must be exhausted. Every effort must be made to develop strategies encouraging peace-building activities. Preventive diplomacy is most important. Incentives to eliminate the conditions that have given rise to the abuses should be offered to the abusive state. Once intervention has taken place, the perpetrators of the human rights abuses must be brought to international criminal justice.

Canada must encourage the international community to adopt norms that trigger armed intervention and that dictate by whom,

---

[65] See in general J. Welsh, *At Home in the World, Canada's Global Vision for the Twenty-First Century* (2004).

since it would be better to do this in a multilateral convention than to leave it to customary international law. Violations of human rights that prompt intervention should be clear and well documented by the UN Commission on Human Rights on an expedited basis[66] or by a UN-appointed Commission of Inquiry.[67] This procedure would avoid any suspicion of ulterior motives on the part of the intervening states.

It is to Canada's credit that it has sponsored the creation of the International Commission on Intervention and State Sovereignty, which produced the report *The Responsibility to Protect*. The recommendations contained in this report[68] are supported by the Canadian government, which is trying to persuade the international community to adopt them.[69] Achieving this goal would probably require enlarging the mandate of the Security Council by amending Article 39 of the UN Charter, specifically giving it the power to authorize intervention in a state with military action or peacekeepers in the case of massive violations of human rights, even when international peace and security are not endangered. Such an amendment would be in keeping with the preamble and Article 1(3) of the UN Charter, which refer to the respect for human rights as one of the goals of the organization. As already mentioned, the UN High-Level Panel on Threats, Challenges and Change supports resort to the Security Council when dealing with the collective international responsibility to protect.[70]

CONCLUSIONS

What should be done when a state supports terrorism and is willing to supply WMD to terrorist groups or when it violates the fundamental human rights of its people and the United Nations is incapable or unwilling to confront it? Recent intervention in Iraq

[66] See, for example, UN Economic and Social Council Resolution 1235 (XLII), 6 June 1967.

[67] As in the case of the Darfur region of Sudan. See SC Resolution 1564, UN Doc. S/RES/ 1564 (18 September 2004) at para. 12; and *Report of the International Commission of Inquiry on Darfur to the Secretary General*, 27 January 2005, and *Report of the Secretary General*, 31 January 2005, Doc. S/2005/ 57.

[68] *Responsibility to Protect, supra* note 55.

[69] See Prime Minister Paul Martin at the Francophonie summit in Ouagadougou in Burkina Faso in November 2004.The Canadian government is preparing a review of Canada's foreign policy to be released in 2005.

[70] *More Secure World, supra* note 34.

reveals evolving attitudes on the part of some states with respect to the use of force in anticipatory-preventive self-defence or in protecting human rights. Yet, post-Cold War interventions do not demonstrate a ready acceptance of a general right of unilateral armed humanitarian intervention. Although some countries and individuals have expressed disapproval of US action in the second Gulf War as another example of its unilateral interventionist imperialist approach to world affairs, one must acknowledge that only America has the power and the resources to defend the international community against terrorism and to sanction massive violations of human rights on which there is more or less universal agreement.

The better approach, as suggested by Canada and the UN panel, is to obtain the authorization of the UN Security Council, pursuant to an amended Chapter VII or construed broadly beyond the concept of a breach of, or threats to, international peace and security to cover massive violations of human rights. This authorization would lend a degree of legitimacy to armed intervention and allow for sharing the costs and risks. It would also reduce suspicion that an intervening state may be furthering a self-serving agenda. The issue is not to by-pass the Security Council but rather to make it work better. However, as the recent events in the Darfur region of Sudan and, before that, in Rwanda and other places have demonstrated, wide support has not been forthcoming.[71] Thus, in certain extreme circumstances, unilateral armed intervention by a state or coalition of states without UN approval should be legal and legitimate, provided that the protection of human rights is the dominant motive. The intervention should be driven by altruistic motives to address the suffering of a foreign people and not primarily to further the economic gain or geopolitical security interest of the intervening state.

Today, international law is moving forward by slowly overcoming the principle of state sovereignty in an attempt to be relevant to a post-Cold War world when the violation of human rights constitutes a threat to an orderly international society. Little by little, international law is adopting normative moral principles that promote values of human dignity and justice as well as systemic stability.

---

[71] For instance, so far in the Darfur region of Sudan, the African Union has taken no military action against the government of Sudan to stop it from participating in gross violations of human rights. See the sources outlined in note 67 of this article.

Neither the lexicon of a just war nor that of terrorism seem to reflect accurately the current state of world affairs. If terrorists or massive violators of human rights cannot be brought to justice peacefully, resort to force may be the only effective response to apprehend them. However, when directing international efforts to eradicate terrorism or massive abuses of human rights, the United States must do so wisely, not as a hegemonic power but as a senior partner sharing in global power and working out problems through the United Nations whenever possible.

Above all, it is important that states not become like the terrorists and violators of human rights and weaken a just cause by the use of unjust means. They must work together to deal with the underlying causes of terrorism and human rights abuses. To eliminate both requires long-term action. Peace is gained by justice, not by the force of arms. Terrorism and human rights abuses can only be effectively challenged through a concerted multilateral collective approach and not through the politics of unilateralism. To gain support, allies must be defined more by shared interests than by shared values. Therefore, it is hoped that in the future, the United States will move towards global leadership rather than global domination and will fully support action by the United Nations, as it has done lately in the case of humanitarian assistance arising from the 26 December 2004 tsunami.[72] By acting in this way, the United States will restore its credibility as an international presence for stability and security and give an ethical dimension to its imperial tendencies.

As US president Harry Truman declared when the United Nation was founded: "We have to recognize — no matter how great our strength — that we must deny ourselves the license to do always as we please."[73] This notion is more relevant now than ever before, as the United States remains the sole superpower in the world. Even though the unilateral military intervention in Iraq by the Coalition of the Willing, without the authorization of the United Nations, appears to be neither legal nor legitimate, it has had a positive effect by bringing to the fore the need to widen the mandate of the Security Council rather than letting it evolve by re-interpretation. As acknowledged by the UN high-level panel, a

---

[72] See Z. Brzezinski, *The Choice, Global Domination or Global Leadership* (2004). With respect to unilateralism versus multilateralism, see R. Kagan, *Of Paradise and Power: America and Europe in the New World Order* (vintage ed., 2003–4) at 144.

[73] Quoted in *More Secure World, supra* note 34 at Part 4: "A More Effective United Nations for the Twenty-First Century" and synopsis at 64.

new international customary norm is emerging, which recognizes that there is a collective international responsibility to protect, exercisable by the Security Council to authorize military action as a last resort in the event of massive violations of human rights. Thus, international law is evolving in the right direction. Let us hope that this new emerging norm will soon become widely accepted and, when necessary, will be acted upon by all of the members of the United Nations.

Sommaire

L'intervention armée unilatérale face au terrorisme, au neo-impérialisme et aux violations massives des droits de l'homme: le droit international évolue-t-il dans la bonne direction?

L'intervention militaire unilatérale en Iraq par les États-Unis et ses alliés sans l'approbation du Conseil de Sécurité qui repose sur la légitime défense préventive contre la menace d'actes de terrorisme et sur la responsabilité de protéger la population iraquienne contre la violation massive des droits de l'homme par Saddam Hussein pose la question de savoir si cette intervention est compatible avec les données actuelles du droit international. Les principes de non intervention et de non ingérence énoncés aux paragraphes 4 et 7 de l'artice 2 de la Charte des Nations Unies et qui ont leur source dans la règle de l'égalité souveraine des États conservent-t-ils encore toute leur force? Dans l'état actuel du droit international, il est clair que l'intervention américaine en Iraq n'est ni légale ni légitime. Seul le Conseil de Sécurité avait le droit d'autoriser une telle intervention en vertu du Chapitre VII de la Charte des Nations Unies à moins que l'intervenant invoque le droit de légitime défense reconnu par l'article 51 de cette Charte ou par le droit international coutumier strictement interprété. Quant au droit d'ingérence, le droit international coutumier évolue dans la bonne direction puisqu'il commence à reconnaître l'existence d'une responsabilité internationale de protection des personnes qui sont les victimes de violations massives des droits de l'homme. En effet, les droits de l'homme font naître à l'égard de l'État des obligations internationales qui conditionnent l'exercice de sa compétence territoriale. Il s'agit d'une conséquence directe de la singularité substantielle des droit de l'homme et de leur caractère objectif. Cependant, ici encore, l'intervention américaine devait être approuvée par le Conseil de Sécurité car seule l'organisation des Nations Unies a le droit de sanctionner les atteintes aux libertés fondamentales perpétrées à l'intérieur même d'un État.

Summary

The Legality and Legitimacy of Unilateral Armed Intervention in
an Age of Terror, Neo-Imperialism, and Massive Violations of Human Rights: Is International Law Evolving in the Right Direction?

*With the end of the Cold War, the United States has emerged as the sole
remaining superpower whose ambition is to create a new open and integrated world order based on principles of democratic capitalism. To ensure
its hegemony, the United States is prepared to resort to military action with
or without UN approval when its international and national security interests are at stake. The intervention in Iraq by the Coalition of the Willing is
a good example of this policy and raises the question of its legality and
legitimacy under contemporary international law. May or must a state resort to military intervention against a state sponsoring terrorism or depriving its nationals of their internationally recognized human rights? The
so-called "Bush doctrine" of anticipatory or preventive self-defence against a
state accused of supplying weapons of mass destruction to a foreign terrorist
organization, which was one of the reasons advanced by the Coalition of the
Willing for intervening in Iraq, meets neither the conditions laid out in
Article 51 of the UN Charter nor those of customary international law.
Thus, at the present stage of development of international law, the Bush
doctrine is not even* lege ferenda. *It is not an extension of the customary
international law right of pre-emptive self-defence. Only with the approval
of the Security Council pursuant to Chapter VII of the UN Charter or when
it takes place within the strict confines of self-defence, can armed intervention be legitimate.*

*The second reason for intervening in Iraq given by the Coalition of the
Willing is based on humanitarian considerations, which raises the question
whether the protection of human rights can be assured from the outside.
Here, international law is evolving in the right direction since the international community is prepared to adopt the concept of responsibility to protect, which justifies the use of force to protect and enforce human rights as
an exception to Article 2(4) and (7) of the UN Charter. Again, such intervention is legal only when approved by the Security Council acting pursuant to Chapter VII on the ground that human right crises do not fall
"essentially within the jurisdiction of any state." However, the international
community, with the exception of the Coalition of the Willing, is not yet
prepared to support a right of unilateral military intervention as a last
resort when the Security Council is incapable and unwilling to do so. This
includes intervention motivated by the non-democratic form of government of the targeted state. Although the primary responsibility to deal with*

human right crises rests with the United Nations based on the responsibility to protect, it is argued that one should not rule out unilateral military action based on a customary international law right of intervention to meet the gravity and urgency of the situation provided the intervening state fully observes the necessary precautionary principles governing such type of intervention. The conclusion is that terrorism and human rights abuses can only be effectively challenged through a concerted multilateral collective approach not through the politics of unilateralism.

La CIJ, l'avis consultatif et la fonction judiciaire: entre décision et consultation

PIERRE-OLIVIER SAVOIE

INTRODUCTION

Avant même que ne soit rendu le dernier avis consultatif de la CIJ sur la licéité d'un mur construit par Israël autour des territoires palestiniens,[1] le gouvernement d'Israël avait clairement indiqué qu'il ne s'y conformerait pas, position maintenue le jour du jugement.[2] Est-ce là une raison de déplorer que l'avis ait été rendu? L'absence de consentement d'Israël ou d'autres raisons liées à la compétence, la recevabilité ou, généralement, à l'intégrité judiciaire de la Cour auraient-elles dû mener celle-ci à décliner de rendre l'avis? Ces questions sur l'autorité et la légitimité des avis consultatifs sont avec nous depuis maintenant deux siècles.[3] En droit interne comme en droit international, l'irritant de l'avis consultatif est le fruit de la montée de l'État démocratique et de la séparation des pouvoirs entre l'exécutif, le législatif et le judiciaire. Ainsi, on considère souvent que la seule fonction légitime du pouvoir judiciaire serait de se prononcer sur des différends nés et réels. En droit international, l'avis consultatif irrite aussi parce qu'il

Pierre-Olivier Savoie, B.C.L./L.L.B. Hons. (McGill, 2005). L'auteur tient à remercier les professeurs René Provost, Armand de Mestral, Frédéric Bachand, et Fabien Gélinas, ainsi que Alexandra Popovici et Eveyln Gitzel Campos Sánchez pour leurs précieux commentaires.

[1] *Conséquences juridiques de l'édification d'un mur dans le territoire palestinien occupé*, avis consultatif du 9 juillet 2004 (*Conséquences juridiques de l'édification d'un mur*), en ligne : <http://www.icj-cij.org>.

[2] "Sharon orders Israeli barrier construction continued," CNN, 11 juillet 2004, en ligne: <http://www.cnn.com/2004/WORLD/meast/07/11/israel.barrier/>.

[3] C'est aux États-Unis, en 1793, que s'est posé pour la première fois la question de la compatibilité des avis consultatifs avec la fonction judiciaire. Voir généralement Stewart Jay, Most humble servants: the advisory role of early judges, New Haven, Conn., Yale University Press, 1997.

porterait atteinte à la souveraineté de l'État qui n'y a pas consenti et dont les droits pourraient être affectés par celui-ci dans le futur.[4] L'avis sur les *Conséquences juridiques de l'édification d'un mur* semble constituer une excellente occasion pour réexaminer l'apport des avis consultatifs de la CIJ. Cependant, il existe déjà une littérature abondante sur l'utilité des avis consultatifs à l'intérieur du système des Nations Unies et du droit international. C'est pourquoi notre approche vise à mesurer l'utilité des avis consultatifs en examinant leur fonctionnement au sein de plusieurs systèmes juridiques. À notre connaissance, la dernière étude comparatiste exhaustive au regard des avis consultatifs est celle de Manley O. Hudson dans son cours à l'Académie du droit international.[5]

Il y a quatre-vingts ans, l'évaluation que faisait Manley Hudson des premières années de la procédure consultative devant la CPJI était plutôt positive.[6] Cet enthousiasme découlait entre autres du fait que la CPJI venait de rendre huit avis en deux ans et qu'elle avait par le fait même contribué à rétablir dans une certaine mesure la paix et la sécurité internationales. Par exemple, un des avis avait été accepté comme obligatoire par les deux parties au conflit, ce qui avait contribué à la résolution d'un différend opposant la France au Royaume-Uni.[7] Essayant aussi de convaincre un lectorat américain

[4] Voir *Statut de la Carélie orientale*, avis consultatif, CPJI série B (no 5) à la p. 27 (*Affaire de la Carélie*): aucun État n'est tenu "de soumettre ses différents avec les autres États, soit à la médiation, soit à l'arbitrage, soit enfin à n'importe quel procédé de solution pacifique sans son consentement."

[5] Manley O. Hudson, "Les avis consultatifs de la Cour Permanente de Justice Internationale" (1925), 8 RCADI 341 (Hudson, "Les avis consultatifs"). Voir aussi, Manley O. Hudson, "Advisory Opinions of National and International Courts" (1924), 37 Harv.L.Rev. 970 (Hudson, "Advisory Opinions"); Kenneth James Keith, *The Extent of the Advisory Jurisdiction of the International Court of Justice*, Leyden, A.W. Sijthoff, 1971 aux pp. 16–18; Dharma Pratap, *The Advisory jurisdiction of the International Court*, Oxford, Clarendon Press, 1972 aux pp. 263–67.

[6] Hudson, "Advisory Opinions," *supra* note 5.

[7] *Requête pour avis consultatif sur les décrets de nationalité promulgués en Tunisie et au Maroc (zone française) le 8 novembre 1921*, avis consultatif, CPJI série B (no 4) qui opposait la France et la Grande-Bretagne, à savoir si le conflit entre les deux États relevait, aux yeux du droit international, d'une question considérée comme relevant purement d'une question interne, selon les allégations françaises. Après une procédure à peu près similaire à un litige contentieux, la France a accepté le jugement qui réfutait ses thèses et a conclu un accord avec la Grande-Bretagne pour soumettre le litige à l'arbitrage. Les deux États ont conclu un accord avant que les procédures arbitrales ne soient engagées. Voir aussi Hudson, "Advisory Opinions," *supra* note 5 aux pp. 994–95.

plutôt froid à l'action judiciaire en l'absence de "controverse," Manley Hudson voyait les avis consultatifs comme donnant la chance aux tribunaux de prévenir et non seulement de guérir les problèmes juridiques de la société.[8] En un sens, Manley Hudson fit figure avant son temps de défenseur des modes alternatifs de résolution des conflits.

Un certain malaise par rapport à la pratique des avis consultatifs ne tarda cependant pas à s'établir dans la doctrine internationale.[9] On peut même dire qu'il précéda l'adoption de la pratique, comme le démontre le débat du comité international des juristes chargé de la rédaction du Statut de la CPJI.[10] Les critiques viennent essentiellement en deux temps. D'abord, l'avis consultatif est généralement considéré comme une fonction suspecte pour un tribunal. Pour préserver son intégrité, celui-ci devrait seulement exercer des fonctions à "caractère judiciaire." En l'absence d'un différend né entre deux ou plusieurs parties, on questionne le bien-fondé de l'avis, qui s'apparenterait moins au jugement d'un tribunal qu'à l'opinion juridique que pourrait rendre un procureur général ou n'importe quel avocat. Cette critique est présente autant en droit international qu'en droit interne. Ensuite, la position classique du droit international, selon laquelle les parties contractent leurs obligations, serait incompatible avec des avis généraux qui pourraient contraindre à l'avance les acteurs qui n'auraient pas accepté d'être ainsi liés. Ces deux critiques nous semblent mal fondées en théorie. D'une part, c'est une vision trop statique de la fonction judiciaire que d'affirmer que tout ce qui va au-delà de la décision du juge dans un conflit né entre deux parties peut dangereusement porter atteinte au caractère judiciaire d'un tribunal, même international. Ces critiques font fi de la constante évolution du rôle du juge et de la fonction judiciaire en droit interne comme en droit international (I). D'autre part, une vision trop classique du droit international ne reflète en rien la réalité puisque les États membres de l'Organisation des Nations Unies se sont liés à cette fonction consultative de la CIJ.[11] De plus, autant

---

[8] Hudson, *ibid.*

[9] Charles de Visscher, "Les avis consultatifs de la Cour internationale de justice" (1929), RCADI 1 (de Visscher, "Les avis consultatifs"); D.W. Grieg, "The Advisory Jurisdiction of the ICJ and the Settlement of Disputes between States" (1966), 15 ICLQ 332.

[10] Voir les propos de Elihu Root et John Bassett Moore cités au début de la section suivante, *infra* notes 19 et 20.

[11] Charte des Nations Unies, art. 96 (Charte).

en droit interne qu'en droit international,[12] la vraie source de la norme juridique, qui est par ailleurs constamment remodelée par les actions des acteurs,[13] demeure la force persuasive et l'adhésion des acteurs à cette norme. C'est pourquoi les mauvais jugements[14] sont évoqués "sans insister sur le[ur]s conclusions"[15] et que les extraits convaincants d'avis "non-obligatoires"[16] sont cités à répétition par la Cour dans sa propre jurisprudence.[17] Les avis consultatifs de la CIJ seraient donc légitimes lorsqu'ils permettent de poser des jalons nécessaires au fonctionnement de la société internationale (II). Ce sont les deux propositions que nous nous proposons d'examiner dans ce texte qui constitue un examen de ce qu'est un avis consultatif selon une analyse comparatiste du droit et une application de cette analyse à la jurisprudence consultative de la CIJ.

LA FONCTION JUDICIAIRE DE LA CIJ RELATIVE AUX DEMANDES D'AVIS

Créée par l'article 14 du Pacte de la Société des Nations[18] (SdN), la fonction consultative de la première vraie juridiction internationale permanente fut remise en question avant même sa naissance.

---

[12] Sur l'idée que le droit international constitue un meilleur reflet de ce qu'est le droit que le droit interne, voir Lon L. Fuller, "A Reply to Critics" dans rev. ed., New Haven, Conn., Yale University Press, 1969 aux pp. 232–36.

[13] Voir R.A. Macdonald, "Normativité, pluralisme et sociétés démocratiques avancées: l'hypothèse du pluralisme pour penser le droit," dans Carole Younès et Étienne Le Roy (dir.), *Médiation et diversité culturelle: pour quelle société?*, Paris, Karthala, 2002 à la p. 21.

[14] *Sud-Ouest africain, deuxième phase*, arrêt 18 juillet 1966, [1966] Rec. CIJ 3. Le professeur Bowett a aussi parlé "d'aberration."

[15] *Conséquences juridiques pour les états de la présence continue de l'Afrique du Sud en Namibie nonobstant la résolution 276 (1970) du Conseil de sécurité*, avis consultatif 21 juin 1971, [1971] CIJ Rec. 16 à la p. 49 (*Conséquences juridiques pour les états*).

[16] Voir Jean Salmon, "L'autorité des prononcés de la Cour internationale de Justice, Travaux du Centre national de recherches de logique, Arguments d'autorité et arguments de raison en droit, Bruxelles, Éd. Nemesis, 1988 à la p. 21 (Salmon, "L'autorité des prononcés").

[17] Charles de Visscher, *Aspects récents du droit procédural de la Cour internationale de Justice*, Paris, Pedone, 1966 à la p. 195 (de Visscher, *Aspects récents*): "Tout comme les arrêts, les avis consultatifs contribuent à la formation d'un corps de jurisprudence homogène; la Cour y puise librement; elle fait référence à ses avis tout comme à ses arrêts, utlisant les uns comme les autres dans ses rédactions."

[18] Le Statut de la Cour était muet sur la fonction consultative de la Cour. Elle tirait cette fonction de l'article 14 du Pacte jusqu'à ce que le Statut soit révisé en 1929: "Le Conseil est chargé de préparer un projet de Cour permanente de

On a qualifié la fonction consultative de la CPJI comme étant, selon le Juge John Bassett Moore, "obviously not a judicial function"[19] ou encore, selon Elihu Root, "a violation of all judicial principles."[20] Encore est-il que les propos de Root ne visaient que les opinions rendues sur des différends internationaux déjà nés entre deux ou plusieurs États. De plus, il acceptait l'argument selon lequel le Conseil de la SdN pourrait référer une question à la Cour si les parties au différend refusaient de le faire, à la condition que l'équivalent d'une procédure contradictoire soit adoptée.[21]

Les déclarations à l'emporte-pièce de John Bassett Moore et Elihu Root semblent refléter une conception trop statique de la fonction judiciaire. La fonction judiciaire est en évolution depuis des millénaires et elle a aussi connu d'importants développements depuis l'établissement de la CPJI (A). L'idée d'avis consultatif, quoique plus récente que la fonction judiciaire, a également connu une évolution non moins significative (B). Les critiques de Moore et de Root sont basées sur la vieille conception de l'avis consultatif, celle où les juges sont consultés en privé par l'exécutif ou le souverain, une façon de faire qui heurte le caractère judiciaire tel que conçu par la séparation des pouvoirs dans les États démocratiques. Il existe bon nombre d'avantages, mais aussi certains inconvénients aux avis consultatifs. Ces supposés inconvénients semblent cependant surtout découler de critiques valables à l'encontre de l'ancienne conception des avis consultatifs (C). Cette première partie vise donc à établir, sur une base comparative, l'idée de l'avis consultatif comme mode alternatif de résolution des conflits ainsi que comme mode alternatif de prévention des conflits.

L'ÉVOLUTION DE LA FONCTION JUDICIAIRE DANS LE TEMPS

Avant de se plonger dans les conceptions historiques, classiques et contemporaines de la fonction judiciaire, une typologie des modes

---

justice internationale et de le soumettre aux Membres de la Société. Cette Cour connaîtra de tous différends d'un caractère international que les Parties lui soumettront. Elle donnera aussi des avis consultatifs sur tout différend ou tout point, dont la saisira le Conseil ou l'Assemblée."

[19] John Bassett Moore, "Organisation of the Permanent Court of International Justice" (1922), 22 Colum. L.Rev. 507.

[20] Le représentant américain Elihu Root au Comité des juristes durant les réunions préparatoires sur la rédaction du Statut de la CPJI: *Minutes of the Advisory Committee of Jurists* (1920), aux pp. 584–85, cité dans Keith, *supra* note 5 à la p. 16.

[21] *Ibid.*

d'ordonnancement social peut être utile.[22] On peut procéder à l'allocation des droits et des ressources selon neuf modes différents. Ceux-ci peuvent être divisés en trois catégories, chacune étant basée sur le degré d'imposition ou de consensualisme qui lui est inhérent: les modes horizontaux sont fondamentalement consensuels (coutume, contrat et médiation); les modes dits verticaux sont basés sur la décision unilatérale d'un tiers (directive managériale, consultation et décision judiciaire); et les modes diagonaux sont basés sur un mécanisme de décision institutionnel supposément neutre (le marché, le hasard et le vote).[23] Ce sont principalement, mais pas uniquement, les modes verticaux qui vont nous intéresser ici. On considère généralement la fonction judiciaire comme se limitant à la décision par une tierce partie, plus particulièrement à la décision raisonnée d'un tiers à la suite d'un débat contradictoire. L'hypothèse explorée ci-dessous est que la fonction judiciaire peut incorporer non seulement les trois modes verticaux, mais également d'autres modes, comme la médiation. Cette fonction judiciaire a des hautes tendances à la verticalité, mais il peut y avoir des ascendants horizontaux variables dépendamment du système et de son époque. C'est pourquoi l'idée selon laquelle les avis consultatifs choquent le caractère judiciaire de la CIJ semble un peu simpliste.

Commençons avec le droit antique. En droit romain, il est vrai que le iudex tranchait le litige. Il ne tranchait cependant pas celui que les parties avaient présenté, mais bien celui que le praetor avait reformulé.[24] Si on pense à la Common Law après la conquête normande, le juge ne tranche pas, mais pose la question au jury local.[25] Dans ce dernier cas, le juge n'est pas le tiers jugeant, puisqu'il ne décide pas. On sort donc des modes d'ordonnancement purement

---

[22] Voir généralement Lon L. Fuller, *The Principles of Social Order: Selected Essays of Lon L. Fuller,* Portland, Or., Hart, 2001; et Henry M. Hart et Albert M. Sacks, *The Legal Process: Basic Problems in the Making and Application of Law,* nouvelle édition préparée par William N. Eskridge, Jr., et Philip P. Frickey, Westbury, N.Y., Foundation Press, 1994.

[23] Voir Roderick A. Macdonald, "Legislation and Governance" dans Willem J. Witteveen et Wibren van der Burg, dir., *Rediscovering Fuller: Essays on Implicit Law and Institutional Design,* University of Amsterdam Press, Amsterdam, 1999 à la p. 279; Roderick A. Macdonald et Pierre-Olivier Savoie, "Une phénoménologie des modes alternatifs de résolution des conflits: résultat, processus et symbolisme" dans Christoph Eberhardt, dir., *Liber Amicorum Étienne Le Roy,* Paris, Karthala (à paraître, 2005).

[24] H. Patrick Glenn, Legal Traditions of the World, Oxford, Oxford University Press, 2000 aux pp. 118–19.

[25] *Ibid.* aux pp. 206–10.

verticaux: il y a là un élément de médiation lorsque le juge reformule le problème et ses solutions possibles au profit des parties. Dépendamment des circonstances, il peut s'agir d'une médiation plutôt hiérarchique ou verticale, mais le juge agit quand même en dehors du cadre de la décision du tiers.

Continuons avec l'idée classique de la fonction judiciaire. Celle-ci servirait à régler un différend né entre deux ou plusieurs parties,[26] de façon rapide, économique et juste, autant que possible.[27] En l'absence de "controverse actuelle," certains systèmes juridiques ne reconnaissent d'ailleurs pas de droit à l'action en justice, comme le droit fédéral américain.[28] La question théorique a souvent été considérée comme allant à l'encontre de la fonction du juge international.[29] Au-delà de cette fonction primordiale de trancher le litige lorsque les parties ne peuvent s'entendre, le juge doit aussi protéger les parties contre le harcèlement découlant des actions abusives ou sans fondement. Une fonction incidente du rôle du juge et du jugement est aussi de démontrer l'efficacité du droit en encadrant la création et la mise en œuvre du droit. Finalement, les actions civiles donnent l'opportunité aux juges de non seulement remplir leur fonction d'application, mais aussi de clarification, d'interprétation, et de développement du droit, un rôle généralement attribué plus principalement aux cours d'appel.[30] Même si les exigences d'une bonne administration de la justice ne peuvent être directement

---

26 J.A. Jolowicz, "On the Nature and Purpose of Civil Procedural Law" dans *On Civil Procedure*, Cambridge, Cambridge University Press, 2000 aux pp. 59–80.

27 Une littérature plus qu'abondante existe sur l'accès à la justice en droit interne, mais on peut aussi noter certains efforts de la CIJ pour accélérer sa procédure, par exemple dans la réforme de son Règlement.

28 *Maryland Casualty Co. c. Pacific Coal & Oil Co.*, 312 U.S. 271 (1941).

29 L'incompétence d'un tribunal arbitral pour cause que la tâche demandée était l'interprétation théorique d'un traité et non le règlement d'un différend est la conclusion à laquelle en est arrivée la Commission de conciliation italo-britannique établie par le traité de paix de 1947 entre les deux États: *Cases of Dual Nationality* (1954) 14 R.S.A. 27 à la p. 34. À propos du fait que cette position est une vue anachronique de la fonction judiciaire, voir Lon L. Fuller, *The Anatomy of Law*, New York, Praeger, 1968 aux pp. 133–74.

30 En droit international, un des plus grands défenseurs de ce rôle de développement du droit international par le juge fut certainement Hersch Lauterpacht. Voir Gérald Fitzmaurice, "Hersch Lauterpacht — The Scholar as Judge. Part I" (1961), 37 B.Y.B.I.L. 1 aux pp. 14–23 et aussi l'opinion individuelle du juge Lauterpacht dans *Procédure de vote applicable aux questions touchant les rapports et pétitions relatifs au territoire du sud-ouest africain, avis consultatif*, [1955] Rec. CIJ 67 à la p. 91.

transposées du droit interne au droit international,[31] toujours est-il que celles-ci sont assez similaires. C'est ce que démontre le prononcé de la CIJ sur les principes essentiels de l'accès à un tribunal dans la *Demande de réformation du jugement nº 158 du Tribunal Administratif des Nations Unies:*

le droit d'avoir accès à un tribunal indépendant et impartial établi par la loi; le droit d'obtenir une décision de justice dans un délai raisonnable; le droit d'avoir, dans ces conditions raisonnables, la faculté de présenter sa cause au tribunal et de commenter les thèses de l'adversaire; le droit à l'égalité au tribunal et de commenter les thèses de l'adversaire; le droit à l'égalité avec celui-ci dans la procédure; et le droit d'obtenir une décision motivée.[32]

Dans cette vision classique, nous retrouvons l'idée de la décision judiciaire pure où la seule tâche des juges est celle de trancher le différend. Cependant, il s'immisce parfois entre les parties et le juge un acteur qui porterait atteinte à la pureté du principe du contradictoire ainsi qu'à celui de l'égalité des armes. Cet acteur, dont la position va même jusqu'à être assimilée à celle de juge,[33] formule au tribunal ses propres conclusions "impartiales," de fait et/ou de droit, après la clôture des audiences. Il s'agit des institutions de l'avocat-général à la Cour de justice des communautés européennes[34] (CJCE), du commissaire du gouvernement auprès du Conseil d'état français[35] ou des divers ministères publics européens. Même si la Cour européenne des droits de l'Homme (CEDH) a commencé à mettre la hache dans ces vieilles institutions, certaines demeurent

---

31 Voir, par exemple, *Demande de réformation du jugement nº 158 du Tribunal Administratif des Nations Unies, avis consultatif,* [1973] Rec. CIJ 166 à la p. 179, par. 34 (*Demande de réformation du jugement nº 158*).

32 *Ibid.* à la p. 209, par. 92; voir aussi *Demande de réformation du jugement nº 273 du Tribunal Administratif des Nations Unies,* [1982] Rec. CIJ 325 aux pp. 338–40, par. 29–32 (*Demande de réformation du jugement nº 273*).

33 Par exemple, les avocats généraux de la CJCE possèdent les mêmes immunités que les juges. Protocole sur le statut de la Cour de justice, tel que modifié le 19 avril 2004 (JO L 132 du 29.4.2004, pp. 1 et 5, et JO L 194 du 2.6.2004, p. 3 — rectificatif), art. 8.

34 Traité instituant la Communauté européenne, art. 222 (ex-art. 166): "L'avocat général a pour rôle de présenter publiquement, en toute impartialité et en toute indépendance, des conclusions motivées sur les affaires qui, conformément au statut de la Cour de justice, requièrent son intervention."

35 Voir Nicolas Rainaud, *Le commissaire du gouvernement près le Conseil d'État*, Paris, LGDJ, 1996.

et continuent de nous rappeler la pluralité des possibilités de l'organisation et de la fonction judiciaire.[36]

Dans la prochaine section sur l'évolution des avis consultatifs dans le temps, nous verrons comment la fonction judiciaire en droit romain et dans la Common Law était déjà loin d'être statique. Encore aujourd'hui, les juges exercent des fonctions beaucoup plus larges que la décision judiciaire pure, que les théoriciens du droit ont d'ailleurs rejeté comme étant impossible puisque la différence entre la décision judiciaire et la décision managériale en est une de degré et non de nature.[37] Les charges judiciaires, au-delà du rôle d'arbitre de la procédure contradictoire, sont surtout liées à la décision managériale du juge dans son rôle de gestionnaire des cas,[38]

---

[36] Voir Florence Benoît-Rohmer, "Le commissaire du gouvernement auprès du Conseil d'État, l'avocat général auprès de la Cour de justice des Communautés européennes et le droit à un procès équitable: Observations sous l'arrêt *Kress* c. *France* rendu par la Cour européenne des droits de l'homme le 7 juin 2001 (req. nᵒ 39594/98)" (2001) 37 RTD eur. 727. À partir de 1991, la CEDH a commencé à trouver incompatibles avec le droit au procès équitable, garanti par l'art. 6 de la Convention européenne des droits de l'homme, les fonctions d'avocats généraux dans certaines juridictions comme la Cour de cassation belge, la Cour suprême du Portugal, la Hof van Cassatie néerlandaise et la Cour de cassation française. Les deux principes en cause étaient l'égalité des armes et celui du contradictoire, puisque l'avocat général prend position, même si de manière "impartiale," et certaines pièces peuvent être soumises à la Cour sans qu'elles ne puissent être discutées par les parties. Dans son arrêt Kress, la CEDH trouve qu'il n'y a pas d'atteinte au principe de l'égalité des armes puisqu'il existe des moyens de répondre aux conclusions du commissaire du gouvernement du Conseil d'état, par exemple par une note au tribunual. Cependant, la participation du commissaire au délibéré est considérée comme incompatible avec le droit à un procès équitable. La CEDH, dans cet arrêt, a donc reculé devant l'uniformisation de l'organisation judiciaire en ne détruisant pas complètement une institution qui a eu, selon Florence Benoît-Rohmer, "une influence certaine sur la formation de la jurisprudence administrative" parce que les "conclusions [des commissaires du gouvernement] sont bien souvent à l'orgine de grandes innovations jurisprudentielles."

[37] Voir Macdonald et Savoie, "Phénoménologie des modes alternatifs de résolution des conflits," *supra* note 23.

[38] Robert F. Peckham, "The Federal Judge as a Case Manager: The New Role in Guiding a Case from Filing to Disposition" (1981), 68 Cal.L.Rev. 770; - "A Judicial response to the Cost of Litigation: Case Management, Two-Stage Discovery Planning and Alternative Dispute Resolution" (1985), 37 Rutgers L.Rev. 253; Judith Resnik, "Managerial Judges" (1982), 96 Harv.L.Rev. 96 374; D. Elliot, "Managerial Judging and the Evolution of Procedure" (1986), 56 U.Chi.L.Rev. 366; Australian Law Reform Commission, "Issues in Case Management," dans Review of the Federal Justice System (Discussion Paper 62), Sydney, Australian Law Reform Commission, 1999.

rôle que joue la CIJ dans sa fixation des délais et de la procédure,[39] des auditions ou encore relativement à la nomination de chambres. Aux États-Unis, c'est en matière de relations ethniques que la pratique gestionnaire atteint son apogée alors que les tribunaux imposent des plans d'intégration raciale dans les écoles et imposent l'obligation de faire rapport au tribunal sur la mise en œuvre de ces plans.[40] Plus généralement, ce nouveau rôle de gestionnaire découle d'une demande pour une justice plus efficiente, où efficience essaie généralement de rimer avec rapidité. Afin de désengorger les tribunaux étatiques,[41] on a essayé de rediriger les parties ailleurs, parfois en affublant le système judiciaire de nouvelles fonctions telles la médiation.[42] D'ailleurs, les commissions arbitrales du dix-neuvième siècle visant à résoudre les conflits inter-étatiques étaient beaucoup plus des commissions conciliatoires qu'arbitrales au vu du fait qu'il y avait un nombre pair d'"arbitres" représentant également chaque pays. Autant en droit international qu'en droit interne, on se pose des questions sur la compatibilité de ces fonctions autres que la "pure décision" avec le caractère "judiciaire" d'un tribunal. Par exemple, la prolifération d'organes quasi-judiciaires,[43] l'institution de procédures rapides et l'encouragement à user de la médiation pour parvenir à un règlement sont vus par certains comme des formes de justice à rabais avec des garanties procédurales formelles diminuées[44]

---

[39] Un exemple du rôle de la Cour comme gestionnaire est son encadrement de la visite sur le site du barrage Gabcikovo-Nagymaros en 1997 durant le litige entre la Slovakie et la Hongrie. Pour une description détaillée des négociations et du rôle de médiateur de la Cour dans la visite, voir Peter Tomka et Samuel S. Wordsworth, "The First Site Visit of the International Court of Justice in Fulfilment of Its Judicial Function" (1998), 92 AJIL 133.

[40] Voir Nathan Glazer, "The Judiciary and Social Policy" dans L. Theberge, dir., *The Judiciary in a Democratic Society*, Lexington, MA, Lexington Books, 1979 à la p. 67; François Ost, "Juge-pacificateur, juge-arbitre, juge-entraîneur. Trois modèles de justice" dans Philippe Gérard, François Ost et Michel van de Kerchove, dir., *Fonction de juger et pouvoir judiciaire*, Bruxelles, Facultés universitaires Saint-Louis, 1983, 1 aux pp. 47 et s.

[41] Voir généralement Derek C. Bok, "A Flawed System of Law Practice and Training" (1983), 33 J. Legal Ed. 570 et Charles Jarosson, "Les modes alternatifs de règlement des conflits: présentation générale," [1997] RIDC 325.

[42] Voir, par exemple, Louise Otis, "La justice conciliationnelle: l'envers du lent droit" (2001), 3(2) Éthique publique 63.

[43] Comme le comité de révision des demandes de réformation de jugement des tribunaux administratif de l'ONU.

[44] Richard L. Abel, "The Contradictions of Informal Justice" dans Richard L. Abel, dir., *The Politics of Informal Justice*, vol. I, New York, Academic Press, 1982, 267;

où les habitués du système continuent de sortir gagnants plus souvent qu'autrement.[45] On peut opposer à cela la nécessité de procédures nouvelles et différentes qui, même si elles ne sont pas identiques aux procédures traditionnelles, sauront combler de nouveaux besoins adéquatement.[46]

Il n'y a pas de parallélisme parfait entre les problèmes de la fonction judiciaire en droit interne et en droit international. D'abord parce que les juridictions internationales ne sont pas aussi chargées que les juridictions nationales et aussi parce que d'aucuns estiment que le prestige de la CIJ n'est pas suffisamment établi pour trop s'écarter de son rôle premier de trancher les litiges.[47] Quoiqu'il en soit, en examinant la question des avis consultatifs, on pourra quand même constater que ces questions trouveront ci-dessous un écho familier.

L'ÉVOLUTION DES AVIS CONSULTATIFS DANS LE TEMPS

L'argument selon lequel l'avis consultatif entre dans la fonction judiciaire d'un tribunal parce qu'il s'agit d'un acte d'interprétation du droit est techniquement correct. Il obscurcit cependant les sources et raisons d'être de l'avis en droit. L'avis a toujours eu une place plus ou moins grande dans le domaine juridique, même si certaines pratiques anciennes nous paraissent aujourd'hui assez malsaines.

Au temps d'Hadrien, le droit romain avait élevé la *responsa* des jurisconsultes au rang de source directe en lui conférant l'officialité

Owen M. Fiss, "Against Settlement" (1984), 93 Yale L.J. 1073; "Out of Eden" (1985), 94 Yale L.J. 1669; M.J. Bailey, "Unpacking the 'Rational Alternative': A Critical Review of Family Mediation Movement Claims" (1989), 8 Can.J. Fam.L. 61; P.E. Bryan, "Killing Us Softly: Divorce Mediation and the Politics of Power" (1992), 40 Buffalo L.Rev. 441; Harry T. Edwards, "Alternative Dispute Resolution: Panacea or Anathema" (1986), 99 Harv.L.Rev. 668; Laura Nader, "Controlling Processes in the Practice of Law: Hierarchy and Pacification in the Movement to Re-Form Dispute Ideology" (1993), 9 Ohio St.J.Disp.Res. 1.

[45] Marc Galanter, "Why the 'Haves' Come Out Ahead: Speculations on the Limits of Legal Change" (1974), 9 L. & Soc.Rev. 95.

[46] En ce qui concerne le rôle des tribunaux administratifs vis-à-vis celui des cours supérieures au Canada, voir *MacMillan Bloedel c. Simpson*, [1995] 4 R.C.S. 725 (dissidence de L'Heureux-Dubé, McLachlin, Major et Iaccobucci).

[47] Edvard Hambro, "The Authority of the Advisory Opinions of the International Court of Justice" (1954), 3 ICLQ 2 aux pp. 22–23; Grieg, *supra* note 9; Michla Pomerance, "The Advisory Role of the International Court of Justice and Its 'Judicial' Character: Past and Future Prisms" dans A.S. Muller, D. Raic et J.M. Thuranszky, dir., *The International Court of Justice: Its Future Role After Fifty Years*, The Hague, Martinus Nijhoff, 1997 à la p. 271.

requise.[48] On retrouve la *responsa* également dans la tradition talmudique en tant que réponse rabbinique à un problème juridique à propos duquel un différend n'est pas nécessairement né.[49] Ces opinions, d'une grande autorité, sont non seulement indirectement envisagées par la Torah,[50] mais sont même parfois perçues comme une source supérieure aux codes.[51]

C'est surtout la pratique consultative des juges britanniques jusqu'au dix-huitième siècle qui choque notre conception de la fonction judiciaire.[52] Leur position de serviteurs du monarque fait en sorte qu'on ne retrouve pas de séparation entre le pouvoir judiciaire et celui de l'exécutif ou du législatif, une division des branches du gouvernement qui est d'abord apparue dans la constitution américaine à la fin du dix-huitième siècle. En tant que serviteurs du monarque, les juges ne se limitaient pas à juger les litiges, mais agissaient aussi comme conseillers juridiques du roi. Ainsi, il était reconnu que le roi pouvait consulter ses juges sur toute question juridique, qu'il s'agisse d'un projet de loi ou même de l'issue possible d'un procès à venir. Au dix-septième siècle, les Stuart abusèrent grandement de ce pouvoir en Angleterre. Les juges furent utilisés pour valider des hausses d'impôt contre le gré du Parlement et pour justifier la légalité du report pendant plus de dix ans de la réunion de la Chambre des communes.[53] Dans le cas d'un homme condamné pour la rédaction d'un sermon diffamant supposément James 1er, le roi voulu convoquer ensemble tous les juges pour obtenir à l'avance leur opinion sur la possibilité d'obtenir une condamnation. Face à l'opposition du Lord Chief Justice Coke, le roi consulta simplement les juges individuellement. Comme cette pratique de consultation était reconnue par la tradition, Coke ne pouvait qu'opposer, *a posteriori*,

---

[48] Thierry Revet, "Rapport introductif" dans Thierry Revet, dir., *L'inflation des avis en droit*, Paris, Economica, 1998, 1 aux pp. 3–4.

[49] Glenn, *supra* note 24 aux pp. 90–91.

[50] Deut. 17:9: "Si tu as à juger un cas qui te dépasse, affaire de meurtre, contestation ou voie de fait, un litige quelconque dans ta ville, tu partiras et tu monteras au lieu choisi par Yahvé ton Dieu, tu iras trouver les prêtres lévites et le juge alors en fonction. Ils feront enquête et ils te feront connaître la sentence." On a donc là une articulation ancienne des avis consultatifs obligatoires.

[51] M. Elon, *Jewish Law: History, Sources, Principles*, vol. III, trad. B. Auerbach et M. Sykes, Philadelphie/Jérusalem, The Jewish Publication Society, 5754/1994 à la p. 1458.

[52] Pour une excellente analyse de cette pratique et du refus américain de suivre ce précédent, voir Jay, *supra* note 3.

[53] *Ibid.*

l'argument qu'il fut plus approprié que les juges soient consultés ensemble. Cette pratique continua jusqu'au milieu du dix-huitième siècle et finit par disparaître sans vraiment d'explication.[54] Durant cette période, les juges continuèrent à cumuler plusieurs fonctions dans l'administration et certains firent même partie du cabinet, le dernier étant Lord Chief Justice Mansfield à la fin du dix-huitième siècle. La pratique consultative pour les projets de loi de la Chambre des Lords continua jusqu'au début du vingtième siècle[55] et il faut attendre jusqu'en 1977 pour que le comité judiciaire de la Chambre des Lords annonce l'incompatibilité des avis consultatifs avec sa fonction judiciaire.[56]

Aux États-Unis, en 1793, cinq des six juges de la Cour suprême signèrent une courte lettre expliquant au président George Washington pourquoi ils déclinaient d'être consultés de façon extrajudiciaire:

The Lines of Separation drawn by the Constitution between the three Departments of Government — their being in certain Respects checks on each other — and our being Judges of a Court of last Resort — are Considerations which afford strong arguments against the Propriety of extrajudicially deciding the questions alluded to; especially as the Power given by the Constitution to the President of calling on the Heads of Departments for opinions, seems to have been purposely as well as expressly limited to *executive* Departments.[57]

Cet argument basé sur la séparation des pouvoirs est repris dans la jurisprudence fédérale[58] ainsi que dans la doctrine.[59] Même si la constitution américaine ne prohibe pas les avis consultatifs comme tels, on a interprété l'exigence de "case and controversy" à son article

---

54 *Ibid.*

55 Voir Hudson, "Avis consultatifs," *supra* note 5 aux pp. 393–96. Intrinsèquement, ces avis n'étaient pas de nature publique, même si parfois ils étaient rendus disponibles en raison de leur intérêt public, notamment par le Foreign Office dans le cas de l'avis sur la délimitation de la frontière maritime entre l'Irlande et la Grande-Bretagne en 1925.

56 Jay, *supra* note 3. Voir le dernier chapitre.

57 Letter from the Justices of the Supreme Court to President George Washington, Philadelphie, 8 août 1793, reproduite dans *ibid.* aux pp. 179–80.

58 *Muskrat* v. *United States,* 219 U.S. 346 (1910); *Allen* v. *Wright,* 468 U.S. 737 à la p. 750 (1984).

59 Felix Frankfurter, "A Note on Advisory Opinions" (1924), 37 Harv.L.Rev. 1002; Note, "Advisory Opinions on the Constitutionality of Statutes" (1956), 69 Harv.L.Rev. 1302; Lawrence Tribe, *American Constitutional Law,* 2e éd., Mineola, N.Y., Foundation Press, 1988 aux pp. 73–77.

III comme excluant une telle possibilité. La lettre de 1793 n'est pas seulement la source de la prohibition des demandes d'avis, mais aussi de toute une constellation d'autres doctrines qui tombent sous le chapeau de la justiciabilité: "mootness, ripeness, political questions, the doctrine of independent state grounds, the principle that constitutional questions are reached only as a last resort, and its related doctrine favoring a narrow basis for decision."[60] Cependant, prendre au pied de la lettre l'explication de la séparation des pouvoirs pour comprendre les raisons d'une décision qui tient toujours aujourd'hui n'éclaire pas toute l'affaire. Selon Stewart Jay, ce sont plutôt les événements politiques de l'époque qui ont poussé la Cour à écrire une lettre de refus qui était en substance un avis consultatif donnant raison à une faction politique de l'exécutif du président George Washington.[61] C'est ce qui nous mène à réaffirmer la thèse que les arguments alléguant l'incompatibilité de l'avis consultatif avec le caractère judiciaire se basent sur la pratique ancienne britannique et non sur une conception moderne du juge.

À cette époque, les juges de la Cour suprême rendaient souvent des avis privés à l'exécutif américain. Le juge en chef John Jay fut même secrétaire d'État pendant qu'il siégeait à la Cour suprême. D'ailleurs, lorsque John Marshall fut nommé juge en chef en 1804, il demeura secrétaire d'État pendant le premier mois de son mandat à la Cour suprême.

La demande adressée à la Cour suprême en 1793 concernait les obligations internationales des États-Unis en vertu de traités de secours mutuel avec la France. Considérant l'exécution récente de Louis XVI et l'entrée en guerre subséquente de la France avec l'Angleterre et l'Espagne, une dispute naquit entre différentes factions de l'exécutif vis-à-vis des obligations en droit international envers la France. L'exécutif était unanime en faveur de la neutralité, mais on craignait que la France demande aux États-Unis d'entrer en guerre. C'est la réponse à cette possibilité qui différait, en se basant sur des interprétations opposées de Vattel quant à la répudiation des obligations découlant de traités. Alexander Hamilton, qui supportait aussi l'idée que la politique extérieure devait être dictée seulement par l'exécutif, soutenait d'un côté la répudiation pour cause d'un changement de gouvernement rendant les obligations en vertu du traité "dangerous, useless or disagreeable." Thomas Jefferson, qui croyait qu'on devait référer la question au congrès, invoqua le devoir moral

[60] Jay, *supra* note 3 aux pp. 113-48.

[61] Voir généralement *ibid.*

du respect des obligations, ajoutant qu'il était toujours possible de répudier les obligations "ruinous or destructive to society."[62] Il s'agissait donc là d'une bataille à propos du fédéralisme naissant américain, où Jefferson croyait qu'il combattait les forces qui voulaient restaurer un semblant de monarchie. Fraîchement débarqué, le nouvel ambassadeur français affirma que la France ne demanderait pas aux États-Unis d'entrer en guerre. Cependant, il avait déjà armé plus d'une douzaine de navires américains privés en leur donnant des mandats du gouvernement français pour aborder et piller les navires "ennemis" britanniques et espagnols. La tolérance de ces actes pouvait mettre les États-Unis *de facto* en guerre et l'ambassadeur britannique faisait de fortes pressions contre l'administration américaine pour que cessent les prises. C'est dans ce contexte que l'avis sur les obligations des États-Unis en droit international fut demandé et refusé. La lettre conclut en s'excusant de devoir ainsi répondre, mais aussi en se consolant à propos de la capacité décisionnelle du président: "your Judgement will discern what is Right, and that your Usual Prudence, Decision and Firmness will surmount every obstacle to the Preservation of the Rights, Peace, and Dignity of the United States."[63] Il s'agit donc là d'un avis consultatif comme tel qui prévoit que c'est à l'exécutif de décider, ce qui permit à l'opinion de Hamilton d'avoir le dessus. De plus, l'avis consultatif n'exclut pas du tout l'idée que d'autres avis consultatifs ne soient rendus dans le futur, contrairement à l'interprétation qui en a été donnée par la suite. Par exemple, quelques années plus tard alors qu'il était gouverneur de l'État de New York, l'ancien juge en chef John Jay, qui signa la lettre du 8 août 1793, demanda un avis consultatif à la Cour suprême de son État. Tout en mettant l'emphase sur l'importance de la séparation des pouvoirs dans sa demande, il ne voyait clairement pas d'incompatibilité absolue entre les deux choses.

Aujourd'hui, la pratique consultative existe encore aux États-Unis dans nombre d'états où le pouvoir est établi de façon statutaire.[64] Cela reflète autant la pratique américaine d'avant 1793 que celle

---

[62] *Ibid.* aux pp. 122–23.

[63] Letter from the Justices of the Supreme Court, *supra* note 57.

[64] Hudson, "Avis consultatifs," *supra* note 5; Hudson, "Advisory Opinions," *supra* note 5; Note, "Advisory Opinions on the Constitutionality of Statutes" (1956), 69 Harv.L.Rev. 1302 à la p. 1313; Edsall, "The Advisory Opinion in North Carolina" (1949), 27 N.C.L.Rev. 297; Field, "The Advisory Opinion – An Analysis" (1949), 24 Ind.L.J. 203; Clovis & Updegraff, "Advisory Opinions" (1928), 13 Iowa L.Rev. 188; Note, "Judicial Determinations in Nonadversary Proceedings" (1959), 72 Harv.L.Rev. 723; Hugo Dubuque, "The Duty of Judges as Constitutional Advisers"

d'après, excepté au niveau fédéral. Au-delà des États-Unis, en 1925 Hudson a examiné en détail le Royaume-Uni, le Canada (et les provinces), l'Autriche, la Colombie, le Costa-Rica, la Tchécoslovaquie, la Finlande, le Honduras, l'Irak, le Nicaragua, le Panama, le Salvador, la Suède, la Norvège et la Bulgarie.[65] En 1971, Keith mentionnait aussi la Libye, l'Inde, la Birmanie, l'Algérie, le Cameroun, la République centrafricaine, le Congo Brazzaville et le Dahomey.[66] On peut aussi ajouter la France où le Conseil constitutionnel rend l'équivalent d'avis consultatifs en procédant à un contrôle de constitutionnalité "obligatoire," dans le cas de lois organiques,[67] ou "facultatif," relativement aux lois ordinaires[68] et aux engagements internationaux non-ratifiés de la France.[69] Dans l'Hexagone, l'avis est aussi envisagé relativement à l'extradition.[70] Pour Hudson, l'idée derrière la liste était d'établir un principe général de droit international afin de justifier la pratique, surtout face à l'opposition des juristes américains. Il semble cependant que le seul principe général que l'on puisse vraiment tirer de cette analyse est que l'octroi statutaire de la fonction consultative n'est pas considéré comme allant à l'encontre du caractère judiciaire d'un tribunal.

Outre le système de droit fédéral américain, il existe d'autres systèmes où les cours ne rendent pas d'avis consultatifs. En Australie, la High Court a jugé qu'une telle tâche se situe à l'extérieur de la fonction judiciaire.[71] La Cour constitutionnelle allemande a brièvement possédé le pouvoir statutaire de rendre des avis consultatifs

---

24 Am.L.Rev. 369; F.W. Grinnell, "Duty of the Court to Give Advisory Opinions" 2 Mass.L.Q. 542.

65 Hudson, "Avis consultatifs," *supra* note 5 aux pp. 393 et s.; M.O. Hudson, "The Second Year of the Permanent Court of International Justice" (1924), 18 AJIL 1 aux pp. 25–29.

66 Keith, *supra* note 5 à la p. 16, n. 18.

67 Constitution française, art. 61(1). Voir Bernard Mathieu et Michel Verpeaux, *Droit constitutionnel*, Paris, Presses universitaires de France, 2004 aux pp. 593 et s.; Francis Hamon et Michel Troper, *Droit constitutionnel*, 28e éd., Paris, LGDJ aux pp. 759 et s.

68 Constitution française, art. 61(2).

69 *Ibid.* art. 54.

70 Revet, *supra* note 48 aux pp. 142 et 173. Selon les articles 14–16 de la loi du 10/03/1927, le ministère public peut demander à la chambre d'accusation de la cour d'appel un avis concernant l'extradition. En cas d'avis défavorable à l'extradition, le gouvernement est lié. En cas d'avis favorable, le gouvernement ne l'est pas.

71 *Re Judiciary and Navigation Act* (1921), 29 C.L.R. 257.

après la seconde guerre mondiale. On le lui a retiré en 1955 après que, par souci de cohérence, elle ait commencé à appliquer les prononcés de ses avis comme obligatoires dans les litiges réels subséquents, ce que certains ont vu comme portant atteinte au droit des parties à ce qu'on ne préjuge pas de leur différend.[72] Au Royaume-Uni, Lord Diplock écrivait en 1977 à propos de la Chambre des Lords que "the jurisdiction of the court is not to declare the law generally or to give advisory opinions; it is confined to declaring contested legal rights, subsisting or future, of the parties represented in the litigation before it and not those of anyone else."[73] C'est là un changement dans la pratique britannique où les avis étaient initialement ancrés dans la tradition puis dans la législation.[74]

En droit international, outre l'article 96 de la Charte des Nations Unies qui confère à la CIJ une fonction consultative, la pratique est très répandue. Parmi les autres juridictions qui possèdent la compétence consultative, on peut noter la Cour interaméricaine des droits de l'homme,[75] le Tribunal du Droit de la Mer,[76]

---

[72] H.G. Schermers et Denis Waelbroeck, *Judicial Protection in the European Communities*, 4ᵉ éd., Deventer, Kluwer, 1976 au par. 661; Robert Kovar, "La compétence consultative de la Cour de justice et la procédure de conclusion des accords internationaux par la communauté économique européenne" dans *Mélanges offerts à Paul Reuter: Le droit international: unité et diversité*, Paris, Pedone, 1981, 357.

[73] *Gouriet* v. *Union of Post Office Workers*, 3 W.L.R., [1977] 300, 332 (H.L. 1977) (C.A.).

[74] Loi pour l'amélioration de l'administration de la Justice dans le Privy Council de Sa Majesté, William IV, c. 41, art. IV (1833).

[75] Convention américaine relative aux des droits de l'homme, 22 novembre 1969, entrée en vigueur le 18 juillet 1978, R.T. O.E.A., nᵒ 36, 1, art. 64: "1. Les États membres de l'Organisation pourront consulter la Cour à propos de l'interprétation de la présente Convention ou de tout autre traité concernant la protection des droits de l'homme dans les États américains. De même les organes énumérés au Chapitre X de la Charte de l'Organisation des États Américains, réformée par le Protocole de Buenos Aires, pourront consulter la Cour au sujet de questions relevant de leur compétence particulière. 2. Sur la demande de tout État membre de l'Organisation, la Cour pourra émettre un avis sur la compatibilité de l'une quelconque des lois dudit État avec les instruments internationaux précités." Voir Jo M. Pasqualucci, *The Practice and Procedure of the Inter-American Court of Human Rights*, Cambridge, Cambridge University Press, 2003, en particulier la partie I, "The Advisory Jurisdiction of the Inter-American Court" aux pp. 27–80 (Pasqualucci, *The Practice and Procedure of the Inter-American Court*).

[76] Convention des Nations Unies de 1982 sur le droit de la mer, 10 octobre 1982, 21 I.L.M. 1261, art. 181: "La Chambre pour le règlement des différends relatifs aux fonds marins donne des avis consultatifs, à la demande de l'Assemblée ou du Conseil, sur les questions juridiques qui se posent dans le cadre de leur activité. Ces avis sont donnés dans les plus brefs délais." Celle-ci n'a encore jamais rendu d'avis consultatif.

la CEDH,[77] la CJCE[78] et la future Cour de Justice de l'Union Africaine.[79]

Avant d'examiner plus en détail les avantages et les inconvénients de la procédure consultative, il est nécessaire de s'arrêter pour essayer de la décrire dans la multiplicité de ses formes. D'abord, la fonction est aujourd'hui statutaire puisque celle émanant de la tradition en Common Law a été abolie ou été substituée par un fondement législatif. La législation spécifiera *qui* (compétence *ratione personae*) peut demander l'avis et *à quel sujet* (compétence *ratione materiae*).

Selon l'article 96 de la Charte, l'Assemblée générale, le Conseil de sécurité et l'Assemblée générale ainsi que certains organes spécialisés des Nations Unies peuvent demander des avis consultatifs.[80] Les

---

77 Convention européenne des droits de l'homme, 4 novembre 1950, 213 R.T.N.U. 222, art. 47: "(1)La Cour peut, à la demande du Comité des Ministres, donner des avis consultatifs sur des questions juridiques concernant l'interprétation de la Convention et de ses Protocoles. (2) Ces avis ne peuvent porter ni sur les questions ayant trait au contenu ou à l'étendue des droits et libertés définis au titre I de la Convention et dans les Protocoles ni sur les autres questions dont la Cour ou le Comité des Ministres pourraient avoir à connaître par suite de l'introduction d'un recours prévu par la Convention. (3) La décision du Comité des Ministres de demander un avis à la Cour est prise par un vote à la majorité des représentants ayant le droit de siéger au Comité." Voir Andrew Drzemczewski, "Advisory Jurisdiction of the European Human Rights Court: A Procedure Worth Retaining?" dans *The Modern World of Human Rights: Essays in Honour of Thomas Buergenthal*, San José, Costa Rica, Inter-American Institute of Human Rights, 1996, 493 à la p. 493.

78 Voir Schermers et Waelbroeck, *supra* note 72; Kovar, *supra* note 72; Rachid Kheitmi, "La fonction consultative de la Cour de Justice des Communautés Européennes" (1967), 3 R.T. dr. Eur. 553.

79 Protocole de la Cour de Justice de l'Union Africaine, Maputo, 10–12 juillet, 2003 (non en vigueur), en ligne: <http://www.africa-union.org>, art. 44(1): "La Cour peut donner un avis consultatif sur toute question juridique, à la demande de la Conférence, du Parlement, du Conseil exécutif, du Conseil de Paix et de Sécurité, du Conseil économique, social et culturel (ECOSOCC), des institutions financières ou de tout autre organe de l'Union autorisé par la Conférence."

80 Certaines propositions ont été faites à l'effet de permettre au secrétaire-général de pouvoir demander des avis. Voir Stephen Schwebel, "Authorizing the Secretary-General of the United Nations to request Advisory Opinions of the International Court of Justice" (1984), 78 AJIL 869. L'American Bar Association s'est aussi prononcé en faveur d'une fonction consultative élargie où la CIJ recevrait des demandes des cours suprêmes nationales concernnant le droit international: American Bar Association, Summary of the House of Delegates, 1982 Midyear Meeting 12 (Chicago, 1982), tel que cité dans Louis B. Sohn, "Broadening the Advisory Jurisdiction of the International Court of Justice" 77 (1983), AJIL 124

deux principaux organes politiques peuvent demander un avis sur "toute question juridique"[81] alors que les organes spécialisés le peuvent sur "des questions juridiques qui se poseraient dans le cadre de leur activité."[82] La CPJI quant à elle pouvait être saisie par le Conseil ou l'Assemblée de la SdN sur "tout différend ou tout point."[83]

La Cour interaméricaine est probablement la juridiction internationale avec la compétence consultative *ratione personae* la plus étendue.[84] Tous les États membres de l'OEA, même ceux qui n'ont pas ratifié la Convention interaméricaine des droits de l'homme, ainsi qu'un très grand nombre de ses organes peuvent demander un avis.[85] La Cour interaméricaine n'a cependant pas la compétence pour rendre des avis consultatifs de son propre chef, même si certains estiment que ce serait une compétence idéale, à tout le moins dans le contexte de l'évaluation de la compatibilité des réserves avec la Convention interaméricaine des droits de l'homme.[86]

La CEDH possède probablement la compétence consultative la plus restreinte. On peut même se demander s'il est possible de

---

à la p. 126. Depuis que le niveau d'occupation de la Cour a repris de la vigueur, ces demandes se font beaucoup moins audibles: James Crawford, "The International Court of Justice, Judicial Administration and the Rule of Law" dans J.P. Gardner et Chanaka Wickeremasinghe *et al.*, *The International Court of Justice: Process, Practice and Procedure,* London, British Institute of International and Comparative Law, 1997, 112 à la p. 113.

[81] Charte, art. 96(1).

[82] *Ibid.* art. 96(2).

[83] Pacte de la Société des Nations, art. 14.

[84] Pasqualucci, *The Practice and Procedure of the Inter-American Court, supra* note 75 à la p. 80.

[85] Selon le c. VIII de la Charte de l'OEA (et non plus le c. X depuis le Protocole de 1985 de Cartagena de Indias): l'Assemblée générale; la Réunion de consultation des ministres des relations extérieures; les Conseils; le Comité juridique interaméricain; la Commission interaméricaine des droits de l'homme; le Secrétariat général; les conférences spécialisées, et les organismes spécialisés.

[86] Andrés E. Montalvo, "Reservations to the American Convention on Human Rights: A New Approach" (2001), 16 Am. U. Int'l L.Rev. 269 à la p. 271; contra *Reports of the Inter-American Commission on Human Rights (Art. 51 American Convention on Human Rights) (1997),* Avis consultatif OC-15/97, Inter-Am. Ct. H.R.(Sér. A) no 15, Opinion de M. le juge Cançado Trindade au par. 37. De plus, on peut noter qu'initialement le projet de la Cour de Justice de l'Union Africaine contenait une disposition (art. 4(1)) permettant à tout organe de l'OUA de demander un avis, ce qui aurait clairement inclus la Cour. Ce projet semble avoir été abandonné. Voir Pasqualucci, *supra* note 75 à la p. 37, n. 54, mais comparer avec le présent Protocole de la Cour de Justice de l'Union Africaine, *supra* note 79.

formuler une question à laquelle la CEDH acceptera de répondre. Il faut qu'il s'agisse de "questions juridiques concernant l'interprétation de la Convention et de ses Protocoles," mais celles-ci "ne peuvent porter ni sur les questions ayant trait au contenu ou à l'étendue des droits et libertés définis au titre I de la Convention et dans les Protocoles ni sur les autres questions dont la Cour ou le Comité des Ministres pourraient avoir à connaître par suite de l'introduction d'un recours prévu par la Convention."[87] En juin 2004, la CEDH a refusé de rendre ce qui aurait été son premier avis parce que celui-ci aurait pu trancher à l'avance des questions risquant d'être soulevées dans le futur.[88]

La compétence de la CJCE pour statuer à titre préjudiciel sur des questions de droit européen à la demande de cours nationales peut certainement être assimilée à l'idée d'avis consultatif.[89] Elle peut aussi être qualifiée de succès: "Almost all the major principles established by the ECJ were decided in the context of a reference

---

[87] Convention européenne des droits de l'Homme, *supra* note 77, art. 47. Voir Drzemczewski *supra* note 77.

[88] Voir Communiqué de presse du Greffe, "Première décision sur la compétence de la Cour pour rendre un avis consultatif," 2 juin 2004, en ligne: <http://www. echr.coe.int/Fr/Press/2004/juin/D%C3%A9cisionsurledemande d'avisconsultatif.htm>. Le Comité des ministres du Conseil de l'Europe avait demandé à la Cour de l'éclairer à savoir si la Commission des droits de l'Homme de la Communauté des États Indépendants (formée d'anciennes républiques soviétiques) était "une autre instance internationale d'enquête ou de règlement" au sens de l'art. 35(2)(b) de la Convention européenne des Droits de l'Homme. Une réponse positive aurait rendu irrecevable devant la CEDH les requêtes essentiellement similaires ayant été précédemment examinées par la Commission des droits de l'Homme de la CEI. La Cour s'est trouvée incompétente parce qu'au moins un État signataire de la Convention européenne des droits de l'Homme avait également ratifié la Convention des droits de l'Homme et des Libertés Fondamentales de la CEI. C'est en raison de la "faiblesse" de la protection des droits de l'homme dans la CEI que la demande avait été faite, avec l'espérance que la CEDH allait exclure la commission de la CEI de la portée de l'art. 35(2)(b).

[89] Version consolidée du traité instituant la communauté européenne, Journal officiel n° C 325 du 24 décembre 2002, en ligne: <http://europa.eu.int>, art. 234(1) (ex-art. 177): "La Cour de justice est compétente pour statuer, à titre préjudiciel: a) sur l'interprétation du présent traité; b) sur la validité et l'interprétation des actes pris par les institutions de la Communauté et par la BCE; c) sur l'interprétation des statuts des organismes créés par un acte du Conseil, lorsque ces statuts le prévoient." Voir aussi Paul Craig et Gráinne de Búrca, *EU Law: Text, Cases, and Materials*, 2ᵉ éd., Oxford, Oxford University Press, 1998 aux pp. 406 et s.; Josephine Steiner, Lorna Woods et Christian Twigg-Flesner, *Textbook on EC Law*, 8ᵉ éd., Oxford, Oxford University Press, 2003 aux pp. 544 et s.

to that Court for a preliminary ruling under article 234."[90] Lorsque qu'une cour nationale est confrontée à une question de droit européen qui n'est pas claire, elle *peut*[91] ou *doit*,[92] dépendamment de la question soulevée, saisir la Cour de justice avant de pouvoir rendre jugement. Il faut aussi mentionner que le traité entre l'Union européenne et les membres de l'Association européenne de libre-échange (Norvège, Liechtenstein et Islande), qui soumet ces derniers à certaines règles du marché européen, octroie au tribunal national le *pouvoir*, mais non le *devoir* de soumettre des questions de droit européen à l'intention de la Cour de l'AELE.[93] L'idée, qui en est une visant l'uniformisation, est similaire à la proposition de l'American Bar Association de permettre aux cours suprêmes nationales de demander un avis consultatif à la CIJ sur des questions de droit international.[94] Dans les deux cas, le succès de la procédure — à tout le moins lorsqu'elle n'est pas obligatoire — dépend de la confiance des juridictions nationales envers l'organe

---

[90] Steiner *et al., ibid.* à la p. 544. Voir aussi G.F. Mancini et D.T. Keeling, "From CILIFT to ERT: the Constitutional Challenge Facing the European Court" (1991), 11 Y.B.E.L. 1 aux pp. 2–3: "In the doctrines of direct effect and supremacy are ... the 'twin pillars of the Community's legal system,' the reference procedure laid down in Article 177 [now Article 234] must surely be the keystone in the edifice; without it the roof would collapse and the two pillars would be left as a desolate ruin, evocative of the temple at Cape Sounion — beautiful but not of much practical utility."

[91] Traité instituant la communauté européenne, *supra* note 89 à l'art. 234(2): "Lorsqu'une telle question est soulevée devant une juridiction d'un des États membres, cette juridiction peut, si elle estime qu'une décision sur ce point est nécessaire pour rendre son jugement, demander à la Cour de justice de statuer sur cette question."

[92] *Ibid.* art. 234(3): "Lorsqu'une telle question est soulevée dans une affaire pendante devant une juridiction nationale dont les décisions ne sont pas susceptibles d'un recours juridictionnel de droit interne, cette juridiction est tenue de saisir la Cour de justice."

[93] Agreement between the EFTA States on the Establishment of a Surveillance Authority and a Court of Justice (ESA/Court Agreement) (main part), 2 mai 1992, en ligne: <http://www.eftacourt.lu/esacourtagreement.asp>, art. 34: "The EFTA Court shall have jurisdiction to give advisory opinions on the interpretation of the EEA Agreement. Where such a question is raised before any court or tribunal in an EFTA State, that court or tribunal may, if it considers it necessary to enable it to give judgment, request the EFTA Court to give such an opinion. An EFTA State may in its internal legislation limit the right to request such an advisory opinion to courts and tribunals against whose decisions there is no judicial remedy under national law."

[94] Voir *supra* note 80.

international. Au surplus, ce type de procédure permet non seulement le développement du droit, mais aussi un certain accès indirect des personnes physiques ou morales à des institutions dont la saisine leur est généralement difficile ou impossible.[95]

Selon l'article 53(1) de la *Loi sur la Cour suprême du Canada*,[96] c'est le gouverneur en conseil qui peut saisir la Cour à propos de "toute question importante de droit ou de fait touchant a) l'interprétation des lois constitutionnelles, b) la constitutionnalité ou l'interprétation d'un texte législatif fédéral ou provincial ... [et] d) les pouvoirs du Parlement canadien ou des législatures des provinces, ou de leurs gouvernements respectifs, indépendamment de leur exercice passé, présent ou futur" ou "toute autre question importante de droit ou de fait touchant toute autre matière, que celle-ci soit ou non, selon la Cour, du même ordre que les matières énumérées au paragraphe (1)."[97] Chacune des provinces canadiennes permet à son lieutenant-gouverneur en conseil de saisir sa Cour d'appel provinciale à propos de questions similaires.[98] C'est donc l'organe politique désigné (exécutif du gouvernement ou encore l'assemblé ou le conseil d'une organisation internationale) qui peut saisir une cour de justice à propos de questions permises par la loi habilitante. En droit interne, il doit généralement s'agir de questions "importantes."[99]

Quant au Conseil constitutionnel français, dans le cadre de son examen "facultatif" des lois ordinaires ou des obligations internationales de la France,[100] il peut être saisi à la demande du président de la République, du Premier ministre, des présidents des assemblées ou encore d'un certain nombre de parlementaires (soixante

---

[95] Le renvoi préjudiciel à la CJCE a permis à des personnes de contester indirectement des normes européennes par la voie de l'art. 234 alors que la voie de saisine normale par la voie de l'art. 230 est très difficile. Voir Craig et de Búrca, *supra* note 89 à la p. 407.

[96] *Loi sur la Cour suprême du Canada*, L.R.C. 1985, c. S-26.

[97] *Ibid.* art. 53(2).

[98] Par exemple, pour le Québec, voir Loi sur les renvois à la Cour d'appel, L.R.Q., c. R-23, art. 1: "Le Gouvernement peut soumettre à la Cour d'appel, pour audition et examen, toute question quelconque qu'il juge à propos, et, sur ce, la Cour les entend et les examine."

[99] En plus de la *Loi sur la Cour suprême*, voir aussi celle ayant octroyé la compétence consultative à la Cour suprême du Massachusetts ainsi que les autres états américains mentionnés dans Hudson, "Advisory Opinions," *supra* note 5.

[100] Voir *supra* notes 67–70.

députés *ou* soixante sénateurs).[101] La dernière possibilité donne la chance à l'opposition de saisir le Conseil, établissant ainsi un élargissement significatif de la procédure.

La rédaction de la loi peut également octroyer une discrétion à l'organe juridictionnel de donner ou non l'avis. C'est le cas de l'article 65 du Statut de la Cour qui établit que la CIJ "peut" donner des avis consultatifs.[102] C'est là un contraste avec l'obligation de juger connue dans certains systèmes.[103] Que la loi octroie ou non la discrétion explicite, le tribunal prendra généralement le soin d'examiner les objections à ce que celui-ci rende l'avis en raison d'une possible atteinte à son caractère judiciaire.[104]

LES AVANTAGES ET INCONVÉNIENTS DE LA PROCÉDURE CONSULTATIVE

Les avantages (1) et inconvénients (2) inhérents à l'avis consultatif se présentent comme une évaluation nécessaire afin d'ensuite

101 Constitution française, art. 61(2); Voir Association française des constitutionnalistes, *Vingt ans de saisine parlementaire du Conseil constitutionnel*, Aix-en-Provence — Paris, Economica — Presses de l'université Aix-Marseille, 1995.

102 Dans sa jurisprudence, la Cour a toujours affirmé, quoique avec un peu plus de vigueur depuis 1962, que ce libellé lui octroyait la discrétion de répondre ou non. Voir aussi Philippe Sands et Pierre Klein, *Bowett's Law of International Institutions*, 5ᵉ éd., Londres, Sweet & Maxwell, 2001 à la p. 364; Abdul G. Koroma, "Assertion of Jurisdiction by the International Court of Justice" dans Patrick Capps, Malcolm Evans and Stratos Konstadinidis, dir., *Asserting Jurisdiction: International and European Legal Perspectives*, Oxford, Hart Publishing, 2003, 189 à la p. 198; Hans Kelsen, *The Law of the United Nations*, New York, Frederick A. Praeger/London Institute of World Affairs, 1950 à la p 549; A.P. Fachiri, *The Permanent Court of International Justice*, Oxford/Londres, 1932 à la p. 80; Pratap, *supra* note 5 aux pp. 142 et s.; Grieg, *supra* note 9 aux pp. 332–33 et 339; M. Sibert, *Traité de droit international public*, t. II, Paris, 1951 à la p. 542; L. Delbez, *Les principes généraux du contentieux international*, Paris, 1962 à la p. 78.

103 Voir Code civil du Bas-Canada, art. 11: "Le juge ne peut refuser de juger sous prétexte du silence, de l'obscurité ou de l'insuffisance de la loi"; et Code Civil Japonais de 1875 (Loi du 8 juin 1875 sur l'administration de la justice et les sources du droit privé, "Décret Dajokwan nº 103 du 8 juin VIIIe année de Meiji"), art. 3: "Dans les affaires civiles, à défaut de loi écrite, on doit juger selon les coutumes, à défaut de coutumes, par la recherche de la raison et de l'équité."

104 C'est le cas de toute la jurisprudence consultative de la CIJ. Dans certains cas la Cour examine d'office les questions de compétence et de recevabilité même si elles ne sont pas soulevées par les parties comme dans *Applicabilité de l'obligation d'arbitrage en vertu de la section 21 de l'accord du 26 juin 1947 relatif au siège de l'Organisation des Nations Unies*, avis consultatif 26 avril 1988, [1988] CIJ Rec.12 [*Applicabilité de l'obligation d'arbitrage*]. En droit national, voir *Renvoi sur la sécession du Québec*, [1998] 2 R.C.S. 217 (*Renvoi sur la sécession*).

pouvoir les appliquer à la jurisprudence et à la pratique de la CIJ en la matière. La comparaison avec le droit interne peut être un point de départ utile même si les avantages et inconvénients varient entre le droit interne et le droit international parce que les sujets de droit diffèrent et aussi parce que la structure organisationnelle est différente de la structure gouvernementale traditionnelle.[105] Les critiques par rapport à la juridiction consultative dans les deux univers juridiques tendent d'ailleurs à se dissiper en raison d'une tendance importante dans les deux systèmes: l'assimilation de la procédure contentieuse dans les demandes d'avis consultatif (3). En partant des constats de cette section, nous analyserons ensuite la pratique de la CIJ dans la partie suivante de ce texte.

Les avantages de la procédure consultative

Les possibilités spécifiques découlent évidemment de la créativité des rédacteurs de la disposition qui octroie la compétence consultative. À un niveau plus général, l'avantage principal des avis consultatifs en droit interne est de permettre de vérifier la constitutionalité d'une loi,[106] en particulier lorsque plusieurs tribunaux inférieurs sont saisis d'une contestation similaire.[107] Cela permet d'éviter des années d'incertitudes juridiques en attendant que les cas fassent leur chemin jusqu'à la cour d'appel de dernière instance.[108] L'absence d'avis consultatifs aux États-Unis fait en sorte que certaines personnes agiraient en se fiant à des lois qui éventuellement pourront être jugées inconstitutionnelles. Une utilisation judicieuse des avis consultatifs pourrait permettre d'éviter cette

---

[105] Hermann Mosler, "Political and Justiciable Legal Disputes: Revival of an Old Controversy?" dans Bin Cheng et D.E. Brown, dir., *Contemporary Problems of International Law: Essays in Honour of Georg Schwarzenberger*, 1988 aux pp. 228–29.

[106] Note, "Advisory Opinions on the Constitutionality of Statutes" (1956), 69 Harv.L.Rev. 1302 à la p. 1304, n. 11.

[107] Au Canada, le gouvernement fédéral a récemment saisi la Cour suprême d'un renvoi sur un projet de loi sur le mariage homosexuel compte tenu du fait que les cours d'appel de plusieurs provinces venaient d'invalider la définition fédérale du mariage qui se limite à l'union entre un homme et une femme. Pour une typologie plus spécifique des différentes utilités de l'avis consultatif devant la Cour suprême du Canada, voir François Chevrette et Grégoire Charles N. Webber, "L'utilisation de la procédure d'avis consultatif devant la Cour suprême du Canada : Essai de typologie" (2003) 82 R.B. Can. 757.

[108] Peter Hogg, *Constitutional Law of Canada*, Loose-leaf ed., Toronto, Carswell, 2003 à la p. 8–19.

fâcheuse conséquence tout en préservant les sauvegardes du système adversatif.[109] La procédure consultative permet également d'obtenir des réponses sur l'interprétation de la loi en l'absence du droit d'agir en justice, en l'absence d'un litige né ou lorsqu'une question n'est simplement pas justiciable, par exemple dans ce dernier cas à savoir s'il est constitutionnel pour les sénateurs américains de voter par procuration.[110] Les avis permettent aussi de développer le droit, une considération à ne pas négliger en droit international. La Cour interaméricaine des droits l'homme a probablement connu ses plus grands moments grâce à ses prononcés consultatifs qui ont su éclaircir beaucoup de questions importantes[111] comme ses prononcés sur la place des réserves dans le système de la Convention interaméricaine,[112] l'universalité des droits de l'homme,[113] la nécessité de la démocratie pour protéger les droits de l'homme[114] ou encore *habeas corpus* comme une garantie judiciaire ne pouvant être suspendue.[115] Dans sa décision relativement à la compatibilité de la Cour pénale internationale avec la constitution française, le Conseil constitutionnel s'est d'ailleurs permis de préciser les conditions mettant en jeu la responsabilité internationale d'un chef d'État.[116] Au Québec, l'avis de la Cour d'appel sur les

---

[109] Note, "Advisory Opinions on the Constitutionality of Statutes" (1956), 69 Harv.L.Rev. 1302 à la p. 1313.

[110] *Ibid.* à la p. 1305, n. 18.

[111] Jo M. Pasqualucci, "Advisory Practice of the Inter-American Court of Human Rights: Contributing to the Evolution of International Human Rights Law" (2002) 38 Stan. Int'l L.J. 241; A.H. Robertson et J.G. Merrills, *Human Rights in the World*, 4ᵉ éd., Manchester, Manchester University Press, 1996 aux pp. 218–26; Thomas Buergenthal, "The advisory practice of the Inter-American Court of Human Rights" (1985) 79 AJIL 1; Drzemczewski, *supra* note 77; Mary Caroline Parker, ""Other Treaties": The Inter-American Court of Human Rights Defines its Jurisdiction" (1983) 33 Am. U. L.Rev. 211.

[112] *The Effect of Reservations on the Entry into Force of the American Convention on Human Rights (art. 74 et 75) (1986)*, Avis consultatif OC-7–86, Inter-Am. Ct. H.R. (sér. A), nᵒ 7.

[113] *The Effect of Reservations on the Entry into Force of the American Convention on Human Rights (1982)*, Avis consultatif OC-1/82, Inter-Am. Ct. H.R. (sér. A) nᵒ 2 au par. 40.

[114] *The Word 'Laws' in Article 30 of the Inter-American Convention on Human Rights (1986)*, Avis consultatif OC-6/86, Inter-Am. Ct. H.R. (sér. A) nᵒ 6 aux par. 27, 32, 38.

[115] *Habeas Corpus in Emergency Situations (art. 27(2), 25(1) et 7(6) American Convention on Human Rights) (1987)*, Avis consultatif OC-8/87, Inter-Am. Ct. H.R. (sér. A) nᵒ 8 au par. 11.

[116] Décision du 25 janvier 1999.

amendements au système de justice pénal pour les adolescents[117] porte entre autres sur la valeur normative des déclarations de l'Assemblée générale de l'ONU et des travaux préparatoires de conventions,[118] sur la signification de la primauté de l'intérêt de l'enfant dans le Pacte des droits civils et politiques et la Convention relative aux droits de l'enfant,[119] ainsi que sur la compatibilité de peines pour adultes à des mineurs et de l'incarcération d'adolescents dans des pénitentiers pour adultes au regard de ces deux traités.[120] On retrouve tous ces avantages à divers degrés dans la pratique consultative de la CIJ.

Les inconvénients de la procédure consultative

L'inconvénient principal de la pratique consultative est que le caractère adversatif et concret d'une vraie controverse serait absent, ce qui nuirait au caractère judiciaire de la décision qui gagne à être éclairée par un débat contradictoire. Par exemple, cela peut créer des problèmes dans la recherche des faits, surtout si dans le cas d'un litige pendant, l'une des parties est en possession d'informations essentielles permettant d'évaluer ses prétentions.[121] Deuxièmement, la pratique consultative porterait atteinte au caractère judiciaire ou même au prestige d'une cour puisqu'il s'agit d'une fonction généralement entreprise par l'exécutif, le procureur général en particulier.[122] Ce ne serait pas à un organe judiciaire de

---

117 *Renvoi relatif au projet de loi C-7 sur le système de justice pénale pour les adolescents,* [2003] J.Q. nº 2850 (C.A.Q.) (*Renvoi relatif au projet de loi C-7*).

118 *Ibid.* aux par. 99–100: au vu des "droits fondamentaux souverains" des États, "tant les travaux préliminaires à la rédaction, signature et ratification d'une convention internationale que les analyses subséquentes de l'application de cette convention par les États signataires n'ont donc aucun effet contraignant, même sur le plan international."

119 *Ibid.* au par. 133. Même si la Convention indique que l'intérêt supérieur de l'enfant doit être une "considération primordiale" (art. 3(1)), il est possible d'avoir d'autres visées, comme la protection du public.

120 *Ibid.* aux par. 159–74 et 182–91.

121 L'absence de faits suffisants pour décider d'une question est l'une des catégories de cas pour lesquelles la Cour suprême du Canada refuse de se prononcer: *McEvoy* c. *Procureur général du Nouveau-Brunswick,* [1983] 1 R.C.S. 704; *Reference re Waters and Water-Powers,* [1929] R.C.S. 200; *Renvoi relatif à la taxe sur les produits et services,* [1992] 2 R.C.S. 445; *Renvoi sur la rémunération des juges de la Cour provinciale de l'Île du Prince Édouard,* [1997] 3 R.C.S. 3 (Renvoi sur la rémunération des juges).

122 Hogg, *supra* note 108 aux pp. 8–15 et 8–16.

donner une simple opinion juridique. Ce qui soulève le problème subséquent de l'incertitude de la valeur de l'avis. Est-il obligatoire ou non? Après avoir réaffirmé la constitutionnalité de la *Loi sur la Cour suprême du Canada* à propos des avis consultatifs, le Conseil Privé a ajouté qu'il ne s'agissait cependant pas d'une fonction judiciaire et que celle-ci n'avait aucun caractère décisionnel: "the answers are only advisory and will have no more effect than the opinions of law officers."[123] Même si selon la lettre de la loi les avis consultatifs ne devraient pas peser autant que les jugements[124] et n'auraient qu'une "force morale" malgré leur "autorité,"[125] il en va autrement en pratique autant dans les juridictions nationales[126] qu'internationales.[127] Cette absence de force de loi formelle peut aussi mener certaines parties ayant un intérêt dans l'affaire à boycotter la procédure afin de délégitimer l'avis.[128] D'aucuns estiment cependant que l'autorité des avis consultatifs, qui doit être conservée à tout prix pour maintenir le prestige d'un organe juridictionnel, surtout en droit international où ceux-ci sont plus vulnérables,

---

123 *A.-G. Ont.* v. *A.-G. Can. (Reference Appeal)*, [1912] A.C. 571; réaffirmé dans le *Renvoi sur la sécession, supra* note 104 au par. 30.

124 *Interprétation des traités de paix conclus avec la Bulgarie, la Hongrie et la Roumanie,* première phase, avis consultatif du 30 mars 1950, [1950] CIJ Rec. 65 à la p. 71 (*Interprétation des traités de paix*): "La réponse de la Cour n'a qu'un caractère consultatif: comme telle, elle ne saurait avoir d'effet obligatoire." Voir aussi Manley O. Hudson, *The P.C.I.J., 1920–1942,* New York, Macmillan, 1943 à la p. 512, selon qui l'opinion de la cour n'a qu'une valeur morale.

125 Nguyen Quoc Dinh, *Droit international Public,* 9e éd., par Alain Pellet et Patrick Daillier, Paris, LGDJ, 2002.

126 Hogg, *supra* note 108 à la p. 8–17.

127 Jean Salmon, "Quels sont les destinataires des avis" dans Laurence Boisson de Charzounes et Philippe Sands, dir., *International Law, the International Court of Justice and Nuclear Weapons,* Cambridge, Cambridge University Press, 1999, 28 à la p. 31; Jean Salmon, "L'autorité des prononcés," *supra* note 16; Hambro, *supra* note 47 aux pp. 21–22. Ce qui en dérange certains: Grieg, *supra* note 9. Pour l'opinion que ces avis sont obligatoires, voir de Bustamente, *La Cour permanente de Justice internationale,* Paris, 1925 à la p. 256; Démètre Negulesco et Gérard Geouffre de Lapradelle (1928), 34 Annuaire de l'institut du droit international aux pp. 409 et s., 441; de Visscher, "Les avis consultatifs" *supra* note 9 aux pp. 25, 27; de Visscher, *Aspects récents, supra* note 17.

128 Le gouvernement du Québec a refusé de participer aux procédures relatives au *Renvoi sur la sécession, supra* note 103. Le gouvernement d'Israël a refusé d'aborder le fonds dans l'avis sur le mur. On peut aussi noter le refus de l'U.R.S.S. de participer d'une façon ou d'une autre dans l'*Affaire de la Carélie, supra* note 4.

est sapée par les dissidences.[129] La Cour suprême du Canada, contrairement à la CIJ, a réussi à rendre des opinions unanimes dans
les avis les plus politiquement chargés qu'on lui a soumis: ces avis
sont signés "La Cour." Contrairement à la Cour suprême des États-
Unis ou au Tribunal constitutionnel allemand, les décisions du
Conseil constitutionnel français ne sont jamais accompagnées d'opinions dissidentes ou concurrentes, parce que dans les "pays latins"
l'attention portée aux divisions au sein de la Cour est perçue comme
portant atteinte à "l'autorité de la justice."[130] D'autres inconvénients
sont que les questions "politiques" n'entreraient pas dans la compétence d'un tribunal habilité à donner un avis consultatif soit sur
"toute question *juridique*" ou sur toute question de "droit ou de
fait." Cette objection à la compétence est généralement rejetée
puisque, selon la juridiction, il est toujours[131] ou généralement[132]
possible d'évaluer en termes juridiques une question politique.
Notons que dans son récent avis sur les amendements au système
de justice pénal pour les adolescents, la Cour d'appel du Québec a
accepté de se prononcer sur la compatibilité de ceux-ci avec la Convention relative au droit de l'enfant et le Pacte des droits civils et
politiques, même si une telle analyse n'avait que des conséquences
morales ou politiques.[133] De plus, une situation de grande tension

129 Manley O. Hudson, "The 28th Year of the World Court" (1950), 44 AJIL 1 aux
pp. 20–21 où l'auteur déplore le langage qui critique trop vertement la position de la majorité; Hambro, *supra* note 47 aux pp. 20–22.

130 Francis Hamon et Michel Troper, *Droit constitutionnel*, 28e éd., Paris, LGDJ, 2003
aux pp. 764–65. Cette "dépersonnalisation" de l'organe juridictionnel est reflétée dans le fait qu'on ne connaît le nom des conseillers d'état qui ont participé aux délibérations "objectives" seulement depuis juin 1995.

131 *Licéité de la menace ou de l'emploi d'armes nucléaires*, Avis consultatif, [1996] Rec.
CIJ 226 (*Licéité de la menace ou de l'emploi d'armes nucléaires*).

132 *Renvoi sur la sécession*, *supra* note 104 à la p. 237. Cependant, pour une question
non juridique, voir *Re Can. Assistance Plan*, [1991] 2. S.C.R. 525 à la p. 545.

133 *Renvoi relatif au projet de loi C-7*, *supra* note 116 au par. 115. La Cour justifie
néanmoins sa décision en évoquant l'hypothèse d'une contestation constitutionnelle subséquente de la loi. Son prononcé sur la compatibilité de la loi avec
le droit international pourrait ainsi être pertinent à savoir si une violation de la
Charte peut être justifiée parce qu'elle demeure dans des "limites qui soient
raisonnables et dont la justification puisse se démontrer dans le cadre d'une
société libre et démocratique" au sens de l'article un de la Charte. Contra, voir
la décision de la CEDH sur ce qui aurait été son premier avis consultatif, *supra*
note 88, et à propos de la défunte compétence consultative de la Cour constitutionnelle allemande, *supra* note 72.

politique peut justement bénéficier d'un éclairage juridique.[134] Un autre inconvénient, qui est aussi un argument visant à forcer un tribunal à décliner de rendre l'avis, est que celui-ci serait inutile et nuirait même à la résolution du problème. Dans le *Renvoi relatif au mariage de personnes de même sexe,* la Cour suprême du Canada a refusé de répondre à une des questions parce qu'une réponse judiciaire avait le potentiel de créer de la confusion alors que le gouvernement fédéral et diverses législatures provinciales étaient déjà sur la voie de l'harmonisation en cette matière.[135] Devant la CIJ, l'argument est surtout valable dans le cadre de l'ONU où différentes majorités institutionnelles peuvent avoir des vues très différentes sur la façon de résoudre un conflit. C'est le cas sur bien des points entre la majorité de l'Assemblée générale et les membres permanents du Conseil de sécurité. Ce à quoi la CIJ a toujours répondu qu'en principe les avis ne doivent pas être refusés parce qu'ils constituent une contribution de l'organe judiciaire principal au fonctionnement de l'organisation.[136] De plus, il ne reviendrait pas à la CIJ d'établir la raison ou l'utilité de l'avis tant que la demande entre dans son champ de compétence. La Cour a toujours évité le rôle d'arbitre entre la majorité de l'Assemblée générale et les membres permanents du Conseil de sécurité.

La difficulté de répondre à des questions ambiguës, qui a poussé la Cour suprême du Canada à décliner de rendre certains avis,[137] est un autre problème. Cette difficulté a simplement poussé la CIJ à réécrire les questions,[138] malgré le fait qu'elle avait déjà énoncé qu'il fallait s'en tenir au strict libellé de la question.[139]

---

134 *Interprétation de l'accord du 25 mars 1951 entre l'OMS et l'Égypte,* Avis consultatif, [1980] Rec. CIJ 73 à la p. 87, par. 33 (*Interprétation de l'accord du 25 mars 1951*).

135 Voir *Renvoi relatif au mariage entre personnes de même sexe,* 2004 CSC 79 aux par. 65–66 et 69–70.

136 *Interprétation des traités de paix, supra* note 123 à la p. 71.

137 *Reference re Education System in Island of Montreal,* [1926] R.C.S. 246; *Renvoi: Compétence du Parlement relativement à la Chambre haute,* [1980] 1 R.C.S. 54; *Renvoi sur la rémunération des juges, supra* note 121.

138 *Licéité de la menace ou de l'emploi d'armes nucléaires, supra* note 131 au par. 20; *Demande de réformation du jugement no 273, supra* note 32 aux pp. 348–49, par. 46–47; *Interprétation de l'accord du 25 mars 1951, supra* note 134 à la p. 88, par. 35: "pour rester fidèle aux exigences de son caractère judiciaire dans l'exercice de sa compétence consultative, la Cour doit rechercher quelles sont véritablement les questions juridiques que soulèvent les demandes formulées dans une requête."

139 *Demande de réformation du jugement no 158, supra* note 31 à la p. 184, par. 41: "lorsqu'elle rend son avis, la Cour est en principe liée par le libellé des questions formulées dans la requête."

De plus, la particulière et maintenant défunte formule de réformation des jugements des tribunaux administratifs de l'ONU et de l'OIT[140] a soulevé d'importantes questions ayant trait à l'inégalité des parties en raison du fait que les fonctionnaires de l'ONU se prévalant d'une demande de réformation, ou contre qui le secrétaire général ou un État s'en prévalaient, n'avaient pas le droit d'ester devant la Cour.[141]

Un tribunal peut aussi être aux prises avec une question consultative qui ne s'est pas matérialisée[142] ou qui est devenue sans objet,[143] ce qui a poussé la Cour suprême du Canada, par exemple, à refuser de rendre certains avis.

Finalement, le fait qu'une question soit théorique ou abstraite serait un inconvénient portant atteinte à la fonction d'un tribunal qui est de régler les différends[144] et pourrait préjuger des droits des justiciables dans des litiges à venir. Dans le contexte d'un système juridique contractualiste comme le droit international, ces considérations seraient encore plus valables.[145]

Cette liste d'inconvénients peut paraître longue. Même si on a toujours répondu à ces objections de façon assez convaincante, ces arguments continuent d'être soulevés, surtout devant la CIJ. L'assimilation de la procédure contentieuse au processus consultatif semble jouer un rôle important afin d'éliminer la plupart de ces inconvénients.

---

[140] Voir généralement Kaiyan Homi Kaikobad, *The International Court of Justice and judicial review: a study of the court's powers with respect to judgments of the ILO and UN administrative tribunals*, La Haye, Kluwer, 2000; Charles N. Brower and Pieter H.F. Bekker, "Understanding 'Binding' Advisory Opinions of the International Court of Justice" dans Nisuke Ando, Edward McWhinney et Rüdiger Wolfrum, dir., *Liber Amicorum Judge Shigeru Oda*, La Haye, Kluwer, 2002 à la p. 351.

[141] *Demande de réformation du jugement no 273, supra* note 32; *Demande de réformation du jugement no 158, supra* note 31.

[142] *A.-G. Ont.* v. *A.-G. Can. (Local Prohibition)*, [1896] A.C. 348 à la p. 370. Voir par contre le *Renvoi sur la sécession, supra* note 103.

[143] *Re Objection by Quebec to Resolution to Amend the Constitution*, [1982] 2. S.C.R. 793 à la p. 806.

[144] *Licéité de la menace ou de l'emploi d'armes nucléaires, supra* note 131, Opinion dissidente de M. le juge Oda.

[145] V.S. Vereschetin, "Is 'Deceptive Clarity' better than 'Apparent Indecision' in Advisory Opinions" dans Emile Yakpo et Tahar Boumedra, *Liber Amicorum Judge Mohammed Bedjaoui*, La Haye, Kluwer, 1999 à la p. 531.

L'assimilation des procédures consultatives et contentieuses

Il n'est pas nouveau qu'on examine la pratique consultative selon son assimilation de la procédure contentieuse.[146] D'ailleurs, le Statut et le Règlement de la CIJ prévoient que la Cour sera guidée par les principes applicables de la procédure contentieuse.[147] Cela permet d'obtenir un réel débat contradictoire lorsque toutes les parties intéressées acceptent de participer.[148] De plus, la CIJ, la Cour suprême du Canada et la Cour interaméricaine possèdent tous des mécanismes pour faire participer les parties intéressées qui n'ont pas le droit d'ester comme tel. Ainsi la CIJ peut donner la permission de participer à la procédure consultative aux États,[149] organisations internationales[150] ou même à des entités au statut incertain comme la Palestine.[151] La pratique et maintenant les règles de procédure[152] de la Cour interaméricaine permettent à des O.N.G. et même à des particuliers de soumettre des observations écrites dans

---

146 Démètre Negulesco, "L'Évolution de la Procédure des Avis consultatifs de la Cour permanente de justice internationale" (1936), 57 RCADI 5. Voir aussi Mario Prost et Julien Fouret, "Du rôle de la Cour internationale de Justice: peau neuve ou peau de chagrin?" (2003), 16–2 R.Q.D.I. 191.

147 Statut de la Cour internationale de justice, art. 68 (Statut); Règlement de la Cour internationale de justice, art. 102–103 (Règlement).

148 Cela a toujours été le cas, excepté dans deux instances: l'avis sur l'interprétation des traités entre la Finlande et la Russie relativement dans l'*Affaire de la Carélie, supra* note 4, où l'U.R.S.S. a complètement refusé de participer (1923) et l'avis sur le mur où Israël a refusé de participer sur le fond (2004).

149 Dans les avis concernant l'ensemble de la communauté internationale, la Cour donne généralement le droit d'ester à tous les États membres des Nations Unies ainsi qu'aux États non-membres qui sont parties au Statut de la Cour. Dans les avis concernant une organisation internationale spécialisée, ce sont les États membres de l'organisation qui ont généralement le droit d'ester.

150 Si elles ne sont pas invitées, celles-ci peuvent demander la permission de soumettre des observations écrites et de participer à la procédure orale en vertu de l'art. 66(2) du Statut de la Cour. Voir Geneviève Guyomar, *Commentaire sur le Règlement de la Cour internationale de Justice*, Paris, Pédone, 1973 à la p. 458; Shabtai Rosenne, *The Law and Practice of the International Court*, 1920–1996, Vol. IV, La Haye, Martinus Nijhoff, 1997 aux pp. 1728–33.

151 *Conséquences juridiques de l'édification d'un mur dans le territoire palestinien occupé*, ordonnance du 19 décembre 2003 au par. 4, en ligne: <http://www.icj-cij.org>.

152 2001 Rules of Procedure of the Inter-American Court of Human Rights, art. 63(3): "The President may invite or authorize any interested party to submit a written opinion on the issues covered by the request. If the request is governed by Article 64(2) of the Convention, he may do so after prior consultation with the Agent."

le cadre d'avis consultatifs.[153] En plus de mécanismes similaires, la *Loi sur la Cour suprême du Canada* permet aussi de nommer un type d'*amicus curiae*[154] particulier afin de représenter une partie intéressée qui refuse de participer. Face à un tel refus, la CIJ est prise au dépourvu. L'institution du juge *ad hoc,* maintenant transposée à l'avis consultatif,[155] qui doit assurer que soient représentées les vues d'un État dont les droits sont en jeu,[156] n'est d'aucun recours si cette partie boycotte la procédure, comme dans le cas de l'avis sur les *Conséquences juridiques de l'édification d'un mur.* Il pourrait donc être utile de songer à la possibilité d'*amicus curiae* dans les avis consultatifs de la CIJ lorsqu'un État ayant un intérêt refuse de se présenter. L'*amicus* soulèverait assurément des exceptions préliminaires, mais en toute intelligence il traiterait assurément du fond aussi, ce qu'Israël n'a pas fait dans le plus récent avis de la Cour. Certains États objecteront assurément que quelqu'un d'autre ne peut parler en leur nom. Mais ce serait là méconnaître la flexibilité inhérente des avis consultatifs dans leur procédure qui, même si elle se rapproche de la procédure contentieuse, demeure différente, se rapprochant de la consultation de par l'ouverture des tribunaux à l'opinion de divers acteurs ayant un intérêt dans l'affaire. On pourrait aussi penser à nommer d'office un juge *ad hoc,* mais l'*amicus curiae* semble plus primordial, puisqu'il est nécessaire de soulever les arguments dans un premier temps, si on veut qu'ils soient considérés.

La plupart des inconvénients associés à la procédure consultative sont d'ailleurs inhérents à la tâche de trancher un litige en disant ou en créant le droit. La question du caractère politique est

---

[153] Voir Pasqualucci, *supra* note 75 aux pp. 74–75. Dans l'avis consultatif *Right to Information on Consular Assitance (1999),* Avis consultatif OC-16/99, Inter-Am. Ct. H.R. (sér. A) no 16, la Cour a reçu un mémoire d'un citoyen mexicain dans le couloir de la mort en Ohio qui alléguait ne pas avoir reçu d'assistance consulaire. Dans *The Enforceability of the Right to Reply or Correction (1986),* Avis consultatif OC-7/86, Inter-Am. Ct. H.R. (sér. A) no 7, dix médias ou organisations pour la défense des intérêts des médias ont soumis des opinions à la Cour.

[154] Loi sur la Cour suprême, *supra* note 75, art. 53(7): "La Cour a le pouvoir discrétionnaire de commettre d'office un avocat, en l'absence de toute autre représentation, relativement à un intérêt auquel il est porté atteinte." Elle s'en est prévalu dans la *Renvoi sur la sécession, supra* note 103.

[155] Règlement, art. 102–103.

[156] Nicolas Valticos, "Pratique et éthique d'un juge ad hoc à la Cour internationale de justice" dans Nisuke Ando, Edward McWhinney et Rüdiger Wolfrum, dir., *Liber Amicorum Judge Shigeru Oda,* La Haye, Kluwer, 2002 à la p. 107.

l'équivalent de savoir si un litige est justiciable ou non, une considération dont les tribunaux doivent toujours tenir compte. L'inégalité entre les parties est un problème inhérent[157] même si son degré est variable. La question de l'obligatoriété de l'avis peut sembler différente, mais autant en droit interne qu'en droit international on peut faire face au refus de se conformer à un jugement[158] comme on peut trouver des cas où les parties acceptent comme obligatoire le résultat d'un avis consultatif. La difficulté de pouvoir établir certains faits en l'absence de la coopération d'un État ou d'une partie est un problème particulièrement difficile, mais qui semble pouvoir être résolu la plupart du temps.[159] L'absence de consentement est une raison qui continue d'être invoquée et qui vaut seulement pour le droit international. Nous l'aborderons dans la section qui suit pour conclure que les États doivent s'adapter à une communauté internationale où le consentement des États à l'acte juridictionnel s'effrite pour le mieux.

En conclusion, il n'y aurait aucune raison de considérer l'avis consultatif comme n'étant pas une fonction judiciaire utile et légitime si quelques conditions de base sont remplies: les jugements doivent être rendus par la Cour et non par les juges à titre individuel, les procédures doivent être publiques et accessibles aux intéressés, la décision doit être bien publicisée et cette décision devrait être motivée.[160] Ainsi, l'avis consultatif semble, à bien des égards, pouvoir être assimilé à une décision judiciaire.

La nécessité et l'utilité de la fonction consultative de la CIJ

Il semble que les avis consultatifs de la CIJ sont aussi nécessaires qu'utiles, même s'il peut y avoir certaines limites à leur utilité, limites qui sont engendrées surtout par les limites de la fonction judiciaire elle-même. Les avis sont nécessaires pour deux raisons (A).

---

[157] Galanter, *supra* note 45.

[158] Voir James Brown Scott, "The Legal Nature of International Law" (1907), 1 AJIL 831 à la p. 831; Colter Paulson, "Compliance with Final Judgments of the International Court of Justice since 1987" (2004) 98 AJIL 434.

[159] C'est seulement dans l'*Affaire de Carélie, supra* note 4, que la CPJI a estimé qu'il manquait des informations essentielles. Dans l'avis sur le Sahara occidental et l'avis sur la Namibie, la Cour a estimé qu'elle avait reçu suffisamment d'information pour pouvoir se prononcer. Dans l'avis sur le Mur, la Cour a également estimé qu'il y avait suffisamment d'information.

[160] Hudson, "Advisory Opinions," *supra* note 5 à la p. 1000.

D'abord, la restriction au droit d'ester devant la Cour aux seuls États[161] empêcherait l'organe judiciaire principal des Nations Unies de résoudre un nombre important de problèmes qui surgissent à l'intérieur de ses champs d'action, mais qui ne concernent pas nécessairement des litiges entre seuls États (1). Ensuite, la nécessité du consentement des États à la procédure contentieuse met un frein à la fonction judiciaire qui est de trancher un litige lorsque la négociation achoppe ou s'éternise (2). Dans un deuxième temps, en ce qui concerne leur utilité (B), les avis qui en principe sont destinés seulement à l'organisation demanderesse, ont servi à faire progresser la société internationale à plusieurs titres. Nous aborderons spécifiquement le développement du droit des organisations et le contrôle des leurs actes (1), le développement du droit international en général (2), ainsi que les limites des avis rendus par la CIJ (3).

LEUR NÉCESSITÉ

Sans les avis consultatifs, l'organe judiciaire principal des Nations Unies ne serait qu'un tribunal arbitral permanent. Cette possibilité existe déjà en l'institution voisine de la CIJ à La Haye: la Cour permanente d'arbitrage. À l'origine, l'objectif de la CPJI était d'institutionnaliser le règlement des différents entre États en encourageant ceux-ci à accepter une juridiction permanente. Cette approche a toujours connu des résultats quelque peu mitigés. Même si le nombre de déclarations acceptant la compétence de la Cour est aujourd'hui relativement élevé avec soixante-trois,[162] les acceptations ne sont pas nécessairement pour l'ensemble du droit international[163] et la plupart des États acceptent la compétence de la Cour seulement vis-à-vis des États qui acceptent les mêmes obligations qu'eux. De plus, on a vu par le passé des clauses d'acceptation où les États se réservaient le pouvoir de déterminer si le litige était principalement lié à leur intérêt national, ce qui aurait eu pour effet d'exclure la compétence de la Cour.[164] Aussi, certains

---

[161] Statut, art. 34.

[162] En date du 31 juillet 2002: Greffe de la Cour internationale de Justice, *Annuaire 2001–2002*, La Haye, CIJ, 2002 à la p. 124 (Annuaire 2001–2002). Depuis 1951, treize États qui avaient accepté la compétence de la Cour l'ont retiré: Afrique du Sud, Bolivie, Brésil, Chine, Colombie, El Salvador, États-Unis d'Amérique, France, Guatemala, Iran, Israël, Thaïlande et Turquie.

[163] Statut, art. 36(2).

[164] Telle était la Déclaration américaine examinée dans *Activités militaires et paramilitaires au Nicaragua et contre celui-ci* (*Nicaragua c. États-Unis d'Amérique*), compétence et recevabilité, arrêt, [1984] CIJ Rec. 392.

États modifient parfois leurs déclarations pour éviter que certains litiges soient portés devant la Cour. Dans l'affaire de *l'Estai,* l'Espagne cherchait réparation pour l'arrestation en eaux internationales d'un de ses chalutiers que le Canada accusait de surpêche. La Cour s'est toutefois trouvée incompétente en raison de la réserve canadienne du 10 mai 1994 qui exclut de la compétence de la Cour les mesures de gestion et de conservation adoptées par le Canada pour les navires pêchant dans la zone de réglementation de l'Organisation des pêches de l'Atlantique Nord-Ouest.[165] On peut aussi noter le cas de l'Australie, qui veut éviter que le Timor oriental ne puisse saisir la Cour de leur différend à propos de la délimitation de la mer territoriale et de la zone économique exclusive entre les deux États.[166] En même temps, le problème de la personnalité juridique internationale attribuée initialement seulement aux États empêcherait d'autres sujets comme les organisations internationales, les organisations non-gouvernementales, les entités *sui generis* comme la Palestine et les individus de pouvoir faire valoir leurs intérêts quand ceux des États sont en jeu. Dans une certaine mesure, la pratique consultative de la Cour a su manœuvrer autour de certains de ces écueils classiques d'un droit international contractualiste.

Du droit d'ester devant la cour

Il y a trois façons par lesquelles l'avis consultatif peut aider à "contourner" le fait que seuls les États peuvent ester devant la Cour. D'abord, l'Assemblée générale ou le Conseil de sécurité peuvent s'enquérir sur "toute question juridique."[167] Deuxièmement, les organes spécialisés peuvent être autorisés par l'Assemblée générale

---

165 *Compétence en matière des pêcheries* (*Espagne* c. *Canada*), arrêt du 4 décembre 1998, CIJ Rec. 432 aux par. 54 et 56: "les États peuvent formuler des réserves excluant la compétence de la Cour pour des motifs divers; il arrive qu'ils le fassent, précisément, parce que la conformité au droit de leur position ou de leur politique est perçue comme étant aléatoire ... Que les États acceptent ou non la juridiction de la Cour, ils demeurent en tout état de cause responsables des actes portant atteinte aux droits d'autres États qui leur seraient imputables. Tout différend à cet égard doit être réglé par des moyens pacifiques dont le choix est laissé aux parties conformément à l'article 33 de la Charte."

166 Déclaration du ministre australien des affaires étrangères, Alexander John Gosse Downer, 22 mars 2002, reproduite dans *Annuaire 2001–2002, supra* note 162 à la p. 125.

167 Charte, art. 96(1). On peut noter que tous ces avis ont été demandés par l'Assemblé générale, à l'exception de celui de 1971, qui a été demandé par le Conseil de sécurité. Les avis de ce type sont les suivants: *Certaines dépenses des Nations Unies (art. 17, par. 2 de la Charte),* avis consultatif 20 juillet 1962, [1962] CIJ Rec.151

à obtenir un avis "sur des questions juridiques qui se poseraient dans le cadre de leur activité."[168] Troisièmement, plusieurs conventions ou chartes d'organisations prévoient la possibilité de demander un avis consultatif — parfois qualifié d'obligatoire — à la CIJ.[169] Malgré leur droit de demander des avis, les organisations internationales n'ont toujours pas le droit d'ester devant la Cour. La permission de soumettre des exposés écrits et de participer à la

---

(*Certaines dépenses des Nations Unies*); *Compétence de l'Assemblée générale pour l'admission d'un État aux Nations Unies*, avis consultatif 3 mars, [1950] Rec. CIJ 4; *Conditions de l'admission d'un État comme membre des Nations Unies (art. 4 de la Charte)*, avis consultatif 28 mai 1948, [1948] Rec. CIJ 57; *Conséquences juridiques pour les états, supra* note 15; *Conséquences juridiques de l'édification d'un mur, supra* note 1; *Interprétation des traités de paix, supra* note 124; *Interprétation des traités de paix conclus avec la Bulgarie, la Hongrie et la Roumanie, deuxième phase*, avis consultatif 18 juillet 1950, [1950] CIJ Rec. 221; *Licéité de la menace ou de l'emploi d'armes nucléaires, supra* note 130; *Procédure de vote applicable aux questions touchant les rapports et pétitions relatifs au territoire du sud-ouest africain*, avis consultatif 7 juin, [1955] Rec. CIJ 67 (*Procédure de vote applicable*); *Réparation des dommages subis au service des Nations Unies*, avis consultatif 11 avril 1949, [1949] CIJ Rec.174; *Réserves à la convention pour la prévention et la répression du crime de génocide*, avis consultatif 28 mai 1951, [1951] CIJ Rec. 15; *Sahara occidental*, avis consultatif 16 octobre 1975, [1975] CIJ Rec. 12; *Statut international du sud-ouest africain*, avis consultatif 11 juillet, [1950] Rec. CIJ 128.

168 Charte, art. 96(2). Les avis de ce type sont les suivants: *Applicabilité de la section 22 de l'article VI de la convention sur les privilèges et immunités des Nations Unies*, avis consultatif du 15 décembre 1989, [1989] CIJ Rec.177; *Licéité de l'utilisation des armes nucléaires par un État dans un conflit armé*, avis consultatif du 8 juillet 1996, [1996] CIJ Rec 66; *Différend relatif à l'immunité de juridiction d'un rapporteur spécial de la Commission des droits de l'homme*, avis consultatif, 29 avril 1999, [1999] CIJ Rec. 62.

169 Règlement, art. 103 et 104 qui font référence à un "organe ou une institution" "autorisé à demander un avis" "conformément à ses dispositions" (103) et au "plus haut fonctionnaire de l'organe ou institution autorisé à demander l'avis" (en plus de la référence au secrétaire général des Nations Unies) (104). Les avis de ce type sont les suivants: *Applicabilité de l'obligation d'arbitrage, supra* note 103; *Composition du comité de la sécurité maritime de l'organisation intergouvernementale consultative de la navigation maritime*, avis consultatif 8 juin 1960, [1960] CIJ Rec. 150 (*Composition du comité de la sécurité maritime*); *Demande de réformation du jugement n° 158, supra* note 31; *Demande de réformation du jugement n° 273, supra* note 32; *Demande de réformation du jugement n° 333 du Tribunal administratif des Nations Unies*, avis consultatif 27 mai 1987, [1987] CIJ Rec. 18 (*Demande de réformation du jugement n° 333*); *Effet de jugements du Tribunal administratif des Nations Unies*, Avis consultatif du 13 juillet 1954, [1954] CIJ Rec. 47; *Interprétation de l'accord du 25 mars 1951, supra* note 133; *Jugements du Tribunal administratif de l'OIT sur requêtes contre l'UNESCO*, avis consultatif du 23 octobre 1956, [1956] CIJ Rec. 77.

procédure orale doit être accordée chaque fois par la Cour. Cette permission peut être accordée d'office sans que les organisations n'aient à la demander[170] ou encore la Cour peut statuer sur la demande formelle d'une organisation de participer.[171] La Cour donne la permission de "participer" et n'utilise pas le mot "ester" vis-à-vis des organisations internationales. Le critère qu'utilise la Cour est qu'une organisation doit être "susceptible de fournir des renseignements."[172] Cependant, les décisions en ce sens ne sont pas raisonnées et on ne peut qu'accumuler les précédents sans pouvoir se baser sur une justification permettant de comprendre l'action. En octroyant les droits de "participation," la Cour agit là en s'inspirant de sa procédure contentieuse,[173] puisqu'il n'existe pas de dispositions spécifiques sur la participation des organisations internationales dans le cadre des avis consultatifs. Dans la pratique, la Cour agit de façon pragmatique afin d'assurer que les intérêts en jeu puissent être débattus. Lorsqu'il s'agit d'un avis consultatif concernant une organisation internationale spécifique, celle-ci est toujours invitée à soumettre des renseignements, qu'il s'agisse du Secrétaire-général de l'ONU ou encore du conseiller juridique d'une organisation spécialisée. Dans le cas de questions concernant la communauté internationale dans son ensemble, la Cour a démontré une certaine ouverture à entendre des acteurs autres que les États ou encore le conseiller juridique du secrétaire général, quoique cette pratique manque de constance. En 1954, la Fédération des associations de fonctionnaires internationaux n'a pas été trouvée susceptible de fournir des renseignements dans l'affaire relative à l'*Effet de jugements du Tribunal administratif des Nations Unies*.[174] En 1962, dans l'affaire relative au *Statut international du sud-ouest africain*, la Cour a accepté de "recevoir des conclusions de droit," mais pas d'exposé des faits, de la part de la Ligue internationale des Droits de l'Homme, qui ne s'est finalement pas prévalue de l'autorisation.[175] En 1971, le Greffe avait d'abord refusé la participation de l'Organisation de l'Unité africaine sur la question de la Namibie, mais la Cour a ensuite permis que ses vues soient

---

[170] Statut, art. 66(2); Règlement, art. 69(1).

[171] Statut, art. 66(3); Règlement, art. 69(2).

[172] Statut, art. 66(2).

[173] Statut, art. 68; Règlement, art. 102.

[174] Guyomar, *supra* note 150 à la p. 358.

[175] *Annuaire 1962–1963*, La Haye, CIJ, 1963. Guyomar, *ibid.*

plaidées par le Nigeria.[176] En 2004, la Palestine s'est vue octroyer d'office le droit de participer à toute la procédure consultative dans l'avis sur les *Conséquences de l'édification d'un mur.*[177] Dans la même procédure, l'Organisation de la conférence islamique[178] et la Ligue des États Arabes ont également obtenu la permission de participer après en avoir fait la demande.[179] Dans *Conséquences juridiques de l'édification d'un mur,* c'était la première fois qu'une entité autre qu'une organisation internationale obtenait le droit de "fournir des renseignements"[180] et donc de participer de façon pleine et entière à une procédure consultative devant la Cour. On pourrait qualifier cette ordonnance d'exceptionnelle, puisque la situation de la Palestine, un État à naître, est particulière, sinon unique. La présence de la mission permanente de la Palestine à l'ONU depuis près de trente ans a sûrement milité en sa faveur. La permission octroyée par la Cour à une organisation non gouvernementale de participer à un titre ou à un autre n'a jamais été répétée depuis 1962. Il pourrait être utile que la Cour s'aventure encore sur cette voie dans le futur, comme l'a fait la Cour interaméricaine.[181]

Ces possibilités n'aident pas les quelque 2 000 personnes qui contactent la Cour annuellement pour déposer une requête contre un État[182] et qui se font réciter l'article 34 du Statut par le Greffe de la Cour. Le problème de la participation des personnes physiques a été soulevé de façon particulière dans le cas de réformation des jugements de tribunaux administratifs des Nations Unies et de l'OIT. En réaffirmant la position que les individus ne peuvent ester devant la Cour, celle-ci s'est trouvée face au problème de l'inégalité des parties parce que les fonctionnaires des Nations Unies en cause ne pouvaient directement transmettre leurs vues à la Cour. La

---

176 *Conséquences juridiques pour les états, supra* note 15.

177 *Conséquences juridiques de l'édification d'un mur,* ordonnance du 19 décembre 2003, *supra* note 150 au par. 4.

178 *Conséquences juridiques de l'édification d'un mur dans le territoire palestinien occupé,* ordonnance du 22 janvier 2004, communiqué de presse 2004/02, en ligne: <http://www.icj-cij.org>.

179 *Conséquences juridiques de l'édification d'un mur dans le territoire palestinien occupé,* ordonnance du 15 janvier 2004, communiqué de presse 2004/01, en ligne: <http://www.icj-cij.org>.

180 C'est le terme généralement utilisé par la Cour. Celui de "conclusions de droit" est exceptionnel.

181 Voir *supra* notes 152 et 153.

182 *Annuaire 2001–2002,* surpra note 162 à la p. 324.

pratique permet au secrétaire général de l'ONU — qui est la partie adverse aux intérêts du fonctionnaire — de représenter ses propres vues. Les États, qui ont parfois un intérêt dans ces affaires, y ont aussi droit. Pour pallier à cet important problème, la Cour n'a pas tenu de procédure orale à trois reprises. Elle s'en est tenu à la procédure écrite seulement parce que les représentants du fonctionnaire n'auraient pu plaider leur cause.[183] Vu que le secrétaire général de l'ONU avait toujours convenu de transmettre par écrit les vues du fonctionnaire, la Cour a estimé que l'inégalité des parties n'était pas un obstacle insurmontable à l'accomplissement de sa fonction judiciaire en toute intégrité, même si les vues du fonctionnaire étaient transmises par sa partie adverse.

En octroyant le droit de "fournir des renseignements" à tous les États intéressés, à certaines organisations ou d'autres entités appropriées, la Cour a su élargir son accès afin d'assurer une consultation plus adéquate sur les questions qui lui sont référées. Il serait assurément trop onéreux pour les ressources de la Cour de permettre à n'importe quelle ONG de "fournir des renseignements" dans des avis consultatifs, mais la prérogative décisionnelle de l'organe qui consulte peut utilement être exercée de façon souple afin d'assurer la représentation des points de vue importants. L'autorisation à l'endroit de la Palestine dans l'avis sur les *Conséquences juridiques de l'édification d'un mur* en est un exemple éloquent.

Le problème du consentement nécessaire des États

Sans les avis consultatifs, certains différends inter-étatiques ayant un intérêt allant au-delà des relations purement bilatérales entre États seraient demeurés en dehors de la juridiction de la CIJ. Lorsque sont réunies les conditions de vote nécessaires pour obtenir une majorité à l'Assemblée générale, au Conseil de sécurité ou dans un organe spécialisé approprié, l'avis consultatif devient un outil fort utile pour obtenir un prononcé contre un État qui refuse de se plier au droit international. On peut penser au processus de décolonisation de la Namibie ou celui du Sahara occidental ainsi qu'au mur construit par Israël autour des territoires palestiniens. Les États impliqués dans ces situations ont souvent opposé leur droit souverain à ce que les différends les concernant ne puissent être examinés sans leur consentement, suivant le célèbre prononcé de la CPJI dans l'avis

---

183 *Demande de réformation du jugement n° 158, supra* note 31; *Demande de réformation du jugement n° 273, supra* note 32; *Demande de réformation du jugement n° 333, supra* note 169.

sur la *Carélie orientale*: "Il est bien établi en droit international qu'aucun État ne saurait être obligé de soumettre ses différends avec les autres États soit à la médiation, soit à l'arbitrage, soit enfin à n'importe quel procédé de solution pacifique, sans son consentement."[184]

Comme toute règle générale, c'est dans ses exceptions que l'on apprécie sa portée. Les avis consultatifs de la CIJ constituent une importante exception au principe du consentement des États à la juridiction internationale. La nature de cette nuance s'apprécie dans sa qualification. La CIJ n'a pas complètement fermé la porte à l'argument selon lequel l'absence de consentement d'un État pourrait mener la Cour à décliner de rendre un avis. Mais la CIJ a aussi su se garder les mains libres en qualifiant l'argument du consentement comme découlant de sa discrétion de rendre ou non les avis demandés, en vertu du libellé de l'article 65 du Statut de la Cour, qui énonce que la Cour "peut" rendre des avis consultatifs. La Cour a donc refusé de qualifier la question du consentement des États comme relevant de sa compétence consultative, ce qui aurait eu pour conséquence de contraindre la Cour à se déclarer incompétente devant toute demande d'avis où un État affecté directement n'y aurait pas consenti. L'avantage de cette distinction est d'augmenter la discrétion de la Cour en matière de consentement et d'ainsi donner pleinement effet aux possibilités de règlement des différends qui découlent des avis consultatifs.

Pour en arriver à cette position, la CIJ a suivi une route interprétative quelque peu sinueuse puisque certains États ont continué de plaider, jusqu'en 1975, qu'une atteinte au principe du consentement rendait la Cour incompétente.[185] Cette incertitude découle du contexte juridique dans lequel fut rendue l'affaire de la *Carélie orientale*, où la CPJI refusa de rendre un avis consultatif parce que l'URSS n'avait pas consenti à ce que soit soumis son différend avec la Finlande concernant l'interprétation de traités de paix. Le Statut de la CPJI n'établissait pas de distinction entre la compétence de la Cour de rendre l'avis et les motifs d'irrecevabilité qui "pourraient" la convaincre de ne pas se prononcer, comme le font présentement l'article 96 de la Charte et l'article 65 du Statut de la Cour. Dans

---

184 *Affaire de la Carélie, supra* note 4 à la p. 27

185 *Sahara occidental, supra* note 167 à la p. 20, par. 20–21 où la Cour déboute l'Espagne sur ce point. En 2003, Israël a cependant plaidé l'absence de consentement comme relevant de l'opportunité judiciaire. Voir l'Exposé Écrit du gouvernement de l'État d'Israël dans *Conséquences juridiques de l'édification d'un mur, supra* note 1 aux pp. 81–86.

cette affaire, la Cour mentionne le fait que l'URSS avait refusé de participer à la procédure, s'y était objecté depuis le début et n'y avait donc pas consenti. Il faut toutefois noter que l'URSS n'était pas membre de la Société des Nations. C'est là un élément important quant à l'évolution de la relation entre le principe du consentement et les avis consultatifs de la Cour. Deuxièmement, dans l'affaire de la *Carélie*, la Cour a ajouté que sans l'URSS, certains éléments de faits relatifs à l'interprétation des traités ne pourraient être élucidés et qu'il s'agissait là d'une autre raison pesant dans la décision. On ne sait cependant pas de quels éléments de fait il s'agissait. L'URSS possédait-elle des documents que la Finlande ne pouvait fournir? Le texte russe des accords était-il indisponible? S'agissait-il seulement d'obtenir l'interprétation de l'URSS? Toujours est-il qu'il y a là trois éléments qui mènent la Cour à conclure qu'elle ne peut exercer sa fonction judiciaire sans préjudice pour celle-ci: (1) l'absence de consentement; (2) un avis concernant un État non-membre de la SdN; et (3) une insuffisance de faits. La Cour n'ayant pas départagé ces éléments selon leur importance, il relève du domaine de la spéculation d'essayer de déterminer si l'un d'entre eux est suffisant pour décliner ou si c'est l'ensemble des trois qui est nécessaire. On ne sait pas plus non plus si cette décision est discrétionnaire ou non.

En adhérant à la Charte des Nations Unies, il semblerait que les États aient consenti par le fait même à la compétence consultative de la Cour dès lors que sont remplies les exigences de l'article 96 de la Charte. Pour que la Cour puisse être valablement saisie d'une demande d'avis, il faudrait seulement qu'il s'agisse (1) d'une question juridique; (2) demandée par un organe habilité; (3) dans le champ de ses compétences (si applicable).[186] Ainsi, si le prononcé dans l'affaire de la *Carélie orientale* tenait encore relativement au consentement, il reviendrait à la Cour de l'appliquer de façon discrétionnaire, puisque aucun État membre des Nations Unies ne pourrait opposer son absence de consentement à ce que la Cour rende un avis consultatif. L'avis sur l'*Interprétation des traités de paix, première phase* semble avoir non seulement confirmé ce raisonne-

---

[186] Il semble que le champ de compétences concernant la question posée s'appliquerait même aux deux organes politiques principaux. C'est la position de Kelsen et c'est aussi la position que la Cour semble implicitement admettre dans son plus récent avis: Hans Kelsen, *The Law of the United Nations*, New York, Frederick A. Praeger/London Institute of World Affairs, 1950, à la p 549; *Conséquences juridiques de l'édification d'un mur*, *supra* note 1 aux par. 16–35.

ment, mais aussi l'avoir poussé plus loin en déclarant qu'aucun État, membre ou non membre, ne peut s'opposer à un avis en vertu du principe de consentement :

La réponse de la Cour n'a qu'un caractère consultatif: comme telle, elle ne saurait avoir d'effet obligatoire. Il en résulte qu'aucun État, Membre ou non membre des Nations Unies, n'a qualité pour empêcher que soit donnée suite à une demande d'avis dont les Nations Unies, pour s'éclairer dans leur propre action, auraient reconnu l'opportunité.[187]

La Cour semble cependant avoir senti le besoin de faire marche arrière à propos du principe du consentement. En 1971, la Cour a mis l'accent sur le fait que l'Afrique du Sud était membre des Nations Unies contrairement à l'URSS dans l'affaire de la *Carélie orientale* et donc que cette affaire n'était pas pertinente en l'espèce.[188] Cette voie se confirme et s'explicite en 1975. La Cour reconnaît d'abord que la situation de l'Espagne est similaire à celle de l'URSS parce qu'ils s'objectent tous deux à l'avis consultatif.[189] La Cour réaffirme, cependant, la différence fondamentale du fait que l'Espagne est membre des Nations Unies et donc soumise à l'article 96 de la Charte.[190] De plus, la Cour ajoute une nouvelle précision en concluant qu'une atteinte à son caractère judiciaire pourrait la mener à exercer sa discrétion de ne pas répondre s'il y a une atteinte suffisamment grave au principe du consentement:

Ainsi le défaut de consentement d'un État intéressé peut, dans certaines circonstances, rendre le prononcé d'un avis consultatif incompatible avec le caractère judiciaire de la Cour. Tel serait le cas si les faits montraient qu'accepter de répondre aurait pour effet de *tourner*[191] le principe selon lequel un État n'est pas tenu de soumettre un différend au règlement judiciaire s'il n'est pas consentant. La situation dans laquelle la Cour se trouve n'est cependant pas celle qui est envisagée plus haut. Il existe dans la présente affaire une controverse juridique mais c'est une controverse qui a surgi lors des débats de l'Assemblée générale et au sujet de problèmes

---

[187] *Interprétation des traités de paix, supra* note 124 à la p. 71.

[188] *Conséquences juridiques pour les états, supra* note 15 à la p. 23, par. 31.

[189] *Sahara occidental, supra* note 167 à la p. 23, par. 29.

[190] *Ibid.* au par. 30.

[191] La phrase est un peu mal tournée si on recherche la clarté. La version anglaise, même si ce n'est pas la version officielle, éclaire cependant l'idée: "would have the effect of circumventing the principle that a State ..."

traités par elle. *Il ne s'agit pas d'une controverse née indépendamment, dans le cadre de relations bilatérales.*[192]

En faisant référence au débat sur la décolonisation, la Cour situe la controverse dans le cadre des activités de l'ONU, ce qui lui permet d'écarter l'élément de "relations bilatérales" qu'elle attribue à l'affaire de la *Carélie*. La Cour est capable d'atteindre cette conclusion même si, deux paragraphes auparavant, elle cite l'extrait de l'affaire de l'*Interprétation des traités de paix, première phase,* cité plus haut, qui indique que ni les membres ni les non-membres ne peuvent empêcher la procédure consultative. Retournant quelques pas en arrière à l'*Interprétation des traités de paix, première phase,* il est légitime de se demander s'il ne s'agissait pas là de telles questions *bilatérales.* Ces questions n'étaient-elles pas justement issues d'une dispute bilatérale reliée à l'application d'une clause d'arbitrage concernant la relation entre deux États? Il est vrai qu'il existait plusieurs permutations de ces relations bilatérales entre la Bulgarie, la Hongrie et la Roumanie, d'un côté, et les puissances occidentales signataires de l'autre côté. Plusieurs relations bilatérales semblables ne deviennent cependant pas une question dont est automatiquement saisie l'ONU. De plus, la Cour s'est bornée à ne pas définir la question autour des droits humains, alors que le litige de fond concernait justement les violations des droits humains par la Bulgarie, la Hongrie et la Roumanie. Ainsi, il nous semble qu'en appliquant *Sahara occidental* rétroactivement, l'*Interprétation des traités de paix, première phase* aurait pu être décidé autrement.

Dans son dernier avis, la Cour essaie de réconcilier l'*Interprétation des traités de paix, première phase* et *Sahara occidental.* Elle affirme d'abord que l'avis de 1950 concerne le fait que le consentement n'est pas une question de compétence, mais une question liée à l'opportunité de rendre l'avis et que l'avis de 1975 explique que l'intégrité judiciaire est menacée seulement "dans le cadre de relations bilatérales."[193] Elle conclut ainsi, au regard du mur érigé par Israël autour des territoires palestiniens: "L'avis est demandé à l'égard d'une question qui intéresse tout particulièrement les Nations Unies, et qui s'inscrit dans un cadre bien plus large que celui d'un différend bilatéral."[194] On peut cependant se demander dans quelle mesure il est réellement possible qu'une question

---

[192] *Sahara occidental, supra* note 167 à la p. 25, par. 33–34 (nos italiques).

[193] *Conséquences juridiques de l'édification d'un mur, supra* note 1 au par. 47.

[194] *Ibid.* au par. 50.

soit purement bilatérale dès lors qu'elle fait l'objet d'une demande d'avis consultatif et donc qu'elle soit appuyée par la majorité des membres de l'organe demandeur. Ou encore pourquoi est-ce qu'une controverse "née indépendamment dans le cadre de relations bilatérales," mais qui dégénère en conflit multilatéral, ne pourrait faire l'objet d'une demande d'avis selon une lecture stricte de *Sahara occidental.* Le prononcé quelque peu radical dans l'avis sur l'*Interprétation des traités de paix, première phase,* semble non seulement plus adapté à l'interdépendance des États mais révélateur de la pratique réelle de la CIJ.

La Cour actuelle n'a jamais décliné de rendre un avis en vertu de son pouvoir discrétionnaire. Ainsi, on peut se demander s'il existe vraiment ces "raisons décisives"[195] — qui incluraient un contournement du principe du consentement — reconnues dans la jurisprudence de la Cour comme étant nécessaires pour que celle-ci utilise sa discrétion et refuse de rendre l'avis.[196] Les arguments utilisés par la Cour semblent même parfois laisser croire qu'elle trouvera toujours le moyen de rendre l'avis.[197] Nous devons cependant être en désaccord avec les conclusions de Robert Kolb et de Georges Abi-Saab concernant la fin de la discrétion de la Cour.

---

[195] *Jugements du tribunal administratif de l'O.I.T.,* avis consultatif du 23 octobre 1956, [1956] C.I.J. Rec. 77 à la p. 86; *Certaines dépenses des Nations Unies, supra* note 167 à la p. 155; *Conséquences juridiques pour les États, supra* note 15 à la p. 27; *Sahara Occidental, supra* note 167 à la p. 21; *Demande de réformation du jugement n⁰ 273, supra* note 32 à la p. 347; *Applicabilité de la section 22 de l'article VI de la convention sur les privilèges et immunités des Nations Unies, supra* note 168 à la p. 191.

[196] Georges Abi-Saab, "On discretion: Reflections on the nature of the consultative function of the International Court of Justice" dans Laurence Boisson de Chazournes et Philippe Sands, dir., *International Law, the International Court of Justice and Nuclear Weapons,* Cambridge, Cambridge University Press, 1999 à la p. 36; Robert Kolb, "De la prétendue discrétion de la Cour internationale de justice de refuser de donner un avis consultatif" (2000) 12 RADIC 799.

[197] Voir *Applicabilité de la section 22 de l'article VI de la convention sur les privilèges et immunités des Nations Unies, supra* note 168 à la p. 191, par. 38. L'argument sur le fait que la réserve de la Roumanie porte sur l'application de la Convention et que l'avis porte sur l'applicabilité de celle-ci semble être un sophisme d'un point de vue théorique, même si le résultat est bienvenu. On essaie de faire une fausse distinction entre fond et forme. On ne peut pas dire, comme la Cour le soutient, qu'un différend sur le fond implique qu'il n'y a pas de différend sur le for où appliquer ce droit, surtout dans le contexte contractualiste du droit international. Cependant, la Cour aurait pu régler la question de la même façon que dans *Sahara occidental* en invoquant le fait que la question de la disparition de M. Mazilu avait été maintes fois discuté et qu'il s'agissait d'une question intéressant au moins cet organe subsidiaire autorisé, si ce n'est l'Organisation.

D'abord, la discrétion est inhérente à l'acte judiciaire. L'action humaine est empreinte de discrétion et on ne peut l'automatiser. Ensuite, il est utile de rappeler que la Cour a déjà affirmé avoir trouvé des raisons décisives qui lui permettraient de ne pas rendre un avis, même si elle a préféré rendre l'avis quand même pour les meilleurs intérêts de l'ONU afin de maintenir la crédibilité du Tribunal administratif des Nations Unies.[198] Ces raisons décisives ne sont pas liées au consentement, mais le fait qu'elles aient été évoquées rend possible que les différents arguments d'irrecevabilité comme l'absence suffisante de faits, qui sont non-limitatifs[199] et doivent être appréciés au regard du contexte de chaque affaire,[200] pourront un jour être acceptés par la Cour.

Dans l'affaire de *Réformation du jugement n° 273*, ces raisons décisives provenaient d'une inégalité suffisamment grave entre les parties pour qu'elle porte atteinte au caractère judiciaire de la Cour. L'instigation de la procédure de réformation d'un jugement concernant un différend entre un fonctionnaire de l'ONU et l'Organisation était au cœur du problème. D'abord, la procédure de réformation avait été entachée d'irrégularités formelles lors de l'examen de la demande des États-Unis au comité de révision qui envoie ces demandes à la CIJ. Ensuite, les motifs de réformation invoqués ne correspondaient pas aux chefs de réformation reconnus. Finalement, on avait refusé de permettre à l'avocat du fonctionnaire, M. Mortished, de faire valoir ses points contre la réformation, alors que durant cette séance, les États-Unis, en tant qu'instigateur de la demande de réformation, avaient non seulement profité de leur présence sur le comité pour faire valoir leur point de vue, mais avaient également participé au vote.

En ne faisant pas usage de sa discrétion de décliner de rendre des avis, la CIJ rappelle implicitement que le consentement juridictionnel ne peut être autant pris pour acquis que par le passé. Que la Cour qualifie le consentement des États comme une question d'opportunité et non de compétence démontre également l'évolution juridique en faveur d'une diminution du rôle de la souveraineté des États dans la détermination de la justiciabilité des

---

[198] *Demande de réformation du jugement n° 273, supra* note 32 à la p. 347, par. 45.

[199] Manley O. Hudson, "Les avis consultatifs", *supra* note 5 à la p. 357; Abi-Saab, *supra* note 196 à la p. 43; Kolb, *supra* note 196 à la p. 810.

[200] *Interprétation des traités de paix, supra* note 124 à la p. 71; *Réserves à la convention sur la prévention et la répression du génocide, supra* note 167 à la p. 19; *Conséquences juridiques pour les États, supra* note 15 aux pp. 24–27; *Licéité de la menace ou de l'emploi d'armes nucléaires, supra* note 131 à la p. 235.

différends. Cette évolution continue de confirmer l'effritement de la souveraineté absolue comme l'avait déjà démontré le prononcé de la Cour dans l'*Avis sur la réparation des dommages subis au service des Nations Unies* à l'effet que même les États non-membres doivent reconnaître la personnalité juridique de l'ONU,[201] une tendance normale dans une société internationale où même les non-membres reconnaissent l'utilité et la nécessité de l'association et par conséquent de la réduction de leur souveraineté.[202]

LEUR UTILITÉ

Cette dernière section a pour but d'offrir un bref examen de l'utilité des avis au regard de la jurisprudence consultative de la CIJ. Avant d'établir les champs de contributions spécifiques des avis, il semble nécessaire de se demander qui sont les destinataires des avis afin d'évaluer leur utilité. La justification des avis est qu'il s'agit d'abord et avant tout d'une contribution de l'organe judiciaire principal au fonctionnement de l'Organisation afin d'éclairer

[201] *Réparation des dommages subis au service des Nations Unies, supra* note 167 à la p. 185: À savoir si l'ONU peut demander réparation en son propre nom vis-à-vis d'un État non-membre, la Cour est unanime à l'effet que l'organisation "possède un droit de protection fonctionnelle à l'égard de ses agents." Elle ajoute: "À cet égard, la Cour est d'avis que cinquante États, représentant une très large majorité des membres de la communauté internationale, avaient le pouvoir, conformément au droit international, de créer une entité possédant une personnalité internationale objective — et non pas simplement une personnalité reconnue par eux seuls — ainsi que la qualité de présenter des réclamations internationales." D'ailleurs, aucun des États s'étant prononcé sur la question ne s'est objecté à ce que l'Organisation puisse agir dans certaines circonstances à l'égard d'un État non-membre: *Réparation des dommages subis au service des Nations Unies,* "Observations écrites du Gouvernement français sur l'avis consultatif demandé à la Cour internationale de Justice," [1949] CIJ Mémoires 15 à la p. 15; "Letter from the Secretary of State of the United States of America to the Registrar of the International Court of Justice," [1949] CIJ Mémoires 19 à la p. 21; *ibid.* "Exposé Oral de M. Fitzmaurice" (9 mars 1949) [1949] CIJ Mémoires 110 aux pp. 129–30.

[202] Le représentant du secrétaire général, M. Feller explique que tous les États (sauf l'Espagne qui n'a pas droit d'être membre ainsi que des États minuscules comme Monaco et Andorre) ont entrepris des démarches pour devenir membres de l'Organisation, à l'exception de la Suisse, qui avait par ailleurs reconnu la personnalité juridique de l'Organisation: *Réparation des dommages subis au service des Nations Unies,* "Exposé oral de M. Feller" (7 mars 1949) [1949] CIJ Mémoires 70 à la p. 74. Par ailleurs, celui-ci plaide qu'il n'y a "no ncessity here for determining whether a non-member State is bound by any specific provision of the Charter," ce qui aurait été le cas si un État non-membre s'était prononcé contre le fait que l'avis soit rendu en vertu de l'art. 96 de la Charte.

juridiquement l'organe demandeur dans ses actions.[203] La Cour affirme qu'elle n'a pas non plus à examiner l'utilité de l'avis, puisque c'est là une question d'appréciation,[204] ni encore le résultat du vote sur l'avis.[205] La Cour n'a démontré aucun intérêt à essayer de voir quel camp lui envoyait la balle. À l'opposé de cette tendance, dans son opinion dissidente dans l'avis sur la *Licéité ou menace de l'utilisation des armes nucléaires*, le Juge Oda considère illégitime la demande parce qu'à son avis des ONG se sont servies des États membres du groupe des 77 comme paravent pour faire avancer leur militantisme anti-nucléaire.[206] En réalité, on pourrait dire que les destinataires de l'avis sont justement les États qui ont voté en faveur de l'avis, puisqu'ils essaient généralement d'ainsi valider une position qu'ils ont déjà, qu'elle soit supportée ou non par des groupes externes. Il est bien rare que l'on soumette réellement une question à propos de laquelle on ne puisse prévoir la réponse dans une certaine mesure. D'ailleurs, les avis consultatifs n'ont jamais réellement créé de commotion juridique, excepté pour les États qui s'opposaient à ce qu'un avis soit donné. Outre les demandes de réformation, les avis se sont toujours généralement conclus dans la logique du "demandeur." Ce qui soulève le problème des questions rédigées de façon tendancieuse.[207] Même si en principe la Cour affirme qu'elle doit s'en tenir au libellé des questions,[208] elle n'hésite pas à réécrire celles-ci[209] et à ajouter des points qu'elle considère essentiels, comme en matière contentieuse d'ailleurs.[210] À un autre niveau, c'est la communauté internationale qui peut être

---

[203] *Réserves à la convention pour la prévention et la répression du crime de génocide, supra* note 167 à la p. 19; *Conséquences juridiques pour les états, supra* note 15 à la p. 24, par. 32; *Sahara occidental, supra* note 167 à la p. 37, par. 72; *Conséquences juridiques de l'édification d'un mur, supra* note 1 au par. 60.

[204] *Sahara occidental, ibid.* à la p. 37, par. 73; *Licéité de la menace ou de l'emploi d'armes nucléaires, supra* note 131 à la p. 237, par. 17; *Conséquences juridiques de l'édification d'un mur, supra* note 1 au par. 61.

[205] *Licéité de la menace ou de l'emploi d'armes nucléaires, supra* note 131.

[206] *Ibid.* Dissidence de M. le Juge Oda.

[207] *Conséquences de l'édification d'un mur, supra* note 1; *Licéité de la menace ou de l'emploi d'armes nucléaires, supra* note 131.

[208] *Supra* note 139.

[209] *Supra* note 138.

[210] *Affaire des plates-formes pétrolières (Iran c. États-Unis d'Amérique)*, arrêt du 6 novembre 2003 (fonds), en ligne: <http://www.icj-cij.org>. Voir sur cette question Antoine Ollivier et Pierre-Olivier Savoie, "La Cour internationale de Justice" (2004), 17–1 R.Q.D.I. 213 à la p. 253.

vue comme destinataire.[211] Mais vu la technicité des avis, il faut plutôt s'attendre à ce que les lecteurs les plus attentifs soient *la doctrine.*[212]

En pensant à tous ces destinataires, la CIJ doit bien balancer la complexité de l'acte judiciaire consultatif tout en faisant progresser le droit international et les relations inter-étatiques. Même si c'est bien souvent du bout des lèvres, comme le démontre certaines de ses contributions au droit des organisations (1). Même si certains estiment que le rôle du juge devrait être de trancher les différends plutôt que de se lancer dans le développement du droit international (2). Même s'il y a des limites à ce que la procédure consultative peut accomplir (3).

Le développement du droit des organisations et le contrôle de l'illégalité des actes des organisations

Considérant que les organes et organisations demandeurs sont les principaux destinataires des avis, il est normal que la plus importante contribution de la Cour en matière consultative se situe au niveau du développement du droit des organisations. D'abord, la Cour a contribué de façon importante à l'élaboration et à la répartition des compétences de l'ONU et à l'intérieur de celle-ci. Ensuite, même si la Cour continue de dire le contraire, elle a contribué à contrôler les actions des organisations internationales et de leurs organes.

La première contribution importante de la Cour se situe évidemment au niveau de la personnalité juridique de l'ONU, qui permet à celle-ci de négocier avec les États sur un pied de quasi égalité.[213] L'autre contribution de la Cour est l'interprétation des dispositions de la Charte ou des différentes conventions établissant les pouvoirs d'une organisation internationale. Dans le cadre des différends ou des questions soulevées par les instances spécifiques, la Cour n'a pas seulement expliqué les dispositions, mais bel et bien réparti les compétences, reconnu la pratique et également contrôlé la légalité des actions des organisations et de leurs organes. L'exemple le plus évident est l'annulation du vote concernant la composition du Comité de la sécurité maritime de l'Organisation intergouvernementale

211 *Licéité de la menace ou de l'emploi d'armes nucléaires, supra* note 131, Déclaration de M. le Président Bedjaoui, au par. 8.

212 *Ibid.* Opinion individuelle de M. le Juge Ranjeva.

213 *Réparation des dommages subis au service des Nations Unies, supra* note 167.

consultative de la navigation maritime.[214] L'assemblée générale de l'organisation s'étant donnée une discrétion dans l'élection des membres du Comité là où le texte de la Convention n'en donnait pas, la Cour a déclaré cet acte illégal. L'élection eut lieu de nouveau, cette fois en conformité avec l'avis. Celui-ci avait été demandé en vertu d'un article de la Convention disposant que les questions de droit peuvent être portées devant la CIJ pour avis consultatif. L'interprétation et l'élaboration des actions et pouvoirs de l'Assemblée générale et du Conseil de sécurité dans le cadre de la Charte soulèvent des questions plus complexes.[215] D'une part, la Cour soutient qu'elle ne peut procéder à la révision des résolutions:

Dans les systèmes juridiques des États, on trouve souvent une procédure pour déterminer la validité d'un acte même législatif ou gouvernemental, mais on ne rencontre dans la structure des Nations Unies aucune procédure analogue. Certaines propositions présentées pendant la rédaction de la Charte et qui visaient à remettre à la Cour internationale de Justice l'autorité suprême d'interpréter la Charte, n'ont pas été adoptées; l'avis que la Cour s'apprête à donner ici est un avis *consultatif.* Comme il a été prévu en 1945, chaque organe doit donc, tout au moins en premier lieu, déterminer sa propre compétence.[216]

Et elle ajoute:

Il est évident que la Cour n'a pas de pouvoirs de contrôle judiciaire ni d'appel en ce qui concerne les décisions prises par les organes des Nations Unies dont il s'agit [le Conseil de sécurité et l'Assemblée générale]. Ce n'est pas sur la validité de la résolution 2145(XXI) de l'Assemblée générale ou des résolutions connexes du Conseil de sécurité ni sur leur conformité avec la Charte que porte la demande d'avis consultatif. Cependant, dans l'exercice de sa fonction judiciaire et puisque des objections ont été formulées, la Cour examinera ces objections dans son exposé des motifs, avant de se prononcer sur les conséquences juridiques découlant de ces résolutions.[217]

---

214 *Composition du comité de la sécurité maritime, supra* note 169.

215 Michael C. Wood "The Interpretation of Security Council Resolutions" (1998) 2 Max Planck Y.B. UN L. 73; Elihu Lauterpacht, "Judicial Review of the Acts of International Organisations" dans Laurence Boisson de Chazournes et Philippe Sands, dir., *International Law, the International Court of Justice and Nuclear Weapons,* Cambridge, Cambridge University Press, 1999 à la p. 92.

216 *Certaines dépenses des Nations Unies, supra* note 167 à la p. 168.

217 *Conséquences juridiques pour les états, supra* note 15 à la p. 45, par. 89.

La Cour dit une chose — qui peut être supportée par le fait que l'organe judiciaire principal ne s'est pas vu nommée "gardienne de la Charte" comme la Cour suprême des États-Unis est la gardienne de la Constitution — mais elle semble bel et bien faire autre chose. La différence entre "examiner" la légalité et "contrôler" la légalité existe-t-elle vraiment? On peut d'ailleurs saisir la CIJ d'une demande d'avis consultatif qui demande l'équivalent d'un contrôle judiciaire des actions d'un des autres organes de l'organisation. Il est vrai que la Cour n'a jamais invalidé une action d'un des deux organes politiques principaux. D'autre part, elle en a validé bon nombre. Ainsi, elle a reconnu que les dépenses autorisées par l'Assemblée générale au Moyen-Orient étaient bien des "dépenses de l'organisation," que ces résolutions concernaient le maintien de la paix — et non des "mesures préventives ou coercitives contre un État, comme il est prévu au chapitre VII" — et qu'elles "n'empiétaient [pas] sur les prérogatives conférées au Conseil de sécurité."[218] Elle a aussi reconnu que l'Assemblée générale avait la compétence pour mettre fin au mandat de l'Afrique du Sud en Namibie parce que son pouvoir de recommandation ne l'empêche pas d'adopter des résolutions ayant le caractère de décisions.[219] Comme elle n'avait pas le pouvoir d'obliger l'Afrique du Sud à se retirer, l'Assemblée générale a légalement porté la question à l'attention du Conseil de sécurité[220] et celui-ci a légalement exigé le retrait en vertu de ses pouvoirs sous les articles 24 et 25 de la Charte.[221] Notons aussi que la Cour a reconnu la légalité de la demande d'avis consultatif sur les *Conséquences de l'édification d'un mur* en affirmant que l'Assemblée générale pouvait bel et bien se saisir de cette question en vertu de la résolution Dean Acheson[222] puisque le Conseil de sécurité avait été bloqué par un veto sur cette exacte question peu de temps auparavant.[223] Cette pratique est à tout le moins l'exemple de la définition des compétences de ces organes, si elle ne peut être considérée comme un contrôle judiciaire *de facto*. Il est vrai que la Cour a plié l'échine devant le Conseil de sécurité dans la procédure

---

218 *Certaines dépenses des Nations Unies, supra* note 167 à la p. 167.

219 *Ibid.* à la p. 50, par. 106.

220 En vertu de l'art. 11(2) de la Charte.

221 *Conséquences juridiques pour les états, supra* note 15 à la p. 51, par. 106–108.

222 *Union pour le maintien de la paix*, Résolution 377(V), AG NU, 1951.

223 *Conséquences juridiques de l'édification d'un mur, supra* note 1 au par. 20.

contentieuse,[224] mais peut-être saura-t-elle un jour s'affirmer de façon stratégique — possiblement dans sa procédure consultative — comme l'a fait la Cour suprême des États-Unis au début de son histoire[225] afin de forger et d'assurer la place et les pouvoirs du gouvernement fédéral au milieu des États essayant de saper les pouvoirs fédéraux.

Le développement du droit international

Si on se fie à Hersch Lauterpacht, le rôle de juge à la CIJ n'inclut pas seulement de répondre strictement à la question qui est posée:

in order to reply to that question, the Court is bound in the course of its reasoning to consider and to answer a variety of legal questions. This is of the very essence of its judicial function which makes it possible for it to render Judgments and Opinions *which carry conviction and clarify the law.*[226]

Les vingt-cinq avis consultatifs se sont montrés des terrains assez fertiles dans ce genre de développement. Il est évidemment impossible de discuter en détail de tous ces développements, mais voici une liste qui sera suivie de quelques observations concernant les prononcés du dernier avis relativement au droit à la légitime défense. Parmi les sujets développés depuis près de soixante ans, on compte le droit des organisations (révision d'actions, élaboration des compétences et transition d'une organisation internationale à une autre),[227] le droit à l'autodétermination dans son contexte classique[228]

---

224 *Questions d'interprétation et d'application de la convention de Montréal de 1971 résultant de l'incident aérien de Lockerbie (Jamahiriya arabe libyenne c. États Unis d'Amérique),* mesures conservatoires, ordonnance du 14 avril 1992, [1992] CIJ Rec. 114.

225 *Marbury* v. *Madison,* 5 U.S. (1 Cranch) 137 (1803), qui concerne l'importance du contrôle judiciaire pour assurer la suprématie de la constitution, qui en l'occurrence est la Charte, même si les interprétations varient dans sa qualification tout au long du spectre allant de la constitution mondiale à un traité multilatéral comme un autre.

226 Opinion individuelle de M. le juge Lauterpacht, *supra* note 30; Fitzmaurice, *supra* note 30 à la p. 18. Voir aussi Prost et Fouret, *supra* note 146 (nos italiques).

227 *Procédure de vote applicable, supra* note 167.

228 *Statut international du sud-ouest africain, supra* note 167; *Procédure de vote applicable, supra* note 167; *Conséquences juridiques pour les états, supra* note 15; *Sahara occidental, supra* note 167.

et post-colonial,[229] l'interprétation des traités (on peut noter en particulier les exigences de bonne foi dans la dénonciation d'un traité[230] ou encore la teneur des réserves acceptables à un traité[231]), la valeur des résolutions de l'Assemblée générale relativement à la preuve d'une coutume,[232] la nature des normes comme les obligations *erga omnes*,[233] le droit international humanitaire[234] et son interaction avec les droits de l'homme,[235] les immunités de juridictions,[236] ou encore les réparations découlant de la responsabilité internationale.[237]

Le problème majeur relatif au développement du droit international est que la Cour développe rarement les idées qu'elle défend. Elle ne cite pas de sources et fait souvent des affirmations sans justification adéquate. Ainsi, la Cour ne va généralement pas reconnaître un point de vue contraire dans la doctrine par rapport à une de ses affirmations ou relativement aux prétentions des parties. Cette problématique est bien reflétée par l'affirmation un peu à l'emporte pièce selon laquelle "[l]'article 51 de la Charte reconnaît ainsi l'existence d'un droit naturel de légitime défense en cas d'agression armée par un État contre un autre État. Toutefois, Israël ne prétend pas que les violences dont il est victime soient imputables à un État étranger."[238] L'article 51 parle seulement du "droit naturel de légitime défense" en cas "d'agression armée," ce qui n'implique pas selon une interprétation stricte qu'il faille que cette dernière provienne d'un État, ni que le droit naturel s'exerce si et seulement si il y a attaque armée.[239] Par ailleurs, la Cour a manqué l'occasion de se prononcer sur les résolutions 1368 et 1373 du Conseil de sécurité qui retirent la nécessité d'attaque prove-

229 *Conséquences juridiques de l'édification d'un mur, supra* note 1.

230 *Interprétation de l'accord du 25 mars 1951, supra* note 134.

231 *Réserves à la convention pour la prévention et la répression du crime de génocide,* avis, *supra* note 167.

232 *Licéité de l'utilisation des armes nucléaires par un État dans un conflit armé, supra* note 168.

233 *Conséquences juridiques de l'édification d'un mur, supra* note 1.

234 *Ibid.; Licéité de la menace ou de l'emploi d'armes nucléaires, supra* note 131.

235 *Conséquences juridiques de l'édification d'un mur, supra* note 1; *Licéité de la menace ou de l'emploi d'armes nucléaires, supra* note 131.

236 *Différend relatif à l'immunité de juridiction d'un rapporteur spécial de la Commission des droits de l'homme, supra* note 168.

237 *Conséquences juridiques de l'édification d'un mur, supra* note 1.

238 *Ibid.* au par. 139.

239 *Ibid.* Opinion individuelle de Mme la juge Higgins aux par. 33–34.

nant d'un autre État,[240] si cette nécessité existait réellement. La déclaration de la Cour sur la teneur de l'article 51 ne répondrait donc pas à la question à laquelle elle s'attaquait, soit le supposé droit de légitime défense d'Israël contre des groupes terroristes.

Malgré ces limitations, et aussi en raison de ces limitations, c'est souvent dans les opinions individuelles qu'on peut retrouver les développements les plus intéressants, à conditions qu'ils soient convaincants. À cet effet, relativement à la procédure contentieuse, l'opinion du Juge Simma dans l'*Affaire des plates-formes pétrolières* mérite d'être soulignée. Au regard du droit comparé des juridictions de common law et des juridictions civilistes française, suisse, allemande et québécoise, il propose un principe général du droit selon lequel les personnes commettant conjointement un préjudice qui ne peut être attribué individuellement, sont toutes considérées entièrement responsables et il indique que ce principe devrait être applicable à la responsabilité des États.[241]

Les limites des avis consultatifs

Cinq aspects reflètent les limites de la procédure consultative de la Cour. D'abord, la CIJ n'a pas su ou n'a pas pu jouer le même rôle que la CPJI dans le maintien de la paix et de la sécurité internationale. Les avis de la CPJI ont tous été acceptés par le conseil de la SdN et certains ont même été acceptés comme obligatoires par les parties.[242] La raison de ce changement est assurément une société internationale plus diversifiée où les États n'ont plus des intérêts aussi uniformes.[243] Deuxièmement, une autre limite provient des questions trop politiques qui devraient plutôt être résolues par voie de négociation.[244] Cependant, le prononcé selon lequel même les

---

240 *Ibid.* Opinion individuelle de M. le juge Kooijmans aux par. 35–36.

241 *Affaire des plates-formes pétrolières*, *supra* note 213, Opinion individuelle de M. le juge Simma aux par. 63 et s. En l'espèce, cela permettrait de trouver l'Iran responsable d'avoir miné des bateaux américains même s'il est impossible de prouver si c'est en fait l'Iran ou l'Irak qui a miné ce bateau spécifique. Les deux États avaient cependant participé à part plus ou moins égale aux attaques contre des navires neutres durant la guerre des pétroliers dans le golfe persique au début des années 1980.

242 Hudson, *The P.C.I.J., 1920–1942*, *supra* note 124 à la p. 512.

243 Voir C.J. Chacko, "The Possible Expansion of the Advisory Jurisdiction of the International Court of Justice" dans M.K. Nawaz, dir., *Essays on International Law In Honour of Krishna Rao, Leyden*, Sijthoff, 1976 à la p. 214.

244 Pomerance, *supra* note 47.

situations les plus tendues politiquement peuvent bénéficier utilement d'un éclairage juridique semble toujours aussi convaincant.[245]
Troisièmement, l'absence de faits nécessaires à l'évaluation des
prétentions des parties semble une limite importante qui peut gê-
ner la Cour. Cependant, considérant la disponibilité de l'information aujourd'hui par rapport aux circonstances de 1923 lorsque la
CPJI a décidé l'affaire de la *Carélie,* il semble que ce point soit presque devenu sans objet. Dans l'avis sur les *Conséquences de l'édification
d'un mur,* le juge Buergenthal estime que la Cour aurait dû user de
sa discrétion et décliner de rendre l'avis parce qu'Israël n'a pas
présenté ses arguments et des informations dont elle disposait relativement à sa lutte contre le terrorisme. Cependant, pour repren-
dre la logique du juge Buergenthal, il semble plutôt que le problème
est que la Cour ne s'est pas penchée sur ces arguments et informations qui étaient disponibles à la Cour dans les différents rapports
de l'ONU déposés en l'instance.[246] Quatrièmement, la Cour devra
continuer d'essayer de maintenir sa crédibilité, son intégrité et son
prestige et cela peut limiter les questions auxquelles elle se considère apte à répondre. Ce problème peut se présenter sous diverses
formes, qui demeurent difficiles à prédire. Finalement, une de ces
formes d'atteinte à sa fonction judiciaire a mené la Cour à répéter
que les demandes de réformation n'étaient pas appropriées pour
son fonctionnement en raison de l'inégalité inhérente des parties.
C'est ce qui a mené à l'abolition de la pratique.

L'AVIS: HYBRIDE ENTRE LA DÉCISION JUDICIAIRE ET LA CONSULTATION

Nous avons proposé au début que l'avis consultatif pouvait être
vu comme une forme de mode alternatif de résolution des conflits.
Au-delà des problèmes potentiels liés à la fonction judiciaire de la
Cour, un autre irritant est qu'ils ne mettent pas terme au conflit,
comme le bon vieux jugement exécutoire. Serait-ce là un problème
puisque le droit judiciaire devrait avoir pour but de démontrer l'efficacité du droit? En réalité, l'exécution d'un jugement est également soumise à bien des aléas. Le créancier peut toujours se sauver.
Sa faillite peut nous faire un pied de nez. À cet effet, on peut rappeler les paroles du président américain Andrew Jackson à la suite

---

245 *Interprétation de l'accord du 25 mars 1951, supra* note 134 au par. 33.

246 *Conséquences juridiques de l'édification d'un mur, supra* note 1, Déclaration de M. le
juge Buergenthal au par. 7.

d'une décision de la Cour suprême: "John Marshall has made the decision; now let him execute it!"[247]

Les avis consultatifs — tout comme les arrêts — ne sont qu'une étape préalable à l'acceptation par les parties d'une certaine finalité ou stabilité dans le cadre d'un conflit, d'une relation. Le fait que les avis ne soient pas "exécutoires" ou qu'ils soient teintés de politique, n'en fait pas une forme juridique ou judiciaire moindre, seulement différente. En tant que processus d'ordonnancement social, l'avis demeure un hybride entre la consultation et la décision judiciaire et s'ajoute ainsi au débat lié à l'émergence, à la confirmation ou à la disparition de la norme. C'est une forme décisionnelle peut-être un peu moins définitive que le jugement entre deux parties, mais celle-ci a l'avantage d'ouvrir plus largement le débat en permettant à un plus grand nombre d'acteurs d'intervenir. De plus, la Cour gère ce mode décisionnel plus souple de façon acceptable puisque les avis de la CIJ respectent les principes fondamentaux de la décision judiciaire: la procédure est publique, l'avis est donné par la Cour au complet, le jugement est motivé,[248] et le jugement est lu en public et largement diffusé.[249] On est donc bien loin des pratiques consultatives qui faisaient dire à Elihu Root que celles-ci constituent "a violation of all judicial principles." Malgré ses imperfections, comme toute fonction judiciaire, la procédure consultative, même devant la CIJ, a su se tailler une place plus qu'honnête dans la jungle du droit international.

Summary

The ICJ, Advisory Opinions, and the Judicial Function: Between Adjudication and Consultation

Legal commentators have not always considered advisory opinions as a legitimate judicial function. Under both national and international law, it is often considered that only ripe controversies can be legitimately decided by a court of law. Under international law, advisory opinions are also criticized for undermining sovereignty when consent is not obtained from all states affected by the matter. By examining the International Court of Justice's (ICJ) advisory opinions in light of comparative law, the author argues that

---

247 Cité dans Scott, *supra* note 158 à la p. 831.

248 Règlement, art. 107(2).

249 Règlement, art. 107(1).

this criticism underestimates the evolution of the judicial function, as much in international as in national law. The advisory opinion is a mode of social ordering that stands somewhere between consultation and adjudication. The advisory opinion not only adopts most of adjudication's characteristics but also has the added flexibility of consultation because it can consider a wider spectrum of opinions than can adversary procedures. The ICJ's advisory opinions can almost be assimilated to adjudication. Considering that they have also greatly contributed to the development of international law, the ICJ's advisory opinions remain an integral and legitimate part of the court's judicial function.

Sommaire

La CIJ, l'avis consultatif, et la fonction judiciaire: Entre décision et consultation

En droit interne comme en droit international, on considère souvent que la seule fonction légitime du pouvoir judiciaire serait de se prononcer sur des différends nés et réels. Ainsi, l'avis consultatif a toujours été considéré comme une fonction suspecte pour un tribunal. En droit international, l'avis consultatif irrite aussi parce qu'il porterait atteinte à la souveraineté de l'État qui n'y a pas consenti et dont les droits pourraient être affectés par celui-ci dans le futur. En examinant en particulier les avis consultatifs de la CIJ au regard du droit comparé, l'auteur estime que ces critiques font fi de la constante évolution du rôle du juge et de la fonction judiciaire en droit interne comme en droit international. L'avis consultatif est un mode d'ordonnancement social qui se situe entre la décision judiciaire et la consultation. L'avis adopte la plupart des caractéristiques de la décision judiciaire mais possède aussi la flexibilité de la consultation, permettant ainsi de considérer un plus grand éventail d'opinions que la procédure contradictoire. Les avis consultatifs de la CIJ sont presque assimilables à la décision judiciaire. Considérant au surplus leur contribution au développement du droit international, ils demeurent une partie intégrante et légitime de la fonction judiciaire de la Cour.

Compliance Committees and Recent Multilateral Environmental Agreements: The Canadian Experience with Their Negotiation and Operation

HUGH ADSETT, ANNE DANIEL, MASUD HUSAIN, AND TED L. MCDORMAN

Introduction

The development of compliance procedures and mechanisms under multilateral environmental agreements (MEAs) has been described as "[o]ne of the most significant developments in the field of international environmental law."[1] All recent MEAs have included a provision calling for the establishment of procedures and mechanisms (a committee) designed to encourage and enhance compliance with MEAs. The first such provision appeared as Article 8 of the Montreal Protocol on Substances That Deplete the Ozone Layer (Montreal Protocol): "The Parties, at their first meeting, shall consider and approve procedures and institutional mechanisms for

Hugh Adsett is Counselor, Permanent Mission of Canada to the United Nations in New York, formerly Deputy Director, Environmental Law, Department of Foreign Affairs, Ottawa. He was a member of the Basel Convention and Espoo Convention compliance committees. Anne Daniel is General Counsel, Department of Justice, Legal Services, Environment Canada, Ottawa. She is a member of the Basel Convention compliance committee and chair of the Legal Drafting Group under the Stockholm Convention. Masud Husain is Deputy Director, Criminal and Security Law, formerly Deputy Director, Environmental Law, Department of Foreign Affairs, Ottawa. He was a member of the Espoo Convention and LRTAP compliance committees. Ted L. Mcdorman is Professor, Faculty of Law, University of Victoria, Victoria, BC, Canada. From 2002–4, he was "academic-in-residence" at the Bureau of Legal Affairs, Department of Foreign Affairs, Ottawa. He was a member of the Espoo Convention compliance committee. The authors would like to thank their colleagues Cam Carruthers, Alain Tellier, and Jean-Louis Wallace for their helpful comments on preliminary drafts. The views expressed in this article are personal and do not necessarily reflect those of the government of Canada.

1 Philippe Sands, *Principles of International Environmental Law*, 2nd edition (Cambridge: Cambridge University Press, 2003) at 205.

determining non-compliance with the provisions of the Protocol and for treatment of Parties found to be in non-compliance."[2] An interim non-compliance procedure, involving an Implementation Committee, was established in 1990,[3] followed by the permanent non-compliance procedure adopted in 1992,[4] with revisions added in 1998.[5] The Implementation Committee, which is referred to as being "unprecedented in international environmental law,"[6] is credited, while working in "uncharted territory,"[7] with a role in making the Montreal Protocol one of the most successful MEAs.[8] This new mechanism and its apparent success has led to the inclusion of like clauses in other international instruments requiring the creation of similar bodies. Treaty provisions owing their parentage to Article 8 of the Montreal Protocol appear in:

- Article 3(3) of the 1991 Protocol to the 1979 Convention on Long Range Transboundary Air Pollution Concerning the Emissions of Volatile Organic Compounds or Their Transboundary Fluxes (VOC Protocol),[9] and Article 7 of the 1994 Protocol to the 1979

---

[2] Montreal Protocol on Substances That Deplete the Ozone Layer, 16 September 1987, entered into force 1 January 1989, reprinted in (1987) 26 I.L.M. 154. The Montreal Protocol is to the Vienna Convention for the Protection of the Ozone Layer, 22 March 1985, entered into force 22 September 1988, reprinted in (1985) 26 I.L.M. 1529. The Vienna Convention and the Montreal Protocol website are available at <www.unep.org/ozone/>.

[3] Decision II/5 of the Second Meeting of the Parties, reproduced in UNEP Ozone Secretariat, *Handbook for the International Treaties for the Protection of the Ozone Layer* (6th ed., 2003), available at <www.unep.org/ozone/> at 183.

[4] Decision IV/5 of the Fifth Meeting of the Parties, reproduced in UNEP Ozone Secretariat, *supra* note 3 at 184 and 295–97 [Montreal Protocol, Non-Compliance Procedure].

[5] Decision X/10 of the Tenth Meeting of the Parties, reproduced in UNEP Ozone Secretariat, *supra* note 3 at 185–86 and 295–97.

[6] Martti Koskenniemi, "Breach of Treaty or Non-Compliance? Reflections on the Enforcement of the Montreal Protocol" (1992) 3 Y.B. Int'l Env. L. 123 at 133.

[7] Stephen O. Anderson and K. Madhara Sarma, *Protecting the Ozone Layer: The United Nations History* (London: Earthscan Publications, 2002) at 275.

[8] *Ibid.* at 274.

[9] Protocol to the 1979 Convention on Long Range Transboundary Air Pollution Concerning the Emissions of Volatile Organic Compounds or Their Transboundary Fluxes, 18 November 1991, entered into force 29 September 1997, reprinted in (1992) 31 I.L.M. 568 [VOC Protocol]. The 1991 VOC Protocol is to the Convention on Long-Range Transboundary Air Pollution, done 13 November 1979, entered into force 16 March 1983, reprinted in (1979) 18 I.L.M. 1442

Convention on Long Range Transboundary Air Pollution on Further Reduction of Sulphur Emissions (LRTAP Convention) (Oslo Protocol);[10]

- Article 11 of the 1996 Protocol to the Convention on the Prevention of Marine Pollution by Dumping of Wastes and Other Matter (Protocol to the London Dumping Convention);[11]
- Article 18 of the 1997 Protocol to the United Nations Framework Convention on Climate Change (Kyoto Protocol to the UNFCCC);[12]
- Article 17 of the 1998 Convention on the Prior Informed Consent Procedure for Certain Hazardous Chemicals and Pesticides in International Trade (Rotterdam Convention);[13]

[LRTAP Convention]. The LRTAP Convention and its protocols website is <www.unece.org/env/lrtap/>. Article 3(3) is set out in note 127 in this article.

[10] Protocol to the 1979 LRTAP Convention on Further Reduction of Sulphur Emissions, 14 June 1994, entered into force 5 August 1998, reprinted in (1998) 33 I.L.M. 1540 [Oslo Protocol]. Article 7 is set out in the text at note 130 in this article. The establishment of the LRTAP compliance committee has a bit of a twist. See the section entitled "LRTAP Convention" later in this article.

[11] Protocol to the Convention on the Prevention of Marine Pollution by Dumping of Wastes and Other Matter, 7 November 1996, not yet in force, reprinted in (1997) 36 I.L.M. 1. The 1996 protocol is to the Convention on the Prevention of Marine Pollution by Dumping of Wastes and Other Matter, 29 December 1972, entered into force 30 August 1975, reprinted in 1046 U.N.T.S. 120 [London Dumping Convention]. The London Dumping Convention and its protocol website is at <www.londonconvention.org>. Article 11 is set out in the text at note 196 in this article.

[12] Protocol to the United Nations Framework Convention on Climate Change, 11 December 1997, not yet in force, reprinted in (1998) 37 I.L.M. 22. The Kyoto Protocol is to the United Nations Framework Convention on Climate Change, done 9 May 1992, entered into force 24 March 1994, reprinted in (1992) 31 I.L.M. 849 [UNFCCC]. The Kyoto Protocol and the UNFCCC website is at <www.unfccc.int/>. Article 18 reads:

> The Conference of the Parties serving as the meeting of the Parties to this Protocol shall, at its first session, approve appropriate and effective procedures and mechanisms to determine and to address cases of non-compliance with the provisions of this Protocol, including through the development of an indicative list of consequences, taking into account the cause, type, degree and frequency of non-compliance. Any procedures and mechanisms under this Article entailing binding consequences shall be adopted by means of an amendment to this Protocol.

[13] Convention on the Prior Informed Consent Procedure for Certain Hazardous Chemicals and Pesticides in International Trade, 11 September 1998, entered into force 24 February 2004, reprinted in (1999) 38 I.L.M. 1 [Rotterdam Convention]. The Rotterdam Convention website is at <www.pic.int>. Article 17 is set out in the text at note 187 in this article.

- Article 15 of the 1998 Convention on Access to Information, Public Participation and Decision-Making and Access to Justice in Environmental Matters (Aarhus Convention);[14]
- Article 34 of the 2000 Cartagena Protocol on Biosafety to the Convention on Biological Diversity (Cartagena Protocol);[15]
- Article 17 of the 2001 Stockholm Convention on Persistent Organic Pollutants (Stockholm Convention);[16] and
- Article 21 of the International Treaty on Plant Genetic Resources for Food and Agriculture (ITPGRFA).[17]

Under two other MEAs, the 1989 Convention on the Control of Transboundary Movement of Hazardous Wastes and Their Disposal (Basel Convention)[18] and the Convention on Environmental Im-

[14] Convention on Access to Information, Public Participation and Decision-Making and Access to Justice in Environmental Matters, 25 June 1998, entered into force 30 October 2001, reprinted in (1999) 38 I.L.M. 517 [Aarhus Convention]. The Aarhus Convention website is at <www.unece.org/env/pp/welcome.html>. Article 15 reads:

> The Meeting of the Parties shall establish, on a consensus basis, optional arrangements of a non-confrontational, non-judicial and consultative nature for reviewing compliance with the provisions of this Convention. These arrangements shall allow for appropriate public involvement and may include the option of considering communications from members of the public on matters related to this Convention.

[15] Cartagena Protocol on Biosafety to the Convention on Biological Diversity, 29 January 2000, entered into force 11 September 2003, reprinted in (2000) 39 I.L.M. 1027 [Cartagena Protocol]. The Cartagena Protocol is to the Convention on Biological Diversity, done 5 June 1992, entered into force 29 December 1993, reprinted in (1992) 31 I.L.M. 822 [CBD]. The Cartagena Protocol website is at <www.biodiv.org/biosafety/>. Article 34 is set out in the text at note 176 in this article.

[16] Stockholm Convention on Persistent Organic Pollutants, 22 May 2001, entered into force 17 May 2004, reprinted in (2001) 40 I.L.M. 532 [Stockholm Convention]. The Stockholm Convention website is at <www.pops.int>. Article 17 is set out in the text at note 191 in this article.

[17] International Treaty on Plant Genetic Resources for Food and Agriculture, 3 November 2001, entered into force 29 June 2004 [ITPGRFA]. The treaty text is available at <www.fao.org/ag/cgrfa/>. Article 21 reads:

> The Governing Body shall, at its first meeting, consider and approve cooperative and effective procedures and operational mechanisms to promote compliance with the provisions of this Treaty and to address issues of non-compliance. These procedures and mechanisms shall include monitoring, and offering advice or assistance, including legal advice or legal assistance, when needed, in particular to developing countries and countries with economies in transition.

[18] Convention on the Control of Transboundary Movement of Hazardous Wastes and Their Disposal, 22 March 1989, entered into force 5 May 1992, reprinted in

pact Assessment in a Transboundary Context (Espoo Convention),[19] compliance committees have been created without the existence of explicit treaty provisions. In June 2004, an amendment to the Espoo Convention was adopted by the Meeting of the Parties, which, when it enters into force, will add a provision providing the basis for the work of the compliance committee.[20]

One other MEA needs to be noted: the 1973 Convention on International Trade in Endangered Species of Wild Fauna and Flora (CITES).[21] CITES has developed a compliance process that is unique and that does not, *per se*, involve a compliance committee structure such as the one utilized in the Montreal Protocol or that has been adopted and envisioned in any of the earlier-noted MEAs.[22]

Canada has been a strong supporter of the compliance committee experiment and has worked hard to ensure that a compliance provision is included in new MEAs and that negotiations leading to the committees being established are pursued in a timely manner. For example, at the 2003 Intergovernmental Negotiating Committee meeting under the Stockholm Convention, Canada pushed for early work on the creation of the compliance mechanism, although,

---

(1989) 28 I.L.M. 657 [Basel Convention]. The Basel Convention website is at <www.basel.int>.

[19] Convention on Environmental Impact Assessment in a Transboundary Context, 25 February 1991, entered into force 10 September 1997, reprinted in (1991) 30 I.L.M. 802 [Espoo Convention]. The Espoo Convention website is at <www.unece.org/env/eia/welcome.html>.

[20] Decision III/7, "Second Amendment to the Espoo Convention," in *Report of the Third Meeting of the Conference of the Parties*, Doc. ECE/MP.EIA/6, 13 September 2004, Annex VII, available at the Espoo Convention website, *supra* note 19. The amendment will add a new Article 14 bis to the convention, which is set out in the text at note 153 in this article and see the section entitled "Espoo Convention" later in this article.

[21] Convention on International Trade in Endangered Species of Wild Fauna and Flora, 3 March 1973, entered into force 1 July 1975, reprinted in 993 U.N.T.S. 243 [CITES]. The CITES website is at <www.cites.org>.

[22] The CITES Secretariat has been working on the Guidelines on Compliance with the Convention, which were presented for state party comment at the forty-ninth Meeting of the Standing Committee, April 2003. *Guidelines on Compliance with the Convention*, Doc. SC 49, Doc. 16, available at the CITES website, *supra* note 21. A revised version with state party comments is found in *Guidelines on Compliance with the Convention*, Doc. SC 50, Doc. 27, available at the CITES website, *supra* note 21. See generally Rosalind Reeve, *Policing International Trade in Endangered Species: The CITES Treaty and Compliance* (London: Earthscan Publications, 2002).

in the end, developing countries, for reasons unrelated to the compliance issue, were not prepared to discuss the matter.[23] While the argument has been made that experience under an MEA is necessary in order to identify the compliance issues that can arise and, therefore, the nature of the mechanism best attuned to deal most effectively with these matters, Canada has supported the view that it is better to establish compliance committees as soon as it is practicable in order to let the committee work alongside of the state parties to the MEAs as they confront implementation and compliance issues.

The purpose of this article is to reflect on Canada's experience in the negotiation and operation of MEA compliance committee structures. As noted, there has been a compliance committee operating pursuant to the Montreal Protocol since 1990,[24] and committees have been operating under the LRTAP Convention[25] and the Espoo Convention.[26] These established committees will receive

---

[23] See *Report of the Intergovernmental Negotiating Committee for an Internationally Legally Binding Instrument for Implementing International Action on Certain Persistent Organic Pollutants on The Work of Its Seventh Session*, Doc. UNEP/POPS/INC.7/ 28, 18 July 2003, at paras. 126–31, available at the Stockholm Convention website, *supra* note 16. A more pointed report of the meeting is provided in "Summary of the Seventh Session of the Intergovernmental Negotiating Committee for an Internationally Legally Binding Instrument for Implementing International Action on Certain Persistent Organic Pollutants" (21 July 2003) 15(81) Earth Negotiations Bulletin 8–9, available at <www.iisd.ca/chemical/pops7>.

[24] Montreal Protocol, Non-Compliance Procedure, *supra* note 4. For the most recent report of the Montreal Protocol Implementation Committee, see *Report of the Implementation Committee under the Non-Compliance Procedure for the Montreal Protocol on the Work of Its Thirty-First Meeting*, Doc. UNEP/OzL.Pro/ImpCom/31/3, 13 November 2003, available on the UNEP Ozone Secretariat website, *supra* note 2. See also Anderson and Sarma, *supra* note 7 at 274–89.

[25] Decision 1997/2, *Concerning the Implementation Committee, Its Structure and Functions and Procedures for Review of Compliance*, Doc. ECE/EB.Air/53, Annex III, available on the LRTAP website, *supra* note 9 [LRTAP Convention, Structure and Functions of Implementation Committee]. Revisions were made in 2001, see Doc. ECE/EB.Air/75, annex v. For the most recent report of the LRTAP Implementation Committee, see *The Sixth Report of the Implementation Committee*, Doc. ECE/EB.Air/2003/1 and Doc. ECE/EB.Air/2003/1/Add.1, 2 October 2003, available on the LRTAP website, *supra* note 9.

[26] Decision II/4, "Review of Compliance," in *Report of the Second Meeting of the Conference of the Parties*, Doc. ECE/MP.EIA/4, 7 August 2001, Annex IV, available on the Espoo Convention website, *supra* note 19. Revisions were made and a consolidation of the Structure and Functions of the Implementation Committee and Procedures for Review of Compliance, adopted in 2004. See Decision III/2, "Review of Compliance," in *Report of the Third Meeting of the Conference of the Parties, supra*

special attention in this article since they provide insights into the work and future of the other compliance committees. In 2002, a compliance committee was established under the Basel Convention,[27] and, in 2004, another was established under the Cartagena Protocol.[28] In 2001, procedures and mechanisms for compliance under the Kyoto Protocol were agreed to by the parties to the UNFCCC for eventual adoption by the parties to the Kyoto Protocol,[29] but since the Kyoto Protocol is not yet in force, the compliance committee has not yet been established. Negotiations of compliance committee processes are still underway but well advanced for the Rotterdam Convention[30] and, to a lesser extent,

---

note 20 [Espoo Convention, Structure and Functions of the Implementation Committee]. For the most recent report of the Espoo Convention Implementation Committee, see *Report of the Fifth Meeting of the Implementation Committee*, Doc. MP.EIA/WG.1/2004/4, 8 April 2004, available on the Espoo Convention website, *supra* note 19.

[27] Decision VI/12, "Establishment of Mechanism for Promoting Implementation and Compliance," in *Report of the Sixth Conference of the Parties of the Basel Convention*, Doc. UNEP/CHW.6/40, 10 February 2003 [Basel Convention, Mechanism for Promoting Implementation and Compliance], available on the Basel website, *supra* note 18.

[28] Decision BS-I/7, "Establishment of Procedures and Mechanisms on Compliance under the Cartagena Protocol on Biosafety," in "Report of the First Meeting of the Conference of the Parties Serving as the Meeting of the Parties to the Protocol on Biosafety," Doc. UNEP/CBD/BS/COP-MOP/1/15, 14 April 2004, available on the Cartagena Protocol website, *supra* note 15.

[29] Pursuant to Article 18 of the Kyoto Protocol, *supra* note 12, the Seventh Conference of the Parties (COP) to the UNFCCC in 2001 adopted Procedures and Mechanisms Relating to Compliance under the Kyoto Protocol as Decision 24/CP.7, reprinted in *Report of the Seventh Conference of the Parties of the Climate Change Convention*, Doc. FCCC/CP/2001/13 Add.3, 21 January 2002 [Kyoto Protocol, Procedures and Mechanisms Relating to Compliance]. The question remains whether the first COP serving as the Meeting of the Parties (MOP) to the Kyoto Protocol will adopt the compliance mechanism as a decision, an amendment to the protocol, or both. See note 53 later in this article. For a brief review of the Kyoto compliance procedures, see Farhana Yamin and Joanna Depledge, *The International Climate Change Regime: A Guide to Rules, Institutions and Procedures* (Cambridge: Cambridge University Press, forthcoming), chapter 12. A draft of this book is available at <www.ids.ac.uk/ids/env/climatechange.html> and references are to this draft. Regarding compliance and the Kyoto Protocol generally, see Jacob Werksman, "Compliance and the Kyoto Protocol: Building a Backbone into a 'Flexible' Regime" (1998) 9 Y.B. Int'l Env. L. 48–101.

[30] The most recent draft of a decision and annex for the establishment of a compliance committee under the Rotterdam Convention is in *Report of the Intergovernmental Negotiating Committee for the Rotterdam Convention on its Tenth Session*, Doc.

under the Stockholm Convention[31] and the Protocol to the London Dumping Convention.[32] No discussions have yet taken place regarding the elaboration of a compliance committee structure under the ITPGRFA, although these are planned for the fall of 2004. At the time of writing, all of the above MEAs, except for the Protocol to the London Dumping Convention and the Kyoto Protocol have entered into force, and Canada is a party to all except the Cartagena Protocol.

Excluded from direct discussion in this article is the Aarhus Convention compliance procedure, which was established in 2002,[33] since Canada is not a party to the Aarhus Convention and has not participated in the negotiations on the establishment of the mechanism. Interestingly and exceptionally, the United States made a formal statement regarding the Aarhus Convention compliance mechanism, noting that the United States does "not consider the compliance rules adopted ... to be a precedent for compliance procedures in other regional or multilateral environment agreements."[34]

Also excluded from direct discussion is the Kyoto Protocol compliance mechanism. While the Kyoto Protocol has a compliance provision with the Montreal Protocol as its parentage, the mechanism subsequently agreed upon is impressively complex and unquestionably unique to the Kyoto Protocol. For example, structurally, the compliance committee has a plenary and two

---

UNEP/FAO/PIC/INC.10/24, 21 November 2003, Annex VIII, available on the Rotterdam Convention website, *supra* note 13 [Rotterdam Convention, Draft Non-Compliance Procedures].

31 See the Stockholm Secretariat report *Synthesis of Views on Non-Compliance*, Doc. UNEP/POPS/INC.7/21, 20 February 2003, prepared for the seventh meeting of the Stockholm Convention intergovernmental negotiating committee, available on the Stockholm Convention website, *supra* note 16.

32 See *Report of the Twenty-Fifth Consultative Meeting of the Parties to the London Dumping Convention*, Doc. LC 25/16, 7 November 2003, paras. 4.1–4.10 available on the London Dumping Convention website, *supra* note 11.

33 Decision I/7, "Review of Compliance," in *Report of the First Meeting of the Conference of the Parties*, Doc. ECE/MP.PP/2, 17 December 2002, available on the Aarhus Convention website, *supra* note 14 [Aarhus Convention, Structure and Functions of the Compliance Committee). For the most recent report of the Aarhus Convention Compliance Committee, see *Report of the Second Meeting of the Implementation Committee*, Doc. MP.PP/C.1/2003/4, 15 October 2003, available on the Aarhus Convention website, *supra* note 14.

34 "Statement by the Delegation of the United States with Respect to the Establishment of the Compliance Mechanism," in *Report of the First Meeting of the Conference of the Parties, supra* note 33, Annex, para. 5 [Statement of the United States].

branches, the facilitative branch and the enforcement branch, with separate functions tied to specific provisions of the protocol.[35] While it has been described as "the strongest and institutionally most sophisticated non-compliance procedure adopted by an MEA to date,"[36] in many respects, it is unlike the compliance committee structures and mandates adopted or contemplated under other MEAs.

Before looking at each of the MEAs in turn, a few words are necessary on the international legal "situation" of compliance procedures, followed by an overview of the key issues involved in the mandates of compliance committees.

COMPLIANCE MECHANISM COMMONALITIES AND INTERNATIONAL LAW

In addition to the similar committee mandates and structures[37] found under the six MEAs that are in operation or in an advanced negotiating state (Montreal Protocol, LRTAP Convention, Espoo Convention, Basel Convention, Cartagena Protocol, and the Rotterdam Convention),[38] there are a number of other commonalities shared by these MEAs, which have or are contemplating compliance mechanisms. The first commonality is the relationship between compliance committees and the Conference of the Parties (COP).[39] Established by the relevant convention or protocol, the COP is the plenary organ on which all of the state parties are represented and which, depending on the underlying convention or protocol, has the mandate to carry out various administrative and organizational tasks related to the convention or protocol.[40]

---

[35] Kyoto Protocol, Procedures and Mechanisms Relating to Compliance, *supra* note 29, paras IV and V; and see Yamin and Depledge, *supra* note 29 at 12–13 to 19.

[36] Yamin and Depledge, *supra* note 29 at 12-10.

[37] To be discussed in the next section of this article, entitled "Overview of Compliance Committee Structure Issues."

[38] Excluded from detailed discussion are the compliance procedures under CITES, *supra* note 22, the Aarhus Convention, *supra* note 33, and the Kyoto Protocol, *supra* note 29.

[39] While Conference of the Parties (COP) will be used throughout this contribution, as evidenced in note 40, for some MEAs the plenary organ is referred to as the Meeting of the Parties (MOP), the Executive Body, or the Governing Body.

[40] For an excellent review of COPs under MEAs, see Robin R. Churchill and Geir Ulfstein, "Autonomous Institutional Arrangements in Multilateral Environmental Agreements: A Little-Noticed Phenomenon in International Law" (2000)

Pursuant to MEAs, it is the COPs that have the mandate to adopt compliance mechanisms.[41] Moreover, a task inevitably within the hands of a COP is the "continuous review and evaluation of the implementation of" the underlying convention or protocol.[42] Thus, MEA compliance committees are subject to the direction and supervision of the COP.

The second commonality among MEA compliance mechanisms is the emphasis that the purpose of the compliance procedures is to be facilitative and non-confrontational with the desire being to assist states to attain or maintain compliance with the obligations in the underlying convention or protocol.[43]

---

94 Am. J. Int'l L. 623–59. See also the listing in Sands, *supra* note 1 at 109–11. Regarding the conventions and protocols discussed in this contribution, see Montreal Protocol, *supra* note 2, Article 11, which establishes the MOP; Basel Convention, *supra* note 18, Article 15, which establishes the COP; LRTAP Convention, *supra* note 9, Article 10, which establishes the Executive Body; Protocol to the London Dumping Convention, *supra* note 11, Article 18, which, when the protocol enters into force, will establish the Meeting of the Contracting Parties that will take over from the consultative meetings of the contracting parties established under the London Dumping Convention, *supra* note 11, Article XIV(4); Espoo Convention, *supra* note 19, Article 11, which establishes the MOP; Rotterdam Convention, *supra* note 13, Article 18, which establishes the COP; Cartagena Protocol, *supra* note 15, Article 29, which allows for the COP established by Article 23 of the CBD, *supra* note 15, to serve as the MOP for the Cartagena Protocol; Stockholm Convention, *supra* note 16, Article 19, which establishes the COP; Kyoto Protocol, *supra* note 12, Article 13, which allows for the COP established by Article 7 of the UNFCCC, *supra* note 12, to serve as the MOP for the Kyoto Protocol; and the ITPGRFA, *supra* note 17, Article 19, which establishes the Governing Body.

41 Montreal Protocol, *supra* note 2, Article 8; VOC Protocol, *supra* note 9, Article 3(3); Oslo Protocol, *supra* note 10, Article 7; Protocol to the London Dumping Convention, *supra* note 11, Article 11; Rotterdam Convention, *supra* note 13, Article 17; Cartagena Protocol, *supra* note 15, Article 34; Stockholm Convention, *supra* note 16, Article 16; Kyoto Protocol, *supra* note 12, Article 18; and the ITPGRFA, *supra* note 17, Article 21.

42 Rotterdam Convention, *supra* note 13, Article 18(5). Similar language is located in: Montreal Protocol, *supra* note 2, Article 11(4)(a); Basel Convention, *supra* note 18, Article 15(5); LRTAP Convention, *supra* note 9, Article 10(2); Protocol to the London Dumping Convention, *supra* note 11, Article 18(1); Espoo Convention, *supra* note 19, Article 11(2); Cartagena Protocol, *supra* note 15, Article 29(4); Stockholm Convention, *supra* note 16, Article 19(5); Kyoto Protocol, *supra* note 12, Article 13(j); and the ITPGRFA, *supra* note 17, Article 19.3.

43 See Oslo Protocol, *supra* note 10, Article 7(2); Protocol to the London Dumping Convention, *supra* note 11, Article 11(2); Cartagena Protocol, *supra* note 15, Article 34; ITPGRFA, *supra* note 17, Article 21; Basel Convention, Mechanism for Promoting Implementation and Compliance, *supra* note 27, paras. 1 and 2;

The third commonality is that the compliance procedures are without prejudice to the dispute settlement provisions that exist in the underlying convention or protocol.[44] Of the eight MEAs discussed in this article, only the 1996 Protocol to the London Dumping Convention provides for compulsory and binding third-party adjudication for disputes arising under the underlying protocol or convention.[45] Six of the MEAs, however, do provide state parties with the opportunity to opt into compulsory and binding third party adjudication, using either arbitration or the International Court of Justice for disputes arising between state parties that have both agreed to use compulsory adjudication.[46] Canada has not consented to third party adjudication by exercising this option under any of these MEAs. Two commentators, after reviewing the relationship between formal dispute settlement and compliance mechanisms,

---

and Espoo Convention, Structure and Functions of the Implementation Committee, *supra* note 26, para. 12. The Kyoto Protocol, Procedures and Mechanisms Relating to Compliance, *supra* note 29, para. I, is a bit different: "The objective of these procedures and mechanisms is to facilitate, promote and enforce compliance with the commitments under the Protocol."

[44] See Cartagena Protocol, *supra* note 15, Article 34; Montreal Protocol, Non-Compliance Procedure, *supra* note 4, preamble; LRTAP Convention, Structure and Functions of Implementation Committee, *supra* note 25, para. 12; Rotterdam Convention, Draft Non-Compliance Procedures, *supra* note 30, para. 27; Basel Convention, Mechanism for Promoting Implementation and Compliance, *supra* note 27, para. 27; Kyoto Protocol, Procedures and Mechanisms Relating to Compliance, *supra* note 29, para. XVI; and Espoo Convention, Structure and Functions of the Implementation Committee, *supra* note 26, para 12.

For a detailed analysis of the legal relationship between the Montreal non-compliance procedures and formal dispute settlement, see Koskenniemi, *supra* note 6 at 155–61. More generally on the relationship between international dispute settlement and MEA compliance mechanisms, see M.A. Fitzmaurice and C. Redgwell, "Environmental Non-Compliance Procedures and International Law" (2000) 31 Netherlands Y.B. Int'l L. 35 at 43–52. These authors wryly note that the without prejudice wording "scarcely penetrates the surface" of the relationship (at 51).

[45] Protocol to the London Dumping Convention, *supra* note 11, Article 16.

[46] See Vienna Convention on Protection of the Ozone Layer, *supra* note 2, Article 11, which applies to the Montreal Protocol pursuant to Article 14 of the protocol, *supra* note 2; Rotterdam Convention, *supra* note 13, Article 20; Basel Convention, *supra* note 18, Article 20; CBD, *supra* note 15, Article 27, which applies to the Cartagena Protocol pursuant to Article 32 of the protocol, *supra* note 15; Stockholm Convention, *supra* note 16, Article 18; and Espoo Convention, *supra* note 19, Article 15. See also UNFCCC, *supra* note 12, Article 14, which applies to the Kyoto Protocol pursuant to Article 19 of the protocol, *supra* note 12.

have concluded that compliance mechanisms "are subordinate" to formal dispute settlement processes.[47]

For international lawyers, these commonalities help "situate" compliance procedures and provide an answer to the question — to what are parties agreeing when they adopt a treaty provision to establish a compliance mechanism? Most importantly, compliance procedures do not replace formal third-party state-to-state dispute settlement, the activation of which is carefully guarded by states. In the absence of language that clearly and unambiguously usurps explicit dispute resolution provisions elsewhere in the treaty, there is no force in an argument that compliance procedures step into the role of formal dispute settlement, even if the formal dispute settlement process cannot function because the parties concerned have not agreed to its activation. Referring to the Basel Convention's compliance procedure relationship with dispute settlement, one knowledgeable commentator indicated:

The purpose of Article 20 [of the Basel Convention] is to provide a procedure to settle disputes between parties. On the other hand, the purpose of the compliance mechanism is to provide a tool to assist parties in complying with the Convention. In other words, the mechanism and the dispute settlement system differ in their purposes, and coexist without prejudicing each other.[48]

A sophisticated reviewer of the Montreal Protocol non-compliance process stated:

The *travaux préparatoires* of the NCP [Montreal Protocol compliance procedure] as well as the composition and functions of the Implementation Committee and, a fortiori, the Meeting of the Parties, make it clear that neither can, or is expected to, work as a judicial body, assessing the performance of the parties' obligations with a view of determining whether or not there has been a wrongful act triggering state responsibility. A dispute about whether some particular type of non-performance is a wrongful act is, by its very nature, a dispute about the interpretation or application of the treaty and capable of being resolved only within the [dispute settlement] procedures."[49]

---

47 Fitzmaurice and Redgwell, *supra* note 44 at 64.

48 Akiho Shibata, "The Basel Compliance Mechanism" (2003) 12 Rev. Eur. Comm. Int'l Env. L. 183 at 196.

49 Koskenniemi, *supra* note 6 at 144 [footnote deleted] and see also 145.

The non-judicial nature of compliance committee structures, from an international legal perspective, is further indicated by: the general lack of procedural safeguards for the parties involved in the process; the minimal consideration of burden of proof issues; and the fact that the outcomes of the compliance process are principally recommendations to a COP.[50] In addition, absent explicit wording in the underlying convention or protocol, the interpretation of treaty obligations is ultimately a matter for individual state parties and not for a compliance committee or a COP,[51] and the decisions of COPs are not enforceable as international legal obligations (typically COP decisions are not internationally legally binding).[52] Interestingly, confronting concerns about the legal nature of compliance mechanisms, Article 18 of the Kyoto Protocol provides: "Any [compliance] procedures and mechanisms under this Article entailing binding consequences shall be adopted by means of an amendment to this Protocol."[53]

Thus, absent express language, state parties to an MEA containing a compliance procedure have not yielded to compliance mechanisms authority that ordinarily resides in adjudicative dispute settlement processes or that is otherwise available to state parties regarding the determination of a convention or protocol breach. Moreover, state parties have not yielded to compliance mechanisms the ability to adopt remedies (countermeasures, as detailed in the

---

[50] See notes 75–76 in this article. Note that Yamin and Depledge, *supra* note 29 at 12-10, refer to aspects of the Kyoto Protocol compliance regime as "quasi-judicial."

[51] Respecting COPs and the interpretation of the underlying convention or protocol, see Churchill and Ulfstein, *supra* note 40 at 641–42.

[52] See Jutta Brunnée, "COPing with Consent: Law-Making under Multilateral Environmental Agreements" (2002) 15 Leiden J. Int'l L. 1 at 32, where it is concluded that COP decisions "do not appear to be binding in a formal sense." She goes on to note that the "distinction between COP decisions that are, technically speaking, legally binding and those that are not may well be more apparent than real" (at 33). Generally, this article provides a sophisticated view of the working of COPs. Koskenniemi, *supra* note 6 at 146 and 152, notes that under the Montreal Protocol "the Meeting of the Parties cannot make binding decisions." See also O. Yoshida, "Soft Enforcement of Treaties: The Montreal Protocol's Noncompliance Procedure and the Functions of Internal International Institutions" (1999) 10 Colorado J. Int'l Env'l L. & Pol. 95 at 118–20. A different perspective, although not necessarily a different result, is provided by Churchill and Ulfstein, *supra* note 40 at 639–42.

[53] Regarding Kyoto Protocol, *supra* note 12, Article 18, see Brunnée, *supra* note 52 at 23–29; and Yamin and Depledge, *supra* note 29 at 12-10 to 19.

international law of state responsibility[54] or remedies under treaty law[55]) that may exist for such breaches.[56] In no significant manner does this fact circumscribe the value of compliance procedures. It is generally recognized that the development of compliance procedures in MEAs has arisen because the "traditional rules of international law concerned with material breach of treaty obligations and with state responsibility ... [were] ... inappropriate — and, indeed, unable — fully to address problems of environmental treaty compliance."[57]

OVERVIEW OF COMPLIANCE COMMITTEE STRUCTURE ISSUES

The structures and mandates of the compliance committees under the six MEAs in operation or in an advanced negotiation state (Montreal Protocol, LRTAP Convention, Espoo Convention, Basel Convention, Cartagena Protocol, and the Rotterdam Convention),[58] with which Canada has been directly engaged all involve balance, negotiation, and compromise respecting three main elements:

- the composition of the committee and its manner of working;
- the "triggering" of the compliance mechanism; and
- the measures that the committee can take and/or recommend be taken.

Each of the compliance processes under the six MEAs has dealt with these issues in a different manner. These differing solutions

---

54   For a discussion of countermeasures in state responsibility in the context of MEA compliance, see Koskenniemi, *supra* note 6 at 141–57; and Fitzmaurice and Redgwell, *supra* note 44 at 52–59.

55   For a discussion of treaty law remedies in the context of MEA compliance, see Koskenniemi, *supra* note 6 at 137–41; and Fitzmaurice and Redgwell, *supra* note 44 at 59–62.

56   This is not to say that the mere presence of a process for formal dispute settlement necessarily excludes the possibility of a compliance process utilizing countermeasures. See Koskenniemi, *supra* note 6 at 156. Rather, the position is that state parties have not yielded to (consented to) compliance mechanisms as the necessary authority.

57   Fitzmaurice and Redgwell, *supra* note 44 at 37 and, more generally on the reasons for the establishment of compliance procedures, at 39–43. See also Churchill and Ulfstein, *supra* note 40 at 644–46.

58   Excluded from detailed discussion are the compliance procedures under CITES, *supra* note 22, the Aarhus Convention, *supra* note 33, and the Kyoto Protocol, *supra* note 29.

are because each MEA is unique, which leads to varied approaches to the issues, and because the experiences emerging from the compliance committee operations inform the compliance committee structures of the next MEA. In short, there is a "limited" experiential building process occurring.

An important limitation on the experiential building process is that each MEA has a different grouping of state parties, and the negotiation of compliance mechanisms, depending on occurrence, may engage differing states. The LRTAP Convention experience, for example, only engages those states within the United Nations Economic Commission for Europe (which includes Canada and the United States). As already noted, since Canada is not a party to the Aarhus Convention, it does not participate in the compliance discussions. With respect to the compliance procedures adopted for the Cartagena Protocol, while influential during their negotiation, at the time of their final adoption at COP/MOP-1 (when the final compromises were made) Canada was not a party to the protocol and thus had to rely on like-minded parties to pursue its interests. It is a difficult issue of balance in determining whether a compliance procedure should be constructed taking into account the views of non-parties to the underlying convention or protocol in order to minimize the impediments to potential ratification by those states. While views can differ on where the balance should lie, it is difficult to perceive any long-term benefit in erecting significant barriers to ratification by non-parties unless there are substantive reasons to do so.

COMPOSITION OF THE COMMITTEES AND THEIR MANNER
OF WORKING

The composition of the committee refers to the question of whether committee members are states or appointed individuals. The manner of working refers to whether the committee is open or closed to the public, including states not represented on the committee, and the nature of the voting process for adoption of reports and decisions by the committee. The tension on these issues arises from differing views on the extent to which compliance committees are able to stray from their purpose of facilitating and helping states to attain and maintain compliance and to be more investigatory and evaluative of state behaviour. Curiously, on these issues, recent compliance committee structures have shunned the successful experiences of the compliance committees under the

Montreal Protocol and the LRTAP Convention. For example, while the early compliance committees had states as members (individuals representing and appointed by states),[59] more recent MEAs have gone to nominated individuals appointed by the COPs.[60] The individuals are, however, not sitting in their personal capacities in a manner akin to judges but rather are to "serve objectively and in the best interest of the Convention."[61]

The concern about appointed individuals is that they would make the compliance committees not directly accountable to the state parties of an MEA, which are in the position of providing facilitative assistance, and they may appear to be (and operate as) quasi-judicial, confrontational bodies. Another issue concerns accessibility to the public. The successful committees under the Montreal Protocol and the LRTAP Convention have been closed to the public,[62] whereas more recent committee structures have been open, except where a compliance matter engaging a specific state is being discussed.[63]

"TRIGGERING" THE COMPLIANCE MECHANISM

A sensitive issue in the negotiation of MEA compliance procedures is who should be able to bring a compliance matter respect-

---

[59] See Montreal Protocol, Non-Compliance Procedure, *supra* note 4, para. 5; LRTAP Convention, Structure and Functions of Implementation Committee, *supra* note 25, para. 1; and Espoo Convention, Structure and Functions of the Implementation Committee, *supra* note 26, para. 1(a).

[60] Basel Convention, Mechanism for Promoting Implementation and Compliance, *supra* note 27, para. 3; Cartagena Protocol, Procedures and Mechanisms on Compliance, *supra* note 28, para. II(2); and Rotterdam Convention, Draft Non-Compliance Procedures, *supra* note 30, para. 2.

[61] Basel Convention, Mechanism for Promoting Implementation and Compliance, *supra* note 27, para. 5; and Rotterdam Convention, Draft Non-Compliance Procedures, *supra* note 30, para. 3. The wording under the Cartagena Protocol is "serve objectively and in a personal capacity." Cartagena Protocol, Procedures and Mechanisms on Compliance, *supra* note 28, para. II(3). This is further noted in notes 178–79 in this article. Members of the Kyoto Protocol compliance committee will "serve in their individual capacities." Kyoto Protocol, Procedures and Mechanisms Relating to Compliance, *supra* note 29, para. II(6).

[62] Neither the Montreal Protocol, Non-Compliance Procedure, *supra* note 4, para. 5, nor the LRTAP Convention, Structure and Functions of Implementation Committee, *supra* note 25, para. 1, make reference to the committee meetings being open and, therefore, are closed pursuant to the operating rules of procedure.

[63] See Basel Convention, Mechanism for Promoting Implementation and Compliance, *supra* note 27, para. 16.

ing a specific state before the committee. This question is referred to as the "trigger" issue. The sensitivity of the "trigger" issue is self-evident — a state party to an MEA may find it embarrassing, politically damaging, and/or insulting to have to answer to a compliance committee for its actions or inaction.[64] Moreover, publicizing or seeking to shame a non-compliant state may elicit a negative or stubborn reaction from the state that may be counter-productive to attaining compliance. Finally, for the same reason that states are generally unwilling to consider third-party involvement in disputes, states may also be unwilling to have alleged compliance matters brought to an international forum since it results in the loss of control over the process and results. Alternatively, it has been argued that a broad triggering mechanism ensures a higher degree of compliance with the underlying MEA by providing more opportunities to require an allegedly non-complying party to account for its actions or inaction.

The one area of common ground on this issue is that a state party to an MEA can self-trigger, which means that a state can indicate that it feels it is, or will be, in a position of non-compliance and can seek advice or assistance through the compliance procedures to attain or re-attain compliance.[65] The state's self-trigger is consistent with the facilitative and non-confrontational mantra of compliance mechanisms. Self-identification of non-compliance, in one form or another, has been the manner in which almost all examples of specific party non-compliance have been brought before the operating compliance committees. An issue that arises from a state party's self-trigger is whether this event acts, or may be used by a state, as a *de facto* exemption or waiver from MEA obligations. Compliance committees have to be on guard to prevent this situation from occurring.

[64] Shibata, *supra* note 48 at 189, noted that in the Basel Convention compliance negotiations "for the majority of parties, the issue of 'non-compliance' or 'compliance difficulties' ... [was] ... politically sensitive, resulting in countries being very cautious about discussing their own compliance issues in an international forum."

[65] See Montreal Protocol, Non-Compliance Procedure, *supra* note 4, para. 4; LRTAP Convention, Structure and Functions of Implementation Committee, *supra* note 25, para. 4(b); Espoo Convention, Structure and Functions of the Implementation Committee, *supra* note 26, para. 4(b); Basel Convention, Mechanism for Promoting Implementation and Compliance, *supra* note 27, para. 9(a); Cartagena Protocol, Procedures and Mechanisms on Compliance, *supra* note 28, para. IV(1)(a); Kyoto Protocol, Procedures and Mechanisms Relating to Compliance, *supra* note 29, para. VI(1)(a); and Rotterdam Convention, Draft Non-Compliance Procedures, *supra* note 30, para. 11(a).

Other possible triggering entities for bringing a specific state before a compliance committee are: another state; the secretariat of
the underlying protocol or convention;[66] the committee itself; or a
non-state actor (that is, a non-governmental organization). All of
these possible triggers involve carefully calculating the balance between the perceived enhanced compliance with convention or protocol obligations versus an affront to state sovereignty. The careful
calculus is to provide sufficient "pressure" to have states decide to
comply with obligations rather than turn away from them. This
reality of international law and politics — namely, that there is little
enforcement power and that public confrontation may be counter-
productive — are usually bitter pills for many non-state actors to
swallow.

As an acceptance that international dispute settlement is a rarity
and that, in some senses, compliance committees can be seen or
used as dispute avoidance techniques or "soft" dispute settlement,
most compliance mechanisms under MEAs recognize the ability of
one state party to bring before a compliance committee the actions
or inactions of another state party.[67] Nevertheless, the argument is
sometimes made that a state-to-state trigger is the very antithesis of
a non-confrontational process and has no place as a compliance
committee trigger.[68] Others argue that without this trigger the value

66 All of the MEAs noted herein either create their own secretariats or make use of
existing secretariats. See Montreal Protocol, *supra* note 2, Articles 1(3) and 12,
which uses the Secretariat established by the Vienna Convention for the Protection of the Ozone Layer, *supra* note 2, Article 7; Basel Convention, *supra* note 18,
Article 16; LRTAP Convention, *supra* note 9, Article 11, which uses the Secretariat of the Economic Commission of Europe; Protocol to the London Dumping Convention, *supra* note 11, Article 19, which, when the protocol enters into
force, will make the International Maritime Organization the Secretariat; Espoo
Convention, *supra* note 19, Article 13, which uses the Secretariat of the Economic Commission of Europe; Rotterdam Convention, *supra* note 13, Article
19; Cartagena Protocol, *supra* note 15, Article 31, which uses the Secretariat
established by the CBD, *supra* note 15, Article 24; Stockholm Convention, *supra*
note 16, Article 20; and the ITPGRFA, *supra* note 17, Article 20.

67 Montreal Protocol, Non-Compliance Procedure, *supra* note 4, para. 1; LRTAP
Convention, Structure and Functions of Implementation Committee, *supra* note
25, para. 4(a); Espoo Convention, Structure and Functions of the Implementation Committee, *supra* note 26, para. 4(a); Basel Convention, Mechanism for
Promoting Implementation and Compliance, *supra* note 27, para. 9(b); Kyoto
Protocol, Procedures and Mechanisms Relating to Compliance, *supra* note 29,
para. VI(1)(b); and Cartagena Protocol, Procedures and Mechanisms on Compliance, *supra* note 28, para. IV(1)(b).

68 For example, the party-to-party trigger is bracketed in the Rotterdam Convention, Draft Non-Compliance Procedures, *supra* note 30, para. 11(b).

of the mechanism is lessened. Interestingly, thus far, no state party has "triggered" a compliance matter against another state party.

The idea that the secretariat of an underlying protocol or convention can bring a matter respecting a specific party to a compliance committee raises concerns of placing the secretariat in an investigatory role and possibly compromising a secretariat's impartiality. However, MEA secretariats may be receiving information from parties and others and be well positioned to notice possible compliance problems. In contemplating a secretariat trigger, the difficult issue is determining upon what information the Secretariat can exercise its trigger mandate, and, for this reason, the MEA compliance mechanisms that contain a secretariat trigger have qualifications upon what basis the secretariat can be a trigger.[69]

The so-called compliance committee self-trigger, where a compliance committee on its own initiative decides to look at alleged non-compliance by a state party, raises concerns, for instance, of how impartial the committee can be when its credibility for starting the process is in question. Where a compliance committee is mandated to receive information from states and the committee can act on the basis of this received information, the concern about the committee self-trigger is lessened. Among the MEAs under review, only the Espoo Convention compliance mechanism explicitly creates a committee self-trigger that is unconnected to receiving reports from state parties.[70] In addition, there is a distinction between the committee trigger in the context of an individual party and the committee undertaking an examination of systemic non-compliance matters, either on its own initiative or at the request of the COP. Several of the MEAs allow for the compliance committee to examine systemic compliance matters.[71]

---

[69] See Montreal Protocol, Non-Compliance Procedure, *supra* note 4, para. 3; LRTAP Convention, Structure and Functions of Implementation Committee, *supra* note 25, para. 5; and Basel Convention, Mechanism for Promoting Implementation and Compliance, *supra* note 27, para. 9(c).

The Espoo Convention compliance mechanism does not contain an explicit secretariat trigger, however, the secretariat can put information regarding compliance before the committee. Espoo Convention, Structure and Functions of the Implementation Committee, *supra* note 26, para. 6(c). This is discussed in the section entitled "Espoo Convention" later in this article.

[70] Espoo Convention, Structure and Functions of the Implementation Committee, *supra* note 26, para. 5.

[71] See Basel Convention, Mechanism for Promoting Implementation and Compliance, *supra* note 27, para. 21; Cartagena Protocol, Procedures and Mechanisms

The proposition that a non-state actor can activate a compliance committee to deal with alleged non-compliance by a state is often suggested but, with the exception of the Aarhus Convention,[72] it has not been adopted in any MEA compliance structure. Since the Aarhus Convention is essentially about non-state actor participation in domestic environmental matters, it is not unreasonable that non-state actors are involved in the compliance processes under this MEA,[73] although questions have been raised about the "efficacy" of the Aarhus Convention compliance procedures' engagement of non-state actors.[74] The argument in favour of a non-state actor "trigger" concerns the enhancement of compliance with the underlying MEA since non-state actors may be vigilant in a way that states or state-accountable organs (MEA secretariats and compliance committees) may not be.

The other side of the equation engages several points. A non-state actor "trigger" can be seen as being inconsistent with the facilitative nature of compliance mechanisms by inevitably making the process one that is adversarial and confrontational, particularly since a non-state actor is unaccountable to the public in the same manner as a state. For many states with sophisticated political, administrative, and legal systems, where non-state actors have ample opportunity to influence and challenge government decisions on environmental matters, there may be little appetite to provide non-state actors that have been unsuccessful domestically with an avenue to continue the challenge before an international body (compliance committee) — particularly one that subjects national decision-making to the vagaries of the international community. Since compliance committees are creatures of their COPs, non-state actors have the opportunity to address the COP and make their "case" that a specific matter should either be referred to a

---

on Compliance, *supra* note 28, para. III(1)(d); LRTAP Convention, Structure and Functions of Implementation Committee, *supra* note 25, para. 3(d); and Montreal Protocol, Non-Compliance Procedure, *supra* note 4, para. 14.

[72] Aarhus Convention, Structure and Functions of the Compliance Committee, *supra* note 33.

[73] See Aarhus Convention, Structure and Functions of the Compliance Committee, *supra* note 33, paras. 17–23. There are a number of safeguards of the "public trigger" including that state parties can, for a period of years, limit application of the trigger to them. More generally on public participation and international environmental treaties, see Jonas Ebbesson, "The Notion of Public Participation in International Environmental Law" (1997) 8 Y.B. Int'l Envt'l L. 51–97.

[74] See Statement by the United States, *supra* note 34, paras. 7–8.

compliance committee or dealt with directly, thus an indirect avenue exists for non-state actors to pursue non-compliance matters.

The trend in compliance structures is for there to be a state party self-trigger, a state-to-state trigger, and a carefully circumscribed secretariat trigger. There are clear limits to the benefits of an overly broad approach to triggering since, ultimately, the coercive power of MEA compliance mechanisms is primarily "name and shame," which relies on the named state party to take action. This outcome is less likely where a confrontational process is used rather than a non-confrontational process. Moreover, the existing practice, where state self-trigger is the primary means by which a matter comes before a compliance committee is indicative of the lack of appetite or even the usefulness of more robust trigger opportunities.

MEASURES THE COMMITTEE CAN TAKE AND/OR RECOMMEND
BE TAKEN

As the earlier discussion indicates, composition and triggering of a compliance committee are process issues that are primarily policy rather than legal matters, although the international legal interest is that composition and triggering outcomes may lead to expectations and the operation of compliance committees that are legally suspect. The significant international legal issue that arises from compliance mechanisms involves the legality (legal basis) of measures that the committees can take or that they can recommend to the COP and that a COP may take.

As a matter of process, of the completed and operating compliance mechanisms, only the ones under the Basel Convention and the Cartagena Protocol provide that certain measures may be taken directly by the compliance committee.[75] Beyond the limited, direct measures that these two committees can take, MEA compliance committees are mandated to make recommendations, as deemed appropriate or necessary, to the COP.[76] The Basel Convention and

---

[75] Basel Convention, Mechanism for Promoting Implementation and Compliance, *supra* note 27, para. 19; and Cartagena Protocol, Procedures and Mechanisms on Compliance, *supra* note 28, para. VI(1).

[76] Montreal Protocol, Non-Compliance Procedure, *supra* note 4, para. 9; LRTAP Convention, Structure and Functions of Implementation Committee, *supra* note 25, para. 9; Espoo Convention, Structure and Functions of the Implementation Committee, *supra* note 26, para. 9; Basel Convention, Mechanism for Promoting Implementation and Compliance, *supra* note 27, para. 20; and Cartagena Protocol, Procedures and Mechanisms on Compliance, *supra* note 28, para. VI(1)(d) and (2).

the Cartagena Protocol are indicative of the recent practice of allowing the compliance committee to take certain actions and thus providing them with a certain autonomy from the COP. They have also being given the mandate to recommend "additional measures" to the COP for COP action.[77]

The facilitative and non-confrontational nature of compliance mechanisms evidences that the principal measures that a compliance committee can take, or recommend be taken, are ones designed to assist a non-compliant state to attain or re-attain compliance with convention or protocol obligations. Thus, as explicitly noted in the Basel Convention and the Cartagena Protocol compliance mechanism, advice and development of compliance action plans are available to assist non-compliant states.[78] Assistance, either technical or financial, is also noted as a possible additional measure in the Basel Convention and the Cartagena Protocol compliance mechanism[79] as well as in the Montreal Protocol's Indicative List of Measures That Might Be Taken by a Meeting of the Parties in Respect of Non-Compliance with the Protocol (Indicative List of Measures).[80] There are several conundrums about providing technical and financial assistance to non-complying states. First, there is a concern that some states may see the compliance process as an avenue to access technical and financial assistance, which it most clearly is

---

[77] See Basel Convention, Mechanism for Promoting Implementation and Compliance, *supra* note 27, paras. 19 and 20; and Cartagena Protocol, Procedures and Mechanisms on Compliance, *supra* note 28, para. VI. This is the pattern being employed in the Rotterdam Convention, Draft Non-Compliance Procedures, *supra* note 30, paras. 17 and 18; and expected under the Protocol to the London Dumping Convention and the Stockholm Convention. In this regard, the Kyoto Protocol compliance mechanism is significantly different than the mechanisms under the other MEAs since the two branches of the committee clearly have the authority to take direct measures respecting a non-compliant party. See Kyoto Protocol, Procedures and Mechanisms Relating to Compliance, *supra* note 29, paras. XIV and XV.

[78] Basel Convention, Mechanism for Promoting Implementation and Compliance, *supra* note 27, para. 19(a) and (c); and Cartagena Protocol, Procedures and Mechanisms on Compliance, *supra* note 28, para. VI(1)(a) and (c).

[79] Basel Convention, Mechanism for Promoting Implementation and Compliance, *supra* note 27, para. 19 (b); and Cartagena Protocol, Procedures and Mechanisms on Compliance, *supra* note 28, para. VI(1)(b).

[80] Indicative List of Measures That Might Be Taken by a Meeting of the Parties in Respect of Non-Compliance with the Protocol, at para. A, adopted at the Fourth Meeting of the Parties to the Montreal Protocol, reproduced in UNEP Ozone Secretariat, *supra* note 3 at 297 [Montreal Protocol, Indicative List of Measures].

not designed to be. Second, there is something counter-intuitive about "rewarding" a non-compliant state with technical and financial assistance, while a state struggling to comply using its own resources is not so "rewarded." In some respects, both of these conundrums can discourage rather than encourage state party compliance. Nevertheless, in many situations, non-compliance is a matter of a lack of resources, and the compliance process can identify this situation as the underlying cause of the non-compliance and make recommendations about technical and financial assistance.

Where the international legal and political issues become most intense is when questions arise about the possibility of "punitive" measures against non-compliant states. The efficacy of punitive measures in compliance processes that embrace as their approach facilitation and non-confrontation is open to debate, as is the effectiveness of punitive measures, however envisioned, in inducing compliance from non-compliant states. The Montreal Protocol's Indicative List of Measures provides for two punitive measures:

- issuing cautions; and
- suspension, in accordance with the applicable rules of international law concerning the suspension of the operation of a treaty, of specific rights and privileges under the protocol, whether or not it is subject to time limits, including those concerned with industrial rationalization, production, consumption, trade, transfer of technology, the financial mechanism, and institutional arrangements.[81]

Whatever the policy merits or demerits of a "caution" or a "cautionary statement,"[82] as a matter of international law, "there is nothing to prevent states from expressing their collective dissatisfaction ... or agreeing on a general procedure for expressing such criticism."[83]

What is legally more intricate is whether a COP can decide to suspend "rights and privileges" available to a state party under a protocol or convention as a response to non-compliant behaviour.[84]

---

81 Montreal Protocol, Indicative List of Measures, *supra* note 80, paras. B and C.

82 The language in the Basel Convention, Mechanism for Promoting Implementation and Compliance, *supra* note 27, para. 20 (b).

83 Koskenniemi, *supra* note 6 at 145.

84 It is worth noting that Patricia Birnie and Alan Boyle, *International Law and the Environment*, 2nd edition (Oxford: Oxford University Press, 2002) at 208, state, without elaboration, that the outcome of a compliance procedure can include

Even though the parties to the Montreal Protocol adopted the Indicative List of Measures, which contain paragraph C, it does not
resolve the question of the international legality of the use of a
measure that suspends "rights and privileges" available under the
protocol. Indeed, paragraph C of the Indicative List of Measures
specifically notes that suspension of rights and privileges is to be
"in accordance with the applicable rules of international law concerning the suspension of the operation of a treaty,"[85] leaving the
question of the international legality of any measure taken to be
assessed on a case-by-case basis.

The wording "in accordance with the applicable rules of international law concerning the suspension of the operation of a treaty"
leads directly to Article 60 of the Vienna Convention on the Law of
Treaties,[86] which deals with possible treaty suspension and termination in the face of the material breach of a treaty. Absent material breach, which means either treaty repudiation or violation of a
provision central to the operation of a treaty,[87] Article 60 has no
application. As one authority has noted, "Article 60 was not to imply that treaty partners could never react to a non-material breach,
only that such reaction was not covered under the law of treaties"
and that for non-material breach it is to the law of state responsibility and countermeasures that recourse exists.[88] Clearly, the Article
60 material breach threshold is very high.[89] Moreover, the Article
60 remedy is suspension or termination of a treaty as a whole, rather
than the suspension of specific rights and privileges arising from

---

"suspension of treaty rights and privileges" pending attainment of full compliance by a state. Note also Churchill and Ulfstein, *supra* note 40 at 646–47, who
make a similar statement, although in a different context.

85 This wording is also found in the Aarhus Convention, Structure and Functions
of the Compliance Committee, *supra* note 33, para. 35(g), and was on the table
during the Basel Convention compliance negotiations, see Shibata, *supra* note
48 at 185.

86 Vienna Convention on the Law of Treaties, 23 May 1969, entered into force 27
May 1980, reprinted in 1155 U.N.T.S. 331.

87 *Ibid.* at Article 60(3).

88 Koskenniemi, *supra* note 6 at 140. See also Fitzmaurice and Redgwell, *supra* note
44 at 60.

89 Jan Klabbers, "The Substance of Form: The Case Concerning the Gabčíkovo-
Nagymaros Project, Environmental Law, and the Law of Treaties" (1997) 8 Y.B.
Int'l Envt'l L. 32 at 37, colourfully asserted that "Article 60 simply does not
work. It does not mean what it says, and does not say what it means."

the treaty.[90] It is recognized that, in the context of an MEA, it is most likely counter-productive to suspend or terminate a party's treaty rights and privileges through Article 60.[91]

The question of whether a COP has the authority to suspend the "rights and privileges" of a state party for a non-material breach is dependent on the underlying convention or protocol. While the argument can be made that a COP may have "implied powers" that are somewhat equivalent to that of an international organization and that this authority may include the suspension of specific rights and privileges,[92] it does not accord fully with the more limited nature of the authority given to a COP (which is a "meeting" or "conference" of the parties) by the underlying convention or protocol, in particular, the adoption of measures that interfere with a party's "rights and privileges."[93]

A useful way to look at the legal capacity of a COP to suspend specific treaty-created "rights and privileges" is to split "rights" from "privileges." By being a party to a convention or protocol, a state is afforded certain rights, such as participatory rights (for example, voting, access to information, receiving notifications from the Secretariat, and the opportunity to access certain types of financial resources). These rights can be said to be core benefits of treaty membership that exist without the intercession of a COP or other MEA body. There are, in many cases, also certain privileges (for example, the receipt of financial and technical assistance, the hosting of meetings, the manner of calculating inventories, and the participation on the bureau), which can be said to be benefits that may be available to a state party at the discretion of a COP. One authority reviewing the Montreal Protocol states unequivocally:

The Meeting of the Parties may suspend the rights of an allegedly defaulting party only if there has been a prior wrongful act by that party. Whether or not a party's behaviour has been "wrongful" can only be assessed from the perspective and through the criteria provided by general international

[90] See Fitzmaurice and Redgwell, *supra* note 44 at 59; and Anthony Aust, *Modern Treaty Law and Practice* (Cambridge: Cambridge University Press, 2000) at 236–39.

[91] Regarding the usefulness of Article 60 of the Vienna Convention on the Law of Treaties and MEAs, see Birnie and Boyle, *supra* note 84 at 194–95.

[92] See Churchill and Ulfstein, *supra* note 40 at 646–47; and Brunnée, *supra* note 52 at 16.

[93] See Yoshida, *supra* note 52 at 119.

law. The non-compliance mechanism, not being a mechanism to produce such assessments, cannot be used to determine wrongfulness.[94]

Absent explicit language in the underlying convention or protocol, a COP cannot adopt a "punitive" measure that suspends a "right" of a state party under a convention or protocol, but a COP could adopt a measure that involves suspending or denying a benefit provided under the underlying protocol or convention whose conferral is within the discretion of the COP. Such a COP discretionary "measure" would be clearly within its mandate, and such a measure would avoid the adoption of punitive measures based on the findings of either material breach or wrongfulness leading to questions about the legal effect of COP decisions and the authority of the compliance mechanism to interpret the treaty text.

For the same reasons, without explicit treaty wording, a COP cannot adopt other types of punitive measures (coercive countermeasures) against a non-compliant state party that are outside the confines of the collective expression of criticism or the specific "rights and privileges" provided to state parties by the underlying convention or protocol. Thus, for example, a COP cannot impose a trade embargo against all or selected products (unrelated to the underlying MEA) from a state that is not complying with an MEA.[95] Similarly, a COP cannot impose a penalty of damages against a state that is not complying with an MEA. The continued debate during the negotiation of MEA compliance structures and mandates about inclusion of punitive measures, beyond cautions or matters clearly within the discretion of a COP, is premised either on a misapprehension of existing international law or as a bargaining chip to be discarded in order to attain advantage on another matter.

[94] Koskenniemi, *supra* note 6 at 145.

[95] Such a trade embargo, having no foundation in international law, as for example a counter-measure, would also appear to be a breach of obligations existing on member states arising from the General Agreement on Tariffs and Trade, 1994 (GATT 1994), which was administered by the World Trade Organization (WTO). Pursuant to Article II(4) of the Agreement Establishing the World Trade Organization, 15 April 1994, entered into force 1 January 1995, GATT 1994 is a renaming of the General Agreement on Tariffs and Trade, 1947, as amended. Both the GATT 1947, as amended (GATT 1994) and the Agreement Establishing the WTO are reprinted in GATT Secretariat, *The Results of the Uruguay Round of Multilateral Negotiations: The Legal Texts* (Geneva, 1994) at 485 and 6. See also the WTO website at <www.wto.org>.

OPERATING COMPLIANCE COMMITTEES

MONTREAL PROTOCOL

As previously noted, the Implementation Committee under the Montreal Protocol was established in 1992.[96] The story of the development of the Implementation Committee has been set out in other sources;[97] moreover, there has been much discussion of the subsequent work of the committee.[98] A curious note on the development of the Implementation Committee was that the original, interim version did not contain a state party self-trigger, but relied instead only on a state-to-state trigger.[99] It appears to have been the Soviet Union that first proposed the state self-trigger in 1991,[100] which was subsequently adopted, albeit amid concerns that the self-trigger might be used as a *de facto* exemption or waiver from obligations in the Montreal Protocol.[101] Canada was a major proponent of the review of the Implementation Committee, which was called for in 1997[102] and which led to some alteration in the workings of the Implementation Committee in 1998.[103] Also in 1998, the committee articulated its framework for dealing with possible non-compliance with the emphasis being on working with the delinquent state to re-attain compliance.[104]

---

[96] Decision IV/5 of the Fifth Meeting of the Parties, *supra* note 4.

[97] See Koskenniemi, *supra* note 6 at 129–34; and Yoshida, *supra* note 52 at 101–4.

[98] See Anderson and Sarma, *supra* note 7 at 274–89; and Yoshida, *supra* note 52 at 109–21 and 127–39.

[99] See Decision II/5 of the Second Meeting of the Parties, *supra* note 3.

[100] *Submission of the Soviet Union to the Third Meeting Ad Hoc Working Group of Legal Experts on Non-compliance with the Montreal Protocol*, Doc. UNEP/OzL.Pro/WG.3/CRP.1, 6 November 1991, available on the UNEP Ozone Secretariat website, *supra* note 3.

[101] *Report of the Third Meeting of the ad hoc Working Group of Legal Experts on Non-Compliance with the Montreal Protocol*, Doc. UNEP/OzL.Pro/WG.3/3/3, 9 November 1991, para. 25, available on the UNEP Ozone Secretariat website, *supra* note 3, notes:

> After discussion the working group approved a slightly amended version of the paragraph and placed it as paragraph 4 of the new text in Annex I. The meeting was of the view that self-reporting was not intended to introduce additional flexibilities into the non-compliance procedure or as a means of circumventing protocol obligations.

[102] Decision IX/35 of the Ninth Meeting of the Parties, reproduced in the UNEP Ozone Secretariat, *supra* note 3 at 184–85.

[103] Decision X/10 of the Tenth Meeting of the Parties, *supra* note 5.

[104] See *Report of the Implementation Committee under the Non-Compliance Procedure for the Montreal Protocol on the work of its Twentieth Meeting*, Doc. UNEP/OzL.Pro/

In 2003, the Implementation Committee reported that twenty-three states (out of a total of 183 state parties) had not completed their annual reporting requirements set out in Article 7(3) and (4) of the Montreal Protocol.[105] In addition, baseline and base-year data requirements had yet to be complied with by a number of states.[106] The chair of the Implementation Committee noted that data reporting had improved from previous years.[107] The major compliance challenge under the Montreal Protocol is having state parties meet their obligations regarding the phase-out or control measures respecting ozone-depleting substances (ODS).[108] In 2003, the Implementation Committee indicated that a number of state parties had not met their obligations on reducing or freezing consumption of controlled substances and that an explanation together with a plan of action were requested.[109] It is interesting that only one state (St. Vincent and the Grenadines) had failed to respond

---

ImpCom/20/4, 9 July 1998, paras. 31–33, available on the UNEP Ozone Secretariat website, *supra* note 3, and set out in condensed form in Anderson and Sarma, *supra* note 7 at 284.

105 See Decision XV/14, "Data and Information provided by the Parties in Accordance with Article 7 of the Montreal Protocol," para. 2, in *Report of the Fifteenth Meeting of the Parties to the Montreal Protocol on Substances that Deplete the Ozone Layer* [*Report of the Fifteenth Meeting*], Doc. UNEP/OzL.Pro. 15/9, 11 November 2003, available on the UNEP Ozone Secretariat website, *supra* note 3.

106 See Decision XV/16, "Non-Compliance with Data Reporting Requirements under Article 7," and Decision XV/18, "Non-Compliance with Data Reporting Requirements for the Purpose of Establishing Baselines," in *Report of the Fifteenth Meeting, supra* note 105.

107 *Report of the Fifteenth Meeting, supra* note 105, paras. 132–33. For more on compliance with the reporting obligations in the Montreal Protocol, see Anderson and Sarma, *supra* note 7 at 275–78; and Yoshida, *supra* note 52 at 127–30.

108 See Yoshida, *supra* note 52 at 130–33; and Anderson and Sarma, *supra* note 7 at 278–80. There have been a number of amendments adding substances to the Montreal Protocol: the London Amendments, 29 June 1990, entered into force 10 August 1992; the Copenhagen Amendment, 25 November 1992, entered into force 14 June 1994; the Montreal Amendment, 17 September 1997, entered into force 19 November 1999; and the Beijing Amendment, 3 December 1999, entered into force 25 February 2002. All are reprinted in UNEP Ozone Secretariat, *supra* note 3 at 358–82 and are available on the UNEP Ozone Secretariat website, *supra* note 3.

109 See *Report of the Fifteenth Meeting, supra* note 105, para. 135 and relevant decisions.

to a similar request for a plan of action made in 2002 and this fact resulted in a further request being made in 2003.[110]

While fully discussed elsewhere,[111] the Russian Federation's non-compliance with control measures in the mid-1990s needs to be noted. The Russian Federation self-triggered the Implementation Committee when it indicated it would not be able to comply with certain phase-out obligations. In 1995, the Implementation Committee recommended, and the MOP adopted, a decision:[112] requesting further information from the Russian Federation; permitting trade in controlled substances to specifically named states but requiring the Russian Federation to prevent the re-export from those states;[113] and recommending access to international assistance be made available to the Russian Federation to enable attainment of compliance. The questions by the Russian Federation about the legality of the MOP decision and, in particular, the legality of the trade paragraph were not pursued since the Russian Federation concentrated on accessing international financial support and bringing itself into compliance.[114]

The Montreal Protocol Implementation Committee has been the model for the compliance mechanisms established under other MEAs. However, there are several features of the Montreal Protocol that have made it possible for the Implementation Committee to be particularly effective. The most important feature is that the MOP, to which the Implementation Committee reports, has direct access to significant funds (the Multilateral Fund), which can be used to assist state parties in complying with the obligations of the protocol.[115] The financial assistance aspects of the protocol are so

---

[110] *Report of the Fifteenth Meeting, supra* note 105, para. 139; and Decision XV/42, "Non-Compliance with the Montreal Protocol by Saint Vincent and the Grenadines," in *Report of the Fifteenth Meeting, supra* note 105.

[111] See, for example, Yoshida, *supra* note 52 at 135–39; Duncan Brack, *International Trade and the Montreal Protocol* (London: Earthscan Publications, 1996) at 103–5; Anderson and Sarma, *supra* note 7 at 282–84; and Werksman, *supra* note 29 at 71–73.

[112] Decision VII/18 of the Seventh Meeting of the Parties, reproduced in UNEP Ozone Secretariat, *supra* note 3 at 214–15.

[113] Decision VII/18, *supra* note 112, at para. 8, does not explicitly indicate that exports to other state parties were prohibited. Note Brack, *supra* note 111 at 104.

[114] This is well described by Werksman, *supra* note 29 at 73.

[115] Montreal Protocol, *supra* note 2, Articles 10 and 11(4)(e). For the most recent report of the Multilateral Fund, see *Report of the Executive Committee [of the*

fully integrated into the compliance process that major environment funding agencies such as the United Nations Development
Programme (UNDP) and the Global Environment Facility (GEF)
participate in the meetings of the Implementation Committee and
even advocate on behalf of non-complying states. This financial
capacity of the MOP to deal directly with non-complying state parties (not only in giving funds but also in withholding funds) is a key
compliance inducement and, among the MEAs discussed in this
article, a unique feature.

A second "indirect" incentive feature of the Montreal Protocol
arises from the prohibition on parties to trade substances controlled
under the Montreal Protocol with non-parties.[116] This trade element has been described as follows:

> One unique feature of the Montreal Protocol's NCP [non-compliance pro-
> cedure] is its ability to use trade pressures, which is tied directly to the
> protocol's general ban on trade in regulated substances between parties
> and non-parties. This feature allows the NCP to treat the ability to trade in
> regulated substances as a privilege granted by the Montreal Protocol and to
> incrementally suspend that privilege in order to encourage compliance.[117]

MOP decisions involving non-compliance parties commonly include
a warning that a failure of a party to return to compliance in a
timely manner may result in the COP considering measures "consistent with item C of the indicative list of measures" and that
"[t]hese measures may include the possibility of actions available
under Article 4, such as ensuring that the supply of CFCs (that is,
the subject of the non-compliance) is ceased and that exporting
Parties are not contributing to a continuing situation of non-compliance."[118] The essence of the warning appears to be that a non-
compliant party would be classed as a "State not Party to this
Protocol" (a non-party) for the purposes of imports and exports
under Article 4 with the result that parties would not be able to

---

Multilateral Fund] to the Fifteenth Meeting of the Parties, Doc. UNEP/OzL.Pro.15/
8, 29 September 2003, available on the UNEP Ozone Secretariat website, *supra*
note 3. For some general comments on the Multilateral Fund, see Sands, *supra*
note 1 at 355–56 and 1031–32.

[116] Montreal Protocol, *supra* note 2, Article 4.

[117] Werksman, *supra* note 29 at 72.

[118] See Decision XV/42, *supra* note 110, at para. 5.

trade with the non-compliant party.[119] There is uncertainty whether the MOP has the authority to declare that a party is "a State not Party to the Protocol."[120] There is no indication in Article 4(9), or explicitly in any other provision of the Montreal Protocol, of the MOP having such authority. No use of Article 4 in this manner has yet to be adopted by the MOP.

The nature of the Montreal Protocol obligations is also a feature that has assisted with compliance matters. The principal obligations in the protocol relate to limits on the production, use, and trade in controlled substances[121] and reporting.[122] These obligations are largely unconditional and there are formulae for the calculation of control levels. The question of compliance/ non-compliance is relatively straightforward as indicated by an Australian representative who stated:

Non-compliance is a question of fact. It is not a political question nor, in the simple framework of the Protocol's phase-out obligations, can it often be a question of law. The role of the Implementation Committee should be to determine at least questions of fact relating to non-compliance.[123]

A final feature of the Montreal Protocol is that its scope is modest, dealing with a handful of banned substances with replacement substances having become available and affordable over the phase-out period. Hence, compliance, reporting, and monitoring has not been particularly onerous on parties. However, the difficulty in meeting targets for methyl bromide indicates that it is not all clear sailing within the Montreal Protocol.[124]

---

[119] Montreal Protocol, *supra* note 2, Article 4(9) reads:

> For the purposes of this Article, the term "State not Party to this Protocol" shall include, with respect to a particular controlled substance, a State ... that has not agreed to be bound by the control measures in effect for that substance.

[120] See *Report of the Work of the Ad Hoc Working Group on Legal and Technical Experts*, Doc. UNEP/OzL.Pro/WG.4/1/3, 18 November 1998, at paras. 41–42, available on the UNEP Ozone Secretariat website, *supra* note 3.

[121] See Montreal Protocol, *supra* note 2, Articles 2 and 3 and the amendments thereto in the London Amendment, the Copenhagen Amendment, the Montreal Amendment, and the Beijing Amendment, *supra* note 108.

[122] The reporting obligation is in Montreal Protocol, *supra* note 2, Article 7.

[123] *Submission by Australia to the Ad Hoc Working Group of Legal and Technical Experts*, Doc. UNEP/OzL.Pro/WG.4/1/1/Add.2, 18 May 1998, paragraph 8, available on the UNEP Ozone Secretariat website, *supra* note 3.

[124] Methyl bromide was the subject of an Extraordinary Meeting of the Parties to the Montreal Protocol in March 2004. See *Report of the First Extraordinary Meeting*

LRTAP CONVENTION

The compliance mechanism for the LRTAP Convention, which is known as the Implementation Committee, was established in 1998 by a decision of the COP, known in LRTAP Convention parlance as the Executive Body.[125] The curiosity is determining what authority the Executive Body has since no such authority was given to the Executive Body in the LRTAP Convention.[126] In as early as 1991, the VOC Protocol to the LRTAP Convention called for the creation of "a mechanism for monitoring compliance."[127] In the Oslo Protocol to the LRTAP Convention, which was completed in 1994, explicit direction was set out to establish an Implementation Committee.[128] However, the Executive Body created the Implementation Committee prior to the entry into force of the Oslo Protocol and by a decision of states that included states not party to the Oslo Protocol. It is clear, however, that the working group that developed the proposal for the Implementation Committee anchored their work on Article 7 of the Oslo Protocol.[129] Article 7 reads:

1. An Implementation Committee is hereby established to review the implementation of the present Protocol and compliance by the Parties with their obligations. It shall report to the Parties at sessions of the Executive Body and may make such recommendations to them as it considers appropriate.

---

of the Parties to the Montreal Protocol, Doc. UNEP/OzL.Pro.ExMP/1/3, 27 March 2004, available on the UNEP Ozone Depletion website, *supra* note 3, and a succinct overview in "Summary of the Extraordinary Meeting of the Parties to the Montreal Protocol" (29 March 2004) 19(34) Earth Negotiations Bulletin 7–8, available at <www.iisd.ca/ozone/exmp/>.

125 LRTAP Convention, Structure and Functions of the Implementation Committee, *supra* note 25.

126 Regarding the authority of the Executive Body under the LRTAP Convention, see LRTAP Convention, *supra* note 9, Article 10.

127 VOC Protocol, *supra* note 9, Article 3(3) states:

The Parties shall establish a mechanism for monitoring compliance with the Present Protocol. As a first step based on information provided pursuant to Article 8 or other information, any Party which has reason to believe that another Party is acting in a manner inconsistent with its obligations under this Protocol may inform the Executive Body to that effect and, simultaneously, the Parties concerned. At the request of any Party, the matter may be taken up at the next meeting of the Executive Body.

128 Oslo Protocol, *supra* note 10, Article 7(1).

129 *Report of the Fifteenth Session of the Executive Body,* Doc. ECE/EB.AIR/53, 7 January 1998, at para. 47, available on the LRTAP Convention website, *supra* note 9.

2. Upon consideration of a report, and any recommendations, of the Implementation Committee, the Parties, taking into account the circumstances of a matter and in accordance with Convention practice, may decide upon and call for action to bring about full compliance with the present Protocol, including measures to assist a Party's compliance with the Protocol, and to further the objectives of the Protocol.

3. The Parties shall, at the first session of the Executive Body after entry into force of the present Protocol, adopt a decision that sets out the structure and functions of the Implementation Committee as well as procedures for its review of compliance.

4. The application of the compliance procedure shall be without prejudice to the provisions of article 9 of the present Protocol.[130]

Moreover, the Executive Body urged the parties to the VOC Protocol to utilize the Implementation Committee created by the Executive Body.[131] The parties to the VOC Protocol subsequently adopted a decision to use the Implementation Committee,[132] as did the parties to the Oslo Protocol.[133] Subsequent LRTAP Convention protocols have made specific reference to the role of the Implementation Committee.[134]

The LRTAP Convention and its protocols, like the Montreal Protocol, create essentially two types of obligations: the obligation to report on the emission of identified substances and the obligation to meet thresholds reducing the emissions of identified substances.[135] Despite the somewhat uncertain provenance of the Implementation Committee, the committee commenced its work in 1998

---

[130] Oslo Protocol, *supra* note 10, Article 7.

[131] Decision 1997/2, *Concerning the Implementation Committee, Its Structure and Functions and Procedures for Review of Compliance, supra* note 25, at para. 4.

[132] Decision 1997/3, *Compliance Monitoring for the VOC Protocol,* Doc. ECE/EB.AIR/53, Annex IV, available on the LRTAP Convention website, *supra* note 9.

[133] Decision 1998/6, *The Review Foreseen Under Article 8 of the 1994 Oslo Convention,* Doc. ECE/EB.AIR/59, Annex I, available on the LRTAP Convention website, *supra* note 9.

[134] See the 1998 Protocol on Heavy Metals, 24 June 1998, entered into force 29 December 2003, Article 9; the 1998 Protocol on Persistent Organic Pollutants, 24 June 1998, entered into force 23 October 2003, Article 11; and the 1999 Protocol to Abate Acidification, Eutrophication and Ground-Level Ozone, 30 November 1999, not yet in force, Article 9. These protocols are available on the LRTAP Convention website, *supra* note 9.

[135] For a good overview of the workings of the LRTAP Convention and its various protocols, see Sands, *supra* note 1 at 324–36.

and has been very active in dealing with non-compliance matters regarding both types of obligations.

The Implementation Committee initially focused on compliance with reporting obligations either as a result of requests by the Executive Body to review compliance with certain protocols[136] or by the authority given to the Implementation Committee to "review periodically compliance by the Parties with the reporting requirements of the protocols."[137] In a short period, the Implementation Committee has developed a process for dealing with reporting obligations. The committee started by naming the non-compliant states in an initial report. If these states continue to be in non-compliance with reporting obligations, their names will be placed in bold and become the subject of a decision of the Executive Body requesting the provision of data within a specified time. For those states that still do not comply with their reporting obligations, a letter is sent from the Chair of the Implementation Committee to the states, noting the seriousness of their continued non-compliance. Those states that continue to be in non-compliance are then the subject to a further decision of the Executive Body, by which the body "expresses serious concern" with continued non-compliance and "strongly urges" the states to comply within a specified timeframe or draw up a timetable with the Secretariat.[138] These Executive Body decisions are to be communicated to the foreign ministries of the non-compliant states. Following these admonitions, if a state party remains in non-compliance, that state will be the subject of another Executive Body decision calling on the head of the delegation to visit the Secretariat and establish a precise timetable.[139]

This "name-and-shame" and slow escalation of pressure has achieved the desired results in relation to reporting requirements.

136 See the *Third Report of the Implementation Committee,* Doc. ECE/EB.AIR/2002/2, 29 September 2000, at para. 31, available on the LRTAP Convention website, *supra* note 9. The authority for this is the LRTAP Convention, Structure and Functions of the Implementation Committee, *supra* note 25, para. 3(d).

137 LRTAP, Structure and Functions of the Implementation Committee, *supra* note 25, para. 3(a).

138 See the *Fourth Report of the Implementation Committee,* Doc. ECE/EB.AIR/2001/3, 3 October 2001, at para. 45(i), available on the LRTAP Convention website, *supra* note 9.

139 See the *Fifth Report of the Implementation Committee,* Doc. EB.AIR/2002/2, 30 September 2002, at para. 30, available on the LRTAP Convention website, *supra* note 9.

In the six years that reporting has been subject to compliance review, reporting under the various protocols in force has gone from a mid-80 per cent compliance rate to a high 90 per cent range (for three of the protocols, the compliance rate has reached 99 per cent, 99 per cent, and 98 per cent).[140] It is worth noting that there is little excuse for non-compliance with reporting obligations as the various protocols provide a significant amount of leeway in how emission estimates are to be calculated.

The Implementation Committee has become engaged with compliance in regard to emission reduction obligations by specific state parties in three ways: (1) through requests by the Executive Body to review compliance with certain protocols;[141] (2) by the Secretariat bringing before the Implementation Committee information on the alleged non-compliance by specific state parties;[142] and (3) where parties have self-identified that they either are, or may be, in non-compliance.[143] It took five years of dealing with reporting matters and the development of a modest track record regarding several specific situations respecting emission reductions in order to build a level of confidence with the work of the Implementation Committee.

Where the Secretariat initiates, or a state party self-initiates, the Implementation Committee process regarding non-compliance with emission reduction obligations, the committee proceeds by seeking to establish the facts as to whether there has been non-compliance. Where a state self-initiates and declares it is in non-compliance, such as Norway's self-initiation in 1991 of non-compliance with the VOC Protocol,[144] the value of the Implementation Committee evaluating or determining whether the state (for example, Norway) was non-compliant may be questioned. A different situation exists where a state self-initiates expressing the view that it may be in non-compliance, as was the situation expressed by Slovenia in 2000 regarding the Oslo Protocol.[145] Yet even in this case, the bigger question is how to achieve compliance rather than an examination of past non-compliance. The Norway situation, where a developed

---

[140] *Sixth Report of the Implementation Committee,*" *supra* note 25, at para. 17.

[141] LRTAP, "Structure and Functions of the Implementation Committee," *supra* note 25, para. 3(d).

[142] *Ibid.* at paras. 5 and 3(b).

[143] *Ibid.* at paras. 3(b) and 4(b).

[144] *Fourth Report of the Implementation Committee, supra* note 138, at paras. 3–10.

[145] *Third Report of the Implementation Committee, supra* note 136, at paras. 3–13.

state has stated that it will remain in non-compliance with an emis-sion reduction requirement for the immediate future, has created a significant challenge for both the Implementation Committee and the Executive Body.

In 2002, the Secretariat brought before the Implementation Com-mittee information of possible non-compliance by Ireland, Greece, and Spain with respect to their emission reduction obligations under the 1988 Protocol to the LRTAP Convention Concerning the Control of Nitrogen Oxides (NOx Protocol)[146] and Luxem-bourg and Spain respecting their emission reduction obligations under the VOC Protocol.[147] With the exception of Luxembourg, none of the states have been very forthcoming in supplying infor-mation to the Secretariat or the Implementation Committee on these matters.[148] It is clear that the Secretariat's identification of possible non-complying states has not been well received by those states, to the point that the states have largely ignored both the requests and deliberations of both the Implementing Committee and the Executive Body.

While the activities and measures of the Implementation Com-mittee and the Executive Body have been quite successful in reduc-ing non-compliance with reporting obligations, there has been less success in regard to non-compliant behaviour respecting emission reduction obligations. The situation in which state parties have announced that they will not be meeting emission reduction obli-gations for a number of years has sparked a debate about the possi-bility of more stringent measures being taken. At the 2003 session of the Executive Body, it was reported that

[a] number of Parties suggested that a stronger compliance regime with mandatory consequences might better encourage Parties to meet their obligations under the protocols and suggested that the Implementation Committee and the Working Group on Strategies and Review should con-sider this for the future. Others pointed out that this was a sensitive and technically difficult issue and expressed their reservations.[149]

---

146 Protocol to the LRTAP Convention Concerning the Control of Nitrogen Oxides, 31 October 1988, entered into force 14 February 1991, reprinted in (1988) 28 I.L.M. 214, and available on the LRTAP Convention website, *supra* note 9.

147 *Fifth Report of the Implementation Committee, supra* note 139, at paras. 22–50.

148 See the *Sixth Report of the Implementation Committee, supra* note 25, at paras 29–62.

149 *Report of the Twenty-First Session of the Executive Body*, Doc. ECE/EB.AIR/79, 21 January 2004, at para. 21, available on the LRTAP Convention website, *supra* note 9.

The chair of the Implementation Committee replied that "the Implementation Committee had had some preliminary discussions on further measures that might be used to encourage or put pressure on Parties to move into compliance. However, he cautioned that introducing a mandatory compliance regime could only be achieved through a legally binding instrument."[150] Such a view is consistent with the original proposal of the working group that established the Implementation Committee. In the report of this group, it was noted that "it was understood by the delegations that ... the Executive Body's decisions concerning compliance were not legally binding unless a provision in the protocol in question rendered them so."[151] It remains to be seen if the Executive Body will decide to seek more stringent, possibly legally binding measures against non-compliant state parties.

ESPOO CONVENTION

The Espoo Convention compliance committee, called the Implementation Committee, was created by the MOP in 2001.[152] As there is no explicit provision in the Espoo Convention calling for the establishment of a compliance committee, reliance was placed upon Article 11(2)(f), which reads:

The Parties shall keep under continuous review the implementation of this Convention, and, with this purpose in mind, shall: ...

(f) Consider and undertake any additional action that may be required for the achievement of the purposes of this Convention.

A more explicit treaty basis for the Implementation Committee has since been developed with the adoption at the June 2004 MOP of an amendment to the Espoo Convention, which adds a new Article 14 bis:

(1) The Parties shall review compliance with the provisions of this Convention on the basis of the compliance procedure, as a non-adversarial and assistance-oriented procedure adopted by the Meeting of the Parties. The review shall be based on regular reporting by the Parties. The Meeting of Parties shall decide on the frequency of regular reporting required by the Parties and the information to be included in those regular reports.

150 *Report of the Twenty-First Session of the Executive Body, supra* note 149 at para. 24.
151 *Report of the Fifteenth Session of the Executive Committee, supra* note 129 at para. 48.
152 Espoo Convention, Structure and Functions of the Implementation Committee, *supra* note 26.

(2) The compliance procedure shall be available for application to any protocol adopted under this Convention.[153]

To address any concern that adopting this amendment might call into question the legal legitimacy of the MOP's 2001 decision to establish the Implementation Committee, the MOP decision adopting the amendment explicitly confirms the validity of the earlier establishment of the Implementation Committee and the actions taken thereunder.[154]

The Espoo Convention Implementation Committee has not yet received a submission on a substantive issue regarding possible noncompliance. The committee has, however, been occupied with reviewing the structure and functions of the committee itself in order to clarify any ambiguities and, in particular, in response to the request of the MOP that the committee consider the role of the public *vis-à-vis* the Implementation Committee.[155] As a result, the Implementation Committee made a number of recommendations, including making reports available to the public and having open meetings, which have been adopted by the MOP as amendments to the constitutive document of the Implementation Committee.[156] The committee discussed, but ultimately decided not to recommend, either the creation of a public trigger or provision for direct and active participation of the public in committee meetings.[157]

An issue that was perhaps not anticipated when the Implementation Committee was created, but which has henceforth required the attention of the committee, was the question of how to deal with unsolicited information from the public, including nongovernmental organizations (NGOs). As there is no public trigger

---

[153] Decision III/7, *supra* note 20, at para. 3(f).

[154] The decision also confirms that parties shall continue to be eligible to participate in the convention's compliance activities, regardless of whether the second amendment has entered into force for that party or not. See Decision III/7, *supra* note 20, paras. 1 and 2.

[155] Decision II/4, *supra* note 26, para. 4 states:

Decides to review the structure and functions of the [Implementation] Committee at the third meeting of the Parties, bearing in mind the possible involvement of the public and requests in this context the Implementation Committee to prepare the necessary proposals for the third meeting of the Parties.

[156] Decision III/2, *supra* note 26.

[157] *Report of the Third Meeting of the Implementation Committee*, Doc. MP.EIA/WG.1/2003/8, 10 July 2003, paras. 13–15, available on the Espoo Convention website, *supra* note 19.

under the Espoo Convention Implementation Committee, it is necessary to examine closely the scope of the committee trigger: "Where the Committee becomes aware of possible non-compliance by a Party with its obligations, it may request the Party concerned to furnish necessary information about the matter."[158] There is some uncertainty as to how the committee is meant to "become aware" of possible non-compliance, given that the Espoo Convention does not contain a reporting obligation.[159] However, while discussion of this issue commenced as a theoretical one,[160] by the time the Implementation Committee met in October 2003 there was a practical significance as two letters from a NGO regarding a possible compliance matter had been sent to the Espoo Convention Secretariat, who in turn brought them forward to the committee.[161] Since the committee agreed that the information provided was insufficient to demonstrate whether the activity described fell within the scope of the convention, it was not necessary to decide on threshold issues, including the fundamental question of whether the Implementation Committee could examine information provided by a NGO.[162] However, a follow-up letter was received, and it became necessary to address the issue directly. A majority of the Implementation Committee took the view that the information provided should not be examined, since "considering unsolicited information from NGOs and the public relating to specific cases of non-compliance

---

[158] Espoo Convention, Structure and Functions of the Implementation Committee, *supra* note 26, para 5. For obvious reasons, the scope of the self- and party-to-party triggers are not relevant to the issue of "unsolicited" information.

[159] These lacunae should be addressed when the second amendment enters into force, as a new provision in the convention will allow the MOP to establish reporting requirements. See Decision III/7, *supra* note 20.

[160] As part of its review of public involvement with the Implementation Committee, the committee reported that:

> If the Committee received unsolicited information, it might review the need for a procedure for processing such information. The Committee would then report back to the Parties at their fourth meeting on how the Committee might deal with unsolicited information.

Report of the Third Meeting of the Implementation Committee, supra note 157, para. 10.

[161] *Report of the Fourth Meeting of the Implementation Committee,* Doc. MP.EIA/WG.1/2003/3, 17 December 2003, para. 4, available on the Espoo Convention website, *supra* note 19.

[162] See *Report of the Fourth Meeting of the Implementation Committee, supra* note 161, paras. 8–10.

was not within the Committee's existing mandate."[163] A minority took the view that, as there were no restrictions on how the committee might "become aware" of an instance of possible non-compliance, the committee should examine the information further.[164] Although a majority of the Implementation Committee took the view that considering unsolicited information from NGOs and the public was not within its mandate, the issue of how to deal with unsolicited information remains. Even the issue of whether criteria should be developed to provide guidance on how to deal with unsolicited information is likely to prove to be controversial, since developing criteria may eventually lead to accepting unsolicited information as a basis for the committee's powers of self-initiation. As a result, the decision adopted by the third MOP in 2004 simply "requests the Committee to consider developing criteria for dealing with information other than submissions from Parties."[165]

RECENTLY ESTABLISHED COMPLIANCE MECHANISMS

BASEL CONVENTION[166]

The Basel Convention's compliance mechanism, the Committee, was created by the COP in December 2002.[167] Without an explicit provision in the Basel Convention calling for the establishment of a compliance mechanism, the COP based its authority to establish the Committee on the general authority given to the COP to keep under continuous review and evaluation the effective implementation of the convention.[168] Interestingly, although the Basel Convention's Article 19 provides for "verification," meaning that a party can inform the Secretariat of a possible breach by another party,[169] there were different views during the negotiations of the compli-

---

[163] *Report of the Fifth Meeting of the Implementation Committee, supra* note 26, para. 7 and see more generally paras. 5–8.

[164] *Report of the Fifth Meeting of the Implementation Committee, supra* note 26, para. 7.

[165] Decision III/2, *supra* note 26, at para. 7.

[166] For a detailed review of the negotiations leading to the completion of the Basel Convention compliance mechanism, see Shibata, *supra* note 48.

[167] Basel Convention, Mechanism for Promoting Implementation and Compliance, *supra* note 27.

[168] Basel Convention, *supra* note 18, Article 15(5)(c) and (e).

[169] Basel Convention, *supra* note 18, Article 19 reads:

Any Party which has reason to believe that another Party is acting or has acted in breach of its obligations under this Convention may inform the Secretariat thereof,

ance mechanism as to whether or not parties were implementing this provision. In the end, no reference exists in the compliance mechanism to Article 19.

The thorny issue of Committee members (individual versus states) was resolved by requiring individuals to be nominated by parties, elected by the COP, and to "serve objectively and in the best interest of the Convention."[170] Regarding "triggers," there was agreement on a state party self-trigger, a party-to-party trigger, and a narrow Secretariat trigger.[171] The party-to-party trigger is qualified. It is available only when one party has concerns or is affected by a failure to comply with, or implement obligations by, another party "with whom it is directly involved under the Convention."[172] The Secretariat trigger is limited to situations where a party fails to comply with reporting obligations under Article 13(3) of the convention.[173]

During negotiations of the mechanism, there was a lengthy debate about measures. First, this issue was tied up in a "package" with the issues of triggers and Committee membership. Second, there was some debate about whether the Committee, without further reference to the COP, could apply any measures. Finally, there was a debate about the measures the COP could impose. On this point, there was little interest in punitive measures, and some considered "a caution" — which was accepted ten years earlier by the Montreal Protocol state parties — too strong, particularly those countries that had not supported a party trigger. Such countries also had difficulties with words that implied a "determination of non-compliance" — a finding that they felt was best left to legal processes. The compromise language (proposed by Canada) of "a cautionary statement" is the strongest weapon in the Committee's arsenal.[174]

The Committee met once in 2003 to deal with organizational and procedural issues and has met once in 2004. The Committee is attempting to establish its initial working arrangements in order to put flesh on the bones of the compliance procedures and to

---

and in such an event, shall simultaneously and immediately inform, directly or through the Secretariat, the Party against whom allegations are made. All relevant information should be submitted by the Secretariat to the Parties.

170 Basel Convention, Mechanism for Promoting Implementation and Compliance, *supra* note 27, paras. 3 and 5.

171 *Ibid.* at para. 9.

172 *Ibid.* at para. 9(b).

173 *Ibid.* at para. 9(c).

174 *Ibid.* at para. 20(b).

consider the general (systemic) review of compliance matters.[175] No submissions have been received by the Committee to date.

CARTAGENA PROTOCOL

The provision in the Cartagena Protocol calling for the creation of a compliance mechanism is Article 34, which provides:

> The Conference of the Parties serving as the Meeting of the Parties to this Protocol shall, at its first meeting, consider and approve cooperative procedures and institutional mechanisms to promote compliance with the provisions of this Protocol and to address cases of non-compliance. These procedures and mechanisms shall include provisions to offer advice or assistance, where appropriate. They shall be separate from, and without prejudice to, the dispute settlement procedures and mechanisms established by Article 27 of the Convention.[176]

Pursuant to this provision, in 2004, at the first COP, serving as the MOP (COP/MOP), compliance procedures were adopted and a Compliance Committee was established.[177]

The adopted procedures share a number of features with other MEA compliance procedures, thus maintaining the same general approach of a limited committee, triggers for individual cases, and some form of "measures" that can be taken by the COP/MOP. One notable variation is that members of the Compliance Committee are "to serve objectively and in a *personal* capacity."[178] This point was adopted despite significant opposition, in part because the "friends of the chair" process, which was used to develop a compromise text, excluded key opposing countries.[179]

A party self-trigger and a party-to-party trigger were agreed upon, with the qualification that a party triggering against another party is to be "affected or likely to be affected" by the alleged non-

---

[175] See "Statement by the Chair of the Committee," *in Report of the Second Session of the Open-ended Working Group*, Doc. UNEP/CHW/OEWG/2/12, 16 December 2003, Annex V, available on the Basel Convention website, *supra* note 18.

[176] Cartagena Protocol, *supra* note 15, Article 34. The convention referred to in Article 34 is the CBD, *supra* note 15.

[177] Cartagena Protocol, Procedures and Mechanisms on Compliance, *supra* note 28.

[178] *Ibid.* at para. II(3) [emphasis added].

[179] See "Summary of the First Meeting of the Conference of the Parties to the Convention on Biological Diversity Serving as the Meeting of the Parties to the Cartagena Protocol on Biosafety" (1 March 2004) 9(289) Earth Negotiations Bulletin at 8, available at <www.iisd.ca/biodiv/bs-copmop1/>.

compliance.[180] Part of the compromise on the party-to-party trigger was the inclusion of language drawn from the Basel Convention compliance procedures allowing the Compliance Committee to screen out *de minimis* or ill-founded submissions.[181]

As always, the issue of the measures that may be taken respecting a non-compliant state party by the COP/MOP received substantial debate. While one group favoured punitive measures, such as trade sanctions, others pointed out that there was no legal basis in the protocol for such measures, and still others felt that this would be too adversarial. Ultimately, the COP/MOP decided upon financial and technical assistance; technology transfer; training and other capacity-building measures; issuing a caution to the concerned party; and requesting the Executive Secretary to publish cases of non-compliance.[182] Respecting more punitive or persuasive measures, the decision was made to review the issue in the future. This mandate is set out as follows:

[I]n cases of repeated non-compliance, take such measures as may be decided by the Conference of the Parties serving as the meeting of the Parties to the Protocol at its third meeting, and thereafter in accordance with Article 35 of the Protocol, within the framework of the review process provided for in Section VII below.[183]

Those who feared punitive sanctions look with concern at the review provision. Other observers consider that this deferral actually constitutes the death knell for punitive sanctions.

"IN PROCESS" COMPLIANCE MECHANISMS

ROTTERDAM CONVENTION[184]

The compliance mechanism for the 1998 Rotterdam Convention is still under negotiation, although it is well advanced. At the 2003 meeting of the Intergovernmental Negotiation Committee

---

[180] Cartagena Protocol, Procedures and Mechanisms on Compliance, *supra* note 28, para. VI(1).

[181] *Ibid.* at para. VI(1). The Basel provision is Basel Convention, Mechanism for Promoting Implementation and Compliance, *supra* note 27, para. 18.

[182] Cartagena Protocol, Procedures and Mechanisms on Compliance, *supra* note 28, para. VI(2)(a),(b) and (c).

[183] *Ibid.* at para. VI(2)(d).

[184] For a recent overview of the Rotterdam Convention, see T.L. McDorman, "The Rotterdam Convention on the Prior Informed Consent Procedure for Certain

(INC), a negotiating text was discussed in a working group with some progress made in moving the document towards an agreed text. Nevertheless, the negotiating text,[185] which will be forwarded to the first COP, which is to be held in September 2004, contains square brackets around a number of the "usual suspect" key areas such as triggering the compliance mechanism and measures that can be taken.[186]

The provision in the Rotterdam Convention calling for the creation of a compliance mechanism is Article 17, which reads:

> The Conference of the Parties shall, as soon as practicable, develop and approve procedures and institutional mechanisms for determining non-compliance with the provisions of this Convention and for treatment of Parties found to be in non-compliance.[187]

There are three points to be noted respecting this wording. First, there is no time requirement for the creation of the compliance mechanism — the provision simply indicates "as soon as practicable." Second, the provision calls for developing procedures and mechanisms "for determining non-compliance." Third, the procedures and mechanisms are to deal with the "treatment of Parties found to be in non-compliance." Viewed out of context, these last two points could be read as suggesting that a compliance committee has an authority equivalent to a third-party adjudicative dispute settlement body for determining breaches and providing for remedies. The better view, however, is that the provision was designed to create an alternative to, and be a "softer" form of, formal dispute settlement to which state parties had not consented to be imbued with formal dispute settlement authority.

This fact is reflected in the contents of the negotiating text, which emphasizes the facilitative and non-confrontational nature of the mechanism being developed[188] and is consistent with the guiding principles underlying other compliance mechanisms.[189]

Hazardous Chemicals and Pesticides in International Trade: Some Legal Notes" (2004) 13 Rev. Eur. Comm. & Int'l Env'l L. 187–200.

185 Rotterdam Convention, Draft Non-Compliance Procedures, *supra* note 30.

186 See *ibid.* at paras. 11 and 18.

187 Rotterdam Convention, *supra* note 13, Article 17.

188 Rotterdam Convention, Draft Non-Compliance Procedures, *supra* note 30, para. 17.

189 See text accompanying note 43 in this article.

The compliance committee structure adopted for the Basel Convention in 2002 has had a significant impact on the discussions of the compliance procedures under the Rotterdam Convention. This impact occurred since the Basel Convention has over 155 parties and the Rotterdam discussions, which were conducted prior to the entry into force of the convention in February 2004, were open to all states. Thus, many of the participants experienced the Basel Convention negotiations and compromises.

STOCKHOLM CONVENTION[190]

The provision in the Stockholm Convention that calls for the creation of a compliance mechanism is Article 17, which is identical to the wording of the relevant wording in the Rotterdam Convention. Article 17 reads:

The Conference of the Parties shall, as soon as practicable, develop and approve procedures and institutional mechanisms for determining non-compliance with the provisions of this Convention and for treatment of Parties found to be in non-compliance.[191]

The same considerations regarding the Rotterdam Convention's provision apply to this one. The provision is best understood as creating an alternative to, and as being a "softer" form of, a formal dispute settlement.[192]

Unlike under the Rotterdam Convention, where significant discussion has taken place regarding the development of a compliance mechanism, under the Stockholm Convention there has been little negotiation. The Stockholm Convention Secretariat prepared a compilation of state views on compliance, including a synthesis of views in preparation for the 2003 session of the INC.[193] While several states, including Canada, called for compliance discussions

---

[190] Regarding the Stockholm Convention, see David Downie and Terry Fenge, eds. *Northern Lights against POPs: Combatting Toxic Threats in the Arctic* (Montreal: McGill-Queen's University Press, 2003).

[191] Stockholm Convention, *supra* note 16, Article 17.

[192] See text accompanying notes 187–89 in this article.

[193] *Compilation of Views on Non-Compliance*, Doc. UNEP/POPS/INC.7/INF/8, 25 February 2003 and *Synthesis of Views on Non-Compliance*, *supra* note 31, available on the Stockholm Convention website, *supra* note 16.

during the 2003 session,[194] other states, notably the Group of 77 and China, took the view that more pressing issues such as the financial mechanism, technical assistance, and technology transfer should be the focus of the session's attention and that compliance discussion should be postponed until the first meeting of the Stockholm Convention COP, which was scheduled for May 2005.[195] The result of this delay is that it may be some time before a compliance committee is operational under the Stockholm Convention.

PROTOCOL TO THE LONDON DUMPING CONVENTION

Article 11 of the Protocol to the London Dumping Convention provides:

(1) No later than two years after entry into force of this Protocol, the Meeting of the Contracting Parties shall establish those procedures and mechanisms necessary to assess and promote compliance with this Protocol. Such procedures and mechanisms shall be developed with a view to allowing for the full and open exchange of information in a constructive manner.

(2) After full consideration of any information submitted pursuant to this Protocol and any recommendations made through procedures and mechanisms established under paragraph 1, the Meeting of the Contracting Parties may offer advice, assistance or co-operation to Contracting Parties and non-Contracting Parties.[196]

Since 1998, when Canada tabled its first compliance paper, compliance has been a topic of discussion at the Consultative Meeting of the London Dumping Convention.[197] Canada chaired the ad hoc working group that set out the key elements of a compliance mechanism discussed in 2003 by the Consultative Meeting.[198] An inter-sessional correspondence group, co-chaired by the United

---

194 "Summary of the Seventh Session," *supra* note 23 at 8; and see *Report of the Seventh Session of the Stockholm Convention, supra* note 23 at para. 128.

195 "Summary of the Seventh Session," *supra* note 23 at 8; and *Report of the Seventh Session of the Stockholm Convention, supra* note 23 at paras. 127 and 130.

196 Protocol to the London Dumping Convention, *supra* note 11, Article 11.

197 *Development of Compliance Arrangements: Compliance under the London Convention 1972 and the 1996 Protocol, Submitted by Canada,* Doc. LC 20/4, 24 September 1998.

198 *Report of the Twenty-Fifth Consultative Meeting of Parties, supra* note 32 at paras. 3.3 et seq. and Annex 2.

States and the Netherlands, is to prepare a first draft of a compliance procedure, including options, for the November 2004 Consultative Meeting.

The recurring issues — committee composition, triggers for individual cases of non-compliance, and measures by the committee and/or the meeting of contracting parties to the protocol — are contentious. As the London Dumping Convention is not a UNEP treaty, where negotiators have a greater familiarity with the range of compliance mechanisms in UNEP and elsewhere, discussions on compliance have been fairly novel to a number of the participants. Further complicating matters institutionally is the relationship that is to exist between the compliance committee and the Scientific Group on Dumping, the scientific and technical advisory body to the Consultative Meeting of the London Dumping Convention,[199] where the Protocol to the London Dumping Convention requires a "subsidiary body" to review national reports[200] and the progress by state parties claiming a transnational compliance period for certain protocol obligations.[201]

CONCLUSIONS

The compliance mechanism phenomenon is borne of the reality that a new approach to the observation of treaty obligations was seen as being necessary regarding MEAs. Canada's aggressive promotion of compliance mechanisms for MEAs is based on a number of premises: that the international community's environmental interests are best served by enhancing global adherence to environmental obligations; that the effectiveness of an MEA is difficult to assess without a clear idea of the degree of state compliance; that MEA compliance committee structures are "dispute avoidance mechanisms" with an important role in preventing and assisting states in dealing with environmental challenges at an early stage before damage or disputes arise; and that, by ensuring that all states are held accountable if they fail to fulfil their obligations, states that are compliant will not be disadvantaged.

The experience with compliance mechanisms in MEAs is modest. Only under the Montreal Protocol and the LRTAP Convention

---

[199] For the most recent report of the Scientific Group on Dumping, see *Report of the Twenty-Fifth Consultative Meeting of Parties, supra* note 32 at paras. 5.1–5.27.

[200] Protocol to the London Dumping Convention, *supra* note 11, Article 9(5).

[201] *Ibid.* at Article 26.

has there been significant practice, and, while more experience exists under CITES, the compliance procedures are not comparable to those under other MEAs.[202] This will change in the next few years as the compliance mechanisms under the Espoo Convention, the Basel Convention, the Cartagena Protocol, and the Aarhus Convention engage in more work. These will soon be followed by the compliance mechanisms under the Rotterdam Convention, the Stockholm Convention, the ITPGRFA, and, at some point, under the Protocol to the London Dumping Convention. The compliance mechanism under the Kyoto Protocol, when established, will also add to the wealth of compliance committee experience.

MEA compliance mechanisms are to operate in a manner that respects the integrity of the underlying treaty or protocol. In order to maintain treaty integrity, there must be a clear basis in the underlying treaty or protocol text for a compliance mechanism or a COP to impose punitive consequences or adopt punitive measures respecting non-compliant behaviour.[203] The distinction maintained in MEAs between formal international dispute settlement and compliance mechanisms makes it clear that state parties are not turning over to compliance mechanisms authority or jurisdiction over disputes normally vested in international dispute settlement procedures and this includes the possibility of non-treaty-sanctioned measures. This is not to conclude that in the face of non-compliant behaviour by a state party that no action can be taken. Rather, the conclusion is that, to assure the integrity of the MEA (the text of the treaty), imposition of consequences (most particularly punitive measures) must be based explicitly in the wording of an MEA or clearly be a matter within the discretion of the COP.

While the Montreal Protocol Implementation Committee is the parent of the MEA compliance mechanisms and seen as a significant success, the success of the parent does not assure the success of the children. This is particularly the case where key factors for the success of the parent may not exist for the children. Under the Montreal Protocol, determination of compliance or non-compliance for the key obligations is relatively direct in so far as numeric benchmarks are established and national reports can be used to assess performance against the benchmarks. These types of numeric emission reduction obligations are not found in the Espoo Convention, the Basel Convention, the Cartagena Protocol, the Protocol to the

202 See text accompanying note 22 in this article.
203 See text accompanying notes 84–95 in this article.

London Dumping Convention, the Rotterdam Convention, the ITPGRFA, or even the Aarhus Convention. It is, however, the model in the LRTAP Convention, the Kyoto Protocol, and, to a lesser extent, in the Stockholm Convention. The nature of the compliance/non-compliance question on key control obligations will be different for those treaties that do not follow the Montreal Protocol and the LRTAP Convention obligation model. The question of compliance/non-compliance may engage more judgment, more fact examination, and more treaty interpretation, which are all matters that a state party may contest or find unwelcome.

Similarly, the principal obligations in the Montreal Protocol (as well as the LRTAP Convention, the Kyoto Protocol, and the Stockholm Convention) are essentially international (to the global community) rather than transactional (and likely more bilateral) in nature. While this element is important in other MEAs, the obligations in the Espoo Convention, the Basel Convention, the Cartagena Protocol, the Rotterdam Convention, the ITPGRFA, and the Protocol to the London Dumping Convention are more transactional in nature. For these treaties, non-compliance with many obligations will directly affect another state party and thus make it more likely that non-compliance will be associated with treaty breach and risk conflating the non-compliance process with formal dispute settlement. While compliance mechanisms may be used by state parties as a means for the settlement of disputes, it is a decision for specific disputants to make and cannot really be credibly forced on unwilling state parties without bringing the legitimacy of compliance processes into question and, thus, undermining their effectiveness. The vision of some of the compliance mechanisms as "soft dispute settlement" may come to fruition under specific MEAs, but this result is by no means a certainty without significant state party acceptance.

Related to the above point is the experience under the LRTAP Convention of non-responses from European states identified by the Secretariat as possibly being in non-compliance of substantive (not reporting) obligations.[204] The non-responses appear to indicate unhappiness by state parties with the "triggering" of compliance processes in a manner that can be seen as confrontational, which can reduce the overall effectiveness of a compliance mechanism. This is not to suggest that confrontational triggering (party-to-party, secretariat, or committee) should be abandoned — only

[204] See notes 146–48 in this article.

that use of, and expectations of, outcomes from such triggers need to be carefully evaluated.

It is also worth noting that both the Montreal Protocol and the LRTAP Convention enjoy broad state party support for their underlying obligations regarding the reduction and elimination of production and use of designated substances. This support can be contrasted with the differences of views of state parties that exist concerning the Cartagena Protocol, for example, which is primarily aimed at preventing the movement of living modified organisms or regulating such movement. Such a fundamental disagreement, unresolvable during negotiations, is not one that should or can be resolved by a compliance mechanism, and attempts could undermine the compliance mechanisms.

The key feature for promoting compliance with the Montreal Protocol is the existence of MOP-controlled access to funds that can be used as a compliance incentive through distribution or withholding. None of the other MEAs, except the Kyoto Protocol,[205] have an equivalent feature. Without this feature, the compliance mechanisms in MEAs rely on "name and shame" to induce compliance. The effectiveness of "name and shame" can be circumscribed by state party indifference or, as suggested by Norway's reaction under the LRTAP Convention, calculation of cost benefits.[206] Over exuberance in using "name and shame" may devalue its effectiveness, which is something of which all MEA compliance mechanisms need to be wary.

Clearly, "name and shame" involves a careful calculus. The compliance mechanisms under both the Montreal Protocol and the LRTAP Convention have "earned" their successes by slowly creating among state parties a level of trust and acceptance. In particular, they have focused on systemic issues of reporting to build the information base and confidence in the mechanism before embarking on non-compliance with control obligations. The new compliance mechanisms that primarily rely on "name and shame" would be well advised to make themselves aware of this aspect of the experiences under the established compliance processes and, to the extent feasible, be wary of going too far, too fast.

Canada is and has been a strong supporter of the development and operation of workable and effective MEA compliance mechanisms with the perspective that the international community's

---

205 Kyoto Protocol, *supra* note 12, Article 11.

206 See note 144 in this article.

environmental interests are best served by enhancing global adherence to obligations in MEAs. However, one should neither set the expectations for MEA compliance mechanisms too high, for fear of condemning them to be evaluated as a failed experiment; nor too low, lest they be abandoned as being without merit. "Name and shame" and, where possible, providing incentives, can make a difference in attaining compliant behaviour by state parties with MEA obligations. The effectiveness of "name and shame" is based on the credibility of the mechanism both for the "named" state in order to induce them to accept "blame" and take action and for complying states who must be comforted that they are not being disadvantaged by their compliant behaviour. The credibility of compliance mechanisms is not to be achieved by an overtly judicial approach. Hence, compliance mechanisms should not pursue court-like approaches to issues. Equally, the credibility of compliance mechanisms is not to be achieved by a blinkered, unwavering attachment to meeting environmental goals. Ultimately, compliance mechanisms seek to induce compliant behaviour and this action requires a compliance committee to embrace, wherever possible, a non-confrontational, non-judicial approach to its work to ensure that there is significant engagement with the alleged non-compliant state party. Ultimately, it is a compliant outcome that is the goal and measurable result and not the virtue of an allegation or the fullness of the process.

Sommaire

Les comités de surveillance et les accords multilatéraux récents sur l'environnement

Dans le but d'améliorer et d'encourager le respect des obligations découlant des accords multilatéraux sur l'environnement (AME), les États ont convenu de créer des comités de surveillance pour tous les accords récents. Le Canada est très favorable à l'expérience des comités de surveillance. Il participe activement dans les négociations et le fonctionnement d'un bon nombre de ces comités. L'article traite de trois points. Premièrement, il examine la nature juridique internationale des comités de surveillance des AME. Deuxièmement, il aborde les questions clés relatives à la structure de ces comités. Enfin, l'article décrit le développement et le fonctionnement des comités de surveillance tels que prévus par le Protocole de Montréal, la Convention sur le transport à grande distance des polluants atmosphériques, la Convention sur l'évaluation de l'impact sur l'environnement dans un contexte transfrontière, la Convention de Bâle, le Protocole sur la biosécurité, la Convention de Rotterdam, la Convention de Stockholm et la Convention de Londres sur l'immersion des déchets.

Summary

Compliance Committees and Recent Multilateral Environmental Agreements

In order to enhance and encourage compliance with obligations in multilateral environmental agreements (MEAs), states have agreed to the creation of compliance committees for all of the recent MEAs. Canada has been a strong supporter of the compliance committee experiment and an active participant in the negotiation and operation of numerous MEA compliance committees. This article does three things. First, it examines the international legal nature of the MEA compliance committees. Second, the key issues of the structure of the committees are explored. Finally, the article looks at the development and operation of compliance committees pursuant to: the Montreal Protocol; the LRTAP Convention; the Espoo Convention; the Basel Convention; the Cartagena Protocol; the Rotterdam Convention; the Stockholm Convention; and the Protocol to the London Dumping Convention.

Of Questionable Legality: The Military Use of Cluster Bombs in Iraq in 2003

INTRODUCTION

> The production, sale and use of [cluster bombs] are incompatible with international human rights and humanitarian law.[1]

The legality of the 2003 invasion and subsequent occupation of Iraq by coalition forces remains highly controversial. Of similarly dubious legality, however, is the question of the use of certain weapons by these forces — namely, the use of cluster bombs. Both the British and American governments have confirmed the use of cluster weapons: the British during *Operation Telic*, in particular, against military objectives in and around Basra,[2] and the United States during *Operation Iraqi Freedom*.[3] Yet as the opening quotation

Dr. Karen Hulme, School of Law, University of Essex, England. I would like to acknowledge the valuable comments from colleagues Francoise Hampson and Geoff Gilbert, and Dominic McGoldrick (University of Liverpool).

[1] The United Nations Commission on Human Rights: Sub-Commission on Prevention of Discrimination and Protection of Minorities, *International Peace and Security as an Essential Condition for the Enjoyment of Human Rights, Above All, the Right to Life*, Res. 1996/16, UNCHR OR, 34th Mtg, UN Doc. E/CN.4/Sub.2/1996/L.11/Add.3 [Sub-Commission for the Protection and Promotion of Human Rights]. The sub-commission is now referred to as the UN Sub-Commission for the Protection and Promotion of Human Rights. The recorded vote was fifteen in favour, one against, with eight abstentions.

[2] For confirmation in Parliament of the use of cluster weapons, see United Kingdom, H.L., Parliamentary Debates, 5th ser., vol. 650, col. 6 (23 June 2003) (Lord Bach, the Parliamentary Under-Secretary of State, Ministry of Defence) [Parliamentary Debates, Lord Bach]; see also United Kingdom, H.C., Parliamentary Debates, sess. 2002–3, vol. 402, col. 1075 (3 April 2003) (Geoffrey Hoon, Secretary of State for Defence).

[3] See Lieutenant General T. Michael Moseley, U.S. Air Force, *Operation Iraqi Freedom — By the Numbers*, Assessment and Analysis Division, 30 April 2003, available

suggests, some commentators believe that cluster bombs are already prohibited by international law. Therefore, the question becomes whether, in using this weapon, user states such as the United Kingdom and the United States have violated fundamental rules of armed conflict.

For as long as there have been wars, there have been limitations on the permissible methods and means of waging these wars. The laws of armed conflict govern the specific situation of armed hostilities — both inter-state and intra-state hostilities. Codified in the latter half of the nineteenth century and the twentieth century, the laws of war have also witnessed many developments. Before the two world wars, international law had already prohibited the use of treacherous and cruel weapons, such as poisonous gas.[4] In a major development in 1977, following the Vietnam conflict, in particular, two protocols were enacted to supplement the 1949 Geneva Conventions (Geneva Protocol I and Geneva Protocol II).[5] The situation of international armed conflict continues to be governed by Geneva Protocol I, and non-international armed conflict by Geneva Protocol II. The two instruments clearly specify the most basic and fundamental limitations applicable to *all* weapons. They codify the existing customary rules as well as incorporating much needed new developments. It was during the negotiation of the protocols, however, that it became apparent that the specific regulation of individual conventional weapons was needed. It was agreed by the participants that this regulation should be undertaken separately. Consequently, the International Committee of the Red Cross (ICRC) convened two further diplomatic conferences of government experts — one at Lucerne in 1974 and the other in Lugano in 1976 — which concerned the regulation of certain conventional weapons. Finally, in 1980, the delegates adopted the 1980 United

---

online <http://www.globalsecurity.org/military/library/report/2003/uscentaf_oif_report_30apr2003.pdf> [*Operation Iraqi Freedom*].

4 1925 Geneva Protocol for the Prohibition of the Use in War of Asphyxiating, Poisonous or Other Gases, and of Bacteriological Methods of Warfare, 17 June 1925, 1930 U.K.T.S. 24 (entered into force 8 February 1928).

5 Protocol Additional to the Geneva Conventions of 12 August 1949, and Relating to the Protection of Victims of International Armed Conflicts, 8 June 1977, 1977 16 I.L.M. 1391–441 (entered into force 7 December 1978) [Geneva Protocol I]; Protocol Additional to the Geneva Conventions of 12 August 1949, and Relating to the Protection of Victims of Non-International Armed Conflicts, 8 June 1977, 1977 16 I.L.M. 1442–9 (entered into force 7 December 1978) [Geneva Protocol II].

Nations Convention on Prohibitions or Restrictions on the Use of Certain Conventional Weapons Which May Be Deemed to Be Excessively Injurious or to Have Indiscriminate Effects (Conventional Weapons Convention),[6] together with three protocols. The original three protocols placed restrictions on the use of certain anti-personnel weapons, namely non-detectable fragments (Protocol I), mines, booby traps, and other devices (Protocol II), and incendiary weapons (Protocol III). It was not until 1995 that a fourth protocol was adopted, which concerned the use of blinding laser weapons.[7]

However, two major developments occurred in the years following due to mounting public pressure on the issue of landmines. First, in 1996, state parties to the 1980 Conventional Weapons Convention adopted further limitations on the use of mines, amending the earlier Protocol II.[8] Second, outside the 1980 Conventional Weapons Convention regime, states met in Ottawa in 1997 to adopt a comprehensive prohibition on the use and possession of anti-personnel mines.[9] In line with similar developments in other forums, including judgments of the International Criminal Tribunal for the Former Yugoslavia, states party to the 1980 Conventional Weapons Convention agreed, in 2001, to extend the application of that treaty to the situation of non-international armed conflict.[10]

---

6   United Nations Convention on Prohibitions or Restrictions on the Use of Certain Conventional Weapons Which May Be Deemed to Be Excessively Injurious or to Have Indiscriminate Effects, 10 April 1981, 19 I.L.M. 1523–36 (entered into force 2 December 1983) [Conventional Weapons Convention]. The three protocols were adopted at the same time as, and annexed to, the convention, see Protocol on Non-Detectable Fragments [Protocol I]; Protocol on Prohibitions or Restrictions on the Use of Mines, Booby-Traps and Other Devices [Protocol II]; and Protocol on Prohibitions or Restrictions on the Use of Incendiary Weapons [Protocol III].

7   Protocol IV on Blinding Laser Weapons to the United Nations Convention on Prohibitions or Restrictions on the Use of Certain Conventional Weapons Which May be Deemed to be Excessively Injurious or to Have Indiscriminate Effects, 30 January 1996, 35 I.L.M. 1218 (entered into force 30 July 1998).

8   1996 Amended Protocol II on Prohibitions or Restrictions on the Use of Mines, Booby-Traps and Other Devices, 3 June 1997, 35 I.L.M. 1206 (entered into force 3 December 1998) [Amended Protocol II on Mines].

9   1997 Ottawa Treaty on the Prohibition of the Use, Stockpiling, Production and Transfer of Anti-Personnel Mines and on Their Destruction, 3 December 1997, 36 I.L.M. 1507 (entered into force 1 March 1999) [Ottawa Treaty].

10   1980 Conventional Weapons Convention, *supra* note 6, Amendment Article 1 (21 December 2001), available online at <http://www.icrc.org>. The amendment

146   *Annuaire canadien de Droit international 2004*

The consequence of the 2001 amendment was that — at least for those state parties — certain weapons' limitations are applicable regardless of the classification of the conflict as international or non-international. Finally, in November 2003, state parties to the Conventional Weapons Convention adopted a fifth protocol governing explosive remnants of war.[11]

Specific treaty limitations are not the end of the story, however. Weapons must also conform to a number of humanitarian principles in order to remain lawful. The first principle is the prohibition of weapons causing unnecessary suffering to combatants and the second is the prohibition on indiscriminate warfare.[12] In regard to the second principle, indiscriminate warfare, weapons would, practically speaking, violate this prohibition if they were to be either (1) inherently indiscriminate in their effects or (2) used in an indiscriminate manner. The first criterion clearly provides grounds for a ban. As a consequence, if a weapon is banned, there is no need for its possession, and, thus, the act of possession can also be banned. Since the second category of indiscriminate warfare places restrictions only on the use of weapons, it follows that the possession of such weapons would remain lawful. Of course, common sense dictates that states have a duty to ensure that their weaponry conforms to international legal requirements. As a consequence, a state developing or procuring a new weapon must ensure its legality before it can use it on the battlefield. Albeit common sense, this principle was confirmed at Geneva in 1977 as Article 36 of Geneva Protocol I. Accordingly, the provision stipulates:

> In the study, development, acquisition or adoption of a new weapon, means or method of warfare, a High Contracting Party is under an obligation to determine whether its employment would, in some or all circumstances, be prohibited by this Protocol or by any other rule of international law applicable to the High Contracting Party.

Cluster weapons have a lengthy battle history. Their first deployment dates back to the 1960s when the United States dropped some

---

was brought into force on 18 May 2004 following the deposit of the twentieth instrument of ratification. As of July 2005, the 2001 amendment had forty-two ratifications, of the ninety-seven state parties.

[11] Protocol V on Explosive Remnants of War to the Conventional Weapons Convention, text available online at <http://untreaty.un.org>. See also online <http://www.icrc.org> [Protocol V on Explosive Remnants].

[12] See also the principle of proportionality.

285 million bomblets on Cambodia, Vietnam, and Laos during the Vietnam conflict.[13] These weapons have been used in both international and internal conflicts such as those in the Falklands, the Gulf, by Russian forces in Chechnya, by both parties to the Eritrea-Ethiopia war, by Nigerian forces in Sierra Leone, by government forces in the Sudanese civil war,[14] and, of course, in the recent conflicts in Kosovo and Afghanistan. Today, cluster weapons form part of the arsenal of many states. Since comprehensive prohibitions on the use of anti-personnel mines were enacted in 1996–7, the controversy surrounding the use of cluster weapons has intensified. The link that is often made is that, due to their high propensity for failure, a large proportion of what would otherwise be legitimate "dumb" bombs are turned into ultra-sensitive anti-personnel mines. This controversy was heightened during the Afghanistan conflict in 2001, where the US cluster bombs were frequently mistaken for food aid packages of the same colour.[15] Even without this added danger, the campaign to limit the use of cluster munitions has recently gained in strength, leading to the adoption of a new legal instrument in the form of a fifth protocol to the 1980 Conventional Weapons Convention. One particular issue remains, however. Despite the emergence of new, more sophisticated technologies, the United Kingdom and the United States are still using older, less reliable versions of cluster munitions. A question that arises, therefore, is whether the new instrument will put a halt to this use, and, if so, whether it will be sufficient to eliminate the controversy surrounding cluster munitions.

As a consequence of the recent use of cluster weapons in Iraq and their generally controversial nature, this article will analyze the legality of such weapons in light of current weapons limitations. Once the science and effects of the weapon have been demonstrated, the analysis will proceed to the question of its current legality on the battlefield of both international and non-international armed conflict. The analysis will not, however, be concerned with

---

13 See "Analysis: Why Use Cluster Bombs?" *BBC News Online* (8 August 2000), available online at <http://news.bbc.co.uk> (BBC quotes US Pentagon estimates).

14 "Cluster Bombs: The Hidden Toll," *The Guardian* (8 August 2000), available online at <http://www.guardian.co.uk>.

15 See Richard Norton-Taylor and Lucy Ward, "Appeals to Halt Cluster Bombs," *The Guardian* (8 November 2001), available online at <http://www.guardian. co.uk>. The same problem was later encountered in Iraq. See Will Knight, "Cluster Bomb Use Sparks Fear for Iraqi Civilians," *New Scientist* (3 April 2003), available online at <http://www.newscientist.com>.

compliance with human rights instruments. As a consequence, should there be grounds for suggesting that cluster weapons violate the prohibition on unnecessary suffering then this outcome would be cause for a ban. Similarly, if cluster weapons can be described as inherently indiscriminate weapons, which thus violate the indiscriminate warfare principle, then this would also be cause for a ban. If, on the other hand, the weapons are *prima facie* discriminate but have been on occasion used in an indiscriminate manner, then it would follow that the weapons are lawful and subject only to limitations on use. The question of future limitations on use — should these be warranted — would then specifically address the adoption of Protocol V on Explosive Remnants to the 1980 Conventional Weapons Convention.

CLUSTER BOMBS DEFINED

TECHNICAL ASPECTS

There are many different types of cluster weapons. Some models are relatively simple, such as those containing landmines, while others can be more complex. Included among the more technical versions are those that employ an incendiary capacity so as to ignite nearby flammable materials and those containing fuel-air explosives. In addition, some versions can contain depleted uranium or chemical warfare agents.[16] Among the more simple "bomb" variety of cluster weapons, the design of the bombs can range from a basic spherical shape to cylindrical or dart-shaped. The various types of cluster bombs, however, all have one thing in common: their basic design.

All cluster weapons work from the basic premise that one larger unit is used to take the many smaller, individual "sub-munitions" to the target zone. Saturation of the target zone with explosive devices can then be achieved with only a relatively small number of the main bomb units. The cluster bomb, therefore, comprises two stages: (1) a container or dispenser, which is approximately 500 millime-

---

[16] Any use of chemical weapons would be prohibited by the 1993 Convention on the Prohibition of the Development, Production, Stockpiling and Use of Chemical Weapons and on Their Destruction, 13 January 1993, 32 I.L.M. 800 (entered into force 29 April 1997) [Chemical Weapons Convention]. The Chemical Weapons Convention makes no distinction as to the level of conflict and now prohibits the use of chemical weapons "in all circumstances" even against non-parties, including in attack and defence and situations of internal armed conflict (see Article I(1)(b)).

ters in diameter by 2,000–3,500 millimeters in length, which houses (2) the multiple smaller, individual sub-munitions. These individual sub-munitions may also be referred to as "grenades" if ground launched and "bomblets" if air-delivered. The number of individual sub-munitions that can be packed inside the larger shell casing varies. Some models will employ only fifty to 200 sub-munitions, while others have been known to utilize up to as many as 1,800 individual sub-munitions.[17] The new Israeli-manufactured variant, which was used by British forces in Iraq during *Operation Telic,* involves only forty-nine sub-munitions. By design, therefore, cluster weapons are area weapons and, as such, are not dependent upon pinpoint accuracy, as are so-called "smart weapons," but instead are dependent on sheer volume and saturation of the target zone.

According to British Ministry of Defence figures, approximately seventy cluster weapons were dropped by British forces around Baghdad, Iraq, in 2003.[18] These were British-made weapons of the type RBL-755, which employ 147 cylindrical-shaped sub-munitions.[19] This weapon is an older-version cluster bomb (introduced into conflict in the 1970s) with a problematic history of use in numerous conflicts, including Kosovo in 1999.[20] As is usual with cluster weapons, this model employs both an anti-*matériel* feature and an anti-personnel feature for maximum effectiveness against "mixed" targets on the battlefield. A mixed target would be a convoy with both armoured (hard-skinned) and non-armoured (soft-skinned) military vehicles. The anti-*matériel* aspect involves a shaped charge contained in the centre of the cluster sub-munition, which

17 For the range of cluster bomb types and descriptions of each, see Federation of American Scientists, "Cluster Bombs," available at <http://www.fas.org/man/dod-101/sys/dumb/cluster.htm> [FAS]. The CBU-75 Sadeye employs 1,800 bomblets only 1 pound each in weight. In each sub-munition are imbedded 600 razor-sharp steel shards. It has an impact radius of approximately twelve meters. Accordingly, a single Sadeye bomb can cover an area more than double that of a standard 2,000 pound bomb. See generally the Global Security organization, available online at <http://www.globalsecurity.org.>

18 *Operations in Iraq: First Reflections* (London: UK Ministry of Defence, 2003) at 24 [*Operations in Iraq*].

19 For a detailed analysis of these weapons, see William M. Arkin, Joost R. Hiltermann, and Michael McClintock, "Ticking Time Bombs," available online at <http://www.hrw.org/hrw/reports/1999/nato2/nato995–01.htm>.

20 The R variant was a redesigned BL-755, following the 1991 Gulf conflict. The RBL-755 entailed fitting a radar proximity sensor kit to existing BL-755 stocks. The new variant can be dropped from a higher altitude and, thus, reduces the risk of attack of the aircraft during delivery and deployment of the weapons.

with sufficient speed on impact with the target will pierce through even armoured vehicles up to depths approaching 250 millimeters. This effect is in addition to the anti-personnel aspect of casing fragmentation. Upon explosion, the sub-munition's pre-scored metal casing is designed to fragment into hundreds or thousands of tiny metal pieces, which is akin to a grenade explosion. When the sub-munition detonates, the metal fragments will generally be scattered in a circular motion with a radius approaching forty meters.[21] The fragmentation aspect of the weapon is designed to be effective against personnel out in the open or at least not protected by armoured vehicles or buildings. With the dual combination of anti-personnel and anti-*matériel* features, the cluster bomb unit is generally most effective against dispersed or mobile mixed targets, situated in the open, or targets such as military encampments and other military positions with a mix of buildings, vehicles, and persons present.

US forces have also employed cluster bombs of type CBU-87 combined effects munition (CEM), which are popular because they contain an additional third feature: an incendiary capacity. This type of cluster bomb was extensively used by American forces during *Operation Desert Storm* in the 1991 Gulf conflict[22] and more recently during the conflicts in Afghanistan (2001) and Iraq (2003).[23] Upon detonation, the bomblets not only employ the molten metal slug to pierce hard-skinned targets and the fragmentation of the casing to disable personnel but they also have the capacity to ignite any combustible materials inside the vehicles or outside in the environment. According to available figures, a fully loaded CBU-87 would cost approximately US $14,000 to produce, which, of course, could then be used to saturate a large area, disabling enemy hard and soft targets.[24] Compared to the cost of a single laser-guided smart bomb, which costs upwards of US $19,000, the value of cluster bombs becomes clearer. Also listed in the US inventory of weapons

---

21 International Committee of the Red Cross (ICRC) Mines-Arms Unit, *Explosive Remnants: Cluster Bombs and Landmines in Kosovo* (Geneva: ICRC, 2000) at 7, available online at <http://www.icrc.org/web/eng/siteengo.nsf/htmlall/p0780/$File/ICRC_002_0780.PDF!Open> [*Explosive Remnants*].

22 See FAS, *supra* note 17.

23 See "Fatally Flawed: Cluster Bombs and Their Use by the United States in Afghanistan," *Human Rights Watch Report*, December 2002, at 15–6 ["Fatally Flawed"]. See also *Operation Iraqi Freedom*, *supra* note 3 at 11.

24 See C. Dickey, "Seeds of Carnage," *Newsweek* (2 August 1999), at 29 ["Seeds of Carnage"].

used during the 2003 engagement in Iraq are a substantial number (some 182) of the Vietnam-era *Rockeye* cluster weapons.[25] The
inventory simply lists the CBU-99 *Rockeye* model, which employs
247 sub-munitions of type Mk-118 — a basic anti-tank bomb.

The British RBL-755 sub-munition, like most cluster weapon models, is usually remotely delivered to the target zone either by mortar,
rocket, or aircraft. Essentially, the sub-munitions are ejected from
the main bomb dispenser either when released from the aircraft or
fired by the rocket. Once the sub-munitions are clear of the dispenser, they deploy parachutes, designed to slow the decent of the
sub-munitions to the target zone. At the same time, the timer inside each sub-munition will commence, and, once a sub-munition
reaches a set air speed, the detonator will become fully armed.[26] In
this particular model, the anti-*matériel* charge will be fired when the
sub-munition impacts with the target, causing an electrical charge
to ignite the detonator. However, the optimum conditions for firing the charge occur when the sub-munition lands with sufficient
speed and force on a vertical impact. If the sub-munition lands in
soft terrain or water, therefore, the sub-munition may fail to detonate.[27] Consequently, the sub-munition would remain live. In addition, however, cluster weapons may fail to detonate (1) if faulty or
damaged mechanical parts were used in the manufacturing process; (2) if the weapon spent long periods of time in storage; (3) if
there have been inadequate precautions taken during the transportation of the weapons; and (4) if there are personnel mistakes
during the loading and flight.[28] Cluster bombs are particularly susceptible to failure under (2) and (3) because, unlike most other
weapons, cluster weapons are shipped from the manufacturer ready
for use.[29] Most other weapons require assembly and/or fusing on
site. Furthermore, where the sub-munition employs a parachute in
order to slow the speed of its descent and to project the correct tra-
jectory for detonation, any failure of, or damage to, the parachute

---

[25] See *Operation Iraqi Freedom, supra* note 3.

[26] For a thorough account, see Rae McGrath, *Cluster Bombs: The Military Effectiveness and Impact on Civilians of Cluster Munitions* (London: UK Working Group on
Landmines, in association with Landmine Action, 2000) at 21.

[27] *Explosive Remnants, supra* note 21 at 7.

[28] See McGrath, *supra* note 26 at 25–7. These are viewed as being among the more
common reasons for failure of cluster weapons as listed by the non-governmental
organization.

[29] For further information, see <http://www.globalsecurity.org>.

will have a significant impact on the reliability and effectiveness of the weapon. Finally, a simple, but considerable, problem, which was highlighted by the organization Landmine Action, is the possibility of a mid-air collision of sub-munitions. When so many sub-munitions are released simultaneously from a single dispenser, the potential for in-air collisions is clear and, hence, the potential for damage to be caused to the fusing mechanism of the sub-munitions. In sum, there are many reasons for the failure of cluster weapons. And it is this issue that causes the military use of cluster weapons to be highly questionable.

According to the manufacturers of these weapons, the reliability requirement for some of the older versions is that no less than 95 per cent of the sub-munitions produced would be effective.[30] This listing gives a manufacturer-accepted dud rate of up to 5 per cent. In the 1990–1 Gulf conflict, however, the actual failure rate may have been as high as 30 per cent.[31] Therefore, the greatest problem posed by cluster weapons is often not their actual military use but rather the propensity of the weapons to fail — in short, their continuing effects *after* the military necessity has passed and, indeed, even *after* the conflict has ended. Furthermore, this propensity for failure cannot be termed an accident, since it forms part of the manufacturing process as well as the military calculation. One of the key advantages of cluster weapons from a governmental viewpoint is their relative affordability in comparison with other weapons. Although exact figures are not generally available, cluster sub-munitions cost approximately US $30–60 each. Unfortunately, it appears that the major consequence of the relatively inexpensive production costs of cluster weapons and the other deployment issues is an increased tendency for failure. While there have no doubt been improvements in the manufacture of cluster weapons since the "95-per cent-effective" figure was widely quoted, there remain two problems. First, there are still problems with the failure rate of more modern cluster weapons — albeit not as high as a 5 per cent failure rate. And second, the older "95-per cent-effective" weapons are still being used today. As a consequence, for every one of the older version cluster bombs used, there will be up to eight duds (based on

---

[30] Although this figure no longer appears to be included on websites of the various manufacturers, it has been noted by a number of sources including Human Rights Watch, "NATO's Use of Cluster Munitions in Yugoslavia" (11 May 1999), available online at <http://www.hrw.org/backgrounder/arms/cluso511.htm> ["Cluster Munitions in Yugoslavia"].

[31] *Ibid.*

an RBL-755, carrying 147 bomblets). Certainly, evidence from recent conflicts indicates that the 5 per cent failure rate is probably a conservative estimate. The real rate may be closer to 10–20 per cent. As a consequence of the high failure rate of cluster weapons, some newer versions have been designed with a secondary fusing system to detonate the sub-munition should the primary fuse fail. The Israeli-made L20 is such a weapon. British forces used the L20 for the first time in Iraq in 2003, exclusively in and around Basra. According to British Ministry of Defence information, some 2,000 L20 cluster bombs were used during the campaign, each housing forty-nine sub-munitions (type M-85).[32] The sub-munitions are again cylindrical in shape but are smaller than the older RBL-755s, measuring only fifty-five millimeters in length by thirty-five millimeters in diameter. Despite having the added technical advantage, however, of a back-up fifteen-second self-destruct mechanism — the L20 still has an estimated failure rate of approximately 2 per cent. Such a rate once again reflects this weapon's manufacturing and deployment faults, which far outstrips the failure rate of other weapons.[33]

HEALTH AND ENVIRONMENTAL EFFECTS OF CLUSTER WEAPONS

The effect on the health of the local inhabitants and on the environment from the use of cluster weapons is beyond doubt. It is estimated that sub-munitions have caused more than 1,600 civilian deaths, including 400 Iraqis and 1,200 Kuwaitis, and a further 2,500 injured in just the first two years following the 1990–1 Gulf conflict.[34] Similarly, according to Human Rights Watch, approximately 11,000 people have been killed or injured in Laos since 1973 as a result of live cluster sub-munitions and landmines.[35] In fact, many non-governmental organizations (NGOs) argue that cluster weapons should be considered to pose an even greater human danger than landmines. This is so because unlike landmines, which require approximately 140 kilograms[36] of pressure for anti-tank mines

---

[32] See Parliamentary Debates, Lord Bach, *supra* note 2.

[33] Part of the increased failure rate of cluster weapons is due to the weapon's design — of using a large volume of mini-bombs as opposed to fewer, but larger tonnage, bombs to achieve the same area coverage.

[34] "Cluster Munitions in Yugoslavia," *supra* note 30.

[35] *Ibid.*

[36] Generally the weight of a single person would not cause anti-tank mines to detonate, however, a civilian vehicle may, and, therefore, even anti-tank mines are not without civilian casualties.

to detonate and three kilograms for anti-personnel mines, failed cluster sub-munitions can detonate with as little pressure as a change in temperature. Furthermore, due to the bright colours and fascinating shapes of cluster sub-munitions, they are particularly attractive to children. As a result, children under the age of fourteen are almost five times more likely to be killed by cluster bombs than landmines.[37] Finally, since the metal fragments are designed to scatter over a distance of forty meters, cluster weapons are more likely than landmines to lead to the death or injury of *several* people.

A further problem is the scale of area that is affected by cluster weapons. Due to the very nature of the weapon and its mode of delivery, an attack with cluster weapons ensures that a large number of sub-munitions are dispersed over a sizeable area. Dependent upon the altitude of release and detonation, a single cluster weapon with some 200 munitions can saturate an area one square kilometer in dimension.[38] In addition, some dispensers are fitted with a programmable spinning device, which further increases the dispersal range of the sub-munitions. Furthermore, it is possible that a larger target area will be affected than was intended, and certainly if the location of impact cannot be pinpointed accurately, a broader area will need to be swept to ensure the safety of the population.

In addition, the presence of unexploded ordnance will undeniably hamper the post-conflict recovery of the country and impede the restoration of vital services, such as the water supply and electricity grids. The return of farmers to their fields will be significantly delayed, and sources of safe drinking water will be reduced. This propensity for failure also leads to exacerbated problems in the clean up and restoration of the environment following the close of hostilities. Certainly, the heavy metal components of failed cluster weapons will degrade (including copper, lead, zinc, mercury, and cadmium) and will contaminate the ground and the water supply if not cleared, but left to rot *in situ*. And, clearly, the greater the number of failed weapons, the greater the contamination that will

37 See the Preparatory Committee for the 2001 Review Conference of the United Nations Convention on Certain Conventional Weapons, *Statement of the International Committee of the Red Cross*, Geneva (14 December 2000), available online at <http://www.icrc.org>.

38 This is the figure given by the North Atlantic Treaty Organization (NATO) in July 2000 to a number of UK Members of Parliament. See All-Party Parliamentary Landmine Eradication Group, "UK House of Commons Cluster Munitions: Note of Meeting with NATO," reprinted in Virgil Wiebe, "Footprints of Death" (2000) 22 Mich. J. Int'l L. 85 at 153.

be caused. According to the official figures supplied by the North Atlantic Treaty Organization (NATO), the estimated operational failure rate for cluster sub-munitions employed during the 1999 Kosovo conflict was approximately 10 per cent. As a consequence, some 30,000 unexploded cluster sub-munitions remained on the battlefield *after* the cessation of hostilities.[39] Given the soft, wet ground conditions and the Yugoslav forces' use of vegetation as cover in Kosovo, it is likely that an even greater number in fact failed. Even assuming a failure rate of a mere 5 per cent, and based on estimates of 24–30 million sub-munitions used against Iraqi troops in the 1990–1 Gulf conflict, one can conclude that at least 1.5 million unexploded sub-munitions were abandoned on the Gulf battlefield.[40] The actual failure rate of cluster weapons during this conflict may have been as high as 25–30 per cent. These are very sizeable proportions of unexploded ordnance, which if not removed will endanger the population and the environment alike for some time to come.

Cluster munitions also pose increased dangers in their removal. Unlike many types of anti-personnel mines (APM) that may be de-activated, the only method of removing cluster weapons is by deto-nation *in situ*. This is further complicated by the fact that mapping out the location of, and removing, cluster sub-munitions is a long and hazardous process. Massive flooding in Mozambique recently highlighted these problems only too well, forcing the re-mapping of unexploded sub-munitions and adding years to the recovery schedule of the country.[41]

Certainly, by design, most weapons will cause harm to people, and most, if not all, weapons will cause a level of harm to the envi-ronment. Furthermore, most weapons will be susceptible to failure in wartime. However, with cluster weapons, it is the fact that the states using them have knowledge of their high failure rate that causes them to be a legally questionable weapon of war. In other words, even with the knowledge of the high propensity for failure of the sub-munitions, states nevertheless continue to use cluster weapons in conflict and so can be said to intend the post-conflict consequences of the weapon's failure.

---

39   *Explosive Remnants, supra* note 21 at 10.

40   "Cluster Munitions in Yugoslavia," *supra* note 30.

41   See Michael Dynes, "Mines Will Pose Threat as Water Recedes" (4 March 2000), available online at <http://www.times-archive.co.uk/news/pages/tim/2000/03/04/timfgnafro3004.html>.

SUMMARY

From this analysis, it can be shown, first, that cluster bombs have been used on the battlefield for more than forty years and that any health and environmental effects are, therefore, a foreseeable consequence of use; second, that due to the nature of the weapon, cluster bombs may present a legal problem both at the point of use and in the long term, leaving a lasting human and environmental legacy; and, third, that despite public and military concerns, these weapons remain in the arsenal of states and have been used by British and American forces in the recent conflict in Iraq. Having established the problems raised by cluster bombs, the following section will seek to examine their legality under the current provisions of the laws of armed conflict.

APPLICATION OF THE LAWS OF ARMED CONFLICT

The function of the law of armed conflict is to place limits on warfare with respect to who can legitimately take up arms in combat and to what methods or means of warfare such persons can employ. Today, the laws have reached a very sophisticated stage, having evolved particularly from the late nineteenth century onwards. Much customary practice and principle has been codified into treaty law, particularly in the 1949 Geneva Conventions and the 1977 Geneva Protocols I and II to these conventions.

One of the first such principles to be codified is found in Article 22 of the 1899 Hague Convention (II) with Respect to the Laws and Customs of War on Land,[42] which governs the limitation of arms during conflict. Simply phrased, the rule stipulates that war *cannot* be fought with any and every means available. First incorporated in the 1874 Project of an International Declaration Concerning the Laws and Customs of War, which was adopted by the Conference of Brussels,[43] the concept was also later included in Article 22 of the 1907 Convention (IV) Respecting the Laws and Customs of War on Land, which governs the laws of land warfare.[44]

---

[42] Hague Convention II with Respect to the Laws and Customs of War on Land, see Regulations Concerning the Laws and Customs of War on Land, Annex, 29 July 1899, 26 Martens Nouveau Recueil (ser. 2) 949 (entered into force 4 September 1900).

[43] Project of an International Declaration Concerning the Laws and Customs of War, 27 August 1874, A.J.I.L. Supplement 1 (1907) (has not entered into force).

[44] Regulations Respecting the Laws and Customs of War on Land, annexed to the 1907 Convention IV Respecting the Laws and Customs of War on Land, Hague,

There is no doubt that the frequent repetition of the principle evidences its fundamentality, but, on the other hand, it may also evidence the fact that it was being breached during these years — one example being the use of chemical weapons. Finally, the customary principle of limitation was stated in Article 35(1) of the 1977 Geneva Protocol I, which states: "In any armed conflict, the right of the Parties to the conflict to choose methods or means of warfare is not unlimited." Yet it is the rigid application of the principle that ensures the limitation of cruel or disproportionate arms on the battlefield. As a consequence, certain weapons have been subjected to specific treaty limitations or even prohibitions on their use in armed conflict. Others may nevertheless be limited by the basic customary law principles of proportionality and discrimination as well as the prohibition on unnecessary suffering.

Finally, recent developments have narrowed the distinction in regard to a weapon's legality in (1) international armed conflict and (2) non-international armed conflict. In a landmark judgment, the International Criminal Tribunal for the Former Yugoslavia in *Prosecutor v. Dusko Tadic* recognized that weapons prohibited, at customary law, as being inhumane in international armed conflict must also be prohibited in situations of internal conflict.[45] According to the tribunal, any other conclusion would be "preposterous."[46] As a consequence, the prohibition on certain "inhumane" weapons is now absolute. Further measures, under certain treaty regimes, have also been adopted, extending weapons prohibitions or limitations to internal armed conflict.

In the following two sections of this article, the legality of the use of cluster weapons will be analyzed, whether as a result of (1) a specific treaty prohibition or limitation relating to that weapon or (2) other rules or principles of humanitarian law.

TREATY-SPECIFIC WEAPONS PROHIBITION OR LIMITATION

There is no specific treaty prohibition on the use of cluster weapons. However, a proposal was made in as early as the 1970s to

18 October 1907, (1910) U.K.T.S. 9, Cd. 5030 (entered into force 26 January 1910) [Hague Convention IV]. The convention is generally taken to be customary law. See *Trial of the Major War Criminals before the International Military Tribunal,* Nuremberg, Vol. XXII, I.M.T. Secretariat 497.

45 *Prosecutor v. Dusko Tadic* (1996), Case No. IT-94-1 (International Criminal Tribunal for the Former Yugoslavia), 35 I.L.M. 32 at para. 119, available online at <http://www.un.org/icty/judgement.htm>.

46 *Ibid.*

include a prohibition on the use of cluster weapons in (what would later become known as) the 1980 Conventional Weapons Convention.[47] The Lucerne Conference in 1974 was convened by the ICRC to consider proposals for the prohibition of certain anti-personnel weapons. Among the governments that opposed the prohibition of cluster weapons were the United States and the United Kingdom. These states attempted to downplay the weapon's deadly effects.[48] Such opposition at Lucerne, however, did not prevent a group of thirteen states from proposing a prohibition on the use of anti-personnel cluster weapons at the second conference in 1976, convened in Lugano.[49] Although ultimately defeated, the proposal stipulated that "[a]nti-personnel cluster warheads or other devices with many bomblets which act through the ejection of a great number of small-calibre fragments or pellets are prohibited for use."[50] The proponents of the prohibition argued that cluster munitions have wide area coverage and, hence, could affect combatants and civilians indiscriminately.[51] In addition, it was stated that due to the multiple wounds that are inflicted in an attack by cluster weapons they would cause unnecessary suffering. These are not dissimilar to the arguments still being advanced today. As it was, however, the proposal, as drafted, would only have prohibited anti-personnel cluster weapons and not the anti-*matériel* or combined effects cluster weapons that are causing such heavy human casualties today. Ultimately, the proposed prohibition was defeated.

ANALOGY WITH ANTI-PERSONNEL LANDMINES

There remains the possibility, however, that cluster weapons fall within the existing restrictions on the use of landmines. Many commentators suggest that unexploded cluster weapons are akin to

---

[47] Although originally adopted with only international armed conflict in mind, the convention and its protocols were extended in 2001 to include applicability in situations of non-international armed conflict. The extension was achieved by way of amendment to Article 1 of the convention and is subject to state consent in the normal way. See Conventional Weapons Convention, *supra* note 6.

[48] See International Committee of the Red Cross, *Conference of Government Experts on the Use of Certain Conventional Weapons*, Official Statement (Lucerne, 1975) at 54.

[49] These states were Algeria, Austria, Egypt, Lebanon, Mali, Mauritania, Mexico, Norway, Sudan, Sweden, Switzerland, Venezuela, and Yugoslavia.

[50] Proposal CDDH/IV/201 (II), O.R. Vol.XVI, 615.

[51] See Wiebe, *supra* note 38 at 154–6.

landmines.[52] The two weapons would appear to share similar human and environmental effects. Yet, is this too simplistic an approach or is it the case that recent limitations governing landmines also refer to cluster weapons? There are currently three instruments regulating the use of APMs: two protocols (1980 Protocol II on Prohibitions or Restrictions on the Use of Mines, Booby-Traps and Other Devices (Protocol II on Mines) and the 1996 Amended Protocol II on Prohibitions or Restrictions on the Use of Mines, Booby-Traps and Other Devices (Amended Protocol II on Mines)) to the 1980 Conventional Weapons Convention[53] and the 1997 Ottawa Treaty on the Prohibition of the Use, Stockpiling, Production and Transfer of Anti-Personnel Mines and on Their Destruction (Ottawa Treaty).[54] The Ottawa Treaty has been widely accepted by states[55] and, as its title suggests, incorporates a comprehensive prohibition on the use of anti-personnel mines due to their post-war human and environmental effects.

In order to make the analogy, two types of cluster weapons must be distinguished. First, there are a number of cluster bombs that contain mines. Such models include the GATOR family of cluster bombs that deliver scatterable mines.[56] A key aspect of the GATOR cluster bombs is the random-delay function. Should the mines not

---

[52] See the working paper submitted by Y.K.J. Yeung Sik Yuen to the Sub-Commission on the Promotion and Protection of Human Rights, UN ESCOR, *Human Rights and Weapons of Mass Destruction, or with Indiscriminate Effect, or of a Nature to Cause Superfluous Injury or Unnecessary Suffering*, UN Doc. E/CN.4/Sub.2/2002/38 (27 June 2002) at para. 116 [*Human Rights and Weapons*].

[53] The first is Protocol II on Prohibitions or Restrictions on the Use of Mines, Booby-Traps and Other Devices, 10 October 1980, 19 I.L.M. 1529 (formed part of the original convention), *supra* note 6 [Protocol II on Mines]; the second is Amended Protocol II on Mines, *supra* note 8.

[54] Ottawa Treaty, *supra* note 9.

[55] In July 2005, the number of ratifications stood at 144. A number of important states are, however, missing from the list including the United States, Russia, China, India, Pakistan, and Israel.

[56] There are other variations that have been designed to include anti-personnel mines and, as such, the use, manufacture, or stockpiling of these by state parties will also contravene the 1997 Ottawa Treaty. According to Landmine Action, other examples of minelaying cluster weapons include Chile's CB-770 cluster bomb; China's Type 84 Minelaying Rocket System; Germany's MW-1 Multipurpose Weapon containing MUSPA mines; Russia's PROSAB-250 cluster bomb with PFM-1 mines; and the US CBU-89/B bomb containing BLU-92/B mines. See Richard Lloyd, "Civilians Face Persistent Threat from Cluster Bombs," *Jane's Defence Weekly* (13 December 2000).

explode on contact, they will be armed and explode at delayed intervals. This function is the key component of the mine, which is commonly used and specifically designed as an area denial weapon. The second category of cluster bombs for present purposes includes those that do not contain mines. Clearly, any treaty regime prohibiting or limiting the use of anti-personnel mines will also apply to the GATOR family of cluster weapons. Further references to cluster weapons will, therefore, refer to the latter category that does not ordinarily contain mines.

Despite efforts to the contrary, cluster weapons in general are not included within the prohibition or limitations on mines. The 1997 Ottawa Treaty is comprehensive in scope — applying to both international and non-international armed conflicts — and in its prohibition, it applies not only to the use but also to the stockpiling, production, and transfer of APMs.[57] However, for state parties, Article 2(1) of the Ottawa Treaty refers simply to "[a] *mine designed* to be exploded by the presence, proximity or contact of a person and that will incapacitate, injure or kill one or more persons" [emphasis added]. Cluster bombs do not share this design. As such, cluster bombs cannot be described as *mines* since these weapons are not primarily delayed-action-explosive devices. Similarly, cluster weapons cannot be read into the limitations on landmines contained in the two protocols to the 1980 Conventional Weapons Convention. These protocols (Protocol II on Mines and Amended Protocol II on Mines) define "mines" in largely the same way, as "a *munition placed* under, on or near the ground or other surface area and *designed* to be exploded by the presence, proximity or contact of a person or vehicle."[58] The two protocols also include "other devices" within their ambit. However, from the definition provided, cluster weapons would not be covered under this categorization either since "other devices" are defined as meaning

manually-emplaced munitions and devices including improvised explosive devices designed to kill, injure or damage and which are actuated manually, by remote control or automatically after a lapse of time.[59]

---

57 See Ottawa Treaty, *supra* note 9 at Article 1.

58 Amended Protocol II on Mines, *supra* note 8 at Article 2(1) [emphasis added]. For the definition of "mines" in the original Protocol II, see Protocol II on Mines, *supra* note 53 at Article 2(1), which refers to "any" munition and adds the words "detonated or" before "exploded."

59 Amended Protocol II on Mines, *supra* note 8 at Article 2(5) [emphasis added]. The definition contained in the original protocol was similar in containing

In addition, state practice does not support the suggestion that cluster weapons are included within the two definitions and, therefore, within the provisions limiting their use. While it is certainly the case that during the Ottawa negotiations some NGOs did attempt to broaden the proposed ban so as to include cluster weapons, these attempts failed. In this regard, Neil Thorns, the spokesman for the British Red Cross commented: "[I]f cluster bombs had been included, it was very doubtful that Britain or any of the major powers would have signed. We had to compromise."[60] Steve Goose, of Human Rights Watch, has also pointed out that the governments that were present at the Ottawa conference refused even to discuss the proposal regarding cluster weapons.[61] It was clear in Ottawa, therefore, that any attempt to expand the proposed prohibition to include cluster bombs would have derailed the whole process. Furthermore, it is clear that the United States rejected any inclusion of cluster weapons within the definition of anti-personnel mines in the 1997 Ottawa Treaty by seeking to insert a requirement that devices be "primarily" designed to function as mines — which cluster weapons are clearly not.[62] This condition brought the Ottawa prohibition in line with the definition of APMs contained in the Amended Protocol II on Mines. Therefore, although the effects of dud sub-munitions are arguably akin to landmines, states have not so far included cluster weapons within these two specific treaty prohibitions.

The Ottawa Treaty established a landmark prohibition, namely the agreement by over one hundred states not just to dispose of their stockpiles of anti-personnel mines but also to clear mines from affected states.[63] Such mines have been used for decades with deadly effect and have created a lasting legacy. Millions have been injured or killed by mines. Unlike cluster weapons, however, anti-personnel mines have a very simple delivery system — they can be manually emplaced or scattered by rocket. The inexpensiveness of the mines and the ease of delivery accounted for their popularity among insurgency groups and militia. Hence, mines became a

---

reference to manually emplaced devices. See Protocol II on Mines, *supra* note 53 at Article 2(3).

[60] "Seeds of Carnage," *supra* note 24 at 30.

[61] *Ibid.*

[62] Ultimately, the United States refused to ratify the Ottawa Treaty, *supra* note 9.

[63] Ottawa Treaty, *supra* note 9 at Articles 1(2), 4, and 5.

global problem. Cluster weapons, on the other hand, do not pose a similar proliferation problem. Cluster weapons require a relatively sophisticated delivery system and so have not fallen into the hands of insurgency groups on the same scale. Cluster weapons do not, therefore, pose such problems on the scale that APMs previously have. Yet there is no denying that cluster weapons have caused grave health and environmental problems. Although these problems may not yet be on the same scale as those caused by landmines, this possibility still remains if their use continues. With this in mind, the question becomes: since cluster weapons in general do not fall within the prohibitions and limitations on mines, do they breach other laws and customs of armed conflict?

LIMITATION BY OTHER RULES OR PRINCIPLES OF HUMANITARIAN LAW

Cluster weapons may raise legality issues at the point of use as well as post-conflict on both the civilian population and the military. In the following section, the legality of cluster weapons will be tested according to their effects on civilians and combatants, for whom different laws and considerations apply.

Limitations Due to Effects on Combatants

Although the principal aim of warfare is to *weaken* the military forces of the enemy, it is not permissible for a party to use any and every means at its disposal. This rule evolved historically to prevent unfair combat and cruel weapons designed to kill, often horribly, and not to disable. Today, the principle is to be found within the customary prohibition on causing unnecessary suffering or superfluous injury. The principle evolved solely out of military pragmatism, in that if one party uses cruel weapons and tactics against its enemy, it can be sure of retaliation in kind. And in the modern era, the cruel deaths and suffering of soldiers might reduce both the military and public support for the war effort and, of course, may increase costs to the state, particularly in pension and healthcare provisions.

Principle of Unnecessary Suffering

The prohibition on weapons that cause unnecessary suffering has consistently been included within treaty law governing armed conflict, including the 1868 St. Petersburg Declaration Renouncing the Use, in Time of War, of Explosive Projectiles under 400 Grammes Weight,[64] Article 23(e) of both the 1899 Hague Convention II and the 1907 Hague Convention IV,[65] and Article 35(2) of the 1977 Geneva Protocol I, such that "[i]t is prohibited to employ weapons, projectiles and material and methods of warfare of a nature to cause superfluous injury or unnecessary suffering." The principle undoubtedly forms part of customary international law in regard to applicability in international armed conflicts and requires a judgment of the degree of suffering that is "superfluous" or "unnecessary."[66] Referring to it as the Guiding Principle, the United Kingdom, in its 2004 *Manual of the Law of Armed Conflict*, commences its section on "Weapons" with the Article 35(2) prohibition. The UK military manual then specifies a number of points in application of the guiding principle. The manual states: "[T]he correct criterion is whether the use of a weapon is of a nature to cause injury or suffering greater than that required for its military purpose."[67] The manual then continues with the statement that in calculating the

legality of use of a specific weapon, it is necessary to assess:
a. its effects in battle;
b. the military task it is required to perform; and
c. the proportionality between factors (a) and (b).[68]

---

[64] 1868 St. Petersburg Declaration Renouncing the Use, in Time of War, of Explosive Projectiles under 400 Grammes Weight, 11 December 1868, (1907) 1 A.J.I.L. Supplement 95–6 (entered into force 11 December 1868) [St. Petersburg Declaration].

[65] The original French text of the Hague Convention IV, *supra* note 44, used the phrase "superfluous injury," while the English text referred instead to "unnecessary suffering." To avoid doubt, the English text now refers to both.

[66] In regard to the applicability of the prohibition on causing unnecessary suffering in situations of non-international armed conflict, first, it might fall within the Tadic principle in being the reason for a particular weapons prohibition at the level of international armed conflict, and, second, the prevention of unnecessary suffering would appear to fall within the general principle of humanity incorporated in the preamble to the 1977 Geneva Protocol II and at paragraph 1 of Common Article 3 to the 1949 Geneva Conventions.

[67] M. Bothe, Karl Josef Partsch, and Waldemar A. Solf, *New Rules for the Victims of Armed Conflicts: Commentary on the Two 1977 Additional Protocols to the Geneva Conventions of 1949* (The Hague: Martinus Nijhoff Publishers, 1982) at 196; reprinted in UK Ministry of Defence, *The Manual of the Law of Armed Conflict* (Oxford: Oxford University Press, 2004) at 103.

[68] *Ibid.*

Finally, the manual addresses the point that even if the use of a weapon can be deemed generally lawful under this calculation, its use in certain ways or circumstances may, however, still be unlawful. This final point of course covers the actual use of the weapon as opposed to its designated function. Overall, the test of "unnecessary suffering" is an objective one, which is based on all of the factors. It is not simply, therefore, a question of the subjective suffering of the victim.[69] In sum, the principle requires that means and methods are not used that would entail a degree of suffering beyond that necessary for the military purpose of the attack.

Clearly, in military operations, there will often be a choice of available weaponry. Taking military needs into account, therefore, a weapon will generally be judged to cause "unnecessary suffering" if the humanitarian *disadvantages* of using a particular weapon clearly outweigh the military advantages of using *that* weapon over any other weapons that are practically available for use.[70] Thus, if there were an alternative weapon offering a similar military advantage, humanitarian considerations would appear to dictate that that weapon be used.

Cluster weapons are anti-personnel weapons as well as anti-*matériel*. The main advantage of cluster munitions is said to be their use against a diffuse and mobile target. However, the earlier assertion by the UK government, among others, that cluster weapons are effective against heavy armour appears to have been retracted. In April 1999, the foreign secretary, Robin Cook, said: "There is a use of cluster bombs but in this context what the term refers to are anti-tank weapons. Each of the clusters in them is designed to penetrate heavy armour. If your target is a collection of a number of tanks, it makes sense to use a weapon that can disable many of the

---

[69] In trying to set universal measuring tools for the principle, the ICRC has created criteria for "unnecessary suffering." Cluster weapons might in the future therefore be shown to breach Criterion 1: specific disease, specific abnormal physiological state, specific and permanent disability, or specific disfigurement. The criteria are not binding however. See Robin M. Coupland, "The SIrUS Project: Towards a Determination of Which Weapons Cause 'Superfluous Injury or Unnecessary Suffering,'" in Helen Durham and Timothy L.H. McCormack, eds., *The Changing Face of Conflict and the Efficacy of International Humanitarian Law* (London: Martinus Nijhoff Publishers, 1999) at 99. The ICRC also appears to have taken the decision to stop using the test.

[70] See ICRC, *Weapons That May Cause Unnecessary Suffering or Have Indiscriminate Effects: Report on the Work of Experts* (Geneva, 1973), 13.

tanks and not just one of them."[71] By June 2000, however, the Official Ministry of Defence report, *Kosovo: Lessons from the Crisis*, referred only to the effectiveness of cluster weapons against soft-skinned military vehicles.[72] Furthermore, according to the fourteenth report of the Select Committee on Defence, the Ministry of Defence had acknowledged as far back as 1991, following its experience in the Gulf conflict, that the BL-755 cluster bomb was "no longer credible against modern main battle tanks."[73] These weapons are beneficial, therefore, where the target comprises a large number of soft-skinned vehicles and/or personnel. The anti-*matériel* slug will penetrate the top of lightly armoured vehicles, while the anti-personnel aspect of fragmentation can easily disable enemy personnel.

Cluster weapons, therefore, have a dual purpose on the battlefield, and, since they are delivered in large numbers, these minibombs have an extensive dispersal range. A single cluster bomb can saturate an area of one square kilometer, disabling a large number of targets with one (mother) bomb. In effect, this means that the disablement of large numbers of targets would be achieved with fewer weapons. Hence, in theory, delivery is achieved with fewer passes by the air force and, hence, less danger to air force personnel. For a similar military advantage, the military suggests, more single munitions would need to be deployed with the obvious disadvantages to air force personnel having to hang around a hot zone with their payload.

It is possible, however, that cluster munitions fall within the current prohibition, due particularly to the characteristic of fragmentation. If the explosion of the sub-munition does not disable the personnel targeted, it is inevitable that those within range — some thirty to forty meters from the ground point of impact — will be

---

71 United Kingdom, H.C., *Kosovo: Interim Report, Minutes of Evidence*, House of Commons Foreign Affairs Committee, 7th Report, vol. 329 (1998–99) at question 156 (speaker: Rt. Hon. Robin Cook, Secretary of State for Foreign Affairs), available online at <http://www.publications.parliament.uk/pa/cm199899/cmselect/cmfaff/188/9041404.htm>.

72 UK Ministry of Defence, *Kosovo: Lessons from the Crisis*, presented to Parliament by the Secretary of State for Defence by Command of Her Majesty, June 2000, Cm 4724, June 2000, available online at <http://www.mod.uk/publications/kosovo_lessons/contents.htm>.

73 See United Kingdom, H.C., *Fourteenth Report of the House of Commons Select Committee on Defence*, Lessons of Kosovo, 23 October 2000, available online at <http://www.parliament.the-stationery-office.co.uk/pa/cm199900/cmselect/cmdfence/347/34714.htm#n340>.

peppered with metal shards. If the metal fragments do not cut
straight through limbs, they become embedded in tissue causing
damage to organs, internal bleeding, and usually infection. The
flying shards can also cause blindness. Indeed, a higher volume of
smaller fragments has been reported to cause greater bodily damage than a smaller number of larger pieces of metal.[74] Clearly, however, the seriousness of the injury is dependent upon which organs
of the body are affected and the degree of damage caused to them.[75]
In addition, such multiple cluster bomb injuries have the potential
to over-stretch any available medical facilities, which would in turn
mean a delay in treatment, causing the injuries to worsen. As a consequence, the mortality rate would also increase. In its application
to the International Court of Justice in 1999, the Federal Republic
of Yugoslavia attempted to argue the illegality of cluster weapons
under this very principle. Unfortunately, the case will now not be
heard due to the court's recent ruling on its lack of jurisdiction.[76]

---

[74] See B.D. Burns and S. Zuckerman, *The Wounding Power of Small Bomb and Shell
Fragments*, R.C. no. 350 of the Research and Experiments Department of the
Ministry of Home Security (London: 1943). When under discussion at the
Lucerne conference, for the 1977 Geneva Protocols, experts were of contradictory opinions — some experts expressed the opinion that multiple injuries were
not necessarily a very serious factor. Reprinted in O.R. Vol. XVI, Doc. CDDH/
ʻIV/SR.12, 26 February 1975, paras. 24–28.

[75] According to the ICRC in a 1973 report "the risk of death rose with the number
of organs affected." See ICRC, *Weapons That May Cause Unnecessary Suffering or
Have Indiscriminate Effects* (Geneva: ICRC, 1973) at para. 146, reprinted in O.R.
Vol. XVI, Doc. CDDH/IV/SR.12, 26 February 1975 at para. 27.

[76] The Federal Republic of Yugoslavia (FRY) also argued in its original application
that the use of cluster weapons amounted to genocide. The ten cases listed were:
*Legality of the Use of Force, (Yugoslavia v. Belgium), (Yugoslavia v. Canada), (Yugosla-
via v. France), (Yugoslavia v. Germany), (Yugoslavia v. Italy), (Yugoslavia v. Netherlands), (Yugoslavia v. Portugal), (Yugoslavia v. United Kingdom), (Yugoslavia v. Spain),
(Yugoslavia v. United States of America)*, 1999, nos. 104–14, (1999) 38 I.L.M. 950,
available online at <http://www.icj-cij.org/icjwww/idecisions.htm>. The cases
against the United States and Spain were dismissed earlier due to lack of jurisdiction. In December 2004, the remaining cases were unanimously dismissed
due to lack of jurisdiction. See the judgment of 15 December 2004, on the International Court of Justice's (ICJ) Internet site. The lack of jurisdiction flowed
from the Security Council's decision in 1992 that the FRY should not be taken
to continue the obligations of the former Socialist Federal Republic of Yugoslavia. See SC Res. 777, UN SCOR, 47th Sess., UN Doc. S/RES/777. From that point,
the FRY that emerged from the break-up of the larger country was not a member
of the United Nations. As such, the FRY was also not a member of the Statute of
the International Court of Justice and, hence, could not lodge cases with the ICJ
in that way. On 27 October 2000, the new president, Mr. Koštunica, sent a letter

However, there is little to suggest that these effects on combatants are greater than the injury caused by other bombs or grenades — most having a fragmentation capacity. Although the risk of incapacitation arguably increases with the use of cluster weapons, the mortality rate may arguably be reduced since the injuries would not be as severe. This assessment, therefore, brings us to the issue of whether there is an alternative weapon readily available for use. In an assessment of the conformity of cluster bombs with the prohibition of causing unnecessary suffering, there are of course two alternative weapons to consider. The first is the category of general-purpose bombs and missiles that might be used against a similar collection of dispersed hard and soft-skinned targets. The second is actually a sub-category of cluster bombs that incorporate a back-up fuse.

The alternative weapon to cluster bombs would be larger tonnage bombs that may be less effective against a more dispersed target. The standard "dumb" bomb tends to be the 1,000-pound general-purpose bomb or, as an alternative, the 540-pound and 250-pound miniature versions.[77] The general-purpose bomb is a dumb bomb employing no guidance system. Dropped from the air, the effectiveness of these weapons relies on the accuracy of the pilot. Approximately 50 per cent of the bomb's weight is explosive material, the blast effects of which will cause considerable damage. In addition, the thick shell casing will fragment on detonation. In the second alternative, states might use "smart" weapons — so-called because they utilize a guidance system. Smart weapons are much more expensive to purchase than dumb bombs, including cluster weapons. The Paveway III (GBU-24) is a laser-guided bomb weighing 2,000 pounds, while the Paveway II (GBU-12) is a 500-pound bomb. There is a vast difference in the production costs of the two variants — the Paveway III costing approximately US $55,600 per unit and the Paveway II some US $19,000 per unit. There are more options in guidance technology, such as the JDAM (joint direct attack munition), which utilizes global positioning satellite technology.[78] Again, JDAMs range from 250 pounds to 2,000 pounds

---

to the secretary-general of the United Nations requesting admission of the FRY to membership of the United Nations based on Security Council Resolution 777.

[77] See the Internet site of the UK Royal Air Force, which is available at <http:// www.raf.mod.uk/ and www.globalsecurity.org>.

[78] There is also an enhanced version of the Paveway, which uses global positioning satellite technology (GPS) and can be guided in bad weather from the weapon's own on-board system or from the ground. See *ibid.*

and can be air-to-surface or surface-to-surface, used by both the air force and navy. Finally, there are missiles. The Maverick is a tactical air-to-surface guided missile used by the United States and the United Kingdom. A single aircraft can carry a payload of six Mavericks and so engage multiple targets in a single mission. The Maverick can be fitted with a number of guidance packages, including an electro-optical television guidance system, which allows the pilot to guide the missile to the target from a screen in the cockpit. Those in the service of the Royal Air Force are fitted with infra-red imaging, which improves the missile's capability by night and in poor weather.[79] Furthermore, the Maverick is fitted with a "launch-and-leave" capability. Once locked on to the target and launched, the missile will guide itself to the target, freeing up the pilot to attack other targets or manoeuvre out of the range of anti-aircraft artillery. It is certainly likely that the blast and fragmentation effects of all of these larger tonnage bombs or missiles, however, will equal or surpass the effects of cluster weapons. As a consequence, cluster weapons appear generally to conform to the prohibition on unnecessary suffering, tending as they do to disable the enemy rather than inevitably leading to death as could be envisioned in an attack with alternative, larger tonnage weapons. Therefore, with respect to their effectiveness against a large and dispersed target, it may be that cluster weapons entail a strong military advantage that outweighs other such munitions.

In regard to the sub-category of cluster weapons that utilize a back-up fuse (the Israeli-made L20), the failure rate is widely quoted as being just 2 per cent. If the choice of weapon were between older versions of cluster bombs or such newer versions, might it be possible that the use of the former would breach the prohibition on causing unnecessary suffering? In other words, if the state has a choice between two types of cluster bombs, one with a lower failure rate, would a state be in violation of this principle if it chose to use the version with the higher failure rate? However, before this assessment could be made, the lower projected failure rate would need to be verified under battle conditions. And although often described as having a mere 2 per cent failure rate, it might, however, simply be too early to assess the actual failure rate of these newer weapons on the battlefield. It is worth remembering that in 1975 members of the armed forces boasted that the new RBL-755 was virtually guaranteed not to result in duds. This premise was, of

[79] *Ibid.*

course, proven to be wrong when during the Falklands conflict in 1982 a failure rate of approximately 10 per cent was witnessed.[80] To quote Rae McGrath of the organization Landmine Action in regard to the much-vaunted 5 per cent failure rate of these older versions, "there is no recorded combat usage that would indicate a failure rate of five per cent and virtually all statistical and anecdotal evidence points to a far higher percentage failure rate."[81] By comparison, therefore, there is little to suggest that the lower estimate of a 2 per cent failure rate for the newer Israeli cluster bombs will be more reliable. Consequently, it is arguably not the case that cluster weapons would breach the prohibition of unnecessary suffering in regard to combatants, when compared to (1) the alternative dumb or smart bombs or (2) newer, apparently more reliable cluster bombs.

Limitations Due to Effects on Civilians

The law of armed conflict makes a distinction between civilian and military persons and objects. Accordingly, the 1868 St. Petersburg Declaration stipulated that "[t]he only legitimate object which States should endeavour to accomplish during war is to weaken the *military forces* of the enemy."[82] In international armed conflict, Article 43 of the 1977 Geneva Protocol I, together with Article 4A(1)(2)(3) and (6) of the Geneva Convention III Relative to the Treatment of Prisoners of War,[83] define those who are to be considered as combatants. In sum, the term "combatants" involves members of the armed forces and other militia fulfilling certain conditions. The result is non-combatant immunity. Today, this distinction is incorporated in the principle of discriminate warfare — the principle whereby it is legitimate for the armed forces to target only (enemy) military objectives.

The prohibition on the targeting of non-combatants has been in existence for almost as long as warfare itself and is recognized by

---

[80] See Letter from John Spellar, MP, Minister of State to Harry Cohen, MP (28 May 2000), MoD Ref. Doc. D/Min(AF)/JS PQ1886K/00/M, in McGrath, *supra* note 26 at 28 (the 10 per cent figure is not given, but the minister admits that 106–7 bombs were used and some 1,492 unexploded sub-munitions were removed from the Falklands following the conflict).

[81] *Ibid.* at 29.

[82] St. Petersburg Declaration, *supra* note 64 at para. 3 [emphasis added].

[83] 1949 Geneva Convention (III) Relative to the Treatment of Prisoners of War, 12 August 1949, 75 U.N.T.S. 135.

most cultures. The primary humanitarian consideration for civilians is due to their non-involvement in the war, namely the fact that they are "innocents." Military considerations would lie in saving valuable ammunition, in not attacking unarmed civilians, and in the avoidance of unnecessary retribution. After all, the routine massacring of the local civilian population would only increase popular resistance to the conflict, strengthen the war effort, and swell the military ranks of the enemy.

Principle of Discriminate Warfare

The principle of discrimination or distinction was codified in Article 48 of the 1977 Geneva Protocol I, which requires state parties to distinguish at all times between the civilian population/civilian objects and military persons or objectives. Consequently, legitimate actions are those directed only against the latter. The terms "civilians and civilian population" are defined negatively, as any person not belonging to one of those categories mentioned in Article 43 ("combatants").[84] Geneva Protocol II contains essentially the same distinction between civilian and military persons and objects.[85] As a consequence, civilians in both internal and international armed conflicts are protected against direct conflict. They are not a military target and, hence, should not be attacked. Unfortunately, however, civilians will often be harmed indirectly in the bombing and resulting destruction. The military are, however, under an obligation to keep the number of collateral casualties to a minimum.[86] Similarly, civilian objects are defined negatively in Article 52(1) as "all objects which are *not* military objectives" [emphasis added]. Although no specific list was included in Geneva Protocol I, military objectives would be those "objects" that make an "effective" contribution to military action and, dependent upon the ambient

---

[84] Geneva Protocol I, *supra* note 5 at Article 50(1).

[85] Geneva Protocol II, *supra* note 5 at Article 4(1). See also *ibid.* at Article 13, which directs in more basic terms only that civilians shall not be the object of attack. The concept can also be discerned from Common Article 3 of the 1949 Geneva Conventions.

[86] This is known as the rule of proportionality in attack and can be found at Geneva Protocol I, *supra* note 5 at Article 51(5)(b), such that "an attack which may be expected to cause incidental loss of civilian life, injury to civilians, damage to civilian objects, or a combination thereof, which would be excessive in relation to the concrete and direct military advantage anticipated." The rule is also part of customary law and as such should be equally applicable to internal armed conflict, however, it will not be considered further.

circumstances, offer a "definite" military advantage.[87] These objectives would be so due to the particular nature, location, purpose, or use of the object. Clearly, attacks directed at targets that do not fulfil the criteria in Article 52(2) are unlawful.

Consequently, it follows that *weapons* are prohibited should they breach the principle of indiscriminate warfare. Practically speaking, one suggests, therefore, that weapons may violate the prohibition if they (1) are inherently indiscriminate or (2), while being capable of being discriminating, are, however, used in an indiscriminate way. Violation of the first proposition must give rise to an automatic ban, violation of the second to the possibility of regulation.

The customary prohibition of discrimination has also been included within Geneva Protocol I in Article 51(4). Accordingly, the provision prohibits indiscriminate attacks, defined to include those employing a *means* (or method) of combat the effects of which cannot be limited to military objectives. More specifically, subparagraph (a) refers to *weapons* not directed at a specific military objective, subparagraph (b) to *weapons* that *cannot* be directed at a specific military objective, and subparagraph (c) to *weapons* with effects that cannot be limited as required by the protocol. As recognized in the commentary to Geneva Protocol I, which is authored by M. Bothe, K. Partsch, and W. Solf, Article 51(4) provides the first definition of the principle.[88] Clearly, the principle forms part of customary law and, as such, is universally binding. The definition, however, may represent only treaty law. However, the fact that the protocol has some 163 state parties as of July 2005 may make this point moot. Yet while the United States refuses to ratify the treaty, it remains a valid one, which is particularly true in the case of subparagraph (c), which merges other violations of the protocol into the prohibition. Clearly, rules protecting the natural environment may fall within this provision with respect to the *effects* of weapons, as may the principle of proportionality contained in Article 51(5). It is clearly on the basis that because of their effects certain weapons *cannot* be strictly limited in geographical or temporal dimensions to the military objective targeted and so will strike civilians and

---

[87] *Ibid.* at Article 52(2). The listing approach can be found in Hague Convention IX of 1907 Concerning Bombardment by Naval Forces in Time of War, 18 October 1907, 2 A.J.I.L. Supplement 146 (entered into force 26 January 1910) at Article 2, which includes "military works, military or naval establishments, depots of arms or war matériel, workshops or plant which could be utilized for the needs of the hostile fleet or army, and the ships of war in the harbour."

[88] Bothe, Partsch, and Solf, *supra* note 67 at 305.

combatants — or solely civilians in the post-conflict period — without distinction. Therefore, for both subparagraphs (b) and (c), it is the actual weapon that cannot discriminate and not its manner of use (as in subparagraph (a)). Consequently, while subparagraphs (b) and (c) can generally be viewed as outlining a prohibition on inherently indiscriminate weaponry, subparagraph (a), on the other hand, prohibits the indiscriminate use of what would otherwise be a discriminatory weapon. In criticism of the language used in Article 51(4), it is of little aid in the assessment of area weapons, where the specific military objective may be multiple diffuse targets.

Inherently indiscriminate weapons

For present purposes, an inherently indiscriminate weapon is one, the effects of which are incapable of distinguishing between military objectives and civilian persons/objects. An example is biological weaponry that once released cannot be controlled so as to target only military objectives.[89] Can the same categorization be made for cluster weapons? Often referred to as "steel rain" or the "rain of death,"[90] cluster weapons are viewed by the UK and US armed forces as the weapon of choice in attacking diffuse and/or mobile targets in the open. However, they are not always used out in the open. Cluster weapons are also notoriously inaccurate. Many cluster submunitions, particularly the older varieties, rely on the wind for descent. As a result, the impact zone (footprint) is generally much greater than the original target. Furthermore, it can be said that the higher the altitude of deployment, the more inaccurate the targeting. At greater altitudes, the risk of missing the target altogether is also high.

According to figures given to Human Rights Watch, cluster munitions accounted for only 4 per cent of the total number of air-delivered weapons used by the coalition in the 2003 Iraq conflict.[91]

---

89 Note there is a specific treaty regime prohibiting such weapons, the 1972 Convention on the Prohibition and Development, Production and Stockpiling of Bacteriological (Biological) and Toxin Weapons and Their Destruction (London, Washington, Moscow), 10 April 1971, 11 I.L.M. 309 (entered into force 28 March 1975).

90 Paul Wiseman, "Cluster Bombs Kill in Iraq, Even after Shooting Ends," *USA Today* (10 December 2003).

91 See Human Rights Watch, *Off Target: The Conduct of the War and Civilian Casualties in Iraq* (New York: Human Rights Watch, 2003) at 56 [*Off Target*].

The figures for ground-delivered cluster munitions have not been released by the United States. During the 2003 invasion, British air forces dropped seventy cluster bombs of the type RBL-755, containing 147 bomblets (totalling 10,290 bomblets), mostly in the vicinity of Baghdad, and fired some 2,000 L20 artillery-delivered shells, mostly around Basra.[92] These sub-munitions have upwards of a 5 and 2 per cent dud rate respectively. Therefore, as a result of the use of cluster weapons by British forces, there would, on these figures, have been approximately 2,500 unexploded cluster sub-munitions in Iraqi civilian areas during and after the end of the hostilities. In addition, and contrary to other efforts taken by the United States and the United Kingdom in minimizing the failure rate of cluster weapons (see discussion later in this article), US ground forces employed multiple-launch rocket systems (MLRS) in Iraq in 2003 for longer-range targets. These systems employ twelve rockets, each of which can carry 644 M77-type cluster sub-munitions. With an attack of six rockets, which was apparently standard in Iraq, the MLRS would release some 3,864 sub-munitions over an area of one-kilometer radius.[93] According to Human Rights Watch, and quoting official US governmental sources, the MLRS system "leaves shockingly large quantities of duds" — a failure rate of 16 per cent.[94] Add to the weapon's level of inaccuracy its high propensity for failure and the question becomes: are the effects of these weapons inevitably indiscriminate?

Thus, one must consider whether cluster weapons are inherently indiscriminate due to (1) their inaccuracy or (2) their failure rate. The starting point for the legal analysis is the provisions of Geneva Protocol I and their interpretation. How, therefore, do the effects of cluster weapons compare with the prohibitions outlined in Article 51 of Geneva Protocol I? One aspect is that of "blind" weapons. While this term is not specifically adopted in the provision, it certainly formed part of the discussion predating the adoption of the final text of Article 51(4)(b) regarding weapons that *cannot* be directed at a specific military objective. And, hence, according to the official commentaries to Geneva Protocol I, an example of "blind" weapons for Article 51(4)(b) would include "long-range

---

[92] *Operations in Iraq, supra* note 18 at 24. Human Rights Watch use the figure of 2,100 shells, but the source for this figure is unclear.

[93] *Off Target, supra* note 91 at 83.

[94] Report submitted to the US Congress by the Office of the Under Secretary of Defense for Acquisition, Technology and Logistics, in *ibid.* at 84.

missiles which cannot be aimed exactly at the objective,"[95] possibly due to having "only a rudimentary guidance system."[96] To this example, one can surely add those weapons with no guidance system. The notion is that such inaccurate weapons systems cannot discriminate effectively between military and civilian objects. In recognition of this notion, the United Kingdom, in its 2004 military manual, similarly emphasizes that the principle of discrimination "operates as an effective prohibition on the use of weapons that are *so inaccurate* that they cannot be directed at a military target."[97] As such, the United Kingdom suggests that the Scud rocket, which was used by Iraqi forces during the Persian Gulf War in 1990–1, and the V-1 flying bomb provide further examples. Weapons with little or no guidance system may therefore breach the rule on discrimination, according to the official commentaries to the 1977 Geneva Protocols. The problem, however, is where to draw the line. Just how inaccurate does a weapon need to be in order to be classified as indiscriminate?

An unguided long-range missile might be more obviously indiscriminate than a bomb dropped from the air. If we assume accuracy in the pilot's aim, then the bomb has more chance of hitting its intended military objective than does the unguided long-range missile. So what can one make then of the potential accuracy of an unguided missile consisting of over two hundred mini-bombs or of two hundred unguided mini-bombs dropped from an aircraft? How accurate are these multiple-cluster sub-munitions? With the limited exception of the new CBU-105 sensor-fused weapon, which uses infra-red heat-seeking sensors,[98] there is no disputing that cluster weapons are "dumb" weapons that are dependent upon nothing more than a favourable wind. Such factors did not, however, stop British forces from using such older-style cluster weapons in Kosovo in 1999 and in Baghdad in 2003.

The second aspect to consider is the issue of the failure rate of cluster weapons. In their commentary on Geneva Protocol I, Bothe et al. also refer to unmarked minefields as offending against

95 Jean S. Pictet, ed., *The Geneva Conventions of 1949: Commentary, IV Geneva Convention Relative to the Protection of the Civilian Persons in Time of War* (Geneva: ICRC, 1958) at 621.

96 See Bothe, Partsch, and Solf, *supra* note 67 at 305.

97 *Manual of the Law or Armed Conflict, supra* note 67 at 104 [emphasis added].

98 See generally the Federation of American Scientists, which is available online at <http://www.fas.org/man/dod-101/sys/dumb/cbu-97.htm>.

sub-paragraphs (b) and (c) of Article 51(4).[99] These minefields, the authors suggest, are "blind" as to time, adding a temporal dimension to the principle of distinction. Certainly, the vast majority of criticism of cluster weapons is due to their continuing threat to the civilian population. According to figures released by UNICEF, unexploded weapons such as failed cluster weapons have injured over one thousand children since the end of the Iraqi conflict.[100] Compiling data from reliable sources, the British group calling themselves Iraq Body Count has listed over 200 deaths in Iraq from cluster bombs, both during and after the end of hostilities.[101] Of this number, the group indicates that 137 deaths were as a result of unexploded or dud cluster bombs and that approximately half were children. In Kirkuk alone, UNICEF reports, 133 children were killed or injured by unexploded ordnance during the last two weeks of April, and, in Mosul, as many as twenty incidents per day were reported.[102]

Furthermore, Human Rights Watch has observed that the environmental conditions in Iraq — sand, wind, and marshes — are likely to have exacerbated the failure rate of cluster bombs.[103] This statistic is highly conceivable since impacting in soft ground conditions has been evidenced to increase the likelihood of detonation failure. Windy conditions are also likely to increase the risk of submunitions colliding mid-air and failing as a result. Similarly, wet ground conditions are said to have exacerbated the weapon's failure rate in Yugoslavia during the 1999 Kosovo conflict. Using NATO's own figures that the failure rate estimated for cluster bombs used in Kosovo was some 10 per cent, approximately 30,000 unexploded cluster munitions were left on the battlefield after the cessation of hostilities.[104] Furthermore, in the 1990–1 Gulf conflict, the dud rate was estimated to be much higher, possibly up to

---

99 Bothe, Partsch, and Solf, *supra* note 67 at 308.

100 UNICEF, News Release / Communiqué, "In Iraq Unexploded Munitions become Child's Play," 17 July 2003, available online at <http://www.unicef.org/media/media_12056.html>.

101 John Sloboda and Hamit Dardagan, "How Many Civilians were Killed by Cluster Bombs?" 6 May 2003, available online at <http://www.iraqbodycount.net>.

102 UNICEF, *supra* note 100. The calculation includes deaths by other types of unexploded ordnance.

103 *Cluster Munitions: A Foreseeable Hazard in Iraq,* Human Rights Watch Briefing Paper, March 2003, available online at <http://www.hrw.org> [*Cluster Munitions a Foreseeable Hazard*].

104 *Explosive Remnants, supra* note 21 at 10.

30 per cent.[105] Even based on conservative estimates of only a 5 per cent failure rate would mean that up to 1.5 million unexploded bomblets were left on the battlefield of Kuwait and Iraq after the 1990–1 Gulf War.[106] If the actual failure rate were closer to 30 per cent, it would mean that nine million unexploded sub-munitions were left. However, given that the same negative environmental conditions would also have affected the weapon's reliability in the first Gulf conflict as the second, one can conclude that such effects were clearly foreseeable.

Furthermore, if these weapons continue to cause casualties after the end of hostilities, then in reality the victims can only be civilian in nature. In Iraq, for instance, there is evidence that 221 injuries were sustained between 1–11 April 2003 in the al-Hilla area as a result of dud British sub-munitions and that there were 109 civilian injuries in the al-Najaf area after the main battle had ended.[107] Similarly, Human Rights Watch reports thirty-eight civilians killed and 156 injured following the American use of cluster munitions on 31 March 2003 at Nadir.[108] In addition to burn injuries from the explosions, civilians are also at risk from the hundreds of metal fragments released. Several reports from Iraq, for example, describe the horrific scene of civilians covered in bloody bandages, with limbs cut to pieces by the metal shards.

Yet what of the yellow colouring of the older-style cluster munitions? Have states acted sufficiently in distinguishing these older versions of cluster sub-munitions from the terrain to ensure the safety of the civilian population? Clearly, cluster weapons are not designed to function as a booby trap or similar device, but with their yellow colouring it has been proven that they are particularly attractive to children. They are also the same colour as aid packages dropped by the United States, for example, in Afghanistan in 2002. For these reasons, it cannot be successfully argued that the colouring of the weapons is sufficient to legitimize the weapon. If anything, their added attraction for children may exacerbate their unsafe nature.

Are cluster weapons, therefore, inherently indiscriminate weapons because (1) they are inaccurate or (2) they cannot discriminate

105 "Cluster Munitions in Yugoslavia," *supra* note 30.

106 *Ibid.*

107 See *Off Target, supra* note 91 at 106–7.

108 *Ibid.* at 81. See also Laura Kink, "Baghdad's Death Toll Assessed," *Los Angeles Times* (18 May 2003).

between military and civilian targets on the ground? Certainly, state practice does not appear to support either conclusion at present. Other than Yugoslavia, few states appear to have complained openly about the military use of cluster weapons. According to Human Rights Watch, at least fifty-seven states stockpile cluster weapons.[109] On the other hand, there was, of course, an attempt by some states in the 1970s to prohibit the use of anti-personnel cluster weapons. This attempt failed.[110] More recently, state parties to the 1980 Conventional Weapons Convention have again resisted a prohibition on cluster weapons. It is doubtful that this action (or rather inaction) by states indicates state *opinio juris* that cluster weapons do not breach the prohibition on indiscriminate weaponry. It may, more simply, indicate a lack of interest by states in the topic. Certainly, at the UN level, the UN Sub-Commission on the Promotion and Protection of Human Rights has classified cluster weapons as "weapons of mass destruction or of indiscriminate effect" in two resolutions of 1996 and 1997.[111] Commissioned to provide a working paper to the sub-commission on *Human Rights and Weapons of Mass Destruction, or with Indiscriminate Effect, or of a Nature to Cause Superfluous Injury or Unnecessary Suffering* in 2002, Y.K.J. Yeung Sik Yuen's opinion was simply that cluster weapons are indiscriminate.[112] Yueng Sik Yuen repeated this conclusion in his 2003 supplementary working paper.[113] Similarly, the European Parliament and the ICRC have demanded a moratorium on the use of cluster weapons. However, even among those states that do not support the use of cluster weapons, for example Australia, the position seems to be that of legality. To quote the Australian defence minister's comments

---

[109] Steve Goose, "Cluster Munitions: Towards a Global Solution," in *Human Rights Watch World Report 2004* (New York: Human Rights Watch, 2004).

[110] Proposal CDDH/IV/201 (II), O.R. Vol.XVI, 615. These thirteen sponsoring states were Algeria, Austria, Egypt, Lebanon, Mali, Mauritania, Mexico, Norway, Sudan, Sweden, Switzerland, Venezuela, and Yugoslavia.

[111] Sub-Commission on the Protection and Promotion of Human Rights, *supra* note 1. The sub-commission also includes within this designation nuclear weapons, chemical weapons, fuel-air bombs, napalm, biological weaponry, and cluster bombs.

[112] See *Human Rights and Weapons, supra* note 52 at paras. 107–18.

[113] See the working paper submitted by Y.K.J. Yeung Sik Yuen to the Sub-Commission on the Promotion and Protection of Human Rights, UN ESCOR, *Human Rights and Weapons of Mass Destruction, or with Indiscriminate Effect, or of a Nature to Cause Superfluous Injury or Unnecessary Suffering,* UN Doc. E/CN.4/Sub.2/2003/ 35 (2 June 2003).

to Parliament in 2003, his country does "not use [cluster weapons] because of the risks."[114] While he fails to detail what these perceived risks entail, he does, however, continue by stating that cluster weapons are not outlawed.

More recently, the Canadian Department of National Defence has announced the destruction of its stockpile of Rockeye cluster bombs.[115] The report suggests, on the one hand, that these stocks procured during the Cold War are now "surplus to Canadian Forces requirements."[116] On the other hand, however, the report continues to remark that "the bomblets did not always explode on impact, leaving unexploded ordnance in an area of conflict and creating a minefield that was dangerous to the Canadian Forces, our allies, and innocent civilians."[117] This quote appears to be a clear signal that the Canadian government views this particular version of cluster weapons, at least, as being landmines in all but name. Consequently, the report states that "any future use of the Rockeye would contravene the 1997 Ottawa Accord, which prohibits the use and sale of anti-personnel mines. Canada, as signatory of the Ottawa Accord, is obligated to destroy its inventory of Rockeye cluster bombs."[118] Since the Rockeye is not an anti-personnel mine *per se*, this position by the Canadian government is rather remarkable. The Rockeye was produced in the 1950s and used in massive number in the Vietnam conflict. The American forces also used it more recently in the Iraq conflict in 2003. Although there does not appear to be a confirmed failure rate for the Rockeye cluster bomb, it almost certainly has a higher failure rate than the RBL-755s. Thus, possibly due to its role as host nation to the 1997 Ottawa Treaty, the Canadian government has decided to take a firmer stance on the issue of such cluster weapons. Certainly, however, this decision is a very valuable piece of state practice on the broader issue of the legality of the whole class of cluster weapons.

The effects of cluster weapons are abundantly clear. Those older weapons systems with a proven failure rate of at least 5 per cent,

114 See Australia, Commonwealth, Senate, *Parliamentary Debates* (20 March 2003), No. 3 at 9873.

115 See Canadian Department of National Defence, Backgrounder, "Disposal of Rockeye Cluster Bombs at CFAD Dundurn" (27 July 2004), available online at <http://www.forces.gc.ca/site/newsroom/view_news_e.asp?id=1439>.

116 *Ibid.*

117 *Ibid.*

118 *Ibid.*

therefore, can arguably be classified as inherently indiscriminate. It is due to the military's own advantage — use against a diffuse target — coupled with this in-built propensity for failure that the older cluster munitions should be categorized as indiscriminate. State practice, of course, does not clearly substantiate this conclusion, but there have certainly been a number of efforts by states to prohibit such weaponry. As for the newer weapons, which boast only a 2 per cent failure rate, the question is a little more difficult. One might still suggest that this failure rate is still too high to remain lawful. As suggested earlier, it may also be too early to sing the praises of the L20, at least until its actual performance on the battlefield can be fully assessed and the boasted 2 per cent failure rate confirmed.

Discriminate weapons used in an indiscriminate manner

Although there is evidence that cluster weapons are inherently indiscriminate and so unlawful under the previous section, this view is not universally held. This article will now turn, therefore, to consider the issue of the use of an otherwise discriminatory weapon in an indiscriminate manner. This aspect of legality involves a close analysis of the actual military uses of a particular weapon on the battlefield. Since it is not always possible, however, to gain an absolutely accurate account of events, the events documented in this article must, therefore, be read in light of this general qualification. Whether the use of a certain weapon violates this aspect of the principle of discrimination is dependent upon the location and type of military objective targeted. Therefore, an assessment must be made on a case-by-case basis. If the objective were positioned within, or within the vicinity of, a town or other populated place, then targeting that objective with area weapons or non-guided weapons would, *prima facie,* appear to be in violation of the provision. Hence, it will not be in every circumstance that such inaccurate weapons will violate the provisions on indiscriminate warfare — violation instead will depend on the presence of civilians. For this reason, there are specific treaty limitations on the use of anti-personnel mines and incendiary weapons when attacking military objectives located in a city, town, or village.[119] The principle remains that the military must choose the optimum weapon for

---

[119] See respectively Amended Protocol II on Mines, *supra* note 8 at Article 3(9) and Protocol III to the 1980 Conventional Weapons Convention, *supra* note 6 at Article 2(3).

the task, and using such weapons in the vicinity of civilians is likely to be viewed as breaching the discrimination provision. On the other hand, if a military objective were located some distance away from the civilian population, its attack with non-guided or area weapons would have a sounder basis in law.

Where military objectives are clearly separated from the civilian population and at some distance away from it, the use of cluster weapons would appear to be consistent with international law. This would be so in regard to the immediate effects of cluster weapons at least. Where both military personnel and civilians are present, however — such as might occur in a town — it is highly questionable whether the use of cluster weapons would remain lawful. Of course, this is not to suggest that military targets in towns or other populated areas cannot be attacked. For example, during the 2003 Iraq conflict, Iraqi forces often took positions within populated areas. Such incidences included the hiding of tanks or anti-aircraft weaponry in gardens, schools, and date groves positioned within civilian areas.[120] This tactic would appear to be a clear violation by Iraq of the principles contained in Article 58(b)(c) of Geneva Protocol I, which are precautions to be taken against the effects of attacks and which prohibit the locating of military objectives within or near densely populated areas. Although Iraq is not party to the protocol, such provisions undoubtedly fall within the range of customary law obligations. However, this fact does not necessarily mean that the coalition response on these occasions was within the laws of armed conflict. Certainly, a military objective could be attacked in such circumstances, but the issue concerns whether such objectives could be attacked with cluster weapons. Where this occurred, therefore, it is arguable that the coalition forces were in violation of this principle because the cluster weapons used, particularly by the British forces, could not be discriminate in such circumstances. Of course, the more "hi-tech" American versions may be able to discriminate, and thus it is not the case that all munitions in the cluster weapons family would violate this principle.

In compliance with humanitarian law, both the UK and US military forces were issued with a no-strike list involving thousands of buildings, including schools, mosques, hospitals, and historic sites.[121]

---

[120] *Off Target, supra* note 91 at 91.

[121] See the interview with Lieutenant Colonel Eric Wesley, in *ibid.* at 92. In particular, note Articles 52 and 53 of Geneva Protocol I, *supra* note 5, which form part of customary international law.

In addition, the US ground forces reported that they strove to keep cluster weapon strikes to a distance of at least 500 meters (sometimes reduced to 300 meters) away from these civilian targets.[122] Despite these efforts, Human Rights Watch documents what it describes as the "widespread use of cluster munitions in populated areas."[123] Talking to reporters on 25 April 2003, US General Richard Myers, chairman of the Joint Chiefs of Staff, admitted that the US use of cluster weapons had caused one civilian casualty.[124] In fact, the number of casualties and injured is considerably higher, possibly stretching into the thousands.[125] Many of the civilian deaths and injuries occurred as a result of cluster weapons landing in homes in populated areas of targeted villages and cities.[126] For example, in an attack on Basra on 23 March, there were reportedly seventy-seven civilians killed and 366 wounded.[127] On 24 March, in an attack on Nasiriyya, a further ten were reportedly dead and 200 injured.[128] Nasiriyya saw some of the most intense fighting, which, according to Human Rights Watch, resulted in over one thousand civilian casualties.[129] On 26 March at Abu Sukhair (a village near Najaf), cluster bomblets were found in people's homes with twenty-six civilians reportedly killed and sixty wounded.[130] Again the evidence of Human Rights Watch documents that 254 civilians were killed in Najaf as a result of the fighting and some 381 injured.[131] Cluster munitions, the doctors suggested, caused most of these incidents. On 1 April at al-Hilla, some eleven civilians were reportedly dead, nine of them children,[132] while between 23 March and

122 *Off Target, supra* note 91 at 94.

123 *Ibid.* at 97

124 Wiseman, *supra* note 90.

125 Sloboda and Dardagan, *supra* note 101.

126 *Off Target, supra* note 91 at 121.

127 "Gulf War 2: The Bombs That Devastated Ordinary Homes: In Your Name," *The Mirror* (24 March 2003); and Oliver Burkeman, "Battle for Key City Leads to 'Massacre of Children' Claim," *The Guardian* (24 March 2003).

128 James Meek, "War in the Gulf: Marines Losing the Battle for Hearts and Minds," *The Guardian* (25 March 2003).

129 *Off Target, supra* note 91, Appendix C at 132.

130 *Ibid.* at 105–7; "US Launches Probe after Reports of Missile Hitting Civilian Target in Baghdad," *Evening Times (Glasgow)* (29 March 2003) at 6.

131 *Off Target, supra* note 91, Appendix B at 130.

132 "Children Killed and Maimed in Bomb Attack on Town," *Belfast Telegraph* (2 April 2003); and *Off Target, supra* note 91 at 105–7.

11 April, Human Rights Watch documented some nineteen casualties and 515 injured in al-Hilla due to the use of cluster bombs.[133]
On 1 April, in the villages of Nadr, Djifil, Akramin, Mahawil,
Mohandesin, and Hail Asker, a further 200 were reportedly
wounded and sixty-one were killed.[134] On 8 April, while US air forces
were reportedly targeting anti-aircraft batteries in a park in
Baghdad's al-Hurriyah neighbourhood, cluster bombs were reportedly found in houses, gardens, trees, and fields. One farmer apparently lost his wheat harvest to cluster munitions.[135] In a late night
attack using cluster munitions on 24 April, US forces were possibly
targeting paramilitary troops at Hadaf and cluster bombed the girls'
primary school in al-Hilla. Two civilians were reportedly dead and
thirteen injured in the attack.[136] Targeting populated areas will inevitably result in civilian casualties, including those deaths that are
due to unexploded ordnance such as those identified by the Iraqi
Red Crescent. The Red Crescent has documented dozens of sites
contaminated with unexploded ordnance, including industrial areas, playgrounds, schools, and civilian houses in urban residential
areas.[137] In one report, it was stated that ambulances were not able
to enter many populated areas for fear of hitting unexploded sub-
munitions.[138]

Similarly, during the Afghanistan conflict in 2001–2, the United
States used older-style cluster weapons against inhabited villages
and other populated areas, causing many civilian casualties. Human Rights Watch documented three such attacks at Ainger, a village east of Kunduz, Ishaq Suleiman, a village of 12,000 inhabitants
northwest of Herat, and Qala Shater, a neighbourhood of some
4,800 people to the northeast of Herat.[139] Although the villages were

---

[133] *Off Target, supra* note 91, Appendix A at 129.

[134] Robert Fisk, "Wailing Children, the Wounded, the Dead: Victims of the Day
Cluster Bombs Rained on Babylon," *The Independent* (3 April 2003).

[135] "Iraqis – and U.S. Troops – Stumble across Bomblets," *USA Today* (12 November
2003). According to *USA Today*, a mine-clearance team that works for the US
State Department took a look at the field of waist-high stalks and decided it was
too dangerous to clear.

[136] *Off Target, supra* note 91 at 59. The report indicates that the US forces used at
least one CBU-103, but Landmine Action, a UK-based NGO, has stated that
pictures from al-Hilla show unexploded BLU-97. "Iraq Civilians under Fire,"
Amnesty International (8 April 2003).

[137] *ICRC Annual Report 2003* (Geneva: ICRC, 2004) at 266.

[138] *Off Target, supra* note 91 at 105.

[139] See "Fatally Flawed," *supra* note 23 at 21–3.

in relatively close proximity to either a military base or Taliban soldiers, the civilian casualties were caused by the use of the inaccurate, older-style cluster weapons.

The older-style cluster bombs utilize up to 200 bomblets per cluster bomb unit. As a result, with such a large number of these older bomblets, it is inconceivable that they could be directed at a specific military objective located within a populated area (as required by Article 51 (4) (b) (c) of Geneva Protocol I). A 500-meter minimum distance between civilian areas and targets as introduced by the American and British forces during the conflict, while a welcome development at least in the use of cluster weapons, has been overwhelmingly proven to be wholly inadequate. During *Operation Telic* in Iraq in 2003, for example, the British Royal Air Force dropped some 10,290 individual cluster bomblets in and around Baghdad — the capital city of Iraq with a peacetime population of over five million. Again, these were the older-style cluster bombs, which the Ministry of Defence admitted had a failure rate of 5 per cent. Moreover, the evidence of Human Rights Watch suggests that British ground forces used L20 cluster weapons "extensively" in populated areas, such as Basra.[140] Although the British forces were targeting military objectives (mostly Iraqi tanks) in and around Basra, Human Rights Watch reported many civilian casualties due to the choice of using cluster weapons in populated areas. According to Human Rights Watch, the Basra areas of Hay al-Muhandissin al-Kubra, al-Mishraq al-Jadid, and Hay al-Zailun were hit between 23 and 25 March during the hours of 12:00 PM, 3:00 PM, and the evening respectively.[141] At these times and in populated areas, the British ground forces should have foreseen civilian casualties from the immediate effects of the use of cluster weapons. Although the Israeli-manufactured L20 has a lower sub-munition capacity (only forty-nine per weapon) and failure rate (estimated at approximately 2 per cent), the use of over 2,000 such weapons would produce almost 2,000 duds. Certainly, with such high figures, the civilian population was at risk of injury or death from (1) the initial attack and (2) the unexploded munitions that would remain after the attack. Although fewer sub-munitions were deployed in each unit, the weapon contained no additional guidance system and, as such, the use of these weapons in populated or built-up areas — as admitted by the defence ministers — would violate the principle of

---

[140] See *Off Target, supra* note 91 at 48 and 80.
[141] *Ibid.* at 90.

discriminate warfare.[142] Furthermore, it has been suggested that the much-quoted lower failure rate may in fact make the user state less hesitant in deploying them in populated areas, encouraging greater use of the perceived "safer" weapon.[143]

From this evidence, which is albeit admittedly limited, it is certainly possible to conclude that the British and American use of cluster bombs — in particular, the older versions — against many targets within populated areas during the 2003 Iraq conflict were in violation of the principle of the discriminate use of a weapon.

CONSEQUENCES OF BREACH

In the previous sections, this author has suggested, with a great degree of certainty, that the older-style cluster munitions (in particular, the RBL-755) are inherently indiscriminate weapons and, hence, violate the prohibition on indiscriminate warfare. Flowing from this categorization is the conclusion that the use of these weapons is already prohibited by international law. Hence, there is no need for their possession, stockpiling, or transfer. Similarly, as a consequence, violator states are required by general international law to make recompense to those states where such weapons have been used.[144] More specifically, compensation provisions within the 1977 Geneva Protocol I (Article 91) would be applicable. This provision may, therefore, require violator states to compensate individual victims. Furthermore, the use of such weaponry may constitute a war crime under the Geneva Conventions and the Rome Statute of the International Criminal Court.[145] Alternatively, there appears to be evidence to suggest the indiscriminate use of cluster weapons during recent conflicts — including the 2003 Iraq conflict by UK and US forces — when such weapons were used against targets within populated areas. Again, the indiscriminate *use* of weapons would constitute a war crime under these provisions.

While many within the international community will not agree with the first proposition, classifying these weapons as inherently

142 See Richard Norton-Taylor, "Basra Troops used Cluster Bombs," *The Guardian* (30 May 2003).

143 See *Off Target, supra* note 91 at 112–13.

144 *Chorzów Factory Case (Germany v. Poland)* (1928) P.C.I.J., Ser.A, No. 17 at 29.

145 In particular, see Geneva Protocol I, *supra* note 5 at Article 85(3)(b); and 1998 Rome Statute of the International Criminal Court, 17 July 1998, 37 I.L.M. 999 (entered into force 1 July 2002) at Article 8. For example, the United Kingdom ratified the Rome Statute on 4 October 2001.

indiscriminate weapons, many will concur on the latter. The question becomes, therefore, what limitations are required to maintain the legality of cluster weapons under the principle of discriminate warfare? There are of course a number of measures that, if undertaken, would alleviate the needless civilian deaths and injuries from unexploded cluster bombs. First, it would be a valuable first step for states to draft a protocol to the 1980 Conventional Weapons Convention, specifically prohibiting the use of cluster weapons within populated areas. Since the design and mode of delivery of cluster weapons means that they cannot be targeted with pinpoint accuracy, they should not be used to target facilities located in the vicinity of civilians. Legal precedents already exist in regard to the use of air-delivered incendiary weapons or remotely delivered mines, the use of which are prohibited in all circumstances against military objectives located within a concentration of civilians.[146] There may also be a need to define further what the concept of "vicinity" might entail in regard to particular weapons and the minimum safe distances between targeted military objectives and concentrations of civilians. This would not necessarily be the same for other similar weapons, but would at least provide an additional safeguard on the ground. Second, with respect to the failure rate of cluster weapons, the use of modern versions with heat-seeking capability (discussed later in this article) is to be welcomed. While this author has some difficulty perceiving at present a lawful use of cluster weapons in any military scenario, the major sticking point is the proven failure rate. If this high failure rate could be eliminated, the legality of cluster weapons in (discriminating) military uses would be secured. As a consequence, there is little prospect of a treaty banning cluster weapons. There is certainly not sufficient political will at present for such a measure. Furthermore, even if such a treaty could be drafted in the present political climate, there is no guarantee that the major user states would ratify. The safer way forward, therefore, may be in a limitation on the use of cluster weapons in populated areas and in securing improvements in the design and reliability of these weapons.

Progress has very recently been made, however, in the form of limitations on the use of weaponry having post-conflict effects, which may impact upon the legality of cluster weapons in the future. These limitations are contained in the 2003 Protocol V on

146 See Protocol II on Mines, *supra* note 53 (and Amended Protocol II on Mines, *supra* note 8) and Protocol III, *supra* note 6 to the 1980 Conventional Weapons Convention.

Explosive Remnants of War (Protocol V on Explosive Remnants) to the 1980 Conventional Weapons Convention. Primarily, the protocol, which has yet to enter into force, concerns the problem of the clean-up of unexploded or failed munitions. Yet how effective the protocol will be in practice in preventing or limiting the incidence of unexploded ordnance remains to be seen.

2003 PROTOCOL V ON EXPLOSIVE REMNANTS

The laws of armed conflict do not generally address the issue of cleaning up spent military ordnance and other debris left on the battlefield after engagements. Advances in this area include the obligations accepted under the 1996 Amended Protocol II on Mines to the 1980 Conventional Weapons Convention and the 1997 Ottawa Treaty. In these two documents, states have agreed to limited responsibility for the post-conflict removal of unexploded anti-personnel mines. However, a sense of obligation for the removal of unexploded ordnance and debris in general appears to be absent. Clearly, these issues may be addressed in a specific peace treaty, but, if they are not addressed, the general rule under international law appears to be that the burden lies where it falls — upon the "host" state (the state in which the debris is located). Consequently, there is no general obligation on the state using weapons in wartime to clear away the spent weapons debris from another country. Obviously, there are good reasons why the "user" state (the state using the weapon) cannot be expected to carry out removal obligations in the host state. First, there is the issue of state sovereignty, since the user state cannot enter or remain on the territory of the host state for such purposes. Second, there is the issue of *de facto* occupation: the user state may no longer be in control of the territory where the debris is located. Third, there will be human rights obligations binding on the host state, which it is the host state's responsibility to ensure. For example, ensuring the right to life may require the host state to remove dangerous ordnance.

Furthermore, there also appears to be no general obligation for the user state to pay for the removal of unexploded ordnance or military debris or for damage caused by the debris. War imposes a tremendous financial burden on states; so much so that few states — the one notable exception being Kuwait in 1991 — will at the close of hostilities have the financial resources to clear the debris. It is clear, however, that if the debris is not removed, the long-term human and environmental consequences from the debris will only increase. It is in this regard that the latest protocol to the 1980 Conventional Weapons Convention marks a fundamental step.

On 28 November 2003, state parties to the 1980 Conventional Weapons Convention adopted the text of a draft protocol concerned with alleviating the problem of explosive remnants of war (ERW). The adopted text forms Protocol V on Explosive Remnants to the 1980 convention and requires twenty ratifications to enter into force.[147] The scope of the protocol includes both internal and international conflicts, due to the Amendment of Article 1 of the 1980 Conventional Weapons Convention in 2001, and applies to explosive remnants of war on land, including the internal waters of state parties. The first point to note about the protocol is that unlike the other four protocols to the Conventional Weapons Convention it does not concern a specific weapon. Consequently, there is no absolute prohibition on the use of cluster weapons or any other weapon producing ERW. There is also a noticeable change in language. The very strict requirements of the earlier protocols have been replaced by much weaker and heavily qualified obligations. Whereas Amended Protocol II on Mines prohibits their use in "all circumstances,"[148] makes state parties "responsible"[149] for all mines, requires "effective advance warning"[150] to civilians, and obliges clearance of mines "without delay,"[151] the new protocol merely "encourages"[152] states "to endeavour"[153] to carry out the obligations only "as far as practicable,"[154] "as soon as feasible,"[155] and "to the maxi-

---

147 To date, Protocol V on Explosive Remnants, *supra* note 11, has received only eight ratifications, that of Sweden, Lithuania, Sierra Leone, Croatia, Germany, Finland, Ukraine, and India.

148 Amended Protocol II on Mines, *supra* note 8 at Article 3(3): "It is prohibited in all circumstance to use any mine, booby-trap or other device which is designed or of a nature to cause superfluous injury or unnecessary suffering."

149 *Ibid.* at Article 3(2).

150 *Ibid.* at Article 3(11). This obligation is, however, qualified by the phrase, "unless circumstances do not permit."

151 *Ibid.* at Article 10(1).

152 Protocol V on Explosive Remnants, *supra* note 11 at Article 9, regarding the generic preventive measures.

153 *Ibid.* at Part 1(a) and 3 of the Technical Annex.

154 *Ibid.* at Article 4 regarding recording, retaining, and transmission of information on the location of ERW.

155 *Ibid.* at Articles 3, 5, 6, 7, and Part 1 of the Technical Annex.

mum extent possible."[156] However, there are greater concerns aside
from its watered down language. Due to the insertion of Article
1(4), the bulk of the protocol is limited only to future ERW, consequently unexploded ordnance (UXO) already *in situ* are largely
ignored.

The new Protocol V on Explosive Remnants applies to explosive
remnants of war, which are defined in Article 2(4) as including
"unexploded ordnance and abandoned explosive ordnance." In
defining "unexploded ordnance," Article 2(2) states that

[u]nexploded ordnance means explosive ordnance that has been primed,
fused, armed, or otherwise prepared for use and used in an armed conflict. It may have been fired, dropped, launched or projected and should
have exploded but failed to do so.

The provision stipulates further that "explosive ordnance" refers
to "conventional munitions containing explosives," albeit with the
exception of mines, booby traps, and other devices (as defined in
the 1996 Amended Protocol II on Mines).[157] Clearly, under Article
2(2), the definition of "unexploded ordnance" is wide enough to
include failed cluster weapons, and, hence, state parties would bear
the responsibilities as set out in the protocol.[158] Dependent on
whether the state concerned is a user state or a host state, the "responsibilities" under the protocol require the state to fulfil one of
two substantive obligations. First, state parties in control of territory containing explosive remnants of war are obliged to mark and
clear, remove, or destroy ERW as soon as is feasible (Article 3(2)),
with priority being given to areas "posing a serious humanitarian
risk." In accordance with Article 3(3), the host state is to undertake
risk assessment in order to prioritize clearance activities and reduce the risks of ERW to the civilian population. Hence, the
protocol's emphasis is on the speedy return of the country to nor-
mality and a reduction in the number of civilians killed by
unexploded ordnance after the end of hostilities. Furthermore,
Article 5 requires the host state to take

all feasible precautions in the territory under their control affected by
explosive remnants of war to protect the civilian population, individual
civilians and civilian objects from the risks and effects of explosive remnants of war.

156 *Ibid.* at Article 4 and Part 2 of the Technical Annex.
157 *Ibid.* at Article 2(1).
158 *Ibid.* at Article 3(1).

Unlike the other provisions of the protocol, Article 5 contains no reference to the end of hostilities and so appears to entail obligations for the host state during conflict. Such measures, the protocol stipulates, are necessary to protect the civilian population. "Feasible precautions" are defined as those precautions "which are practicable or practicably possible, taking into account all circumstances ruling at the time, including humanitarian and military considerations."[159] Consequently, the possible precautions, such as warnings, risk education to the civilian population, marking, fencing, and monitoring of territory affected by explosive remnants of war are subject to military considerations.[160]

A major difference between the earlier obligations under the 1996 Amended Protocol II on Mines and Protocol V on Explosive Remnants is the timeframe for clearance. Under Amended Protocol II on Mines, Article 10(1) requires the host state to clear mined areas "without delay after the cessation of active hostilities." According to Article 3(2) of Protocol V on Explosive Remnants, however, the timeframe with respect to ERW is lengthened to "after the cessation of active hostilities and as soon as feasible." As a consequence, the obligation is weakened. One possible reason for this discrepancy is the technological differences between the clearance of unexploded ordnance and mines. Certainly, since Protocol II and Amended Protocol II to the 1980 Conventional Weapons Convention require that mines be detectable, their clearance is a simpler task than other weapons causing ERW, such as cluster bombs. Although cluster bombs are also detectable, they can be much more sensitive and, hence, pose greater risks in clearance. Thus, an affected state may require additional time to acquire the technology and train personnel to undertake the task. Other than for this reason, it is not immediately apparent as to why the obligation under Protocol V on Explosive Remnants is reduced.

Where the user state is not in control of the affected territory, its obligations under the protocol are reduced. Here a state party (and party to the conflict) is to provide, *inter alia*, "technical, financial, material or human resources assistance ... to facilitate the marking and clearance, removal or destruction of such ERW," but only "where feasible."[161] This duty is similar to that imposed in previous protocols to the 1980 Conventional Weapons Convention, and it

---

159 *Ibid.* at Article 5.

160 *Ibid.*

161 *Ibid.* at Article 3(1).

recognizes the principle of state sovereignty of the state in control of the affected territory. Unlike the assistance demanded by Amended Protocol II on Mines,[162] however, Protocol V on Explosive Remnants obliges state parties to provide such assistance only "where feasible."[163] This point clearly reduces the strength of the obligation. On the other hand, however, this discrepancy in language may be explained by the broadened list of aid that should be provided. While Amended Protocol II on Mines obliges the user state to provide both technical and material assistance, Protocol V on Explosive Remnants recognizes the need for financial and human resource assistance in the clearance of ERW. In order to fulfil its obligations, the user state may consider the first part of the protocol's Technical Annex. Although implementation of the Technical Annex is only on a voluntary basis, states that do "have regard" to it would find that it suggests a number of practical steps for the user state to undertake to facilitate clearance by the host state.[164] Such practical requirements include recording information concerning the ordnance used and the storage of this information in a manner that allows it to be retrieved and subsequently released.[165] Clearly, in order for a state to record information on the use of potentially failing weapons, it requires knowledge of (1) the location of the areas targeted, (2) the approximate number of weapons used, and (3) the type and nature of the ordnance used.[166] In deciding which information to release, the user state can legitimately take into account "security interests and other obligations."[167] Finally, the release of such information should be granted "as soon as possible."[168] These obligations arise only under the voluntary Technical Annex.

It is clear from previous state practice that states using such weapons do not always record the location of their deployment. For example, it was recently highlighted by Human Rights Watch in a paper on the use of cluster weapons in Iraq in 2003, that the United

---

[162] Amended Protocol II on Mines, *supra* note 8 at Article 10(2)(3), where the state "shall provide ... technical and material assistance necessary to fulfil such responsibilities."

[163] Protocol V on Explosive Remnants, *supra* note 11 at Article 3(1).

[164] *Ibid.* at Article 4(3).

[165] See *ibid.*, Part 1.a and b of the Technical Annex.

[166] *Ibid.*, Part 1.a of the Technical Annex.

[167] *Ibid.*, Part 1.c of the Technical Annex.

[168] *Ibid.*, Part 1.c.iv of the Technical Annex.

States had failed to keep records regarding its use of ground-launched cluster munitions.[169] This admission was provided by an unnamed US defence official and has severe repercussions for the civilian population, ground troops, and UXO clearance missions. Obligations of accurate mapping were included within the scheme of Amended Protocol II on Mines for remotely delivered mines. Accordingly, it is prohibited for a state party to use remotely delivered mines unless they are recorded in accordance with paragraphs 1(a)(i) and 1(b) of the Technical Annex.[170] These provisions are specific to the use of remotely delivered mines. Cluster weapons, however, are delivered in a similar manner, contain a large number of duds, and there is little doubt that such duds pose a similar danger to that of landmines. Why then does Article 4 of Protocol V on Explosive Remnants place only a weak obligation on state parties to record such information? As a result, such an imperative obligation is replete with qualifications, resulting in an obligation to record and retain information on the use of explosive ordnance "to the maximum extent possible and as far as practicable" (Article 4(1)). Article 4(2) further weakens the obligation by subjecting the transfer of that information to the affected state to the "parties' legitimate security interests."

The problem of unexploded ordnance is global. It affects all conflict zones. As a consequence, states have learned the important role of cooperation in the sharing of information, technology, and other assistance. In regard to all state parties to the new protocol, therefore, there will be obligation to cooperate in the provision of assistance to affected states. This principle is pivotal, and it develops concepts that are found in the previous protocols. A new aspect to the protocol, however, is the specific recognition of the role of NGOs in the provision of ERW clearance. Accordingly, Article 3(5) stipulates that

[h]igh Contracting Parties shall co-operate, where appropriate, both among themselves and with other states, relevant regional and international organisations and non-governmental organisations on the provision of, *inter alia*, technical, financial, material and human resources assistance including, in appropriate circumstances, the undertaking of joint operations necessary to fulfil the provisions of this Article.

---

[169] Human Rights Watch, "Iraq: Clusters Info Needed from U.S.," press release (29 April 2003).

[170] Amended Protocol II on Mines, *supra* note 8 at Article 9(1).

Finally, Article 9 and Part 3 of the voluntary Technical Annex are of interest with respect to the limitation of the use of cluster weapons. Article 9 "encourages" generic preventive measures to minimize the occurrence of UXO. This is an obligation of common but differentiated responsibilities for states "bearing in mind the different situations and capacities."[171] As a consequence, state parties "should to the extent possible and as appropriate endeavour"[172] to ensure, *inter alia,* that production processes are designed to achieve the greatest reliability of munitions. Most surprisingly, this obligation, although contained in the voluntary annex, is not further qualified by any specific reference to cost. Cost may of course be included within the concept of common but differentiated responsibilities. In addition to quality control measures and quality assurance standards, paragraph (a)(v) of Part 3 requires high reliability standards. The current rule for landmines is that "no more than ten per cent of activated mines will fail to self-destruct within 30 days." Consequently, the required reliability rate for landmines is 99.9 per cent.[173] Similarly, under Article 6 of Amended Protocol II on Mines, remotely delivered landmines are subject to a very strict regime, including stringent rules governing effective self-deactivation and self-destruct mechanisms and effective advance warning of the civilian population. Unlike the Amended Protocol II on Mines, no specific reliability requirement was established for cluster weapons under the new protocol, but the reliability requirements of Part 3 are a tentative first step in that direction.

Clearly, the current Israeli-manufactured L20 cluster weapon may in fact be consistent with the provisions of the new protocol. With its back-up fifteen-second self-destruct mechanism, its use may result in fewer duds. Having said this, however, there is still an estimated 2 per cent failure rate even for such weapons. More importantly, the United States has taken two further steps in this direction: first, with the decision in December 2001 that any submunitions produced after 2005 will be required to be 99 per cent reliable.[174] Unfortunately though, this mandate does allow for the

171 Protocol V on Explosive Remnants, *supra* note 11 at Article 4(3).
172 *Ibid.* at Part 3 of the Technical Annex.
173 See *ibid.*, Part 3.a. of the Technical Annex.
174 See *Cluster Munitions a Foreseeable Hazard, supra* note 103, and Secretary of Defense William Cohen, "Memorandum for the Secretaries of the Military Departments, Subject: Department of Defense Policy on Submunition Reliability (U)," 10 January 2001.

continued use by US forces of existing stocks of the older, less reliable cluster weapons in the meantime. What may be required, therefore, to ensure discriminate warfare by cluster weapons is some mechanism to guarantee greater accuracy in targeting. This is the second step taken by the United States, which it has achieved with its CBU-105 sensor-fused weapon.[175] The 105 model saw its first combat use in Iraq in 2003. Each munition employs forty armour-piercing explosives.[176] The dispenser splits in mid-air to release ten smaller units, their descent being controlled by small parachutes, similar to the older CBU models. As the ten smaller units approach the ground, they split again to eject four armour-piercing explosives. What is special about these cluster sub-munitions, however, is that they use infra-red heat-seeking sensors and can be steered in flight. The heat-seeking capability of the sub-munitions means a greater strike rate against such objectives as tank engines and other vehicles. Furthermore, if no target is detected, the sub-munitions will explode automatically after a pre-set period of time.[177] This capability, of course, complies with the requirements of reliability for ERW under the new protocol, but it may cause a problem if civilian persons are present when the weapon self-destructs. If the self-destruct delay is sufficiently short then the risk of civilian harm should be minimal, bearing in mind that it would still be unlawful to attack military objectives disproportionately and indiscriminately.

The reception received by the new protocol has been rather muted. Organizations such as Human Rights Watch and the ICRC view it as a weak instrument that achieves little by way of concrete obligations of UXO prevention and removal. It is certainly not an instrument that prohibits any particular weapon — say cluster weapons — due to their propensity for high failure rates. It is more of an instrument of general application and, although heavily qualified, may aid in the post-conflict removal of UXO. It is certainly politically neutral in tackling the problem. As in earlier treaties, the obligations on the host state are greater than those on the user state, but this fact should not diminish the responsibilities of the user state in the provision of financial, technical, material, and human resource assistance. It is true that the protocol does not specifically

---

175 The cluster weapons are delivered by means of a wind-corrected munition dispenser (WCMD) and the individual sub-munitions are hockey-puck shaped. The United States used six such weapons in Iraq.

176 See *Off Target, supra* note 91 at 60.

177 See generally Federation of American Scientists, *supra* note 98.

prohibit or limit the use of cluster weapons in armed conflict, but this was clearly something that the negotiating states could not achieve.

CONCLUSIONS

The issue of the limitation of cluster weapons has been on the agenda for over thirty years, almost as long as these weapons have been in use, but no treaty limitation or prohibition has been successfully negotiated. There appears to be insufficient state willingness to limit or prohibit a weapon that many states possess and have come to regard as extremely useful — particularly in targeting a mobile or dispersed military objective. Is it arguable, therefore, that state practice is amending the customary prohibition on indiscriminate warfare so as to exclude cluster bombs? This development would be highly unwelcome and one that the states themselves would not admit to. To this author, however, the terms of Article 51(4) of Geneva Protocol I are clear, and they suggest the prohibition of most types of cluster weapons.

Regardless of the lack of such specific prohibitions, this article questions whether the existing laws of armed conflict already contain sufficient limitations on the use of such weapons to afford effective civilian and environmental protection. At the least, it is suggested that the United Kingdom and the United States were both in violation of the customary principle relating to indiscriminate warfare when they used certain cluster weapons against targets in the Iraqi cities of Baghdad and Basra in 2003. Finally, while clean-up operations commenced in Iraq very quickly following the end of the conflict, civilians continue to be harmed by uncleared ERW, including unexploded cluster bombs. The future is uncertain for the 2003 Protocol V on Explosive Remnants, but one can only hope that once it is in force it will crystallize an obligation in the psyche of military forces to reduce ERW and carry out post-conflict clean-up of other military debris.

Sommaire

De licéité douteuse: l'utilisation des bombes à dispersion à des fins militaires en Iraq en 2003

Au cours du siècle dernier, les lois régissant les conflits armés ont limité ou interdit l'utilisation d'un certain nombre d'armes, principalement à cause de leurs effets cruels ou de leur nature indifférenciée. Parmi celles-ci, mentionnons les armes chimiques et biologiques, les mines antipersonnel et les lasers aveuglants. Plus récemment, il y a eu une grande controverse concernant l'utilisation des bombes à dispersion par les États. Ces armes sont produites localement à peu de frais, mais ne sont guère fiables. L'utilisation des armes à dispersion est condamnée depuis le conflit armé au Vietnam, et leur licéité est plutôt douteuse. La question en la matière n'est pas tellement s'il y a lieu de créer des nouveaux instruments de limitation, voire même de prohibition, mais plutôt de déterminer si les lois existantes régissant les conflits armés sont suffisantes pour répondre aux préoccupations concernant la protection des personnes et de l'environnement.

Summary

Of Questionable Legality: The Military Use of Cluster Bombs in Iraq in 2003

Over the past century, the laws of armed conflict have limited or prohibited the use of a number of weapons, principally due to their cruel effects or indiscriminate nature. Among the examples are chemical and biological weapons, anti-personnel mines, and blinding laser weapons. In recent years, one of the most controversial armaments used by states has been the cluster bomb. Cluster weapons are inexpensively produced area weapons with a high propensity for failure. The source of constant condemnation since the Vietnam conflict, the legality of cluster weapons remains highly questionable. With such weapons, the question is not so much whether there is a need to create new instruments of limitation, or indeed prohibition, but whether the existing laws of armed conflict are already sufficient to address any human and environmental concerns.

A Return to *Communitarianism?* Reacting to "Serious Breaches of Obligations Arising under Peremptory Norms of General International Law" under the Law of State Responsibility and United Nations Law

MARK TOUFAYAN

> [M]y final thesis is that the future of international law is one with the future of international organization. Concretely, this means that progress towards clarity and effectiveness in a supranational legal order will depend less upon the formulation and reformulation of general principles, or upon codification, than upon arrangements for the supranational administration of specific common interests.[1]
>
> — Percy Elwood Corbett

INTRODUCTION

The idea that a human being bears responsibility to intercede to aid another human being in danger reaches far back to the drafters of the Code of Hammurabi, the Talmud, the Koran, and the Christian Bible. Both common law and civil law traditions have also struggled with the concept of a "duty to rescue." For such influential figures as Gentili, Grotius, Suarèz, and Vattel, all of whom were deeply rooted in the scholastic, humanist, and natural law traditions where all people owe obligations to God and their fellow humans, there could have been no question that genocidal acts

---

Mark Toufayan, LL.B., B.C.L. (McGill); LL.M. in International Legal Studies (NYU School of Law). A draft version of this article was presented at the Inaugural Emerging Human Rights Scholarship Conference hosted by the Center for Human Rights and Global Justice at New York University School of Law on 31 October 2003. The author wishes to thank Don McRae, editor-in-chief of the *Yearbook*, for having authorized the presentation of this article at the conference as well as Philip Alston, Thomas Franck, and James Cockayne for their helpful comments on earlier drafts. Any shortcomings, however, are strictly his own.

[1] P.E. Corbett, *Law and Society in the Relations of States* (New York: Harcourt, 1951) at 12–13.

perpetrated by a sovereign could and must be stopped by others through the use of force in a just war. A somewhat similar idea finds modern expression in Article I of the Convention on the Prevention and Punishment of the Crime of Genocide (Genocide Convention), where the contracting parties "confirm that genocide, whether committed in time of peace or in time of war, is a crime under international law which they undertake to prevent and punish."[2]

To be sure, the translation of the just war tradition and its underlying idea of punishment through the use of force into contemporary international law does not present the same attractiveness today. In fact, since the advent of the Charter of the United Nations (UN Charter),[3] the doctrine has been tailored on numerous occasions to avoid the excesses of military conflagration. Yet over and above what may be seen as an over-simplistic argument appealing to the obligation of all states to preserve the welfare of peoples by protecting them from unjust tyrants,[4] a fundamental question remains: must states carry out this obligation within existing (or newly created) structures of cooperation of international institutions, or can it be discharged at will by states *uti singuli* by resort to unilateral or collective measures?[5]

---

[2] Convention on the Prevention and Punishment of the Crime of Genocide, GA Resolution 260(A)(III), UN GAOR, 3rd Sess., Supp. No. 1921, 9 December 1948, 78 U.N.T.S. 227 [Genocide Convention].

[3] Charter of the United Nations, 26 June 1945, Can. T.S. 1955 No. 7 [UN Charter].

[4] Thus, proceeding from the assumption that nations are no less subject to the law of nature than are individuals, Vattel concluded that what one man owes to other men, each nation, in turn, owes to all other nations: "Since Nations are bound mutually to promote the society of the human race, they owe one another all the duties which the safety and welfare of that society require ... and protect an unfortunate people from an unjust tyrant." See E. de Vattel, *The Law of Nations on the Principles of Natural Law*, trans. C. Fenwick, 1964, (Philadelphia: T and J.W. Johnson, 1758) at xii.

[5] This question was left open by Secretary General Kofi Annan upon revealing his five-point action plan to prevent genocide, which includes (1) preventing armed conflict that usually provides the context for genocide; (2) protecting civilians in armed conflict including a mandate for UN peacekeepers to protect civilians; (3) ending impunity through judicial action in both national and international courts; (4) information gathering and early warning through a UN Special Advisor for Genocide Prevention making recommendations to the UN Security Council on actions to prevent or halt genocide; and (5) swift and decisive action along a continuum of steps, including military action. For the full text of the recommendations, see Press Release SG/SM/9197, available online at <http://www.un.org/News/Press/docs/2004/sgsm9245.doc.htm> (date accessed: 16 October 2004). The Genocide Convention itself is ambiguous

In any discussion on what is perhaps clumsily referred to here as a state's "responsibility" to the international community as a whole, this question conserves its prominence. It represents the focal point of this article, which is divided as follows. The first section considers the implications of the duty to prevent genocide for individual states through the lens of the recently codified law of state responsibility, which provides the logical framework for discussing the consequences of breaches of international legal obligations. It is argued that the new draft articles of 2001, with their emphasis on "serious breaches of obligations arising under peremptory norms of general international law" rather than on obligations *erga omnes*, and on the vague requirement of "state cooperation" to put an end to serious breaches, are ill-suited to provide for the taking of effective preventive measures by "not-directly affected" states.[6] The second part then moves the discussion "outside the box," so to speak, and casts our juristic gaze upon the United Nations, which remains arguably to this day the only collective expression of humanity and sole repository of legitimacy in international relations. Having concluded that contemporary international law imposes a subsidiary legal obligation on the United Nations to act pre-emptively against genocide, I finally address in the third section the issue of constitutional reform of the present collective security system for the effective protection of community interests, particularly in light of the

---

as perfunctory references to prevention are all that remain of the considerably more extensive proposals in the Secretariat draft. Thus, to weaken the preventive effect of the treaty, a modification of the more substantial provisions of the earlier draft relating to actions to be taken by the UN was introduced in the final text by omitting the legal obligation of the contracting parties to "do everything in their power" to assist the UN in its measures to suppress or prevent acts of genocide. See on this point *Fifth Report on State Responsibility by Mr. Roberto Ago, Special Rapporteur ("Content of the obligation breached")*, UN Doc. A/CN.4/291 and Add.1 and 2, reprinted in *Yearbook of the International Law Commission 1976*, vol. 2, Part 1, New York, 1976, at 48 ff [*Fifth Report of Roberto Ago*].

6 This expression can be attributed to Grotius: "Kings ... have the right of demanding punishments not only on account of injuries committed against themselves or their subjects, but also on account of injuries which do not directly affect them but excessively violate the law of nature or of nations in regard to any person whatsoever." See H. Grotius, *De jure belli ac pacis libri tres*, Book II, ed. by Carnegie, trans. F. Kelsey, 1625, Chapter XX at XL. I prefer this expression to that of "non-injured states" retained by the ILC in its 2001 draft, for the latter misconceives the fact that all states are injured, some because they have undergone damage affecting their subjective rights, others because they have suffered harm that involves a non-material, legal feature (infringement of a right).

recent recommendations of the secretary general's High Level Panel on Threats, Challenges and Change.[7] Of course, the issues discussed in this article are also highly relevant when it comes to questions of responsibility of the UN and of its member states *stricto sensu* such as: who is responsible for the inactivity of UN peacekeeping forces when facing impending genocide;[8] what is the responsibility, if any, of states whose nationals are sent as contributing troops; and who is responsible for the inactivity of forces of so-called "coalitions of the able and willing" carrying on UN-authorized operations?[9] Additional questions also emerge where the United Nations, through the passivity of the Security Council, fails to act altogether. Who then is responsible for the council's *largesse* where one or some of its members block a resolution authorizing recourse to force or put limitations on funding?[10] Specific problems thus appear to exist where the Organization is

[7] See *A More Secure World: Our Shared Responsibility*, Report of the Secretary-General's High-Level Panel on Threats, Challenges and Change, at paras. 248–49 and 256, available online at <http://www.un.org/secureworld/report2.pdf> (date accessed: 9 December 2004) [*More Secure World*].

[8] It has been generally accepted that the UN would normally be liable to third parties for damages incurred as a result of *acts* performed by it or by its agents acting in their official capacity. See, for example, on this point *Difference Relating to Immunity from Legal Process of a Special Rapporteur of the Commission on Human Rights*, Advisory Opinion, [1999] I.C.J. Rep. 62 at 88–89, para. 66; L. Condorelli, "Le Statut des Forces de l'ONU et le Droit International Humanitaire" (1995) 78 Rivista di Diritto Internazionale 881 at 897; C.F. Amerasinghe, *Principles of the Institutional Law of International Organizations* (Cambridge: Cambridge University Press, 1996) at 241, footnotes 51 and 52 and references therein. There is no reason why an *omission* to act should not similarly attract the UN's liability when the latter has a duty to act.

[9] As the latter type of operation is not the same as a UN operation *stricto sensu*, this essentially raises the question to what extent a coalition *omission* to act that causes damage to third parties is attributable to the UN as the "authorizer" of the operation.

[10] It would appear that under general international law, a state is not automatically responsible for the conduct of an international organization to which it belongs. See the resolution adopted by the Institut de droit international on 1 September 1995, "Les Conséquences Juridiques pour les États Membres de l'Inexécution par des Organisations Internationales de leurs Obligations envers des Tiers" (1996-II) 66 Ann. inst. dr. int 1, at 448, Article 6(a); and R. Higgins, "Provisional Report: The Legal Consequences for Member States of the Non-Fulfilment by International Organizations of Their Obligations toward Third Party" (1995-I) 66 Ann. inst. dr. int 249 at 281–83. For a thorough analysis of possible legal grounds for such responsibility, see P. Klein, *La responsabilité des organisations internationales dans les ordres juridiques internes et en droit des gens* (Bruxelles: Bruylant, 1998) at 430–520.

the bystander to genocide, and member states are said to be "responsible" either by virtue of their direct involvement in its conduct (the Permanent Five)[11] or of their membership therein.[12] Hardly any research has been undertaken concerning such controversial attribution issues, but to discuss them in this article would clearly not do justice to the complexity of the topic and should therefore be avoided.[13]

COMMUNITARIANISM STRAPPED INTO THE BILATERALIST STRAITJACKET

The juxtaposition of the traditional bilateralist structure of international law alongside the notion of "community interest" embedded in such multilateral treaties as the Genocide Convention has

---

11 According to certain commentators, a purely political act such as a vote is sufficient to establish the complicity of a state with respect to the illegal acts of another. See B. Graefrath, "Complicity in the Law of State Responsibility" (1996) 29 Rev. B.D.I. 370 at 374; J. Quigley, "Complicity in International Law: A New Direction in the Law of State Responsibility" (1986) 57 Brit. Y.B. Int'l L. 77 at 86–87. By extension, it might be argued that the vote by a state within the decision-making organs of an international organization, to the extent that it allows the adoption by the latter of a decision contrary to international law may constitute an act of complicity with the international organization for which responsibility would be borne both by the "voting" state and the organization. See on this point E. Butkiewicz, "The Premises of International Responsibility of Inter-Governmental Organizations" (1981–2) 11 Pol. Y.B. Int'l L. 117 at 125; Klein, *supra* note 10 at 468–70, 489–90; Amerasinghe, *supra* note 8 at 258–59.

12 Such a possibility was alluded to in passing by Special Rapporteur Giorgio Gaja in his first report on responsibility of international organizations presented to the International Law Commission (ILC). See *First Report on Responsibility of International Organizations by Mr. Giorgio Gaja, Special Rapporteur,* ILC, 55th Sess., UN Doc. A/CN.4/532 (May 2003), at 5, para. 8, and 17, para. 33.

13 Questions of attribution of conduct were recently debated within the ILC in its work on the controversial topic of responsibility of international organizations. At its 2,610th meeting, which was held on 4 June 2004, the commission considered the report of the chairman of the Drafting Committee and adopted on first reading the following draft articles: Article 4 (general rule on attribution of conduct to an international organization), Article 5 (conduct of organs or agents placed at the disposal of an international organization by a state or another international organization), Article 6 (excess of authority or contravention of instructions), and Article 7 (conduct acknowledged and adopted by an international organization as its own). The draft articles are accessible online at <http://www.un.org/law/ilc/sessions/56/56docs.htm> (date accessed: 31 July, 2004). See also *Second Report on Responsibility of International Organizations by Mr. Giorgio Gaja, Special Rapporteur,* ILC, 556th Sess., UN Doc. A/CN.4/541 (May 2004). Questions of attribution of responsibility will be addressed in the special rapporteur's third, fourth, and fifth reports.

certainly had a crucial impact on such basic foundational questions as the basis of obligation and notions of sovereignty and consent. It should be recalled that international law does not generally oblige states to adopt a certain conduct towards some abstract "common interest" but only in relation to the particular state or states to which a specific obligation under treaty or customary law is owed.[14] No doubt the relativism inherent in the traditional structures and processes of international law has been secured by a thorough and pervasive emphasis on strict consensualism. For Bruno Simma, this traditional morally and value-impoverished law has been "a severe obstacle standing in the way of stronger solidarity in international relations."[15] Yet the fact that mankind is in a position today to destroy itself has led to a rising awareness by states of their mutual interest in safeguarding and promoting those human values that belong to the very foundation of international law.[16] It also appears to have led to some kind of "acknowledgment that they all have a responsibility to the general global welfare"[17] — an idea reminiscent of Emile Durkeim's *conscience collective*.[18]

[14] B. Bollecker-Stern, *Le préjudice dans la théorie de la responsabilité internationale* (Paris: Pédone, 1973) at 50 ff, particularly at 58; P. Weil, "Towards Relative Normativity in International Law?" (1983) 77 A.J.I.L. 413 at 431; M. Virally, "Le Principe de Réciprocité en Droit International Contemporain" (1967) 122 Rec. des Cours 1 at 26; and C. Chinkin, *Third Parties in International Law* (Oxford: Clarendon Press, 1993) at 1–7.

[15] B. Simma, "Bilateralism and Community Interest in the Law of State Responsibility," in Y. Dinstein and M. Tabory, eds., *International Law at a Time of Perplexity: Essays in the Honor of S. Rosenne* (Dordrecht: Kluwer Academic Publishers, 1989) at 822 ff.

[16] R.-J. Dupuy, *La communauté internationale entre le mythe et l'histoire* (Paris: Economica, 1986) at 180; J. Charney, "Universal International Law" (1993) 87 A.J.I.L. 529 at 530 ff. Louis Henkin characterizes this development as a move from state values to human values and from a liberal state system to a welfare system. See L. Henkin, "Human Rights and State Sovereignty" (1995) 25 Ga. J. Int'l & Comp. L. 31 at 34–35.

[17] R. St.-J. Macdonald, "The Principle of Solidarity in Public International Law," in C. Dominicé, R. Patry, and C. Reymond, eds., *Études de droit international en l'honneur de Pierre Lalive* (Bâle: Francfort-sur-le-main, 1993) at 295, 301. See also G.M. Abi-Saab, "International Law and the International Community: The Long Road to Universality," in R. St-J. Macdonald, ed., *Essays in Honour of Wang Tieya* (Dordrecht: Martinus Nijhoff, 1994) at 97 ff.; and P. Allott, *Eunomia: New Order for a New World* (New York: Oxford University Press, 1990) at 254–57, 285–88.

[18] E. Durkheim, *The Division of Labour in Society* (New York: Free Press, 1964) at 73. A central tenet of Durkheim's work is that society is held together by certain shared sentiments and beliefs. The solidarity and cohesion of society is

The recognition that a small number of values and principles are common to every state is, of course, not novel in international law. From such values flow several concepts and mechanisms to foster community interests such as *jus cogens* norms. This notion became essential for the understanding of international law at a time when it was again realized that the individual and arbitrary agreement of states could not be the highest value in international society, as this would enhance dangers that strike at the very heart of the common goal of survival of mankind. It is posited on the underlying "Grotian" idea of a pattern for living broadly consonant with one universal precept accepted by all, even skeptics: the natural urge of all of us to self-preservation.[19] The common goal of preserving peace and protecting peoples and individuals presupposes then the recognition of some basic human and moral values and rules, which, in turn, determine the basic obligations of states, without or against their will, by the mere fact of them being members of international society.[20] Obligations *erga omnes* (literally, "towards all") are precisely of this kind.

One cannot overlook that there are prominent criticisms that have been voiced against this development. They have cautioned

---

threatened by a breach of these common sentiments, which consequently necessitates a collective response against the offender in order to repair and reinforce the injured conscience. This basic aspect of Durkheim's much broader theory helps explain to some extent the functioning of positive morality in international society.

[19] For a thoughtful account of Grotius's theory of self-preservation and human sociability in his work on the law of nations, see B. Kingsbury, "A Grotian Tradition of Theory and Practice?: Grotius, Law and Moral Skepticism in the Thought of Hedley Bull" (1997) 17 Q.L.R. 3.

[20] Alberico Gentili is celebrated for the pragmatic pluralism of his concept of an international society open to all organized political communities and based upon essential minimal rules for coexistence and the pursuit of common interests. This idea also finds echo in modern legal scholarship. See H. Bull, *The Anarchical Society: A Study of Order in World Politics*, 1st ed. (New York: Columbia University Press, 1977) at 13, 16–18, 22; T.M. Franck, *The Power of Legitimacy among Nations* (New York: Oxford University Press, 1990) at 189–94, 195–98; L. Henkin, "The Mythology of Sovereignty," in Macdonald, ed., *Essays in Honour of Wang Tieya*, *supra* note 17 at 354–55, 358–59; C. Tomuschat, "Obligations Arising for States without or against Their Will" (1993-IV) 241 Rec. des Cours 195 at 211; Charney, *supra* note 16 at 531; F. Tesón, "International Obligation and the Theory of Hypothetical Consent" (1990) 15 Yale J. Int'l L. 84 at 112–18; and A. Bleckmann, "General Theory of Obligations under Public International Law" (1996) 38 Germ. Y.B. Int'l L. 26 at 32.

that such "laws of higher normativity,"[21] which really prescribe ideal standards of state conduct rather than describe existing practice,[22] will channel friction between formally equal sovereigns and lead to "the dislocation of the normative structure of international law and the perversion of its functions."[23] Certainly, it is correct to assert that the diversity among states may lead to different understandings of the values and role of such "higher laws." Yet there also seems to be ground for optimism today regarding the development of common values that are by no means limited to expressing the interests of a few hegemonic states. Let us mention world peace, a healthy environment, economic integrity, and sustainable development. It is hardly conceivable that these values and interests could be understood as mere iterations of one particular "Western" bias. At the very least, they may serve as points of reference for developing a minimal set of common values, if indeed we are serious about making peace in international relations and the individual enjoyment of human rights a realistic prospect.[24]

THE DUTY TO PREVENT GENOCIDE: AN *ERGA OMNES* OBLIGATION PAR EXCELLENCE

It is in the *Case Concerning the Barcelona Traction, Light and Power Company* that the International Court of Justice (ICJ) drew the now

---

21 This language is borrowed from O. Schachter, "Entangled Treaty and Custom," in Dinstein and Tabory, *supra* note 15 at 733–35.

22 H. Chodosh, "Neither Treaty or Custom: The Emergence of Declarative International Law" (1991) 26 Tex. Int'l L.J. 87; B. Simma and P. Alston, "The Sources of Human Rights Law: Custom, Jus Cogens, and General Principles" (1992) 12 Aus. Y.B. Int'l L. 82 at 98–99; T. Meron, "On a Hierarchy of International Human Rights" (1986) 80 A.J.I.L. 1 at 19–20.

23 Weil, *supra* note 14 at 442. Weil, who can hardly be recognized as an enthusiastic supporter of the concept of obligations *erga omnes,* nevertheless acknowledged in his 1992 General Course at the Hague Academy of International Law that they have become a key component of the conceptual apparatus of contemporary international law, which is more receptive to respectable ethical considerations than traditional international law ever was. I share Chinkin's view that the fears and scepticism voiced by Weil are only justified "if international law is to be confined within the parameters of the statist model" and not "if it is to develop to regulate activities of States ... with respect to a broader range of subject-matter, reflecting international community (not exclusively statist) concerns and morality." See Chinkin, *supra* note 14 at 293.

24 J.A. Frowein, "Reactions by Not Directly Affected States to Breaches of Public International Law" (1994-IV) 248 Rec. des Cours 344 at 365; M. Ragazzi, *The Concept of International Obligations Erga Omnes* (Oxford: Oxford University Press,

well-known distinction between obligations of a state arising solely *vis-à-vis* another state and obligations "towards the international community as a whole" (*erga omnes*).[25] The latter were "by their very nature the concern of all States," and all states could be held to have a "legal interest" in their observance and in the protection of the substantive rights involved.[26] This language parallels the court's earlier Advisory Opinion in the *Case Concerning Reservations to the Convention on the Prevention and Punishment of the Crime of Genocide,* where accent was put on a "common interest" of states outside any "individual advantages" or "perfect contractual balance between rights and duties."[27] Despite the court's rather generous characterization of many obligations relating to genocide as applicable *erga omnes,*[28] it is astonishing to note the absence of any discussion in "mainstream" scholarship on how this concept can be operationalized outside the treaty regime set up by the Genocide Convention, specifically when it comes to the appropriate mode(s) of response to its breach.[29] The recent completion of the International Law

---

1997) at 187; Tomuschat, *supra* note 20 at 214–15; W. Jenks, "The Will of the World Community as the Basis of Obligation in International Law," in J. Basdevant, ed., *Hommage d'une Génération de Juristes au Président Basdevant* (Paris: A. Pédone, 1960) 1 at 15.

[25] *Case Concerning the Barcelona Traction, Light and Power Company (Belgium* v. *Spain),* Second Phase, [1970] I.C.J. Rep. 3 at 32, paras. 33, 34 [*Barcelona Traction* case].

[26] *Ibid.* For an analysis of compliance with, and enforcement of, these obligations, see C.J. Tams, *Enforcement of Erga Omnes Obligations* (Cambridge: Cambridge University Press, 2005); K. Zemanek, "New Trends in the Enforcement of Erga Omnes Obligations" (2000) 4 Max. Plank Y.B. UN L. 1.

[27] *Case Concerning Reservations to the Convention on the Prevention and Punishment of the Crime of Genocide,* Advisory Opinion, [1951] I.C.J. Rep. 15 at 46–47 (dissenting opinion of Judges Guerrero, McNair, Read, and Hsu Mo) [*Reservations to the Genocide Convention* case].

[28] These are the prohibition against the commission of genocide as well as the obligations of prevention and punishment. See *Barcelona Traction* case, *supra* note 25 and the *Case Concerning the Application of the Convention on the Prevention and Punishment of the Crime of Genocide (Bosnia and Herzegovina* v. *Yugoslavia (Serbia and Montenegro)) (Preliminary Objections),* Judgment of 11 July 1996, [1996] I.C.J. Rep. 4 at 24–25, para. 31. See also Judge Oda's declaration, *ibid.* at 35–36, para. 4.

[29] The convention recognizes the impact on state interests of a violation purely internal to one state, yet fails to provide effective enforcement mechanisms for the prevention of genocide. Taken literally, this would lead to the absurd conclusion that the contracting parties' obligations remain unenforceable. Although the matter is still highly debated within academic circles and the ILC, human rights treaties generally have not been viewed as "self-contained regimes" and

Commission's (ILC) work on the codification of the law of state responsibility has however given impetus to a careful examination of this question.

GENOCIDE PREVENTION REVISITED UNDER THE LAW
OF STATE RESPONSIBILITY

The point has of course been long known to international lawyers, who marveled at the idea: *erga omnes* obligations entail the corresponding right of every other state bound by the same customary or conventional rule to take measures against a state breaching the most important community interests.[30] The exact contours and parameters of this right remained however uncertain, by and large due to the unwillingness of states to commit themselves to clear-cut definitions. The existence of a right of "not directly affected states" to take action in the wake of internal human rights abuses has now been "officially" endorsed by the ILC.[31] According

---

therefore do not exclude *ab initio* recourse to general international law to sanction their breach through inter-state measures. See on this point *Study on the "Function and Scope of the Lex Specialis Rule and the Question of 'Self-Contained Regimes'": Preliminary Report by Mr. Martti Koskenniemi, Chairman of the Study Group,* ILC, 56th Sess., UN Doc. ILC (LVI)/SG/FIL/CCCRD.1/Add.1 at 27–28 [unpublished text; on file with author]; *Fourth Report on State Responsibility by Mr. Gaetano Arangio-Ruiz, Special Rapporteur,* UN Doc. A/CN.4/444/Add. 1–3, reprinted in *Yearbook of the International Law Commission 1992,* vol. 2, Part. 1, paras. 97–127, New York, 1995, UN Doc. A/CN.4/SER.A/1992/Add.1 (Part 1); A. Cassese, *International Law* (Oxford: Oxford University Press; 2001) at 208; M.T. Kamminga, *Inter-State Accountability for Violations of Human Rights* (Philadelphia: University of Pennsylvania Press, 1992) at 179–83; B. Simma, "Self-Contained Regimes" (1985) 16 Neth. Y.B. Int'l L. 111 at 129–35; Frowein, "Reactions by Not Directly Affected States," *supra* note 24 at 400.

30 See C. Dominicé, "The International Responsibility of States for Breaches of Multilateral Obligations" (1999) 10 E.J.I.L. 353 at 354–55, 359; J. Crawford, P. Bodeau, and J. Peel, "The ILC's Draft Articles on State Responsibility: Toward Completion of a Second Reading" (2000) 94:4 A.J.I.L. 660 at 672–73.

31 See State Responsibility: Titles and Texts of the Draft Articles on Responsibility of States for Internationally Wrongful Acts Adopted by the Drafting Committee on Second Reading, ILC, 53rd Sess., UN Doc. A/CN.4/L.602/Rev.1 (26 July 2001), Part III, Articles 48(1)(b) and 54 [Draft Articles on Second Reading]. Article 54 is a savings clause and represents the compromise reached within the commission in view of the reluctance to include a provision expressly recognizing and regulating the practice of countermeasures in the collective interest. Article 48(1)(b) (to which Article 54 refers) deals with the invocation of responsibility in the collective interest, in particular, with respect to breaches of human rights obligations owed to the international community as a whole, giving effect to the court's dictum in

to State Responsibility: Titles and Texts of the Draft Articles on Responsibility of States for Internationally Wrongful Acts Adopted by the Drafting Committee on Second Reading (Draft Articles on State Responsibility), which were adopted in 2001, such action is strictly targeted towards conduct amounting to a "serious breach of an obligation arising under a peremptory norm of general international law."[32] New Article 40(2) defines a "serious breach" as one involving a gross or systematic failure by the responsible state to fulfil the obligation.[33] This definition implies that isolated or minor infringements that are not intentional and do not reveal "a consistent pattern of reliably attested violations of fundamental human rights"[34] do not authorize enforcement measures.[35] This rule, we are told, is consistent with state practice, despite its admittedly sparse and embryonic nature.[36] The main reason for limiting

---

the *Barcelona Traction* case. See on this point *Third Report on State Responsibility by Mr. James Crawford, Special Rapporteur,* ILC, 52nd Sess., UN Doc. A/CN.4/507/ Adds.4 (2000) at 391–94 [*Third Report of James Crawford*]; D. Alland, "Countermeasures of General Interest" (2002) 13:5 E.J.I.L. 1221 at 1232–33.

32 Draft Articles on Second Reading, *supra* note 31 at Article 40(1).

33 The commentary indicates that "gross" refers to the intensity of the violation or its effects, meaning flagrant violations. A "systematic" violation is one carried out in an organized and deliberate way. See *Report of the International Law Commission on the Work of Its Fifty-Third Session,* UN GAOR, 56th Sess., Supp. No. 10, UN Doc. A/56/10 (November 2001) at 285, para. 8 [*Report on Fifty-Third Session*]. No procedures are indicated in the draft for determining when such a breach has occurred.

34 This language is borrowed from the *Procedure for Dealing with Communications Relating to Violations of Human Rights and Fundamental Freedoms,* 27 May 1970, ECOSOC Resolution 1503 (XLVIII), 48 UN ESCOR, Supp. (No. 1A) 8, UN Doc. E/4832/Add.1 (1970).

35 *Report of the International Law Commission on the Work of Its Thirty-Seventh Session,* UN Doc. A/40/10, reprinted in *Yearbook of the International Law Commission 1985,* vol. 2, Part 2 at 27, New York, 1986, UN Doc. A/CN.4/SER.A/1985/Add.1 (Part 2). See also *Responsibilities of States: Commentaries and Observations by Governments,* ILC, 50th Sess., UN Doc. A/CN.4/488 (1998) at 95–102; *Sixth Report on the Content, Forms and Degrees of International Responsibility (Part 2 of the Draft Articles),* by Mr. Willem Riphagen, Special Rapporteur, UN Doc. A/CN.4/389 and Corr. 1, reprinted in *Yearbook of the International Law Commission 1985,* vol. 2, Part 1, commentary on Art. 5(2)(e)(iii), New York, UN Doc. A/40/100 (1985); M. Akehurst, "Reprisals by Third States" (1970) 44 Brit. Y.B. Int'l L. 1 at 15; B. Conforti, "Cours Général de Droit International Public" (1988-IV) 212 Rec. des Cours 9 at 196–201; Kamminga, *supra* note 29 at 168–71.

36 *Third Report of James Crawford, supra* note 31 at 391-400. Citing no fewer than eight incidents, Special Rapporteur Crawford argues that state practice regarding

reaction to these cases appears to be a desire to defend the normative integrity of the international legal system against patterns of
behaviour that go against its most "fundamental" tenets, whatever
these may be.[37]

It is noteworthy that the ILC deliberately eliminated any reference in the new draft to obligations "owed to the international community as a whole" (or *erga omnes* obligations) from Part 2, Chapter
III, on the "Content of the International Responsibility of a State"
(Articles 40 and 41),[38] confining them to the following provisions in
Part 3, Chapter I, on "Implementation of the International Responsibility of a State" (namely Articles 42(1)(b), 48(1)(b), and 54,
which refers to Article 48(1)(b)). Though considered from different angles, one from the viewpoint of scope and priority and the
other from the viewpoint of content,[39] obligations "arising under a
peremptory norm of general international law" mentioned in Article 40 are of course equally "owed to the international community as a whole," as mentioned in Article 48(1)(b). Yet this in no

---

collective countermeasures suggests the following observations: (1) no distinction based on the legal source (conventional or customary) of the collective
obligation that was violated appears to exist, and (2) responses are generally
made only in opposition to severe violations of collective obligations, notably
breaches of human rights obligations owed to the international community as a
whole that affect only the nationals of the responsible state. See also E. Zoller,
Peaceful Unilateral Remedies: An Analysis of Countermeasures (New York: Transnational
Publishers, 1984) at 117; L.-A. Sicilianos, *Les reactions décentralisées à l'illicite* (Paris:
L.G.D.J., 1990) at 110–75; O. Yousif Elagab, *The Legality of Non-Forcible Counter-
Measures in International Law* (Oxford: Clarendon Press, 1988) at 56–57; H. Thierry,
"L'Évolution du droit international. Cours général de droit international public"
(1990-II) 222 Rec. des Cours 9 at 104–7; P.-M. Dupuy, "Observations sur la pra-
tique récente des sanctions de l'illicite" (1983) 87 Rev. D.I.P. 505 at 537–38;
Frowein, "Reactions by Not Directly Affected States," *supra* note 24 at 416–20.

[37] *Report on Fifty-Third Session*, *supra* note 33 at 283, para. 3, and 285, para. 8. See
also M. Spinedi, "From One Codification to Another: Bilateralism and
Multilateralism in the Genesis of the Law of Treaties and the Law of State Responsibility" (2002) 13:5 E.J.I.L. 1099; G. Abi-Saab, "The Uses of Article 19"
(1999) 10:2 E.J.I.L. 339 at 350.

[38] Article 40 of the new draft thus seems to have moved some distance from its
immediate predecessor, Article 41, which was aligned very faithfully on the old
Article 19 of the draft produced by then Special Rapporteur Roberto Ago in
the late 1970s, terming a "serious breach" the breach of an "international obligation so essential for the protection of fundamental interests of the international community."

[39] See *Report on Fifty-Third Session*, *supra* note 33 at 281, para. (7) (Commentary to
Part Two, Chapter III) and the *Third Report of James Crawford*, *supra* note 31, at 7,
para. 374.

way justifies the absolute normative equivalence that the ILC seems to have set up between the one and the other. Indeed, "obligations *erga omnes* and those resulting from peremptory norms form two concentric circles, the first of which is larger than the second," and confusing them risks harming the "conceptual clarity of the whole system of 'serious' breaches of international law."[40] In particular, one is left guessing today whether the right of all states to invoke responsibility against a perpetrator state under Article 48(1)(b) is concerned only with the fact that the obligation breached was *erga omnes* or whether in the ILC's conception the generality of this right to action presupposes that the obligation *erga omnes* in question also has a peremptory nature.[41] The matter is all the more confusing since the ICJ recently assimilated the consequences of violations of *erga omnes* obligations to those of a "serious breach of an obligation arising under a peremptory norm of general international law" under draft Article 41(2) on state responsibility, namely the duties of "not-directly affected" states not to recognize the illegal situation brought about by a "serious breach" and not to give assistance to the wrongdoer.[42]

Inadequacy of the Concept of "Serious Breaches" for Prevention

The question raised above becomes highly relevant in a discussion on the *prevention* of genocide insofar as the only *erga omnes* obligation relating to genocide recognized to date as having a peremptory

[40] L.-A. Sicilianos, "The Classification of Obligations and the Multilateral Dimension of the Relations of International Responsibility" (2002) 13(5) E.J.I.L. 1127 at 1137.

[41] This question arises from the confusion created by the commission's view that "the core cases of obligations *erga omnes* are those non-derogable obligations of a general character which arise either directly under general international law or under generally accepted multilateral treaties (e.g. in the field of human rights). They are virtually coextensive with peremptory obligations (arising under norms of *jus cogens*). For if a particular obligation can be set aside or displaced as between two States, it is hard to see how that obligation is owed to the international community as a whole."
See *Report on Fifty-Third Session, supra* note 33 at 281, para. (7) (Commentary to Article 48) and the *Third Report of James Crawford, supra* note 31 at 49, para. 106(a).

[42] See *Legal Consequences of the Construction of a Wall in the Occupied Palestinian Territory*, Advisory Opinion, [2004] I.C.J. Rep. 136 at 200, para. 159, accessible online at <http://www.icj-cij.org/icjwww/idocket/imwp/imwpframe.htm> (date accessed: 29 May 2005) [*Legal Consequences of the Construction of a Wall*]. See also the separate opinion of Judge Kooijmans (at 231, para. 41).

nature is the prohibition against its commission. It deserves a particular development here since the field of application *ratione personae* of an obligation *erga omnes* — towards all — appears to be confused with the binding force of the rule under which it is said to "arise" — the non-derogable nature of a peremptory obligation.[43] From a policy viewpoint, it would appear somewhat artificial to oppose, in terms of illegal and legal, enforcement action to *prevent the commission* of a "serious breach"[44] to reactive measures to *ask for its cessation*.[45] This is a semantical distinction and not an ontological

---

[43] The problem emerges from the transposition of a concept relating to the theory of nullity of *legal* acts — non-derogability — to the area of wrongfulness of "material" *conduct*. This convergence has given rise to an equivalence that I cannot dwell on in this article. Suffice it to say that it is not the bindingness of the norms that countermeasures in the collective interest would defend but the essential nature of the principles they contain. This has led commentators such as Alland to argue that when it comes to peremptory norms, countermeasures of general interest could not possibly look like suitable consequences. See D. Alland, *Justice privée et ordre juridique international. Étude théorique des contre-mesures en droit international public* (Paris: Pédone, 1994) at para. 290.

[44] Or, as its predecessor was called, an "international crime of state." As Eric Wyler has indeed been able to verify, there is essentially only a "cosmetic" or terminological modification between yesterday's "crime" on the one hand and, on the other, the serious breach of an obligation arising under a peremptory norm of international law in the final text of the draft articles. The confirmation of the identity between the two concepts is to be found in the fact that we remain attached to a combination of two aggravating factors, one which Wyler calls "circumstantial severity" and having to do with the perpetrator's conduct, and the other specifically normative and called "substantive severity." See E. Wyler, "From 'State Crime' to Responsibility for 'Serious Breaches of Obligations under Peremptory Norms of General International Law'" (2002) 13:2 E.J.I.L. 1147 at 1151–54; and also A. Pellet, "Le nouveau projet de la C.D.I. sur la responsabilité de l'État pour fait internationalement illicite: 'requiem' pour le crime?" in L. Chand Vohrah, ed., *Man's Inhumanity to Man: Essays on International Law in Honour of Antonio Cassese* (The Hague: Kluwer, 2003) at 655.

[45] The commentary to Draft Article 40 suggests that "serious breaches" include aggression, slavery, genocide, racial discrimination, apartheid, torture, and violation of "the basic rules of international humanitarian law" and of the right to self-determination — a list in almost all respects identical to that of the former category of "international crimes." See *Report on Fifty-Third Session*, *supra* note 33 at 283–84. Dinah Shelton has suggested reservations about the prominence given to peremptory norms in Article 40 rather than to obligations *erga omnes*, whose wider ambit would have allowed for a broader range of claims to be made. See D. Shelton, "Righting Wrongs: Reparations in the Articles on State Responsibility" (2002) 96:4 A.J.I.L. 833 at 841–44. Indeed, the ICJ's dictum in the *Barcelona Traction* case, *supra* note 25 at para. 34, that obligations *erga omnes* result, *inter alia*, "from the principles and rules concerning the basic rights of the human person, *including* protection from slavery and racial discrimination" clearly suggests that

one, for in the end both types of measures are aimed at safeguarding lives in imminent danger, which is an integral component of prevention. This was not however the view adopted by the ILC in 1996, according to which only certain grave violations of human rights such as genocide could qualify as "international crimes," thus giving rise to a special regime of aggravated responsibility and the resort to countermeasures by all other states.[46] The entitlement to react was thus bound up specifically (and only) with the commission of a crime — a concept defined explicitly in terms of substantive severity.[47] This amounted implicitly to saying that in the case of breaches of obligations, whether conventional or customary,

---

there are several other principles and rules relating to human rights that give rise to this type of obligations. The commission's emphasis on peremptory norms certainly restricts the domain within which the invocation of state responsibility in the general interest will operate in the future.

[46] But as Simma validly argues, "if we take the concept of obligations *erga omnes* at face value, the breach of such obligations ought to lead to injury on the part of all other States without the 'crimes' concept having to come into play." See B. Simma, "From Bilateralism to Community Interest in International Law" (1994-VI) 250 Rec. des Cours 234 at 314 and from the same author, "International Crimes: Injury and Countermeasures." Comments on Part 2 of the ILC Work on State Responsibility," in A. Cassese, J.H.H. Weiler, and M. Spinedi, eds., *International Crimes of State. A Critical Analysis of the ILC's Draft Article 19 on State Responsibility* (Berlin and New York: Walter de Gruyter, 1989) at 299.

[47] If in order to inflict injury upon all states and thus lead to the taking of countermeasures, breaches of obligations *erga omnes* have to assume the format of "international crimes," those obligations whose breach does not fall within this category nor entails any material injury in the traditional bilateralist sense would presumably remain unenforceable. Thus, for instance, if a state commits over a long period of time sporadic but flagrant human rights violations revealing a state policy to wipe out an entire ethnic group, but which fall short of the critical "quantity and quality" threshold of genocide, the concept of "international crime" would bar other states from taking countermeasures immediately to enforce compliance. The substitution of this concept with that of "serious breaches of obligations under peremptory norms of general international law" represents the compromise reached by the commission between reservations about collective countermeasures in the general interest and the inappropriateness of allowing gross breaches of human rights to continue without allowing any state to intervene. See on this last point *First Report on State Responsibility by Mr. James Crawford, Special Rapporteur,* UN Doc. ILC, 50th Sess., UN Doc. A/CN.4/490/ Add.2 (1998) at para. 43, 61; Crawford, Bodeau, and Peel, *supra* note 30 at 672–73 and, more generally, C. Annacker, "The Legal Regime of Erga Omnes Obligations in International Law" (1993–4) 46 Austrian J. Pub. & Int'l L. 131 at 148, 157. This development in the law of responsibility certainly avoids the problematic terminology of "crimes," but not the substantive implications of limiting reactions to this category of breaches.

established for the protection of fundamental human rights that
constituted an "ordinary" wrongful act, the responsibility relationship was established exclusively with the state directly injured.[48] Yet
in cases of human rights violations that have not reached the "gravity threshold" of genocide,[49] no such state simply exists.

Whether the commission's position has undergone any significant change under the new draft is not entirely clear. This is particularly so since the criterion of "severity" of the breach, though
appearing in Articles 40 and 41, which concern specifically violations of peremptory norms, is by contrast absent from Articles 48
and 54, which concern obligations *erga omnes*. It could be argued
that the fact that "not directly affected states" are recognized today
as having the right to react to "serious breaches of obligations under peremptory norms of international law" does not depend exclusively on the *quantitative* seriousness of the wrongful act, which
the ILC's commentary unfortunately seems to suggest,[50] but rather
on the type of obligation infringed — one "arising under a peremptory norm"[51] — and the nature of the violation, which has to

---

[48] This interpretation is confirmed by the consideration that the majority of the
ILC members were of the opinion at the time that general international law
prohibited only gross violations of human rights (genocide, apartheid, slavery,
and so on). Breach of customary obligations concerning the protection of fundamental human rights accordingly coincided for them with the category of
international crimes.

[49] For an analysis of the "threshold of gravity," see J. Salmon, "Les obligations quan-
titatives et l'illicéité," in L. Boisson de Chazournes and V. Gowlland-Debbas, eds.,
*The International Legal System in Quest of Equity and Universality/L'Ordre juridique
international, un système en quête d'équité et d'universalité, Liber Amicorum Georges Abi-
Saab* (The Hague: Kluwer Law International, 2002) at 311 ff.

[50] This, at least, is the impression one is left with when reading the ILC commentary to draft Article 40, which states: "The word 'serious' signifies that *a certain
order of magnitude of violation is necessary* in order not to trivialize the breach and
it is not intended to suggest that any violation of these obligations is not serious
or is somehow excusable. But relatively less serious cases of breach of peremptory norms can be envisaged, and it is necessary to limit the scope of this chapter
to the more serious or systematic breaches." See *Report on Fifty-Third Session, supra* note 33 at 285, para. 7 [emphasis added]. It really does not help the special
rapporteur to argue that this distinction between serious and less serious cases
of breach of peremptory norms is supported by state practice, especially when
no evidence of such practice is given.

[51] It is noteworthy that in its commentary on Article 19, which it adopted in 1976,
the ILC had expressly stated its understanding "that the category of international
obligations admitting of no derogation [which can be said to "arise under a peremptory norm of international law" as well as being of an *erga omnes*

be "serious."[52] Breaches of human rights obligations are "serious" because of the criteria adopted, whether the "gross" nature of the breach is measured by the yardstick of its intensity, its damaging effects, its "systematic" (organized and deliberate) nature, or a combination of these.[53] In this regard, the concept of "serious breaches of obligations so essential for the protection of fundamental interests of the international community" in Article 41 of the 2000 draft would have been preferable as it referred to a single concept that was used to cover cases concerning both states that had been designated as "injured" and states that, although not "injured" in the classical sense, nonetheless had a right to act in defence of these obligations.

Unless we assume that the taking of preventive measures is entirely ill conceived under the new Draft Articles on State Responsibility, it would be unreasonable as a matter of legal principle to wait until a state breached its obligation not to commit genocide

---

nature] is much broader than the category of obligations whose breach is necessarily an international crime," the latter being the precursor of the new category of "serious breaches." See *Yearbook of the International Law Commission 1976*, vol. 2, Part 2, New York, 1976, 118 at 119–20. See also G. Gaja, "Should All References to International Crimes Disappear from the ILC Draft Articles on State Responsibility?" (1999) 10:2 E.J.I.L. 365 at 367; Ragazzi, *supra* note 24 at 189 ff. This position was to change, however, in the 2001 draft where the ILC considers that the serious breach of *any* obligation arising under a peremptory rule entails a special regime of responsibility, including rights and obligations for all states.

52 These are in fact the two conditions identified by the ILC to distinguish between "ordinary" and "serious" breaches. See *Report on Fifty-Third Session, supra* note 33 at 282, para. (1). It is noteworthy that it was already the commission's view in 1976 that infringements relating to human rights had to, in order to give rise to a special regime of aggravated responsibility, be particularly grave in the specific case, that is, a circumstantial gravity. The criteria indicated by the commission (which were cumulative) related to the intensity and repetition of the breach: the breach had to be "massive," "flagrant," "persistent," "systematic," and "large scale." See *Fifth Report of Roberto Ago, supra* note 5 at 53, para. 150 and the *Yearbook of the International Law Commission 1976*, vol. 2, Part 2, New York, 1976, at 110, para. 34 and 120, paras. 70–71.

53 My contention appears to be in line with the commission's own determination in the 2001 draft that the scope and number of individual violations is but one of the factors that may establish the "seriousness" of a breach, the others being the intent to violate the norm and the gravity of consequences of the violations for the victims. See on this point *Report on Fifty-Third Session, supra* note 33 at 285, para. 8. Thus, the "severity" of the breach now apparently covers both "substantial severity" and "circumstantial severity" and for infringements of human rights to reach the threshold of "severity," they must be particularly grave also in the latter sense of the term.

before taking enforcement measures.[54] The unfortunate assumption that the legal determination of genocide must precede any opportunity to respond is what led in 1994 to the appalling spectacle of US State Department spokespersons and UN officials using verbal gymnastics to avoid using the term "genocide" while hundreds of thousands of Rwandans were being slaughtered. Genocide first occurs on a small scale, as if to see if the rest of the world will do anything. For intervention to be effective, whatever form it ultimately takes, it must come months before full-scale genocide begins, not after.[55] Since the system of aggravated responsibility for "serious breaches of obligations arising under a peremptory norm of general international law" was clearly aimed above all at guaranteeing international legality, the emergence of obligations regarded as being essential by the international community should imply the special treatment of any important breach of such obligations in order to safeguard this embryonic international *ordre public.*

Ambiguity Surrounding State Cooperation to Counter "Serious Breaches"

Genocide prevention clashes with the course set by the ILC on the codification of the law of state responsibility in another important way. It raises the question, which was noted in passing by

---

54 The suitability of countermeasures as preventive measures that ought to be conceived as instrumental appears to have been emphasized by the ICJ in its valuable discussion in the *Case Concerning the Gabčíkovo-Nagymaros Project (Hungary* v. *Slovakia),* [1997] I.C.J. Rep. 7 at para. 87. The court referred, in passing, to "one other condition for the lawfulness of a countermeasure, namely that its purpose must be to induce the wrongdoing state to comply with its obligations under international law, and that the measure must therefore be reversible." Thus, countermeasures are part of a "dynamic" process of obtaining cessation and reparation for wrongful conduct; they do not involve freestanding rights. This is a useful clarification, and like Part 2 of the new Draft Articles on State Responsibility, completely leaves out questions of punishment or reprisal. See on this point, G.M. Abi-Saab, "De la Sanction en Droit International: Essai de Clarification," in J. Makarczyk, *Theory of International Law at the Threshold of the Twenty-First Century: Essays in Honour of Krzysztof Skubiszewski* (The Hague: Kluwer Law International, 1991) at 67–70; P.-M. Dupuy, "The International Law of State Responsibility: Revolution or Evolution?" (1989) 11 Mich. J. Int'l L. 96; Elagab, *supra* note 36 at 46; O. Schachter, "International Law in Theory and Practice. General Course of Public International Law" 178 (1982) Rec. des Cours 9 at 182–84; M. Spinedi, "International Crimes of State: The Legislative History," in Cassese, Weiler, and Spinedi, *supra* note 46 at 71–77.

55 See generally A.J. Kuperman, *The Limits of Humanitarian Intervention: Genocide in Rwanda* (Washington, DC: Brookings Institution Press, 2001).

Special Rapporteur James Crawford in his fourth report,[56] of the
role of regional and international organizations in authorizing or
coordinating states' responses to "serious breaches of obligations
arising under peremptory norms."

Here, two conceptually different visions have traditionally con-
fronted each other in the literature. The so-called "institutionalist"
view holds that international institutions bear sole responsibility
for community enforcement of such obligations. Accordingly, the
United Nations would be the only appropriate forum within which
to take measures to prevent genocide.[57] One might take the following two jurisprudential examples to illustrate this point. In the *Case
Concerning East Timor (Portugal v. Australia),*[58] the ICJ remained non-
persuaded that the UN organs had acted forcefully through resolutions to define and protect the rights of the Timorese people.[59]
The court appears — at least implicitly — to have taken the view
that enforcement of *erga omnes* obligations is a collective one acting
through the United Nations,[60] although in finding that the Security Council had not acted in an imperative fashion towards East
Timor it suggested that the concept is, at best, of limited value and,

56 *Fourth Report on State Responsibility by Mr. James Crawford, Special Rapporteur,* UN
Doc. ILC, 53rd Sess., UN Doc. A/CN.4/517 (2001) at 27–28, paras. 71–73 [*Fourth
Report of James Crawford*].

57 It was thus, on the one hand, arguments associated with the logic of the system
(the response of the "organized" international community to acts seriously threatening its fundamental values) and, on the other, a finding drawn from the practice of UN organs in response to situations constituting international crimes,
that led then Special Rapporteur Riphagen to conclude that the consequences
of international crimes could be dealt with only within the framework of the
structures and mechanisms of the UN. See *Fourth Report on the Content, Forms and
Degrees of International Responsibility (Part 2 of the Draft Articles), by Mr. Willem
Riphagen, Special Rapporteur,* UN Doc. A/CN.4/SER.A/1982/Add.1, reprinted
in *Yearbook of the International Law Commission 1983,* vol. 2, Part 1, New York, 1982
at 11, para. 60 [*Fourth Report of Willem Riphagen*].

58 *Case Concerning East Timor (Portugal v. Australia),* Judgement of 30 June 1995,
[1995] I.C.J. Rep. 90 [*East Timor* case].

59 *Ibid.* at 103–4. Thus, in the absence of such binding resolutions imposing an
obligation on states not to recognize Indonesian authority over East Timor, Australia was under no obligation to refrain from dealings with Indonesia over East
Timor.

60 Annacker, *supra* note 47 at 139. For a view that considers the UN to be the sole
recipient of *erga omnes* rights of protection, see A.J.J. De Hoogh, "The Relationship between *Jus Cogens,* Obligations *Erga Omnes* and International Crimes: Peremptory Norms in Perspective" (1991) 42 Austrian J. Pub. & Int'l L. 183 at
208–11.

at worst, ineffectual.[61] More recently, after noting that many of Israel's obligations in the occupied Palestinian territories under human rights and humanitarian law and various United Nations resolutions had an *erga omnes* character,[62] the court invited the UN organs to consider what further action was required to bring an end to the illegal situation.[63] The case is, however, of limited value as the court did not issue a formal ruling on this point. Rather, it found (in a surprisingly axiomatic way) that a violation of *erga omnes* obligations entailed an obligation for third states party to the fourth Geneva Convention Relative to the Protection of Civilian Persons in Time of War[64] to ensure compliance by Israel with international humanitarian law.[65] It is thus the very vulnerability and essentially

[61] P.D. Coffman, "Obligations Erga Omnes and the Absent Third State" (1996) 39 Germ. Y.B. Int'l L. 285 at 306–7, 314–15. A tentative explanation why the court adopted its reasoning with respect to the enforcement of *erga omnes* obligations may lie in a lack of consensus over the exact contours and scope of the right of self-determination generally and its relationship to other norms of international law such as non-intervention, territorial integrity, and the prohibition against genocide. A better approach, I would suggest, was adopted by the ICJ in the *Namibia* case where it observed that the termination of the mandate and the declaration of the illegality of South Africa's presence in Namibia were "opposable to all states in the sense of barring *erga omnes* the legality of a situation which is maintained in violation of international law." See *Legal Consequences for States of the Continued Presence of South Africa in Namibia (South-West Africa) Notwithstanding Security Council Resolution 276 (1970)*, Advisory Opinion, [1971] I.C.J. Rep. 16 at 56 [*Namibia* case].

[62] *Legal Consequences of the Construction of a Wall, supra* note 42 at 199, paras. 155–57.

[63] *Ibid.* at 200, para. 160 and 202, para. 163(3)E. If one reads the object of the request for the Advisory Opinion as a need for the General Assembly to obtain assistance from the Court for the proper exercise of its functions under the UN Charter, it is only logical that a specific paragraph of the *dispositif* is addressed to the General Assembly. That the same paragraph is also addressed to the Security Council is logical as well in view of its primary responsibility in matters of international peace and security.

[64] Geneva Convention Relative to the Protection of Civilian Persons in Time of War, 12 August 1949, 6 U.S.T. 3516, 75 U.N.T.S. 287 [Fourth Geneva Convention].

[65] *Legal Consequences of the Construction of a Wall, supra* note 42 at 200, para. 159. Two judges of the court took issue with this aspect of the court's opinion. At para. 40 of his separate opinion, Judge Kooijmans questioned why a violation of an obligation *erga omnes* by one state should necessarily lead to an obligation for third states. Judge Higgins was more categorical, arguing at para. 37 of her opinion that the concept deals with the very specific issue of jurisdictional *locus standi* and had nothing to do with imposing substantive obligations on third parties to a case. While leaving resolution of this question for another day, it must at least be conceded that the cogency of the court's reasoning on this point is rather

fluctuating nature of the United Nations's commitment to the defence of collective interests and the inconsistent way it condemns some breaches of obligations arising under peremptory norms while ignoring others of equal severity that stifles the possibility of pursuing their enforcement exclusively through the institutional framework.[66]

On the opposite side of the scale, it has been argued that the right to ensure fulfilment of these obligations should first and foremost be attributed to individual states, vested individually or collectively, considering the increasing failures of the Security Council to channel the political will to take action in such cases.[67] Such institutional enforcement is also said to be too ineffective and unrealistic given the decentralized nature of international society.[68] Yet for an unbearably long time there simply did not arise any tangible, operational "sense of community" that reacted forcefully enough to the unspeakable atrocities committed in the Former Yugoslavia, Kosovo, and Rwanda. The scanty interventions by

---

weak, for the obligation of states to "ensure respect" for humanitarian law is not a legal consequence of the violation of *erga omnes* obligations but rather a duty flowing from Article I of the Fourth Geneva Convention of 1949.

66 See N.H. Jorgensen, *The Responsibility of States for International Crimes* (Oxford: Oxford University Press, 2000) at 137, 213, and 218. The recognition of the exclusive power of the Security Council to establish the existence of a serious breach would prove particularly problematic in this connection, since it would inevitably imply that situations presenting all the constituent features of such a breach might no longer be treated as such because of an abstention of the council.

67 Annacker, *supra* note 47 at 140–41, 157–61. Thus, according to the late Philip Jessup, "it would seem that the only possible argument against the substitution of collective measures under the Security Council for individual measures by a single state would be the inability of the international organization to act with the speed requisite to preserve life." See P.C. Jessup, *A Modern Law of Nations: An Introduction* (New York: MacMillan, 1948) at 170. See also G. Gaja, "Obligations Erga Omnes, International Crimes and Jus Cogens: A Tentative Analysis of Three Related Concepts," in Weiler, Cassese, and Spinedi, *supra* note 46 at 273–74, and particularly footnote 17.

68 During the debates that preceded the adoption of the Vienna Convention on the Law of Treaties, 23 May 1969, 1155 U.N.T.S. 331, Georg Schwarzenberger had invoked the idea that the enforcement of peremptory norms in the legal order was not realistic since international society was deprived of a supranational authority that could sanction them. See G. Schwarzenberger, "International *Jus Cogens?*" (1965) 43 Tex. L. Rev. 455 at 467–69. See also Annacker, *supra* note 47 at 148, 160; C. Gray, *Judicial Remedies in International Law* (Oxford: Oxford University Press, 1987) at 212–15; Gaja, "Obligations Erga Omnes, International Crimes and Jus Cogens," *supra* note 67 at 273.

Tanzania in Uganda in 1979 to end Idi Amin's reign, by India in East Pakistan in 1971 to protect the Bengalis, and by Vietnam in Cambodia to overthrow Pol Pot's regime in 1978–9 demonstrate that other than altruism or self-interest, there is simply no incentive for states today to take effective action when a single state oppresses its own citizens.[69] This lack of motivation is further exacerbated by the concern over the "international vigilantism" inherent in allowing each state to unilaterally determine the existence of situations involving human rights violations regardless of any subjective material injury[70] — the hazards of which, though considerable, nonetheless do not seem necessarily greater than the arbitrary exercise of discretionary power by the Security Council.

Perhaps surprisingly, neither of these two positions appears to correspond to the current state of international law on the subject. It should be noted that an earlier version of the 1996 Draft Articles on State Responsibility permitted resort in such cases to individual countermeasures by all states, quite conveniently labelled "injured,"[71] subject however to very complicated and politically unacceptable

[69] T.J. Farer, "An Inquiry into the Legitimacy of Humanitarian Intervention," in L. Fisler-Damrosch and D.J. Scheffer, *Law and Force in the New International Order* (Boulder: Westview Press, 1991) at 192; A. Cassese, "La Communauté Internationale et le Génocide," in D. Bardonnet *et al.*, eds., *Le droit international au service de la paix, de la justice et du développement. Mélanges Michel Virally* (Paris: Pédone, 1991) at 187–92.

[70] D.N. Hutchinson, "Solidarity and Breaches of Multilateral Treaties" (1988) Brit. Y.B. Int'l L. 151 at 202 (quoting Bruno Simma for the term "a sort of international vigilantism." See Simma, "International Crimes: Injury and Countermeasures," *supra* note 46 at 299). It could be argued that to guard against the possibility that a state might be subjected to countermeasures based on a spurious legal claim that it has breached an obligation toward the international community as a whole, the chapter on countermeasures, in new Article 54, has limited the right of any state entitled to invoke the responsibility of another state under Article 48(1) to "lawful measures." The ILC commentaries indicate that the reference to this expression rather than "countermeasures" is deliberate; it permits practice to evolve in this area. See *Report on Fifty-Third Session*, *supra* note 33 at 355; and D.J. Bederman, "Counterintuiting Countermeasures" (2002) 96:4 A.J.I.L. 817 at 827–28.

[71] The old Article 40 of the 1996 draft, the predecessor to new Article 48, did not distinguish between states in cases of breach of bilateral obligations and those in cases of breach of *erga omnes* obligations and treated all of them as "injured." This terminology posed problems because not all states were equally injured in the traditional usage of that word. Some suffered direct harm whereas others simply "suffered" from the fact that an obligation to which they had subscribed had been breached and therefore the integrity of the rule was threatened. The ILC's fiction of the "injured state" has received its share of

collective procedures put forth by then Special Rapporteur Gaetano
Arangio-Ruiz, which not only involved compulsory adjudication by
the ICJ but also the General Assembly and the Security Council.[72]
The various UN organs were to collaborate on building up a genuine international criminal trial of the wrongful state, first accused
by the Security Council or the General Assembly and then judged
by the ICJ, so as to become subject to the special provisions governing the consequences of a guilty finding against a state.[73] These
proposals have been completely eliminated in the new draft,[74] partly

---

criticism and subsequently been confined to those states directly affected by a
breach (as defined in new Article 42). For a sharp critique, see, for example, P.
Allott, "State Responsibility and the Unmaking of International Law"(1988) 29
Harv. J. Int'l L. 1. One must laud the sagacity of Special Rapporteur Crawford
who, noting that this "equal" treatment of states was not conducive to developing public international law (rather than what he calls a "private spectre of international law"), has argued that it is important to distinguish between the primary
beneficiaries (the right holders) and those states with a legal interest in compliance, "irrespective of how or whether the breach has affected [them]." To do so,
according to him, would be "the first step in disentangling the tangle article 40
... creates, by which, for example, any state in the world can take countermeasures for a breach of human rights even though the victim of that breach does
not want the countermeasures to be taken, and may actually be harmed by them."
See J. Crawford, "Responsibility to the International Community as a Whole"
(2001) 8 Ind. J. Global Legal Studies 303 at 320–21.

72 *Seventh Report on State Responsibility, by Mr. Gaetano Arangio Ruiz, Special Rapporteur,*
UN Doc. A/CN.4/469 and Add.1 and 2, reprinted in *Yearbook of the International
Law Commission 1995,* vol. 2, Part 1, New York, 1995 at 46 ff, paras. 245 ff [*Seventh Report of Gaetano Arangio-Ruiz*]. For a critique of these proposals for their
obvious political unrealism, see P.-M. Dupuy, "Implications of the Institutionalization of International Crimes of States," in Weiler, Cassese, and Spinedi, *supra*
note 46 at 182.

73 Under the same provisions, the "guilty" state would additionally be subject to
countermeasures decided collectively but implemented individually by each state
injured by the perpetration of the crime. The complexity of the machinery contemplated would undoubtedly justify reproducing in its entirety draft Article 19
of the second part of the articles proposed by Special Rapporteur Arangio-Ruiz,
but for considerations of space and emphasis I shall refrain from doing so. The
text of this article is reproduced in the *Yearbook of the International Law Commission
1995, supra* note 72 at 46, note 117. For a summary of the debates at the ILC
leading to its rejection, see *ibid.* at 55, para. 305.

74 All that is left now is a "without prejudice" clause. See Draft Articles on Second
Reading, *supra* note 31 at Article 46 and 59. On the circumstances of the dis-
carding of this part of the draft by the ILC, see A. Pellet, "Can a State Commit a
Crime? Definitely, Yes!" (1999) 10 E.J.I.L. 425 at 429 and P. Klein, "Responsibility for Serious Breaches of Obligations Deriving from Peremptory Norms of International Law and United Nations Law" (2002) 13:5 E.J.I.L. 1241 at 1252–53.

because of the fear of widening the expression "threat to international peace and security" to encompass "international crimes," which would have brought all obligations for the protection of fundamental interests of the international community within the scope of Chapter VII of the UN Charter in order to secure their enforcement.[75] Paradoxically, the council's dynamic practice of intervening in cases of internal conflict and concomitant *ad hoc* enlargements of the concept of "threat to peace" may well have led to the same result. In any event, the newly adopted provisions grant *priority* rather than *exclusivity* to the "UN super-system" over the general *régime* of consequences of internationally wrongful acts.[76] Theoretically, it would no doubt be possible to subordinate action under Article 54(2) of the new draft articles to one *duly taken* under Chapter VII, but this would not be flexible enough to deal with all humanitarian crisis situations.

It is new draft Article 41(1) that stipulates some of the rather limited consequences of the existence of "serious breaches" for not-directly affected states: they shall "cooperate" to bring them to an end through lawful means and not recognize or help maintain situations resulting from them.[77] The reference to a duty of cooperation was absent from old draft Article 14(3) of 1984, which subjected the exercise of rights and obligations "unless otherwise provided for by an applicable rule of general international law, *mutatis mutandis* to the procedures embodied in the UN Charter with respect to the maintenance of international peace and security."[78] In his brief

---

75 The other reasons being, more generally, the unsuitability of existing UN mechanisms for implementing a system of aggravated responsibility and, more specifically, the relativity of the qualifications likely to be applied by the Security Council and the legitimacy of the latter as a body acting in the name of the international community. On this point, see Klein, *supra* note 74 at 1247–50. See also S.M. Villalpando, *L'émergence de la communauté internationale dans la responsabilité des États* (Paris: P.U.F., 2005) at 415–50.

76 Draft Articles on Second Reading, *supra* note 31 at Article 46 and 59.

77 It is noteworthy that the ambiguity (mentioned earlier) of the nature of the obligation breached (obligations arising under peremptory norms in Article 40 and obligations owed to the international community as a whole in Article 48), combined with the related problem of the threshold of seriousness of breaches (which only appears in Article 40) leads to the following absurd result: the serious breach of a small number of peremptory obligations entails the fairly mild "particular consequences" enumerated in Article 41. At the same time, a breach (whether serious or not) of a broader range of obligations — *erga omnes* — creates the notably more serious consequences appearing in Articles 48 and 54 (the taking of countermeasures or "lawful measures").

78 See *Report of the International Law Commission on the Work of Its Thirty-Seventh Session*, UN Doc. A/40/10, reprinted in *Yearbook of the International Law Commission*

commentary to Article 14, then Special Rapporteur Riphagen stated
that in addition to particular circumstances and arrangements, the
"not-directly injured" state "should exercise its new rights and perform its new obligations *within the framework of the organized community of States.*"[79] It is not clear what was meant by that formula.
Probably he was referring to the United Nations, not as an international organization acting within its specific competences but rather
as a "material organ" of the international community as a whole,
for the text of the commentary does not speak of action *within or
through an international organization.*

Much like with Riphagen's proposal, one wonders what the ad-
dressees of new draft Article 41(1) are expected to do to comply
with their new duty of cooperation. The ILC commentaries do not
add much, explaining that "because of the diversity of circumstances
which could possibly be involved, the provision does not prescribe
in detail what form this cooperation should take," nor "what measures States should take in order to bring an end to those breaches."[80]
What is made clear is that the proposal of the drafting committee in
2000 to only allow for coordinated countermeasures through an
international or regional organization was abandoned,[81] and the
reference to "lawful means" was apparently meant to rule out the
use of force.[82] This is in fact corroborated by the commentaries to
the 2001 draft, which mention, using phraseology similar to
Riphagen's: "Cooperation *could* be organized in the framework of
a competent international organization, in particular the United

---

1985, vol. 2, Part I, Article 14(3), New York, 1986, UN Doc. A/CN.4/SER.A/
1985/Add.1 (Part I) [*Report on Thirty-Seventh Session*].

79 *Ibid.* at 14, para. 10 (commentary to Draft Article 14) [emphasis added]. Simma
has observed that Riphagen's draft Article 14 had tried to "develop community
reactions without really leaving the field of traditional bilateralism" and concluded by expressing his concern that "these new conceptions are being grafted
upon international law without support through, and any attempt at, adequate
institution-building." See Simma, "International Crimes: Injury and Countermeasures," *supra* note 46 at 305, 315 respectively.

80 *Report on Fifty-Third Session, supra* note 33 at 286–87.

81 *Report of the International Law Commission on the Work of its Fifty-Second Session*, UN
GAOR, 55th Sess., Supp. No. 10, UN Doc. A/55/10 (2000) at 112–113, paras.
366–68, 116, para. 381.

82 Arguably, the strong procedural safeguards surrounding countermeasures would
be applicable *mutatis mutandis* to whatever "solidarity measures" states envisage
taking. These are found in new draft Articles 49-53. This would take care, at least
in part, of the concern voiced by many that the consequences of the category of
"serious breaches" allow for reactions by individual states acting without regard

Nations. However, paragraph 1 also envisages the possibility of non-institutionalized cooperation."[83] Essentially, what is called for in the face of serious breaches is "a joint and coordinated *effort* by all states to counteract the effect of these breaches."[84] The ILC concludes that "[p]aragraph 1 seeks to strengthen existing mechanisms of cooperation, on the basis that all states are called upon to make an appropriate response."[85] No specific mode of response has therefore been ruled out *ab initio.*

These perfunctory remarks raise, however, more questions than they answer. First, it is not clear whether the ILC intended to exclude unilateralism altogether. One might argue that the latter is the antithesis of cooperation and yet, in view of the whole drafting history of draft Article 41(1), which carefully avoided the question of who would be entitled to instigate such action, would it not be going too far to infer such a wide-ranging prohibition from the simple

---

to the position of the "international community as a whole" — a legitimate concern in the face of the very alarming recent wanton use of force by certain states (on grounds of self-defence) on the basis of their own subjective determination of alleged violations by other states. Alland has argued, however, that these principles can operate only *a posteriori*, when the well foundedness of the countermeasures are evaluated to see if they are justified. The result, according to him, is that "such countermeasures are unsuited to any *a priori* legal conditioning: subjecting their exercise to pre-conditions is a contradictory undertaking that amounts quite simply to precluding countermeasures." See Alland, *supra* note 31 at 1234–35.

[83] *Report on Fifty-Third Session, supra* note 33 at 287, para 2. In the same vein, the commission had already asserted that obligations incumbent on all states under Article 53 (former Article 41) of the 1996 draft articles "would arise for each State as and when it formed the view that a crime had been committed. Each state would bear responsibility for its own decision, although it may be added, there may be cases in which the duty of non-recognition or the duty of non-assistance, for example, might flow from mandatory resolutions of the Security Council or other collective actions duly taken." See *Report of the International Law Commission on the Work of Its Forty-Eighth Session,* UN GAOR, 51st Sess., Supp. No. 10, UN Doc. A/CN.4/SER.A/1996/Add.1 (Part 2), reproduced in *Yearbook of the International Law Commission 1996,* vol. 2, Part. 2, New York, 1996 at 71, para. 4 [*Report on Forty-Eighth Session*].

[84] *Report on Fifty-Third Session, supra* note 33 [emphasis added]. To make things even more confusing, the ILC had stated in its commentary to Article 40 that "the serious breaches dealt with in this chapter are likely to be addressed by the competent international organizations including the Security Council and the General Assembly." See *ibid.* at 286, para (9).

[85] *Ibid.* at 287, para 2. See also P.-M. Dupuy, "The Place and Role of Unilateralism in Contemporary International Law" (2000) 11(1) E.J.I.L. 19 at 24–25.

text of the article?[86] Second, assuming that unilateralism is not completely ruled out, does international law impose a duty on each and every state to cooperate with another state unilaterally taking countermeasures?[87] Does the duty extend to all states belonging to a regional organization when one of its members takes countermeasures, giving rise to something akin to a "collective self-defence"?[88] Further, no mention is made of how to face the many problems that a non-institutionalized cooperation could give rise to. What should be done, for instance, when states, all moved by a *bona fide* intent to bring a serious breach to an end, disagree on the appropriateness or scale or duration of enforcement measures? In this respect, draft Article 41(1), despite its *semblance* of *communitarianism*, remains an enigma awaiting subsequent developments in international law and international relations.[89]

86 Gattini argues that such an inference cannot be made given "the complete silence of the commentary on this point, and the explicit statement of the Chairman of the Drafting Committee that the paragraph was 'not intended to exclude unilateral actions by states'." See A. Gattini, "A Return Ticket to 'Communitarisme.' Please" (2002) 13:5 Eur. J. Int'l. L. 1181 at 1187.

87 Draft Article 53 of the first version of 1996 draft was no more explicit, stating that "[a]n international crime committed by a State entails an obligation for every other State: ... (d) to cooperate with other States in the application of measures designed to eliminate the consequences of the crime." The very brief commentary to this provision referred in particular to the cooperation of states in implementing sanctions adopted by the Security Council. It added, however, that "apart from any collective response of States through the organized international community, the Commission believes that a certain minimum response to a crime is called for on the part of all States." See *Report on Forty-Eighth Session*, *supra* note 83 at 170. To what form of "minimum response" was the ILC alluding remains a mystery.

88 One can recall here Article 5 of the North Atlantic Treaty Organization Treaty, which states in part:

The Parties agree that an armed attack against one or more of them in Europe or North America shall be considered an attack against them all and consequently they agree that, if such an armed attack occurs, *each of them*, in exercise of the right of individual or collective self-defence recognised by Article 51 of the Charter of the United Nations, *will assist the Party or Parties so attacked by taking forthwith, individually and in concert with the other Parties, such action as it deems necessary*, including the use of armed force, to restore and maintain the security of the North Atlantic area" [emphasis added].

Perhaps Special Rapporteur Riphagen had something similar in mind when he maintained that reaction to an international crime was "comparable to a measure of collective self-defence." See *Report on Thirty-Seventh Session*, *supra* note 78 at 14, para. 9.

89 The ILC Commentary itself reveals that the commission was not certain whether it codified or developed international law: "It may be open to question whether

BACK TO THE FUTURE: TOWARDS AN INSTITUTIONALIZED
REACTION TO SERIOUS BREACHES?

The reader may be left feeling bewildered and frustrated once
again for failing to receive clear indications about the measures
third states may take when breaches of *erga omnes* obligations relating to genocide occur. I would submit that no clearer indications
could be gained from intensive legal research. The answer cannot
be more precise because the Genocide Convention itself is ambiguous and because the practice that creates custom varies tremen-
dously. Some would even qualify it as so selective that it cannot
create legal rules, which they would argue must be the same for all
similar situations. If only every state in the world would systematically and regardless of other considerations invoke the responsibility of the "violating" state as soon as it deems a violation of obligations
relating to genocide to have occurred, and would claim cessation
of the breach, then of course much would be gained. However,
political and legal considerations are inevitably intermingled. Even
in abstract statements states do not want to restrict their freedom
in responding to future cases where, to recall the words of Lassa
Oppenheim, the "balance of power," economic and political interests, and sometimes also humanitarian expediency may suggest different reactions. The new Draft Articles on State Responsibility may
well have a postmodern structure and texture, but at least for the
provisions on enforcement measures in the collective interest, they
reflect as much the imperative of realist power politics.

It seems quite revealing that the ILC should ultimately have decided to put unilateral responses by states at the forefront of the
question of invocation of responsibility for the most serious breaches
of international law. In doing so, it clearly moved away from the
idea of systematically institutionalizing responses to such wrongful
acts. But while the argument that new draft Article 48 could be
used for spurious ends to justify unilateral intervention remains a
serious one,[90] it should nonetheless be given limited weight. The
concrete possibility — or perhaps the greater probability — of a
genuine coordinated reaction to violations of the "international

---

general international la at present prescribes a positive duty of cooperation, and
paragraph 1 in that respect may reflect the progressive development of international law." See *Report on Fifty-Third Session, supra* note 33 at 287, para. 3.

[90] M. Koskenniemi, "Solidarity Measures: State Responsibility as a New International Order?" (2002) 71 Brit. Y.B. Int'l L. 337 at 349–50, 355. See also J.I.

public order" undeniably exerts a visible influence on the way in which states employ self-help and countermeasures today. States have traditionally been and are still wary to open a Pandora's box that would allow every state to become a "surrogate prosecutor" on behalf of the international community.[91] Arguably, this is precisely why such individual and collective initiatives have been almost completely replaced today with the "authorization model,"[92] whereby individual states assume the role of agents of the community after securing the approval of the Security Council.[93] One can recall the interventions in the Kuwait crisis and, recently, in Somalia, Haiti, Rwanda, East Timor, Albania, and Sierra Leone. This has had the benefit of checking the abuse of power and promoting stability and determinacy in international relations — a most welcomed addition to the plethora of measures aimed at safeguarding so-called "overriding interests." It follows that before the progressive codification

---

Charney, "Third States Remedies in International law" (1989) 10 Mich. J. Int'l L. 57 at 101 (noting that "a substantial expansion of international law remedies to give third states a significant role ... might erode, rather than enhance, obedience to the rule of law," and suggesting that third-state remedies under customary international law "may be appropriate in the case of a few subjects of international law under limited circumstances").

91 Simma and Pulkowski thus argue that "[f]ar from obsessively policing human rights violations across the world, states' attitude towards human rights violations is all too often characterized by a remarkable lack of vigor to counter such treaty breaches." See B. Simma and D. Pulkowski, "*Leges Speciales* and Self-Contained Regimes," in J. Crawford and A. Pellet, *Le droit de la responsabilité des États* (Paris: Pédone, 2005).

92 Simma, "Bilateralism and Community Interest," *supra* note 46 at 267–68. See also D. Sarooshi, *The United Nations and the Development of Collective Security: The Delegation by the UN Security Council of Its Chapter VII Powers* (Oxford: Clarendon Press, 1999) at 12–13, 153–63 and, more specifically, B. Simma, "Does the UN Charter Provide an Adequate Basis for Individual or Collective Responses to Violations of Obligations Erga Omnes?" in J. Delbrück, ed., *The Future of International Law Enforcement, New Scenarios-New Law?* (Berlin: Duncker and Humblot, 1993) at 139; N. Blokker, "Is the Authorization Authorized? Powers and Practice of the UN Security Council to Authorize the Use of Force by 'Coalitions of the Able and Willing'" (2000) 11(3) E.J.I.L. 541.

93 H. Kelsen, *Principles of International Law* (New York: Rinehart, 1952) at 25; J.A. Frowein, "Collective Enforcement of International Obligations" (1987) 47 ZaöRV 67 at 76–77; J. Delbrück, "The Impact of the Allocation of International Law Enforcement Authority on the International Legal Order," in J. Delbrück, ed., *Allocation of Law Enforcement Authority in the International System: Proceedings of an International Symposium of the Kiel Institute of International Law, March 23 to 25, 1994* (Berlin: Duncker and Humblot, 1995) at 135, 154.

of anti-genocide norms can be paralleled by the widespread refinement and expansion of unilateral individual or collective enforcement measures aimed at prevention, states must remove themselves from the "genocidal" impulse of *realpolitik* and move towards a "true sense of community." They must come to believe and decide effectively from the community perspective that not only is international action to prevent genocide not at risk of becoming unruly but also that it is actually in their best interest.

Political considerations aside, however, the idea of a *duty*, and not merely a right, of "not directly affected states" to enforce compliance by a state with its obligations relating to genocide — quite apart from questions as to its existence — certainly overestimates the capacity of states in general to identify signs of imminent genocide and of weaker ones to employ measures to prevent human rights abuses.[94] More importantly, it may well lead to complete anarchy if no effective institutional mechanisms are established or existing structures used to replace reciprocity and control the execution by all states of their "duty to prevent."[95] In this respect, the overly technical and apolitical bilateralist approach to community enforcement, fruit of Dionizio Anzilotti's fervent imagination and still defended by some commentators,[96] fails to grasp the revolutionary political impact of the establishment of an institutional

---

[94] To provide for such a duty also presupposes a higher degree of solidarity among states than in case of the dispensing of rights of protection that may be exercised or not, according to factual expediency. This is certainly questionable in the current state of flux in international relations.

[95] Frowein, "Reactions by Not Directly Affected States," *supra* note 24 at 423, 431–33.

[96] According to Michael Byers, "there are two parts to every *erga omnes* rule. First, as with ordinary rules, each *erga omnes* rule contains a series of rights and corresponding obligations concerning its substantive content. *It is these rights and obligations which form the principle bilateral relationships between any of the many pairs of States which are subject to that rule.* Secondly each State has, in the words of the Court, a 'corresponding right of protection'" [emphasis added]. He further writes: "[E]ach State not only has rights and obligations in respect of the substantive content of the *rule*, giving rise to State responsibility vis-à-vis injured States in the event of a violation, but it is also subject to a series of additional, bilateralised rights and obligations." See M. Byers, *Custom, Power and the Power of Rules: International Relations and Customary International Law* (Cambridge: Cambridge University Press, 1999) at 197 [emphasis added]. The conversion from the language of obligation to that of rules is quite unfortunate and appears to imply that all responsibility relations can be assimilated today to bundles of classical bilateral right-duty inter-state relations (an assumption contradicted by the ICJ in the *Barcelona Traction* case). To the contrary, the substantive *erga omnes* rights at the primary level

apparatus such as the United Nations to deal with genocide.[97] Far
from assuming a static view of the international legal system, the
choice of collectively authorized measures over unilateral ones to
prevent genocide is merely an attempt to escape a regression to
unilateral decisions involving community interests.[98]

Entrusting the defence of peremptory norms of general international law to unilateral responses by states is problematic for another reason. It fails to take account of the discretionary nature of
the latter: it means bringing the bindingness of these norms under
the will of states since the latter may agree to allow a situation to be
asserted against themselves (or, more appropriately, the international community as a whole) through inaction, even though it was
created following an internationally wrongful act in breach of an
obligation arising under a peremptory norm. This "selectivity" of
state practice (where states respond to one incident but not to another),[99] in a sense, is to allow derogation from what has been defined as non-derogable. Thus, also at a strictly practical level, the
question arises whether it really makes sense today to have community interests to prevent genocide implemented by what Denis

<hr>

of the relationship (at the level of the substantive content of the rule) are held
by individuals, not states, though it may be argued that other states do have a
right to expect performance of these obligations. States have the corresponding
erga omnes obligations towards those individuals or groups not to violate these
rights. Thus, the primary rights and obligations do not exist between states, but
rather between states and individuals or groups. At the secondary level of the
relationship (procedural aspect of the rule), these same *erga omnes* obligations
are owed to "the international community as a whole," and each state has a corresponding right of protection, which is opposable *erga omnes* — that is, the right
to make claims against the state in case of breach. There is a fear that Byers's
essentially bilateralist depiction of the concept of *erga omnes* obligations that, it
should be recalled, is grafted onto the notion of "community interest" will turn
out to be too weak to come to terms with the full implications of such a concept,
particularly for any future prospect of an organized, institutional reaction to
their breach. On the third party rights of individuals at the primary level of the
relationship, see Chinkin, *supra* note 14 at 13–15, 120–33.

97 C. Tomuschat, "International Crimes by States: An Endangered Species," in K.
Wellens, ed., *International Law: Theory and Practice, Essays in Honour of Eric Suy*
(The Hague: Martinus Nijhoff, 1998) at 265.

98 V. Gowlland-Debbas, "The Limits of Unilateral Enforcement of Community
Objectives in the Framework of United Nations Peace Maintenance" (2000) 11(1)
E.J.I.L. 361 at 385–86.

99 See on this point the *Third Report of James Crawford, supra* note 31 at 17–18, para.
396.

Alland calls the "private-justice"[100] nature of the rules and enforcement mechanisms provided by the law of state responsibility.[101]

COMMUNITARIANISM UNLEASHED: "THINKING OUTSIDE THE ILC TOOLBOX"

As mentioned earlier with regard to the limited number of fundamental obligations seeking to uphold basic community interests, the "international community as a whole" is the bearer of the corresponding rights to demand compliance by states with their commitment to refrain from perpetrating genocidal acts. Traditionally, this concept has been perceived as comprising exclusively sovereign states — the latter being until today the primary subjects of international law and the main actors in the law-making process — while international law has lended the necessary normative structure to this community.[102] However, human rights norms and the rising awareness of the "community interest" in the survival of mankind have evolved to challenge this notion to take into account the needs and fears of all human beings and actors and to attempt to cope with the "odious scourge" of genocide.[103] As Christian Tomuschat has put it, "it would be wrong to assume that States as a mere juxtaposition of individual units constitute the international community. Rather, the concept denotes an overarching system which embodies a common interest of all States and, indirectly, of mankind."[104]

Tomuschat's point is well taken, but it raises the intriguing question of when, if ever, state responsibility can be incurred to the

---

[100] Alland, *supra* note 31 at 1234 ff.

[101] See in this sense P.-M. Dupuy, "A General Stocktaking of the Connections between the Multilateral Dimension of Obligations and Codification of the Law of State Responsibility" (2002) 13(5) E.J.I.L. 1053 at 1078; Simma, "Bilateralism and Community Interest," *supra* note 46 at 249. Indeed, the very essence of human rights comes from the fact that, by being beyond the interplay of reciprocity, they are *by definition* resistant to a strictly bilateral perception, and in any case are not inter-state things, since the beneficiary of the right is an individual, independent of ties of nationality.

[102] H. Mosler, "The International Society as a Legal Community" (1974) 140 Rec. des Cours 1 at 32; M. Virally, "Panorama du droit international contemporain. Cours général de droit international public" (1983-V) 183 Rec. des Cours 1 at 28.

[103] R.-J. Dupuy, "Communauté internationale et disparités de développment" (1979) 165 Rec. des Cours 9 at 220.

[104] Tomuschat, *supra* note 20 at 227.

determining "body" referred to as "the international community as a whole."[105] In particular, do genocidal acts create a new legal relationship between an offending state and a certain legal entity called the "universal international community," as once contemplated by the late Roberto Ago?[106] This question, far from being a toy for academics, will help clarify whether the mere existence of a breach of an *erga omnes* obligation relating to genocide could trigger "automaticity" of United Nations action. And if this were the case, one might further ask whether the right of member states to take unilateral or collective countermeasures in such cases subsists or effectively becomes extinguished. It is to these questions that my reflections in the following two sections will be entirely devoted.

THE "INTERNATIONAL COMMUNITY AS A WHOLE" PERSONIFIED?: THE INSTITUTIONAL MIRAGE OF THE UNITED NATIONS

The solution retained by the ILC, according to which only the state specifically affected by a serious breach is "injured," entails, in a sense, considering that in the absence of such a state either the subjective rights infringed are that of individuals and, hence, that

105 In 1970, Roberto Ago explained that "international treaty law [provided] that *in certain cases* a particular internationally wrongful act may be source of new legal relations, not only between the guilty State and the injured State, but also between the former State and other States or, especially, between the former State and organizations of States." He also stressed that the development of international organization had led, "as early as the League of Nations, but more particularly with the United Nations ... to consideration of the possibility for a State committing an internationally wrongful act *of a certain kind and of a certain importance* to be ... subject to the faculty, or even the duty, of the Organization and its members to react against the internationally wrongful conduct by applying sanctions collectively decided upon." See *Second Report on State Responsibility, by Mr. Roberto Ago, Special Rapporteur,* UN Doc. A/CN.4/233, reprinted in *Yearbook of the International Law Commission 1970,* vol. 2, Part 1, New York, 1970 at 184 (UN Doc. A/8010/Rev.1 (A/25/10)) [emphasis added].

106 Although in 1970, Ago denied the presence of such a personified international community, he considered such a possibility by linking the personification of the international community to the degree of institutionalization of international relations present at any given time. See *ibid.* at 177–97. However, he subsequently backed away from his initial stance, describing the emergence of "[s]omething which already exists to some extent today ... namely that the *entity called the international community,* distinct from its members who have rights and obligations, is able to enter into legal relationship with its members. It is not all States, but rather the international community, that is envisaged as the possible bearer of a right of reaction to this particularly serious form of internationally wrongful act ... The whole idea of obligations *erga omnes* is bound up ... with the fact of recognition of the existence of that community as such." See R. Ago,

the latter are subjects of international law or that the subject injured is the international community as such, which implies the personification of the latter.

This, at least, has been the approach favoured by the ICJ. In the case *Legal Consequences for States of the Continued Presence of South Africa in Namibia (South-West Africa) Notwithstanding Security Council Resolution 276*, for example, the court underscored that "the injured entity is a people which must look to the international community for assistance,"[107] thus portraying the latter as an institutional arrangement called upon to shoulder the ultimate responsibility for the fate of the community of the people of Namibia. Similarly, in *United States Diplomatic and Consular Staff at Tehran (United States of America v. Iran)*, the court felt its duty to draw "the attention of the entire community ... to the irreparable harm that may be caused by events of the kind now before the Court. Such events cannot fail to undermine the edifice of law carefully constructed by mankind over a period of centuries."[108] The court's judgment here seems to appeal to the international community as a guardian of fundamental interests, the protection of which "is vital for the security and well-being of the complex international community of the present day."[109] The difficulty, however, is that the "international community" is, in the words of Charles de Visscher, "un ordre en puissance dans l'esprit des hommes; dans les réalités de la vie internationale, elle en est encore à se chercher, elle ne correspond pas à un ordre effectivement établi."[110] Therefore, the United Nations, if only because it is not established through absolute universal membership

---

"Obligations Erga Omnes and the International Community," in Weiler, Cassese, and Spinedi, *supra* note 46 at 238 [emphasis added]; See also on this same point Annacker, *supra* note 47 at 157; Tomuschat, *supra* note 20 at 224, 227, 236. For a comprehensive discussion of Ago's ideas on this point, see Spinedi, "From One Codification to Another," *supra* note 37 at 1115–19.

[107] *Namibia* case, *supra* note 61 at 56. See also Special Rapporteur Crawford's analysis of the South West Africa cases before the ICJ to the effect that the beneficiaries of the obligation invoked by Ethiopia and Liberia were the people of South West Africa themselves, and that "[a] legal system which seeks to reduce the legal relations between South Africa, the people of the territory, and the two applicant States to a bilateral form is deficient." See *Third Report of James Crawford, supra* note 31 at 37–38, 40, para. 85.

[108] *United States Diplomatic and Consular Staff at Tehran (United States of America v. Iran)*, [1980] I.C.J. Rep. 3 at 43.

[109] *Ibid.*

[110] C. de Visscher, "Positivisme et 'Jus Cogens'" (1971) 75 Rev. D.I.P. 5 at 8.

and does not reflect all "commonly-held societal values," cannot be equated with the personified international community.[111] Yet can it be said by the same token that the institutional mirage of the United Nations, which long encouraged the promoters of the concept of international crime, has completely dissolved without a trace? As Bruno Simma has remarked, the first permanent imprint of community interests on international relations is to be seen in a stronger "organization" of international society.[112] The traditional pattern of bilateralism has thus been replaced today in the field of international peace and security by a community mechanism where a centralized institution, namely the Security Council, is entrusted not only with the responsibility but also with the duties, pursuant to Article 24(1) of the UN Charter, to ensure the realization of community interests common to all states.[113] In a sense, one can see *erga omnes* obligations as a Janus-faced concept, with the enforcement of community interests and the centralization of the enforcement function in an international organization with a worldwide mandate representing different sides of the same coin. The emergence of the United Nations from the ashes of the Armenian genocide and the Jewish Holocaust is arguably a specific illustration of this concept. According to the judgment of the then participant states, a specific area, namely genocide prevention, could not be sufficiently dealt with through their individual efforts, and

111 *Fourth Report of James Crawford, supra* note 56 at 13, para. 37; P. Weil, "Le droit international en quête de son identité : Cours général de droit international public" (1992-VI) 237 Rec. des Cours 9 at 308–11; *Namibia* case, *supra* note 61 at 241, para. 33 (dissenting opinion of Fitzmaurice J.). Contrast this with the statement of Mohammed Bedjaoui J. in his declaration appended to the 1996 Advisory Opinion on Nuclear Weapons to the effect that "the progress made in terms of the institutionalization, not to say integration and 'globalization' of international society is undeniable" and referring to "an objective conception of international law, a law more readily seeking to reflect a collective juridical conscience and respond to the social necessities of States organized as a community." *Case Concerning the Legality of the Threat and Use of Nuclear Weapons,* Advisory Opinion, [1996-I] I.C.J. Rep. 3 at 270 (para. 12), 271 (para. 13).

112 Simma, "Bilateralism and Community Interest," *supra* note 46 at 235–37. See also S. Rosenne, "Bilateralism and Community Interest in the Codified Law of Treaties," in W. Friedmann, L. Henkin, and O. Lissitzyn, eds., *Transnational Law in a Changing Society: Essays in Honor of Philip C. Jessup* (New York: Columbia University Press, 1972) at 208.

113 Simma, "Bilateralism and Community Interest," *supra* note 46 at 256 ff. See also B. Graefrath, "On the Reaction of the "International Community as a Whole": A Perspective of Survival," in Weiler, Cassese, and Spinedi, *supra* note 46 at 253–55.

collective action through the establishment of a collective security machinery was necessary.

Indeed, the very nature of what the ILC calls "obligations arising under peremptory norms of international law" (which are essentially *erga omnes* obligations) indicates the close relationship between the concept and the United Nations and, more generally, between the future ramifications and implications of the normative density of the concept and the process of "institutionalization" of the international community.[114] Thus, in institutionalized systems such as the United Nations, the international organization will normally be entrusted with the legal right of reacting in the name of the community to uphold the foundational principles of the international legal order.[115] The extent to which this premise holds true will however largely depend on the future organic development of the United Nations and, more broadly, on the sociological reality of the constitutional *ambiente* of the international community.[116]

That being said, the fact that all UN member states are in possession of a legal interest in the fulfilment of *erga omnes* obligations relating to genocide cannot be considered sufficient ground to conclude upon the existence of an additional general and distinct interest of the United Nations itself.[117] Even though it is argued in this article that the realization of collective interests must be ensured by means of a robust organizational response intended to supplement state action, an independent legal interest for the United Nations cannot be said to accrue to it from the mere fact that an *erga omnes* obligation is breached towards the collectivity of states.[118] Furthermore, since the United Nations did not participate in the

---

[114] G.M. Abi-Saab, "Cours Général de Droit International Public" (1987-VII) 207 Rec. des Cours 15 at 93; R. Ago, "Obligations Erga Omnes and the International Community," *supra* note 106 at 238; Simma, "Bilateralism and Community" in Dinstein and Tabory, *supra* note 15 at 844.

[115] R. Provost, "Reciprocity in Human Rights and Humanitarian Law" (1994) 65 Brit. Y.B. Int'l L. 384 at 384–85; Simma, "Bilateralism and Community Interest," *supra* note 46 at 244; Tomuschat, *supra* note 20 at 218.

[116] On this point, see G.M. Abi-Saab, ""La communauté internationale" saisie par le droit — Essai de radioscopie juridique," in G.M. Abi-Saab *et al.*, eds., *Boutros Boutros-Ghali, amicorum discipulorumque liber: paix, développement, démocratie,* vol. I (Brussels: Bruylant, 1998) at 106.

[117] A.J.J. De Hoogh, *Obligations Erga Omnes and International Crimes: A Theoretical Inquiry into the Implementation and Enforcement of the International Responsibility of States* (The Hague: Kluwer Law International, 1996) at 106.

[118] *Ibid.* at 108. See also *Reparation for Injuries Suffered in the Service of the United Nations,* Advisory Opinion, [1949] I.C.J. Rep. 174 at 179 [*Reparations* case].

elaboration of the Genocide Convention and is not party to it,[119] an independent legal interest would be held to exist only to the extent that an express provision stipulates specific rights for the organization regarding the supervision or enforcement procedures established in the treaty.[120] Article VIII of the Genocide Convention would seem to provide this basis. It stipulates: "Any Contracting Party may call upon the competent organs of the United Nations to take such action under the Charter of the United Nations as they consider appropriate for the prevention and suppression of acts of Genocide."[121] This, however, militates against the existence of an independent legal interest of the United Nations since any action for the prevention of genocide cannot be taken by the competent organs on their own volition on the basis of the convention but rather must be taken on the basis of the UN Charter.[122] This means that the United Nations could only claim a general legal interest related to a breach of *erga omnes* obligations if, *qua organization*, it would be affected by a particular breach on the basis of its constituting document.[123]

[119] Article 35 of the Vienna Convention on the Law of Treaties between States and International Organizations or between International Organizations, UN Doc. A/CONF.129/15; (1986) 25 I.L.M. 543, stipulates that a treaty obligation arises for a third organization only "if the parties to the treaty intend the provision to be the means of establishing the obligation (on the organization) and the ... third organization expressly accepts that obligation in writing." Neither of these conditions seems to be met in the case of Article I of the Genocide Convention.

[120] De Hoogh, *Obligations Erga Omnes and International Crimes, supra* note 117 at 111.

[121] While this provision at least psychologically imposes a certain responsibility upon the UN, it has in effect been of little practical value since very little use of it has been made. It appears that in an effort to halt the genocide, the Bosnian government requested assistance from the UN Security Council, to no avail. See the letter dated 13 July 1992 from the permanent representative of Bosnia-Herzegovina to the Security Council, UN SCOR, UN Doc. S/24266 (1992), cited in N.M. Procida, "Ethnic Cleansing in Bosnia-Herzegovina, A Case Study: Employing United Nations Mechanisms to Enforce the Convention on the Prevention and Punishment of the Crime of Genocide" (1995) 18 Suffolk Transnat'l L. Rev. 655 at 675. The council was also challenged to take measures to prevent genocide in Rwanda in 1994 and in effect was called upon to act by the Czech Republic in accordance with Article VIII, but failed and dawdled as hundreds of thousands were killed. More recently in September 2004, the UN secretary-general pleaded with Security Council members and secured a resolution ordering Sudan to stop the violence in its Darfur region and threatening to impose an oil embargo if it failed to act.

[122] See M. Toufayan, "Deployment of Troops to Prevent Impending Genocide: A Contemporary Assessment of the UN Security Council's Powers" (2002) 40 Can Y.B. Int'l L. 195 at 220–21.

[123] De Hoogh, *Obligations Erga Omnes and International Crimes, supra* note 117 at 111–12. See also *Reparations* case, *supra* note 118 at 178–80.

A number of provisions of the UN Charter bear witness to the existence of such a legal interest on the part of the United Nations in the performance by member states of their *erga omnes* obligations to respect fundamental human rights.[124] Since genocide is "contrary to moral law and to the spirit and aims of the United Nations,"[125] its prevention will always remain at the very heart of an organization shaped by community interests. The historical lack of effective enforcement action by the Security Council to prevent widespread human rights abuses, institutionalized in the structural impediment of the veto and exacerbated by the Cold War, had rendered a UN response unreliable. However, since the end of the Cold War, the revitalization of the Security Council has undoubtedly established it as the most dynamic element within the UN institutional framework.[126] It has been argued that through its numerous resolutions under Chapter VII, the council has in effect taken massive and systematic breaches of *erga omnes* obligations for the protection of basic human rights as the decisive or sole basis of its determinations of "threats to international peace and security" under Article 39 of the UN Charter.[127] Of course, it cannot be said that the Security Council's practice exhibits the consistency necessary to conclude that the existence of a rule of customary law indicating that any "serious breach by a State of an obligation arising under a peremptory norm of general international law" will *ipso facto* be considered a threat to international peace and security.[128] Nevertheless, the organization is clearly in possession of an independent legal interest regarding the enforcement by states of their *erga omnes* obligations relating to genocide.

UNITED NATIONS VERSUS STATE ACTION AND THE "CONSTITUTION-ALIZATION" OF THE GLOBAL COLLECTIVE SECURITY SYSTEM

Once it is accepted that the fulfilment of *erga omnes* obligations relating to genocide may be enforced by preventive measures within the framework of UN law, the question naturally comes to mind

---

[124] Toufayan, *supra* note 122 at 201–11.

[125] Genocide Convention, *supra* note 2 at preamble

[126] See generally F.L. Kirgis, "The Security Council's First Fifty Years" (1995) 89 A.J.I.L. 506.

[127] Toufayan, *supra* note 122 at 229–45.

[128] De Hoogh, *Obligations Erga Omnes and International Crimes*, *supra* note 117 at 119–22. See also Toufayan, *supra* note 122 at 241–42.

whether the United Nations itself, and particularly the Security Council, has a distinct legal obligation to prevent genocide. No such duty can be expressly derived from the text of the UN Charter. It could nevertheless be argued that the duty imposed on states under Article I of the Genocide Convention further extends to the United Nations. This argument inevitably underlies a particular conception of the global collective security system and entails specific implications for a state's ability to take enforcement measures. According to this view, the United Nations is regarded nowadays as "the concrete organization of the community model of interstatal society existing in political reality."[129] The UN Charter has been almost universally recognized, despite its imperfections, as the common law and *Grundgesetz* (constitutional document) of an international political community within which international law would operate.[130] As Simma points out, it has undoubtedly

---

[129] M. Lachs, "Quelques réflexions sur la communauté internationale," in D. Bardonnet *et al., Le droit international au service de la paix, de la justice et du développement, supra* note 69 at 352. According to Giorgio Gaja, the action taken by the Security Council in the cases of Southern Rhodesia, Iraq, Former Yugoslavia, Somalia, and Haiti was "une forme de réaction de la communauté internationale organisée à des violations d'obligations essentielles," including obligations arising from human rights and humanitarian law. See G. Gaja, "Réflexions sur le Rôle du Conseil de Sécurité dans le Nouvel Ordre Mondial: À propos des Rapports entre Maintien de la Paix et Crimes Internationaux des États" (1993) 97 Rev. D.I.P. 297 at 313. See also P.-M. Dupuy, "Après la Guerre du Golfe ..." (1991) 95 Rev. D.I.P. 621 at 635 (describing the involvement of the Security Council in the implementation of Iraqi responsibility in the aftermath of the Gulf war as that of the "organized international community"). For a specific reference to the "organized international community" in the jurisprudence of the ICJ and the work of the ILC, see respectively *South West African cases (Ethiopia v. South Africa; Liberia v. South Africa),* Second Phase, [1966] I.C.J. Rep. 6 at 467 (dissenting opinion of Judge Padilla Nervo); *Third Report on the Content, Forms and Degrees of International Responsibility (Part 2 of the Draft Articles), by Mr. Willem Riphagen, Special Rapporteur,* UN Doc. A/CN.4/SER.A/1982/Add.1, reprinted in *Yearbook of the International Law Commission 1982,* vol. 2, Part 1, New York, 1983 at 48 and 49, paras. 5 and 14 [*Third Report of Willem Riphagen*].

[130] The language is borrowed from Sir Humphrey Waldock. See H. Waldock, "General Course on Public International Law" (1962) 106 Rec. des Cours 1 at 19. For academic support for this view, see T.M. Franck, "Is the U.N. Charter a Constitution?" in J.A. Frowein, K. Scharioth, I. Winkelmann, and R. Wolfrum, eds., *Negotiating for Peace: Liber Amicorum Tono Eitel* (Berlin: Springer-Verlag, 2003) at 95; R. St-J. MacDonald, "Fundamental Norms in Contemporary International Law" (1987) 25 Can. Y.B. Int'l L. 115 at 119 ff; Tomuschat, *supra* note 20; Simma, "Bilateralism and Community Interest," *supra* note 46 at 260; H. Kelsen, *The Law of the United Nations: A Critical Analysis of Its Fundamental Problems* (London: Stevens and Sons, 1951) at 106–10; A. Verdross and B. Simma, *Universelles*

achieved the translation of the concept of "international community" from an abstract notion to something approaching institutional reality.[131] The General Assembly and the Security Council
have behaved, and in fact still do behave, as if they had a perfectly
valid mandate to act on behalf of states as the representatives or
agents of this community.[132] Recent UN practice has also demonstrated the increased vigilance of the Security Council in authorizing collective humanitarian intervention *primarily* to protect
civilian populations against mass murder rather than upon a determination that the situation constitutes a "threat to international
or regional peace and security" based on a finding of regional

---

Volkerrecht. Theorie und Praxis, 3rd ed. (Berlin: Duncker & Humblot, 1984; A.
Ross, *Constitution of the United Nations* (NewYork: Rinehart, 1950); H.M. Kindred
et al., eds., *International Law: Chiefly as Interpreted and Applied in Canada*, 6th ed.
(Toronto: Emond Montgomery, 2000) at 19, para 9; B. Fassbender, "The United Nations Charter as Constitution of the International Community" (1998)
36 Colum. J. Transn'l L. 529; N. Onuf, "The Constitution of International Society" (1994) 5 E.J.I.L. 1 at 16–17. The number of authors taking the idea of
the UN Charter as a "constitution" seriously and trying to apply it consistently
to practical questions of the international legal order such as genocide is,
however, still very limited. For an assessment of the contributions of the ICJ to
the interpretation of the UN Charter as a constitutional order, see C. de Visscher,
Problèmes d'interprétation judiciaire en droit international public (Paris: Pédone, 1963)
at 140 ff.

131 Simma, "Bilateralism and Community Interest," *supra* note 46 at 235–37. It is
interesting to note that in an opinion appended to a case of the ICJ, the latter
has been characterized as the "principal judicial organ of the international
community" whereas Article 92 of the UN Charter defines it as "the principal
judicial organ of the United Nations." See *Case Concerning the Arbitral Award of
31 July 1989 (Guinea-Bissau v. Senegal)*, [1975] I.C.J. Rep. 53 at 121, para. 5
(dissenting opinion of Judges Aguilar Mawdsley and Ranjeva); See also *East
Timor* case, *supra* note 58, "Counter-Memorial of Australia," [1995] I.C.J.
Pleadings 1 at 97–98, where Australia contended that "East Timor's rights imply
a duty *on behalf of the international community (i.e. the United Nations)* but not on
behalf of individual States such as Australia." The very term "international
community" is frequently used interchangeably with the name of the
Organization today.

132 Tomuschat, *supra* note 20 at 330. See also P. Daillet and A. Pellet, *Droit International Public*, 5th ed. (Paris: L.G.D.J., 1994) at 394, where the authors state: "*Si
des précautions sont prises pour garantir la représentation objective de l'ensemble des
États dans une structure institutionelle ... il devient impossible de distinguer la "communauté internationale" de l'organisation internationale qui agit en son nom. Mais ce
n'est que dans la mesure où la personnalité juridique de la communauté internationale s'affirmerait à l'encontre de celle de l'organisation qui exprime sa
volonté, que l'on pourrait admettre que cette communauté dispose d'une certaine capacité propre d'exercice de ces droits*" [emphasis added].

instability.[133] Basing itself on Articles 2(6) and 39 of the UN Charter, the Security Council has even taken the view that non-member states can be bound by decisions under Chapter VII. What we are essentially witnessing through this development is a new vision by states and the council of the organization's mandate as being the guarantor of international peace and security on behalf of the "international community as a whole."[134] Thus, the UN system of collective security has metamorphosed today into a regime for the enforcement of obligations *erga omnes.*

Undoubtedly, the core *erga omnes* obligation to prevent genocide has acquired today a special status not only in international human rights law but also more generally in the international legal order and international relations. As such, it belongs, together with the obligation to "respect and ensure respect" for humanitarian law, to a select group of norms and principles held by the international community to be — dare we say — of a constitutional nature and thus of cardinal importance for the promotion of "elementary considerations of humanity."[135] As it was emphasized earlier, all states are bound by these obligations merely by being members of this community, even if they have not consented to the formation of the norm. One may therefore argue that it is in fact the "international community of states as a whole" that is burdened to prevent genocide. However, so long as this obligation is incapable of being

---

133 Toufayan, *supra* note 122 at 229–45, and references therein.

134 Tomuschat, *supra* note 20 at 256; P.-M. Dupuy, "Sécurité Collective et Organisation de la Paix" (1993) 97 Rev. D.I.P. 626 at 671.

135 This language is borrowed from the *Corfu Channel case (United Kingdom v. Albania)*, [1949] I.C.J. Rep. 4 at 24. The substantive notion of constitutional norms of the international society here defended is akin to the one put forward by Georges Scelle. According to this author:

> [L]es normes constitutives ou constitutionelles ... sont reconnues à un moment donné, dans une société determinée, comme étant les bases de toutes les autres prescriptions normatives et constructives, parce qu'essentielles a la vie même et au progrès de la société ... Toute collectivité intersociale, y compris la communauté universelle du Droit des Gens repose, comme les collectivités mieux intégrées et notamment les collectivités étatiques, sur un ensemble de règles constitutives essentielles à leur existence, à leur durée, à leur progrès ... une constitution au sens large, mais au sens juridique.

See G. Scelle, *Précis de droit des gens: Principes et systématiques* (Paris: Sirey, 1934) at 7. For a defense of the constitutional nature of the obligation to "respect and ensure respect" for humanitarian law, see L. Condorelli and L. Boisson de Chazournes, "Common Article 1 of the Geneva Conventions Revisited: Protecting Collective Interests" 837 Int'l Rev. Red Cross (31 March 2000) 67 at 69.

carried out through unilateral or collective measures, its execution will inevitably require some form of institutional reaction if the concept of *erga omnes* obligations is not to be confined to a bogus category associated with a high level of rhetoric.[136] Would it not be fair to say, then, that by acting on behalf of states in the past to uphold fundamental norms of the "community interest order,"[137] the United Nations has specifically assumed this obligation today?[138]

There is, however, a second, more important reason for drawing this obligation to the United Nations. It is now increasingly accepted that universal or peremptory rules of international law are appli-

---

[136] V. Starace, "La responsabilité résultant de la violation des obligations à l'égard de la communauté internationale" (1976) 153 Rec. des Cours 265 at 289; C. Eagleton, "International Organization and the Law of Responsibility" (1950) 76 Rec. des Cours 319 at 323, 401, 423.

[137] This point has been noted by several scholars, although recent events in the Balkans crisis may not paint such a comforting picture. See namely Gaja, "Réflexions sur le role du Conseil de Sécurité," *supra* note 129 at 314 ff; O. Schachter, "United Nations Law in the Gulf Conflict" (1991) 85 A.J.I.L. 452; and P.-M. Dupuy, "Le Maintien de la Paix," in R.-J. Dupuy, ed., *A Handbook on International Organizations*, 1st ed., (Dordrecht: Martinus Nijhoff, 1998) at 593–98.

[138] As with regard to states, unilateral declarations by international organizations (IOs) may give rise to international legal obligations towards third parties. The elements of clear intention, publicity, and authority to make a statement, derived from the *Nuclear Tests cases (Australia v. France; New Zealand v. France)*, Judgment of 20 December 1974 - Merits, [1974] I.C.J. Rep. 252 at 269–70, para. 43–51, in the case of unilateral declarations of states, constitute the preliminary requirements necessary to bind the organization legally by declarations made by its organs. See also on this point M. Virally, "Unilateral Acts of International Organizations," in M. Bedjaoui, ed., *International Law: Achievement and Prospects* (Paris: UNESCO, 1991), 241 at 256–57; M. Hirsch, *The Responsibility of International Organizations towards Third Parties* (Dordrecht: Martinus Nijhoff, 1995) at 38. In the specific case of genocide, we can cite, among many others, the following unilateral declaration made by the UN secretary-general, the chief administrative organ of the organization pursuant to Article 97 of the UN Charter:

> Of all my aims as Secretary General, there is none to which I feel more deeply committed than that of *enabling the United Nations never again to fail to protecting a civilian population from genocide or mass slaughter* ... The responsibility for the protection of civilians cannot be transferred to others. *The United Nations is the only international organization with the reach and authority to end these practices.* I urge the Security Council to commit itself to this task.

> See K. Annan, *Statement on Receiving the Report of the Independent Inquiry into the Actions of the United Nations during the 1994 Genocide in Rwanda*, 16 December 1999, at 1, available online at <http://www.un.org/News/ossg/sgsm_rwanda.htm> (date accessed: 18 April 2004) [emphasis added]. This statement may in effect be seen as binding the organization in the future towards third parties.

cable *mutatis mutandis* to intergovernmental organizations[139] even if they were not involved in the process of norm-creation.[140] Put bluntly, there is simply no reason why such rules, which are not by their nature unsuitable for international organizations, should not be automatically binding on them. Thus, the United Nations may either derive rights from these rules or be placed under obligations through them.[141] If the United Nations cannot undertake activities in which states, whether members or not, are not allowed to engage in their individual capacity,[142] subject however to use

---

[139] There is growing acceptance among commentators of the existence of international practice supporting such a concept of "universal international law" applicable to IOs — that is, treaty provisions whose global normative reach cannot be explained in terms of treaty law *proper,* or of customary law in the traditional sense. See, in particular, S.I. Skogly, *The Human Rights Obligations of the World Bank and the International Monetary Fund* (London: Cavendish Publishing Limited, 2001), Chapters 4, 5, and 7; É. David, *Droit des organisations internationales* (Brussels: Bruylant, 1997) at 20–25; H. Schermers, *International Institutional Law* (The Hague: Sitjoff and Noordhoff, 1980) at 657.

[140] As international organizations, including the UN, have begun to exercise expanded functions relative to their constituent instruments as originally interpreted, it is only logical to conclude that they must also be deemed subject to a commensurably expanded reach of customary or general international law. See *Report of the International Law Commission on the Work of Its Thirty-Fourth Session (Question of Treaties Concluded between States and International Organizations or between Two or More International Organizations),* UN Doc. A/CN.4/L.341, reprinted in *Yearbook of the International Law Commission 1982,* vol. 2, Part 2, at 56, para. 3 (commentary on Article 53), New York, 1982 (UN Doc. A/37/10 (1982)); É. David, "Le droit international applicable aux organisations internationales," in M. Dony, ed., *Mélanges en hommage à Michel Waelbroeck* (Brussels: Bruylant, 1999) at 3; F. Morgenstern, *Legal Problems of International Organizations* (Cambridge: Grotius, 1986) at 32–36; G. Cahin, *La coutume internationale et les organisations internationales: L'incidence de la dimension institutionnelle sur le processus coutumier* (Paris: Pédone, 2001) at 512–37; M. Virally, "L'O.N.U. devant le droit" (1972) 99 J. Dr. Int'l. 501; Butkiewicz, *supra* note 11 at 118–19; Hirsch, *supra* note 138 at 31. The subject has attracted considerable attention with respect to the applicability of the customary laws of war to the peacekeeping operations of the UN. For an interesting analysis of genocide in former Yugoslavia and the lawfulness of the Security Council's actions, see C. Scott *et al.,* "A Memorial for Bosnia: Framework of Legal Arguments Concerning the Lawfulness of the Maintenance of the United Nations Security Council's Arms Embargo on Bosnia and Herzegovina" (1994) 16 Mich. J. Int'l L. 1 at 112.

[141] G. Tunkin, "The Legal Bases of International Organization Action," in R.-J. Dupuy, ed., *A Handbook on International Organizations,* 1st ed. (Hague Academy of International Law, Dordrecht: Martinus Nijhoff, 1988) at 261–62; De Hoogh, *Obligations Erga Omnes and International Crimes, supra* note 117 at 98, 104, 112.

[142] *Namibia* case, *supra* note 61 at 264 (dissenting opinion of Judge Fitzmaurice); *Reparations* case, *supra* note 118 at 177; Klein, *supra* note 10 at 340–49, 362; De Hoogh, *supra* note 117 at 98.

force through enforcement measures under Chapter VII,[143] then the Security Council can be said to be bound by the norm prohibiting genocide.[144] Extending this argument one step further, one could validly argue that since the duty to prevent genocide can be characterized as a constituent norm of the international legal order "without which the community would cease to exist,"[145] the United Nations is bound by this obligation and cannot dispense with this constitutional minimum.[146] After all, the United Nations was created to promote public order and enhance human welfare. It would therefore "be perverse, even destructive, to postulate a community expectation that international organizations need not conform to the principles of public order."[147]

To be sure, the United Nations might be reluctant to accept a legally binding obligation arising from a treaty — *qua* treaty law — to which it has not given its consent. Although the will of the international community for the United Nations to act to prevent genocide may be shrouded today, perhaps more than ever, by the political goals of its member states relating to international relations and not from a real "sense of community interest," those states' motivation with respect to the implementation of the "duty to prevent" is

[143] B. Martenczuk, "The Security Council, the International Court and Judicial Review: What Lessons from Lockerbie?" (1999) 10 E.J.I.L. 517 at 546.

[144] See in this sense, *Case Concerning the Application of the Convention on the Prevention and Punishment of the Crime of Genocide (Bosnia and Herzegovina v. Yugoslavia (Serbia and Montenegro)) (Request for the indication of additional provisional measures)*, Order of 13 September 1993, [1993] I.C.J. Rep. 325 at 440, para. 100 (separate opinion of ad hoc Judge Lauterpacht).

[145] This language is borrowed from Mosler, *supra* note 102 at 17–19, and G. Jaenicke, "International Public Order," in R. Bernhardt *et al.*, eds., *Encyclopedia of Public International Law*, Max Planck Institute of International Law (Amsterdam: North-Holland, 1987) at 314–18. For comparable language, see H.L.A. Hart, *The Concept of Law* (Oxford: Clarendon, 1961) at 187–89 (on the minimum content of natural law).

[146] In *Prosecutor v. Dusko Tadic (Decision on the Defence Motion for Interlocutory Appeal on Jurisdiction)*, 2 October 1995, Case no. IT-94-1-AR72, reprinted in (1996) 35 I.L.M. 32 at para. 93, the Appeals Chamber of the International Criminal Tribunal for the Former Yugoslavia thus held that Article 1 of the four Geneva Conventions of 1949 is a principle that "lays down an obligation that is incumbent, not only on States, but also on other international entities including the United Nations."

[147] M.H. Arsanjani, "Claims against International Organizations: *Quis custodiet impsos custodes*" (1981) 7 Yale. J. World Pub. Ord. 131 at 134. See also H. Schermers and N. Blokker, *International Institutional Law: Unity within Diversity*, 3rd ed. (The Hague: Martinus Nijhoff, 1995) at 988.

irrelevant. The Genocide Convention, although defective in large respects, conveys clear signals regarding the policy content and underpinnings of authority of the normative concepts attached to the outlawing of genocide as well as the willingness of the international community to ensure the effectiveness of its provisions through inter-state cooperation. Without mechanisms of enforcement, the prohibition against genocide effectively becomes a dead letter and will continuously be honoured in its breach. The convention, like other treaties of a humanitarian character, must therefore be deemed capable of creating rights and obligations both for third states and international organizations.[148] Such a conclusion represents evidence, arguably, of an emerging international consensus on the peremptory or overriding normative effects associated with the core principles and rules pertaining to genocide.

It should be noted that although the establishment of the Yugoslav and Rwanda War Crimes Tribunals was essential for the *ex post facto* attribution of individual responsibility for the atrocities committed, these developments in UN law are clearly insufficient for the effective prevention of genocide. Similarly, the idea that early indication by the Security Council that it is carefully monitoring a conflict and that it is willing to use its powers under the Rome Statute of the International Criminal Court[149] will deter parties from committing genocide remains at the present time pure speculation. Criminal law's deterrent function, which traditionally supports the claim that prompt and appropriate punishment prevents the commission of future offences, has time and time again been found to be of no avail with respect to the crime of genocide.[150] The United Nations must therefore give itself all reasonable means and take all reasonable steps, presumably through its implied powers, to fulfil

---

148 On such effects of human rights treaties, see, in particular, R. Higgins, *Problems and Process: International Law and How We Use It* (Oxford: Clarendon Press, 1994) at 20–22; M.S. McDougal and H.D. Lasswell, *Jurisprudence for a Free Society: Studies in Law, Science and Policy* (Dordrecht: Martinus Nijhoff, 1992) at 163–64.

149 Rome Statute of the International Criminal Court, 17 July 1998, UN Doc. A/CONF.183/9, 37 I.L.M. 999, Articles 13 and 16.

150 See the commentaries of the United Nations Secretariat on Article XII of the draft Genocide Convention (old Article VIII), UN ESCOR, UN Doc. E/447 (1947) at 45–46. See also P. Akhavan, "Justice in the Hague, Peace in the Former Yugoslavia?" (1999) 149 Hum. Rts. Q. 737 at 743–51; D. Wippman, "Atrocities, Deterrence, and the Limits of International Justice" (1999) 23(2) Fordham Int'l L.J. 473 at 476–88; T. Meron, "From Nuremberg to The Hague" (1995) 149 Mil. L. Rev. 107 at 110–11.

its duty to prevent apprehended genocide.[151] Yet this obligation is both *complementary* and *subsidiary*, for it is states that have, at least within the conventional framework, assumed primary responsibility to prevent genocide. They may not exonerate themselves from liability by interposing an international organization between their obligation and its breach.[152]

Although the collective execution of the duty to prevent genocide through existing institutional structures is highly preferable — as it is arguably less partisan and open to abuse — states indeed seem to agree that there is in the present international system a central need for unilateral third party reactions countering gross human rights abuses.[153] The translation of a principle of "subsidiarity" into the allocation of a residual responsibility to the United Nations failing effective action by member states is thus one that best suits the state of contemporary international society pending the emergence of a genuine "international community," which certainly remains today more fantasy than real.[154] And yet

---

[151] B. Fassbender, *UN Security Council Reform and the Right of Veto: A Constitutional Perspective (Legal Aspects of International Organization, vol. 32)* (The Hague: Kluwer Law International, 1998) at 221–77; D. Caron, "The Legitimacy of the Collective Authority of the Security Council" (1993) 87 A.J.I.L. 552 at 562–88.

[152] M. Singer, "Jurisdictional Immunity of International Organizations: Human Rights and Functional Necessity Concerns" (1995–6) 36 Va. J. Int'l. L. 53 at 90; Arsanjani, *supra* note 147 at 132. See also the recent decisions of the European Court of Human Rights in *Matthews v. The United Kingdom,* Judgment (Merits), 18 February 1999, Application no. 24833/94 at para. 32 and *Beer and Regan v. Germany,* Judgment (Merits), 18 February 1999, Application no. 00028934/95 at para. 57.

[153] Frowein, "Reactions By Not Directly Affected States," *supra* note 24 at 423. See also Sir I. Sinclair, "State Crimes Implementation Problems: Who Reacts?" in Weiler, Cassese, and Spinedi, *supra* note 46 at 257; G. Gaja, "Ius *Cogens* beyond the Vienna Convention"(1981-III) 172 Rec. des Cours 280 at 299–301; B. Graefrath, "International Crimes — A Specific Regime of International Responsibility of States and Its Legal Consequences," in Weiler, Cassese, and Spinedi, *supra* note 46 at 161.

[154] To the extent that we might regard "subsidiarity" as fundamentally concerned with the distribution of competences among higher and lower levels of governance (as is the case in the European Union), this is certainly a legitimate claim. I wish, however, to emphasize here the comprehensive reach of "subsidiarity," flowing from its grounding in a notion of the common good as the totality of conditions necessary for the flourishing of every individual in society. Subsidiarity is relevant whenever a community cannot be said to be capable of achieving that common good in a self-sufficient manner. Applying the principle of subsidiarity (broadly understood as suggested here) to the "international community," as with any other level of human association, would

any measure taken by the Security Council in such circumstances indubitably has the effect of limiting a state's room to manoeuvre in terms of individual responses to impending genocide.[155] Under Article 59 of the Draft Articles on State Responsibility, the entitlement of all states to have recourse to countermeasures against serious breaches is said to be "without prejudice to the UN Charter of the United Nations," thus itself constituting a subsidiary competence subordinate to the "constitutional" system of the UN Charter and, more particularly, to the Security Council's Chapter VII powers.[156] Therefore, in order for genocide prevention to be implemented effectively, it is imperative that states do not interfere with a UN response but rather fully cooperate with it, as they have a duty to do under new draft Article 41(1) on state responsibility, so that any decisions made by the organization are duly carried out.[157]

THE FUTURE OF COMMUNITY ENFORCEMENT: A NEED FOR STRUCTURAL REFORM?

Now, coming to the question of reform to the UN collective security system, the longstanding debate — at least since 1994 — over

---

generate a responsibility for that order to intervene and assist, but would prohibit it from taking over what more local communities can accomplish by themselves.

[155] The extent to which states' room for manoeuvre is restricted in such situations has been, however, the object of debate among scholars. See, in particular, De Hoogh, *supra* note 117 at 249–51 and Sicilianos, *supra* note 36 at 135–77.

[156] However, it is not uncommon in practice that states give themselves a power of self-interpretation of the Security Council's resolutions to justify the adoption of "collective" countermeasures with only a remote relation, or none at all, to the UN sanctions, or even measures that might go counter to UN objectives. Hence, the need in having the regulation of "collective countermeasures" in the wake of impending genocide clarified.

[157] It is to be recalled that pursuant to Article 89 of Protocol Additional to the Geneva Conventions of 12 August 1949, and Relating to the Protection of Victims of International Armed Conflicts (Protocol I), 8 June 1977, 1125 U.N.T.S. 3, the high contracting parties have undertaken to act, jointly and separately, *in co-operation with* the United Nations in certain circumstances, namely when and wherever "serious violations" of international humanitarian law occur. The language of this provision parallels Article 56 of the UN Charter whereby "all Members pledge themselves to take joint and separate action *in cooperation with* the Organization for the achievement of the purposes set forth in Article 55" [emphasis added]. According to the wording of Article 56, the member states are only under an obligation to give, jointly or separately, such support to the UN to achieve the purposes delineated in Article 55 as they see fit. Article 56, however, does require member states to cooperate with the UN in a constructive way, and obstructive policies in the national interest are thus excluded.

whether the UN Charter should be amended to permit the organization to espouse a more activist role in the pursuit of genocide prevention appears to be, at least in one respect, a red herring. However one sees it, there is simply no need for such an amendment. The United Nations not only is free to take prevention concerns into account but in fact has, as it was argued earlier, an international legal obligation to do so — not *despite* its constituting instrument but, rather, *because* of it!

An analysis of the ILC's work on state responsibility over the past forty years demonstrates that the concern to institutionalize the response to international crimes was a central one and that assigning a prime role to the United Nations was a constant feature of the proposals formulated in this connection, even if they ultimately were not retained.[158] The ideological and doctrinal risk that the ILC took at the time, and which sadly materialized itself in subsequent events of international life, lay in the fact that it conceived the normative advance constituted by the concept of "state crime" as necessitating a corresponding institutional enhancement[159] but, at the same time, considered that there was no need to amend the UN Charter. Of course, it cannot be denied that Chapters VI and VII of the UN Charter provide means for the prevention of genocide that are far more concrete and effective than anything possible in

---

[158] See *Eighth Report on State Responsibility, by Mr. Roberto Ago, Special Rapporteur ("Content of the Obligation Breached")*, UN Doc. A/CN.4/291 and Add.1 and 2, reprinted in *Yearbook of the International Law Commission 1979*, vol. 2, Part I, New York, 1976 at 43, para. 91. Ago's position was that

> a community such as the international community, in seeking a more structured organization, even if only an incipient "institutionalization" should have turned in another direction, namely towards a system vesting in international institutions other than States the exclusive responsibility, first, for determining the existence of a breach of an obligation of basic importance to the international community as a whole, and thereafter, for deciding what measures should be taken in response and how they should be implemented. Under the United Nations Charter, these responsibilities are vested in the competent organs of the Organization.

See also the debate that took place within the ILC in *Report of the International Law Commission on the Work of Its Twenty-Eighth Session*, 3 May to 23 July 1976, UN Doc. A/CN.4/SER.A/1976 (77.V.4), reprinted in *Yearbook of the International Law Commission 1979*, vol. 2, Part 1, New York, 1976 at 55–91, 239–53; the *Third Report of Willem Riphagen*, *supra* note 129 at 48, paras. (4) and (14); and the *Seventh Report (by) of Gaetano Arangio-Ruiz*, *supra* note 72.

[159] See also in this sense P.-M. Dupuy, "Quarante ans de codification du droit de la responsabilité des États. Un bilan" (2003) 107(3) Rev. D.I.P. 305 at 341–42; B. Graefrath, "International Crimes and Collective Security," in Wellens, *supra* note 97 at 240.

the sphere of international jurisdiction. Yet one cannot help question the suitability of the present constitutional system set up in this document for the task of executing the duty to prevent genocide bestowed upon the organization.[160] The ICJ has recognized that it is both essential to, and an attribute of, international organizations and their international legal personality that they be enabled in some instances to express a position contrary to the will of some of its members.[161] This fact clearly explains why decision-making with a majority of voting members within an organization is indicative of the existence of a *volonté distincte* of the institution.[162] However, within the United Nations, any military enforcement of obligations essential for the safeguard of community interests presupposes a positive decision of the Security Council, which can only act upon a prior characterization of human rights atrocities as a "threat to the peace" and the unanimity among its permanent members.

Such unanimity, unfortunately, will not be forthcoming the further away from the traditional Chapter VII scenario of an inter-state threat or use of force Security Council action moves to sanction additional obligations *erga omnes*.[163] Thus, the concern over the unrepresentativeness of this body and the veto power held by its permanent members as having a disabling effect on the sense of participatory governance by the other members[164] has been displaced

---

160 See, *inter alia,* in this connection Riphagen's questions in *Fourth Report of Willem Riphagen, supra* note 57 at 31 and 32, para. 64.

161 *Case Concerning the Interpretation of the Agreement of 25 March 1951 between the WHO and Egypt,* Advisory Opinion, [1980] I.C.J. Rep. 73 at 111 (separate opinion of Judge Lachs). See also Higgins, *Problems and Process, supra* note 148 at 46; F. Capotorti, "Cours Général de Droit International Public" (1994-IV) 248 Rec. des Cours 10 at 60; M. Lachs, "General Course in Public International Law" (1980) 169 Rec. des Cours 9 at 141; I. Seidl-Hohenveldern, *Corporations in and under International Law* (Cambridge: Grotius, 1988) at 72.

162 M. Rama-Montaldo, "International Legal Personality and Implied Powers of International Organizations" (1970) 44 Brit. Y.B. Int'l L. 111 at 146; Seidl-Hohenveldern, *supra* note 161 at 73. See also P. Cahier, "Le droit interne des organisations internationales" (1963) 67 Rev. D.I.P. 575; P. Reuter, "Principes de droit international public" (1961) 103 Rec. des Cours 425 at 516–17.

163 Simma, "Bilateralism and Community Interest," *supra* note 46 at 312–13. H. Freudenschu, "Article 39 of the UN Charter Revisited: Threats to the Peace and the Recent Practice of the UN Security Council" (1993) 46 Austrian J. Pub. & Int'l L. 1 at 39.

164 In this connection, see, in particular, the debates in the General Assembly on the "question of equitable representation on the Security Council and increasing the number of its Members," October 2001, during the 55th Session, available

today to account for the more troubling idea that these have and likely will hamstring the Security Council in the future. To overcome this obstacle, in the case of failure by the council to act, the General Assembly, as another organ of the "organized international community" in matters of international peace and security, would be obligated to recommend measures and enforce *erga omnes* obligations relating to genocide. These actions could be taken pursuant to an enactment similar to the "Uniting for Peace" resolution of 1950 on Korea[165] and would include the use of force in relation to genocidal situations constituting a threat to international peace and security.

Any future proposal made to revise the Genocide Convention to mandate the implementation of automatic coercive measures by the Security Council within a specified time and manner, if certain genocidal indicators occur, cannot, therefore, stand alone. It must be accompanied by an amendment to the UN Charter, even if the likelihood of this happening is quite low considering the strict requirements of Article 108.[166] One is thus left perplex with the recent conclusion reached by the secretary-general's High-Level Panel on Threats, Challenges and Change that the enlargement of the Security Council is *the* way to enhance the effectiveness of this body without the need for a concomitant change in existing members' veto power configuration.[167] It really seems like the panel was more concerned with shoring up the council's credibility and legitimacy than with proposing reform measures aimed at ensuring timely reactive action in cases of apprehended genocide.[168] If statesmen

---

at <http://www.un.org/News/fr-press/docs/2001/AG1214.doc.htm> (date accessed: 7 October 2003). For a critique on the illegitimacy of the Security Council in cases where the responsibility of states is called into question, see V. Gowlland-Debbas, "Security Council Enforcement and Issues of State Responsibility" (1994) 43 I.C.L.Q. 55 at 71.

[165] Uniting for Peace, GA Resolution 377 (V) A, UN GAOR, 5th Sess., Supp. No. 20, 3 November 1950, at 10, UN Doc. A/1775 (1950).

[166] Under this provision, amendments to the UN Charter require the vote of two-thirds of the members of the General Assembly and ratified in accordance with their respective constitutional processes by two-thirds of the members of the UN, including all the permanent members of the Security Council.

[167] *More Secure World, supra* note 7 at paras. 248–49 and 256.

[168] The panel's recommendations are even more troubling when one considers other excerpts of its report where it stated that the Security Council "was created to be not just a representative but a responsible body, one that had the capacity for decisive action" (*ibid.* at para. 244) and that "the challenge for any reform is

were to ever consider the possibility of an amendment in the future, they should always bear in mind that such constitutional reform offers many advantages: it would lessen the Security Council's
concerns about intervening into the internal affairs of a sovereign
state; it would address many third world countries' concerns that
the United Nations simply represents a continuation of Western
imperialism;[169] it would eliminate the belief that the Security
Council's action is unlikely if its members are uninterested from a
political or economic point of view in the state confronting genocide or if they are on opposing sides of the debate about appropriate measures to prevent genocide; it would guarantee that all
potential genocides are presented to, and considered by, the council, whether the targeted group is Muslim, Jewish, Christian, Tutsi,
Cambodian, Indian, and so on; and, finally, it would ensure that
UN action reflects the principle in Article 2(1) of the UN Charter
that all states are equal sovereigns.[170]

Ultimately, then, in the absence of ineffective decisional institutions for the enforcement of community interests, the choice is
not, as it is too often claimed, between the subjectivism of a decentralized response and the absence of any consequences for the most
serious wrongful acts. Rather, the choice is to be made to strengthen
the United Nations's institutional capacity, thereby obviating a re-
surgence of this false dichotomy in the future.[171] The purpose of
this article has not been so much the making of proposals for

---

to increase both the effectiveness and the credibility of the Security Council
and, most importantly, to enhance its capacity and willingness to act in the face
of threats" (*ibid.* at para. 248). One thus wonders whether the necessity for a
"collective responsibility to protect" strenuously advocated by the Panel can be
met simply by a call upon the permanent members, in their individual capacities,
"to pledge themselves to refrain from the use of the veto in cases of genocide
and large-scale human rights abuses" (*ibid.* at para. 256).

169 A. Roberts and B. Kingsbury, "Introduction: The UN's Roles in International
Society since 1945," in A. Roberts and B. Kingsbury, eds., *United Nations, Divided
World: The U.N.'s Roles in International Relations,* 2nd ed. (Oxford: Oxford Uni-
versity Press, 1993) at 45.

170 *Ibid.* at 55.

171 The constant struggle of international organizations to strike a balance
between obsessive concerns with internal institutional problems and exclusive concentration upon substantive issues of current world politics is well
illustrated by Inis Claude Jr. in his famous book *Swords into Plowshares: The
Problem and Progress of International Organization,* 4th ed. (New York: Random
House, 1984) at 6 ff.

reforming the veto power and bringing other structural changes as an argument that the United Nations has a legally binding subsidiary obligation to take all appropriate measures to prevent genocide. There is no doubt, however, that such initiatives led by governments, non-governmental organizations, corporate bodies, and trans-national civil societies are increasingly necessary to eradicate the culture of impunity and give effect to community values that have crystallized as legal precepts.

CONCLUSION

The ineffectiveness of the inter-state mechanisms provided for in the Genocide Convention to prevent the recurrence of genocide has given impetus to the concept of obligations *erga omnes*, which reflects the "common interests" of the international community to salvage the globe's life support capacity. The *erga omnes* nature of the duty to prevent genocide has been directed precisely at redressing situations such as those of immediately apprehended genocide on the basis that rules of international law should be capable of supporting inter-state claims and allow for effective enforcement opportunities if they are to have any effect. Therefore, it seems obvious that there is a great need today for individual nations, or preferably groups of nations, to counter breaches by states of their *erga omnes* obligations relating to genocide through a decentralized enforcement avenue. This need has been clearly recognized by the ILC in its work on the codification of the Draft Articles on State Responsibility.

The commission has nevertheless turned a blind eye on an important and well-known fact of international life: the inability of the international community to prompt third states to take interest in problems occurring far from their borders. This problem, which is further exacerbated by the factual inequalities between states and the fear that the enforcement of *erga omnes* norms through third-party countermeasures would be hijacked by the most powerful and used to further their own cynical foreign policies, has essentially rendered today any immediate reaction by "not directly affected states" illusory.

At the same time, it has brought to the fore the need for an institutional framework for preventive action, such as the United Nations. This article has demonstrated that the latter in fact has an independent legal interest that is clearly affected when violations of the *erga omnes* obligations relating to genocide occur. Further, as the organized expression of the international community in matters of international peace and security and by acting on its behalf, the United Nations, and particularly the Security Council, has itself assumed today a legally binding subsidiary obligation to prevent genocide in the event that states fail to act promptly. This core obligation, which states themselves consider of cardinal importance to the promotion of "elementary considerations of humanity," cannot simply be waived by the United Nations through inaction. It must call for such constitutional reforms that are deemed necessary to strengthen the Organization and ensure that it has the means to execute its obligation. Should it fail to perform its pledge in the future, it may be called upon to answer responsibility claims,[172] for its silence will be interpreted as complicity in the commission of genocide.

As Michael Reisman perceptively pointed out more than thirty years ago, "the dynamics of the international system are such that an intense myth of human dignity can be extended and exploited without being put into effective and sustained practice."[173] The absence of UN practice in preventing genocide has set a poor precedent and has revealed that the reasons for the failure of international prevention go far beyond any defects in the Genocide Convention. They are deeply rooted in the structure and ideologies of the organization and the political concerns for national self-interest and ideological alliances of its member states. The United Nations is after all an organization of governments, and the crime of genocide generally involves the latter either as active agents or as states condoning or failing to take preventive action within their own territories. The plight of mankind will thus go unheeded so long as contemporary statesmen lack the moral courage and political will to utilize Security Council authority and powers to mount collective humanitarian intervention in situations that offend the world's conscience and our so-called "standards of behaviour." Yet

---

[172] This view is held by Éric David who calls into question the responsibility of different actors, including Belgium and the UN, who were bystanders to the Rwandan genocide for failing to prevent the commission of the crime. See É. David, "Aspects juridiques de la responsabilité des différents acteurs dans les evénements du Rwanda (Avril-Juillet 1994)," in K. Boustany and D. Dormoy, eds., *Génocide(s)* (Brussels: Bruylant, 1999) at 403, and particularly at 430–35, 440.

[173] W.M. Reisman, "Responses to Crimes of Discrimination and Genocide: An Appraisal of the Convention on the Elimination of Racial Discrimination" (1971) 1 Den. J Int'l L. & Pol'y 29 at 64.

one cannot easily shy away from the idea that recognizing the legally binding subsidiary duty of the United Nations to prevent genocide might begin to signal this much-awaited shift in public attitudes towards the belief that the defence of the oppressed must always prevail over frontiers and legal documents. As such, we are bound today not to strive for mere punishment but rather for prevention and to develop and create the institutions required by the normative design of new concepts such as "serious breaches of obligations arising under peremptory norms of international law."

Sommaire

Un retour au communautarisme? Réagir aux "violations graves d'obligations découlant de normes impératives du droit international général" créées par la Loi sur la responsabilité de l'État et le droit onusien

Le débat concernant la prévention du génocide a porté essentiellement sur le ou les moyens de réagir de façon appropriée aux violations particulièrement graves des obligations relatives aux des droits de la personne. En particulier, la question a été soulevée de savoir si les mécanismes onusiens actuels pour le maintien de la paix et de la sécurité internationales doivent être considérés comme des moyens privilégiés — voire même exclusifs — de contraindre les états à respecter leurs obligations en matière de génocide. Se fondant de manière extensive sur les travaux de la Commission de droit international sur la codification du droit de la responsabilité des États, l'auteur soutient que le nouveau projet d'articles, en mettant l'emphase sur les "violations graves d'obligations découlant de normes impératives du droit international général" plutôt sur les obligations erga omnes, ne favorise pas la prise de mesures préventives par les États qui "ne sont pas directement affectés." Paradoxalement, l'institutionnalisation de mécanismes pour la prévention des violations graves des droits de la personne a été réduite au minimum dans le nouveau projet d'articles, l'emphase étant mis sur la vague exigence que les États "coopèrent" afin que cessent les violations graves. Il est suggéré, toutefois, qu'il est nécessaire de prêter un rôle subsidiare aux organes et aux procédures des Nations Unies, malgré les critiques formulées quant à leur efficacité, afin de suppléer à l'action étatique. Les Nations Unies ont en effet un intérêt juridique distinct, auquel portent nettement atteinte les violations d'obligations relatives au génocide. Plus important encore, en agissant au nom de la "communauté internationale organisée" en matière de maintain de la paix et de la sécurité internationale, le Conseil de sécurité lui-même assume de nos jours une obligation subsidiaire de prévenir le génocide. En l'absence d'instances décisionnelles efficaces pour prévenir le génocide, l'article conclut qu'il ne s'agit pas de choisir entre le subjectivisme d'une réponse décentralisée et l'absence de toute conséquence pour les préjudices les plus graves, mais plutôt de renforcer la capacité institutionnelle des Nations Unies de réagir.

Summary

A Return to *Communitarianism?* Reacting to "Serious Breaches of Obligations Arising under Peremptory Norms of General International Law" under the Law of State Responsibility and United Nations Law

Discussion surrounding the prevention of genocide has focused to a large extent on the appropriate mode(s) of reaction to particularly serious breaches of human rights obligations. In particular, the question arose whether existing UN mechanisms aimed at preserving international peace and security should be regarded as a privileged — or even exclusive — means to enforce compliance by states with their obligations relating to genocide. Drawing extensively on the work of the International Law Commission on the codification of the law of state responsibility, the author argues that the new draft articles, with their emphasis on "serious breaches of obligations arising under peremptory norms of general international law" rather than obligations erga omnes, are ill-suited to provide for the taking of preventive measures by "not-directly affected" states. Paradoxically, the institutionalization of mechanisms for preventing gross human rights abuses has been reduced to a minimum in the new draft, with emphasis being laid on the vague requirement that states "cooperate" to bring "serious breaches" to an end. It is suggested, however, that ascribing a subsidiary role to UN organs and procedures is, despite criticisms made as to their adequacy, necessary to supplement state action. The UN has in fact a distinct legal interest that is clearly affected when breaches of obligations relating to genocide occur. More importantly, by acting on behalf of the "organized international community" in matters of international peace and security, the Security Council has itself assumed today a legally binding subsidiary obligation to prevent genocide. The article concludes that in the absence of ineffective decisional institutions for the prevention of genocide, the choice is not between the subjectivism of a decentralized response and the absence of any consequences for the most serious wrongful acts but rather to strengthen the UN's institutional capacity to react.

Global Public Policy
and the World Trade Organization
after *Shrimp/Turtle* and *Asbestos*

MAUREEN IRISH

INTRODUCTION

For much of the history of the General Agreement on Tariffs and Trade (GATT),[1] the national treatment principle has been the guardian of the border between national regulation and international trade obligations. So long as imports were treated at least as favourably as domestic products, national regulators could generally accommodate the diverse needs of public policy without being in breach of a GATT obligation. Now, with the adoption of the Agreement on the Application of Sanitary and Phytosanitary Measures (SPS Agreement)[2] and the Agreement on Technical Barriers to Trade (TBT Agreement)[3] as part of the World Trade

Maureen Irish, Faculty of Law, University of Windsor. I am grateful for comments from my colleague Professor Marcia Valiante, students in her International Environmental Law classes, and students in my International Economic Law classes. I also thank Trenton Johnson, LL.B. (Windsor, 2004), J.D. (University of Detroit Mercy, 2004) and Amy Wilson, LL.B. (Windsor, 2005), J.D. (University of Detroit Mercy, 2005) for assistance with research and footnotes. Any errors remain mine. Research funding was provided by the Canadian-American Research Centre for Law and Policy of the Faculty of Law, University of Windsor and the Law Foundation of Ontario. I was pleased to have the opportunity to discuss the arguments in Assertion 2 at the annual meeting of the Canadian Council on International Law in October 2004.

1 General Agreement on Tariffs and Trade, 30 October 1947, Can. T.S. 1948 No.31, 55 U.N.T.S. 187 (provisionally in force 1 January 1948) [GATT].

2 Agreement on the Application of Sanitary and Phytosanitary Measures, Annex 1A of the Marrakesh Agreement Establishing the World Trade Organization, 15 April 1994, available at <http://www.wto.org>, (1994) 33 I.L.M. 15 [WTO Agreement] [SPS Agreement].

3 Agreement on Technical Barriers to Trade, Annex 1A of the WTO Agreement, *supra* note 2 [TBT Agreement].

Organization (WTO) in 1995, the rules have changed. These two agreements take a market-opening approach that does not depend on the presence or absence of discrimination against imports. Market-access obligations were always part of the GATT, particularly in Article XI, which bans import prohibitions and restrictions. Market access now has a larger role and the national treatment standard is a less reliable guardian. In the new context, GATT Article XX on exemptions assumes increasing importance. This article discusses recent decisions applying Article XX and presents the argument that interpretation should become more balanced in order to promote the development of public policy at the global level.

In 2001, the WTO Appellate Body twice allowed health and environmental interests to take priority over trade obligations. In *European Communities – Measures Affecting Asbestos and Asbestos-Containing Products (Asbestos)*,[4] the product posed a potential risk to human health. The Appellate Body ruled that France's ban on asbestos imports was justified under Article XX of GATT 1994. In *United States – Import Prohibition of Certain Shrimp and Shrimp Products (Shrimp/ Turtle)*,[5] the concern was over shrimp fishing methods that failed to protect certain endangered species of sea turtles. The Appellate Body ruled that the United States's import ban on shrimp caught through objectionable methods was also justified under Article XX. These decisions represent significant developments in the interpretation of WTO legal obligations, acknowledging the importance of non-trade interests and pointing the way towards further accommodation of global public policy. GATT Article XX has always provided exemptions from trade obligations. The two decisions in 2001 rejected overly narrow interpretations of those exemptions.

With the benefits of economic globalization have come fears that private economic actors have increased the power to operate free from regulation. The need to build a global public sphere is quite apparent, and international institutions will respond. Part of this

---

[4] *European Communities – Measures Affecting Asbestos and Asbestos-Containing Products,* Appellate Body Report, Doc. WT/DS135/AB/R, adopted 5 April 2001 [*Asbestos*].

[5] *United States – Import Prohibition of Certain Shrimp and Shrimp Products,* Appellate Body Report, Doc. WT/DS58/AB/R, adopted 6 November 1998 [*Shrimp/Turtle 1998*]; *United States – Import Prohibition of Certain Shrimp and Shrimp Products,* Recourse to Article 21.5 of the DSU by Malaysia, Appellate Body Report, Doc. WT/ DS58/AB/R, adopted 21 November 2001 [*Shrimp/Turtle 2001*].

response involves the debates over exemptions from trade obligations to recognize important non-trade public policies. In this process, the traditional GATT non-discrimination norms have an important continuing role. National treatment, for example, brings the interests of foreigners into account in domestic decision-making and provides an element of even-handedness that should be preserved. In order to find workable solutions, we must retain key elements of the past and concentrate on achieving balance through global public structures.

In this article, I make four assertions, the first two dealing with the interpretation of GATT Article XX and the last two relating to the relationship between national treatment and market access. In order of their appearance, the assertions are as follows:

1. The interpretation of the introductory clause of Article XX should be substantive in order to preserve the even-handedness of the non-discrimination norms of national treatment and most-favoured-nation (MFN) treatment. Article XX should be kept suitable for ongoing analysis of the relationship between trade and non-trade interests.
2. In the interpretation of Article XX, trade interests should not have priority. Rather, interpretation should be balanced in order to provide effective exemptions for the non-trade interests reflected in the paragraphs of the article.
3. The coverage of the national treatment standard should not be expanded in an attempt to protect domestic regulations that block imports. It may be preferable for the development of global public policy to treat certain import bans as breaches of GATT Article XI that would be subject to possible justification under Article XX.
4. The SPS Agreement and TBT Agreement adopt a market-opening approach that will overtake traditional GATT non-discrimination norms in many applications. Exemptions and areas of overlap should be interpreted in harmony with GATT to the extent possible.

The article addresses the interpretation of GATT Articles XX and III in *Shrimp/Turtle* and *Asbestos* against the framework of relevant GATT and WTO decisions. The analysis then proceeds to the TBT and SPS Agreements. The two main cases are summarized in the next part.

THE TWO CASES

SHRIMP/TURTLE

The US import ban at issue in *Shrimp/Turtle* applied to shrimp and shrimp products from countries where the fishing methods failed to protect sea turtles. Initially, Panel and Appellate Body decisions in 1998 found the US measure contrary to GATT. This result was reversed in 2001 when the Panel and the Appellate Body determined that the US measure was justified under Article XX.

The United States adopted the ban due to concern that shrimp fishing methods caused the incidental drowning of sea turtles, recognized as an endangered species. To reduce these losses, the US government developed turtle excluder devices (TEDs), which use a trapdoor mechanism to capture shrimp while deflecting turtles and other large objects out of the fishing nets.[6] Starting in 1987, the United States imposed regulations on shrimp trawlers in its own jurisdiction, requiring the use of TEDs or other control measures to reduce the mortality of sea turtles.[7] In 1991, a ban was established on shrimp imports from several countries in the Caribbean and western Atlantic if the country's regulatory program was not certified as comparable to the US program. These countries had a three-year phase-in period to 1994.[8] In 1996, the import ban was expanded worldwide, following a domestic court decision.[9] The

---

[6] *Shrimp/Turtle 1998,* Panel Report, *supra* note 5 at para. 2.5.

[7] *Ibid.* at para. 2.6.

[8] *Ibid.* at paras. 2.8 and 2.9. Certification required that the country have a comparable regulatory regime and an incidental-taking rate for sea turtles that was comparable to the US rate. Pursuant to guidelines issued in 1991, the foreign regulatory regime would be comparable if it required the use of TEDs or if it included a verifiable scientific program to reduce sea turtle mortality associated with fishing. The guidelines were revised in 1993 to eliminate the second option and simply require the use of TEDs, with some exceptions (para. 2.14). A country could also be certified if its fishing environment for shrimp did not threaten sea turtles (para. 2.7). Revised guidelines in 1996 allowed imports in further circumstances, including imports of shrimp caught in the waters of an uncertified country if the shrimp had been harvested using TEDs (para. 2.12). The US Court of International Trade ruled in late 1996 that this provision for TED-harvested shrimp from the waters of uncertified countries was contrary to the underlying legislation. At the time of the Panel proceedings, this decision was under appeal (para. 2.15 and note 13).

[9] The US Court of International Trade ruled in 1995 that the original guidelines were incorrect in limiting their scope to the Caribbean and western Atlantic region. The court decided that enforcement had to be worldwide (*Ibid.* at paras. 2.10 and 2.11).

dispute was brought by four countries affected by the 1996 expansion, all of which had a phase-in period of four months or less.[10] In the 1998 process, the complaints were brought by India, Pakistan, Thailand, and Malaysia. They argued that the ban was a prohibition on imports contrary to GATT Article XI:1.[11] The United States did not contest that the ban was contrary to Article XI[12] but maintained that it was justified under Article XX. The United States relied principally on the exemption in Article XX(g) for measures "relating to the conservation of exhaustible natural resources if such measures are made effective in conjunction with restrictions on domestic production or consumption." The United States also argued that the ban was necessary to protect animal life and health and, thus, was exempted under Article XX(b).

The 1998 Panel found the US measure inconsistent with Article XI[13] and not justified under Article XX.[14] The Panel began its analysis of Article XX by examining the introductory clause, which the Panel considered was intended to guard against abuse of the exemptions listed in the article.[15] The introductory words state that nothing in the agreement shall be construed to prevent the adoption or enforcement of the exempted measures,

---

[10] India, Pakistan, and Thailand argued that they had a four-month phase-in period (*Ibid.* at paras. 2.10, 3.268, and 7.56). Malaysia argued that its phase-in period was only three months (para. 3.271).

[11] The complainants also argued that the ban involved discrimination in the administration of a quantitative restriction, contrary to GATT Article XIII:1. Since the method of harvesting did not change the nature of the shrimp, they argued that the United States could not accept imports from certified countries while banning imports from non-certified countries. As well, they maintained that the differences in phase-in periods meant that the restrictions were not "similar" for all member countries, as required by Article XIII:1 (*Ibid.* at paras. 3.137–3.142). In addition, India, Pakistan, and Thailand argued that the import ban was contrary to the most-favoured-nation obligation in GATT Article I:1, due in part to the differences in phase-in periods (para. 3.135).

[12] *Ibid.* at para. 3.143. The United States did not accept the complainants' arguments concerning Article I and Article XIII but did not pursue those points in view of its position on Article XI. The United States accepted that the ban was a restriction under Article XI for countries that had not been certified under the US process. As Thailand had been certified (para. 3.136), the admission did not apply to the complaint brought by Thailand.

[13] *Ibid.* at paras. 7.15–7.17. Given this finding, the Panel did not address the arguments concerning Article I and Article XIII.

[14] *Ibid.* at para. 7.62.

[15] *Ibid.* at paras. 7.29, 7.35–7.41.

[s]ubject to the requirement that such measures are not applied in a manner which would constitute a means of arbitrary or unjustifiable discrimination between countries where the same conditions prevail, or a disguised restriction on international trade.

The Panel interpreted the phrase "unjustifiable discrimination" to include measures that undermine the WTO multilateral system and found that the US measure at issue did just that.[16] In the Panel's view, if members were permitted to make access to their markets conditional on the exporting country adopting certain policies, including conservation policies, then market access could be made to depend on compliance with a variety of possibly conflicting requirements for the same products, and the result would lead to the end of the WTO as a multilateral trading system.[17] The Panel further considered that the US measure would normally require international cooperation and found that the United States did not enter into negotiations with the complainants before imposing the ban.[18] In light of its interpretation of the introductory clause of Article XX, the Panel did not address the possible application of Article XX(b) or XX(g) to the US measure.

The 1998 Appellate Body decision reversed the Panel's interpretation of Article XX but still found that the US measure was not justified. The Appellate Body ruled that the Panel should have first analyzed whether the measure was provisionally covered by one of the exemptions in Article XX, before considering the introductory clause.[19] The Appellate Body stated that the Panel's broad test of "undermining the multilateral trading system" was not supported by the words of Article XX. In fact, the Appellate Body noted, unilateralism may be a common feature of measures justified under several of the exceptions listed in Article XX.[20]

The 1998 Appellate Body determined that the US measure was provisionally covered under Article XX(g), as it related to the

---

[16] *Ibid.* at para. 7.44. See also paras. 7.34 and 7.49.

[17] *Ibid.* at para. 7.45.

[18] *Ibid.* at para. 7.56. See paras. 3.98, 3.99, 3.101, and 3.105.

[19] *Shrimp/Turtle 1998*, Appellate Body Report, *supra* note 5 at para. 120: "The standard of 'arbitrary discrimination,' for example, under the chapeau may be different for a measure that purports to be necessary to protect public morals than for one relating to the products of prison labour."

[20] *Ibid.* at para. 121.

conservation of exhaustible natural resources,[21] but then ruled against the US measure under the introductory clause of Article XX. Application of the measure involved "unjustifiable discrimination," according to the Appellate Body, because exporting countries were required to adopt US policy without flexibility to take account of other measures that countries may have chosen for the protection of sea turtles. In practice, countries were required to adopt a regulatory program that was essentially the same as the US one in order to be certified.[22] Other indications of unjustifiable discrimination were the different phase-in periods for different groups of countries[23] and the failure of the United States to engage in serious negotiations with the complaining countries while agreeing to a separate treaty with other shrimp-exporting countries.[24] Inflexibility was also an indication of "arbitrary discrimination," in the Appellate Body's view,[25] as was the lack of a transparent, predictable procedure for the country certification decision.[26] As the Appellate Body found that the application of the US measure constituted both unjustifiable discrimination and arbitrary discrimination, it was not necessary to examine whether the measure involved

[21] *Ibid.* at paras. 134 and 142. The measures were also made effective in conjunction with domestic restrictions, as required by Article XX(g) (para. 145). The main US claim was under Article XX(g), and Article XX(b) was claimed only in the alternative (paras. 125 and 146).

[22] *Ibid.* at paras. 161–65. In response to a question during the hearing, the United States confirmed that, despite wider provisions in the guidelines, US officials decided certification only on the basis of whether a country required TEDs or whether certain limited exceptions applicable to US domestic trawlers applied. See further para. 177, note 181. In addition, the Appellate Body noted that while the dispute was underway, exports from uncertified countries were banned even if the shrimp had been caught using TEDs. The Appellate Body saw this as evidence of the intention to influence the policy of other countries, rather than to protect and conserve sea turtles (para. 165).

[23] *Ibid.* at para.175. The shorter periods meant lower efforts by the United States concerning the transfer of TED technology.

[24] *Ibid.* at paras. 165–72. The United States concluded the Inter-American Convention for the Protection and Conservation of Sea Turtles (1996 U.S.T. Lexis 61) in late 1996 with Brazil, Costa Rica, Mexico, Nicaragua, and Venezuela (para. 169, note 170).

[25] *Ibid.* at para. 177.

[26] *Ibid.* at para. 180. The procedure did not involve a formal opportunity to be heard, written reasons or even specific notification of acceptance or rejection. In connection with this analysis, the Appellate Body referred to the transparency and procedural fairness requirements of GATT Article X:3 and found that they had not been met (paras. 182 and 183).

a disguised restriction on international trade.[27] In the result in 1998, the US measure was contrary to Article XI and was not justified under Article XX.

The matter returned to the WTO in 2000 at the request of Malaysia, which argued that the United States had not brought its system into compliance with GATT following the 1998 ruling. In accordance with Article 21.5 of the Understanding on Rules and Procedures Governing the Settlement of Disputes (DSU),[28] the dispute was referred to a panel composed of the three members of the original panel. After the 1998 decision, the United States kept its import ban in place but issued revised guidelines in 1999. It also attempted to negotiate an agreement on the conservation of sea turtles with countries in the Indian Ocean region. Before the Article 21.5 Panel, Malaysia argued that the measure was still inconsistent with GATT 1994 and that the import ban had to be lifted.

The analysis of the Article 21.5 Panel centred on interpretation of the introductory clause of Article XX, as the United States accepted that the ban was contrary to Article XI and Malaysia accepted that the measure was provisionally justified under Article XX(g).[29] The Panel first addressed the issue of US responsibility concerning negotiations, since the Appellate Body had held that the failure to negotiate seriously with all was part of "unjustifiable discrimination." The Panel viewed this claim as relating to the need to avoid abuse of the Article XX exemptions.[30] Although the objective was to reach a bilateral or multilateral agreement, the Panel ruled that the US responsibility was met through serious, good faith negotiations even though an agreement had not yet been concluded.[31] Concerning flexibility, the Panel ruled that the US

---

[27] *Ibid.* at para. 184.

[28] Understanding on Rules and Procedures Governing the Settlement of Disputes, 1994, Annex 2 to the WTO Agreement, *supra* note 2 [DSU].

[29] *Shrimp/Turtle 2001,* Panel Report, *supra* note 5 at paras. 3.30, 3.43, 5.20, and 5.38. See paras. 5.23 and 5.42.

[30] *Ibid.* at para. 5.50.

[31] *Ibid.* at para. 5.87. The Panel stated that since a multilateral agreement was to be preferred, the unilateral US measure should be seen as provisionally allowed "for emergency reasons" and the extent of serious good faith efforts could be reassessed at any time. Unilateral measures could be definitively accepted if they were part of an international agreement or "if they were taken further to the completion of serious good faith efforts to reach a multilateral agreement" (para. 5.88). At the time of the Panel proceeding, negotiations did not appear to have reached this point.

measure was now sufficiently flexible to comply with Article XX as interpreted by the Appellate Body, since the revised guidelines no longer required that countries adopt US environmental rules in order to be certified, but only a conservation regime "comparable in effectiveness."[32] Application of the US measure, therefore, no longer involved unjustifiable discrimination.[33] As the revised guidelines introduced due process requirements into the certification procedure, the Panel determined that application of the US measure no longer constituted "arbitrary discrimination."[34] Continuing with the rest of the introductory clause in Article XX, the Panel considered that the Article XX(g) exemption would be abused if the US measure were a "disguised restriction on international trade." The US ban, however, was the result of pressure from environmental groups. Noting the US offer of technical assistance to encourage the use of TEDs and the increased opportunity for imports in the revised guidelines, the Panel concluded that the US measure was not applied so as to constitute a disguised restriction on trade.[35] In the result, the US measure was now justified under Article XX, subject to the obligation of ongoing serious good faith efforts to negotiate an agreement.[36]

---

[32] *Ibid.* at paras. 5.102 and 5.104. The United States provided the example of the Northern Prawn Fishery in Australia, where TEDs were found acceptable by US authorities even though they did not conform to all US technical requirements (para. 5.94). Further, the revised guidelines allowed for certification on proof of a comparably effective regulatory program that protected sea turtles from shrimp fishing even without TEDs (para. 5.96). The United States gave the example of Pakistan, which had obtained certification on the basis of TED use and some prohibitions on shrimp trawling (para. 5.100). The Panel concluded that the United States applied the revised guidelines in a manner that considered conditions in the exporting countries (para. 5.102).

[33] Other changes made in the revised guidelines and practice related to imports of TED-caught fish from non-certified countries (*Ibid.* at para. 5.111), a sufficient phase-in period (para. 5.116), and efforts to transfer TED technology (para. 5.120).

[34] *Ibid.* at para. 5.137.

[35] *Ibid.* at paras. 5.143 and 5.144.

[36] *Ibid.* at para. 6.1(b). The Panel concluded that the measure was justified under Article XX "as long as the conditions stated in the findings of this Report, in particular the ongoing serious good faith efforts to reach a multilateral agreement, remain satisfied." This conclusion could be interpreted as including the continuing openness of the US market to imports of TED-caught shrimp from non-certified countries. The US Court of International Trade had decided in July 2000 that this part of the revised guidelines was contrary to the legislation, but had not required the Department of State to change its policy. The matter

The 2001 Appellate Body upheld the findings of the Panel. The Appellate Body confirmed that the US obligation was to negotiate with all, using comparable efforts, resources, and energies,[37] but that the introductory clause of Article XX did not require the successful conclusion of an agreement as a result of those negotiations.[38] The Appellate Body also agreed that the US measure was now sufficiently flexible and no longer involved arbitrary or unjustifiable discrimination. According to the Appellate Body, the United States could condition market access on the exporting country having a regulatory program "comparable in effectiveness" to the US program, as this approach allowed the exporting country to take account of specific conditions in its own territory to achieve the required effectiveness.[39] The changes instituted through the revised guidelines and the ongoing efforts at negotiation meant that, although the US measure breached Article XI, it was justified under Article XX(g).

ASBESTOS

On 1 January 1997, France banned the manufacture and sale of asbestos on its domestic market and banned imports as well. The French decree contained temporary permission for certain uses of asbestos for which no acceptable substitutes were available.[40] In its

---

was under appeal at the time of the Panel proceedings (paras. 5.107–5.109). The United States gave the examples of Australia and Brazil, where shrimp exports from certain fisheries were permitted into the United States even though the two countries were not certified, since they did not require the use of TEDs in all of their fisheries (para. 5.107 and note 232). The Appellate Body in 2001 simply upheld the conclusion of the Panel in the same words, without clarifying the point (*Shrimp/Turtle 2001*, Appellate Body Report, *supra* note 5 at para. 153).

[37] *Shrimp/Turtle 2001*, Appellate Body Report, *supra* note 5 at para. 122

[38] *Ibid.* at paras. 123 and 134. The Appellate Body noted one disagreement with the reasoning of the Panel in this respect. The Panel had stated that the United States bore an especially heavy burden in negotiations, given its scientific, diplomatic, and financial means. The Appellate Body disagreed with this emphasis on the circumstances of a particular country and ruled that the good faith obligation applies to all WTO members equally (para.134, note 97).

[39] *Ibid.* at para. 144. As Malaysia did not appeal the Panel's conclusion that the US measure was not a disguised restriction on international trade, that Panel finding remained undisturbed (paras. 82 and 118, note 68).

[40] *Asbestos*, Panel Report, *supra* note 4 at para. 3.8. The scope of this permission was defined through a list to be updated annually until 2002 when the ban became total. See further para. 3.32.

complaint against the European Communities (EC), Canada argued that the measure was contrary to certain WTO obligations and was not justified under GATT Article XX.[41] The exemption at issue in Article XX(b) provides that nothing in GATT is to prevent the adoption or enforcement of measures "necessary to protect human, animal or plant life or health."

Canada claimed that the measure breached GATT Article III:4,[42] which requires that imports receive "treatment no less favourable than that accorded to like products of national origin in respect of all laws, regulations and requirements affecting their internal sale, offering for sale, purchase, transportation, distribution or use." Canada also claimed that the import ban was a quantitative restriction contrary to GATT Article XI. Pursuant to the Note Ad Article III, the Panel treated the ban as an internal measure enforced against imports at the time of importation and did not pursue the analysis under Article XI.

Concerning Article III:4, the Panel had to decide whether the decree failed to give national treatment to Canadian asbestos exports by favouring "like products" of French origin. Since asbestos could not be produced or sold in France, Canada argued that there were other domestically produced goods that qualified as "like" imports. The Panel addressed both asbestos fibre and products containing asbestos fibre in a cement matrix, which is the most common form in which asbestos was used in France.[43] The Panel found that certain domestically produced substitute fibres were like asbestos fibres since they shared similar end uses.[44] Cement

---

41 Canada is the world's leading exporter of chrysotile asbestos, the main type of asbestos consumed worldwide (*Ibid.* at paras. 3.20, 3.22, and 3.105).

42 *Ibid.* at paras. 8.87–8.100, and 8.159. Canada also based its claim on the TBT Agreement, *supra* note 3. The Panel and the Appellate Body disagreed on the interpretation of the TBT Agreement, and the argument was not fully examined. This issue is summarized after the outline of the Panel and Appellate Body reasoning on Articles III and XX. The Panel dealt with and rejected a further claim by Canada that the decree constituted non-violation nullification and impairment under GATT Article XXIII:1(b) (Panel Report, *Asbestos, supra* note 4 at para. 8.282). The Appellate Body supported the Panel's reasoning on Article XXIII:1(b) (*Asbestos,* Appellate Body Report, *supra* note 4 at para. 192). The initial notification from Canada also mentioned the SPS Agreement, *supra* note 2, but Canada did not pursue this issue in argument (*Asbestos,* Panel Report, *supra* note 4 at para. 1.2; *Asbestos,* Appellate Body Report, *supra* note 4 at para. 3, note 4).

43 *Asbestos,* Panel Report, *supra* note 4 at paras. 3.128 and 8.105.

44 *Ibid.* at paras. 8.124–8.126 and 8.144. The substitute fibres identified by Canada were polyvinyl alcohol, cellulose, and glass. Considering the rules governing

products containing the substitute fibres were like asbestos-cement products, as they shared end uses, external appearance, and tariff classification.[45] In its analysis on the issue of like goods, the Panel declined to take account of the greater risk of cancer associated with asbestos as compared to the substitutes. The Panel reasoned that taking risk into account for the choice of like goods in Article III would undermine and replace an analysis of health risks under Article XX(b).[46] As the substitute fibres and products were not banned by France or subject to the same restrictions as those that applied to asbestos, the Panel concluded that France had violated Article III:4.[47]

The Panel then addressed the EC argument that the measure was justified under Article XX(b) as necessary for the protection of human life and health. Canada argued that chrysotile asbestos encapsulated in a matrix could be used without detectable risk to health and that the ban was unnecessary.[48] According to Canada, any current risk was associated with past use, which the ban did nothing to address.[49] The Panel assessed the scientific evidence, consulting experts pursuant to Article 13 of the DSU, and found that a public official could reasonably conclude that asbestos products posed a health risk.[50] Controlled use, as suggested by Canada, was difficult to apply in the building sector, especially among the service trades and do-it-yourself enthusiasts.[51] France's objective was to halt the spread of asbestos-related risk,[52] and the Panel could

---

burden of proof, the Panel restricted its examination to those products (paras. 8.107 and 8.150).

[45] *Ibid.* at paras. 8.146, 8.148, and 8.150.

[46] *Ibid.* at paras. 8.129–8.132, and 8.149.

[47] *Ibid.* at paras. 8.157 and 8.158.

[48] *Ibid.* at paras. 3.9, 3.54–3.56, and 8.163–8.165.

[49] *Ibid.* at paras. 3.12 and 3.57.

[50] *Ibid.* at para. 8.193.

[51] *Ibid.* at paras. 8.209–8.217. Controlled use requires using low-speed saws with water injection or vacuum systems, using pressure chains to break pipes (paras. 3.296 and 3.489) and wearing a mask (para. 3.56, Canada) or "diver's suit" (para. 3.296, EC – see para. 3.63). Controlled-use practices would be necessary in construction, in building maintenance and services, and in do-it-yourself projects. The tools required could be heavy and time-consuming to set up (para. 3.171, EC). The EC argued that there was no way of monitoring the use of asbestos once it was in the market to make sure that the procedures were followed (para. 3.490).

[52] *Ibid.* at paras. 3.18, 3.59, and 8.185.

not question France's chosen level of protection.[53] The Panel found
that France had no reasonable alternative in light of the objective
and that the measure was justified under Article XX(b).[54]

The Appellate Body upheld the Panel's finding that the decree
was justified under Article XX(b). As the trier of fact, the Panel has
a margin of discretion in assessing the evidence.[55] France had chosen to halt the spread of the risk, as it was entitled to do,[56] and
controlled use was not shown to be effective to achieve that level of
protection.[57] Concerning Article III:4, the Appellate Body disagreed
with the Panel and was "very much of the view" that the health risks
should be considered in the determination of like products.[58] The
risks were part of the physical properties of asbestos.[59] As well, the
health risks associated with asbestos would affect consumers' tastes
and habits.[60] The Appellate Body concluded that Canada had not
demonstrated that the substitute fibres and products were like asbestos fibres and products.[61] Canada, therefore, had failed to prove
that the measure breached Article III:4, and the Panel's finding of
inconsistency was reversed.[62]

Before the Panel, Canada had also presented argument based on
the TBT Agreement. Canada claimed that the measure breached
Article 2.1 of this agreement by failing to provide national treatment,[63]
breached Article 2.2 by creating an unnecessary obstacle to trade,[64]
breached Article 2.4 by failing to use international standards from

---

[53] *Ibid.* at paras. 8.179 and 8.210.

[54] *Ibid.* at paras. 8.222, 8.240, and 8.241.

[55] *Asbestos*, Appellate Body Report, *supra* note 4 at para. 161.

[56] *Ibid.* at para. 168.

[57] *Ibid.* at para. 174.

[58] *Ibid.* at para. 113.

[59] *Ibid.* at paras. 114, 128, 134–36, and 142.

[60] *Ibid.* at paras. 121–23, 130, 139, and 145.

[61] *Ibid.* at para.147. In a concurring statement, one member of the Appellate Body
indicated that this finding did not have to be qualified as a question of Canada's
burden of proof. Given the serious health risks, this member of the Appellate
Body would have made an unqualified finding that these were not like products,
since it was difficult to imagine what other evidence of end uses and consumer
tastes and habits could outweigh the deadly nature of asbestos (paras. 152 and
153).

[62] *Ibid.* at para. 148.

[63] *Asbestos*, Panel Report, *supra* note 4 at paras. 3.266–3.269.

[64] *Ibid.* at paras. 3.273–3.289, 3.298–3.312, and 3.322–3.352.

the International Labour Organization (ILO) and the International Organization for Standardization (ISO),[65] and breached Article 2.8 by failing to base product requirements on performance rather than description.[66] The Panel had to decide whether the French decree was a technical regulation — that is, "a document which lays down product characteristics or their related processes and production methods ... with which compliance is mandatory."[67] The Panel decided that this definition did not include a general ban on a product but was intended only for technical specifications that a product had to meet in order to be marketed.[68] Although the exceptions allowing for temporary use did qualify as "technical regulations,"[69] Canada had not made any claims relating specifically to those exceptions, and the Panel did not continue the analysis on this issue.[70]

The Appellate Body reversed the Panel's reasoning concerning the TBT Agreement. The decree was examined as a whole, since the exceptions had no separate existence apart from the ban.[71] Although the agreement might not apply to a total ban on asbestos fibres alone,[72] the decree in fact regulated products containing fibres and required that they not contain asbestos fibres. This requirement was a negative "product characteristic," and the decree therefore was a technical regulation subject to the agreement.[73] Since the Panel had made no findings on Canada's detailed arguments under the agreement, however, the Appellate Body considered that it did not have a sufficient basis on which to complete the review.[74]

In the result, Canada failed to prove the breach of the national treatment obligation, but the ban on asbestos would have been justified under GATT Article XX in any event. As well, there were insufficient findings at the Panel level for the Appellate Body to

---

[65] *Ibid.* at paras. 3.358–3.361, 3.369–3.372, and 3.377–3.386.

[66] *Ibid.* at paras. 3.388–3.389, and 3.392–3.393.

[67] TBT Agreement, *supra* note 3, Annex I.

[68] *Asbestos,* Panel Report, *supra* note 4 at paras. 8.40, 8.43, and 8.63.

[69] *Ibid.* at paras. 8.64–8.69.

[70] *Ibid.* at para. 8.72. Although the EC had notified the decree to the Committee on Technical Barriers to Trade, the Panel found that the EC was not estopped from arguing against application of the TBT Agreement (para. 8.60).

[71] *Asbestos,* Appellate Body Report, *supra* note 4 at para. 64.

[72] *Ibid.* at para. 71.

[73] *Ibid.* at paras. 72, and 74–76.

[74] *Ibid.* at paras. 81–83.

examine Canada's claims under the TBT Agreement. The Appellate Body used the health risk in its analysis of both justification under Article XX and the determination of like products under Article III.

ASSERTION 1: THE INTERPRETATION OF THE INTRODUCTORY CLAUSE OF ARTICLE XX SHOULD BE SUBSTANTIVE IN ORDER TO PRESERVE THE EVEN-HANDEDNESS OF THE NON-DISCRIMINATION NORMS OF NATIONAL TREATMENT AND MFN TREATMENT. ARTICLE XX SHOULD BE KEPT SUITABLE FOR ONGOING ANALYSIS OF THE RELATIONSHIP BETWEEN TRADE AND NON-TRADE INTERESTS

This part of the article addresses the *Shrimp/Turtle* dispute and presents the assertion that the analysis of Article XX should become more substantive if the even-handedness of the non-discrimination norms is to be preserved. In *Shrimp/Turtle,* the interpretation of Article xx took a procedural turn, emphasizing flexibility, negotiation, and due process rather than the content of the alleged discrimination. The argument in this part is that it is important to address the substance of Article XX and the exemptions in order to establish approaches for the balancing of trade and non-trade interests in GATT and other agreements, such as the SPS Agreement and the TBT Agreement. The sections below address first the analysis of flexibility and, then, other procedural issues including due process and the duty to negotiate. An alternative, substantive argument is presented in the third section. Unilateralism is the final topic, particularly as it appears in the *Shrimp/Turtle* dispute, concerning the treatment of processing and production methods that are not reflected in the physical characteristics of the goods.

ARTICLE XX — FLEXIBILITY

The result of the WTO dispute is that the United States is not in breach of its GATT obligations when it continues to condition access to its market on adoption of certain conservation policies in the territories of exporting countries. Although the Panel and Appellate Body in 2001 found more flexibility in the 1999 US guidelines, this flexibility is only at a level of fairly refined detail. The general policy must still be followed. Sea turtles must be protected, and they must be protected through methods that have an effect comparable to those used in the US domestic system. In order for their exports to have access to the market in the United States, countries must adopt US conservation policy.

In its submissions, Malaysia had argued that it was protecting sea turtles in its own way and that the US provisions interfered in Malaysia's national sovereignty. Malaysia contended that, in fact, it had programs for the protection of sea turtle nesting grounds on its beaches and that, in Malaysia, the nesting season for turtles does not overlap with the shrimp season. According to Malaysia, any incidental catch of sea turtles related to fish trawling in general, not specifically to shrimp trawling, and Malaysia had prohibited the use of fishing nets with large mesh sizes in order to reduce turtle mortality.[75] Malaysia noted that one of the scientists consulted by the 1998 Panel had praised Malaysia's efforts to protect nesting stocks of turtles, describing the Malaysian system as "one of the best conservation programmes for marine turtles anywhere in the world."[76] Now, as a result of the WTO dispute, if Malaysia wishes to export shrimp or shrimp products to the United States, US standards will apply, and they may distort Malaysia's priorities, as the 2001 Panel noted.[77] Malaysia can avoid these standards only by refraining from exporting to the United States.

In response, the United States had maintained that the Article XX exemptions were intended for the recognition of important non-trade policies, such as the conservation of endangered species, and noted that the same expert mentioned by Malaysia considered that the most significant threat to sea turtles came from fishing.[78] Throughout the case, the United States argued that it should be able

---

[75] *Shrimp/Turtle 1998,* Panel Report, *supra* note 5 at paras. 3.7–3.10; *Shrimp/Turtle 2001,* Panel Report, *supra* note 5 at paras. 3.124–3.131; *Shrimp/Turtle 2001,* Appellate Body Report, *supra* note 5 at para. 145 at note 106. In the 1998 Panel proceedings, India, Pakistan, and Thailand also noted that they had their own programs for the protection of sea turtles (*Shrimp/Turtle 1998,* Panel Report, *supra* note 5 at paras. 3.4–3.6 and paras. 3.11–3.16). India, in particular, mentioned the costs of TEDs and submitted that these had to be considered in context. While TEDs might be inexpensive by US standards, they would be very expensive to the average owners of fishing vessels in India. As well, in India, the larger fish that were also caught in shrimp nets were of economic value and would be lost if TEDS were used (*Shrimp/Turtle 1998,* Panel Report, *supra* note 5 at paras. 3.81–3.82). See further Thailand's arguments that the 1999 guidelines lacked flexibility since TED use was still the standard applied by US authorities: *Shrimp/Turtle 2001,* Panel Report, *supra* note 5 at para. 4.107.

[76] *Shrimp/Turtle 2001,* Panel Report, *supra* note 5 at para. 3.162.

[77] *Ibid.* at para. 5.103

[78] *Shrimp/Turtle 1998,* Panel Report, *supra* note 5 at para. 3.152; *Shrimp/Turtle 2001,* Panel Report, *supra* note 5 at para. 3.163

to prevent its market from causing a further threat to endangered species and that GATT did not require the United States to become an unwilling partner in the extinction of sea turtles.[79] In 2001, the Panel and Appellate Body agreed, finding that the US measure was covered by the exemption in GATT Article XX(g).

The reasoning of the *Shrimp/Turtle* decisions centres around the interpretation of the introductory words of GATT Article XX, which govern the specific paragraphs of the article:

Subject to the requirement that such measures are not applied in a manner which would constitute a means of arbitrary or unjustifiable discrimination between countries where the same conditions prevail, or a disguised restriction on international trade, nothing in this Agreement shall be construed to prevent the adoption or enforcement by any Member of measures.

The 1998 Appellate Body addressed the coercive effect of the US measure by finding a requirement of flexibility in the avoidance of "arbitrary or unjustifiable discrimination."[80] Initially, the Appellate Body speaks of this as relating to "[o]ther specific policies and measures that an exporting country may have adopted for the protection and conservation of sea turtles"[81] — wording that seems to defer to the exporting country and that would be wide enough to cover programs for something other than shrimp fishing. The Appellate Body then says that the United States cannot apply to other countries the same uniform standard that it applies at home without "taking into consideration different conditions which may occur in the territories" of the exporting countries — a phrase that effectively removes the choice for exporting countries.[82] By the time

---

[79] *Shrimp/Turtle 1998,* Panel Report, *supra* note 5 at para. 3.145.

[80] *Shrimp/Turtle 1998,* Appellate Body Report, *supra* note 5 at para. 161. ("Perhaps the most conspicuous flaw in this measure's application relates to its intended and actual coercive effect on the specific policy decisions made by foreign governments.")

[81] *Ibid.* at para. 163.

[82] *Ibid.* at para. 164. The Appellate Body linked this analysis to the ban on imports from uncertified countries even if the shrimp had been caught using TEDs. The Appellate Body concluded that the measure was intended to influence other WTO members to adopt "essentially the same comprehensive regulatory regime as that applied by the United States to its domestic shrimp trawlers" (para. 165). The Appellate Body stated that "discrimination results not only when countries in which the same conditions prevail are differently treated, but also when the application of the measure at issue does not allow for any

the Appellate Body concludes its analysis of "unjustifiable discrimination" and addresses "arbitrary discrimination," the problem is
that the measure requires countries to "adopt a comprehensive
regulatory program that is essentially the same as the United States's
program, without inquiring into the appropriateness of that program for the conditions prevailing in the exporting countries."[83]
On this analysis of flexibility, the exporting countries are not the
judges of the appropriateness of the US measure for local conditions, and they are not the ones who choose whether to focus on
nesting beaches or shrimp trawling.

The 2001 Appellate Body decision addresses flexibility in a similar manner. The Appellate Body states that the difference between
requiring essentially the same regulatory regime and requiring only
a regime comparable in effectiveness is that the increased flexibility "allows the exporting Member to adopt a regulatory programme
that is suitable to the specific conditions prevailing in its territory,"[84]
wording that appears to give some choice to the exporting country.
The Appellate Body then notes provisions in the revised US guidelines that refer to programs of comparable effectiveness concerning shrimp trawl fishing and to other measures, including the
protection of nesting beaches, all of which are to be taken into
account in the certification process.[85] The Appellate Body concludes
that the revised guidelines demonstrate sufficient flexibility to allow for the conditions in Malaysia.[86] It may be noted, however, that
the same guidelines still indicated that the United States was "presently aware of no measure or series of measures that can minimize
the capture and drowning of sea turtles ... that is comparable in
effectiveness to the required use of TEDs."[87] As well, the examples
of additional flexibility cited before the Panel in 2001 involved
Pakistan, which had been certified on the basis of a combination of

---

inquiry into the appropriateness of the regulatory program for the conditions
prevailing in those exporting countries" (*ibid.*).

[83] *Ibid.* at para. 177.

[84] *Shrimp/Turtle 2001*, Appellate Body Report, *supra* note 5 at para. 144.

[85] *Ibid.* at paras. 146 and 147.

[86] *Ibid.* at para. 144. Before the 2001 Panel, the representative of the United States
stated that there was nothing in the Malaysian program that would make it impossible for the United States to grant certification, should Malaysia decide to
apply (*Shrimp/Turtle 2001*, Panel Report, *supra* note 5 at para. 5.101).

[87] *Shrimp/Turtle 2001*, Panel Report, *supra* note 5 at Annex, II.B.(a)17.

TED requirements and prohibitions on shrimp trawling[88] and shrimp from certain fishing grounds in Australia, which could be imported into the United States on the basis of the low presence of sea turtles in the area (Spencer Gulf) or a requirement of TED use (Northern Prawn fisheries).[89] No example was given of imports found acceptable on the basis of the exporting country's program to protect nesting beaches. The United States still sets the standard, and exporting countries are not the judges.[90]

This coercive effect is what should be expected once we accept that the US measure is covered by Article XX(g) and that Article XX measures can be unilateral. There is no point in creating reverse coercion and forcing the United States to be, in its view, an unwilling instrument of the extinction of sea turtles. If the measure is justified under Article XX, then the importing country sets the standard. The phrasing in the Appellate Body decisions that at first appears to acknowledge choice by exporting countries might soften the blow initially but does not change the situation. Even in this dispute, when the countries involved all agreed on the basic policy of protecting sea turtles, the actual flexibility was illusory.

This interpretation of "arbitrary or unjustifiable discrimination" was novel in *Shrimp/Turtle* and presents some problems. As the facts in *Shrimp/Turtle* demonstrate, flexibility is not a terribly demanding standard. If this is the main sort of review that an importing country will have to meet under the introductory clause of Article XX, that review will not accomplish a great deal. The language used in the introductory wording appears to call for a review that is more onerous and more in line with the goal of controlling protectionism and trade restrictions in masquerade. There is nothing in the words of Article XX that explicitly requires flexibility. The *Shrimp/Turtle* approach was a specific interpretation of the introductory clause for the facts of this dispute, but it should not be seen as the main or only interpretation.

A major difficulty raised by the requirement of flexibility is the question of how it fits with the GATT obligation of national treatment. While there can be questions about what actually constitutes national treatment in particular conditions, a uniform tax or standard applied to both domestic and imported goods would usually meet Article III. The measure needs to be judged in context to see

---

[88] *Ibid. at* para. 5.100

[89] *Ibid.* at paras. 3.137, 3.138, 5.94, 5.100, and 5.124.

[90] *Ibid.* at para. 3.171 (Malaysia), para. 4.107 (Thailand).

whether it imposes a greater tax burden on imports or otherwise treats them less favourably than domestic goods,[91] but uniformity is generally the opposite of discrimination in GATT law and there is no call for flexibility. If a domestic measure breaches Article III and the importing country relies on Article XX for an exemption, the background might be quite different from the facts in *Shrimp/ Turtle*. The domestic measure may have nothing to do with the conditions in the country of export. Flexibility concerning these conditions may be quite irrelevant to the dispute. In this context, a prohibition on "arbitrary or unjustifiable discrimination" must have some other meaning.[92]

Even for measures that do relate to conditions in the country of export, flexibility is still directed at only a limited set of circumstances. *Shrimp/Turtle* involved a border measure and was not argued as an Article III dispute, but it was noted that, at various times, shrimp caught using TEDs that met the US domestic standard would nevertheless be barred if they were from a non-certified country.[93] Under Article III:4 of GATT, imported products are entitled to treatment that is "no less favourable" than the treatment accorded like products of national origin. It does not take much to imagine facts that would transform the *Shrimp/Turtle* dispute into one about internal sale, transportation, distribution, or use of imported products within the wording of Article III:4. In that case, as discussed later in this article concerning Assertion 3, two lines of reasoning

[91] *Dominican Republic – Measures Affecting the Importation and Internal Sale of Cigarettes*, Appellate Body Report, Doc. WT/DS302/AB/R, adopted 19 May 2005, para. 94.

[92] In the *Asbestos* dispute, for example, it was not argued that the EC had to make its import ban flexible in order to meet the requirements of Article XX.

[93] Throughout the 1998 process, TED-caught shrimp from non-certified countries was, in practice, banned from the US market due to domestic court decisions (*Shrimp/Turtle 1998*, Appellate Body Report, *supra* note 5 at paras. 5.165). In contrast, during the 2001 process, shrimp from non-certified countries was permitted to enter the United States pursuant to the revised guidelines, despite a decision of the US Court of International Trade to the contrary. That decision had not been implemented in departmental practice, pending an appeal (*Shrimp/ Turtle 2001*, Panel Report, *supra* note 5 at paras. 2.18, 3.121, 3.147, 4.83, 4.104, and 5.109–5.111; *Shrimp/Turtle 2001*, Appellate Body Report, *supra* note 5 at paras. 25, 64, 93–95, and 151). On appeal to the Court of Appeals for the Federal Circuit and the US Supreme Court, the decision of the Court of International Trade was later reversed and the departmental guidelines were upheld (Sean D. Murphy, ed., "Contemporary Practice of the United States Relating to International Law" (2003) 97 Am. J. Int'l L. 681 at 691–92).

are possible for the analysis of such a measure. On one line of reasoning, the production or processing method (PPM) does not
change the nature of the product, and all shrimp, imported and
domestic, must receive the same favourable level of treatment. A
measure that discriminated against imports for failure to meet a
PPM applying to domestic goods would breach Article III:4. The
alternate line of reasoning considers the PPM as the "treatment"
imposed by the importing country and looks to see whether imported goods receive treatment that is at least as favourable as the
treatment granted to domestic products — that is, whether potential imports have the same opportunity of complying with the PPM
as domestic goods do. In both lines of reasoning, on whatever is
being judged, the GATT value is uniformity to ensure even-handedness. If there is a breach of Article III and if the importing member claims a justification under one of the paragraphs of Article
XX, it is hard to see why the introductory words of that article should
be interpreted so as to encourage flexibility. Why should the underlying policy change to, in effect, the opposite of uniformity?

The Panel in 1998 made a potentially significant distinction between exported products and the policies adopted by exporting
countries. Referring to the Article XX(e) exemption for the products of prison labour, the Panel noted that this exemption refers to
the products themselves and not to the policy of the exporting country.[94] The 1998 Appellate Body saw the ban on TED-caught shrimp
from non-certified countries as evidence of an intent to coerce other
countries,[95] and flexibility was one of the answers to this perceived
coercion. The Appellate Body states that while it is acceptable for
the United States to apply a uniform standard within its own territory, it is not acceptable to require other WTO members to adopt
essentially the same regulatory program, without taking account of
local differences.[96] It is best to treat *Shrimp/Turtle* as dealing most
specifically with the situation in which the measure at issue certi-
fies the entire regime of an exporting country as complying or not
complying. There should be room for other interpretations of the
introductory words of Article XX, especially if the measure in question lacks the country-certification features of the measure in *Shrimp/
Turtle.*

[94] *Shrimp/Turtle 1998,* Panel Report, *supra* note 5 at footnote 649.

[95] *Shrimp/Turtle 1998,* Appellate Body Report, *supra* note 5 at para. 165. The Appellate Body also said that such coercive intent was "difficult to reconcile with
the declared policy objective of protecting and conserving sea turtles" (*ibid.*).

[96] *Ibid.* at para. 164.

ARTICLE XX — NEGOTIATION AND DUE PROCESS

The 1998 Appellate Body also looked at coercion and unilateralism when it discussed the duty to negotiate. Since the United States had failed to negotiate seriously with the complaining states, the result according to the Appellate Body was that US authorities alone set the policies and decided on certification.[97] This failure to negotiate was a factor in the finding of unjustifiable discrimination contrary to the introductory clause of Article XX, along with differences in the effort made to negotiate with some countries as compared to others, including the complainants. In contrast, the 2001 Appellate Body does not have the same focus on unilateralism when it discusses the duty to negotiate, but it emphasizes instead the need for similar treatment of all exporting nations. In order to meet the requirements of the introductory clause, the negotiations with each country must involve comparable efforts, resources, and energies, according to the Appellate Body in 2001.[98] This latter interpretive approach emphasizes the absence of discrimination and is consistent with the idea that the introductory clause in Article XX has to do with preserving the benefits of national and MFN treatment in the case of exempted measures.[99] It is not clear, however, that the duty has become one simply of non-discriminatory treatment, since both the Panel and the Appellate Body in 2001 state that the United States is subject to an ongoing obligation of good faith negotiation. The Appellate Body upheld and quoted the determination from the Panel report that the US measure "is justified under Article XX of the GATT 1994 as long as the conditions stated in the findings of this Report, in particular the ongoing serious, good faith efforts to reach a multilateral agreement, remain satisfied."[100]

---

[97] *Ibid.* at para. 172.

[98] *Shrimp/Turtle 2001*, Appellate Body Report, *supra* note 5 at para. 122.

[99] In the 1998 Panel, India, Pakistan, and Thailand argued that the differences in the phase-in periods were contrary to Article I:1 and Article XIII:1 (*Shrimp/Turtle 1998*, Panel Report, *supra* note 5 at paras. 3.135 and 3.139).

[100] *Shrimp/Turtle 2001*, Appellate Body Report, *supra* note 5 at paras. 152, 153(b), quoting from *Shrimp/Turtle 2001*, Panel Report, *supra* note 5 at para. 6.1(b). The Panel viewed this as a provisional exemption granted for emergency reasons while negotiations continued, rather than a right to a permanent measure (*Ibid.* at para. 5.88). See Kuei-Jung Ni, "Redefinition and Elaboration of an Obligation to Pursue International Negotiations for Solving Global Environmental Problems in Light of the WTO Shrimp/Turtle Compliance Adjudication between Malaysia and the United States" (2004) 14 Minn. J. Global Trade 111.

Like the requirement of flexibility, the duty to negotiate can be seen as relating specifically to the facts of the *Shrimp/Turtle* dispute. A duty to negotiate, of course, may not be particularly demanding.[101] The importing country cannot guarantee successful negotiations, and there is no requirement that an agreement be concluded.[102] A duty to negotiate is a somewhat weak counterbalance for coercion, since negotiations in any future disputes are now bound to be influenced by the fact that measures unilaterally imposed by an importing country have been found acceptable under Article XX.[103] There is nothing in the introductory words of Article XX that explicitly requires negotiation.[104] In future disputes, particularly those without the country-certification feature of the measure at issue in *Shrimp/Turtle*, the introductory clause of Article XX might not be interpreted as imposing a duty to negotiate.[105]

Similar comments apply to the "due process" interpretation of the prohibition on "arbitrary discrimination" by the Appellate Body in 1998. The Appellate Body stated then that the lack of due process was part of the finding of arbitrary discrimination, involving discrimination against the unsuccessful applicants for certification — although the successful applicants also seem to have received the same lack of due process.[106] The Appellate Body drew the

---

[101] In the 2001 process, Australia argued unsuccessfully that the United States had not met the burden of justification under Article XX, given the progress made on the initiative among Indian Ocean nations (*Shrimp/Turtle 2001*, Appellate Body Report, *supra* note 5 at paras. 49 and 50). See also *Shrimp/Turtle 2001*, Panel Report, *supra* note 5 at para. 4.26, where Australia argued that good faith negotiations should involve possible changes in the "existence or nature" of the import ban, and not just details of implementation.

[102] *Shrimp/Turtle 2001*, Appellate Body Report, *supra* note 5 at paras. 124 and 134. See US argument, *Shrimp/Turtle 2001*, Panel Report, *supra* note 5 at para. 3.117.

[103] See *Shrimp/Turtle 2001*, Panel Report, *supra* note 5 at para. 5.73.

[104] See the argument by Mexico, *Shrimp/Turtle 2001*, Panel Report, *supra* note 5 at para. 4.85.

[105] Note the criticisms of the Appellate Body's approach in Donald M. McRae, "GATT Article XX and the WTO Appellate Body," in Marco Bronckers and Reinhard Quick, eds., *New Directions in International Economic Law: Essays in Honour of John H. Jackson* (The Hague / London / Boston: Kluwer Law International, 2000) 217 at 230–31: "To require that only measures that result from negotiations with other Members fall within the scope of Article XX, or of paragraph (g) of that Article changes the nature of Article XX completely. It would deny the right to invoke exceptions to WTO obligations and supplant Article XX with a rule based on negotiated exceptions" (*Ibid.* at 234).

[106] *Shrimp/Turtle 1998*, Appellate Body Report, *supra* note 5 at paras. 180 and 181.

requirement of due process from GATT Article X:3. In 2001, the Appellate Body decision did not deal directly with the question, since the process problems had been solved in the 1999 revised guidelines.[107] Nevertheless, in the discussion of flexibility to permit certification based on measures such as the protection of nesting beaches, the 2001 Appellate Body decision mentions the requirement of reasons in the revised guidelines if certification is going to be refused.[108] Like flexibility and a duty to negotiate, due process is not expressly contained in the introductory words of Article XX. The due process interpretation of those introductory words seems to be directed mainly to the set of facts in *Shrimp/Turtle* and might not apply in other disputes, particularly since other provisions of the WTO dispute settlement process require consultation before a matter moves forward.

ARTICLE XX — SUBSTANTIVE ANALYSIS

To summarize the analysis so far, it has been argued that the procedural interpretation of the introductory clause of Article XX in *Shrimp/Turtle* should be treated as having limited application and that a more substantive interpretation should be adopted in other disputes to preserve traditional GATT non-discrimination norms. In this next section, it is argued further that the interpretation in the *Shrimp/Turtle* dispute itself should have been substantive and that the same result could have been reached without bypassing those traditional non-discrimination norms. The major challenge for this further argument is that the Appellate Body in *Shrimp/Turtle* was presented with the substantive interpretation, more or less, but rejected it.

Before the 1998 Appellate Body, the United States argued in favour of a substantive approach to the introductory wording of Article XX. The United States argued that whether discrimination was "unjustifiable" in terms of Article XX depended on whether the differing treatment was based on a rationale legitimately connected with the policy of the Article XX exception. The question would be, for example, whether the conservation goal of a measure described in Article XX(g) provided a justification for the discrimination.[109] India, Pakistan, and Thailand argued against this

---

[107] See *Shrimp/Turtle 2001*, Panel Report, *supra* note 5 at paras. 5.126–5.136.

[108] *Shrimp/Turtle 2001*, Appellate Body Report, *supra* note 5 at para. 147.

[109] *Shrimp/Turtle 1998*, Appellate Body Report, *supra* note 5 at paras. 148 and 15.
    This is not exactly the substantive approach that is suggested later in this

approach, saying it would render the introductory words meaningless, since any trade measure meeting the requirements of a listed
exception would be automatically covered by the introductory paragraph.[110] The Appellate Body rejected the US argument, which it
viewed as disregarding the words of Article XX.[111]

The Appellate Body then developed its interpretation of the introductory clause, referring to the context of the language and indications of object and purpose as well as negotiating history. In
the review of negotiating history,[112] the Appellate Body noted that
the drafters intended to prevent protectionism and avoid results
irreconcilable with the aims of other parts of the treaty. The Appellate Body then went on to interpret "arbitrary or unjustifiable discrimination" as implying the duties of flexibility, negotiation, and
due process. This procedural interpretation, however, is not the only
possible way of differentiating the introductory clause from the listed
paragraphs of Article XX. The paragraphs provide various sorts of
links to the exempted policy: "necessary to," "relating to," "imposed
for," "undertaken in pursuance of," "involving," and "essential to."
A measure might be described in one of those paragraphs and yet
still contain elements of discrimination — a word that receives little
attention in the Appellate Body's procedural interpretation. The
introductory clause can be taken as guaranteeing that an exemption
will not be used as an excuse for protectionism. In this view, the
introduction is intended to preserve the non-discrimination norms
and prevent masquerades. Article XX provides exemptions for
breaches of all of the other provisions of GATT, not just Articles I
and III concerning MFN treatment and national treatment. For all
of these possible breaches, the introductory words of Article XX
ensure a review for the non-discrimination norms and disguised
protectionism when a member claims exemption under one of the
listed paragraphs. If a measure breaches Articles I (MFN) or III
(national treatment), the analysis in Article XX should require two
steps, just as it does in the case of any other breach — first the
possible application of one of the paragraphs of Article XX and,
second, the interpretation of the introductory words. If a provisional assessment of the application of a listed paragraph also

---

section, which would consider the member's chosen level of protection as
expressed in the measure and the link between that level and the discrimination.

[110] *Ibid.* at paras. 43 and 44.

[111] *Ibid.* at para.149.

[112] *Ibid.* at para.157.

involves a complete analysis of the discrimination, then the inter-
preter has simply combined the two steps. The Appellate Body stated
that the introductory words of Article XX imposed both substantive and procedural requirements[113] but did not expand on the full
range of substantive interpretations.

In *Shrimp/Turtle,* the United States acknowledged a breach of
Article XI on quantitative restrictions. It would also have been possible to decide that the differing negotiation efforts and phase-in
periods breached Article I or Article XIII, and the lack of due process breached Article X. Whatever the initial breach, assuming Article XX(g) is provisionally met, analysis would turn to the
introductory clause of Article XX. On a substantive interpretation,
it is unlikely that the US measure would have been exempted in
the 1998 process, as the chosen level of environmental protection
does not explain the various types of discrimination. In 2001, once
the problems had been addressed, the US measure could have been
found either in conformity with the other articles cited or exempted
pursuant to Article XX. This approach, which preserves the non-
discrimination norms, would be a more effective way of respecting
the drafters' intent and guarding against protectionism. The Appellate Body's procedural interpretation of the introductory words
of Article XX has the potential for weakening the intended impact
of this clause.

The approach suggested here is similar to the Appellate Body's
reasoning in the *United States – Standards for Reformulated and Conventional Gasoline* (*Reformulated Gasoline*) decision,[114] a dispute that, notably, involved Article III and a measure without country-certification
features. The US measure at issue in that dispute established baselines
for producers and importers of gasoline in order to calculate reductions of contaminants under the US *Clean Air Act.*[115] Existing domestic refiners could establish individual baselines, using one of three
methods. Foreign refiners of gasoline were not given these options.
Imported gasoline was normally judged in accordance with a statutory baseline that was more onerous than the methods available to
domestic refiners. The Panel found a breach of the national treatment obligation of Article III:4, since chemically identical gasoline

113 *Ibid.* at para. 160.

114 *United States – Standards for Reformulated and Conventional Gasoline,* Appellate Body
     Report, Doc. WT/DS2/AB/R, adopted 20 May 1996, DSR 1996:1 at 3
     [*Reformulated Gasoline*].

115 *Clean Air Act,* 42 U.S.C. § 7401 et seq.

could be treated differently depending on whether it was imported or domestically produced. The Appellate Body determined that, while the US measure related to conservation as described in Article XX(g), it was not justified pursuant to the article because it did not meet the requirements of the introductory wording. The Appellate Body was not persuaded that possible difficulties of verification and enforcement in foreign territory were sufficient to explain the unavailability of individual baselines to foreign refiners. The Appellate Body noted that in other areas, such as antidumping laws, the United States relied on information from exporting countries and, as well, there was no record that the United States had tried to negotiate cooperation arrangements with Venezuela or Brazil, which were the countries bringing the complaint. Article III would be met if the statutory baseline were also imposed on domestic refiners, but the legislative record revealed that the legislators were unwilling to demand this burden of US refiners. According to the Appellate Body, the United States "counted the costs"[116] for domestic refiners but disregarded them for foreign refiners, and the resulting discrimination was "foreseen ... not merely inadvertent or unavoidable."[117] The Appellate Body concluded that the US measure constituted unjustifiable discrimination and a disguised restriction on international trade and was therefore not exempted under Article XX.

The decision can be criticized as downgrading Article XX and finding only that the United States had to meet GATT Article III, but this effect is expected of any exemption claim that fails. If, as suggested earlier, the analysis required of "arbitrary or unjustifiable discrimination" in the introductory words of Article XX should relate to whether the claimed exemption justifies the discrimination, then it is preferable for the analysis of Article XX to look explicitly at that question. The Appellate Body in *Reformulated Gasoline* did, in fact, do just that, evaluating the enforcement difficulties and quoting the US environmental argument to the effect that imposing the statutory baseline on domestic refiners would have delayed the start of the program.[118] Analysis under the introductory words of Article XX was not the same as the line of reasoning

---

[116] *Ibid. at* 27.

[117] *Ibid.*

[118] *Ibid. at* 26–27. This was one way of avoiding the discrimination. The other would have been to make the full range of optional methods available to foreign refiners.

that led to the conclusion of a breach of Article III initially. In some instances, the operation and surrounding circumstances of the environmental measure could justify the discrimination. In *Reformulated Gasoline*, the arguments linking the discrimination to the chosen level of environmental protection failed to convince the Appellate Body.

In the disputes prior to *Reformulated Gasoline*, the full substantive review of regulatory motive was done as part of the analysis of paragraph XX(g). If the measure did not pass this analysis, there was no need to consider the introductory words. In *Reformulated Gasoline*, the Appellate Body made it easier to find provisional justification under the paragraph, and attention therefore shifted to the introductory clause. GATT Article XX(g) provides an exemption for measures: "(g) relating to the conservation of exhaustible natural resources if such measures are made effective in conjunction with restrictions on domestic production or consumption." An early precedent was the GATT Panel decision concerning a Canadian requirement that herring and salmon be processed in the country prior to export.[119] The GATT Panel determined that the purpose of paragraph (g) was to ensure that trade commitments did not jeopardize measures that were primarily aimed at conservation — a requirement that the Panel found was not met by the Canadian measure at issue. In two unadopted reports, GATT Panels in the *United States – Restrictions on Imports of Tuna* disputes over US measures restricting imports of tuna harvested in ways considered too harmful to dolphins applied the "primarily aimed at" interpretation of paragraph (g), as part of their reasons for finding against the US measures.[120]

The approach to Article XX(g) changed with the Appellate Body decision in *Reformulated Gasoline*. The Panel had followed the previous decisions and examined whether the less favourable treatment

---

[119] *Canada – Measures Affecting Exports of Unprocessed Herring and Salmon*, GATT Panel Report, adopted 22 March 1988, BISD 35S/98 [*Canada – Unprocessed Herring and Salmon*].

[120] *United States – Restrictions on Imports of Tuna*, GATT Panel Report, 3 September 1991, unadopted, BISD 39S/155, (1991) 30 I.L.M. 1594, para. 5.33 [*Tuna/ Dolphin I*]; *United States – Restrictions on Imports of Tuna*, GATT Panel Report, 16 June 1994, unadopted, (1994) 33 I.L.M. 839, para. 5.27 [*Tuna/Dolphin II*]. See further *United States – Taxes on Automobiles*, GATT Panel Report, 11 October 1994, unadopted, (1994) 33 I.L.M. 1397, paras. 5.59–5.66, especially para. 5.63, rejecting a "least-trade-restrictive" test for paragraph (g)) [*United States – Automobiles*].

accorded to imported gasoline was primarily aimed at conservation. The Appellate Body rejected this approach and stated that the Panel appeared to have interpreted paragraph (g) as if it referred to measures "necessary" for conservation rather than measures "relating to" conservation, in accordance with the wording of the paragraph.[121] The Appellate Body accepted that "relating to" could be construed as meaning "primarily aimed at," as none of the participants in the dispute had made contrary submissions on this point, although the phrase "primarily aimed at" was not in the text. As there was a substantial relationship between the baseline establishment rules and conservation, the Appellate Body stated that the rules "cannot be regarded as merely incidentally or inadvertently aimed at the conservation of clean air in the United States."[122] The measure was provisionally covered by paragraph (g), although, as outlined earlier, the Appellate Body found that it was not ultimately justified under Article XX, since it failed to meet the requirements of the introductory clause.

The approach in *Reformulated Gasoline* treats paragraph (g) as a fairly lenient classification question and leaves the analysis of the discriminatory aspects of the measure to the introductory clause. This is a more natural meaning of the text. It was always odd to say that the US measure in *Tuna/Dolphin* did not relate to conservation. Due to this change, it is now particularly significant that the interpretation of the introductory clause in Article XX be substantive, since that is the point at which the non-discrimination norms are addressed. Article XX(g) should not be read as an exemption for any measure at all with a link to conservation.

The 1998 Appellate Body decision in *Shrimp/Turtle* followed the same pattern of first considering paragraph (g) of Article XX and then addressing the introductory clause. The measure that was examined was the import ban on shrimp harvested in ways that were too harmful to sea turtles. The requirement of TED use was seen as being connected with the conservation of sea turtles. As well, the Appellate Body found that the ban was not disproportionately wide in relation to the policy objective, that the means were reasonably

---

[121] *Reformulated Gasoline,* Appellate Body Report, *supra* note 114 at 15.

[122] *Ibid.* at 18. This interpretation is less demanding than the previous views of paragraph (g), effectively ignoring the word "primarily." See Donald M. McRae, "The Contribution of International Trade Law to the Development of International Law" (1996) 260 Recueil des Cours 99 at 202. For further discussion of the interpretation of the introductory clause in this decision, see later in the text under Assertion 2.

related to the ends, and that the relationship between the means and the ends was "observably a close and real one, a relationship ... every bit as substantial" as the relationship in *Reformulated Gasoline*.[123] As the measure was made effective in conjunction with domestic restrictions,[124] it was provisionally covered by paragraph (g). The Appellate Body then proceeded with an analysis of the introductory clause of Article XX, finding the measure unacceptable in 1998 but justified in 2001 when the procedural problems had been solved. It may be noted that since the interpretation of paragraph (g) is now fairly lenient and since the interpretation given to the introductory clause was only procedural, there was no substantive review of the US measure for compliance with the traditional non-discrimination norms.

It is possible that, on the facts of the *Shrimp/Turtle* dispute, analysis of the MFN principle in connection with an environmental justification would have added nothing new to the discussion that occurred concerning negotiation efforts and phase-in times. The duty of flexibility likely would have been absent. Since paragraph (g) already refers to domestic restrictions, perhaps there would have been no further review of national treatment for the introductory clause. If it applied, a review for national treatment in light of the environmental measure might have led to a fuller discussion of whether TED use was actually "treatment no less favourable" than the treatment of domestic goods in the circumstances, including the costs. Depending on how the national treatment analysis was framed, the "due process" issue might have involved a comparison between domestic and foreign producers. It is not every dispute that will call for a complete substantive review on its facts, but such a review should be kept available for future exemption claims across the full list of paragraphs in Article XX.

It is not necessary to treat the introductory clause of Article XX as a procedural review only, on the assumption that all substantive review takes place in the consideration of the listed paragraphs. The introductory wording has important substantive functions, to prevent protectionism and maintain the non-discrimination norms, at least when discrimination is judged "arbitrary or unjustifiable." The reasoning of the Appellate Body in *Reformulated Gasoline* is one example of a substantive interpretation of the introductory clause, but note that the analysis in that decision also relates to disguised

[123] *Shrimp/Turtle 1998*, Appellate Body Report, *supra* note 5 at para. 141.

[124] *Ibid.* at paras. 143–45.

restrictions on trade.[125] If the interpretation were to focus more narrowly on discrimination, different tests might emerge.[126]

ARTICLE XX — UNILATERALISM

It should be noted that in *Reformulated Gasoline,* unilateralism was not a major concern, nor was there a need for flexibility, despite the fact that the activities to be verified were located in foreign territory. The negotiations envisaged by the Appellate Body were to facilitate extraterritorial information gathering and the enforcement of a uniform standard, rather than the adaptation of standards to reflect local conditions. On the facts in *Shrimp/Turtle,* it would be as if the negotiations were only about information gathering to verify claims that shrimp from uncertified countries had been caught using TEDs.

Reformulated Gasoline *is also instructive in that the measure at issue did not depend on the physical characteristics of the gasoline itself, either imported or domestic, but rather on the baselines for the various producers, which could be expected to have an overall effect on the products. The circumstances of production were key, as was also the case in *Shrimp/Turtle.*[127] In both of these disputes, the link to the product was quite direct. Coercion is likely to be increasingly problematic as the link becomes more distant. In *United States –*

---

125 *Reformulated Gasoline,* Appellate Body Report, *supra* note 114 at p. 23.

126 See, for example, the conclusion of the GATT panel in *United States – Automobiles* that a system of averaging fleets of automobiles by manufacturer breached Article III but met the requirements of the introductory clause of Article XX because it promoted fuel conservation and supported the restrictions on domestic producers: GATT Panel Report, *United States – Automobiles, supra* note 120 at para. 5.65. The US measure was not exempted, however, as it also mandated separate accounting for foreign and domestic fleets and this feature was not justified. See also the rejection of retroactive measures in GATT Panel Report, *Tuna/Dolphin I, supra* note 120 at para. 5.33.

127 See Robert E. Hudec, "GATT/WTO Constraints on National Regulation: Requiem for an 'Aim and Effects' Test" (1998) 32 Int'l Law 619 at 624, stating that the traditional GATT approach to distinctions among products accepts "product distinctions phrased in terms of product qualities themselves, or else ... other characteristics that indirectly govern product qualities, such as characteristics of the production process (slaughterhouse cleanliness) or characteristics of the producer (possession of a license certifying requisite skills)." For historical background on unilateral trade measures taken for environmental or humanitarian reasons, see Steve Charnovitz, "Exploring the Environmental Exceptions in GATT Article XX" (1991) 25/5 J. World Trade 37; Steve Charnovitz, "The Moral Exception in Trade Policy" (1998) 38 Va. J. Int'l L. 689.

Prohibition of Imports of Tuna and Tuna Products from Canada,[128] the US ban on tuna imports from Canada was a response to Canada's arrest of US tuna boats fishing in a disputed area that Canada claimed within its 200-mile fisheries jurisdiction. The US assertion of an Article XX(g) defence in favour of greater multilateral environmental efforts was unsuccessful.[129] As part of the reasoning, the Panel indicated that this sort of retaliation for a non-trade issue was not the type of measure included in Article XX.[130] The 2001 Appellate Body in *Shrimp/Turtle* accepted that the United States could consider Malaysia's program for the protection of nesting beaches for sea turtles in connection with the certification decision, but the link between nesting beaches and the shrimp is rather tenuous. If the situation were reversed, would Malaysia be able to block imports of shrimp and shrimp products from countries that did not have, in its view, adequate programs for the protection of nesting beaches for sea turtles? *Shrimp/Turtle* has established that distinctions based on the process of production could be justified under Article XX, but, at some point, it can be expected that the link will be too remote.

In this context, unilateralism arises when an importing country adopts a trade measure that is directed at events occurring outside its territory, particularly if the trade measure attaches negative consequences to those events. In pre-WTO decisions, the first GATT Panel in *United States – Restrictions on Imports of Tuna* (*Tuna/Dolphin*) dealt with the issue of unilateralism, in part, by deciding that paragraphs (b) and (g) of Article XX did not cover measures to protect dolphins outside the territory of the United States.[131] This territorial test was rejected by the second *Tuna/Dolphin* Panel, which held that

---

[128] *United States – Prohibition of Imports of Tuna and Tuna Products from Canada*, GATT Panel Report, adopted 22 February 1982, BISD 29S/91.

[129] The claim was unsuccessful mainly because there were no corresponding restrictions on domestic production or consumption, as required in Article XX(g).

[130] *Ibid.* at para. 4.13. For other instances involving a link to goods that was too distant, see *Belgian Family Allowances*, GATT Panel Report, adopted 7 November 1952, BISD 1S/59; *Border Tax Adjustments*, GATT Working Party Report, adopted 2 December 1970, BISD 18S/97, at para. 14.

[131] *Tuna/Dolphin I*, GATT Panel Report, *supra* note 120 at paras. 5.27 and 5.32. See para. 5.27: "The Panel considered that if the broad interpretation ... suggested by the United States were accepted, each contracting party could unilaterally determine the ... policies from which other contracting parties could not deviate without jeopardizing their rights under the General Agreement. The General Agreement would then no longer constitute a multilateral framework for trade among all contracting parties."

it was not supported by the text or relevant preparatory work of Article XX and that the United States was not barred from protecting dolphins located in international waters.[132] The major difficulty for the Panel in *Tuna/Dolphin II* was country coercion — the use of "trade measures so as to force other contracting parties to change their policies within their jurisdiction, including conservation policies."[133] The reasoning from both of the *Tuna/Dolphin* decisions influenced the Panel in *Shrimp/Turtle 1998*,[134] but the Appellate Body rejected it. In rejecting this reasoning, the Appellate Body was quite specific in referring to country-based programs, not just to activities occurring outside the territory of the importing country. The Appellate Body in *Shrimp/Turtle 1998* said:

> It appears to us, however, that conditioning access to a Member's domestic market on whether exporting Members comply with, or adopt, a policy or policies unilaterally prescribed by the importing Member may, to some degree, be a common aspect of measures falling within the scope of one or another of the exceptions (a) to (j) of Article XX ... It is not necessary to assume that requiring from exporting countries compliance with, or adoption of, certain policies (although covered in principle by one or another of the exceptions) prescribed by the importing country, renders a measure *a priori* incapable of justification under Article XX.[135]

The 1998 Appellate Body concluded that unilateralism may be,[136] to some degree, a common aspect of "one or another" of the exceptions listed in Article XX. Although exporting countries could be required to comply with policies unilaterally prescribed by the importing country, the Appellate Body considered that Article XX nevertheless provides certain exceptions from GATT obligations otherwise applicable, given the importance of the measures covered by the exceptions. If requiring compliance with unilateral policies was not possible under Article XX, according to the Appellate Body,

---

132 *Tuna/Dolphin II*, GATT Panel Report, *supra* note 120 at paras. 5.20 and 5.31–5.33.

133 *Tuna/Dolphin I*, GATT Panel Report, *supra* note 120 at para. 5.26. See *Ibid.* at paras. 5.27, 5.38, and 5.39

134 *Shrimp/Turtle 1998*, Panel Report, *supra* note 5 at paras. 7.45–7.46.

135 *Shrimp/Turtle 1998*, Appellate Body Report, *supra* note 5 at para. 121.

136 John H. Jackson notes how nuanced the language of this paragraph is. He specifically draws attention to the word "may." See John H. Jackson, "Comments on *Shrimp/Turtle* and the Product/Process Distinction" (2000) 11 European J. Int'l L. 303 at 306.

those exceptions would have no effect.[137] The exception for the products of prison labour in Article XX(e), for example, would be in this category.[138]

Future panels will, no doubt, be faced with deciding how far this reasoning extends and whether the policies described in Article XX must have a direct link to the goods affected by the measures in question. In its third party arguments before the *Tuna/Dolphin* panels, Venezuela asked whether Article XX could justify restrictions on imports from countries that lacked recycling programs or food distribution programs for the poor[139] or from low-wage countries or countries where workers were forbidden (or permitted) to smoke or were denied breaks for religious practices.[140] Venezuela questioned whether trade sanctions would become available for "a wide range of purposes clearly not endorsed by even a significant minority of the GATT contracting parties."[141] After *Shrimp/Turtle*, this question is now open — restrained somewhat by flexibility and the duty to negotiate — but likely, for the moment, to depend on interpretation of the specific paragraphs of Article XX on a case-by-case basis.[142]

The conflict arose despite general agreement that sea turtles were threatened and in need of protection. Species of sea turtles are listed as endangered in Appendix I of the Convention on International Trade in Endangered Species of Wild Fauna and Flora (CITES),[143]

---

137 See *Shrimp/Turtle 2001*, Panel Report, *supra* note 5 at para. 5.65; *Shrimp/Turtle 2001*, Appellate Body Report, *supra* note 5 at paras. 137–38.

138 The other listed exceptions provide somewhat less support for the conclusion that unilateral measures are covered. Before the 1998 Panel, the United States argued that the language in Article XX(b) was based on similar language in earlier treaties that had been commonly interpreted as permitting measures for the protection of life or health of animals and plants outside the territory of the Party applying the measure. See *Shrimp/Turtle 1998*, Panel Report, *supra* note 5 at paras. 3.186–3.194.

139 *Tuna/Dolphin I*, GATT Panel Report, *supra* note 120 at para. 4.29

140 *Tuna/Dolphin II*, GATT Panel Report, *supra* note 120 at para. 4.34

141 *Ibid.*

142 In the *EC – Tariff Preferences* decision, the Appellate Body rejected an argument that the Enabling Clause justified a special preference in the GSP system of the EC that provided greater benefits to countries combating drug production and trafficking: *European Communities – Conditions for the Granting of Tariff Preferences to Developing Countries*, Appellate Body Report, Doc. WT/DS246/AB/R, adopted 20 April 2004.

143 Convention on International Trade in Endangered Species of Wild Fauna and Flora, 3 March 1973, Can. T.S. 1975 No.32, (1973) 12 I.L.M. 1088 [CITES].

to which the United States, Malaysia, India, Pakistan, and Thailand are all party.[144] In addition, the conflict arose even though sea turtles migrate through the waters of several countries, including the United States, and the 1998 Appellate Body ruled that there was a sufficient jurisdictional nexus for the US claim of justification under Article XX(g).[145] Given this ruling on jurisdiction, there is some doubt as to whether the *Shrimp/Turtle* reasoning on unilateralism and Article XX applies generally or is limited to facts with some similar territorial connection.

Interpretation of GATT Article XX can be placed in the context of general public international law rules on extraterritoriality, especially for an analysis of trade measures that discriminate on the basis of PPMs in order to promote environmental protection, labour rights, or other human rights. It may be argued that such measures are not, in fact, extraterritorial as they do not regulate persons or conduct outside the territory of the importing state, but merely set out consequences that apply should there be an attempt to import goods into the regulating country.[146] On the other hand, extraterritoriality could be present if the regulating state makes its laws applicable to the outside persons or activities — through intent, substantial and foreseeable effects, or other possible linkages recognized by certain theories of state jurisdiction.[147] If a dispute relates to the protection of basic human rights or the global commons, it should

---

[144] *Shrimp/Turtle 1998*, Panel Report, *supra* note 5 at paras. 3.5, 3.9, 3.14, 3.18, 3.54, and 7.1.

[145] *Shrimp/Turtle 1998*, Appellate Body Report, *supra* note 5 at para. 133. This claim was disputed. Thailand, for example, argued that the most common type of sea turtles found in its waters was very rare in the US and that its future was thus not the responsibility of the United States (*Shrimp/Turtle 1998*, Panel Report, *supra* note 5 at para. 3.40, citing a report from the US National Research Council). See argument at *Shrimp/Turtle 1998*, Panel Report, *supra* note 5 at paras. 3.36–3.46, and 3.157–3.163.

[146] This statement is an over-simplification. For full analysis, see Robert Howse, "Back to Court after *Shrimp/Turtle?* Almost but Not Quite Yet: India's Short-Lived Challenge to Labor and Environmental Exceptions in the European Union's Generalized System of Preferences" (2003) 18 Am. U. Int'l L. Rev. 1333 at 1369–70; Robert Howse, "The Appellate Body Rulings in the *Shrimp/Turtle* Case: A New Legal Baseline for the Trade and Environment Debate" (2002) 27 Colum. J. Envtl. L. 489; Robert Howse and Donald Regan, "The Product/Process Distinction – An Illusory Basis for Disciplining 'Unilateralism' in Trade Policy" (2000) 11(2) Eur. J. Int'l L. 249 at 274–79.

[147] Lorand Bartels, "Article XX of GATT and the Problem of Extraterritorial Jurisdiction: The Case of Trade Measures for the Protection of Human Rights" (2002) 36(2) J. World Trade 353 at 379–82.

be noted that breaches of fundamental human dignity and survival may attract norms that over-ride claims to state sovereignty.[148] As disputes come forward through the WTO process, panels and the Appellate Body may be called upon to consider public international law limits on state jurisdiction and extraterritoriality.

This part of the article has presented the argument that the interpretation of the introductory clause of Article XX should not be limited to procedural matters such as flexibility, due process, and the duty to negotiate. Instead, interpretation should be substantive in order to preserve the even-handedness of the norms of non-discrimination as the WTO deals with the treatment of important non-trade interests in the development of global public policy.

Assertion 2: Trade Interests Should Not Be Given Priority in the Interpretation of Article XX. Rather, Interpretation Should Be Balanced in Order to Provide Effective Exemptions for the Non-Trade Interests Reflected in the Paragraphs of the Article

This part of the article addresses the interpretation of Article XX and presents the argument that trade interests must not receive special priority in this process if Article XX is to provide a mechanism for the balancing of public policy interests. The introductory clause provides that "nothing in this Agreement shall be construed to prevent the adoption or enforcement" of certain measures. To give effect to this intent, there must be room for a decision in favour of the specific non-trade interests reflected in the paragraphs of Article XX.

The first section of this part considers the priority given to trade in the interpretation of the introductory wording. This question has arisen concerning the prohibition on disguised restrictions on international trade. It will also arise over the approach to "arbitrary and unjustifiable discrimination," if this phrase is interpreted in a substantive way, as suggested earlier under Assertion 1. The second section addresses the "necessity" requirement in paragraph (b) of

---

[148] Donald M. McRae, "The Contribution of International Trade Law to the Development of International Law" (1996) 260 Recueil des Cours 99 at 206: "[T]rade that involves the violation of internationally accepted labour or human rights standards cannot claim to be solely a domestic issue for the States concerned." See further Gabrielle Marceau, "WTO Dispute Settlement and Human Rights" (2002) 13 Eur. J. Int'l L. 753; *European Communities – Conditions for the Granting of Tariff Preferences to Developing Countries*, Appellate Body Report, Doc. WT/DS246/AB/R, adopted 20 April 2004.

Article XX, which covers measures "necessary to protect human, animal or plant life or health." This section contains the argument against using a "least-trade-restrictive" approach in interpretation of this paragraph.

ARTICLE XX — DISGUISED RESTRICTION ON TRADE

This section reviews the substantive interpretation of the intro-ductory clause of Article XX, particularly concerning disguised re-strictions on international trade. The argument presented is that the clause should not be interpreted with a presumption in favour of trade interests and against a finding of exemption. The struc-ture of Article XX does not call for such a narrow approach to exemptions. The analysis can be done without this presumed pri-ority for trade, as is demonstrated in a decision that is discussed in this section. The introductory clause of Article XX is as follows:

Article XX. Subject to the requirement that such measures are not ap-plied in a manner which would constitute a means of arbitrary or unjusti-fiable discrimination between countries where the same conditions prevail, or a disguised restriction on international trade, nothing in this Agree-ment shall be construed to prevent the adoption or enforcement by any Member of measures.

The Appellate Body in *Shrimp/Turtle 1998* gave priority to trade interests when describing its approach to the interpretation of the clause:

[A] balance must be struck between the *right* of a member to invoke an exception under Article XX and the *duty* of that same Member to respect the treaty rights of the other Members. To permit one Member to abuse or misuse its right to invoke an exception would be effectively to allow that Member to degrade its own treaty obligations as well as to devalue the treaty rights of other Members. If the abuse or misuse is sufficiently grave or extensive, the Member, in effect, reduces its treaty obligation to a merely facultative one and dissolves its juridical character, and, in so doing, ne-gates altogether the treaty rights of other Members.[149]

Note that the member claiming use of the exception has both a right to invoke that exception and a duty to respect the treaty rights of other members. Those other members, however, are seen as

---

[149] *Shrimp/Turtle 1998*, Appellate Body Report, *supra* note 5 at para. 156 [emphasis in original].

having only treaty rights to enforce; they do not appear to have the duty to respect the right of the member claiming the exception. This is a one-sided arrangement in which only the member claiming the exception is suspected of misuse or an abuse of a right.[150]

Since the Appellate Body in 1998 determined that application of the US measure in question involved arbitrary and unjustifiable discrimination, it did not need to address the issue of a disguised restriction on international trade. When the dispute returned to the Panel in 2001, the Panel ruled that the problems relating to discrimination had been solved. The Panel therefore had to complete the analysis of the introductory words of Article XX and consider whether the measure was a disguised restriction. The Panel determined that there would be an abuse of Article XX(g) if the measure was only a disguise to pursue trade-restrictive objectives.[151] The Panel stated that the "design, architecture and revealing structure" of the measure could be examined for hidden trade-restrictive objectives and that the text of the measure and guidelines revealed no such objectives.[152] The Panel then considered issues relating to application, noting that the measure was adopted and expanded in response to pressure from environmental groups. The Panel found that, by accepting TED-caught shrimp from non-certified countries[153] and by offering technical assistance to support the use of TEDs, the United States had demonstrated that the measure was

[150] The Appellate Body refers in paragraph 159 to a line of equilibrium and balance between the competing rights. It is not clear that the rights are given equal weight, however, since paragraph 160 returns to the question of the "abuse or misuse" of the exceptions provided in Article XX.

[151] *Shrimp/Turtle 2001,* Panel Report, *supra* note 5 at para. 5.142. See paras. 5.49 and 5.50, where the Panel quotes paragraphs 156 and 159 of Appellate Body Report, *Shrimp/Turtle 1998, supra* note 5.

[152] *Shrimp/Turtle 2001,* Panel Report, *supra* note 5 at para. 5.142. This wording concerning protective application to be discerned from the "design, architecture and revealing structure" of the measure is drawn from *Japan – Taxes on Alcoholic Beverages,* Appellate Body Report, Doc. WT/DS8/AB/R, Doc. WT/DS10/AB/R, and Doc. WT/DS11/AB/R, adopted 1 November 1996, DSR 1996:1, 97 at 120.

[153] Note the statement from the Appellate Body in 1998 that the exclusion of shrimp that had been harvested using methods identical to those employed in the United States was "difficult to reconcile with the declared policy objective of protecting and conserving sea turtles": *Shrimp/Turtle 1998,* Appellate Body Report, *supra* note 5 at para. 165. See also *Shrimp/Turtle 1998,* Panel Report, *supra* note 5 at para. 7.16.

not a disguised restriction on trade.[154] As Malaysia did not appeal this conclusion, the issue was not addressed by the Appellate Body in 2001.[155]

This is the general sort of substantive analysis that is called for in the introductory clause. The only way of doing a procedural or formal analysis of the "disguised restriction" wording would be to consider whether the discrimination was open, published, and not hidden. This consideration was advanced earlier as the approach to take,[156] but it has now been abandoned in favour of substantive analysis. The remaining problem of interpretation is the pro-trade presumption, which risks causing the exemptions to be applied too narrowly.

The Appellate Body gave priority to trade interests in its earlier decision in *Reformulated Gasoline:*

[W]hile the exceptions of Article XX may be invoked as a matter of legal right, they should not be so applied as to frustrate or defeat the legal obligations of the holder of the right under the substantive rule of the *General Agreement.* If those exceptions are not to be abused or misused, in other words, the measures falling within the particular exceptions must be applied reasonably, with due regard both to the legal duties of the party claiming the exception and the legal rights of the other parties concerned.[157]

The Appellate Body thus presumed in favour of the trade interest (the party with the legal right) and against the member claiming the benefit of the exception (the party with the duty).

In *Reformulated Gasoline,* the Appellate Body found that the baseline rules at issue in that dispute met paragraph (g) of Article XX but failed to meet the introductory words. The Appellate Body treated "unjustifiable discrimination" as subsumed under "disguised restriction on international trade" and found that the US measure at issue in the dispute constituted both. The United States

---

[154] *Shrimp/Turtle 2001,* Panel Report, *supra* note 5 at para. 5.143.

[155] *Shrimp/Turtle 2001,* Appellate Body Report, *supra* note 5 at para. 82.

[156] *United States – Prohibition of Imports of Tuna and Tuna Products from Canada,* GATT Panel Report, adopted 22 February 1982, BISD 28S/91 at para. 4.8; *United States – Imports of Certain Automotive Spring Assemblies,* GATT Panel Report, adopted 26 May 1983, BISD 30S/107 at para. 56. The shift to a substantive analysis appears in *Reformulated Gasoline,* Appellate Body Report, *supra* note 114 at 3. See also *Asbestos,* Panel Report, *supra* note 4 at paras. 8.235–8.239.

[157] *Reformulated Gasoline,* Appellate Body Report, *supra* note 114 at 20–21.

had alternate courses of action open to it.[158] Concerning the possibility of individual baselines for foreign refiners, the Appellate Body found that the United States did not adequately explore the possibility of verification using foreign data, with reliance on other information only when that data was not available, as is the US practice in anti-dumping law. Concerning application of the statutory baseline to domestic as well as foreign refiners, the Appellate Body found that the United States chose not to impose on its domestic industry the expences of immediate compliance. The Appellate Body concluded that,

> while the United States counted the costs for its domestic refiners of statutory baselines, there is nothing in the record to indicate that it did other than disregard that kind of consideration when it came to foreign refiners.[159]

According to the Appellate Body, the discrimination "must have been foreseen" and was "not merely inadvertent or unavoidable."[160]

The Appellate Body came to this conclusion on motive despite the fact that the measure was provisionally covered by paragraph (g) of Article XX as relating to conservation. This conclusion must mean that the motives were mixed, although the Appellate Body did not say that explicitly. When dealing with such mixed-motive measures, the Appellate Body's methodology was to look at whether alternate measures were available and whether the costs to foreigners were appropriately considered. This is similar to methodology developed by an earlier panel in *Canada's Landing Requirement for Pacific Coast Salmon and Herring (Landing – Salmon and Herring)*,[161] a dispute under Chapter 18 of the Canada-United States Free Trade

---

[158] The Appellate Body quoted with approval language from the Panel decision below that reflected a "least-trade-restrictive" test developed for the Article XX exceptions that mention necessity: "While the Panel agreed that it would be necessary ... to ascertain the origin of gasoline, the Panel could not conclude that the United States had shown that this could not be achieved by other measures reasonably available to it and consistent or less inconsistent with the General Agreement." *Reformulated Gasoline*, Panel Report, *supra* note 114 at para. 6.26, quoted at *Reformulated Gasoline*, Appellate Body Report, *supra* note 114 at 24.

[159] *Reformulated Gasoline*, Appellate Body Report, *supra* note 114 at 27.

[160] *Ibid.*

[161] *Canada's Landing Requirement for Pacific Coast Salmon and Herring*, Binational Panel Report, United States-Canada Free Trade Agreement, Doc. CDA-89-1807-01, 16 October 1989, 1989 FTAPD LEXIS 6 [*Landing – Salmon and Herring*].

Agreement.[162] Importantly, however, the Panel in *Landing – Salmon and Herring* analyzed Article XX without the strong presumptions in favour of trade rights that appear in *Shrimp/Turtle* and *Reformulated Gasoline.*

The Panel in *Landing – Salmon and Herring* was established after Canada lost a GATT dispute concerning a measure that required salmon and herring to be processed in Canada first before they could be exported.[163] The GATT panel had held this requirement to be an export restraint contrary to GATT Article XI and not exempted under Article XX. In response, Canada had abolished the processing in Canada provision and replaced it with a requirement that the fish had to be landed in Canada for inspection and counting before they could be exported. Canada argued that the measure was justified for reasons of conservation and management of fish stocks. The problem was that domestic sales of fish for Canadian buyers could land directly at processing plants, but fish for export to US buyers would usually have to be unloaded and then loaded again and sent by ship to processing plants in the United States. Some fish for export sales could go overland by truck to Washington state, but fish destined for Alaska and other US plants was subject to the additional loading process. The Panel found this extra commercial burden to be a restriction on sales for export and therefore contrary to GATT Article XI.[164]

Addressing Canada's claim of a conservation justification, the Panel considered that Article XX was intended to prevent the trade interests of one state from overriding the legitimate environmental concerns of another and that governments should have appropriate latitude to implement their own conservation policies.[165] In the Panel's view, a measure with multiple motives could nevertheless reflect a genuine conservation motive and could be worth doing for conservation reasons alone. This was the test applied by the Panel — whether the measure would have been adopted for conservation reasons alone.[166]

[162] Canada-United States Free Trade Agreement, 22 December 1987 and 2 January 1988, Can. T.S. 1989 No.3.

[163] *Canada – Measures Affecting Exports of Unprocessed Herring and Salmon,* GATT panel Report, adopted 22 March 1988, BISD 35S/98.

[164] *Landing – Salmon and Herring,* Chapter 18 Panel Report, *supra* note 161 at para. 6.13.

[165] *Ibid.* at para. 7.05.

[166] *Ibid.* at para. 7.07.

To apply the test in the circumstances of the dispute, the Panel focused on the costs and conservation benefits of the landing requirement. Using methodology similar to that adopted later in *Reformulated Gasoline*, the Panel considered whether there were alternate measures that would accomplish the same objective and whether Canada would have adopted the measure if domestic buyers had had to bear the extra commercial inconvenience and costs.[167] Noting the other possible means of gathering information that were reasonably available in Canadian jurisdiction,[168] the Panel determined that the conservation benefits would not have been sufficient to justify imposing on Canadian buyers an extra landing requirement that covered 100 per cent of the catch. Rather, a certain proportion of the catch could be exempted from the extra landing without impairing the integrity of the data collection process.[169] This proportion, in the Panel's view, would be in the range of 10 to 20 per cent.[170]

The Panel in *Landing – Salmon and Herring* was not analyzing "disguised restriction" but rather deciding whether the landing requirement was primarily aimed at conservation. This was the interpretation that the GATT panel had put on Article XX(g) — an interpretation that has now been overtaken by subsequent WTO cases. The Panel said, however, that its analysis of motive for Article XX(g) was really just "the opposite face" of disguised restriction.[171] It is worth noting that the process in Chapter 18 of the Canada-United States Free Trade Agreement differs from the dispute settlement mechanism of the WTO. Chapter 18 is similar to Chapter 20 of the current North American Free Trade Agreement (NAFTA).[172] The process combines elements of both binding and non-binding dispute settlement. After a Panel decision, the parties must negotiate

---

167 *Ibid.* at paras. 7.09 and 7.10.

168 Here, the Panel adopts a different approach from the one later taken in *Reformulated Gasoline* and says that a country should not have to rely on the cooperation of a foreign country for its conservation policy (*Ibid.* at para. 7.16). See Donald M. McRae, "The Contribution of International Trade Law to the Development of International Law" (1996) 260 Recueil des cours 99 at 205.

169 *Landing – Salmon and Herring,* Chapter 18 Panel Report, *supra* note 161 at para. 7.38.

170 *Ibid.* at para. 7.40

171 *Ibid.* at para. 7.04.

172 North American Free Trade Agreement, 17 December 1992, Can. T.S. 1994 No.2 [NAFTA].

as to the resolution of the dispute, which normally is expected to conform to the Panel's recommendations. If there is no agreement, a remedy may be taken. The Panel in *Landing – Salmon and Herring* produced a hedged decision suitable to this context.[173]

The conservation defence in *Landing – Salmon and Herring* was given significant recognition despite the somewhat suspicious circumstance of the measure being adopted in response to the loss at the GATT Panel. In addition, it should be noted that in looking at the alternatives, the Panel did not use a least-trade-restrictive test that prioritized trade over other interests. Instead, the Panel responded to an argument by the United States that, given reasonable alternatives, Canada had adopted the one chosen for trade restrictive reasons.[174] This approach is more nuanced, one that assumes that the burden of an Article XX exception should be borne by both imports and domestic products.[175]

The *Landing – Salmon and Herring* Panel saw Article XX as being intended to prevent trade interests from impinging on legitimate environmental interests. Article XX, after all, says that "nothing in this Agreement shall be construed to prevent the adoption or enforcement by any Member" of the exempted measures. The Panel took a direct approach to the interpretation of the meaning, without privileging one side or the other. This approach recognized various goals as important, as, in fact, does Article XX.

The *Landing – Salmon and Herring* Panel decision was criticized by David Wirth in a 1994 article for failing to defer to the expert judgment of Canadian governmental scientists.[176] In the article, he examines the role of scientists in risk assessment and risk management and argues in favour of deference to national regulators in environmental and public health matters. This criticism, however, fails to take account of the differences between the tasks assigned to domestic scientists and the role of a trade dispute settlement panel.

173 For the eventual resolution of the dispute, see Ted L. McDorman, "Using the Dispute Settlement Regime of the Free Trade Agreement: The West Coast Salmon and Herring Problem" (1990–91) 4 Canada-U.S. Bus. L. Rev. 177.

174 *Landing – Salmon and Herring*, Chapter 18 Panel Report, *supra* note 161 at para. 7.14.

175 *Ibid.* at para. 7.09 and Panel footnote 14.

176 D.A. Wirth, "The Role of Science in the Uruguay Round and NAFTA Trade Disciplines" (1994) 27 Cornell Int'l L.J. 817. See further *EC – Measures Concerning Meat and Meat Products (Hormones)*, Appellate Body Report, Doc. WT/DS26/AB/R, Doc. WT/DS48/AB/R, adopted 13 February 1998, para. 118, and paras. 112–19 generally [*Beef Hormones*].

A trade panel is not simply reviewing a scientific decision to see whether it conforms to the requirements of domestic administrative law. Panels are given different responsibilities and must make the legal rulings called for in their terms of reference. A standard of deference would not operate as a balancing test, but could constitute a rejection of the trade treaty obligations altogether.[177] The issue of the role of scientific expertise in trade agreements is complex. While the test in *Landing – Salmon and Herring* may not be the only or the best one for deciding on disguised restrictions,[178] the decision illustrates how Article XX can be interpreted without marginalizing non-trade interests.

There are some signs of interpretation that allow more room for the exceptions of Article XX and give less weight to the competing trade interests. The principle of narrow interpretation of an exempting clause was rejected by the Appellate Body in the *EC –*

---

[177] *Landing – Salmon and Herring*, Chapter 18 Panel Report, *supra* note 161 at para. 7:11: "The Panel was aware that each state has the sovereign right to decide upon the particular conservation policies it wishes to employ. But, at the same time, the Panel was required to take account of the obligations that Canada and the United States have accepted, under GATT and the FTA regarding trade-restricting conservation measures. The preamble to GATT Article XX, which expressly prohibits 'disguised' actions on international trade, is an acknowledgement by the Parties that they will submit the purpose of trade-restricting conservation measures to third party scrutiny. By directing the application of this provision, the Panel's terms of reference required the Panel to make its own independent evaluation of the conservation justification in question."

[178] Note the tests used in *Australia – Measures Affecting Importation of Salmon*, Appellate Body Report, Doc. WT/DS18/AB/R, adopted 6 November 1998 [*Australia – Salmon*], concerning Article 5.5 of the SPS Agreement, *supra* note 2. Article 5.5 prohibits arbitrary or unjustifiable distinctions in levels of sanitary or phytosanitary protection if those distinctions result in discrimination or disguised restriction on trade. The Appellate Body upheld the finding of breach and approved the Panel's use of certain warning signals and other factors, including differences in the levels of protection between the salmon products at issue and other products presenting similar risks, the lack of an appropriate risk assessment and the absence of internal controls (paras. 159–78 and 237–40). In *Beef Hormones*, the Appellate Body reversed a Panel finding of breach of Article 5.5 relating, in part, to distinctions between treatment of the hormones at issue and other substances known to be harmful. The degree of difference in the levels of protection was a factor, but it was out-weighed by other factors. There was no evidence that the prohibition had been adopted due to lobbying from the domestic industry, but there was evidence of the depth and extent of public anxiety over the health effects of growth hormones (*Beef Hormones, supra* note 176 at paras. 239–46.)

Measures Concerning Meat and Meat Products (Hormones) (Beef Hormones) decision:

[M]erely characterizing a treaty provision as an "exception" does not by itself justify a "stricter" or "narrower" interpretation of that provision than would be warranted by examination of the ordinary meaning of the actual treaty words, viewed in context and in the light of the treaty's object and purpose, or, in other words, by applying the normal rules of treaty interpretation.[179]

This view was repeated in the *European Communities – Conditions for the Granting of Tariff Preferences to Developing Countries (EC – Tariff Preferences)* decision.[180] Narrow interpretation of exceptions is no more than an interpretive technique to assist with the finding of intent. It should not be used to defeat the clear statement in the introductory wording of Article XX that the other provisions of GATT were not to hinder the policies and measures listed in the specific paragraphs of the article.

To summarize, the 1998 Appellate Body decision in *Shrimp/Turtle* repeated an approach from *Reformulated Gasoline* that prioritizes trade and treats exception claims as if they involve an abuse or a misuse of a right. An earlier Canada-United States trade panel in *Landing – Salmon and Herring* addressed the question of mixed motives and developed the test of whether the conservation benefit of the Canadian measure at issue in that dispute would have been sufficient to justify its adoption if all the burden had fallen on Canadian domestic interests. The approach in *Landing – Salmon and Herring* is the preferred one because it does not give trade interests priority over other important areas of public policy and because it more accurately reflects the language of Article XX. In order to make the exemptions of Article XX effective, there should be no presumption of narrow interpretation.

179 *Beef Hormones,* Appellate Body Report, *supra* note 176 at para.104.

180 *European Communities – Conditions for the Granting of Tariff Preferences to Developing Countries,* Appellate Body Report, Doc. WT/DS246/AB/R, adopted 20 April 2004, para. 98: "In sum, in our view, the characterization of the Enabling Clause as an exception in no way diminishes the right of Members to provide or to receive 'differential and more favourable treatment' … Whatever its characterization, a provision of the covered agreements must be interpreted in accordance with the 'customary rules of interpretation of public international law,' as required by Article 3.2 of the Understanding on Rules and Procedures Governing the Settlement of Disputes."

ARTICLE XX(B) — NECESSARY FOR THE PROTECTION OF HEALTH

This section completes the argument against the priority for trade and places it in the context of the health exception dealt with in the *Asbestos* decision concerning France's import ban on asbestos and products containing asbestos. The section presents the argument against the "least-trade-restrictive" approach to paragraph (b) of Article XX. The traditional non-discrimination norms should be protected through the introductory clause of Article XX, in accordance with its wording, rather than through the interpretation of each listed paragraph. The section includes discussion of a WTO Panel decision that analyzed an Article XX exemption claim without the trade-privileging assumptions.

Article XX(b) provides an exception for the adoption or enforcement of measures: "(b) necessary to protect human, animal or plant life or health." The Appellate Body in *Asbestos* affirmed the decision by the Panel that the ban and restrictions were justified by Article XX(b). The Panel had moved to Article XX after finding a breach of Article III:4, as discussed later in this article under Assertion 3. As the Appellate Body ruled that Canada had not in fact established a breach of Article III, it was not strictly necessary for the resolution of the dispute to continue with Article XX. Since Canada had appealed this part of the Panel's decision, however, the Appellate Body continued with the analysis.[181]

The Appellate Body upheld the Panel's finding that asbestos posed a health risk, a finding that was within the Panel's jurisdiction as the trier of fact.[182] The Appellate Body also agreed with the Panel that France had the right to choose its level of protection — in this case, a halt to the spread of asbestos-related health risks — and that the French measure was designed and apt to accomplish that.[183] Canada had argued that the ban did not meet the requirement in paragraph (b) of being "necessary" because there was no detectable risk involved in chrysotile asbestos cement if proper handling

---

[181] As well, perhaps the Appellate Body considered that Canada might start new procedures to try to prove likeness of the products. See Gabrielle Marceau, "L'affaire '*CE – Amiante*' et la nouvelle jurisprudence de l'Organe d'appel de l'OMC concernant les risques à la santé" (2000) 38 Can. Y.B. Int'l L. 213 at 223–24.

[182] *Asbestos*, Appellate Body Report, *supra* note 4 at para. 163.

[183] *Ibid.* at para. 168.

techniques were followed.[184] Canada said controlled use was a reasonably available alternative that France was obliged to adopt.[185]

The Appellate Body began its analysis of this issue by quoting
from the decision in the *Thailand – Restrictions on Importation of and
Internal Taxes on Cigarettes* (*Thailand – Cigarettes*) dispute on the interpretation of paragraph (b) of Article XX:

> The import restrictions imposed by Thailand could be considered to be
> "necessary" in terms of Article XX(b) only if there were no alternative
> measure consistent with the General Agreement, or less inconsistent with
> it, which Thailand could *reasonably be expected to employ to achieve its health
> policy objectives.*[186]

This is the least-trade-restrictive test, which analyzes various options
that might have been available to a regulating government in order of their level of consistency with GATT provisions. The necessity involved is the necessity of a breach of GATT, rather than the
extent to which the measure advances and supports the chosen
level of health protection. The test has been criticized as too heavily
weighted in favour of trade interests, since it will almost always be
possible to imagine an alternate measure that would be less restrictive of trade.[187]

---

[184] *Asbestos*, Panel Report, *supra* note 4 at paras. 8.163–8.165. See *Ibid.* at paras.
3.50–3.58, 3.120–3.127, and 3.137–3.168. Canada argued that the only risk
came from past use of asbestos, which the measure did nothing to address.
Note that this argument becomes less forceful when the chosen level of protection is defined as a halt in the spread of the risk. If it had been determined that
the goal was to protect the populace from asbestos exposure, Canada's argument over the failure to remedy past uses might have had more weight.

[185] *Asbestos*, Appellate Body Report, *supra* note 4 at para. 169.

[186] *Ibid.* at para. 170, emphasis added by the Appellate Body, quoting from *Thailand
– Restrictions on Importation of and Internal Taxes on Cigarettes*, GATT Panel Report, adopted 7 November 1990, BISD 37S/200, para 75 [*Thailand – Cigarettes*]. In that dispute, Thailand was unsuccessful in its claim for an Article XX(b)
exemption for its restrictions on cigarettes. The GATT Panel found that there
were other options reasonably available to limit smoking, such as non-
discriminatory labelling and bans on advertising, and the practice of restricting
imports while permitting sales of domestic cigarettes was therefore not necessary
(*Ibid.* at para. 81).

[187] Steve Charnovitz, "Exploring the Environmental Exceptions in GATT Article
XX" (1991) 25(5) J. World Trade 37 at 49–50; Robert Howse, "Managing the
Interface between International Trade Law and the Regulatory State: What
Lessons Should (and Should Not) Be Drawn from the Jurisprudence on the
United States Dormant Commerce Clause," in Thomas Cottier and Petros C.

The Appellate Body in *Asbestos* softened the test somewhat by expanding on the availability of alternative measures. Quoting *Korea – Measures Affecting Imports of Fresh, Chilled and Frozen Beef (Korea – Beef)*, a decision concerning Article XX(d), the Appellate Body mentioned the question of the extent to which the alternative measure "contributes to the realization of the end pursued"[188] and also remarked that "'[t]he more vital or important [the] common interests or values' pursued, the easier it would be to accept as 'necessary' measures designed to achieve those ends."[189] As the protection of life is a value of the highest order, the Appellate Body determined that France could not be expected to choose an alternative measure involving a spread of the risk. The Panel had found that controlled use might still result in some risk and that controlled use was not reliably applied in the building service industry or do-it-yourself home repairs. Controlled use, therefore, was not a reasonably available alternative that would meet France's chosen level of protection, and the measure would be exempted under Article XX(b).[190] This analysis is wider than the blunt least-trade-restrictive test of *Thailand – Cigarettes*, but there is still a search for an alternative that would be less restrictive of trade than the measure at issue in the dispute.[191]

The decision in *Korea – Beef* dealt with the interpretation of Article XX(d), which exempts measures:

(d) necessary to secure compliance with laws or regulations which are not inconsistent with the provisions of this Agreement, including those relating to customs enforcement, the enforcement of monopolies operated under paragraph 4 of Article II and Article XVII, the protection of patents, trade marks and copyrights, and the prevention of deceptive practices.[192]

Mavroidis, eds., *Regulatory Barriers and the Principle of Non-Discrimination in World Trade Law* (Ann Arbor: University of Michigan Press, 2000), 139 at 140.

[188] *Asbestos*, Appellate Body Report, *supra* note 4 at para. 172, quoting *Korea – Measures Affecting Imports of Fresh, Chilled and Frozen Beef*, Appellate Body Report, Doc. WT/DS161/AB/R, WT/DS169/AB/R, adopted 10 January 2001, para. 163 [*Korea – Beef*].

[189] *Asbestos*, Appellate Body Report, *supra* note 4 at para. 172, quoting *Korea – Beef*, Appellate Body Report, *supra* note 188 at para. 162.

[190] *Asbestos*, Appellate Body Report, *supra* note 4 at paras. 174 and 175.

[191] *Ibid.* at para. 172.

[192] For early precedents developing the least-trade-restrictive test for Article XX(d), see *United States – Section 337 of the Tariff Act of 1930*, GATT Panel Report, adopted

The wording of paragraph (d) refers to laws and regulations in the domestic sphere, provided they are not inconsistent with GATT. The paragraph does not question the policy choices in those laws and regulations but deals only with the issue of compliance. The paragraph establishes a useful pattern for interpretation of the health exemption in paragraph (b), despite the differences in wording between the two paragraphs. The Appellate Body in *Asbestos* does not question the level of health protection chosen by France but deals only with the issue of what is necessary to support that choice, avoiding an approach that could have been much more intrusive in domestic regulation. It is likely that interpretation of the two paragraphs will continue to operate in parallel, concerning, for example, such issues as reasonable availability of alternative measures.[193] For both, unfortunately, the leading Appellate Body decisions still contain the search for a less-trade-restrictive measure.[194]

7 November 1989, BISD 36S/345; *European Economic Community – Regulation on Imports of Parts and Components*, GATT Panel Report, adopted 16 May 1990, BISD 37S/132.

[193] See *Canada – Measures Relating to Exports of Wheat and Treatment of Imported Grain*, Panel Report, Doc. WT/DS276/R, as upheld by the Appellate Body Report, WT/DS/276/AB/R, adopted 27 September 2004 (Article XX(d) — issue not appealed to Appellate Body), paras. 6.220–6.226 [*Canada – Wheat*]. The Panel stated that reasonable availability could be determined on the basis of the effectiveness of the alternative measure in producing the desired result, the relative administrative, financial and technical burdens and "the trade impact of the alternative measure compared to that of the measure for which justification is claimed"(*Ibid.* at para. 6.226 and Panel footnote 311). To reduce the emphasis of the trade interests, it would be preferable to reduce the weight given to the last-mentioned factor. The *Canada – Wheat* approach can be compared to footnote 3 in the SPS Agreement: "For purposes of paragraph 6 of Article 5, a measure is not more trade-restrictive than required unless there is another measure, reasonably available taking into account technical and economic feasibility, that achieves the appropriate level of sanitary or phytosanitary protection and is significantly less restrictive to trade."

[194] See *Dominican Republic – Measures Affecting the Importation and Internal Sale of Cigarettes*, Appellate Body Report, Doc. WT/DS302/AB/R, adopted 19 May 2005. In its decision, the Appellate Body considers several factors concerning reasonable availability ("the trade impact ... the importance of the interests protected by the measure, ... the contribution of the measure to the realization of the end pursued") but sees the factors as information for the decision on the least-trade-restrictive test (para. 70). See further *United States – Measures Affecting the Cross-Border Supply of Gambling and Betting Services*, Appellate Body Report, Doc. WT/DS285/AB/R, adopted 20 April 2005, paras. 307–08, concerning Article XIV(a) of the General Agreement on Trade in Services, WTO Agreement, *supra* note 2, Annex 1B.

There is no need to judge the necessity of a measure in paragraph (b) in light of the overall notion of enhancement of trade interests and no need to privilege those interests at this stage of the analysis. The basic GATT non-discrimination norms are preserved in the introductory clause of Article XX, which will be addressed if the measure meets the requirements of a listed paragraph. In fact, a general direction to give priority to all other GATT provisions is difficult to apply, since it is hard to know which ones in that group are to have precedence. For the interpretation of paragraph (g), we now decide whether a measure relates to conservation by considering such factors as its effectiveness in promoting conservation and the width of its reach in proportion to the goal sought.[195] We should adopt a similar approach for the interpretation of paragraph (b) and leave the analysis of discrimination to the introductory clause. The link between the measure and the policy objective may be more demanding than in paragraph (g) since the measure must be "necessary." Measures could be assessed to see whether they were essential to the achievement of the chosen level of protection.[196] There could be a review of alternative measures, but these do not have to be assessed in order of their consistency with national treatment and MFN treatment. If the measure passes the necessity test, analysis would then move to the norms set out in the introductory words of Article XX.

The Panel decision in *Argentina – Measures Affecting the Export of Bovine Hides and the Import of Finished Leather* (*Argentina – Bovine Hides*) shows how analysis might proceed if the least-trade-restrictive test is dropped from interpretation of the paragraphs of Article XX.[197] The analysis related to a system of taxation requiring pre-payment of internal sales and income taxes on imported goods.

---

[195] *Shrimp/Turtle 1998*, Appellate Body Report, *supra* note 5 at para. 141.

[196] Disputes dealing with GATT Article XI:2(c) have not adopted a least-trade-restrictive approach in interpreting the reference in that article to import restrictions "necessary to the enforcement" of certain governmental measures. The decisions have examined factors such as whether the products covered in the import restriction were the same as those affected by the governmental measure and whether the import restriction made the measure effective: *Japan – Restrictions on Imports of Certain Agricultural Products*, GATT Panel Report, adopted 22 March 1988, BISD 35S/163 [*Japan – Agricultural Products I*]; *Canada – Import Restrictions on Ice Cream and Yoghurt*, GATT Panel Report, adopted 5 December 1989, BISD 36S/68; *Thailand – Cigarettes*, GATT Panel Report, *supra* note 186 at para. 70.

[197] *Argentina – Measures Affecting the Export of Bovine Hides and the Import of Finished Leather*, Panel Report, Doc. WT/DS155/R, adopted 16 February 2001.

Argentina argued the measure was necessary to fight tax fraud that it alleged was a persistent problem and said Article XX(d) did not contain a least-trade-restrictive test.[198] The Panel did not resolve this question, but found for Argentina that the measure was provisionally within paragraph (d) whether or not a least-trade-restrictive test was used.[199] The measure still was not justified, however, as Argentina did not satisfactorily explain its failure to compensate importers for interest lost because of the pre-payment. Application of the measure thus involved unjustifiable discrimination within the terms of the introductory clause of Article XX.[200] This was not simply a least-trade-restrictive test or a national treatment analysis, but rather an examination of the discrimination through the perspective of what was necessary for tax enforcement.

The interpretation of paragraph (b) of Article XX should not follow a least-trade-restrictive approach that gives priority to trade interests, such as the non-discrimination norms of national treatment and MFN treatment. Discrimination is addressed through the introductory clause of Article XX, which prohibits only "arbitrary or unjustifiable" discrimination, not all trade discrimination. Interpretation should allow room for the important non-trade interests reflected in the listed paragraphs of Article XX, as the drafters of GATT appear to have intended.

ASSERTION 3: THE COVERAGE OF THE NATIONAL TREATMENT STANDARD SHOULD NOT BE EXPANDED IN AN ATTEMPT TO PROTECT DOMESTIC REGULATIONS THAT BLOCK IMPORTS. IT MAY BE PREFERABLE FOR THE DEVELOPMENT OF GLOBAL PUBLIC POLICY TO TREAT CERTAIN IMPORT BANS AS BREACHES OF GATT ARTICLE XI, WHICH WOULD BE SUBJECT TO POSSIBLE JUSTIFICATION UNDER ARTICLE XX

If a country bans certain imports for health reasons, should it matter whether producers in the importing country have also lost business? This part of the article addresses the limits on national treatment as a justification for domestic regulation, as well as the

[198] *Ibid.* at para. 11.299.

[199] *Ibid.* at paras. 11.304–11.308.

[200] Since the Panel found that a system of compensation would make the measure consistent with Article III:2 (*Ibid.* at para. 11.329), a least-trade-restrictive test under paragraph (d) presumably should have disqualified the measure from provisional justification under paragraph (d). It appears that the Panel was not applying a least-trade-restrictive interpretation to paragraph (d).

relationship between national treatment and the exemptions of GATT Article XX. The national treatment obligation in GATT has been a key factor in establishing the dividing line between national regulation and international trade rules. Together, the non-discrimination norms of national treatment and MFN treatment have served the important function of ensuring even-handedness towards imports and domestic products. It is argued in this part that domestic measures recognizing non-trade interests are best protected through the provisions of Article XX, interpreted as suggested in Assertions 1 and 2 earlier in this article, rather than by way of expansive views of the coverage of "like products" and the national treatment standard. The interpretation of "like products" in the *Asbestos* decision is quite wide, using the consumer perspective and conditions of competition. Emphasizing the operation of market forces is, in any case, a problematic strategy for the defence of national decision-making in important areas of public policy such as the protection of health.

The national treatment obligation appears in the TBT Agreement but does not control the full impact of that agreement on domestic regulation. The TBT Agreement and the SPS Agreement contain additional market-opening obligations that are likely to supplant the national treatment norm in many applications. As these market access rules cannot be avoided, the preferable strategy should focus on achieving a balanced interpretation of Article XX, to be available for breaches of Article III and also for breaches of the market access provisions.

The first section of this part discusses like products and national treatment under GATT Article III, in general arguing against taking an expansive view of Article III as a way of protecting national regulatory power. In the second section, it is suggested that the relationship between GATT Articles III and XI should be re-examined to determine whether import bans should be judged under the market access provisions of Article XI rather than primarily as domestic regulation under Article III. In both sections, the analysis focuses on the *Asbestos* decision.

ARTICLE III — LIKE PRODUCTS

Concerning the identification of "like products," this section argues that the Appellate Body in *Asbestos* reached the correct result but for the wrong reason, which gave too much emphasis to the views of consumers in the importing country. The same result could have been achieved through a focus on end use, which would be better suited to an accurate examination of the risks presented. The section discusses the *Asbestos* decision against the background of previous cases dealing with GATT Article III. Further remarks then address the implications of the Appellate Body's emphasis on competition and the consumer viewpoint in relation to the "aim and effects" interpretation of Article III and to measures that distinguish among goods according to their processing and production methods.

In *Asbestos*, Canada alleged a breach of GATT Article III:4, which provides as follows:

III:4. The products of the territory of any Member imported into the territory of any other Member shall be accorded treatment no less favourable than that accorded to like products of national origin in respect of all laws, regulations and requirements affecting their internal sale, offering for sale, purchase, transportation, distribution or use.

The Panel in *Asbestos* had declined to consider health risks at the stage of identifying like products of domestic origin because it did not want to undermine the review under Article XX(b).[201] The Appellate Body disagreed and ruled that those risks should be considered as part of the determination of like products, according to the criteria relating to physical characteristics and to consumers' tastes and habits.[202] The approach taken by the Appellate Body would dispense with the need to examine Article XX in this dispute, since there is no breach of Article III:4 if there are no like products.[203]

In other disputes, taking health risks into account for the determination of like products might not necessarily lead to the same result. Asbestos fibres are acknowledged to be carcinogenic, and, for the cancers concerned, the mortality rate is close to 100 per cent.[204] For other goods, the health risks could be less severe. Imported foods

---

[201] *Asbestos*, Panel Report, *supra* note 4 at paras. 8.128–8.132.

[202] *Asbestos*, Appellate Body Report, *supra* note 4 at paras. 113–16.

[203] In the context of the *Asbestos* appeal, however, the Appellate Body did complete its analysis of Article XX. Note that both the Panel and the Appellate Body accepted that the Note Ad Article III required review of the French measure to be only under Article III and not under Article XI as a quantitative restriction. The relationship between Articles III and XI is discussed in the second section of this part.

[204] *Asbestos*, Panel Report, *supra* note 4 at para. 8.188, quoted in *Asbestos*, Appellate Body Report, *supra* note 4 at para. 114.

306 Annuaire canadien de Droit international 2004

containing peanuts, for example, pose health risks to certain consumers with allergies and those risks vary in intensity. The health risks could be taken into account without necessarily precluding a finding that cookies with peanuts and cookies without peanuts are like products.

If the health risks are less serious than those associated with asbestos, or if the comparable domestic goods also present similar risks, the goods might still be like products, and, assuming a breach of Article III, analysis could proceed to potential justification under Article XX. The Appellate Body is correct to state, therefore, that its approach to the recognition of health risks does not deny all useful effect to Article XX(b). The important question, however, is whether the health risks will be appropriately assessed under the Appellate Body's approach. Article XX(b) of GATT allows an exemption for measures that are "necessary to protect human ... life or health." This exemption is subject to the requirements in the introductory words of the article that the measure not be applied so as to constitute "a means of arbitrary or unjustifiable discrimination ... or a disguised restriction on international trade." The approach of the Appellate Body in *Asbestos* saves this sort of review for the less significant health risks and for cases where the domestic goods also present risks. The more significant health risks, the ones that preclude a finding of "likeness," are dealt with at the initial stages of the analysis, under the criteria for the identification of like products. The Article III process, given priority of place in the Appellate Body's decision, avoids a review concerning necessity, discrimination, and disguised restrictions on trade. The question is whether this result is appropriate and, in particular, whether the Article III process is adequate for this distinction between the health risks that preclude a finding of like products and the other health risks that could go on to full review under Article XX.

The criteria used in *Asbestos* to identify like products are derived from a list in a 1970 GATT Working Party report on *Border Tax Adjustments,* which refers to "the product's end-uses in a given market; consumers' tastes and habits, which change from country to country; the product's properties, nature and quality."[205] In the

205 *Border Tax Adjustments,* Report of the GATT Working Party, adopted 2 December 1970, BISD 18S/97, para. 18 (as suggested criteria for similarity of products). The list is repeated in *Japan – Customs Duties, Taxes and Labelling Practices on Imported Wines and Alcoholic Beverages,* GATT Panel Report, adopted 10 November 1987, BISD 34S/83, para. 5.6 (dealing with Article III:2) [*Japan – Alcoholic Beverages II*], with the additional mention of tariff classification, a factor used in *EEC –*

Appellate Body decision in *Asbestos,* the list is expressed as: "(i) the properties, nature and quality of the products; (ii) the end-uses of the products; (iii) consumers' tastes and habits — more comprehensively termed consumers' perceptions and behaviour — in respect of the products; and (iv) the tariff classification of the products."[206] The Appellate Body found the Panel's analysis of shared end uses inadequate and noted the physical uniqueness of asbestos, in particular, its carcinogenicity. Although the Appellate Body did not have evidence of consumers' tastes and habits, it determined that consumers would likely be influenced by the health risks.[207] The Appellate Body determined that Canada had failed to demonstrate the presence of like products of domestic origin and thus had not established a breach of Article III:4.

The Appellate Body's approach to the interpretation of "like products" in Article III:4 was informed by a general principle derived from Article III:1, which favoured equality of competitive conditions between imported and domestic goods. The approach reflects the stipulation in Article III:1 that internal taxes and certain internal measures "should not be applied to imported or domestic products so as to afford protection to domestic production."[208] In this view, the determination of likeness is "fundamentally, a determination about the nature and extent of a competitive relationship between and among products."[209] According to the Appellate Body, "key elements" indicating such a competitive relationship between products are: "first, the extent to which products are capable of

---

Measures on Animal Feed Proteins, GATT Panel Report, adopted 14 March 1978, BISD 25S/49, para. 4.2 (dealing with, *inter alia,* Article III:2 and III:4). See also *Japan – Taxes on Alcoholic Beverages,* Appellate Body Report, Doc. WT/DS8/AB/R, Doc. WT/DS10/AB/R, Doc. WT/DS11/AB/R, adopted 1 November 1996, DSR 1996:1, 97 at 113 (dealing with Article III:2) [*Japan – Alcoholic Beverages II*]; *Canada – Certain Measures Concerning Periodicals,* Appellate Body Report, Doc. WT/DS31/R, adopted 30 June 1997, DSR 1997:1, 449 at 466 (dealing with Article III:2 and III:8) [*Canada – Periodicals*]. In a dispute concerning Article III:4, products were found to be like because they "have exactly the same physical characteristics, end-uses, tariff classification and are perfectly substitutable" in *United States – Standards for Reformulated and Conventional Gasoline,* Panel Report, Doc. WT/DS2/R, as modified by the *Reformulated Gasoline,* Appellate Body Report, *supra* note 114 at para. 6.9 (finding not appealed to the Appellate Body).

[206] *Asbestos,* Appellate Body Report, *supra* note 4 at para. 101.

[207] *Ibid.* at paras. 122, 130, and 145.

[208] *Ibid.* at paras. 93–100.

[209] *Ibid.* at para. 99. See para. 103.

performing the same, or similar, functions (end-uses), and, second, the extent to which consumers are willing to use the products to perform these functions (consumers' tastes and habits)."[210] The competitiveness perspective is strongly emphasized when the "consumer" criterion is re-stated by the Appellate Body as "the extent to which consumers perceive and treat the products as alternative means of performing particular functions in order to satisfy a particular want or demand."[211]

This emphasis on consumer perception is, however, problematic for issues of health risks allegedly presented by imported goods. If consumers think that the imports are dangerous even though they are not, will the Article III process be adequate for sorting this out? Will negative consumer perceptions make it more likely that the health risk be seen as so serious that the goods are not "like"? If the imports are not like domestic products within the terms of Article III, there will be no further step to an Article XX review involving necessity, non-discrimination, and the absence of disguised restrictions. The danger is that the article III analysis could pay more attention to price and marketing surveys than to scientific evidence about the alleged risk. After *Asbestos,* Article III analysis in these circumstances may not be adequate to preserve traditional GATT norms. In particular, there is nothing in the "like products" criteria to review for discrimination and disguised restrictions on trade, as these considerations arise under Article XX, following a finding of breach.

In *Asbestos,* the health risks could have been fully assessed as part of the physical characteristics of the products and their end use. There was no need to expand the role for consumer perception. The physical characteristics of asbestos are unique, and the extremely serious risks associated with asbestos are well documented. Canada was arguing that the products posed no detectable risk if they were installed and handled following certain precautions, which surely should have been part of their use and commercial application. When asbestos cement blocks cannot be cut without special equipment and cumbersome procedures and when the goods cannot be handled except by operators wearing protective gear,[212] there has to be an effect on end use. It is quite artificial and

---

[210] *Ibid.* at para. 117.

[211] *Ibid.* at para. 101.

[212] *Asbestos,* Panel Report, *supra* note 4 at paras. 3.55 and 3.56 (Canada's submissions); paras. 3.63, 3.171, and 3.296 (EC submissions).

divorced from commercial reality to say that those precautions should appear in the discussion only peripherally as part of the analysis of "necessity" in Article XX(b). When the Appellate Body re-stated the end use criterion as "the extent to which the products are capable of serving the same or similar end-uses,"[213] it omitted an important link to practice that has to do with the functioning of the goods in application.[214] The end use criterion should not be simply about whether asbestos and substitute products both work effectively for the given purposes such as for insulation or brake linings. How they work also needs to be considered, and the extraordinary control measures suggested by Canada for the safe use of asbestos should have been relevant in this context. It is not adequate to view these control measures in the abstract as simply a question of whether consumers were willing to accept the additional related costs.[215] The health risks were so closely linked to the physical aspects of the goods that the Panel's original finding of like products seems odd. The scientific evidence supporting the precautions, which Canada did not deny, and the resulting significant physical differences in commercial application should have been part of the consideration of end use.

If health risks of imported goods are considered in Article III, it is preferable to ground the analysis in the traditional attention to material fact — physical characteristics and end use — rather than competitive relationships and consumer perception, in order to promote an accurate examination of the alleged risk. For risks that are not as serious as those in *Asbestos,* the goods could still be found to be like products, and the analysis will move on to Article XX. We should hope that there are not too many commercial products around that are as dangerous as asbestos. For the majority of products, analysis of health risks should not stop at the Article III "like products" classification but should move on to review under Article XX.

---

213 *Asbestos,* Appellate Body Report, *supra* note 4 at para. 101.

214 For a discussion of the end use factor in tariff classification, including both purpose and function, see Maureen Irish, "Interpretation and Naming: The Harmonized System in Canadian Customs Tariff Law" (1993) 31 Can. Y.B. Int'l Law 89.

215 *Asbestos,* Appellate Body Report, *supra* note 4 at para. 122. Note that the Appellate Body decided to examine the alleged health risks only under the criteria of physical properties and consumers' tastes and habits, not end use (paras. 113 and 122).

The original list of criteria from *Border Tax Adjustments* emphasized material fact: "[E]nd uses in a given market; consumers' tastes
and habits, which change from country to country; product's properties, nature and quality." The emphasis on physical characteristics and end use is similar to criteria for the tariff classification of
goods — appropriately enough, if Article III was intended, at least
in part, to prevent countries from undercutting tariff deals through
internal charges and regulations.[216] In the *Border Tax Adjustments*
list, the mention of "consumers' tastes and habits, which change
from country to country," can be interpreted as ensuring that the
exploration of end use relates to conditions in the country of import. The weight to give to consumers' presumed tastes and habits
has been controversial in past disputes concerning the identification of like goods. In the 1987 GATT Panel decision in *Japan –
Customs Duties, Taxes and Labelling Practices on Imported Wines and
Alcoholic Beverages (Japan – Alcoholic Beverages I)*, the consumer viewpoint was characterized as "subjective." The Panel in that matter
ruled that traditional habits provided no reason for refusing to
consider imported vodka and the domestically produced beverage
shochu to be like products.[217]

It was in *Asbestos* that consumer perceptions were given enhanced
priority and the criterion was expanded to reflect the interpretation that Article III is primarily about the maintenance of competitive conditions. This evolution in the interpretation of Article III is

216 See *Japan – Alcoholic Beverages II*, Appellate Body Report, *supra* note 205 at DSR
1996:1, 97 at 110. Note, however, that Article III applies even in the absence of
tariff bindings for the goods in question: *ibid.*, citing *Brazilian Internal Taxes*,
GATT Panel Report, adopted 30 June 1949, BISD II/181, para. 4; *United States
– Taxes on Petroleum and Certain Imported Substances*, GATT Panel Report, adopted
17 June 1987, BISD 34S/136, para. 5.1.9; *EEC – Regulation on Imports of Parts
and Components*, GATT Panel Report, adopted 16 May 1990, BISD 37S/132,
para. 5.4.

217 *Japan – Alcoholic Beverages I*, *supra* note 205 at para. 5.7. Imported vodka and
shochu were again found to be like products in 1996 in *Japan – Alcoholic Beverages
II*, *supra* note 205 (Panel finding, affirmed on appeal). Both of these analyses
involved the first sentence of Article III:2. See further *Korea – Taxes on Alcoholic
Beverages*, Appellate Body Report, Doc. WT/DS75/AB/R, Doc. WT/DS84/AB/
R, adopted 17 February 1999 [*Korea – Alcoholic Beverages*], especially the Panel
Report in that dispute, WT/DS75/R, WT/DS84/R, at paras. 10.70–10.76,
rejecting a similar defence by Korea under the second sentence of Article III:2,
relating to beverages consumed in traditional-style restaurants. The consumer
perspectives in these disputes did not prevent findings that the national
treatment obligation had been breached.

particularly sensitive in a dispute concerning health risks, which is an area of significant concern for national regulators. It would have been helpful if the Appellate Body had provided more guidance on the relationship between Articles III and XX, instead of referring simply to the rather arid interpretive principle of useful effect, which does not explain why one article has wide application and the other is interpreted narrowly.

The Appellate Body in *Asbestos* added the "competitive conditions" gloss to Article III:4 partly in order to match the overall coverage of Article III:2, which is the other main expression of the national treatment obligation in GATT. Under Article III:4, imports must receive "treatment no less favourable than that accorded to like products of national origin in respect of all laws, regulations and requirements affecting their internal sale, offering for sale, purchase, transportation, distribution or use." Internal taxes and charges are governed by a different paragraph, Article III:2, which provides as follows:

III:2. The products of the territory of any Member imported into the territory of any other Member shall not be subject, directly or indirectly, to internal taxes or other internal charges of any kind in excess of those applied, directly or indirectly, to like domestic products. Moreover, no Member shall otherwise apply internal taxes or other internal charges to imported or domestic products in a manner contrary to the principles set forth in paragraph 1.

Paragraph 1 of Article III provides that internal taxes and measures described in the other paragraphs "should not be applied to imported or domestic products so as to afford protection to domestic production."

Also relevant for the interpretation of Article III:2 is the following Note Ad Article III, paragraph 2:

A tax conforming to the requirements of the first sentence of paragraph 2 would be considered to be inconsistent with the provisions of the second sentence only in cases where competition was involved between, on the one hand, the taxed product and, on the other hand, a directly competitive or substitutable product which was not similarly taxed.

The controls on certain non-fiscal regulations in Article III:4, which is the provision at issue in *Asbestos,* apply only to like products. In contrast, the controls on fiscal regulation in Article III:2 apply to both like products (first sentence) and "directly competitive or substitutable" products (second sentence, as interpreted through the note). Since both taxation and non-tax regulation may be used for the same purposes, the Appellate Body in *Asbestos* reasoned that it would be incongruous to prevent a state from using one form of regulation but not the other in a given set of circumstances.[218] "Like products" in Article III:4, therefore, is broader than "like products" in Article III:2 (first sentence) but not wider than "directly competitive or substitutable" products in Article III:2 (second sentence), according to the Appellate Body.[219] The "accordion" of like-ness[220] stretches to make Article III:4 cover about the same territory as Article III:2.

Japan – Alcoholic Beverages II, the source of the accordion metaphor for the determination of like products, was a decision concerning both sentences of Article III:2. In that dispute, Japan was found to have violated the first sentence through its differential treatment of shochu and vodka, which were held to be like products. As well, Japan was in violation of the second sentence of Article III:2 concerning its tax treatment of other alcoholic beverages. When dealing with the second sentence, the Panel in *Japan – Alcoholic Beverages II* looked to the market place and examined economic data showing changes in demand relative to price changes in the other alcoholic beverages, which were found to be directly competitive with, or substitutable for, shochu. The Appellate Body endorsed the Panel's approach.[221] In *Korea – Taxes on Alcoholic Beverages*, the Panel and Appellate Body decided that goods were "directly competitive or substitutable" by looking at physical characteristics, end use, channels of distribution, and cross-price elasticity, although this last factor

---

[218] Note the following, published before the *Asbestos* decision: "It is worth emphasizing that article III:2, second sentence, prohibits tax differentials between products which, while not 'like,' are 'directly competitive,' but there is no counterpart in article III:4, which covers internal regulations. Accordingly, article III:4 appears to grant more leeway with respect to differential *regulatory* treatment of 'directly competitive' products than differential taxation" [emphasis in original]. Warren H. Maruyama "A New Pillar of the WTO: Sound Science" (1998) 32 Int'l Law. 651 at 674. Presumably, the Appellate Body sought to avoid exactly this distinction.

[219] *Asbestos*, Appellate Body Report, *supra* note 4 at para. 99.

[220] *Ibid.* at para. 96.

[221] *Japan – Alcoholic Beverages II*, Appellate Body Report, *supra* note 205 at 117. See *Japan – Alcoholic Beverages II*, Panel Report, *supra* note 205 at paras. 4.82 and 6.28–6.32. The Panel also mentioned that marketing strategies could be a relevant criterion (para. 6.28), although they were not significant in that decision.

was not found to be determinative.[222] On the evidence presented, the Panel was unable to determine whether soju and vodka were "like products," but the question did not affect the outcome, as the two products were covered in the wider category of "directly competitive or substitutable" goods.[223] The dispute in *Chile – Taxes on Alcoholic Beverages* also involved the second sentence of Article III:2, as there was no claim that the goods were like products. The Panel came to the conclusion that domestically produced pisco and the other alcoholic beverages at issue were "directly competitive or substitutable" based on a list of factors, including physical characteristics, end use, channels of distribution, and studies of prices.[224] If the matter in dispute involves tax regulation, there is actually little point in trying to identify goods that are "like products," since the

[222] *Korea – Alcoholic Beverages*, Panel Report and Appellate Body Report, *supra* note 217. Quantitative analysis of cross-price elasticity is discussed at paras. 121–24, 132–34 in the Appellate Body report.

[223] *Korea – Alcoholic Beverages*, Panel Report, *supra* note 217 at paras. 10.103–10.104. This issue was not appealed to the Appellate Body. In its interpretation of the second sentence of Article III:2, the Appellate Body contrasted the products covered by that sentence that might be "imperfectly substitutable," with the like products covered by the first sentence that would be "perfectly substitutable." See *Korea – Alcoholic Beverages*, Appellate Body Report, *supra* note 217 at para. 118.

[224] *Chile – Taxes on Alcoholic Beverages*, Panel Report, Doc. WT/DS87/R, Doc. WT/DS110/R, as upheld by the Appellate Body Report, Doc. WT/DS87/AB/R, Doc. WT/DS110/AB/R, adopted 12 January 2000 [*Chile – Alcoholic Beverages*]. Chile had argued that pisco was distinct from the imported distilled spirits, since pisco was made from grapes while the spirits (for example, whisky) were made from grain. The Panel noted that some of the imported spirits were also made from grapes and remarked that physical characteristics were more significant concerning "like" products than products alleged to be "directly competitive or substitutable" (Panel Report, paras. 7.50–7.54). In its reasoning, the Panel also mentioned the opinion of a domestic Chilean anti-trust agency that there was competition between domestically-produced pisco and other alcoholic beverages. In the Panel's view, this opinion confirmed the Panel's finding of "directly competitive or substitutable" products (Panel Report, paras. 7.86–7.87). As this finding was not appealed, the relevant list of factors and the treatment of the domestic anti-trust opinion were not examined by the Appellate Body, which upheld the Panel's decision that there was a *de facto* breach of Article III.2. See also *Canada – Periodicals*, *supra* note 205 at 472–73, where the Appellate Body mentioned a domestic governmental Task Force report that acknowledged the competition between US magazines and English-language Canadian magazines, seen as confirming the finding that the goods were "directly competitive or substitutable"; Chi Carmody, "When 'Cultural Identity' was not at Issue': Thinking about *Canada – Certain Measures Concerning Periodicals*" (1999) 30(2) Law & Pol'y Int'l Bus. 231.

outcome will most probably depend on the wider category of "directly competitive or substitutable" products.[225]

In these decisions concerning the second sentence of Article III:2, competitive or substitutable products were determined according to channels of distribution, advertising, points of sale, and prices, including cross-price elasticity calculations used to show latent demand. Now, as a result of the decision in *Asbestos*, it appears that this thinking about competitive conditions may be read into the "like products" test in Article III:4. There has already been some spillover of language from one test to the other. The Panel decision in *Korea – Taxes on Alcoholic Beverages*, which deals with Article III:2, second sentence, states that consumers viewed competitive products as "alternate ways of satisfying a particular need or taste."[226] This wording is then reflected in the *Asbestos* Appellate Body's restatement of the "consumer" criterion for the like-products test as "the extent to which consumers perceive and treat the products as alternative means of performing particular functions in order to satisfy a particular want or demand."[227] It may be noted that none of the economic evidence of competition — prices, marketing, or distribution — calls for a scientific study of the physical properties of the goods themselves or the health risks they might pose. Analysis moves away from the physical facts associated with the goods. Note, as well, that much of the information gathered reflects the behaviour of the sellers, which is only presumed to relate to consumer perceptions. This approach is not the same thing as empowering consumer choice directly through a labelling system to identify a specific health risk or other issue concerning the goods.[228] An examination of market competition is not the only — or even the best — way of assessing the consumer viewpoint. The Appellate Body's discussion of competitive conditions was not essential to its decision to consider health risks as part of the determination of

---

[225] Concerning interpretation of the phrase "like and/or directly competitive products" in Article 6.2 of the Agreement on Textiles and Clothing, see *United States – Transitional Safeguard Measure on Combed Cotton Yarn from Pakistan*, Appellate Body Report, Doc. WT/DS192/AB/R, adopted 5 November 2001, paras. 91, 94–98.

[226] *Korea – Alcoholic Beverages*, Panel Report, *supra* note 217 at para. 10.40. See *Korea – Alcoholic Beverages*, Appellate Body Report, *supra* note 217 at para. 115.

[227] *Asbestos*, Appellate Body Report, *supra* note 4 at para. 101.

[228] See further Douglas A. Kysar, "Preferences for Processes: The Process/Product Distinction and the Regulation of Consumer Choice Preferences" (2004) 118 Harv. L. Rev. 525.

like products and such an approach does not necessarily identify consumers' views on particular issues relating to the goods. One member of the Appellate Body is correct to wonder in a concurring statement whether likeness should be interpreted in this manner in accordance with only the one main identified policy objective of equal competitive conditions between imports and domestically produced goods.

The Appellate Body based its approach to interpretation on the general principle it found expressed in Article III:1, which states that various measures listed elsewhere in Article III "should not be applied to imported or domestic products so as to afford protection to domestic production." The Appellate Body determined that it would "frustrate a consistent application"[229] of this principle to permit the protection of certain domestic products by one measure but not by another. Article III:4 received a wide interpretation, therefore, even though the Appellate Body does not explain why the general principle of Article III:1 should over-ride the more specific language in the other paragraphs or why the general principle must have the same coverage in both paragraphs rather than varying with the content of the specific obligation in each one.

The text of Article III does not require that both Article III:2 and Article III:4 have the same scope. Since complainants might not bother to raise the "like products" argument under Article III.2, the "like products" test is now mostly for Article III:4. In *Asbestos,* the Appellate Body seems to be treating this test as having a meaning that is very close to "directly competitive or substitutable" products. The drafters of GATT, however, did not include these words in Article III:4. They had the example of both phrases in Article III:2 and in the note addendum, but chose to include only a "like products" standard in Article III:4 for non-fiscal regulation. Perhaps they felt that the danger of the national treatment obligations being undermined by clever product descriptions and manipulation was greater for taxation than for other forms of regulation. Perhaps negotiators were mainly worried about undercutting tariff deals and thought a tax was more likely to do this than some other internal regulation. Whatever the reason, some effect should be given to the difference in wording.[230] The approach to "like products" in *Asbestos* comes close to reading these paragraphs together.

[229] *Asbestos,* Appellate Body Report, *supra* note 4 at para. 99

[230] Won-Mog Choi, *"Like Products" in International Trade Law: Towards a Consistent GATT/WTO Jurisprudence* (Oxford: Oxford University Press, 2003) at 111–14. There are differences as well in the standards of discrimination that constitute

Even if consistency between Article III:2 and Article III:4 is accepted as a goal, an approach emphasizing competition and the market is an awkward way to take account of important public policies such as the protection of health. The market could easily overestimate a health risk. It could also under-estimate a risk, when products might still find willing buyers despite health or environmental concerns.[231] The Appellate Body in *Asbestos* considered the perspectives of consumers and sellers in the internal distribution system in the country of import, but not the perspectives of regulators or those who argue in favour of a given general public purpose. Public policy goals are best addressed directly rather than indirectly through the language of competitive markets.[232]

The Appellate Body's treatment of Article III:1 in *Asbestos* builds on its use of Article III:1 in the *European Communities – Regime for the*

---

breach: taxation "in excess of" taxes on like products (Article III:2, first sentence); dissimilar taxation of directly competitive or substitutable products "so as to afford protection to domestic production" (Article III:2, second sentence and the note addendum) and non-fiscal regulation resulting in treatment that is "less favourable" than the treatment of domestic like products (Article III:4).

231 Reinhard Quick and Christian Lau suggest the example of refrigerators banned because they contain chlorofluorocarbons (CFCs): Richard Quick and Christian Lau, "Environmentally Motivated Tax Distinctions and WTO Law: The European Commission's Green Paper on Integrated Product Policy in Light of the 'Like Product-' and 'PPM-' Debates" (2003) J. Int'l Econ. L. 419 at 435–36. If the "like products" test is fundamentally about market competition rather than physical characteristics, the acceptability of such a ban could be made to depend on whether consumers distinguished between refrigerators with CFCs and those without — presumably prior to the imposition of the ban. See further: Marco Bronckers and Natalie McNelis, "Rethinking the 'Like Product' Definition in GATT 1994: Anti-Dumping and Environmental Protection," in Thomas Cottier and Petros C. Mavroidis, eds., *Regulatory Barriers and the Principle of Non-Discrimination in World Trade Law* (Ann Arbor: University of Michigan Press, 2000) 345 at 372–76; Henrik Horn and Joseph H.H. Weiler, "*EC – Asbestos* European Communities — Measures Affecting Asbestos and Asbestos-Containing Products" (2004) 3(1) World Trade Review 129 at 149–50.

232 Robert Howse and Elizabeth Tuerk solve this problem by stating that the Appellate Body was presuming "an *idealised* market-place, one where consumers have full information, and where, at least through tort liability, negative externalities have already to some extent been internalised": Robert Howse and Elizabeth Tuerk, "The WTO Impact on Internal Regulations: A Case Study of the Canada-EC Asbestos Dispute," in Gráinne de Búrca and Joanne Scott, eds., *The EU and the WTO: Legal and Constitutional Issues* (Oxford and Portland, OR: Hart Publishing, 2001) 283 at 301 [emphasis in original]. This abstraction sits somewhat uncomfortably, however, with the other criteria used to identify like products, which relate to an actual rather than an ideal market.

Importation, Sale and Distribution of Bananas (*Bananas*) decision in 1997. In *Bananas*, the Article III:4 claim related to the allocation of import licences in a way that favoured EC-origin bananas. The Appellate Body held that this allocation affected competitive conditions and was in breach of Article III:4. The Appellate Body then mentioned that, unlike the second sentence of Article III:2, Article III:4 does not specifically refer to Article III:1 and so does not require a separate consideration of whether a measure affords protection to domestic production.[233] Article III:1 was still treated as a general principle that informed interpretation of the rest of Article III. As well, in both *Bananas* and *Asbestos*, it was clear that Article III:1 does not add a requirement for proof of injury or declining statistics in order to demonstrate that imports have received less favourable treatment. A long line of previous decisions confirms that GATT is not about ensuring trade volumes but only about effective equality of opportunity.[234] For Article III:4, the general principle of paragraph 1 does not add an injury test. In *Asbestos*, the Appellate Body ruled that it adds an emphasis on competitive conditions that goes to the identification of like products.[235]

In two pre-WTO decisions, Article III:1 was used to support an "aim and effects" test for the identification of like products. This test addressed discrimination among products by "asking whether a difference of treatment is rationally related to a legitimate regulatory

---

233 *European Communities – Regime for the Importation, Sale and Distribution of Bananas*, Appellate Body Report, Doc. WT/DS27/AB/5, adopted 25 September 1997, para. 216 [*Bananas*].

234 *United States – Section 337 of the Tariff Act of 1930*, GATT Panel Report, adopted 7 November 1989, BISD 36S/345 at para. 5.11; *Canada – Import, Distribution and Sale of Certain Alcoholic Drinks by Provincial Marketing Agencies*, GATT Panel Report, adopted 18 February 1992, BISD 39S/27, para. 5.12. See further, concerning Article III:2, *United States – Taxes on Petroleum and Certain Imported Substances*, GATT Panel Report, adopted 17 June 1987, BISD 34S/136, para. 5.1.9 ("Article III:2, first sentence, cannot be interpreted to protect expectations on export volumes; it protects expectations on the competitive relationship between imported and domestic products"); *Japan – Alcoholic Beverages I*, GATT Panel Report, *supra* note 205 at para. 5.16; *United States – Alcoholic and Malt Beverages*, GATT Panel Report, adopted 19 June 1992, BISD 39S/206, para. 5.6 [*United States – Malt Beverages*]; *United States – Measures Affecting the Importation, Internal Sale and Use of Tobacco*, GATT Panel Report, adopted 4 October 1994, BISD 41S, vol.I/131, para. 99.

235 This is not quite the same as for the second sentence of Article III:2, where it adds the test of "the design, the architecture and the revealing structure of a measure" to reflect the specific mention in the sentence (*Japan – Alcoholic Beverages II*, Appellate Body Report, *supra* note 205 at 120).

purpose"[236] other than trade protectionism. The two decisions were *United States – Alcoholic and Malt Beverages*, which was adopted in June 1992, and *United States – Taxes on Automobiles*, which was not adopted, due to opposition from the European Communities.[237] The "aim and effects" test was later rejected by the Appellate Body in 1996.[238] In *United States – Alcoholic and Malt Beverages*, the GATT Panel used Article III:1 to find that there was no breach of Article III:4 for several state restrictions on points of sale, distribution, and labelling, which distinguished between beer with low-alcohol levels and beer with high-alcohol levels. Although the products were similar on the basis of their physical characteristics, the Panel concluded that "there was no evidence ... that the choice of the particular level has the purpose or effect of affording protection to domestic production."[239] The Panel in *United States – Taxes on Automobiles* went further and treated the aim and effects test as if it replaced the *Border Tax Adjustments* criteria altogether for any measures that were not origin specific. The Panel decided that a measure would have "the *aim* of affording protection if ... an analysis of the instruments available ... demonstrated that a change in competitive opportunities in favour of domestic products was a desired outcome and not merely an incidental consequence of pursuit of a legitimate policy."[240] According to the Panel, a measure would have the "*effect*" of affording protection ... if it accorded greater competitive opportunities to domestic products than to imported products."[241] With this approach, the GATT Panel found that a "gas guzzler" tax on sales of automobiles that failed to meet fuel economy requirements did not breach Article III because "the nature and level of the regulatory distinction made at the threshold ... were consistent with the overall purpose of the measure and did not appear to

---

[236] Robert E. Hudec, "GATT/WTO Constraints on National Regulation: Requiem for an 'Aim and Effects' Test" (1998) 32 Int'l Law. 619 at 626.

[237] *United States – Automobiles*, GATT Panel Report, *supra* note 120.

[238] *Japan – Alcoholic Beverages II*, Appellate Body Report, *supra* note 205.

[239] *United States – Malt Beverages*, *supra* note 234 at para. 5.74. There was some historical evidence, however, that the measures authorizing sale of the low-alcohol beer were intended to support the establishment of brewing operations. The measures did not distinguish explicitly between imported and domestic products and their burden did not fall more heavily on the imported beer. See further *ibid.* at paras. 5.25 and 5.26, concerning Mississippi state excise tax on wine.

[240] *United States – Automobiles*, *supra* note 120 at para. 5.10 [emphasis in original].

[241] *Ibid.* [emphasis in original].

create categories of automobiles of inherently foreign or domestic origin."[242] The categories, therefore, did not involve comparisons of "like" products and could be accorded differing treatment, despite the heavier burden of the tax on EC-origin products. The Panel also found that the sport utility vehicles (SUVs) and other light trucks exempted from the gas guzzler tax were not "like" the automobiles subject to the tax because they were not inherently of domestic origin. Since the EC exporters could have exported light trucks to the United States, the conditions of competition had not been altered in favour of the domestic manufacturers. The exemption did not breach Article III:2, even though SUVs were a significant part of total US vehicle sales, and many of the exempted light trucks had the same uses as the passenger vehicles that were taxed.[243] It can be seen that the "aim and effects" test, particularly as it appeared in *United States – Taxes on Automobiles,* gave Article III:1 overriding importance in interpretation and paid less attention to the other paragraphs in Article III. The test also seemed to leave little or no room for the application of Article XX[244] and made it very difficult to prove a breach of Article III, as this would likely have required showing protectionist intent as the sole or at least a major goal of the measure at issue.

In 1996, the Appellate Body decision in *Japan – Alcoholic Beverages II* rejected the "aim and effects" test and returned to the *Border Tax Adjustments* criteria for like products.[245] Paragraph 1 of Article III was seen as articulating only "a general principle that internal measures should not be applied so as to afford protection to domestic production."[246] According to the Appellate Body, this protective application arises automatically from proof of the listed

---

[242] *Ibid. at* para. 5.25.

[243] *Ibid. at* paras. 5.33–5.37. See also paras. 5.11–5.16, concerning a luxury tax on sales of vehicles above a certain price level.

[244] Robert E. Hudec, "GATT/WTO Constraints on National Regulation: Requiem for an 'Aim and Effects' Test" (1998) 32 Int'l Law. 619 at 628–29. See also Won-Mog Choi, *"Like Products" in International Trade Law: Towards a Consistent GATT/WTO Jurisprudence* (Oxford: Oxford University Press, 2003) at 82–83; and discussion in Daniel A. Farber and Robert E. Hudec, "GATT Legal Restraints on Domestic Environmental Regulations," in Jagdish Bhagwati and Robert E. Hudec, eds., *Fair Trade and Harmonization: Prerequisites for Free Trade?* Vol. 2, Legal Analysis (Cambridge, MA: MIT Press, 1996), 59.

[245] See discussion in Debra Steger, "Afterword: The 'Trade and ...' Conundrum – A Commentary" (2002) 96 Am. J. Int'l L.135 at 141–45.

[246] *Japan – Alcoholic Beverages II,* Appellate Body Report, *supra* note 205 at 111.

elements of the first sentence of Article III:2. As the second sentence of Article III:2 contains an explicit reference to the principles of Article III:1, the Appellate Body decided that there must be a separate step in the analysis to examine for protective application. This is not an examination of intent or reasons motivating legislators, but rather a study of the "design, architecture and revealing structure" of the measure itself [247] in order to see whether it alters the competitive conditions in favour of domestic production. In *Japan – Alcoholic Beverages II,* the Appellate Body rejected an approach that seemed to give too much leeway to national decision-making, particularly when it can be expected that much legislation is adopted for mixed motives. It is now possible that the emphasis placed on consumer perception and competitive conditions in the Appellate Body's decision in *Asbestos* has revived the "effects" part of the "aim and effects" test for the determination of like products, which is to be used along with the *Border Tax Adjustments* criteria. In keeping with GATT jurisprudence, any effects test would not be one of actual injury or proof of statistical decline. In *Asbestos,* for example, producers of substitute products apparently did not experience a significant economic benefit after the imposition of the ban.[248] If they had gained business, however, that fact alone should not be proof of a breach of Article III:4. The Appellate Body in *Asbestos* uses the competitive context as part of the determination of like products. The traditional *Border Tax Adjustments* criteria, in fact, serve as shorthand for the same thing, identifying goods most likely to be in competition with each other.

Trade in GATT is about goods, and criteria are needed to attach the rules to relevant goods. To the extent possible, tests that emphasize material facts, such as physical characteristics and end use, create predictability and assist decision-makers in applying the rules in several contexts. Criteria that emphasize material fact, including scientific evidence for the examination of alleged health risks, also provide a shield against decision-making that is too heavily influenced by protectionism. Treating such risks solely as matters of market competition could accord too much weight to the presumed

---

247 *Japan – Alcoholic Beverages II,* Appellate Body Report, *supra* note 205 at 120. Government statements showing protectionist intent were used as an additional factor in *Canada – Periodicals, supra* note 205 at 474–76. See discussion of the use of such statements in *Chile – Alcoholic Beverages,* Panel Report, *supra* note 224 at paras. 7.116–7.120 (compare with Appellate Body Report, generally upholding the Panel's approach, paras. 61–76).

248 *Asbestos,* Panel Report, *supra* note 4 at para. 8.239.

views of the buying public in the importing country. Balance is important in a "world where the commercial interests of foreign states have little or no representation in the political life"[249] of the country of import. In its decision in *Asbestos,* the Appellate Body's attention to the views of consumers risks privatizing what should be a public process and marginalizing the interests of exporters.

Commentators have considered whether the "aim and effects" test should be revived and used in the interpretation of "less favourable" treatment in Article III:4 in order to create a "safe harbour for non-protectionist domestic regulations."[250] As the Appellate Body in *Asbestos* found that Canada failed to prove its argument concerning like products, the Appellate Body did not need to examine the other elements of Article III:4. The "aim and effects" test fits more comfortably with an assessment of "less favourable" treatment in Article III:4 than with the identification of like products. It still suffers, however, from the same objections over the difficulty of determining purpose and the diminished place for Article XX. The debate on the appropriate recognition of non-protectionist regulatory purpose is ongoing.[251] It would be preferable for the debate to focus directly on interpretation of Article XX where possible, but regulatory purpose may continue to be raised in both Article III:4 and the provisions of the TBT Agreement, which are likely to overtake Article III:4 analysis in many applications.[252]

---

[249] Robert E. Hudec, "GATT/WTO Constraints on National Regulation: Requiem for an 'Aim and Effects' Test" (1998) 32 Int'l Law. 619 at 619.

[250] Howse and Tuerk, *supra* note 232 at 305. See discussion in William J. Davey and Joost Pauwelyn, "MFN Unconditionality: A Legal Analysis of the Concept in View of its Evolution in the GATT/WTO Jurisprudence with Particular Reference to the Issue of 'Like Product,'" in Thomas Cottier and Petros C. Mavroidis, eds., *Regulatory Barriers and the Principle of Non-Discrimination in World Trade Law* (Ann Arbor: University of Michigan Press, 2000), 13 at 40.

[251] Frieder Roessler, "Beyond the Ostensible: A Tribute to Professor Robert Hudec's Insights on the Determination of the Likeness of Products under the National Treatment Provisions of the General Agreement on Tariffs and Trade" (2003) 37(4) J. World Trade 771 at 780; Amelia Porges and Joel P. Trachtman, "Robert Hudec and Domestic Regulation: The Resurrection of Aim and Effects" (2003) 37(4) J. World Trade 783.

[252] Gabrielle Marceau and Joel P. Trachtman, "The Technical Barriers to Trade Agreement, the Sanitary and Phytosanitary Measures Agreement, and the General Agreement on Tariffs and Trade: A Map of the World Trade Organization Law of Domestic Regulation of Goods" (2002) 36(5) J. World Trade 811 at 821–22 and 875.

Robert Howse and Elizabeth Tuerk would use a revived "aim and effects" test to deal with the issue of PPMs, including those not reflected in the physical characteristics of the product.[253] They develop this interpretation through the language of the Appellate Body in *Asbestos*, focusing on protectionist results and competitive relationships — thus, the "effects" part of the test. In this view, if the PPM imposed does not result in a heavier burden on imports than on domestic products, then imports as a group have not received less favourable treatment. It is not actually necessary to see this reasoning as an "aim and effects" test or one that looks to regulatory purpose. The crucial step is simply to consider the PPM as "treatment" within Article III:4, even if the treatment relates to PPMs occurring outside the territory of the importing member. There is a strong argument that process-based measures in general must be covered by Article III:4, even those that are not reflected in the physical characteristics of the goods, since, otherwise, Article III:4 would not constrain such measures within the country of import.[254] Proponents of the recognition of PPMs argue that there is nothing setting territorial limits on the use of specific certificates indicating how particular goods were produced.[255] If this is the case, then a measure requiring such certificates could be judged under Article III:4 as to whether it accorded imports with treatment that was not less favourable than the treatment of domestic products.

---

[253] Howse and Tuerk, *supra* note 232 at 297–99.

[254] Robert E. Hudec, "The Product-Process Doctrine in GATT/WTO Jurisprudence," in Marco Bronckers and Reinhard Quick, eds., *New Directions in International Economic Law: Essays in Honour of John H. Jackson* (The Hague/London/Boston: Kluwer Law International, 2000), 187 at 198; Howse and Regan, *supra* note 146 at 254–55.

[255] Robert E. Hudec, "GATT Legal Restraints on the Use of Trade Measures against Foreign Environmental Practices," in Jagdish Bhagwati and Robert E. Hudec, eds., *Fair Trade and Harmonization: Prerequisites for Free Trade?*, Vol. 2, Legal Analysis (Cambridge, MA: MIT Press, 1996) 95 at 119, 151; Howse and Regan, *supra* note 146 at 274–79; Robert Howse, "The Appellate Body Rulings in the *Shrimp/Turtle* Case: A New Legal Baseline for the Trade and Environment Debate" (2002) 27 Colum. J. Envtl. L. 489 at 509–14. Howse argues that specific certificates are to be distinguished from certification based on country of origin, which would raise concerns about extraterritoriality. For analysis in public international law that does not adopt the same distinction, see Lorand Bartels, "Article XX of GATT and the Problem of Extraterritorial Jurisdiction: The Case of Trade Measures for the Protection of Human Rights" (2002) 36(2) J. World Trade 353 at 381–82.

An argument treating PPMs as a "like-products" issue was rejected in the *Tuna/Dolphin* disputes.[256] As these GATT Panel reports were not adopted and as the matter was not examined in *Shrimp/Turtle*, the question is still open. Production processes not affecting physical characteristics are not among the usual criteria for tariff classification and are not included in the *Border Tax Adjustments* list. It is possible that the emphasis on consumers' tastes in the *Asbestos* decision will make consumers' views concerning the social and environmental conditions of production relevant to the determination of like products,[257] but such views could be difficult to isolate and may be an unreliable basis for ongoing regulation. It would be preferable to address the issue directly through Article XX or other exemption clauses, perhaps against a framework of international standards for the assessment of social and environmental conditions.

The treatment of PPMs may be one area in which GATT Article III and its national treatment standards will continue to define the main limits on national regulation. Article III:2 will continue to determine internal taxation questions, but much of the coverage of Article III:4 is likely to be overtaken by the provisions of the SPS Agreement and the TBT Agreement. By its terms, the SPS Agreement does not apply to protect animal or plant life or health outside the territory of the importing member.[258] As discussed under Assertion 4 of this article, many WTO members argue that the TBT Agreement has no application to PPMs that are not reflected in the physical characteristics of products. The resolution of disputes over measures that distinguish according to any production and processing methods not covered by the SPS Agreement or the TBT Agreement would depend on the interpretation of Article III – and Article XX.

---

[256] *Tuna/Dolphin I, supra* note 120; *Tuna/Dolphin II, supra* note 120.

[257] Carlos Lopez-Hurtado, "Social Labelling and WTO Law" (2002) 5(3) J. Int'l Econ. L. 719 at 743.

[258] The definition of "sanitary or phytosanitary measure" in the SPS Agreement, *supra* note 2, Annex A, includes "processes and production methods" as well as "quarantine treatments including relevant requirements associated with the transport of animals or plants, or with the materials necessary for their survival during transport." Some of these measures might be extraterritorial and might not relate to product characteristics: see Marceau and Trachtman, *supra* note 252 at 862.

To summarize, this section presented the argument that the Appellate Body should have emphasized physical characteristics and end use in its decision in *Asbestos* rather than market competition. It is problematic to recognize important areas of public policy such as the protection of health only indirectly through the operation of market forces and the presumed views of consumers.

RELATIONSHIP BETWEEN ARTICLES III AND XI

An alternate approach in *Asbestos* would have been to treat the import ban as an import prohibition or restriction contrary to Article XI:1 of GATT 1994:

XI:1. No prohibitions or restrictions other than duties, taxes or other charges, whether made effective through quotas, import or export licences or other measures, shall be instituted or maintained by any Member on the importation of any product of the territory of any other Member or on the exportation or sale for export of any product destined for the territory of any other Member.

Article XI is the "market access" provision that has been part of GATT since its inception. The article channels protectionism away from quotas and other restrictions and into customs tariffs, which are open and subject to reduction during rounds of trade negotiations. Tariffs impede trade but function in a manner compatible with the operation of pricing, competition, and market forces across borders. Article XI provides that, apart from duties, taxes, or other charges, borders are to be open. A ban on imports of asbestos fibres or asbestos cement, thus, would be a prohibition or restriction that could not be saved by banning competing domestic products. If Article XI applies, national treatment is not a defence, and analysis moves to the issue of justification under Article XX. This section of the article suggests that there is some support, particularly textual support, for the argument that the import bans in *Asbestos* should have been dealt with in this manner under Article XI rather than through the "like products" analysis of Article III.

The *Asbestos* Panel applied Article III instead of Article XI because of the Note Ad Article III in Annex I of the GATT:

Any internal tax or other charge, or any law, regulation or requirement of the kind referred to in paragraph 1 which applies to an imported product and to the like domestic product and is collected or enforced in the case of the imported product at the time or point of importation, is nevertheless to be regarded as an internal tax or other internal charge, or a law, regulation or requirement of the kind referred to in paragraph 1, and is accordingly subject to the provisions of Article III.[259]

Canada had argued that the note covered only measures that applied to imports and domestic products in the same way.[260] In this view, the import ban was distinct and did not apply to domestic products, which were subject to different bans on manufacturing, processing, placing on the market, transfer of title, exportation, and possession for sale.[261] The Panel disagreed, finding that the import ban was merely the "logical corollary" of the domestic bans.[262] The Panel ruled that the requirements of the note had been met, and the measure was to be judged under Article III.

The note itself does not say that other provisions of GATT have no application to a measure covered by the note. The Panel mentioned a further possible argument involving the cumulative application of Articles III and XI, but determined that such a claim was not properly before it in accordance with the terms of reference and that, in any case, Canada had not brought forward a *prima facie* argument for cumulative application.[263] In fact, it is difficult to see how cumulative application could work, since either national treatment is a complete defence or it is no defence at all, and the measure breaches Article XI. The note appears to mean that the Article III analysis has priority, and the measure is not a prohibition or restriction on importation to be judged under Article XI.

The Panel considered Canada's reference to *Canada – Import, Distribution and Sale of Certain Alcoholic Drinks by Provincial Marketing Agencies*, which was decided in 1988.[264] This decision, which dealt with provincial government import and distribution monopolies, found certain measures contrary to Article XI and saw "great force"

---

[259] The parties had agreed that Article III:4 applied to the internal bans on sale, marketing, and transfer (*Asbestos*, Panel Report, *supra* note 4 at para. 8.87).

[260] *Asbestos*, Panel Report, *supra* note 4 at para. 8.89. See the French version of the Note: "Toute taxe ou autre imposition intérieure ou toute loi, réglementation ou prescription visées au paragraphe premier, qui s'applique au produit importé *comme au* produit national similaire" [emphasis added].

[261] See the measure itself, in *Asbestos*, Appellate Body Report, *supra* note 4 at para. 2.

[262] *Asbestos*, Panel Report, *supra* note 4 at para. 8.90.

[263] *Ibid.* at para. 8.100

[264] *Canada – Import, Distribution and Sale of Certain Alcoholic Drinks by Provincial Marketing Agencies*, GATT Panel Report, adopted 22 March 1988, BISD 35S/37 [*Canada – Alcohol 1988*]. See Panel Report, *Asbestos*, *supra* note 4 at para. 8.97.

in the argument that Article III:4 also applied.[265] In the case of a state trading monopoly, it makes sense to expect a blending of "the distinction normally made between restrictions affecting the importation of products and restrictions affecting imported products,"[266] but to say that the two apply cumulatively in other contexts would be to deprive the Note Ad Article III of useful effect. Either national treatment saves the measure or it does not.[267]

On the *Asbestos* Panel's analysis, a ban on imports that reflects a domestic ban on the sale or use of the same goods will be judged under Article III and national treatment is all that is required. This means that a country can decide that it simply wants no part of the goods of a certain type even if those goods are in circulation elsewhere. It can ban alcohol, cigarettes, marijuana, birth control apparatus, abortion medications, pornography, certain books, or goods containing genetically modified organisms[268] and be fully in

[265] *Canada – Alcohol 1988, supra* note 264 at para. 4.26. By the time of the decision in *Canada – Import, Distribution and Sale of Certain Alcoholic Drinks by Provincial Marketing Agencies,* GATT Panel Report, adopted 18 February 1992, BISD 39S/27, Canada had accepted that Article III:4 applied to liquor board practices (para. 5.6), and the Panel found that restrictions on private delivery of beer as well as a system of minimum prices breached Article III:4. The Panel in *Korea – Beef, supra* note 188, accepted that both MFN and national treatment obligations applied in the case of imports by state trading enterprises (para. 753). The question of whether the non-discriminatory treatment stipulated in Article XVII for exports by state trading enterprises was only MFN and not national treatment arose in the Panel decision in *Canada – Wheat, supra* note 193 at paras. 6.44–6.50, but was not resolved by the Panel.

[266] *Asbestos,* Panel Report, *supra* note 4 at para. 8.97, using language from *Canada – Alcohol 1988, supra* note 264 at para. 4.24. The Panel in *Korea – Beef* also noted that this distinction blurs for state trading agencies (para. 766). That Panel found some practices of the state trading agency in question contrary to Article XI — practices relating to tenders and distribution, including calls for tenders that distinguished between grass-fed and grain-fed beef. Other practices were found to be contrary to other GATT Articles, including Article III:4 (see also *Korea – Beef,* Panel Report, *supra* note 188 at para. 705). The Article XI issues were not appealed to the Appellate Body.

[267] The *Asbestos* Panel also referred in para. 8.95 to GATT Panel Report, *United States – Section 337 of the Tariff Act of 1930,* adopted 7 November 1989, BISD 36S/345, which applied Article III:4 and the Note Ad Article III to find that certain border measures enforcing domestic patent law were in breach of US obligations. None of the submissions in that dispute argued that Article XI should have applied instead, presumably due to the general understanding of the Note Ad Article III.

[268] But other WTO agreements may apply, especially the SPS Agreement. See *European Communities – Measures Affecting the Approval and Marketing of Biotech*

compliance with GATT so long as the same products are banned in the domestic market. There is, perhaps, a lingering counter-argument that there must have been some domestic production initially to be banned,[269] but, apart from this consideration, it appears that national treatment is a complete answer. Bans could be imposed for all of the complex reasons of health, culture, morality, and religion implied in the above list, as well as for any other reason at all, and pose no GATT problems so long as national treatment applies. This is the operation of the non-discrimination norm — if there is no discrimination, then there is no breach and no need to consider the exemptions in Article XX.

This debate has been addressed under GATT, in the *Tuna/Dolphin* and *Shrimp/Turtle* disputes, which both concerned a society wanting no part of certain goods because of the way in which they were produced. The question of whether Article III or Article XI applied to such a case was considered in *Tuna/Dolphin,* a dispute dealing with an import ban on tuna caught in a manner judged to be too harmful to dolphins.[270] The United States argued that the

---

Products, Requests for the Establishment of a Panel by the United States (Doc. WT/DS291/23), by Canada (Doc. WT/DS292/17) and by Argentina (Doc. WT/DS293/17), 8 August 2003.

[269] The *Asbestos* Panel noted that the decree was the reason why production in France had ceased (para. 8.91). In a somewhat different context, the Panel in *Canada – Wheat, supra* note 193, noted that an origin-based distinction between domestic and imported products can be found contrary to Article III:4 even without identification and comparison of specific domestic goods. Citing *Argentina – Measures Affecting the Export of Bovine Hides and Import of Finished Leather,* Panel Report, Doc. WT/DS155/R and Corr.1, adopted 16 February 2001, paras. 11.168–11.170 and *United States – Tax Treatment for "Foreign Sales Corporations," Recourse to Article 21.5 of the DSU by the European Communities,* Panel Report, Doc. WT/DS108/RW, as modified by the Appellate Body Report, Doc. WT/DS108/AB/RW, adopted 29 January 2002, paras. 8.132–8.134, the *Canada – Wheat* Panel stated that it was sufficient that there could or would be domestic and imported products that were like (para. 6.164). The issue concerning the application of Article III:4 was not appealed to the Appellate Body. If national treatment is to be a complete answer or defence for measures such as the import ban in *Asbestos,* then the same idea of a notional domestic market should probably be applied. It would be possible to make the acceptability of an import ban depend on the actual level or volume of domestic production halted when the measure was adopted, but such a standard would be difficult to apply. If national treatment is a complete answer, then the fact of the internal ban should probably be enough, even if both imports and domestic production were future contingencies when the measure was adopted.

[270] *Tuna/Dolphin I,* GATT Panel Report, *supra* note 120. See further *Tuna/Dolphin II,* GATT Panel Report, *supra* note 120.

ban was the enforcement at the border of domestic regulations imposed on the US fishing fleet and, thus, was protected by the Note Ad Article III. The Panel rejected this view of the domestic fishing restrictions, stating that they did not actually apply to domestic tuna and that the "Note covers only measures applied to imported products that are of the same nature as those applied to domestic products."[271] As the internal sale of tuna was not regulated, the Panel concluded that the note did not save the measure and the US import ban breached Article XI. The *Shrimp/Turtle* dispute also involved the process of production of the goods. The United States conceded a breach of Article XI[272] and did not argue Article III as a defence. The facts of *Asbestos* differ significantly from these two previous disputes, since the domestic sale and use of asbestos were prohibited. *Asbestos* raises very directly the question of whether national treatment is a complete defence for import bans that support such domestic measures.

The alternate approach to an Article III analysis is to view the import ban as a prohibition or restriction contrary to Article XI and then consider whether an exemption is available under Article XX. The alternate view suggests that Article III may not protect all such bans even if the corresponding domestic regulations do apply to goods. The Appellate Body in *Asbestos* hints at a distinction between regulations and bans in its analysis of the application of the TBT Agreement. The Appellate Body noted that while the agreement might not apply to a total ban on asbestos fibres (para. 71), it would apply to the ban on asbestos cement, since this was a negative technical regulation about what goods must *not* contain and thus met the definition of a "technical regulation" in the agreement (para. 75). The Appellate Body reversed the Panel's interpretation, which had found that the TBT Agreement did not cover the import bans but only the limited exceptions to these bans. In both the Appellate Body and Panel decisions, there was a hesitation about treating a complete ban on a product as a regulation. In a different context, the drafters of the GATT may have similarly assumed that import prohibitions were in a separate category and were not to be considered regulations.

---

271 *Tuna/Dolphin I*, GATT Panel Report, *supra* note 120 at para. 5.11. In para. 5.15, the Panel noted that cargoes could be seized for breach of the domestic fishing restrictions. In case this could be considered as regulating domestic sale, the Panel made an alternate finding that rejected the use of the production method as a factor for the determination of like products.

272 *Shrimp/Turtle 1998*, Panel Report, *supra* note 5 at para. 3.143.

Is it tenable to say that a border measure that sets a number for permissible imports, including "0," is primarily a quantitative measure and should be judged under Article XI rather than Article III? Article XI, by its terms, applies to "prohibitions or restrictions"[273] and would thus seem to cover import bans. The issue of the distinction between Article III and Article XI arose in *Lobsters from Canada*, a dispute between Canada and the United States under Chapter 18 of the 1989 Canada-United States Free Trade Agreement.[274] The United States established a minimum size requirement for live lobsters in interstate and foreign commerce. The effect was that smaller lobster legally caught in Canada could no longer be imported. Canada argued that this was an import restriction contrary to Article XI, while the United States argued that Article III applied instead. The Panel majority agreed that Article III applied rather than Article XI, which the majority stated was for measures that dealt exclusively with imports (para. 7.12.4). The Panel minority, however, was of the view that a measure might be potentially covered by both articles (para. 8.1.4). According to the minority, treating Article XI as something that applies to measures dealing solely with imports would undermine the effect of Article XI and was difficult to reconcile with certain provisions, notably Article XI(2)(c)(i), which presumes the concurrent existence of domestic restrictions:

XI:2. The provisions of paragraph 1 of this Article shall not extend to the following:

---

273 GATT decisions have held that Article XI distinguishes between complete bans ("prohibitions") and partial bans or quotas ("restrictions"): *United States – Prohibition of Imports of Tuna and Tuna Products from Canada*, GATT Panel Report, adopted 22 February 1982, BISD 29S/91 at para. 4.6; *Japan – Agricultural Products I*, GATT Panel Report, *supra* note 196 at para. 5.1.3.1; *European Economic Community – Restrictions on Imports of Dessert Apples, Complaint by Chile*, GATT Panel Report, adopted 22 June 1989, BISD 36S/93 at para. 12.5; *Canada – Import Restrictions on Ice Cream and Yoghurt*, GATT Panel Report, adopted 5 December 1989, BISD 36S/68 at paras. 62–63.

274 *Lobsters from Canada*, Final Report of the Panel, 25 May 1990, 3 T.C.T. 8182 [*Lobsters from Canada*]. See Canada's note to the Final Report: "With respect to the Final Report of the Panel on Lobsters from Canada, the Government of Canada wishes to record its view that the opinion of the minority represents the correct interpretation of the relevant provisions of the FTA and GATT. The government of Canada maintains the position set out in its various submissions in this case." See further Ted L. McDorman "Dissecting the Free Trade Agreement Lobster Panel Decision" (1991) 18 Can. Bus. L.J. 445.

... (c) Import restrictions on any agricultural or fisheries product, imported in any form, necessary to the enforcement of governmental measures which operate:

> (i) to restrict the quantities of the like domestic product permitted to be marketed or produced, or, if there is not substantial domestic production of the like product, of a domestic product for which the imported product can be directly substituted.[275]

The minority would have applied Article XI to a complete prohibition on entry of the product into domestic commerce and Article III to other restrictions.[276] The debate between market access and national treatment norms was directly engaged. The United States argued that Canada's market-access approach "was implicitly asking the Panel to bar governments from imposing equal restrictions on domestic and foreign products whenever doing so would have the effect of restricting imports" (para. 4.2.2.3). Canada argued that the US reliance on national treatment would "render Articles XI and XX practically meaningless" (para. 4.1.1.3).

In my view, the majority's opinion is generally to be preferred, as the measure was not purely a quantitative restriction, but its particular impact was unusual in the facts. As the minority explained, prior to the adoption of the measure, undersized lobsters from Canada were admissible into the United States, even though they would have been too small to be fished in US federal waters. At that time, enforcement involved the production of bills of lading or other documents of origin on challenge to demonstrate that the lobster had been legally caught (paras. 9.5.2 and 9.6.1). Due to limits in the Panel's mandate, the majority did not complete the analysis and determine whether the revised measure actually complied with the national treatment requirement of Article III, which might have been debated.

The majority opinion is not convincing, however, in its view that Article XI is for measures dealing exclusively with imports. As the minority opinion points out, if that interpretation were correct, there would be no need for Article XI(2)(c)(i) concerning agricultural and fisheries products, since any measure that also restricted

---

[275] *Ibid.* at para. 8.3.10.

[276] The minority took a wide view of what constituted a prohibition and found that the US measure was a "complete prohibition on the sale, use or transportation of ... sub-sized lobsters" (para.8.3.3) that prevented them from entering the market, rather than merely imposing conditions on sale within the market, which would have been governed by Article III.

domestic production would be judged under the national treatment standard of Article III:4 instead. The distinction cannot be that Article XI is solely for measures that have no link at all to restrictions on domestic products.

So then what was intended in GATT? To what do the market access provisions of Article XI apply? Most trade lawyers have assumed that Article XI would prohibit the classic sort of quotas from the 1930s, which stipulate that only a given quantity of a named product may be imported. For matters that are solely border measures without accompanying prohibitions or restrictions on domestic products, there is no difficulty in saying that Article XI applies.[277] For hybrid measures, however, involving both a border effect and some similar application to domestic products, the argument must be that quantitative measures are in a distinct category. Otherwise, it is difficult to see the point of Article XI(2)(c)(i) involving a situation with concurrent domestic restrictions.

There is a textual argument based on Article III that supports this way of seeing things. The argument is that a quantitative measure is not a "law, regulation or requirement of the kind referred to in paragraph [III:]1" within the terms of the Note Ad Article III, quoted earlier in this section. In this view, Article III:1 distinguishes between "laws, regulations and requirements affecting the internal sale, offering for sale, purchase, transportation, distribution or use of products" and the internal quantitative restrictions mentioned next in the same sentence. If the "laws, regulations and requirements" were intended to include all quantitative restrictions, there would be no need for paragraph 1 to continue on and list "internal quantitative regulations requiring the mixture, processing or use of products in specified amounts or proportions." These internal quantitative restrictions are mentioned specifically as a separate category, one that is not included in the phrase "laws, regulations and requirements." Article III, in fact, is drafted on the assumption that internal quantitative restrictions are distinct measures to be dealt with under separate provisions, paragraphs 5 to 7, and not under paragraph 4, which applies to the "laws, regulations and requirements." For internal quantitative restrictions, Article III does not impose a national treatment obligation. Rather, such quantitative restrictions must not require that an amount or proportion be

---

[277] See, for example, the trade balancing requirement found in breach of Article XI by the Panel in *India – Measures Affecting the Automotive Sector,* Doc. WT/DS146/R, Doc. WT/DS175/R, adopted 5 April 2002 (appeal by India to the Appellate Body withdrawn).

supplied from domestic sources (Article III:5) and must not be applied so as to afford protection to domestic production (Article III:1 and Article III:5). The obligation imposed by paragraph 5, in fact, could be more onerous than national treatment. A measure stipulating, for example, that domestic and imported cookies must all contain at least 10 per cent domestically produced peanuts might meet the national treatment obligation,[278] but it would not pass paragraph 5. In this interpretation, Article III treats internal quantitative restrictions as a separate category with obligations distinct from those applied to "internal taxes or other internal charges" (para. 2) and to "laws, regulations and requirements affecting ... internal sale, offering for sale"(para. 4). On this view, the Note Ad Article III refers only to the measures covered by paragraphs 2 and 4 of Article III, which would not include quantitative restrictions. Internal quantitative restrictions are governed by paragraphs 5 to 7 of Article III, and external quantitative restrictions, including bans, are governed by Article XI.[279]

If this interpretation were applied to the facts in *Asbestos*, the argument would be that the measure in question was essentially a ban, despite certain temporary exemptions covering uses for which asbestos substitutes were not available. Since the Note Ad Article III does not apply in the case of quantitative restrictions, the measure should have been judged as a prohibition on imports within the terms of Article XI and found in breach. Analysis would then have proceeded to the health justification under Article XX.

This alternate interpretation of Article III is not completely free from problems. Internal quantitative restrictions that do not involve specified amounts or proportions from domestic production and are not described in the first sentence of Article III:5 would be covered by the second sentence and, thus, would be subject to the obligation of Article III:1 that they not afford protection to domestic production. For example, a measure that permitted only 100,000

---

[278] For cookies at least, although not for peanuts.

[279] Note the views of Professor McGovern, which appear consistent with this analysis in some respects: "[W]hile Article III ... permits internal quantitative measures provided both imported and domestic products are included within their scope, Article XI does not allow such action against domestic goods to justify restrictions imposed at the point of importation (save to a limited extent in respect of agricultural goods)." This interpretation thus allows scope for the application of Article XI at the border in the case of quantitative measures. (Edmond McGovern, *International Trade Regulation* (Exeter: Globefield Press, 1995, looseleaf) at para. 8.211).

chairs to be sold on the domestic market, imported or domestic, would have to meet the obligation that it not afford protection to domestic production rather than the national treatment obligation of Article III:4, although the difference may not matter in practice. The current debate over the choice between Article III and Article XI could re-surface over an internal ban that was not accompanied by an import ban. If a country decided that it simply wanted nothing to do with a particular product and banned all internal sale, use, and production without banning imports, would the obligation be simply to avoid affording protection to domestic production (Article III:5, second sentence and Article III:1)? Or would this be equivalent to a prohibition on imports and a breach of Article XI? Such a situation would pose again, in effect, the initial question of whether national treatment should be a complete defence.

This section outlined the alternate interpretation that the import bans in *Asbestos* should have been treated as quantitative measures contrary to Article XI, the "market opening" provision that has been part of GATT since its beginnings. Application of an interpretation favouring Article XI will likely lead to a finding of breach and thus the question of possible exemptions in Article XX. This interpretation may be the preferable approach for regulations that amount to prohibitions or quantitative restrictions, although the distinction between domestic regulations and import restrictions is a fine one. If the domestic requirement is one that the imported product can meet with some adjustments, such as a labelling or packaging requirement, then it is most likely a regulation to be judged pursuant to Article III:4, despite the fact that non-conforming imports will be denied entry. A requirement relating to the method of production, on the other hand, constitutes, in effect, an import ban on non-conforming goods and may be best judged under Article XI. Measures such as the ban on under-sized lobster in *Lobsters from Canada* are difficult to classify as primarily either a domestic regulation or an import prohibition.

For practical purposes, many of the disputes that raise the choice between Article III and Article XI will also involve issues under the SPS Agreement or the TBT Agreement. The provisions of these two agreements may make the GATT analysis redundant in many cases. The prospect of determinations of breach of one of these two agreements, in addition to the analysis under GATT Article XI, underlines the importance of exemption clauses such as Article XX. Article XI and the market-opening provisions of the SPS

Agreement and the TBT Agreement, which are discussed in the next part of this article, impose obligations for which national treatment is not a complete defence.

ASSERTION 4: THE SPS AGREEMENT AND THE TBT AGREEMENT ADOPT A MARKET-OPENING APPROACH THAT WILL OVERTAKE TRADITIONAL GATT NON-DISCRIMINATION NORMS IN MANY APPLICATIONS. EXEMPTIONS AND AREAS OF OVERLAP SHOULD BE INTERPRETED IN HARMONY WITH GATT TO THE EXTENT POSSIBLE

This part examines aspects of the SPS Agreement and the TBT Agreement, both of which were included among the Uruguay Round of multilateral agreements on trade in goods in Annex 1A to the Marrakesh Agreement Establishing the World Trade Organization (WTO Agreement).[280] The analysis presents the last of the four assertions listed in the introduction — that while these two agreements move past traditional GATT non-discrimination norms, they should be coordinated with the GATT general exceptions to the extent possible. The sections below address first the SPS Agreement and then the TBT Agreement. A final section examines issues relating to international standards and harmonization.

The SPS and TBT Agreements reflect a new approach to the relationship between international trade rules and domestic regulation. Instead of relying solely on MFN and national treatment, they adopt market-access obligations that apply in the absence of competing domestic goods and even in the absence of a relevant harmonized international standard. This is the market-opening theme of GATT Article XI — the prohibition on quantitative restrictions — which has been expanded beyond border issues to cover internal domestic regulation. In this context, the experience under GATT Article XX should be used to develop a consistent approach to exemptions and coordinated interpretation whenever possible, since the agreements are part of the overall WTO Agreement. It is likely that analysis relating to the SPS and TBT provisions will replace many of the debates over provisions of GATT, particularly GATT Article III. If there were difficulties in the past of coordination between Article III:2 and Article III:4, the greater concern now should be coordination between GATT and the provisions of these two new agreements.

In *Asbestos*, the Appellate Body had no difficulty in assuming that the obligations of GATT 1994 and the TBT Agreement were

[280] WTO Agreement, *supra* note 2.

cumulative. Although the Appellate Body did not complete its analysis under the TBT Agreement, it was clear that both this agreement and GATT Article III:4 could apply to the facts at issue.[281] The assumption of cumulative operation has even more force between the SPS Agreement and GATT 1994 since measures that conform to the SPS Agreement are presumed to be in accordance with GATT Article XX(b).[282] Should GATT conflict with an obligation in either the SPS Agreement or the TBT Agreement, then the General Interpretative Note to the multilateral agreements on trade in goods[283] stipulates that GATT gives way to the other agreement and the SPS or TBT provision would prevail.[284]

SPS AGREEMENT — MARKET ACCESS

The SPS Agreement covers measures to protect human, animal, or plant health from imported products bringing diseases, pests, additives, contaminants, or toxins into the territory.[285] The measures are to be based on international standards (Article 3.1).[286] Members can have higher levels of protection if these are based on scientific justification or established as a result of a risk assessment pursuant to Article 5 (Article 3.3).[287] The SPS Agreement elabo-

---

[281] Gabrielle Marceau, "L'affaire '*CE – Amiante*' et la nouvelle jurisprudence de l'Organe d'appel de l'OMC concernant les risques à la santé" (2000) 38 Can. Y.B. Int'l L. 213 at 230–31.

[282] SPS Agreement, *supra* note 2 at Article 2.4.

[283] WTO Agreement, *supra* note 2, Annex 1A.

[284] Marceau and Trachtman, *supra* note 252 at 867 ff.

[285] SPS Agreement, *supra* note 2, Annex A, Definitions.

[286] Note the interpretation of this provision by the Appellate Body in *Beef Hormones, supra* note 176. The Appellate Body determined that harmonization was a goal of the SPS Agreement, but that members were not required to conform to the international standards immediately (*Beef Hormones, supra* note 176 at para. 165; see SPS Agreement, *supra* note 2, Preamble, Article 12.4). The Appellate Body elaborated on this interpretation concerning a similar obligation in the TBT Agreement in *EC – Trade Description of Sardines*, Appellate Body Report, Doc. WT/DS231/AB/R, adopted 23 October 2002 [*Sardines*]. In that decision, the obligation to use international standards "as a basis" for domestic technical regulations (TBT Agreement, *supra* note 2 at Article 2.4) was held to mean that, while conformity was not required, the international standard still must be a "principal constituent," "fundamental principle," "main constituent" and "determining principle" of the domestic measure (*Sardines*, Appellate Body Report, para. 245).

[287] See also Article 2.2. In *Beef Hormones*, the Appellate Body noted the footnote to Article 3.3, which ties "scientific justification" to the evaluation of scientific

rates on GATT Article XX(b)[288] and contains obligations drawn from those provisions as interpreted through GATT decisions. Measures are to be applied only to the extent necessary to protect life or health (Article 2.2). Members must avoid arbitrary or unjustifiable discrimination and disguised restrictions on trade (Article 2.3, Article 5.5).[289] Unfortunately, the SPS Agreement also contains an explicit least-trade-restrictive test. SPS measures must not be more trade-restrictive than is required to achieve the chosen level of protection (Article 5.6). As well, members are to recognize the SPS measures of other members if those measures meet the importing member's chosen level of sanitary and phytosanitary protection (Article 4.1).

How would the peanut-containing cookies fare under SPS tests? First, SPS review would apply whether the measures in question were domestic restrictions governed by GATT Article III or border restrictions governed by GATT Article XI. This classification would not be required and it would not be necessary to find competing domestically produced goods to bring the analysis into operation. The SPS Agreement is about market access, not about competition with domestic products or preservation of a negotiated tariff binding. An initial question would be whether the peanuts were "additives, contaminants, toxins or disease-causing organisms in food" within the definition of a sanitary or phytosanitary measure. If they meet this definition, then the necessity test would apply, as would the discrimination and disguised restriction norms and the least-trade-restrictive test. It has been argued earlier that the least-trade-restrictive test was a misreading of the "necessity" requirement in GATT Article XX and that it tends to marginalize other important areas of public policy, narrowing the scope of intended exceptions in GATT Article XX. Even if jurisprudence under GATT 1994 were to take a different approach, the current provisions of the SPS

---

evidence in accordance with the rest of the agreement. The Appellate Body found a general obligation to conduct risk assessments in accordance with Article 5.1 (*Beef Hormones, supra* note 176 at paras. 172–76). See further *Australia – Salmon,* Appellate Body Report, *supra* note 178; *Japan – Measures Affecting Agricultural Products,* Appellate Body Report, Doc. WT/DS76/AB/R, adopted 19 March 1999 [*Japan – Agricultural Products II*]; *Japan – Measures Affecting the Importation of Apples,* Appellate Body Report, Doc. WT/DS245/AB/R, adopted 10 December 2003 [*Japan – Apples*]; Robert Howse, "Democracy, Science, and Free Trade: Risk Regulation on Trial at the World Trade Organization" (2000) 98 Mich. L. Rev. 2329.

[288] SPS Agreement, *supra* note 2, Preamble

Agreement would still require a least-trade-restrictive test and trade interests would have enhanced priority.[290]

Overall, the SPS Agreement would require more detail in the scientific evidence than the proof of risk found sufficient to meet the Article XX(b) exemption in *Asbestos*.[291] International standards could have a significant effect if they exist, since international standards are presumed to be necessary to protect life or health and presumed to be in conformity with the SPS Agreement and GATT 1994 (Article 3.2).

The SPS Agreement deals specifically with the relationship between it and GATT 1994. Article 2.4 provides that measures that conform to the SPS Agreement are presumed to be in accordance

[289] Note that Article 5.5 differs from the introductory words of GATT Article XX. Article 5.5 requires that a member "avoid arbitrary or unjustifiable distinctions in the levels [of sanitary or phytosanitary protection] it considers to be appropriate in different situations, if such distinctions result in discrimination or a disguised restriction on international trade." In *Beef Hormones, supra* note 176, the Appellate Body reversed a Panel finding of breach of this provision. In *Australia – Salmon, supra* note 178, a Panel finding of inconsistency with Article 5.5 was upheld by the Appellate Body.

[290] The least-trade-restrictive test is explained as follows in a footnote to Article 5.6: "[A] measure is not more trade-restrictive than required unless there is another measure, reasonably available taking into account technical and economic feasibility, that achieves the appropriate level of sanitary or phytosanitary protection and is significantly less restrictive to trade." The requirement that the alternate measure be "significantly" less trade-restrictive and the mention of economic feasibility may allow domestic governments extra leeway. On the other hand, Article 5.4 reinforces the trade priority and could restrict governments in their choice of levels of protection: "Members should, when determining the appropriate level of sanitary or phytosanitary protection, take into account the objective of minimizing negative trade effects." In *Australia – Salmon, supra* note 178 and *Japan – Agricultural Products II, supra* note 287, the Appellate Body reversed Panel findings of inconsistency with Article 5.6.

[291] In *Asbestos,* the Appellate Body upheld the Panel's finding of a health risk that reflected the views of the four scientific experts consulted by the Panel as well as the views of certain international organizations including the World Health Organization (*Asbestos,* Appellate Body Report, *supra* note 4 at para. 162). The standard used by the Panel was whether a public health official could reasonably conclude that there was evidence of a risk (*Asbestos,* Panel Report, *supra* note 4 at para. 8.193, see paras. 8.184–8.195) and whether the measure in question was designed and apt to meet that risk (Appellate Body Report, para. 168). This is not as detailed as a risk assessment under Article 5 of the SPS Agreement: see Appellate Body Reports in *Beef Hormones, supra* note 176, *Australia – Salmon, supra* note 178, *Japan – Agricultural Products II, supra* note 287, *Japan – Apples, supra* note 287.

with the provisions of Article XX(b). Article 2.4 does not, of course, say that the SPS Agreement represents the only way of meeting Article XX(b) and it does not explain how the presumption of conformity might be rebutted. Questions of how the two fit together will undoubtedly have to be sorted out in future applications. It is clear, however, that both can apply to the same set of facts. The SPS Agreement could be relevant for any number of GATT breaches, including breaches of Article III or Article XI.[292]

TBT AGREEMENT — NATIONAL TREATMENT AND MARKET ACCESS

The TBT Agreement is not linked to Article XX exemption issues[293] but uses other approaches to encourage harmonization of standards. The agreement adopts the obligations of national treatment and MFN treatment. Technical regulations must grant imported products treatment that is no less favourable than the treatment of like products of national origin and like products from any other member (Article 2.1). A technical regulation contains "product characteristics or their related processes and production methods ... with which compliance is mandatory." It may also deal with "terminology, symbols, packaging, marking or labelling requirements as they apply to a product, process or production method" (Annex 1).

The agreement also adopts a market access approach and contains provisions very similar to those of the SPS Agreement. Technical regulations must not be unnecessary obstacles to trade and must not be more trade-restrictive than necessary to fulfil a legitimate objective (Article 2.2 and Article 2.3).[294] Examples given of such legitimate objectives are national security, prevention of

---

292 In *Japan – Apples,* after finding breaches of various SPS Agreement provisions, the Panel decided not to proceed with analysis of claims under GATT Article XI. This aspect of the Panel decision was not appealed (*Japan – Apples,* Appellate Body Report, *supra* note 287 at para. 4).

293 Some of the introductory wording of Article XX is repeated in the preamble of the TBT Agreement, *supra* note 3, where the environment is specifically mentioned.

294 The opening sentence of Article 2.2 provides that "Members shall ensure that technical regulations are not prepared, adopted or applied with a view to or with the effect of creating unnecessary obstacles to international trade." This wording ("with a view to or with the effect of") comes very close to adopting for this area the "aim and effect" test that was rejected for GATT Article III in *Japan – Alcoholic Beverages II,* Appellate Body Report, *supra* note 205 at 119. Despite the explicit incorporation of the least-trade-restrictive test in the second sentence of Article 2.2, members may wish to argue that the first sentence gives them more leeway and makes their non-protective intent relevant. The opening

deceptive practices, protection of health, and protection of the environment (Article 2.2). International standards are to be used as a basis where relevant (Article 2.4).[295] It is presumed that a technical regulation conforming to an international standard is not an unnecessary obstacle to trade (Article 2.5).[296]

In *Asbestos*, both national treatment and market-access approaches were at issue. Canada alleged that the ban on asbestos breached Article 2.1 of the TBT Agreement by failing to provide national treatment,[297] breached Article 2.2 by creating an unnecessary obstacle to trade,[298] and breached Article 2.4 by failing to use international standards from the ILO.[299] TBT issues were not fully explored

---

sentence is perhaps more explicit in this regard in the French version: "Les Membres feront en sorte que l'élaboration, l'adoption ou l'application des règlements techniques *n'aient ni pour objet ni pour effet* de créer des obstacles non nécessaires au commerce international" (emphasis added). The version in Spanish is as follows: "Los Miembros se asegurarán de que no se elaboren, adopten o apliquen reglamentos técnicos que *tengan por objeto o efecto* crear obstáculos innecesarios al comercio internacional" [emphasis added]. See Robert E. Hudec, "GATT/WTO Constraints on National Regulation: Requiem for an 'Aim and Effects' Test" (1998) 32 Int'l Law. 619; Amelia Porges and Joel P. Trachtman, "Robert Hudec and Domestic Regulation: The Resurrection of Aim and Effects" (2003) 37(4) J. World Trade 783; Maureen Irish, "NAFTA Chapter 9 and the WTO Agreement on Technical Barriers to Trade," in Kevin C. Kennedy, ed., *The First Decade of NAFTA: The Future of Free Trade in North America* (Ardsley, NY: Transnational Publishers, 2004) 57; discussion earlier in the article under Assertion 3.

[295] This provision presents some incongruity, since Annex I to the TBT Agreement defines a "standard," in part, as a "[d]ocument approved by a recognized body, that provides, for common and repeated use, rules, guidelines or characteristics for products or related processes and production methods, *with which compliance is not mandatory*" [emphasis added]. This definition was applied to Article 2.4 in *Sardines*, Appellate Body Report, *supra* note 286 at paras. 217–27.

[296] The TBT Agreement, *supra* note 3, does not require recognition of other members' domestic measures, as is the case in the SPS Agreement. Concerning technical regulations, the TBT Agreement only requires that members give "positive consideration" to recognition if those regulations "adequately fulfil the objectives" of the importing member's own regulations (Article 2.7). Other members' conformity assessment procedures are to be recognized "whenever possible" if those procedures "offer an assurance of conformity with applicable technical regulations or standards equivalent to" the importing member's own procedures (Article 6.1).

[297] *Asbestos*, Panel Report, *supra* note 4 at paras. 3.266–3.269

[298] *Ibid.* at paras. 3.273, 3.275, 3.277, 3.279–3.289, 3.298–3.312, and 3.322–3.352

[299] *Ibid.* at paras. 3.358–3.361, 3.369–3.372, and 3.377–3.386. Canada further argued that the measure breached Article 2.8 by failing to base product

due to differing interpretations by the Panel and the Appellate Body of the definition of "technical regulation" in Annex 1. The definition states that a technical regulation "lays down product characteristics or their related processes and production methods." Since the ban on asbestos fibres did not actually set out any "characteristics" for the fibres to meet, the Appellate Body reasoned that a simple ban on a product in its natural state "might not constitute" a technical regulation.[300] The ban on products containing asbestos, however, did set out a characteristic — the requirement that they be asbestos-free — which qualified, in the Appellate Body's view, as a negative technical regulation.[301] The Appellate Body did not continue with an analysis of the TBT claims, since the Panel had ruled that only the exceptions to the ban qualified as technical regulations and the findings of fact were therefore incomplete.

If the TBT claims had gone ahead, and assuming the EC succeeded in arguing against the ILO standards,[302] then analysis would have proceeded, at least initially, somewhat as under GATT Article III. Concerning national treatment and like products, the same questions would arise under the TBT Agreement as in the *Asbestos* decision. The least-trade-restrictive test is, unfortunately, confirmed and given prominence in TBT Article 2.2.[303] A major difference between the TBT Agreement and GATT Article XX is that the TBT Agreement does not make provision for a breach of national or MFN treatment (Article 2.1), which is nevertheless the least-trade-restrictive means of fulfilling one of the legitimate objectives. In

---

standards on performance rather than descriptive characteristics: paras. 3.388–3.389 and 3.392–3.393.

[300] *Asbestos,* Appellate Body Report, *supra* note 4 at para. 71.

[301] *Ibid.* at para. 76.

[302] The EC argued that the ILO standards were not covered by the definition of a "standard" in the TBT Agreement and were "ineffective or inappropriate" to meet France's legitimate objectives within the terms of Article 2.4. The EC also argued that, in any case, the standards had been used as a basis for the French decree, as this did not require complete conformity with the international standards (*Asbestos,* Panel Report, *supra* note 4 at paras. 3.362–3.368, 3.373–3.376, and 3.387). The United States supported the argument by the EC that these were not relevant international standards for the purpose of Article 2.4 (*Asbestos,* Appellate Body Report, *supra* note 4 at paras. 46–48).

[303] Scientific evidence may be used in application of the test. Article 2.2 of the TBT Agreement, *supra* note 3, states, in part, that "[i]n assessing ... risks, relevant elements of consideration are, *inter alia:* available scientific and technical information, related processing technology or intended end-uses of products."

these circumstances, Article 2.2 might modify and provide an exemption from the obligation of national treatment in Article 2.1,
but the agreement does not say that. It is just as likely that Article
2.2 is a separate obligation that applies in addition to Article 2.1
and is in no way an exemption. It would be incongruous to decide
that something exempted under GATT Article XX(b) as a necessary and least-trade-restrictive measure to protect health was nevertheless a breach of TBT Article 2.1 because Article 2.2 does not
function as an exemption, but this is the most probable conclusion.[304] It is also not clear how the introductory language from
Article XX in the preamble concerning arbitrary or unjustifiable
discrimination and disguised restrictions on trade would affect the
analysis, if at all. Unless the TBT Agreement brings in an international standard or unless the issue relates to the performance of
goods rather than to their description (Article 2.8), the TBT Agreement could produce more confusion than clarity for these disputes. It does not replace GATT analysis, which will also apply on
the same facts.

The TBT Agreement does not contain language dealing with the
relationship between it and GATT 1994. The legitimate objectives
listed in Article 2.2 reflect many of the listed paragraphs of GATT
Article XX. In principle, it seems likely that the same facts could give
rise to arguments under both agreements. Although the provisions
of the two agreements differ, it would be helpful to coordinate interpretation to the extent possible, particularly for the exemptions.

The *EC – Trade Description of Sardines* (*Sardines*) decision proceeded
under the market-access provisions of the TBT Agreement rather
than GATT and involved interpretation of the legitimate objectives.
The complaint was brought against the EC by Peru concerning the
trade description for preserved sardines. The EC regulation at issue reserved the term "sardines" exclusively for a species found
mainly in the waters around Europe and did not make it available
for a different species of sardines found in the Pacific Ocean off
the coasts of Peru and Chile. Peru argued that the EC had breached

---

[304] Even if Article 2.2 does function as an exemption to Article 2.1, a disjunction
could arise in cases governed by GATT Article XX(g) which covers conservation and environmental measures. The phrase "relating to ... conservation" in
GATT Article XX(g) will not have the same interpretation as the necessity and
least-trade-restrictive tests of TBT Article 2.2. Thus, a measure acceptable under
GATT Article XX(g) could nevertheless breach the TBT Agreement, even if
Article 2.2 is construed as a general exemption clause.

TBT Articles 2.4, 2.2, and 2.1 as well as GATT Article III:4. The Appellate Body affirmed Panel findings that the EC regulation was a technical regulation and that the EC had breached Article 2.4 since the regulation contradicted the relevant international standard. The other claims by Peru were not examined by the Appellate Body.

The EC tried unsuccessfully to argue that the international standard was an "ineffective or inappropriate" means for fulfilling the legitimate objectives pursued, as set out in Article 2.4. The legitimate objectives were not the ones listed in Article 2.2, but three additional objectives identified by the EC and accepted by Peru: market transparency, consumer protection, and fair competition.[305] These additional objectives do not directly match either the ones mentioned in Article 2.2 or the list of exemptions in GATT Article XX. Article 2.4 requires the use of international standards — an obligation that is not part of GATT. Having a more extensive list of potential defences available for a breach of Article 2.4 will not necessarily cause overlap problems and conflicts with GATT. A wider list of potential defences could produce such results, however, if they are used for breaches of Article 2.2, which contains the necessity and least-trade-restrictive obligations since these have some counterparts in GATT. This is not to say that any list of exemptions should be restricted solely to those matters mentioned in GATT Article XX. Perhaps ongoing discussions will lead to revisions of the GATT exemptions. Given the potential for overlap, coordinated interpretation should be the goal whenever possible.

Coordinated interpretation is also the best approach for the least-trade-restrictive test, which is included in both the TBT Agreement and the SPS Agreement. In both agreements, the test should be interpreted in light of important common interests, following the Appellate Body's interpretation of GATT Article XX(b) in *Asbestos.* Measures that promote vital or important common interests are more likely to pass the requirement of "necessity" in GATT Article XX(b).[306] In the same way, such measures should be more likely to escape the obligations of the TBT Agreement and the SPS Agreement. This technique of coordinated interpretation would apply to TBT Article 2.2, where the necessity test ("unnecessary obstacle[s] to international trade") and the least-trade-restrictive test ("not ... more trade-restrictive than necessary to fulfil a legitimate objective")

[305] *Sardines,* Appellate Body Report, *supra* note 286 at para. 263.

[306] *Asbestos,* Appellate Body Report, *supra* note 4 at para. 172, citing *Korea – Beef,* Appellate Body Report, *supra* note 188 at para. 162.

both appear in the same provision. In the SPS Agreement, the approach should apply to both the necessity test ("only to the extent necessary to protect, human, animal or plant life or health") in Article 2.2 and the least-trade-restrictive test in Article 5.6 ("not more trade-restrictive than required to achieve ... [the] appropriate level of sanitary or phytosanitary protection"). Support for this interpretation of Article 5.6 can be derived from the opening words of the paragraph: "[w]ithout prejudice to paragraph 2 of Article 3." Article 3.2 presumes that measures conforming to international standards are necessary to protect life or health and are consistent with the SPS Agreement and GATT 1994. The least-trade-restrictive test, then, can be seen as both linked with, and subordinate to, the overall requirement that the measure be necessary for one of the protected purposes — the requirement from which the least-trade-restrictive test developed in previous GATT decisions. Coordination could involve, for example, the approach to the reasonable availability of alternate measures within the terms of the footnote to Article 5.6.[307]

A major area of contention surrounding the TBT Agreement involves measures that distinguish among goods according to their production or processing methods (PPMs). The *Shrimp/Turtle* decision confirmed that such measures can be justified under GATT Article XX, even if the process does not produce a change in the physical characteristics of goods. The US measure at issue in *Shrimp/ Turtle* was justified despite the fact that the physical characteristics of shrimp do not depend on whether they are caught using TEDs. There is significant disagreement over whether the TBT Agreement governs such non-product-related PPMs. A number of members are of the view that the negotiating history of the TBT Agreement demonstrates an intention to cover only PPMs that affect the physical

---

[307] The footnote is as follows: "For purposes of paragraph 6 of Article 5, a measure is not more trade-restrictive than required unless there is another measure, reasonably available taking into account technical and economic feasibility, that achieves the appropriate level of sanitary or phytosanitary protection and is significantly less restrictive to trade." In *Canada – Wheat,* a Panel dealing with GATT Article XX(d) stated that reasonable availability of an alternate measure could be determined on the basis of the effectiveness of that measure in producing the desired result, the relative administrative, financial and technical burdens and "the trade impact of the alternative measure compared to that of the measure for which justification is claimed." Panel Report, *Canada – Wheat, supra* note 193, para. 6.226 and Panel footnote 311 (Article XX(d) issue not appealed to Appellate Body).

characteristics of goods and are therefore product related.[308] During negotiations, several countries opposed non-product-related PPMs as extraterritorial and unilateral. This view may explain why the claims in *Shrimp/Turtle* were brought only under GATT and not the TBT Agreement.

The argument for excluding non-product-related PPMs emphasizes the definitions in Annex I of the TBT Agreement. The definition of a "technical regulation" refers to "product characteristics or their related processes and production methods." The definition of a "standard" refers to "products or related processes and production methods." In the Spanish version, the wording differs slightly between the two definitions. In Spanish, the definition of "reglamento técnico" refers to "las características de un producto o los procesos y métodos de producción *con ellas relacionados*" while the definition of "norma" refers to "los productos o los procesos y métodos de producción *conexos*" [emphasis added]. I am not qualified to say whether the two phrases in italics, both expressed as "related" in English, indicate real differences in intensity. I suggest, however, that the Spanish definition of "reglamento técnico" provides strong support for the argument that the processes and production methods must relate to product characteristics ("ellas") rather than reflect a more general linkage.[309] The SPS Agreement has certain territorial limits, protecting plant, animal, and human health only within the member's own territory.[310] If some non-product-related PPMs are not covered by either the SPS Agreement or the

308 Seung Wha Chang, "GATTing a Green Trade Barrier: Eco-Labelling and the WTO Agreement on Technical Barriers to Trade" (1997) 31(1) J. World Trade 137; Carlos Lopez-Hurtado, "Social Labelling and WTO Law" (2002) 5(3) J. Int'l Econ. L. 719.

309 The wording in the French version also differs between the two definitions, but does not provide the same confirmation of the link to characteristics. In French, the definition of "règlement technique" refers to "les caractéristiques d'un produit ou les procédés et méthodes de production *s'y rapportant*" while the definition of "norme" refers to "des produits ou des procédés et des méthodes de production *connexes*" [emphasis added].

310 See the definition of "sanitary or phytosanitary measure" in SPS Agreement Annex A. But note that the definition includes "processes and production methods; testing, inspection, certification and approval procedures; quarantine treatments including relevant requirements associated with the transport of animals or plants, or with the materials necessary for their survival during transport; provisions on relevant statistical methods, sampling procedures and methods of risk assessment." Some of these measures might apply extraterritorially and might not relate to product characteristics: see Marceau and Trachtman, *supra* note 252 at 862.

TBT Agreement, then such measures are subject only to GATT scrutiny, as in the *Shrimp/Turtle* dispute.

Clearly, there are a number of issues relating to the TBT Agreement that require sorting out. In future disputes, one issue is likely to be whether there is a relevant international standard, as was argued in *Asbestos*. Even without an international standard, the provisions of the agreement will pose problems, as they differ from those of GATT 1994. A coordinated approach to interpretation would be best wherever possible. A major problem is that the TBT Agreement provides a necessity test for environmental measures when WTO decisions have rejected that interpretation of GATT Article XX(g) and require only that the measure be one "relating to" conservation. This area is likely to be contentious in the future.

INTERNATIONAL STANDARDS — GLOBAL REGULATION

Both the SPS Agreement and the TBT Agreement give a prominent place to relevant international standards. International standardization moves regulatory decision-making to the global level, with the objective of producing uniformity. This section addresses first the identification and then the use of international standards in the SPS and TBT Agreements. A crucial question in both agreements is the identification of the international standards. The SPS Agreement lists certain international bodies in its preamble, in Article 3.4, and in Annex A, and then refers to appropriate standards from other relevant international organizations that are open for membership to all WTO members, as identified by the Committee on Sanitary and Phytosanitary Measures (Annex A, 3(d)). The TBT Agreement is less precise about the source of the international standards. In the TBT Agreement, an international body must be open to at least all WTO members (Annex 1), but there is no filtering mechanism such as identification by a committee.

In *Asbestos*, identification of an international standard was at issue under the TBT Agreement, but the question was not resolved. As outlined earlier, Canada argued that a convention and a recommendation from the ILO were the relevant international standards under Article 2.4 of the TBT Agreement.[311] The Panel and Appellate Body did not have to decide the point, due to their differences over whether the measure was a "technical regulation." Some WTO members might be concerned that a link has already been alleged

---

[311] *Asbestos,* Panel Report, *supra* note 4 at paras. 3.358–3.361, 3.369–3.372, and 3.377–3.386; *Asbestos,* Appellate Body Report, *supra* note 4 at para. 17.

between the WTO and the ILO on the setting of labour standards. Similarly, the representatives at the ILO international conference, which adopted the convention and the recommendation in question, might be surprised to find these instruments enforceable through WTO trade remedies.[312] Since the TBT Agreement lacks a filtering mechanism, similar arguments over identification of the standard can be expected in the future.[313]

In several disputes, participants have argued that the matter should be dealt with under the provisions of other international regimes, not the trade rules. In *Tuna/Dolphin,* Venezuela maintained that its fishing fleet was following the recommendations of the Inter-American Tropical Tuna Commission to reduce dolphin mortality and argued that the problem should be handled through that multilateral forum rather than the unilateral US embargo.[314] All of the relevant species of sea turtles in the *Shrimp/Turtle* dispute were listed as threatened with extinction in Appendix I of CITES,[315] and India in the 1998 process argued that nothing in that convention supported an import ban on shrimp or the use of TEDs as a "multilateral environmental standard" for the protection of sea turtles.[316] It can be expected that there will be more of such developments in the future, concerning overlapping multilateral regimes that could produce international standards covered by the TBT Agreement, possibly conflicting with other WTO provisions.[317]

[312] ILO, Convention Concerning Safety in the Use of Asbestos (Convention 162) and ILO, Recommendation Concerning Safety in the Use of Asbestos (Recommendation 172), both adopted at the International Labour Conference on 24 June 1986; see further ILO, Code of Practice on Safety in the Use of Asbestos, Geneva, 1984 (*Asbestos,* Panel Report, *supra* note 4 at para. 3.359, footnotes 475, 476). Canada also referred to Guidelines for On-Site Work from the International Organization for Standardization (International Standard ISO-7337), which covered the use of asbestos cement materials (*Asbestos,* Panel Report, *supra* note 4 at para. 3.359, footnote 477).

[313] Joost Pauwelyn, "WTO Compassion or Superiority Complex?: What to Make of the WTO Waiver for 'Conflict Diamonds'" (2003) 24 Mich. J. Int'l L. 1177 at 1188–189.

[314] *Tuna/Dolphin I, supra* note 120 at para. 4.26; *Tuna/Dolphin II, supra* note 120 at paras. 4.36–4.39. See *Tuna/Dolphin II, supra* note 120 at paras. 2.3–2.4.

[315] Most were also listed as endangered or vulnerable in Appendices I and II of the 1979 Convention on Migratory Species of Wild Animals (available at <http://www.cms.int>) and the IUCN Red List (*Shrimp/Turtle 1998,* Panel Report, *supra* note 5 at para. 2.3).

[316] *Shrimp/Turtle 1998,* Panel Report, *supra* note 5 at para. 3.5.

[317] Gabrielle Marceau, "Conflicts of Norms and Conflicts of Jurisdictions: The Relationship between the WTO Agreement and MEAs and other Treaties"

Once a relevant international standard has been identified, there is a further issue concerning its effect. Article 3.1 of the SPS Agreement provides that members "shall base" their sanitary and phytosanitary measures on international standards, guidelines, or recommendations. In *Beef Hormones*, the Appellate Body rejected the view of the Panel that domestic measures had to conform to certain international standards contained in the Codex Alimentarius.[318] The Appellate Body noted that the treaty language does not require conformity, that harmonization is a goal of the SPS Agreement and not an immediate obligation, and that the standards are only recommendations within the Codex itself.[319] In *Sardines*, a Codex Alimentarius standard had a stronger effect. The provision at issue was TBT Article 2.4, which requires that a relevant international standard be used "as a basis" for the technical regulation. The Appellate Body interpreted this to mean that the international standard had to be a "principal constituent," "fundamental principle," "main constituent," or "determining principle" of the domestic measure.[320] Since the EC regulation contradicted the international standard, the EC was found in breach.

(2001) 35(6) J. World Trade 1081; Joost Pauwelyn, *Conflict of Norms in Public International Law: How WTO Law Relates to Other Rules of International Law* (Cambridge, UK: Cambridge University Press, 2003). In its 1998 decision in *Shrimp/Turtle*, the Appellate Body specifically noted the reference to the TBT Agreement in the Inter-American Convention for the Protection and Conservation of Sea Turtles, the convention that the Appellate Body considered to mark out the "equilibrium line" between GATT exceptions and other GATT obligations: *Shrimp/Turtle 1998*, Appellate Body Report, *supra* note 5 at paras. 169–170 (compare with para. 159). See further the submissions of Australia and reply of the United States in *Shrimp/Turtle 2001*, Panel Report, *supra* note 5 at paras. 4.12–4.26, paras. 3.110–3.114; *Shrimp/Turtle 2001*, Appellate Body Report, *supra* note 5 at paras. 125–30.

318 The Codex Alimentarius Commission was established in 1963 as a joint project of the World Health Organization and the Food and Agriculture Organization of the United Nations (available at <http://www.codexalimentarius.net/web/index_en.jsp>).

319 *Beef Hormones*, Appellate Body Report, *supra* note 176 at para. 163–68. But note that SPS Article 3.1 requires members to base their SPS measures on international guidelines and recommendations, as well as international standards.

320 *Sardines*, Appellate Body Report, *supra* note 286 at para. 245. As in the SPS Agreement, there are other provisions of the TBT Agreement indicating that the drafters did not expect instant harmonization of standards among all WTO members. Article 2.6 speaks only of harmonizing technical regulations "on as wide a basis as possible," and Article 2.9 accepts the possibility of technical regulations that are not in accordance with the relevant international standards.

In *Sardines*, the EC was unsuccessful in arguing that the TBT Agreement did not require members to revise their existing technical regulations to meet the obligations of the agreement.[321] The EC was also unsuccessful in claiming that a "relevant international standard" within Article 2.4 had to be adopted by consensus. This argument related to the explanatory note to the definition of "standard" in Annex 1:

The terms as defined in ISO/IEC Guide 2 cover products, processes and services. This Agreement deals only with technical regulations, standards and conformity assessment procedures related to products or processes and production methods. Standards as defined by ISO/IEC Guide 2 may be mandatory or voluntary. For the purpose of this Agreement standards are defined as voluntary and technical regulations as mandatory documents. Standards prepared by the international standardization community are based on consensus. This Agreement covers also documents that are not based on consensus.

The introductory words of Annex I adopt the definitions of the sixth edition of the International Organization of Standardization (ISO)/International Electrotechnical Commission (IEC) Guide 2, *General Terms and Their Definitions Concerning Standardization and Related Activities* (1991), except as more specifically set out in the annex.[322] After noting that the ISO/IEC guide defines a standard as a document established by consensus, the Appellate Body determined that the last sentence in the explanatory note indicated that consensus was not required for standards under the TBT Agreement.[323]

The decision in *Sardines* confirms that international harmonization is a fairly robust phenomenon. Standards that are voluntary and subject to national choice within the standardizing organization

---

[321] *Sardines*, Appellate Body Report, *supra* note 286 at para. 205. Both the EC regulation and the Codex standard were adopted prior to the entry into force of the TBT Agreement at the beginning of 1995 (*Ibid.* at para. 196).

[322] The International Organization for Standardization (ISO) was founded in 1946 and the International Electrotechnical Commission (IEC) dates from 1906. For background, see Lisa C. Thompson and William J. Thompson, "The ISO 9000 Quality Standards: Will They Constitute a Technical Barrier to Free Trade under the NAFTA and the WTO?" (1997) 14 Ariz. J. Int'l & Comp. L. 155; Kristina Kloiber, "Removing Technical Barriers to Trade: The Next Step toward Freer Trade" (2001) 9 Tul. J. Int'l & Comp. L. 511.

[323] *Sardines*, Appellate Body Report, *supra* note 286 at para. 225.

where they are developed will become binding on WTO members through the SPS and TBT Agreements. These agreements are much more restrictive for national regulation than the GATT Article III approach in which national treatment is a complete answer. In *Sardines*, Peru had also made a claim under GATT Article III:4, which was not addressed given the decision on TBT Article 2.4. The TBT Agreement made Peru's case significantly easier to prove.

The SPS and TBT Agreements represent a significant step towards harmonization and the use of international standards. It may be noted that the harmonization obligation is an ongoing one for international standards as they develop and not solely for standards that existed when the country became a member of the agreements. A great deal of regulatory authority is now imposed on international standardizing organizations, and their activities will need to be followed with care to make sure that decisions reflect the interests of all rather than particular industry groups.[324] As the global regulatory process becomes stronger, there is an increasing need to achieve balance in global public policy.

To summarize this part of the article, the SPS and TBT Agreements have largely replaced traditional GATT non-discrimination norms with enhanced market-opening provisions pursuant to which the national treatment obligation no longer offers a buffer for diversity in domestic regulation.[325] The market-opening provisions apply in the absence of competing domestic products and even in the absence of a relevant harmonized international standard. The SPS and TBT provisions are likely to supplant GATT Article III in many applications. To the extent possible, interpretation of exemptions from the SPS and TBT Agreements should be coordinated with the interpretation of GATT exemptions in order to produce a consistent approach to the recognition of important non-trade interests in global public policy.

Conclusion

This article has discussed recent WTO decisions concerning the recognition of non-trade interests, particularly *Shrimp/Turtle* and *Asbestos*. The argument presented was that some adjustments in

---

[324] David G. Victor, "The Sanitary and Phytosanitary Agreement of the World Trade Organization: An Assessment after Five Years" (2000) 32 N.Y.U. J. Int'l L. & Pol. 865 at 887–88.

[325] Robert E. Hudec, "Introduction: Science and 'Post-Discriminatory' WTO Law" (2003) 26 B.C. Int'l & Comp. L. Rev. 185.

interpretation are needed in order to encourage the development
of approaches and tests suitable for the role of trade agreements as
part of policy-making at the global level. The article made the following four assertions:

*1. The interpretation of the introductory clause of Article XX should
be substantive in order to preserve the even-handedness of the non-
discrimination norms of national treatment and MFN treatment.
Article XX should be kept suitable for ongoing analysis of the relationship between trade and non-trade interests.*

The *Shrimp/Turtle* dispute involved difficult issues of unilateralism
and extraterritoriality as well as the relationship of trade to the
protection of the environment. It is perhaps not surprising that
analysis turned to procedural issues such as flexibility, due process,
and a duty to negotiate. As more disputes come forward concerning the Article XX exemptions, interpretation of the introductory
clause of the article should become more substantive in order to
preserve the even-handedness of the non-discrimination norms and
encourage the development of further approaches to the accommodation of non-trade interests.

*2. Trade interests should not be given priority in the interpretation of Ar-
ticle XX. Rather, interpretation should be balanced in order to provide
effective exemptions for the non-trade interests reflected in the paragraphs
of the article.*

Interpretation of Article XX should recognize the important non-
trade policies reflected in the listed paragraphs of the article. Exemption claims should not be considered abusive and the
paragraphs should not be interpreted narrowly. Since the traditional non-discrimination norms are preserved in the introductory
clause, the paragraphs of Article XX should not be interpreted in
accordance with a "least-trade-restrictive" approach that would give
these norms additional emphasis.

*3. The coverage of the national treatment standard should not be expanded
in an attempt to protect domestic regulations that block imports. It may
be preferable for the development of global public policy to treat certain
import bans as breaches of GATT Article XI that would be subject to
possible justification under Article XX.*

The interpretation of "like products" should emphasize material
fact concerning the goods. Measures adopted for public health

reasons should be justified on a scientific basis rather than through the presumed views of consumers and the operation of market competition.

4. *The SPS Agreement and TBT Agreement adopt a market-opening approach that will overtake traditional GATT non-discrimination norms in many applications. Exemptions and areas of overlap should be interpreted in harmony with GATT to the extent possible.*

Market access and non-discrimination have both been important themes throughout the history of GATT. Article XI, for example, bans quantitative restrictions on imports in order to open markets. The preamble of GATT 1947 states that the agreement is "directed to the substantial reduction of tariffs and other barriers to trade" as well as "to the elimination of discriminatory treatment in international commerce." Prior to the creation of the WTO, domestic regulation of goods was generally reviewed in accordance with the non-discrimination norms, principally the national treatment provisions of Article III. Now, that analysis may persist for some areas, such as internal tax differences and some aspects of PPMs. Other issues are more likely to be determined in accordance with the market access and harmonization obligations of the SPS and TBT Agreements. Coordinated policy concerning exemptions should be the goal for all of the agreements now part of the WTO.

In 1947, the exemptions of GATT Article XX may have been assumed to be generally for public policies determined at a national level. Now, however, social, environmental, and human rights issues are increasingly seen as being of global concern and as part of the common interests of all humanity. As views change, the recognition of non-trade interests should not be principally about protecting national policy-making from international trade obligations. Rather, a major task will involve adapting institutions to facilitate the development of balanced policies and obligations at the global level. GATT 1994 and other agreements under the WTO aegis should be interpreted in light of the changing needs of global public policy.

Sommaire

La politique publique internationale et l'OMC après le différend sur les crevettes, les tortues et l'amiante

La jurisprudence récente de l'Organe d'appel de l'Organisation mondiale du commerce interprète l'article XX du GATT, qui fournit des exemptions pour reconnaître des politiques publiques importantes, telles que la protection de la santé et de l'environnement. L'article analyse cette jurisprudence, ainsi que l'équilibre entre le commerce et d'autres politiques publiques dans les dispositions de l'Accord relatif aux mesures sanitaires et phytosanitaires et l'Accord relatif aux obstacles techniques au commerce.

Summary

Global Public Policy and the WTO after *Shrimp/Turtle* and *Asbestos*

Recent decisions of the Appellate Body of the WTO deal with the interpretation of GATT Article XX, which provides exemptions from trade obligations for important non-trade policies such as the protection of health and the environment. The article discusses those decisions, as well as the balance between trade and non-trade interests in the provisions of the Agreement on the Application of Sanitary and Phytosanitary Measures and the Agreement on Technical Barriers to Trade.

Notes and Comments / Notes et commentaires

The Decision of the International Court of Justice in the *Case Concerning Legality of Use of Force (Serbia and Montenegro v. Canada)*

On 15 December 2004, Canada's third case before the International Court of Justice came to an end with the dismissal at the preliminary objections stage of Serbia and Montenegro's case against Canada and seven other North Atlantic Treaty Organization (NATO) countries.[1] The court was unanimous in the result, but split eight to seven in its reasoning. This comment will review the procedural history of the case, examine the reasoning of the court both at the provisional measures stage and at the preliminary objections stage, and, finally, consider some of the implications of the surprising approach taken by the court.

BACKGROUND

The NATO bombing campaign in the Federal Republic of Yugoslavia[2] (FRY) began on 24 March 1999 and continued until 10 June 1999. The NATO action was the culmination of a series of efforts to stop the acts of repression and serious violations of international humanitarian law committed against Kosovar Albanians by the FRY. These acts included, according to the Commission on Human Rights in 1999, large-scale killings, systematic and planned massacres, summary executions, mass forced exoduses, and the destruction of personal identity documents, records, homes, and property as well as agricultural capacity, all with a view to preventing the return of the Kosovar Albanians. The UN Security Council had

---

[1] *Case Concerning Legality of Use of Force (Serbia and Montenegro v. Canada)*, 15 December 2004, available at <www.icj-cig.org> [*Legality of Use of Force*].

[2] On 5 February 2003, the applicant notified the court that the state of the Federal Republic of Yugoslavia (FRY) had changed its name to Serbia and Montenegro. In this article, the applicant is referred to as the FRY before February 2003 and Serbia and Montenegro thereafter.

condemned the excessive use of force by Serbian police forces against civilians and had demanded, in Resolutions 1160, 1199, and 1203 in 1998,[3] that the FRY stop attacks on the civilian population in Kosovo and take immediate steps to avert a humanitarian catastrophe. This did not happen.

Diplomatic efforts to resolve the crisis continued throughout 1998, culminating in negotiations at Rambouillet, France, in February 1999, from which emerged the draft Rambouillet Accords,[4] which defined the terms of a cease fire and a peace settlement that would include an international presence. While the members of the contact group[5] endorsed the Rambouillet Accords, the FRY was not satisfied. At the conclusion of a second round of talks on 15–19 March in Paris and in the face of the FRY's demands for substantial changes to the draft accords, the co-chairman of the talks concluded that there was no purpose in continuing the talks any further. Also on 19 March, the Kosovo Verification Mission of the Organization for Security and Cooperation in Europe (OSCE) (an unarmed civilian ground verification mission that had been established in October 1998) withdrew, as it had concluded that the situation had deteriorated to such an extent that it could not safely conduct its mission. Indeed, on 5 May 1999, the United Nations High Commissioner for Refugees had stated that its agency had been providing assistance to 500,000 Kosovar Albanians in and outside Kosovo well before the NATO air action began. It was against this backdrop that NATO concluded that military action was necessary to avert a humanitarian catastrophe.

On 25 April 1999, one month after the NATO air action began, the government of the FRY submitted a declaration pursuant to Article 36(2) of the Statute of the International Court of Justice (ICJ Statute),[6] in which it recognized the jurisdiction of the ICJ "in all disputes arising or which may arise *after the signature of the present*

3 UN Security Council Resolutions 1160 (UN Doc. S/RES/1160 (1998) 31 March 1998), 1199 (UN Doc. S/RES/1199 (1998) 23 September 1998), and 1203 (UN Doc. S/RES/1203 (1998) 24 October 1998).

4 See the Interim Agreement for Peace and Self-Government in Kosovo, Rambouillet, France, 23 February 1999 available at <http://www.state.gov/www/regions/eur/fs_990301_rambouillet.html>.

5 France, Germany, Italy, the Russian Federation, the United Kingdom, the United States, and European Community presidency.

6 Statute of the International Court of Justice, annexed to the Charter of the United Nations and forming an integral part of the Charter pursuant to Article 92 thereof [ICJ Statute].

Declaration, with regard to the *situations or facts subsequent to this signature.*[7]

Four days later, on 29 April, the FRY filed applications with the ICJ to institute proceedings in ten separate cases against ten NATO allies[8] for violation of the international obligation banning the use of force and various other violations relating to international humanitarian, human rights, and environmental law. The court chose to summarize the proceedings with the title *Case Concerning Legality of Use of Force.* At the same time, the FRY sought an order for provisional measures,[9] ordering Canada and the other NATO allies to "cease immediately its acts of use of force" and to "refrain from any act of threat or use of force against the Federal Republic of Yugoslavia."[10]

REQUEST FOR PROVISIONAL MEASURES

The request for provisional measures was quickly set down for hearing, and, from 9–11 May 1999, Canada and the other nine NATO countries appeared before the court. As the basis for the court's jurisdiction, the FRY invoked Article 36(2) of the ICJ Statute, as well as Article IX of the Convention on the Prevention and Punishment of the Crime of Genocide (Genocide Convention).[11]

---

[7] Yugoslavia's purported declaration recognizing the compulsory jurisdiction of the court pursuant to Article 36(2) of the ICJ Statute is set out in full at para. 22 of the Order of the Court of 2 June 1999 on provisional measures (*infra* note 17) and reads as follows:

> I hereby declare that the Government of the Federal Republic of Yugoslavia recognizes, in accordance with Article 36, paragraph 2, of the Statute of the International Court of Justice, as compulsory *ipso facto* and without special agreement, in relation to any other State accepting the same obligation, that is on condition of reciprocity, the jurisdiction of the said Court in all disputes arising or which may arise after the signature of the present Declaration, with regard to the situations or facts subsequent to this signature, except in cases where the parties have agreed or shall agree to have recourse to another procedure or to another method of pacific settlement. The present Declaration does not apply to disputes relating to questions which, under international law, fall exclusively within the jurisdiction of the Federal Republic of Yugoslavia, as well as to territorial disputes.

[8] Belgium, Canada, France, Germany, Italy, Netherlands, Portugal, Spain, United Kingdom, and the United States.

[9] Pursuant to Article 73 of the Rules of Court of the ICJ, made pursuant to Article 30 of the ICJ Statute and available at <www.icj-cij.org>.

[10] *Legality of Use of Force, supra* note 1, Application of the FRY, 25 April 1999.

[11] Convention on the Prevention and Punishment of the Crime of Genocide, GA Resolution 260(A)(III), UN GAOR, 3rd Sess., Supp. No. 1921, 9 December 1948, 78 U.N.T.S. 227 [Genocide Convention].

Setting aside cases submitted by special agreement, contentious cases before the court normally base their jurisdiction on the "Optional Clause" in Article 36(2) of the ICJ Statute [12] or on provisions in a treaty vesting jurisdiction in the court as provided in Article 36(1) of the statute. Optional Clause declarations commonly provide either temporal or subject matter limitations on the acceptance of the jurisdiction of the court. The language of the FRY's Optional Clause acceptance of the compulsory jurisdiction of the court, as quoted earlier in this note, was a reservation respecting the *temporal* jurisdiction of the court and was based on numerous precedents. Indeed, as Canada submitted, the FRY's declaration took a familiar form, the so-called double exclusion or "Belgian formula," since jurisdiction is excluded either if the dispute arose before the declaration or if it pertains to situations or facts prior to that date.

Provisional measures, under Article 41 of the ICJ Statute, refer to urgent orders normally made at the outset of a case to preserve the rights of the parties. Such measures may be compared to preliminary injunctions in domestic proceedings. The jurisdictional test applied to requests for provisional measures under the jurisdiction of the court is that of *prima facie* jurisdiction, which, in practice, represents an extremely low threshold that is easily satisfied. Respondents frequently challenge the jurisdiction of the court under one or more of the following three headings: *ratione personae* (personal jurisdiction — that is, jurisdiction with respect to the parties), *ratione materiae* (subject matter jurisdiction), and *ratione temporis* (temporal jurisdiction). In this case, Canada submitted, the FRY's application was flawed in all three respects. Canada also argued that the court should exercise its discretion to refuse provisional measures because they would be fundamentally inappropriate, indeed counter-productive, in light of the conduct of the FRY that had led to the NATO bombing campaign.

On jurisdiction, Canada argued that the optional clause declaration filed by the FRY was a nullity because the court lacked jurisdiction *ratione personae* — the FRY was not a member of the United Nations and therefore not a party to the ICJ Statute. Accordingly, it was not entitled to file an Optional Clause declaration under the

[12] ICJ Statute, *supra* note 6 at Article 36(2), known as the Optional Clause, which allows states, on a purely voluntary basis, to file declarations accepting the compulsory jurisdiction of the court *vis-à-vis* other states accepting the same obligation, in relation to specified categories of legal disputes, including the interpretation of a treaty and "any question of international law."

terms of Article 36(2) of the statute. Further, even if the declaration were valid, it would be inapplicable because of its own temporal restriction to disputes arising after the signature of the declaration — a failure of jurisdiction *ratione temporis*. Finally, Canada argued that the Genocide Convention could not provide a basis for jurisdiction because its subject matter was irrelevant to a request for provisional measures that focused exclusively on the use of force: a failure of jurisdiction *ratione materiae*.

In support of the argument that the declaration was a nullity, Canada relied upon the language of United Nations resolutions in 1992, which had stated that the FRY "cannot automatically continue the membership"[13] of the old Yugoslavia and that both the Security Council and the General Assembly had ruled that the FRY should apply for such membership. Indeed, in 1992, the Arbitration Commission of the Peace Conference of Yugoslavia had determined that the dissolution of the old Yugoslavia was complete and that it "no longer exists."[14] The situation was thus clearly different from that of Russia, where the international community and the United Nations had accepted the continuity of the legal personality of Russia and the Union of Soviet Socialist Republics (USSR).

Since the applicant's own temporal restriction accepted jurisdiction only for disputes that arose after 25 April 1999, it was essential to determine when the dispute in the case "arose." Canada cited the *Mavrommatis* test[15]: "[A] dispute is born as soon as there is a disagreement on a point of law or fact, a conflict of legal views or interests." Furthermore, while the situation was a continuing one, there was a single and indivisible legal dispute. As Canada argued, "[t]here cannot be a new and independent dispute with every bomb that falls."[16]

As for the Genocide Convention, Canada argued that the applicant had failed to make a case that the subject matter of the dispute was plausibly related in any way to the subject matter of the treaty. Not a single relevant act imputed to Canada had been cited in support of the broad assertion that genocidal acts within the

---

[13] Security Council Resolution 777, UN SCOR, 47th Year, UN Doc.S/RES/777 (1992)(Annex 1A); GA Res. 47/1, UN GAOR, 47th Sess., UN Doc. A/RES/47/1 (1992) (Annex 1B).

[14] Arbitration Commission of the Peace Conference of Yugoslavia, *Opinion no. 8 of 4 July 1992*, 1993 (92) I.L.R. 199, at 202.

[15] *Readaptation of the Mavrommatis Jersusalem Concessions,* Judgment no. 10, 1927, P.C.I.J. Series A, No. 26.

[16] *Legality of Use of Force, supra* note 1, Oral Proceedings, at para. 21.

definition of the convention had been committed. The applicant was confusing its allegations regarding genocide with the conduct of the military campaign (*jus in bello*) and the legality of the use of force (*jus ad bellum*). The subject matter of the applicant's request for provisional measures referred exclusively to the use of force and not to genocide.

In reply at the oral proceedings, the applicant took jurisdiction for granted, basing its argument primarily on factual issues related to the effects of the bombing. Ian Brownlie presented a spirited attack on the notion of humanitarian intervention — an attack that was nonetheless irrelevant in light of the serious jurisdictional weaknesses in the case.

ORDER OF THE COURT AT THE PROVISIONAL MEASURES STAGE

The court rejected the request for provisional measures against Canada on 2 June 1999 by a vote of twelve to four.[17] The majority[18] ruled that the applicant had failed to establish even the relatively low threshold of *prima face* jurisdiction that applies at the provisional measures phase. Three of the majority issued separate declarations agreeing with the decision, but with differing reasoning.[19] Four dissenting judges disagreed with the court's reasoning with respect to *ratione temporis* jurisdiction.[20]

OPTIONAL CLAUSE ARGUMENT: JURISDICTION *ratione temporis*

The majority accepted Canada's argument in the alternative on the lack of jurisdiction *ratione temporis*.[21] There was no doubt that the temporal reservation in the purported Optional Clause declaration would be effective if the declaration itself was valid. In this respect, the court cited the principle in the *Fisheries Jurisdiction* (*Spain v. Canada*) case,[22] namely that it "is for each State, in formulating its declaration, to decide upon the limits it places on the jurisdic-

---

17 Order Respecting the Request for the Indication of Provisional Measures, 2 June 1999, [1999] I.C.J. Rep. 259.

18 President Schwebel, Judges Oda, Bedjaoui, Guillaume, Ranjeva, Hercegh, Fleischauer, Koroma, Higgins, Parra-Aranguren, Kooijmans, and Judge ad hoc Lalonde.

19 Judges Oda, Kooijmans, and Higgins.

20 Judges Weeramantry, Shi, and Vereshchetin, and Judge ad hoc Kreća.

21 *Legality of Use of Force*, *supra* note 1, Order of 3 June 1999, at para. 29.

22 *Fisheries Jurisdiction* (*Spain v. Canada*), Jurisdiction, Judgment, [1998] I.C.J. Rep. 432.

tion of the Court." Nor was there any doubt that the reservation could be invoked by Canada since the jurisdiction of the court only exists to the extent to which the jurisdiction accepted by the applicant and respondent states coincides.

The court found that the legal dispute arose between Yugoslavia and Canada well before 25 April 1999 — the day on which the FRY deposited its declaration. The court found that the "legal dispute" concerning the legality of the use of force, taken as a whole, "arose" before the submission of the declaration, notwithstanding the continuation of the bombing campaign after that time. The FRY had not established the fact that new disputes, distinct from the initial dispute, had arisen after 25 April. The purported declaration under Article 36(2) did not, therefore, constitute a basis upon which *prima facie* jurisdiction could be founded, ruled the court.

MEMBERSHIP IN THE UNITED NATIONS: JURISDICTION
RATIONE PERSONAE

Having found a lack of *prima facie* jurisdiction *ratione temporis*, the court found it unnecessary to rule on Canada's principal argument that the FRY was not a member of the United Nations and thus not a party to the Statute of the ICJ at the time of the deposit of its declaration.

GENOCIDE CONVENTION ARGUMENT: JURISDICTION
RATIONE MATERIAE

Finally, on the jurisdictional head of Article IX of the Genocide Convention, the court accepted Canada's argument that the acts imputed by Yugoslavia to Canada were not capable of coming within the provisions of the Genocide Convention. The bombings did not entail the element of intent "to destroy a group as such," as required by the definition of genocide in Article 2 of the Genocide Convention. In so finding, the court cited and followed its approach to *ratione materiae* jurisdiction under a treaty as formulated in the 1996 Judgment on Preliminary Objections in the *Case Concerning Oil Platforms (Islamic Republic of Iran v. United States of America)*,[23] which is described in slightly different language in two passages of that decision. Either the subject matter of the claim must "fall within" the relevant treaty,[24] or, alternatively, it must refer to matters whose

---

[23] *Case Concerning Oil Platforms (Islamic Republic of Iran v. United States of America)*, Preliminary Objection, Judgment, [1996] I.C.J. Rep. (II), 810.

[24] *Ibid.* at para. 16.

"lawfulness can be evaluated" in relation to a provision of the treaty.[25] Under either iteration of the test, there was no *prima facie* jurisdiction under the Genocide Convention.

The court, however, was clear that its decision on jurisdiction at the provisional measures stage was itself provisional. It in no way prejudged the ultimate decision on the jurisdiction of the court or on any questions of admissibility.

JUDGMENT RESPECTING THE OTHER NATO COUNTRIES

With certain variations in reasoning based on whether the country was party to the Genocide Convention (Portugal was not at the relevant time) or whether it accepted the compulsory jurisdiction of the court (France, Germany, and Italy did not), the court made similar findings with respect to jurisdiction under the Optional Clause with respect to seven of the other NATO allies: Belgium, France, Germany, Italy, Portugal, Netherlands, and the United Kingdom.

With respect to Spain and the United States, however, the court removed the case from the list. The court distinguished between those cases in which it "manifestly" had no jurisdiction (that is, Spain and the United States) and those where it merely had no *prima facie* jurisdiction (that is, Canada and the seven other NATO allies). Both Spain and the United States had reservations to Article IX of the Genocide Convention, which deprived the court of jurisdiction. Moreover, the United States did not accept the compulsory jurisdiction of the court under the Optional Clause, and Spain's acceptance is subject to a twelve-month time lapse after the deposit by another country of its acceptance of the jurisdiction of the court.

This is the first case in the court's jurisprudence in which the court has dismissed a request for the indication of provisional measures due to the lack of *prima facie* jurisdiction, but in which it has nonetheless remained seized of the case.[26]

---

25 *Ibid.* at para. 51.

26 See *Legality of Use of Force, supra* note 1, Opinion of Judge Oda, at paras. 25 ff. There have, of course, been cases in which the court found that it did have *prima facie* jurisdiction, only to find later that it did not have jurisdiction to hear the case at a subsequent stage (*Anglo-Iranian Oil Co.,* Preliminary Objection, Judgment, [1952] I.C.J. Rep. 104; and *Interhandel (Switzerland v. United States of America),* [1959] I.C.J. Rep. 6).

PRELIMINARY OBJECTIONS STAGE

The FRY filed its 367-page memorial on 4 January 2000. It was short on legal argument (there were only fifty pages in the memorial) and long on allegations listing each individual bomb that dropped in the spring of 1999. It also included new allegations relating to illegal acts allegedly committed by troops in the United Nations Kosovo Force (KFOR), which was the UN-mandated peace-keeping force. Despite the fact that there were eight respondent countries, the FRY filed only one version of the memorial, making no distinction as to the liability of individual NATO countries.

In the practice of the court, preliminary objections can deal either with jurisdiction as such or with a variety of more procedural defects affecting the "admissibility" of the claim. Canada submitted its written preliminary objections in July 2000. Since the court had made it clear that its ruling at the provisional measures stage was only *prima facie*, it was necessary in Canada's written preliminary objections to repeat the arguments on jurisdiction made at the provisional measures stage as noted earlier in this comment. In addition, Canada made two objections to the admissibility of the claim: first, that new elements related to KFOR were extraneous to the original claim and, second, that the absence of essential third parties (particularly the United States and the United Nations) rendered the claim inadmissible under what is commonly referred to as the "*Monetary Gold*" principle.[27]

For reasons that will become apparent later, it is worth noting that in a footnote to the argument that the purported Optional Clause was a nullity because the FRY was not a party to the ICJ Statute, Canada pointed out that there "has been no attempt in this case to rely on Article 35(2) of the Statute."[28] Article 35(2) provides that *subject to the provisions of treaties in force,* the court may be open to non-parties under conditions laid down by the Security Council, but that, in no case, shall such access place the parties in a position of inequality before the court. The provision appears to leave open the possibility that, in certain cases at least, the court might be open to non-parties that adhere to treaties "in force" containing a clause vesting jurisdiction in the court.

The case then lay dormant for two-and-a-half years while dramatic and ongoing changes in Yugoslavia were underway. The government

---

[27] *Monetary Gold Removed from Rome in 1943,* Judgment, [1954] I.C.J. Rep. 19.

[28] See the Preliminary Objections of Canada in *Legality of Use of Force, supra* note 1 at 2, n. 4, available at <www.icj-cij.org>.

changed, Milosevic was handed over to the International Criminal Tribunal on Yugoslavia, and, most significantly, on 1 November 2000, the FRY was accepted as a new member of the United Nations. Logically, this acceptance would imply that it was not a member of the United Nations when it filed its application before the court in April 1999.

The uncertainty as to the impact of this fact lasted for several years until 18 December 2002. Finally, the agent for the FRY replied to the preliminary objections of Canada and the other NATO respondents with observations noting that the FRY, in 1999, was not a member of the United Nations and "accordingly, it became an established fact that before 1 November 2000, the Federal Republic of Yugoslavia was not and could not have been a party to the Statute of the Court by way of UN membership."[29] Second, with regard to the Genocide Convention, the FRY "did not continue the personality and treaty membership of the former Yugoslavia, and thus specifically, it was not bound by the *Genocide Convention* until it acceded to that Convention (with a reservation to Article IX) in March 2001."[30] However, the observations did not seek the discontinuance of the case, which was the step logically implied by the effective abandonment of the grounds of jurisdiction originally invoked. Instead, they requested that the court decide on its jurisdiction. The significance of this request appears to lie in the other cases in which the FRY is respondent, as discussed later in this comment.

Canada and the other NATO respondents responded to these observations by writing individually to the court in early 2003, suggesting that the case should be dismissed. To the surprise of some, the FRY insisted that it did not consider its observations to constitute a *de facto* withdrawal of the case but rather a request for a ruling by the court on jurisdiction. The NATO respondents met with the agent for Serbia and Montenegro and urged that the applicant consider withdrawing the case. This was not possible — popular sentiment in Serbia and Montenegro against the NATO bombing could not be ignored. Furthermore, Serbia and Montenegro wanted some clarity from the court with respect to its status under various treaties.

ORAL HEARINGS ON THE PRELIMINARY OBJECTIONS

The court convened 19–23 April 2004 in The Hague to hear oral argument. It was not exactly the same court as the one that

---

29 *Ibid.*, Written Observations of FRY of 18 December 2002, at 2, para. (a).

30 *Ibid.* at 2, para. (b).

heard the case at the provisional measures stage. Only eight of the original permanent judges were still in office.[31] There were six new judges on the court,[32] and six were no longer on the bench.[33] Furthermore, Canada was without its ad hoc judge Marc Lalonde, who had sat at the provisional measures stage. This was the result of a ruling by the court on 23 December 2003, rejecting Canada's request that its judge ad hoc should participate, while leaving open the possibility of his participation in subsequent phases of the case. The court justified its position by referring to the presence on the bench of several judges with the nationality of some of the other NATO respondents (Britain, the Netherlands, and France),[34] but it disregarded the fact that the applicant had dropped its earlier objection to the judges ad hoc.

The ruling appears to reflect a curious interpretation of the ICJ Statute. Article 31, which deals with judges ad hoc, refers to "the case" before the court. Serbia and Montenegro had chosen to pursue the matter in the form of eight separate cases. There was only

---

[31] President Shi (China) and Judges Guillaume (France), Higgins (United Kingdom), Kooijmans (Netherlands), Koroma (Sierra Leone), Vereschetin (Russian Federation), Parra-Aranguren (Venezuela)), Ranjeva (Madagascar), Kreća (Judge ad hoc for Serbia and Montenegro).

[32] Owada (Japan), Tomka (Slovakia), Elaraby (Egypt), Buergenthal (United States), Al-Khasawneh (Jordan), and Simma (Germany). However, Judge Simma recused himself from the case pursuant to Article 24(1) of the ICJ Statute. Judge Simma had written an article ("NATO, the UN and the Use of Force: Legal Aspects" (1999) Eur. J. Int'l L. 1) suggesting that the October 1998 threat of air strikes against the FRY breached the Charter of the United Nations, despite NATO's effort to rely on the doctrines of necessity and humanitarian intervention and to conform to the sense and logic of relevant Security Council resolutions. He did acknowledge that there are "hard cases" involving terrible dilemmas in which imperative political and moral considerations leave no choice but to act outside the law. However, his recusal probably relates more directly to advice given to one of the parties at some point before he became a judge.

[33] Judges Weeramantry (Sri Lanka), Schwebel (United States), Oda (Japan), Bedjaoui (Algeria), Herczegh (Hungary), and Fleischhauer (Germany).

[34] Judge ad hoc Kreća noted that the approach of the court implied that all the NATO parties are legally in the same interest. He linked the right to appoint a judge ad hoc to the *jus cogens* sovereign equality of states. He goes on to make a number of novel suggestions on how to deal with a situation such as this where several judges on the court originate in states with the same interest as one of the parties. One of these, inspired by discussions on the 1926 Rules of Court, would be to exclude one or more of these judges. The other would be to allow the appointment of more than one judge ad hoc. Although he argues that such innovations would be consistent with the ICJ Statute, this conclusion is questionable.

one case before the court involving Canada. The court had not joined the cases, and the respondents had opposed any such measure. While at first blush, one might consider that the NATO allies were all in the same interest, there were differences in the legal position of each country with respect to jurisdiction. Furthermore, the assumption that Canada was in the same interest on jurisdictional issues as the three respondents with a national on the bench is open to dispute on a number of grounds.[35]

In the absence of a rebuttal by Serbia and Montenegro of the respondents' preliminary objections on jurisdiction and admissibility, Canada and the other NATO allies were left with no real case to meet before the court. It was, however, necessary at the oral proceedings to review the arguments on jurisdiction and admissibility submitted in Canada's written submission. There were also new issues to be considered: (1) the significance of the court's determination in 2003 (in the *Case Concerning the Application for Revision of the Judgment of 11 July 1996 in the Case Concerning Application of the Convention on the Prevention and Punishment of the Crime of Genocide (Bosnia and Herzegovina v. Yugoslavia)* (*Application for Revision* case) (discussed later in this comment) that the position of the FRY in the 1990s *vis-à-vis* the United Nations was *sui generis*[36] and (2) the significance of the admission of Serbia and Montenegro to the United Nations in 2000. Above all, there was the question of the legal effect of the implied abandonment of the jurisdictional grounds initially relied upon in the applicant's written observations of 18 December 2002.

On this latter point, Canada argued strongly that the court should dismiss the case because the applicant had failed to meet the requirement in Article 38(2) of the Rules of Court[37] of the ICJ that it specify the legal grounds on which the jurisdiction of the court is said to be based. The applicant had abandoned its claim to jurisdiction. There was no dispute before the court and no reason for the parties to be there. In the alternative, Canada argued that the

---

[35] (1) France does not accept the compulsory jurisdiction of the court; (2) the United Kingdom's acceptance of the compulsory jurisdiction of the court included a twelve-month rule, and (3) the Netherlands had an additional possible jurisdictional basis argued by the applicant relating to bilateral treaties.

[36] *Case Concerning the Application for Revision of the Judgment of 11 July 1996 in the Case Concerning Application of the Convention on the Prevention and Punishment of the Crime of Genocide (Bosnia and Herzegovina v. Yugoslavia)*, Preliminary Objections, [2003] I.C.J. Rep. at para. 71 [*Application for Revision* case].

[37] Rules of Court, *supra* note 9.

court lacked jurisdiction for the reasons presented at the provisional measures stage, as outlined earlier in this comment, and developed more fully in its written preliminary objections. All of these arguments allowed the court to maintain consistency with its previous decisions, while avoiding any determinative impact on other cases before the court.

Despite the unusual nature of Serbia and Montenegro's request, its agent, Tibor Varady, presented an articulate plea for the court to provide it with clarity as to its legal status as a result of the complicated situation it had found itself in as a result of the break up of the FRY. He argued, and requested in Serbia and Montenegro's final submissions, that the court should rule on its jurisdiction *ratione personae*, but he took no express position on what the answer to that question should be. By contrast, in the applicant's final submissions, Serbia and Montenegro did take a position with respect to jurisdiction *ratione materiae* and *ratione personae*. As Ian Brownlie has argued orally on these headings of jurisdiction, in its final submissions to the court, Serbia and Montenegro expressly asked it "to dismiss the remaining preliminary objections of the respondent States and to order proceedings on the merits if it finds it has jurisdiction *ratione personae*."[38]

Court's Judgment on the Preliminary Objections

Five-and-a-half years after its decision that there was no *prima face* jurisdiction sufficient to support an order of provisional measures, the court ruled unanimously on 15 December 2004 that it lacked jurisdiction to hear the case. The unanimous nature of the decision applies only as to the *dispositif* — the actual ruling. The court split eight to seven in its reasoning. The majority[39] declined to remove the case from the list *in limine litis* (as a threshold matter) on the basis that the issue of jurisdiction is a legal question independent of the views of the parties. Since Serbia and Montenegro maintained that there was a dispute on the merits, the underlying dispute had not disappeared.

Unexpectedly, however, the majority of the court did not then turn to review the objections made by Canada with respect to jurisdiction *ratione temporis* under the purported Optional Clause

---

[38] *Legality of Use of Force, supra* note 1 at Verbatim Record of the Public Sitting of 23 April 2004, Doc. CR 2004/23, available at <www.icj-cij.org>.

[39] President Shi, Vice President Ranjeva, Judges Koroma, Vereshchetin, Parra-Aranguren, Rezek, Owada, and Tomka.

declaration and with respect to jurisdiction *ratione materiae* under the Genocide Convention. Instead, it examined whether Serbia and Montenegro had access to the court under Article 35 of the ICJ Statute, specifically whether Serbia and Montenegro was a party to the statute. If it were not a party, reasoned the court, Serbia and Montenegro could not have properly seized the court under any title of jurisdiction (subject to a possible exception in Article 35(2), discussed later in this comment), because it did not have the right to appear before the court.[40] This shift in the court's reasoning was unexpected because, in earlier stages of the case, the court had assiduously avoided the issue of UN membership (as it did in the related cases discussed below) and had preferred to rely on considerations of *ratione temporis* and *ratione materiae* jurisdiction.

The court's detailed review of developments in the United Nations between 1992 and 2000 included the position of the UN General Assembly (UNGA), the Security Council, and the Secretariat itself. The UNGA and Security Council resolutions, letters of the Legal Counsel to the United Nations, statements by the FRY, and payment of assessed contributions all underscored "the absence of an authoritative determination by the competent organs of the United Nations defining clearly the legal status of the Federal Republic of Yugoslavia vis-à-vis the United Nations."[41] This confusion definitively came to an end when the FRY was admitted as a new member of the United Nations on 1 November 2000. Whatever its *sui generis* position might have been before that time "could not have amounted to its membership in the Organization."[42] Thus, at the time of the filing of the application on 29 April 1999, Serbia and Montenegro was not a member of the United Nations and not a party to the ICJ Statute and, thus, was not entitled to access to the court under Article 35(1) of the statute.

This, by a process of elimination, left only the possibility that the reference to "treaties in force" in Article 35(2) might entitle Serbia and Montenegro to access to the court for the purposes of Article IX of the Genocide Convention. In a robust exercise of judicial independence, the court considered this provision at considerable length, even though it had not been cited in the applicant's oral or written pleadings. As indicated earlier, Article 35(2) of the ICJ Statute provides that

[40] *Legality of Use of Force, supra* note 1 at para. 45.

[41] *Ibid.* at para. 63.

[42] *Ibid.* at para. 77.

[t]he conditions under which the Court shall be open to other States [that is, States not parties to the Statute] shall, subject to the special provisions contained in treaties in force, be laid down by the Security Council, but in no case shall such conditions place the parties in a position of inequality before the Court.

Article 35(2) had not been central in any of the respondent's oral arguments, though a number had raised it in their written pleadings (notably Belgium, the United Kingdom, Portugal, Germany, and Italy). Canada had mentioned it in passing in the footnote referred to earlier — but only in passing in view of the failure of the applicant to invoke the provision.

The court concluded that the "treaties in force" phrase in Article 35(2) denotes only those treaties in force at the date of entry into force of the ICJ Statute — that is, in 1945. The Genocide Convention entered into force on 12 January 1951, several years after the ICJ Statute. Therefore, "even assuming that Serbia and Montenegro was a party to the *Genocide Convention* at the relevant date, Article 35(2) of the ICJ Statute does not provide it with a basis to have access to the Court."[43] In support of this conclusion, the court cites the interpretive rules in Article 31 of the Vienna Convention on the Law of Treaties, and, in particular, the requirement that interpretation should reflect the "object and purpose" of a treaty. According to the judgment, the object and purpose of Article 35(2) is to regulate access to the court, and it would be inconsistent with that objective to enable non-party states to obtain access to the court through the conclusion of a special treaty to that effect at any time.

The court relied heavily on the *travaux préparatoires* concerning an identical provision in the Statute of the Permanent Court of International Justice (PCIJ Statute), its predecessor. The negotiations at that time demonstrated that the central concern of the drafters was to ensure that the court would have jurisdiction in relation to the complexity of peace treaties connected with the settlement of the First World War — "to cover cases contemplated in agreements concluded in the aftermath of the First World War before the Statute entered into force."[44] The court conceded that the *travaux préparatoires* of the ICJ Statute are "less illuminating," but it considered that its provisions should be interpreted in the same way. As it stated in its conclusion in paragraph 112:

---

43 *Ibid.* at para. 113.

44 *Legality of Use of Force, supra* note 1 at para. 108.

Accordingly Article 35(2), must be interpreted, *mutatis mutandis,* in the same way as the equivalent text in the Statute of the Permanent Court, namely as intended to refer to treaties in force at the date of the entry into force of the new Statute, and providing for the jurisdiction of the new Court.[45]

But the court must have struggled with its interpretation, since it observes that there may be no such prior treaties referring to the jurisdiction of the court.[46]

The court also relied on two cases relating to the equivalent provision in the PCIJ Statute, neither of which is at all conclusive.[47] Finally, it invoked the remarks of two judges when the PCIJ Statute rules were being discussed in 1926, namely that the exception in Article 35 "could only be intended to cover situations provided for by the treaties of peace."[48] Seven of the fourteen permanent judges[49] made a joint declaration, which is discussed at length later in this comment, stating that they "profoundly disagreed" with the reasoning adopted by the court.

Implications of the Decision

Canada and the other NATO respondents obviously achieved the practical result they wanted: jurisdiction has been declined and the case has been removed from the list. The respondents no longer face the prospect of long and costly proceedings on a case that has far-ranging substantive issues but that could nevertheless be characterized as nuisance litigation in view of the very dubious grounds for jurisdiction.

However, for court-watchers the outcome may be of concern. It has implications for other pending cases relating to the Genocide Convention, where jurisdiction has already been confirmed. As the seven judges who authored the joint declaration stated so forcefully, it raises serious questions about the consistency of the court's jurisprudence. Finally, by adopting the most technical of grounds

---

[45] *Ibid.* at para. 112.

[46] *Ibid.* at paras. 99–112.

[47] See *ibid.* at para. 108, referring to *S.S. "Wimbledon"* case ([1923] P.C.I.J., Series A, No. 1, 6) and *Certain German Interests in Polish Upper Silesia* ([1925] P.C.I.J., Series A, No. 6).

[48] *Legality of Use of Force, supra* note 1 at para. 108.

[49] Vice-President Ranjeva and Judges Guillaume, Higgins, Kooijmans, Al-Khasawneh, Buergenthal, and Elaraby.

for denying jurisdiction under the Genocide Convention, it closes a door to jurisdiction under the convention that might conceivably have proven to be useful on some unforeseeable future occasion, and it does so on questionable grounds.

PENDING GENOCIDE CASES

Case Concerning Application of the Convention on the Prevention and Punishment of the Crime of Genocide (Bosnia and Herzegovina v. Yugoslavia (Serbia and Montenegro) (Bosnia Case)

In March 1993, the new State of Bosnia and Herzegovina instituted proceedings in the court against the Federal Republic of Yugoslavia, as it was then called.[50] By 1993, of course, the *sui generis* era that had lasted from 1992 to 2000 was underway, the old Yugoslavia had broken up, and the Security Council had determined in Resolution 777[51] of September 1992 that it had "ceased to exist" as a state. The application stated, by way of introduction, that

[t]he abominable crimes taking place in the Republic of Bosnia-Herzegovina at this time can be called by only one name: genocide. Genocide is the most evil crime a State or human being can inflict upon another State or human being. The sheer enormity of this crime requires that the nations of the world stand together as one, and with a single voice stop the destruction of the Bosnian People.

In contrast to the NATO cases, there was no question of an Optional Clause jurisdiction. The application referred to the Genocide Convention as the basis of jurisdiction,[52] although the conclusions refer as well to a wide variety of instruments, including

---

[50] *Case Concerning Application of the Convention on the Prevention and Punishment of the Crime of Genocide (Bosnia and Herzegovina v. Yugoslavia (Serbia and Montenegro),* Order of 7 October, [1993] I.C.J. Rep. 470 [*Bosnia* case].

[51] Resolution 777, *supra* note 13.

[52] See *Bosnia* case, *supra* note 50, Application of 20 March 1993, at para. 101. In the course of the proceedings respecting provisional measures of protection, the applicant attempted to invoke additional bases of jurisdiction, namely a 1919 treaty, a 1992 letter to the Arbitration Commission of the International Conference for Peace in Yugoslavia, *forum prorogatum,* and the Customary and Conventional International Laws of War and International Humanitarian Law. None of these were considered to provide a *prima facie* basis of jurisdiction, and they were definitively rejected in the Preliminary Objections judgment. See Order of 13 September 1993, respecting Further Requests for the Indication of Provisional Measures, at paras. 26–32 and the Judgment of 11 July 1996 on Preliminary Objections, at para. 41.

370   *Annuaire canadien de Droit international 2004*

the principal humanitarian law conventions and the provisions of the Charter of the United Nations with respect to the use of force.[53]

Since 1993, the *Bosnia* case has had a long and intricate procedural history, during which the court has made findings and observations that are difficult to reconcile with the reasons given in the NATO cases. The court found a *prima facie* basis of jurisdiction in the Genocide Convention in two orders respecting the provisional measures of protection made in 1993. It stated that Article IX of the Genocide Convention "could" be regarded *prima facie* as a special provision contained in a treaty in force, providing standing under Article 35(2) of the ICJ Statute and that "if Bosnia-Herzegovina and Yugoslavia are both parties to the Genocide Convention, disputes to which Article IX applies are in any event prima facie within the jurisdiction ratione personae of the Court."[54]

This was a provisional finding, and it was expressed in tentative terms. Yet the court returned to the issue of *ratione personae* jurisdiction in a judgment of 1996 on preliminary objections, and, on this occasion, its conclusions were definitive and unequivocal.[55] It affirmed, over the objections of the Federal Republic of Yugoslavia, that it had jurisdiction to adjudicate the dispute under Article IX of the Genocide Convention. And it specifically stated, in paragraph 34, that "it has jurisdiction in the present case, both *ratione personae* and *ratione materiae* on the basis of Article IX of the Genocide Convention."

As the court itself has noted, neither party challenged the legal status of the FRY in the preliminary objections. Bosnia obviously had no legal interest in challenging the standing of the party it had brought before the court, and, throughout the 1990s, Yugoslavia had strongly asserted its status as the continuation of the old Yugoslavia and, as such, as a party to the United Nations and the ICJ Statute. However, the court itself was fully aware of what it now calls the "amorphous" legal status of Yugoslavia[56] when these proceedings were launched. Indeed, it referred to the relevant Security Council and General Assembly resolutions in its first provisional measures order and noted that the "solution adopted is not free from legal difficulties" and that "the question whether or not Yugoslavia is a Member of the United Nations and as such a party to the

53 See *ibid.*, Application, at para. 135.
54 *Ibid.*, Order of 8 April 1993, at para. 19.
55 *Ibid.*, Judgment of 11 July 1996 on Preliminary Objections, para. 34.
56 *Ibid.* at para. 73.

ICJ Statute is one which the Court does not need to determine definitively at the present stage."[57] And, while not pressing the point for obvious reasons, Bosnia has alluded to the contested status of the respondent in its own application.[58]

So when it affirmed its jurisdiction *ratione personae* in 1996, the court was fully conscious that the status of Yugoslavia as a party to the statute was both controversial and unresolved. And if Yugoslavia was not a party, a possibility the court had expressly left open, it could *only* be impleaded before the court if Article IX of the Genocide Convention came within the phrase "special provisions of treaties in force" in Article 35(2) of the ICJ Statute — as the court had suggested in its 1993 Order. There is accordingly an inconsistency between this decision and the conclusion, in paragraph 113 of the recent decision in the case against Canada, that Article IX does not afford a basis for access to the court under the ICJ Statute.

The court justified the inconsistency partly on the ground that neither party had contested the status of Yugoslavia in the preliminary objections phase. The judgment refers to arguments made by Italy and especially by Belgium in the parallel NATO cases, inviting the court to "revisit" the provisional finding made in the 1993 Order. Essentially, this invitation was taken up. In relation to the affirmation of *ratione personae* jurisdiction in the 1996 judgment on preliminary objections — which, of course, was in no way provisional — the court simply noted that

[i]n the further proceedings in that case, however, the point was not pursued ... The Respondent however did not raise any objection on the ground that it was itself not a party to the Genocide Convention, nor to the ICJ Statute since, on the international plane, it had been maintaining its claim to continue the legal personality, and the membership in international organizations including the United Nations, of the Socialist Federal Republic of Yugoslavia, and its participation in international treaties. The Court, having observed that it had not been contested that Yugoslavia was party to the Genocide Convention (*I.C.J. Reports 1996 (II)*, p. 610, para. 17) found that it had jurisdiction on the basis of Article IX of that Convention.[59]

As a summary of the course of events, this is unexceptionable. However, it does not provide a real explanation of the court's change

---

[57] *Ibid.*, Order of 8 April 1993, at para. 18.

[58] *Ibid.* at para. 96.

[59] *Ibid.* at para. 9.

of position with respect to *ratione personae* jurisdiction. On a matter of jurisdiction, it should not matter that neither party has raised an objection. There is no burden of proof in relation to jurisdiction. The court must itself be satisfied that it has jurisdiction, and it can raise the question *proprio motu.* These principles are confirmed by the *Fisheries Jurisdiction Case (Spain v. Canada),*[60] where the court noted that "the establishment or otherwise of jurisdiction is not a matter for the parties but for the Court itself." Indeed, the judgment in the NATO cases asserts that in matters of jurisdiction, the court is free to base its decision on grounds of its own choosing.[61] It is therefore difficult to see why the failure of Bosnia to pursue the issue in its preliminary objections, for obvious tactical reasons, would justify a departure from the 1996 ruling that Yugoslavia was subject to the jurisdiction of the court *ratione personae.*

As a practical matter, the court might understandably overlook a possible defect in jurisdiction that neither party has identified in its pleadings. Yet the issue of access to the court was both fundamental and obvious, since the court had already referred to it in its 1993 Order. It was a matter of record. The omission of any reference to it in the 1996 judgment, combined with the express and unqualified statement that the court had jurisdiction *ratione personae* in the matter, could be interpreted fairly as an affirmation of the original suggestion that Article IX could provide a basis of access to the court under Article 35(2) of the ICJ Statute.

The court reaffirmed its jurisdiction on yet another occasion. In 1997, after the rejection of its preliminary objections, Yugoslavia filed counter-claims (since withdrawn) against Bosnia. Under Article 80, paragraph 1, of the Rules of Court, the court "may entertain a counter-claim *only if it comes within the jurisdiction of the Court.*" In an Order of 17 December 1997, the court determined that the counter-claim was admissible under Article 80. A claim brought by an entity with no right of access to the court could not come within its jurisdiction. This ruling implied, therefore, that the court could exercise *ratione personae* jurisdiction over Yugoslavia for the purpose of Article IX of the Genocide Convention.

Throughout these prolonged and complex proceedings, the court had thus treated Yugoslavia as a state with a right of access to the court for the purposes of the Genocide Convention, either by vir-

[60] *Fisheries Jurisdiction (Spain v. Canada), supra* note 21; *Bosnia* case, *supra* note 50 at para. 37.

[61] *Bosnia* case, *supra* note 50 at para. 45.

tue of UN membership — which was always highly implausible in light of the relevant UN resolutions — or, more likely, by virtue of the "treaties in force" proviso of Article 35(2). And yet the recent NATO decisions, including the one respecting Canada, expressly ruled out both of these options.

Application for Revision Case

After its change of regime and admission to the United Nations as a new member in late 2000, Yugoslavia instituted separate proceedings seeking a revision of the 1996 judgment on preliminary objections. This case is referred to by the court as the *Application for Revision* case, which culminated in a judgment of 3 February 2003, holding the application to be inadmissible. The application was rejected because a revision, under Article 61 of the ICJ Statute, requires the existence of a "new fact" that existed at the time the original judgment — that is, in 1996 — but that was only discovered after that time. Obviously, the new developments of 2000 failed to meet the first criterion. They did not constitute new facts for the purposes of Article 61.

Nothing more had to be decided. But the court nevertheless embarked on a far-ranging review of the "amorphous" legal status of Yugoslavia from 1992 to 2000 and its "*sui generis*" relationship to the United Nations. All of this inquiry, of course, was *obiter*. It was also inconclusive, as the court remarked in the NATO cases, "[n]o final and definitive conclusion was drawn by the Court from this descriptive term on the amorphous status of the Federal Republic of Yugoslavia vis-à-vis or within the United Nations during this period."[62] And yet the analysis — in the year preceding the judgment in the NATO cases — did imply that Yugoslavia was properly before the court. The joint declaration cites references in the 2003 decision to Yugoslavia's "right to appear before the Court or to be a party to a dispute before the Court" and to "its position in relation to the Statute" and concludes that

[t]he Court thus previously found in 2003 that the Federal Republic of Yugoslavia could appear before the Court between 1992 and 2000 and that this position was not changed by its admission to the United Nations in 2002.[63]

---

[62] *Legality of Use of Force, supra* note 1 at para. 73.

[63] *Application for Revision* case, *supra* note 36, Joint Declaration, at para. 10.

It is, of course, precisely this proposition that has now been repudiated by the court.

Case Concerning the Application of the Convention on the Prevention and Punishment of the Crime of Genocide (Croatia v. Serbia and Montenegro) (Croatia Case)

To complete the picture, there is another case pending before the ICJ that deals with Serbia and Montenegro and the Genocide Convention, namely the *Croatia* case.[64] This case was filed in 1999 before the status of Yugoslavia had been clarified and rectified. It invokes the Genocide Convention in connection with allegations of ethnic cleansing by Yugoslavia between 1991 and 1995. The respondent has submitted preliminary objections, but, to date, there have been no judgments or orders in the case. The jurisdictional issues, so far as the standing of Yugoslavia before the court during the 1992–2000 period is concerned, appear to be identical to those in the *Bosnia* proceedings.

RELATIONSHIP BETWEEN THE NATO CASES AND THE *BOSNIA* AND *CROATIA* CASES

A number of respondents, including Canada, suggested that Serbia and Montenegro was improperly pursuing the NATO cases only to procure a ruling that it could invoke in its pending litigation with Bosnia and Herzegovina and with Croatia. The thrust of the two points in Serbia's written observations — that it was not a party to the ICJ Statute or the Genocide Convention at the relevant times — was plainly conceived in terms of its interests in these other pending cases and not of its interests in the NATO cases. The respondents urged that the NATO cases should not be used to procure a favourable opinion from the court for use in an entirely separate proceeding. The court responded that "it cannot decline to entertain a case simply because of a suggestion as to the motives of one of the parties or because its judgment may have implications in another case."[65]

This fact may be true, although the seven judges who authored the joint declaration thought this passage "does not adequately

---

64 *Case Concerning the Application of the Convention on the Prevention and Punishment of the Crime of Genocide (Croatia v. Serbia and Montenegro)*, Order of 14 September, [1999] I.C.J. Rep. 1015 [*Croatia* case].

65 See *Legality of Use of Force supra* note 1 at para. 39.

reflect the role of the Court as a judicial institution."[66] In any event, there is something troubling in the way that the court appears to have been induced in the NATO cases into giving the very ruling that Serbia and Montenegro had failed to obtain in the *Application for Revision* case. Once the court had filed its written observations in the NATO cases, it was clear that Serbia and Montenegro had either endorsed or failed to contest all of the principal contentions of its adversaries. There would have been no point in going on with these cases had it not been for the unsettled questions in the *Bosnia* and *Croatia* cases.

At the very least, Serbia has successfully managed, through the NATO cases, to obtain what amounts to an advisory opinion from the court — something that is normally the exclusive prerogative of the organs of the United Nations. In a sense, Serbia and Montenegro was quite candid about this objective. It submitted that only a decision of the court could clarify the "intricate and controversial" issue of the legal status of Yugoslavia during the 1990s. The court responded that its function was not to "engage in the clarification of a controverted issue of a general nature."[67] However, in practical terms, this is precisely what the court has done — except that "muddying the waters" rather than "clarification" might be a better phrase, where the jurisdictional foundations of other proceedings, which have already been settled by a judgment of the court, have once more been put into doubt.

In summary, the recent decision in the NATO cases represents a radical change of position in two senses. On the one hand, the court has chosen not to base its decision on the grounds invoked in its own Orders at the provisional measures stage of these cases — the interpretation of the time clause in the purported Optional Clause declaration and the subject matter scope of the Genocide Convention. At the same time, it has contradicted the approach taken thus far in the *Bosnia* case. As the seven judges stated in paragraph 9 of their joint declaration, the "change of position is all the more surprising as the reasoning now adopted by the Court is at odds with judgments or orders previously rendered by the Court."

The *Bosnia* case has now been set down for hearings to begin on 27 February 2006. These are to be hearings on the merits. There should be no question at this stage of a renewed consideration of

---

[66] *Ibid.*, Joint Declaration of Vice-President Ranjeva and Judges Guillaume, Higgins, Kooijmans, Al-khasawneh, Buergenthal and Elaraby, at para. 13.

[67] *Ibid.* at paras. 36 and 37.

jurisdiction *ratione personae,* which has been conclusively determined in the 1996 judgment and which is *res judicata* between the parties and which the court has reaffirmed in the *Application for Revision* case. What remains to be seen is whether the court will take this opportunity to attempt a reconciliation of the contradictions between its findings in the *Bosnia* case and its findings in the more recent NATO cases. For if no reconciliation is attempted, the impression will be inescapable that the court is proceeding to a judgment on the merits in circumstances where it now has determined, in clear and unequivocal terms, that it has no jurisdiction *ratione personae* over one of the parties.

ISSUE OF JUDICIAL CONSISTENCY

As already pointed out, the court was unanimous on the outcome but sharply divided on the reasons. In fact, the permanent judges were equally divided. Seven out of fourteen[68] authored a joint declaration, which began with a statement that they "profoundly disagree with the reasoning upon which the Judgment rests, in particular the ground upon which the Court has found it has no jurisdiction [that is, Article 35, paragraph 2]."[69] It may be of interest that the seven judges include all of the judges originating in the NATO countries, but it was certainly not a "North-South" ideological split — three of the seven are from the developing world. It was only the adherence of Judge Ad Hoc Kreća, appointed by Serbia and Montenegro, that created a bare majority in favour of the reasons for judgment — although even Judge Kreæa filed lengthy reasons of his own as well.

The fault line that divided the court concerned the importance — or otherwise — of judicial consistency. The majority reasons make light of this issue. Referring to its observations on Article 35(2) in its first provisional measures order in the *Bosnia* case, the court simply notes that the Order "was made in a different case; but as the Court observed in a previous case in which questions of *res judicata* and Article 59 of the ICJ Statute were raised, "[t]he real question is whether, in this case, there is cause not to follow the reasoning and conclusions of earlier cases."[70]

---

68 There are fifteen permanent judges, but Judge Simma did not participate.

69 *Legality of Use of Force, supra* note 1, Joint Declaration, at para. 1.

70 *Ibid.,* Judgment, at para. 97. The quotation refers to *Land and Maritime Boundary between Cameroon and Nigeria (Cameroon v. Nigeria),* Preliminary Objections, Judgment, [1998] I.C.J. Rep. 292 at para. 28). Article 59 of the ICJ Statute, *supra*

The joint declaration sets out a very different philosophy. "Consistency," it states, "is the essence of judicial reasoning. This is especially true in different phases of the same case or with regard to closely related cases."[71] This is the first of three principles proposed in the declaration, which continues as follows:

Second, the principle of certitude will lead the Court to choose the ground which is the most secure in law and to avoid a ground which is less safe and, indeed, perhaps doubtful. Third, as the principal judicial organ of the United Nations, the Court will, in making its selection among possible grounds, be mindful of the possible implications and consequences for the other pending cases.[72]

With respect to the second criterion, the Joint Declaration — differing in this respect from the Canadian view — indicates that it is "far from self-evident" that the *sui generis* position of Yugoslavia from 1992 to 2000 could not have amounted to UN membership.[73] And with respect to the third, the seven judges concluded that the judgment "goes back on decisions previously adopted by the Court," that it cast doubt on whether Yugoslavia was a party to the Genocide Convention during that period, and that

[s]uch an approach could call into question the solutions adopted by the Court with respect to its jurisdiction in the case brought by Bosnia-Herzegovina against Serbia and Montenegro for the application of the Genocide Convention.[74]

There is no principle of *stare decisis* in international jurisprudence. On the other hand, the role of judicial decisions as a source of law is recognized by the court's own statute in Article 38(1)(d). This implies that some weight must be given to the jurisprudence, particularly where recent decisions in closely connected cases are at issue. This provision was not referred to in the joint declaration, but it supports the reasoning of the seven judges who signed it. Indeed, there is a very recent decision of the court that indicates a renewed respect for precedent and consistency. On 10 February

---

note 6, provides that "[t]he decision of the Court has no binding force except between the parties and in respect of that particular case."

[71] *Legality of Use of Force, supra* note 1, Joint Declaration, at para. 3.

[72] *Ibid.*

[73] *Ibid.* at para. 12.

[74] *Ibid.* at para. 13.

2005, the court upheld the preliminary objections of Germany in the *Case Concerning Certain Property (Liechtenstein v. Germany)*.[75] It concluded that it lacked jurisdiction *ratione temporis* because the "real source" of the dispute pre-dated the effective date of the title of jurisdiction invoked by the applicant.[76] In so doing, the court applied the classic tests of *ratione temporis* jurisdiction as set out in its own jurisprudence and that of its predecessor the Permanent Court of International Justice.[77]

What is puzzling is why, in the NATO cases, the court chose to involve itself in a tangle of contradictions, when the matter could have been disposed of much more easily on far simpler and more persuasive grounds — some of which would simply have endorsed its own reasons as set out in the 1999 provisional measures orders. It could, accordingly, have reaffirmed the position that the time clause in the Optional Clause declaration excluded jurisdiction over a dispute that had already crystallized when the declaration was filed and that the true subject matter of the dispute was the use of force and the *jus in bello* — not genocide as it is legally defined. Indeed, whatever view might have been taken of the lawfulness of the use of force against Yugoslavia in 1999, it seems absurd to have characterized it as genocide in any sense of the word.

However, Canada and the other respondents had offered an even simpler solution. Serbia had never contested a single point set out in Canada's written submissions on jurisdiction and admissibility. It had never objected to the formal submission or plea set out in the conclusion to these pleadings, namely that the court had no jurisdiction and that the case was inadmissible. Indeed, everything set out in its very summary written observations pointed inexorably to only one possible conclusion — that, as Canada had contended, though for somewhat different reasons, the court had no jurisdiction. In these unusual if not unique circumstances, it should not

---

[75] *Case Concerning Certain Property (Liechtenstein v. Germany)*, Judgement of 10 February 2005, available at <www.icj-cij.org>.

[76] Article 1 of the European Convention for the Peaceful Settlement of Disputes of 29 April 1957, entered into force between Germany and Liechtenstein on 18 February 1980. See Preliminary Objections of Germany in this case of 27 June 2002, para. 65 on the court website at <www.icj-cij.org>. The court decided that the dispute was ultimately rooted in events that took place in 1945 and not in judicial decisions of the German courts during the 1990s.

[77] See *Legality of Use of Force, supra* note 1, Judgment of 10 February 2005, at paras. 41–46.

have been difficult to fashion a judicial rationale for dismissing the case *in limine litis.*[78] The rules contemplated that the purpose of the oral proceedings was to deal with the issues that divided the parties after the written pleadings were completed, but, in this case, there appeared to be nothing that still divided the parties and no real purpose in pursuing the contentious proceedings to the bitter end.

The court took a strict view of Article 89 of the Rules of Court on discontinuance, which requires a notice in writing from the applicant.[79] At the same time, as the separate opinion of Judge Higgins points out, Serbia had put itself "out of conformity" with the rules by resiling from specified heads of jurisdiction without proffering others; and a request for a judicial decision on jurisdiction in these circumstances "is totally outside the contemplation of the Rules."[80] Further, in her opinion, the "disorderly nature" of this course and Serbia's "incoherent manner of proceeding" warranted a removal of the case from the list "as an exercise of inherent power to protect the integrity of the judicial process."[81]

It is equally troubling — the joint declaration calls it "astonishing"[82] — that the court should have chosen to base its decision on Article 35(2) of the ICJ Statute, when the applicant had never invoked that text as a basis of jurisdiction. In a veiled reference to the *Bosnia* case, Judge Higgins refers to the "remarkable attention given by the Court to Article 35, para. 2," concluding that

going beyond what the Applicant requested in the present case, the Court has devoted some 23 paragraphs to laying the grounds for a finding that Article 35, paragraph 2, of the Statute could not have been an alternative basis for allowing access to the Court in respect of the Genocide Convention so far as Serbia and Montenegro is concerned. *This exercise was clearly unnecessary for the present case. Its relevance can lie, and only lie, in another pending case.* I believe the Court should not have entered at all upon this ground in the present case.[83]

[78] See *ibid.,* Separate Opinion of Judge Kooijmans, at para. 13 and Separate Opinion of Judge Higgins, at paras. 11–16.

[79] *Ibid.* at paras. 30–31.

[80] *Ibid.* at paras. 13–14.

[81] *Ibid.* at paras. 12 and 16.

[82] *Ibid.* at para. 11.

[83] *Ibid.* at para. 17 [emphasis added].

Not only were there simpler and more appropriate ways of dismissing the case; the restrictive interpretation given to the reference to "treaties in force" in Article 35(2) is open to question and might someday come back to haunt the court — assuming, of course, that some weight is once again to be given to the need for consistency. The interpretation is narrower than the actual words would indicate. The negotiating history of a convention may properly be invoked to clarify the scope of ambiguous terms. But it does not follow that the general terms in a multilateral convention of indefinite duration should be restricted to the immediate, practical concerns of the drafters. If the language is general and unqualified, it should be given its full effect.

The court sought to put its interpretation in a traditional context of treaty interpretation by citing the general interpretive rules of Article 31 of the Vienna Convention on the Law of Treaties.[84] It states that a broader interpretation "would be quite incompatible with the object and purpose of Article 35, paragraph 2, namely the regulation of access to the Court by States non-parties to the Statute." This, with respect, rather overstates the case: it would simply broaden the range of situations in which such states might have access.

The precedents invoked by the court for a restrictive interpretation are far from compelling. The *travaux préparatoires* certainly confirm the preoccupation of the drafters with the First World War peace treaties, but they do not demonstrate an intention to *limit* the exception to those treaties. And the remarks of two judges in the course of the meetings of the court when the 1926 rules were being drafted fall well short of the weight that would be accorded to an actual judgment of the court.[85]

The arguments on this question in the separate opinion of Judge Elaraby are also of interest. He argues, first, that the Genocide Convention can be considered a treaty connected with the peace settlement of 1945 by analogy to the collection of treaties connected with the settlement of the First World War. As such, it would come within the exception in Article 35(2) even on the restrictive interpretation adopted by the court. Second, he suggests with the support of scholarly commentary, that the expression "treaties in force" should be broadly construed to encompass multilateral treaties addressing violations of *jus cogens* norms.[86]

---

[84] Vienna Convention on the Law of Treaties, 1155 U.N.T.S. 331.

[85] *Legality of Use of Force, supra* note 1 at para. 108.

[86] *Ibid.*, Separate Opinion of Judge Elaraby, at part III.

There is another fundamental point. The majority analysis comes close to contradicting the principle that the provisions of a treaty must be given some practical effect — the principle of an *effet utile*. The judgment states in paragraph 112, referring to its interpretation that the exception covers only treaties in force at the date of entry into force of the new statute, that "in fact, no such prior treaties, referring to the jurisdiction of the present Court, have been brought to the attention of the Court, *and it may be that none existed*."[87] This statement would leave the provision with no *effet utile* at all.

One is left with the unmistakable impression that the majority must have shifted its ground so radically for reasons that the court has chosen not to identify but that seem not to be directly related to the NATO cases. The dismissal of the case is welcome, but it comes encumbered with reasons that are perplexing. It is to be hoped that some clarification will be provided in the reasons to be given in the final judgment on the merits in the forthcoming *Bosnia* case.

COLLEEN SWORDS AND ALAN WILLIS[88]
Government of Canada

Sommaire

La décision de la Cour internationale de justice dans l'*affaire relative à la licéité de l'emploi de la force (Serbie-et-Monténégro c. Canada)*

Au printemps de 1999, les alliés de l'OTAN ont mené une campagne de bombardements de plusieurs semaines contre la République fédérale de Yougoslavie. Cette campagne a été lancée à la suite de l'échec des négociations de Rambouillet, France, concernant la situation au Kosovo, que les agences des Nations Unies qualifiaient de "crise humanitaire." À la fin d'avril, quelques jours seulement avant le dépôt de sa déclaration en vertu de la clause facultative du Statut de la Cour internationale de justice pour accepter la compétence obligatoire de la Cour, sous certaines réserves, la Yougoslavie a introduit une procédure devant la Cour contre dix alliés de l'OTAN, y compris le Canada. Elle a joint à sa requête une demande en

---

[87] *Ibid.* at para. 112 [emphasis added].

[88] Colleen Swords is Legal Adviser, Foreign Affairs Canada and was Agent for Canada in this case. Alan Willis was Counsel and Advocate for the government of Canada in this case. The views expressed in this comment are those of the authors only and do not necessarily represent the views of the government of Canada.

*indication de "mesures conservatoires" en vertu du Statut pour enjoindre
aux alliés de l'OTAN de cesser leur emploi de la force contre la Yougoslavie.
Celle-ci y invoquait sa nouvelle déclaration et la clause compromissoire de la
Convention sur le génocide comme fondement de la compétence de la Cour.
En juin 1999, la Cour a rejeté la demande de mesures conservatoires au
motif qu'elle n'avait pas la compétence prima facie. Le Canada et les autres
défendeurs ont déposé des exceptions préliminaires relativement à la
compétence de la Cour et à la recevabilité de l'affaire. Les exceptions relatives à la compétence de la Cour sont fondées sur les motifs présentés à
l'étape de la demande en mesures conservatoires, auxquels la Cour avait
souscrit dans une large mesure: premièrement, que la Yougoslavie n'était
pas alors membre des Nations Unies et qu'elle n'avait donc pas le droit de
faire une déclaration en vertu de la clause facultative; deuxièmement, que
la déclaration était valide pour les différends à venir; et troisièmement, que
la question faisant l'objet de différend n'était pas couverte par la Convention sur le génocide et qu'elle ne pouvait donc pas être invoquée pour établir
la compétence de la Cour. À la suite des audiences tenues en avril 2004, la
Cour a statué le 15 décembre 2004 qu'elle n'avait pas compétence dans le
dossier. L'ordonnance est fondée exclusivement sur le fait que la Yougoslavie
n'était pas membre des Nations Unies et n'avait pas le pouvoir d'agir devant
la Cour en 1999. La Cour conclut que l'exception à l'article 35(2) du
Statut de la Cour relativement aux "traités en vigueur" n'autorise pas un
non membre des Nations Unies à comparaître devant la Cour dans une
affaire soulevant la Convention sur le génocide. Selon l'interprétation de la
Cour, cette exception ne s'applique qu'aux traités en vigueur avant 1945.
Ce raisonnement est surprenant, étant donné que la Cour s'est toujours
efforcée d'éviter la question du statut de membre des Nations Unies, tant en
ordonnant des mesures conservatoires qu'en rendant sa décision dans une
procédure très similaire prise par la Bosnie et la Croatie contre la Yougoslavie
en vertu de la Convention sur le génocide. Il reste à voir comment la Cour
réconciliera cet arrêt avec sa jurisprudence antérieure concernant sa
compétence dans la procédure prise par la Bosnie. Dans cette affaire, la
Cour a déjà confirmé sa compétence, et les audiences sur le fond sont prévues
en 2006.*

Summary

The Decision of the International Court of Justice in the *Case Concerning Legality of Use of Force (Serbia and Montenegro v. Canada)*

*In the spring of 1999, the NATO allies conducted a bombing campaign
against the Federal Republic of Yugoslavia for several weeks. The campaign*

*was a response to the failure of negotiations at Rambouillet, France, relat-
ing to a situation in Kosovo that United Nations agencies had characterized as a "humanitarian crisis." In late April, only a few days after filing
an Optional Clause declaration under the Statute of the International Court
of Justice accepting the compulsory jurisdiction of the court subject to reservations, Yugoslavia initiated proceedings in the court against ten NATO
allies, including Canada. The application was accompanied by a request
for the indication of "provisional measures" pursuant to the statute, enjoining the NATO allies from continuing the use of force against Yugoslavia.
Yugoslavia relied upon its new declaration and upon the compromissory
clause of the Genocide Convention as grounds of jurisdiction. In June 1999,
the court refused the request for provisional measures on the ground that it
lacked prima facie jurisdiction. Canada and other remaining respondents
filed preliminary objections on jurisdiction and admissibility. The objections on jurisdiction were based on the grounds that had been advanced at
the provisional measures stage and largely endorsed by the court: first, that
Yugoslavia was not then a member of the United Nations and was therefore
not entitled to make an Optional Clause declaration; second, that the declaration was limited to future disputes; and, third, that the subject matter of
the dispute was not covered by the Genocide Convention, which could therefore not be invoked to establish jurisdiction.*

*Following oral hearings in April 2004, the court ruled in a judgment of
15 December 2004 that it lacked jurisdiction. The ruling was based exclusively on the fact that Yugoslavia lacked United Nations membership and
standing in the court in 1999. The judgment concludes that the exception
in Article 35(2) of the statute relating to "treaties in force" does not entitle a
non-member of the United Nations to appear before the court in a matter
related to the Genocide Convention, which the Court interprets as applying
only to treaties in existence before 1945. This reasoning came as a surprise,
since the court had assiduously avoided the issue of UN membership both in
its provisional measures ruling and in its decisions in closely related proceedings taken by Bosnia and Croatia against Yugoslavia pursuant to the
Genocide Convention. It remains to be seen how the judgment will be recon-
ciled with rulings already made on jurisdiction in the proceedings taken by
Bosnia, where jurisdiction has already been confirmed and where hearings
on the merits are scheduled for 2006.*

The Role of Discipline in the Military

Discipline: Training in the practice of arms and military evolutions; training or skill in military affairs generally; military skill and experience; the art of war; the order maintained and observed among persons under control or command; a system of rules for conduct.

— *Oxford English Dictionary*

In so far as military operations and service are concerned, discipline has two purposes. It serves in time of peace to ensure order within the military system. During conflict, it has a function whereby it operates to ensure conduct that is in compliance with the laws of armed conflict to secure obedience to orders on pain of sanction. Without some system of order to which compliance must be given, an army would rapidly become an unruly mob. George Washington expressed it well: "Discipline is the soul of an army. It makes small numbers formidable, procures success to the weak, and esteem to all."[1] Two hundred years later, Justice William O. Douglas of the United States Supreme Court expressed a similar view: "The military by tradition and by necessity demands discipline; and those necessities require obedience in training and in action. A command is speech brigaded with action, and permissible commands may not be disobeyed."[2] Machiavelli, in discussing the essentials of princedom, wrote: "A prince should therefore have no other aim or thought, nor take up any other thing for his study, but war and its organization and discipline, for this is the only art that is necessary to one who commands."[3] These comments serve as a background to the remarks of Canada's chief justice in the Supreme Court of Canada in 1992:

This article is based on an address to Court Martial Appeal Court of Canada Education Seminar 2003.

[1] George Washington, Letter of Instructions to the Captains of the Virginia Regiments, 29 July 1759.

[2] *Parker v. Levy*, 417 US 733 (1974).

[3] Niccolo Machiavelli, *The Prince* (1532), ch. 14.

The safety and well-being of Canadians depends considerably on the willingness and readiness of a force of men and women to defend threats to the national security. To maintain the armed forces in a state of readiness, the military must be in a position to enforce internal discipline effectively and efficiently. Breaches of military discipline must be dealt with speedily and frequently punished more seriously than would be the case of a civilian engaged in such conduct.[4]

As becomes clear from their writings, the earliest Chinese commentators on military matters were drawing attention to the need for discipline in the armed forces:

In the earliest stages of the Shang and Chou [dynasties, 1523–256 BC], force size was apparently irregular; it was enumerated, constituted and organized to meet the situation and the demand. However, with the vastly augmented scope of conflict in the Warring States and the imposition of universal service obligations, military hierarchy and discipline became essential, as is evident from the emphasis on them in the *Seven Military Classics*.[5]

Selected quotations from these classics might be helpful. Thus, in *The Methods of the Ssu-Ma*, which is from the fourth century BC, it is stated: "The solidarity of a campaign army derives from military discipline that maintains order in formation, does not exhaust the strength of men or horses, and — whether moving slowly or rapidly — does not exceed the measure of the commands."[6] Sun-tzu, too, in his *Art of War* remarks: "The laws (for military organization and discipline) encompass organization and regulations, the Tao[7] of command, and the management of logistics."[8] More detail is to be found in *Wu-tzu:*

Marquis Wu asked: "What measures will ensure the soldiers will be victorious?"
Wu Ch'i replied: "Control is foremost."
Marquis Wu again asked: "Is it not large numbers?
"If the laws and orders are not clear, rewards and punishments not trusted; when sounding the gongs will not cause them to halt or the beating of the

---

4 *R. v. Généreux*, [1992] 1 S.C.R. 259, at 293.

5 Ralph D. Sawyer, *The Seven Military Classics of Ancient China* (1993) at 375.

6 *Ibid.* at 131.

7 "The Tao causes the people to be fully in accord with the ruler: they will die with him; they will live with him and not fear danger." *Ibid.*

8 *Ibid.* at 157.

drum to advance, then even if you have one million men, of what use would they be? What is meant by control is that when stationary (in camp) they observe the forms of propriety and when in action they are awesome. When they advance they cannot be withstood; when they withdraw they cannot be pursued. Their advancing and withdrawing are measured; the left and right flanks respond to the signal flags. Even if broken off from the main order they preserve their formations; even if scattered they will reform lines. They will hold together in peace; they will hold together in danger. Their number can be assembled together, but cannot be forced apart. They can be employed, but they cannot be exhausted. No matter where you can dispatch them, no one under Heaven will be able to withstand them. They are called the troops of a father and son."[9]

Finally, reference might be made to the *Questions and Replies between T'ang T'ai-Tsung and Li Wei-kung:*

The T'ai-tsung said: "The constrained and disciplined army — when it realizes appropriate strategies — flourishes, but when it lacks them perishes. My lord, please compile and record the writings of those through the ages who excelled at constraint and discipline, provide diagrams, and submit them to me. I will select the quintessential ones to be transmitted to later ages."[10]

In ancient India, discipline was also a basic principle governing the behaviour of kings and their forces during war. As is recounted by W.S. Armour,

[n]o one should slay him who goes out to procure forage or fodder, camp followers or those who do menial service. No one should kill him who is skilled in a special art. He is no son of the Vishni race who slayeth a woman, a boy or an old man. Let him not strike who has been grievously wounded. A wounded opponent shall either be sent to his own home, or, if brought to the victor's quarters, have his wounds attended to, and when cured he shall be set at liberty. This is eternal duty. Night slaughter is horrible and infamous. With death our enmity has terminated ... Customs, laws and family usages which obtain in a country should be preserved when that country has been acquired. Having conquered of his foe, let him not abolish or disregard the laws of that country. A king should never do such injury to his foe as would rankle in the latter's heart.[11]

---

[9] *Ibid.* at 214.

[10] *Ibid.* at 359.

[11] See W.S. Armour, *Customs and Warfare in Ancient India, Transactions of the Grotius Society*, vol. 8 (1922) at 71, 75–7, and 81.

In the early days of Islam, somewhat similar rules were laid down concerning the behaviour required during battle. Abu Bakr, the first caliph after the death of the Prophet, commanded his troops: "Let there be no perfidy, no falsehood in your treaties with the enemy. Be faithful to all things, proving yourselves upright and noble and maintaining your word and promises truly."[12] During the Battle of the Camel in 656 AD, the Caliph Ali instructed:

> When ye defeat them, do not kill their wounded, do not behead the prisoners, do not pursue those who return and retreat, do not enslave their women, do not mutilate their dead, do not uncover what should remain covered, do not approach their property except what weapons, beast, male or female slaves you find in their camps; all the rest is to be inherited by their heirs according to the law of God.[13]

By the ninth century, the Islamic law of nations[14] had banned the killing of women, children, the aged, the blind, the crippled, and the helplessly insane. Moreover, while fighting was in progress between the *dar al-islam* (the territory of Islam) and the *dar al-harb* (the rest of the world, also known as the territory of war), Muslims were under legal obligations to respect the rights of non-Muslims, both combatants and civilians, which included the understanding that prisoners of war should not be killed. In fact, the opening chapter of the *Siyar* is entitled "Traditions Relating to the Conduct of War" and states:

> Whenever the Apostle of God sent forth an army or a detachment, he charged its commander personally to fear God, the Most High, and he enjoined the Muslims who were with him to do good [i.e. to conduct themselves properly]. And said: ... Do not cheat or commit treachery, nor should you mutilate anyone or kill children ... The Apostle of God prohibited the killing of women.[15]

Perhaps more important from the point of view of discipline are the comments relating to the "penalties in the territory of war." The following exchange reflects upon the powers of a governor of a city or province within his own army camp, when his army has

---

12 Al Muttaquii, *Book of Kanzul'umman*, vol. 4 (1949) at 472.

13 Mohammad Talaat Al Ghunaimii, *The Muslim Conception of International Law and the Western Approach* (1968) at 140.

14 Majid Khadduri, translated, *The Islamic Law of Nations* (Shaybani's *Siyar*) (1966), sections 29–32, 47, 81, 110–1.

15 *Ibid.*, sections 1 and 29.

entered the territory of war: "I asked: Would he be (competent) to order the cutting off of the hand for theft and enforce the penalty for false accusation ... and to enforce the penalties for zina (adultery or fornication) and (the drinking of wine)? He replied: Yes."[16]

According to the early sixteenth-century writers on the law of war, discipline was strictly enforced in the Roman armies,[17] particularly in regard to conduct within the lines. Ayala, in his study of the law of war, devoted an entire chapter to military discipline, pointing out that

[h]istory tells us how great the importance of military discipline is: so does daily experience; and it is abundantly clear that the conquest of the world by the Roman people was accomplished by nothing else than the training in arms, the discipline of the camp, and the practice of campaigning. Quintilian puts this very well when he says "Rightly considered, the empire of the Roman people has been based until now on military discipline ... It was the sternness of our institutions, our system of military service, our love of toil, our daily exercisings, and our assiduous consideration of questions of war." And so Valerius Maximus said that there was no bond so lasting as that of military discipline, that preeminent adornment and buttress of the Roman power, in whose bosom repose the serene and tranquil blessings of peace ... [W]e cannot have a better instance of what the neglect or maintenance of military discipline means, than that of the Romans; for they who aforetime were superior to all people in their instinct for justice and their military glory, later on, when discipline decayed, were conquered by every one.[18]

As a general comment, Ayala says:

The rigor of discipline varies with authority of commanders ... It is rather by the obedient attitude than by the putting forth of officers' orders that a military situation is kept in healthy condition and that army will be bravest in time of crisis which is the quietest before the crisis.[19]

It is interesting to note that these early writers were more concerned with evidence from Rome than with the military regulations of the

---

16 *Ibid.,* sections 128–31.

17 See, for example, Pierino Bellii, *De Re Militari et Bello Tractatus* (1563) (English translation by Herbert C. Nutting, 1936), Part VIII, ch. I "On the Crimes of Soldiers and Their Punishment," 219–46.

18 Balthazar Ayala, *De Jure et Officiis Bellicis* (1582) (English translation by John Pawley Bate, 1912), Book III, ch. I, 171–6.

19 *Ibid.* at 175. See, for a modern example of this, the discussion later in this text concerning the Canadian Airborne Regiment and its record in Somalia.

princes of Europe. From earliest feudal times, examples are to be found of military codes based on these two principles. An Ordinance of Richard I, promulgated in 1190 and meant to prevent disputes between the soldiers and sailors during the voyage to the holy land, provided "[w]hoever shall slay a man on ship-board, he shall be bound to the dead man and thrown into the sea, If he shall slay him on land he shall be bound to the dead man and buried in the earth." [20] In fact, of Richard I it has been said:

Richard was clearly a fierce disciplinarian. When he arrived, en route for his crusade, at Messina in Sicily, one of his first actions was to erect a gallows outside his camp. When battle seemed likely, he announced that anyone who ran away on foot should lose a foot, and that any knight who deserted would be stripped of the belt which signified his status. The line of battle was to be drawn up following military discipline. [21]

More significant from the point of view of military discipline, as it is understood today, within the lines as well as in the field are the Articles of War of Richard II in 1335:

These are the Statutes, Ordinances and Customs, to be observed in the Army ... Firstly. That all manner of persons, of what nation, state, or condition they may be, shall be obedient to our lord the King, to his constable and mareschall, under penalty of everything they can forfeit in body and goods.

III. that no one be so hardy as to rob and pillage the church, nor to destroy any man belonging to holy church, religious or otherwise, nor any woman, nor to take them prisoners, if not bearing arms; nor to force any woman, upon pain of being hanged ...

VI. that every one be obedient to his captain, and perform watch and ward, forage, and all other things belonging to his duty, under penalty of losing his horse and armour, and his body in arrest to the mareschall, till he shall have made his peace with his lord or master, according to the award of the court ...

VIII. no one shall make riot or contention in the army for debate of arms, prisoners, lodgings, or any other thing whatsoever, nor cause any party or assembly of persons, under pain (the principals as well as the parties) of losing their horses and armour and having their body in arrest ... Any person conceiving himself aggrieved shall make known his grievance to the constable and mareschall, and right shall be done him.

[20] William Winthrop, *Military Law and Precedents* (1886) at 903.

[21] Michael Prestwich, *Armies and Warfare in the Middle Ages — The English Experience* (1996) at 179–80.

IX. that no one be so hardy as to make a contention or debate in the army on account of any grudge respecting time past, or for any thing to come; if in such contest or debate any one shall be slain, those who were the occasion shall be hanged ...

XIII. if any one takes a prisoner, and another shall join him, demanding a part [of the prisoner's worth], threatening that otherwise he will kill him (the prisoner), he shall have no part ... and if he kills the said prisoner he shall be in arrest to the mareschall ...

XV. that for no news or affray whatsoever that may happen in the army, any one shall put himself in disarray in his battail, whether on an expedition or in quarters, unless by assignment of his chieftain, under pain of losing horse and armour.

XVII. that no one be so hardy as to raise a banner or pennon of St. George, or any other, to draw together the people out of the army, to go to any place whatsoever, under pain, that those who thus make themselves captains shall be drawn and hanged, and those who follow them be beheaded, and all their goods and heritages forfeited to the King.

XVIII. that if any one shall take a prisoner, as soon as he comes to the army, he shall bring him to his captain or master; and that his said captain or master shall bring him to our lord the King, constable or mareschall, as soon as he well can, without taking him elsewhere, in order that they may examine him concerning news and intelligence of the enemy, under pain of losing his third to him who may first make it known to the constable ...

XXII. if any one take a prisoner, he shall take his faith, and also his hacinet, or gauntlet, to be a pledge and sign that he is so taken, he shall leave him under the guard of some of his soldiers, under pain, that if he takes him, and does not do as is here directed, and another comes afterwards, and take from him (if not under a guard) as is said, his hacinet or right gauntlet in pledge, he shall have the prisoner, though the first had taken his faith."[22]

The Code of Articles and Military Lawes to be Observed in the Warres propounded by Gustavus Adolphus of Sweden in 1621[23] is more directly concerned with what is today understood as discipline. After laying down a series of provisions relating to the worship of God, prayer, and blasphemy, with accompanying punishments, the code proceeds to deal with disciplinary matters both within the lines and in the field:

17 ... no government can stand firmly, unless it be first rightly grounded; and that the Lawes be rightly observed; We, the King doe hereby make

---

[22] Winthrop, *supra* note 20 at 904.

[23] *Ibid.* at 907.

known unto all our Souldiers and Subjects, as well Nobles as others: that in our presence they presume not to doe any unseemly thing: but that every one give us our due honour, as we ought to receive; who presume to doe the contrary, shall bee punished at our pleasure.

18. Next shall our Officers and Souldiers be obedient to our Generall and Field-Marshal, with others our Officers next under them, in whatsoever they shall command belonging unto our service, upon paine of punishment ...

19. Whosoever behaves not himself obediently unto our great Generall ... shall be kept in irons or in prison until such time as he shall be brought to his answer, before a Councell of Warre, where being found guilty, whether it were wilfully done or not, he shall stand to the order of the Court, to lay what punishment upon him they shall think convenient, according as the person and fact is.

20. And if any shall offer to discredit these great Officers by word of mouth or otherwise, and not be able by proof to make it good, hee shall be put to death without mercy.

21. Whosoever offers to lift up any manner of Armes against them, whether hee doth them hurt or not, shall be punished by death.

22. If any offers to strike them with his hand, whether hee hit or miss, he shall lose his right hand.

25. As every Officer and Souldier ought to be obedient unto our Generall and other great Officers; so shall they in the under Regiments be unto their Colonell, Lieftenant-Colonell, Serjeant-Major, and Quarter-Master, upon paine of the same punishment before mentioned.

26. If any Souldier or Officer ... shall offer any wrong or abuse unto his superior Officer either by word or deed, or shall refuse any duty commanded him, tending unto our service, he shall be punisht according to the importance of the fact.

27. If any Colonell, Lieftenant-Colonell, Serjeant-Major, or Quarter-Master, shall command any thing not belonging unto our service, he shall answer to the complaint before the Court.

28. In like manner if any inferiour Officer ... does challenge any common Souldier to be guilty of any dishonest action; the Souldier finding himself guiltless, may lawfully call the said Officer to make proofe of his word before the Court as his equall.

29. If any Souldier ... shall offer to strike his Officer that shall command him any duty for our service, he shall first lose his hand, and be then turned out of the Quarter. And if it be done in any Fort or place beleaguered after the watch is set, he shall lose his life for it.

30. And if he doth hurt to any of them, whether it be in the field or not, he shall be shot to death.

33. He who shall in anger draw his sword while his Colours are flying, either in Battell or upon the March, shall be shot to death; if it be done in any strength or fortified place, he shall lose his hand, and be turned out of the Quarter.

36. If any shall hinder the Provost Marshall Generall, his Lieftenant or servants, when they are to execute anything that is for our service; who does the contrary, shall lose his life.

37. Leave is given unto the Provost Marshall Generall to apprehend all whatsoever that offend against these Articles of Warre. All other offenders he may likewise apprehend by his owne authority.

44. All Officers shall diligently see that the Souldiers plye their worke, when they are commanded so to doe; he that neglects his duty therein shall be punished according to the discretion of the Court.

45. All Souldiers ought diligently to honour and obey their Officers, and especially being by them commanded upon service; but if at any time they can on the contrary discover that they are commanded upon a service which is to our prejudice in any manner of way; then shall that souldier not obey him what charge soever he receives from him, but is presently to give notice of it.

46. No Colonell or Captaine shall command his souldiers to doe any un-lawful thing; which who so does, shall be punished according to the dis-cretion of the Judges ...

51. He that comes off his watch where he is commanded to keep his Guard, or drinks himselfe drunke upon his watch or space of Sentinell, shall be shot to death.

53. When any march is to be made, every man that is sworn shall follow his Colours; whoever presumes without leave to stay behind shall be punished.

56. He that runnes from his Colours in the field shall dye for it; and if any of his Comrades kill him in the meane time he shall be free.

58. Whatever Regiment shall first charge the enemy and retire afterwards from them before they come to dint of sword with them, shall answer it before our highest Marshal's Court.

59. And if the thing be occasioned by any Officer, he shall be publikley disgraced for it, and then turned out of the Leaguer.

60. But if both Officers and Souldiers bee found faulty alike, then shall the officers be punished as aforesaid. If it bee in the Souldiers alone, then shall every tenth man be hanged; the rest shall bee condemned to carry all the filth out of the Leaguer, until such time as they performe some exploit that is worthy to procure their pardon, after which they shall bee cleer of their former disgrace. But if, at the first, any man can by the testimony of ten men prove himself not guilty of the cowardize, he shall goe free.

72. They that give over any strength unto the enemy, unlesse it be for extremity of hunger or want of Ammunition; the Governour, with all the Officers, shall die for it; all the souldiers shall be lodged without the quarters, without any Colours, they shall be made to carry out all the filth of the Leaguer; thus to continue untill some noble exploit of them be performed, which shall promerit pardon for their former cowardize.

85. Hee that forceth any woman to abuse her, and the matter bee proved, hee shall die for it.

89. No Souldier shall pillage anything from our subjects upon any March, Strength, Leaguer, or otherwise howsoever, upon pain of death.

92. They that pillage or steal either in our Land or in the enemies, or from any of them that come to furnish our Leaguer or Strength, without leave, shall bee punish'd as for other theft.

95. When any Fort or place of Strength is taken, no man shall fall upon the spoyle before that all the places in which the enemy is lodged be also taken in, and that the Souldiers and Burgers have layed down their Armes, and that the quarters be dealt out and assigned to every body; who so does the contrary, shall be punished ...

96. No man shall presume to pillage any Church or Hospitall, although the Strength be taken by assault; except that he be first commanded, or that the Souldiers and Burgers be fled thereinto and doe harme from thence; who dares the contrary, shall be punished ...

97. No man shall set fire upon any Hospitall, Churches, Schools, or Mill; or spoyle them in any way, except he be commanded; neither shall any tyrannize over any Churchman, or aged people, men or women, maides or children, unless they first take arms against them, under paine of punishment at the discretion of the Judges.

116. Whatsoever is not contained in these Articles, and is repugnant to Military Discipline, or whereby the miserable and innocent country may against all right and reason be burdened withall, whatsoever offence finally shall be committed against these orders, that shall the severall Commanders make good, or see severally punished, unless themselves will stand bound to give further satisfaction for it.

119. If any bee found drunken in the enemies Leaguer, Castle, or Towne, before the enemy hath yielded himself wholly up to our mercy, and laid downe his Armes; whosoever shall kill the said drunken Souldier shall be free for it; always provided that good proofe be brought that hee was drunken; and if that Souldier escape for that time with his life, and that it can appear that some dammage or hindrance hath come unto our service by his drunkennesse, then wheresoever he be apprehended he shall die for it; but if no hurt ensued thereof, yet shall be put in irons for the space of one month, living upon his pittance of Bread and Water.

132. No Captaine ... shall hold backe any of his souldiers meanes from him; of which if any complaine, the Captaine shall answer it before the Court, where being found guilty, he shall be punisht as for other Felony; also if any mischance ensue thereupon, as that the Souldiers mutine, be sicke, or endure hunger, or give up any Strength; then shall he answer for all those inconveniences, that hereupon can or may ensue.

The Swedish Articles of Warre then go into great detail as to the constitution of the courts martial that are to be established to ensure the proper obedience of the code and the maintenance of discipline envisaged therein. The judges are required to take an oath of the strictest character, while:

165. No superiour Officer, Colonel or Captain ... shall solicit for any man that is lawfully convicted by the Court, either for any crime or for not observing of these Articles of Warre; unless it be for his very neere kinsman, for whom nature compells him to intercede; otherwise the soliciter shall be held as odious as the delinquent and cashiered from his charge.
166. Whosoever is minded to serve us in these Warres shall be obliged to the keeping of these Articles. If any out of presumption, upon any Strength, in any Leaguer, in the field, or upon any worke, shall doe the contrary, be he Native or be he Stranger, Gentleman or other, Processe shall be made out against him for every time, so long as he serves us in these warres in the quality of a Souldier.
167. These Articles of warre we have made and ordained for the welfare of our Native Countrey, and doe command that they be read every moneth publickly before every regiment, to the end that no man shall pretend ignorance. We further will and command all, whatsoever Officers higher or lower, and all our common souldiers, and all others that come into our Leaguer amongst the souldiers, that none presume to doe the contrary, hereof upon paine of rebellion.

In 1686, James II propounded a code on English military discipline,[24] spelling out detailed instructions regarding the formation and function of courts martial. This instrument was the precursor of James II's Articles of War,[25] which dealt with such matters as the religious duties of soldiers and their fealty to the monarch, and which, in many ways, were a reflection of what was already to be found in the Swedish Articles of Warre. Thus,

[24] *Ibid.* at 919.
[25] *Ibid.* at 920.

Art. VIII. Whosoever shall hold correspondence with any Rebel or Enemy ... or shall give them Advice or Intelligence ... in any manner of way whatsoever, shall suffer Death. And whatever Regiment, Troop or Company shall treat with such rebels or Enemies, or enter into any Condition with them without His Majesties Leave, or Leave of the General, Lieutenant General, or of the Chief Commander in his absence; and the officers of such Regiment, Troop or Company who are found guilty shall die for it; and of the Soldiers who shall consent thereunto, every tenth Man by Lot shall be Hanged, and the rest punished at the Discretion of the General Court-Martial; But whatsoever Officers or Soldiers can prove that they did their utmost to resist and avoid such a Treaty, and were no Partakers of the Crime, they shall not only go free, but shall also be rewarded for their Constancy and Fealty.

Art. X. If any Officer of Soldier shall behave himself disrespectfully towards the General, Lieutenant General, or other Commander of the Army, or speak words tending to his Hurt or Dishonour, he shall be punished according to the Nature and Quality of the Offence by the Judgment of the General Court-Martial.

Art. XV. If any Inferior Officer or Soldier shall refuse to obey his Superior Officer, or shall quarrel with him, he shall be Cashiered, or suffer such Punishment as a Court-Martial shall think fit ...

Art. XVII. All murders and wilful killing of any person shall be punished with Death.

Art. XVIII. All Robbery and Theft committed by any Person in or belonging to the Army, shall be punished with Death, or otherwise as the Court-Martial shall think fit.

There then follows a series of articles that are similar to those in earlier codes relating to mutiny, desertion, cowardice, and the like. Provision is also made for the care of the wounded and sick, while by "Art. XXVI. All Officers whose Charge it is shall see the Quarters kept clean and sweet upon pain of severe Punishment." In addition, "Art. XL. If any trooper or Dragoon shall lose or spoil his Horse, or any Foot Soldier his Arms, or any part thereof by negligence or Gaming, he shall remain in the quality of a Pioneer or Scavenger, till he be furnished at his own Charge, with as goods as were lost; and if he is not otherwise able, the one half of his Pay shall be deducted and set apart for the providing of it till he is re-furnished."

The fact that the importance of discipline in an army was generally recognized, outside of written codes directed at those enlisted,

---

[26] William Shakespeare, *Henry V,* Act III, Scene V.

may be seen in Shakespeare's *Henry V*,[26] when Fluellen refers to the Duke of Exeter who "keeps the pridge most valiantly, with excellent discipline." This is followed immediately by a reference to Bardolph's theft of a pax[27] from a church. Bardolph, a former "comrade" of the king when he was the prince of wales,[28] was sentenced to death, and Pistol pleads for his life. In response, Fluellen says: "[I]f he were my brother, I would desire the duke to use his goot pleasure, and put him to execution; for discipline ought to be used." Moments later, Henry asks Fluellen what men he has lost in the battle, and the following conversation ensues:

Fluellen: ... for my part, I think the duke hath lost never a man, but one that is like to be executed for robbing a church — one Bardolph, if your Majesty know the man ...
King: We would have all such offenders so cut off: and we give express charge that, in our marches through the country, there be nothing compell'd from the villages, nothing taken but paid for, none of the French upbraided or abused in disdainful language; for when lenity and cruelty play for a kingdom, the gentler gamester is the soonest winner."

Although we do have this example of Henry enforcing discipline, there are few other records of military courts dealing with breaches of discipline, and

only one roll survives recording actual cases from a military court. This is from Edward I's Scottish expedition of 1296, and the record gives unique glimpses of daily life in a medieval army. The cases do not reveal more than occasional incidents of insubordination, such as that when John de Averinthe refused to perform watch and ward, or go on a foray when ordered to do so. Another dispute took place over a sum of fifty shillings, intended as wages to pay footsoldiers, which was misappropriated. The impression is, however, that military discipline was reasonably well maintained. A man who dared to go in advance of the banner of the constable and marshal, contrary to a proclamation, was duly arrested. Two men who left their column to go plundering were imprisoned.[29]

During the nineteenth century, attempts were made to draw up laws of war that would serve to govern conduct during modern conflicts, and, once again, the importance of discipline can be seen.

[27] A small piece of plate used during Mass. This is apparently based on a report by Henry's chaplain, Prestwich, *supra* note 21 at 180.

[28] See, for example, William Shakespeare, *Henry IV*, Part I, Act I, Scene II; Act II, Scenes II, IV. .

[29] Prestwich, *supra* note 21 at 180–1.

Francis Lieber is generally considered as the first individual[30] to draw up a code of behaviour for those involved in war. While his *Instructions for the Government of Armies of the United States in the Field*[31] do not actually use the word "discipline," they employ a language that is reminiscent of that found in earlier codes:

Art. 44. All wanton violence committed against persons in the invaded country, all destruction of property not commanded by the authorized officer, all robbery, all pillage or sacking, even after taking a place by main force, all rape, wounding, maiming, or killing of such inhabitants, are prohibited under the penalty of death, or such other severe punishment as may seem adequate for the gravity of the offense. A soldier, officer or private, in the act of committing such violence, and disobeying a superior ordering him to abstain from it, may be lawfully killed on the spot by such superior.

The first major attempt by the powers to establish rules for the conduct of hostilities was the Brussels Conference of 1874, which was responsible for a project of an International Declaration Concerning the Laws and Customs of War.[32] While this instrument does not use the word "discipline," it is clear from the context that it is based on the premise that discipline is of the essence and that those involved in the conflict must not constitute an unruly mob:

Art. 9. The laws, rights, and duties of war apply not only to armies, but also to militia and volunteer corps fulfilling the following conditions:

1. That they be commanded by a person responsible for his subordinates ...
2. That they have a fixed distinctive emblem recognizable at a distance;
3. That they carry arms openly; and
4. That they conduct their operations in accordance with the laws and customs of war.

In accordance with Article 10, if a group of the population of a territory about to be invaded, not having the time to organize themselves in accordance with Article 9, take up arms to oppose the invader, they will only be regarded as "belligerents [— and thus

---

30 See, for example, Richard R. Baxter, "The First Modern Codification of the Law of War" (June 1962) 1(3) Int'l Rev. Red Cross 1.

31 General Orders no. 100 by President Lincoln, 24 April 1863; Dietrich Schindler and Jiri Toman, *On the Laws of Armed Conflicts* (2004) at 3.

32 International Declaration Concerning the Laws and Customs of War, quoted in Schindler and Toman, *supra* note 31 at 21.

entitled to the rights of lawful combatants —] if they respect the laws and customs of war." Although produced by an international conference of state representatives, the Brussels project never came into force. However, it did form the basis of the *Oxford Manual of the Laws of War on Land*, which was adopted by the Institute of International Law in 1880.[33] In the preface to this manual, we find a positive reference to the importance of discipline:

[The Institute] believes it is rendering a service to military men themselves. In fact so long as the demands of opinion remain indeterminate, belligerents are exposed to painful uncertainty and to endless accusations. A positive set of rules, on the contrary, serves the interests of belligerents and is far from hindering them, since by preventing the unchaining of passion and savage instincts — which battle always awakens, as much as it awakens courage and manly virtues, — it strengthens the discipline which is the strength of armies; it also ennobles their patriotic mission in the eyes of the soldiers by keeping them within the limits of respect due to the rights of humanity.

The manual reproduces Articles 9 and 10 of the Brussels project, indicating that the armed forces of a state must be "under the direction of a responsible chief."[34] The manual, having postulated a series of principles to govern the conduct of belligerents, indirectly reiterating the significance of discipline, provides: "Art. 84. Offenders against the laws of war are liable to the punishment specified in the penal law." The manual was never intended to constitute a binding treaty, but it clearly influenced the approach of the delegates to the Hague Conference of 1899, which was responsible for the first internationally accepted Convention with Respect to the Laws and Customs of War on Land, which was then replaced by Convention IV, adopted by the Hague Conference of 1907.[35] This latter convention, as supplemented by the Geneva Conventions of 1949,[36] the Protocols of 1977,[37]and specific treaties dealing with particular

---

[33] *Oxford Manual of the Laws of War on Land,* quoted in Schindler and Toman, *supra* note 31 at 29.

[34] *Oxford Manual of the Laws of War on Land, supra* note 33 at Article 2, 2(a).

[35] Convention with Respect to the Laws and Customs of War on Land and Convention IV, both are reprinted in Schindler and Toman, *supra* note 31 at 55. The two instruments are reproduced side by side for easy reference.

[36] Geneva Conventions of 1949, 12 August 1949, 1125 U.N.T.S. 3, reprinted in Schindler and Toman, *supra* note 31 at 459–689.

[37] Protocol (I) Additional to the Geneva Conventions of 12 August 1949, and relating to the Protection of Victims of International Armed Conflicts, 8 June 1977

weapons, forms the basis of the entire law of war as we know it today.

The preamble to Convention IV indicates its purpose, which can only be achieved if those engaged in hostilities behave in a disciplined manner:

Animated by the desire to serve ... the interests of humanity and the ever-progressive needs of civilization; Thinking it important, with this object, to revise the general laws and customs of war, either with a view to defining them with greater precision or to confining them within such limits as would mitigate their severity as far as possible ... these provisions, the wording of which has been inspired by the desire to diminish the evils of war, as far as military requirements permit, are intended to serve as a general rule of conduct for the belligerents in their mutual relations and in their relations with the inhabitants. It has not, however, been found possible at present to concert regulations covering all the circumstances which arise in practice; On the other hand, the High Contracting Parties clearly do not intend that unforeseen cases should, in the absence of a written undertaking, be left to the arbitrary judgment of military commanders. Until a more complete code of the laws of war has been issued, the High Contracting Parties deem it expedient to declare that, in cases not included in the regulations adopted by them [— and annexed to the convention —], the inhabitants and the belligerents remain under the protection and the principles of the law of nations, as they result from the usages established among civilized peoples, from the laws of humanity, and the dictates of the public conscience.[38]

Seeking to ensure that military forces were in fact properly disciplined, the convention provides[39] that "[a] belligerent party which violates the provisions of the said regulations shall, if the case demands, be liable to pay compensation. It shall be responsible for all acts committed by persons forming part of its armed forces." In addition, Article 1 of the regulations reproduces the provision of the Brussels project and the Oxford manual with respect to the

---

and Protocol (II) Additional to the Geneva Conventions of 12 August 1949, and relating to the Protection of Victims of Non-International Armed Conflicts, 8 June 1977, both reprinted in Schindler and Toman, *supra* note 31 at 711–84.

38 This last paragraph is known as the Martens Clause and is still regarded as a fundamental principle of the law of armed conflict. See, for example, Advisory Opinion of International Court of Justice on *Legality of the Threat or Use of Nuclear Weapons*, I.C.J. Reports 1996, 226, 257, paras. 78–9.

39 Convention IV, *supra* note 35 at Article 3.

qualification of belligerents, requiring that they "be commanded by a person responsible for his subordinates; have a fixed distinctive emblem; carry arms openly; and conduct their operations in accordance with the laws and customs of war." It is implicit in all of these instruments that to be recognized as a proper armed force that is entitled to the rights and subject to the duties arising from the law of armed conflict, a force must be disciplined, and, as a result, the members of such a force must obey the orders of their superiors.

However, as may be seen from a decision of the German Reichsgericht, sitting at Leipzig for the trial of German personnel for war crimes committed during the First World War, this disciplinary obligation has its limits. Among these limitations, perhaps the most famous was considered during the trial arising from the shooting of survivors of the hospital ship *Llandovery Castle* after its illegal sinking by a U-boat. In the course of its judgment, the court stated:

The firing on the boats [containing survivors] was an offence against the law of nations. In war on land the killing of unarmed enemies is not allowed ... similarly in war at sea the killing of shipwrecked people, who have taken refuge in lifeboats is forbidden ... Any violation of the law of nations in warfare is ... a punishable offence, so far as, in general, a penalty is attached to the deed. The killing of enemies in war is in accordance with the will of the State that makes war ... only in so far as such killing is in accordance with the conditions and limitations imposed by the Law of Nations. The fact that his deed is in violation of International Law must be well known to the doer ... In examining the question of the existence of this knowledge, the ambiguity of many of the rules of International Law, as well as the actual circumstances of the case, must be borne in mind, because in war time decisions of great importance have frequently to be made on very insufficient material. This consideration, however, cannot be applied in the case at present before the Court. The rule of International Law, which is here involved, is simple and universally known ...

[The commander's] order [to fire and kill] does not free the [subordinate] accused from guilt. It is true that according to para. 47 of the [German] Military Penal Code, if the execution of an order in the ordinary course of duty involves such a violation of the law as is punishable, the superior officer issuing such an order is alone responsible. According to No. 2, however, the subordinate obeying an order is liable to punishment if it was known to him that the order of the superior involved the infringement of civil or military law ... It is certainly to be urged in favour of the military subordinates that they are under no obligation to question the order of their superior officer, and they can count upon its legality.[40] But no such confidence can be held to exist if such an order is universally known to everybody, including the accused, to be without any doubt whatever against the law. This happens only in rare and exceptional cases. But this case was precisely one of them, for ... it was perfectly clear to the accused that killing defenceless people in the lifeboats could be nothing else but a breach of the law. As Naval officers by profession they were well aware ... that one is not legally authorized to kill defenceless people. They well knew that this was the case here ... They could have gathered, from the order given by [their commander], that he wished to make use of his subordinates to carry out a breach of the law. They should, therefore, have refused to obey. As they did not do so, they must be punished ...

The defence finally points out that the [subordinate] accused must have considered that [the commander] would have enforced his orders, weapon in hand, if they had not obeyed them. This possibility is rejected. If [he] had been faced by a refusal on the part of his subordinates, he would have been obliged to desist from his purpose, as then it would have been impossible for him to attain his object, namely, the concealment of the torpedoing of the *Llandovery Castle* ...

[The subordinate accused] should certainly have refused to obey the order. This would have required a specially high degree of resolution. A refusal to obey the commander on a submarine would have been something so unusual that it is humanly possible to understand that the accused could not bring themselves to disobey. That certainly does not make them innocent ... They had acquired the habit of obedience to Military authority and could not rid themselves of it. This justifies the recognition of mitigating circumstances in determining the punishment.[41]

This issue of discipline as instilled even into senior officers played a role in the decision of the United States Military Tribunal in the *German High Command Trial* in 1948:

[A] distinction must be drawn as to the nature of a criminal order itself. Orders are the basis upon which an army operates. It is basic to the discipline of an army that orders are issued to be carried out. Its discipline is based upon this principle. Without it, no army can be effective and it is certainly not incumbent upon a soldier in a subordinate position to screen the orders of superiors for questionable points of legality. Within certain

---

40 See, however, US Department of the Army, "Lesson Plan" on Teaching the Geneva Conventions of 1949 and Hague Convention no. IV of 1907, AsubjScd 27–1 (8 October 1970).

41 *Llandovery Castel*, (1921) 2 Ann. Dig. 436; reprinted in John Cameron, *The Peleus Trial* (1948), appendix IX, 180–82.

limitations, he has the right to assume that the orders of his superiors and the State which he serves and which are issued to him are in conformity with International Law.

Many of the defendants here were field commanders and were charged with heavy responsibilities in active combat. Their legal facilities were limited.

They were soldiers — not lawyers. Military commanders in the field with far-reaching military responsibilities cannot be charged under International Law with criminal participation in issuing orders which are not obviously criminal or which they are not shown to have known to be criminal under International Law. Such a commander cannot be expected to draw fine distinctions and conclusions as to legality in connection with orders issued by his superiors. He has the right to assume, in the absence of specific knowledge to the contrary, that the legality of such orders has been properly determined before their issuance ...

... The choices which he has for opposition to implementing an illegal order of his superiors are few: (1) he can issue an order countermanding the order; (2) he can resign; (3) he can sabotage the enforcement of the order within a certain limited sphere.

As to countermanding the order of his superiors, he has no legal status or power. A countermanding order would subject him to the severest punishment ...

His second choice — resignation — was not much better. Resignation in wartime is not a privilege generally accorded to officers in an army ... Disagreement with a State policy as expressed by an order affords slight grounds for resignation ...

Another field of opposition was to sabotage the order. This he could do only verbally by personal contacts. Such verbal repudiation could never be of sufficient scope to annul its enforcement.[42]

The tribunal then turned to the issue of discipline in general, with particular reference to its role in the German Army:

War is human violence at its utmost. Under its impact, excesses of individuals are not unknown in any army. The measure of such individual excesses is the measure of the people who compose the army and the standard of discipline of the army to which they belong. The German Army was, in general, a disciplined army. The tragedy of the German Wehrmacht and these defendants is that the crimes charged against them stem primarily from its highest military leadership and the leadership of the Third Reich itself.[43]

[42] *German High Command Trial* (1948) 15 UNWCC, Law Reports of Trials of War Criminals, 1949, 1.73–4.

[43] *Ibid.* at 75–6.

And being highly disciplined, there was an inherent reaction to obey.
It is perhaps apposite to cite at this point what may be the clearest
exposition of the duty to disregard an unlawful order in defiance
of military discipline that has ever been rendered by a military tribunal. In the course of its judgment arising from the Kfar Qasem
massacre, the Israel Military Court of Appeal stated:

The identifying mark of a "manifestly unlawful" order must wave like a
black flag above the order given, as a warning saying "forbidden." It is not
formal unlawfulness, hidden or half-hidden, not unlawfulness that is detectable only by legal experts, that is the important issue here, but an overt
and salient violation of the law, a certain and obvious unlawfulness that
stems from the order itself or of the acts it demands to be committed, an
unlawfulness that pierces the eye and agitates the heart, if the eye be not
blind nor the heart closed or corrupt. That is the degree of "manifest"
illegality required in order to annul the soldier's duty to obey and render
him criminally responsible for his actions ...

A reasonable soldier can distinguish a manifestly illegal order on the
face of it, without requiring legal counsel and without perusing the law
books. These provisions impose legal and moral responsibility on every
soldier, irrespective of rank.[44]

Refusal to carry out a "manifestly unlawful" order does not amount
to a criminal breach of discipline. However, refusal to obey an order on the ground that the conflict in question was unlawful and
that compliance with the order might lead to the commission of a
war crime[45] or that a particular operation would be, when tested
subjectively or personally, distinct from "manifestly" "illegal and
immoral"[46] would constitute such a breach.

In 1929, attempts were made to bring the law more up to date.
Further and more specific recognition of the need for discipline is
to be found in Chapter VIII of the 1929 Geneva Convention on the

---

[44] *Chief Military Prosecutor v. Melinke*, 1958, reprinted in (1985) 2 Palestine Y.B. Int'l
Law 69, 108.

[45] See, for example, the case of Captain Levy who opposed the war in Vietnam and
refused to teach medical corpsmen attached to US Special Forces, contending
that they would commit war crimes, rendering him an accomplice, *Levy v. Resor*,
37 C.M.R. 399 (1967); Anthony D'Amato et al., "War Crimes and Vietnam: The
'Nuremberg Defense' and the Military service Resister" (1969) 57 Cal. Law Rev.
1055; and *Levy v. Parker* 396 U.S. 1204 (1969).

[46] See refusal by Israeli Air Force personnel to carry out air strikes in civilian Palestinian areas, Farrell, "'Refusenik' Pilots Cause Shockwaves in Israel," *The Times
(London)*, 26 September 2003.

Amelioration of the Condition of the Wounded and Sick in Armies in the Field.[47] According to Article 29, "[t]he Governments of the High Contracting Parties shall propose to their legislatures should their penal laws be inadequate, the necessary measures for the repression in time of war of any act contrary to the provisions of the present Convention." Interestingly enough, no similar provision is to be found in the Convention Relative to the Treatment of Prisoners of War,[48] which was adopted at the same conference. On the other hand, it does imply the necessity for discipline among the members of a capturing force:

Art. 2. Prisoners of war are in the power of the hostile Government, but not of the individuals or formation which captured them.

They shall at all times be humanely treated and protected, particularly against acts of violence, from insults and from public curiosity ...

Art. 3. Prisoners of war are entitled to respect for their persons and honour. Women shall be treated with all consideration due to their sex.

While, as has just been noted, the convention does not refer specifically to discipline among the capturing forces, it does refer to discipline in regard to prisoners. Article 18 is concerned with the "internal discipline of camps":

Each prisoner of war camp shall be placed under the authority of a responsible officer. In addition to external marks of respect required by the regulations in force in their own armed forces with regard to their nationals, prisoners of war shall be required to salute all officers of the detaining Power. Officer prisoners of war shall be required to salute only officers of that Power who are their superiors or equals in rank.

The issue of discipline arises again in connection with penal sanctions with respect to prisoners of war:

Art. 45. Prisoners of war shall be subject to the laws, regulations and orders in force in the armed forces of the detaining Power.

Any act of insubordination shall render them liable to the measures prescribed by such laws, regulations, and orders, except as otherwise provided in this Chapter [of the convention].

---

[47] Geneva Convention on the Amelioration of the Condition of the Wounded and Sick in Armies in the Field, 1929, reprinted in Schindler and Toman, *supra* note 31 at 409.

[48] Convention Relative to the Treatment of Prisoners of War, 1929, reprinted in *ibid.* at 421.

Art. 46. ... Officers, non-commissioned officers or private soldiers, prisoners of war, undergoing disciplinary punishment shall not be subjected to treatment less favourable than that prescribed as regards the same punishment, for similar ranks in the armed forces of the detaining Power.

The convention then proceeds to deal in detail with the procedures and treatment to be meted out in application of the disciplinary punishment of such prisoners, and, in this way, disciplinary punishment is distinguished from judicial proceedings. The nearest the convention gets to the issue of discipline in so far as the forces of the detaining power are concerned is by providing generally, in Article 82, that "[t]he provisions of the present Convention shall be respected by the High Contracting Parties in all circumstances." And this mandate requires that those members of the forces of the detaining power responsible for the administration and proper supervision of the prisoner of war camps maintain discipline to ensure the convention is in fact complied with.

Hague Convention IV, together with the 1929 Geneva Conventions and the principles of customary law hinted at in the Martens Clause, provided the law governing the Second World War. The issue of discipline — or the failure to enforce it — became very significant in the *Trial of General Tomoyuki Yamashita*.[49] Yamashita was commanding general of the Japanese Fourteenth Army Group in the Philippines, serving concurrently as military governor, and was formerly commanding general in Singapore and Malaya. He was charged before a United States Military Commission with having

[u]nlawfully disregarded and failed to discharge his duty as commander to control the operations of the members of his command permitting them to commit brutal atrocities and other high crimes against people of the United States and its allies, particularly the Philippines; and he thereby violated the laws of war.

Yamashita was not accused of having himself committed any breach of the laws and customs of war but with having failed as a commander to carry out his duty under the law of war to ensure that the troops under his command observed those laws and customs. In other words, he was charged with having failed to ensure that those under his command exercised the proper discipline expected

---

[49] *Trial of General Tomoyuki Yamashita* (1945) U.N.W.C.C. Law Reports of Trials of War Criminals, vol. 4, .1.

of an organized armed force. In the course of his defence, Yamashita stated:

I put all my effort to get the maximum efficiency and the best methods in the training of troops and the maintaining of discipline, and even during combat I demanded training and maintenance of discipline. However, they were inferior troops, and there simply wasn't enough time to bring them up to my expectations ... We managed to maintain some liaison, but [due to the American bombing] it was gradually cut off, and I found myself completely out of touch with the situation. I believe that under the foregoing conditions I did the best possible job I could have done. However, due to the above circumstances, my plans and my strength were not sufficient to the situation, and if these things happened they were absolutely unavoidable.[50]

This plea was not acceptable to the commission and, in delivering judgment, the president stated:

The prosecution presented evidence to show that the crimes were so extensive and widespread, both as to time and area, that they must either have been wilfully permitted by the accused, or secretly ordered by the accused ... As to the crimes themselves, complete ignorance that they had occurred was stoutly maintained by the accused, his principal staff officers and subordinate commanders, further, that all such acts, if committed, were directly contrary to the announced policies, wishes and orders of the accused. The Japanese Commanders' testified that they did not make personal inspections or independent checks ... to determine for themselves the established procedures by which their subordinates accomplish their missions. Taken at full face value, the testimony indicates that Japanese senior commanders operate in a vacuum, almost in another world with respect to their troops, compared with standards American generals take for granted.[51]

The president might as easily have commented that the "control" exercised by the Japanese fell far below the standards of most armies in the field, not merely American. He continued:

This accused is an officer of long years of experience, broad in its scope, who had extensive command and staff duty in the Imperial Japanese Army in peace as well as war. Clearly, assignment to command military troops is accompanied by broad authority and heavy responsibility. This has been

[50] *Ibid.* at 27.
[51] *Ibid.* at 34–5.

true of all armies throughout recorded history ... [W]here murder and rape and vicious, revengeful actions are widespread offences, and there is no effective attempt by a commander to discover and control the criminal acts, such a commander may be held responsible, even criminally liable, for the lawless acts of his troops, depending upon their nature and the circumstances surrounding them.

Yamashita appealed against his death sentence to the United States Supreme Court. Dismissing the appeal, Chief Justice Stone, speaking for the majority and clearly "having in mind issues arising from a breakdown in discipline," said:

An important incident to the conduct of war is the adoption of measures by the military commander, not only to repel and defeat the enemy, but to seize and subject to disciplinary measures those enemies who, in their attempt to thwart or impede our military effort, have violated the Law of War ... [T]he gist of the charge is an unlawful breach of duty by petitioner as an army commander to control the operations of the members of his command by "permitting them to commit" the extensive and widespread atrocities specified. The question is whether the Law of War imposes on an army commander a duty to take such appropriate measures as are within his power to control the troops under his command for the prevention of the specified acts which are violations of the Law of War ... It is evident that the conduct of military operations by troops whose excesses are unrestrained by the orders or efforts of their commander would almost certainly result in violations which it is the purpose of the Law of War to prevent. Its purpose to protect civilian populations and prisoners of war from brutality would largely be defeated if the commander of an invading army could with impunity neglect to take reasonable measures for their protection. Hence the Law of War presupposes that its violation is to be avoided through the control of the operations of war by commanders who are to some extent responsible for those subordinates.

This is recognized by the Annex to the Fourth Hague Convention of 1907, respecting the laws and customs of war on land. Article 1 lays down as a condition which an army must fulfil in order to be accorded the rights of lawful belligerents, that it must be "commanded by a person responsible for his subordinates,"[52]

and one who must, accordingly, ensure that discipline is maintained.

By way of contrast, it is of interest to note the order to enforce discipline issued by Feldmarschall von Rundstedt as supreme commander of the Army Group South. He was concerned that forces

---

[52] *Ibid.* at 41 and 43.

under his command might support *sonderkomandos* in their activities directed against Jews, communists, and other "enemies of the state":

Ref.: Combatting anti-Reich elements

The investigation and combating of anti-Reich tendencies and elements (Communists, Jews and the like), in so far as these are not incorporated into the enemy army are the *sole* [*sic*] responsibility of the Sonderkommandos of the Security Police and the SD in the occupied areas. The Sonderkommandos have sole responsibility for taking the measures necessary to this end.

Unauthorized action on the part of individual Wehrmacht members or participation of Wehrmacht members in the excesses of the Ukrainian population against the Jews is forbidden, as is watching or photographing the Sonderkommandos' measures.

This prohibition is to be made known to members of all units. The disciplinary superiors of all ranks are responsible for ensuring that this prohibition order is complied with. In the event of a violation, the case in question will be examined to ascertain whether the superior has failed to fulfil his supervisory duty. If this is the case he is to be punished severely.[53]

Experience in the Second World War, as exemplified by evidence presented during the various trials for war crimes that ensued, suggests that the Hague and Geneva law, as it then existed, was inadequate. Consequently, in 1949, four new conventions were adopted at Geneva.[54] Each of these conventions provides, in Article 1, that the "High Contracting Parties undertake ... to ensure respect for the present Convention in all circumstances." Each convention, similarly, contains provisions for the "[r]epression of Abuses and Infractions": "The High Contracting Parties undertake to enact any legislation to provide effective penal sanctions for persons committing, or ordering to be committed, any of the grave breaches of the

---

[53] Ic/AO (Abw.III), 24 September 1941; Ernst Klee, Willi Dressen, and Volker Riess, *The Good Old Days: The Holocaust as Seen by Its Perpetrators and Bystanders* (1988) at 116.

[54] Convention (I) for the Amelioration of the Condition of the Wounded and Sick in Armed Forces in the Field, 12 August 1949; Convention (II) for the Amelioration of the Condition of Wounded, Sick and Shipwrecked Members of Armed Forces at Sea, 12 August 1949; Convention (III) Relative to the Treatment of Prisoners of War, 12 August 1949; and Convention (IV) Relative to the Protection of Civilian Persons in Time of War, 12 August 1949, all are reprinted in Schindler and Toman, *supra* note 31 at 459, 485, 507, 575, resp.

present Convention defined in the following Article,"[55] which inevitably requires the maintenance of proper discipline to ensure that such breaches do not occur. However, it is only Convention III Relative to the Treatment of Prisoners of War that actually uses the term "discipline" and, as with the 1929 convention, only in regard to the behaviour of the prisoners themselves.

To some extent, this lacuna is remedied in Protocol I Additional to the Geneva Conventions of 12 August 1949, and Relating to the Protection of Victims of International Armed Conflicts, which was adopted in 1977.[56] Article 1 commits the parties to ensuring respect for the protocol and, with slight verbal changes, reiterates the provisions of the Martens Clause. In order to give effect to both the conventions and this protocol, Article 80 of the latter provides: "2. The High Contracting Parties and the Parties to the conflict shall give orders and instructions to ensure observance of the Conventions and the Protocol, and shall supervise their execution." This, of course, imposes upon the parties an obligation to ensure that discipline is maintained and, to ensure that this obligation is done, the protocol provides:

Article 82. The High Contracting Parties at all times, and the Parties to the conflict in time of armed conflict, shall ensure that legal advisers are available, when necessary, to advise military commanders at the appropriate level on the application of the Conventions and this Protocol and on the appropriate instruction to be given to the armed forces on this subject.

Article 83. The High Contracting Parties undertake, in time of peace as in time of armed conflict, to disseminate the Conventions and this Protocol as widely as possible in their respective countries and, in particular, to include the study thereof in their programmes of military instruction and to encourage the study thereof by the civilian population so that those instruments may become known to the armed forces and to the civilian population.

The protocol then proceeds to deal with the repression of breaches and provides further:

Article 86. Failure to Act

---

[55] Geneva Convention I, *supra* note 54 at Article 49; Geneva Convention II, *supra* note 54 at Article 50; Geneva Convention III, *supra* note 54 at Art. 129; and Geneva Convention IV, *supra* note 54 at Article 146.

[56] Protocol I Additional, reprinted in Schindler and Toman, *supra* note 31 at 711.

1. The High Contracting Parties and the Parties to the conflict shall repress grave breaches, and take measures necessary to suppress all other breaches, of the Conventions or of this Protocol which result from a failure to act when under a duty to do so.

2. The fact that a breach of the Conventions or of this Protocol was committed by a subordinate does not absolve his superiors from penal or disciplinary responsibility, as the case may be, if they knew, or had information which should have enabled them to conclude in the circumstances at the time, that he was committing or was going to commit such a breach and if they did not take all feasible measures within their power to prevent or repress the breach.

Article 87. Duty of Commanders

1. The High Contracting Parties and Parties to the conflict shall require military commanders, with respect to members of the armed forces under their command and other persons under their control, to prevent and, where necessary, to suppress and to report to competent authorities breaches of the Conventions and of this Protocol.

2. In order to prevent and suppress breaches, the High Contracting Parties and Parties to the conflict shall require that, commensurate with their level of responsibility, commanders ensure that members of the armed forces under their command are aware of their obligations under the Conventions and this Protocol.

3. ... The High Contracting Parties and Parties to the conflict shall require any commander who is aware that subordinates or other persons under his control are going to commit or have committed a breach of the Conventions or of this Protocol, to initiate such steps as are necessary to prevent such violations of the Conventions or this Protocol, and, where appropriate, to initiate the disciplinary or penal action against violations thereof.

Even Protocol II Additional to the Geneva Conventions of 12 August 1949, and Relating to the Protection of Victims of Non-International Armed Conflicts,[57] which is not concerned with the conduct of regular forces, provides in Article 1 for its application to

[a]rmed conflicts which are not covered by ... Protocol I ... and which take place in the territory of a High Contracting Party between its armed forces and dissident armed forces or other organized armed groups which, under responsible command, exercise such control over a part of its territory as to enable them to carry out sustained and concerted military operations and to implement this Protocol.

[57] Protocol II Additional, reprinted in *ibid.* at 775.

These provisions can only have meaning if the commanders ensure that the forces under their control are properly disciplined. The need for this discipline has become clear from the jurisprudence of the ad hoc tribunal established by the United Nations for the prosecution of offences against humanity and the law of armed conflict in the former Yugoslavia.[58] This jurisprudence indicates that discipline in so far as a commander is concerned requires that he exercise proper control over those under his command and that he should ensure that they comply with the requirements of the law of armed conflict — failure to do so will amount to criminal command responsibility.[59] To a very great extent, much of the evidence against accused superiors is to be found in their failure to ensure proper discipline by subordinates under their command or their own failure to punish offences when they occur.

Thus, General Blaškić, commander of the Croatian Defence Council forces in central Bosnia, was charged with, among other offences,

having known or having had reason to know that subordinates were preparing to commit[60] [the various crimes alleged] or that they had done so and that he had not taken the necessary and reasonable measures necessary to prevent the said crimes from being committed or to punish the perpetrators.[61]

In the course of its judgment, the Trial Chamber stated:

[T]he commander need not have any legal authority to prevent or punish acts of his subordinates. What counts is his material ability, which instead of issuing orders or taking disciplinary action may entail, for instance, submitting reports to the competent authorities in order for proper measures to be taken."[62]

---

58 Statute of the International Criminal Tribunal for the Former Yugoslavia, I.L.M. 32 (1993), 1192; Schindler and Toman, *supra* note 31 at 1285.

59 See, for example, Leslie C. Green, "Superior Orders and Command Responsibility: The Fifteenth Waldemar Solf Lecture in International Law" (March 2003) 175 Mil. Law. Rev. 286.

60 It is nowhere made clear how a commander is to "know a subordinate is preparing to commit" an offence. In the English common law, there is a statement relevant to this "only God and the devil know the mind of man"!

61 *The Prosecutor v. Tihomir Blaškić*, No. IT-95-4-T, 3 March 2000 (Trial Chamber Judgment).

62 *Ibid.* at paras. 301, 302, 444, 446, 467–8.

In regard to a number of the incidents in which it was alleged that crimes had been committed, the accused acknowledged this to have been the case, so that his failure to seek out and punish those responsible involved a breach of discipline and obligation on his part. The tribunal pointed out that

[t]he Defence depicted the Croatian troops in Bosnia as bands of "armed villagers," very much influenced by local alliances. The lack of qualified officers, of training and of equipment for the troops as well as an inadequate communication system would explain that such crimes could have been committed. Thus without challenging the accused's *de jure* authority, the Defence submitted that he had no *de facto* authority over his troops ... Yet the accused congratulated himself on several occasions on how perfectly well organised and controlled his troops were ... according to several international observers, the HVO [Croatian forces] were very well organised and very well armed troops ... [having] very precise organisation charts defining everyone's tasks and areas of responsibility. The hierarchy seemed very clear, with each unit having a number, an area of activity and a grade ... [T]he military personnel were generally well trained since they had been trained in the JNA [Yugoslav Army], which provided for two years of military service.

And presumably, therefore, they were a disciplined force and clearly not "bands of armed villagers." Moreover,

[t]he planned nature and, in particular, the fact that all [the] units [involved] acted in a perfectly coordinated manner presupposes in fact that these troops were responding to a single command, which accordingly could only be superior to the commander of each of those units. In this connection, it is worth recalling that that was the opinion expressed by the accused himself.

This fact indicates that those committing the atrocities were in fact behaving in a disciplined manner. In fact, the accused had received a number of reports of disciplinary inquiries on which he failed to take adequate action.[63]

The tribunal clearly acted on the basis that a disciplined officer of superior rank would, especially after receiving notice that atrocities were being committed on a widespread scale in the area of his command, have instituted proper inquiries and proceeded to try those individuals responsible:

[63] *Ibid.* at paras. 488–95.

General B did know of the circumstances and conditions under which the Muslims were detained [and] did not perform his duties with the necessary reasonable diligence. As a commander holding the rank of Colonel [*sic*] he was in a position to exercise effective control over his troops in a relatively confined territory ... [T]he accused did not duly carry out his duty to investigate the crimes and impose disciplinary measures or to send a report on the perpetrators of these crimes to the competent authorities.[64]

In assessing the guilt of a senior officer, it is necessary to examine his professional history in order to ascertain how far he is himself a disciplined soldier:

[T]he Trial Chamber bears in mind ... his keen sense for the soldiering profession which he considers a duty ... It is appropriate to note that several witnesses attested to the professionalism of the accused and his organisational skills. He is a man of duty. He is also a man of authority who barely tolerated non-compliance with his orders ... As a professional soldier who, as he himself explained, took a course on the law of armed conflicts while in the former JNA the accused knew perfectly well the range of his obligations. It is inconceivable that [he] was unable to assess the criminal consequences stemming from the violation of such obligations.[65]

Just as a superior demands discipline from his subordinates, so he must also exercise the discipline that goes with command. The fact that some of the findings of guilt in Blaškić's case were overturned on appeal does not affect the validity of the general reasoning.

Somewhat similar issues regarding the duty of a commander arose in the prosecution of General Krstić,[66] chief of staff/deputy military commander of the Bosnian Serbian Army Drina Corps. He was charged with responsibility for a vast range of offences that had been committed within his area of command, including the atrocities perpetrated at Srebrenica. Here again, we have a senior officer who clearly understands the need to maintain discipline among those under his command, yet, when the need demands, fails to do so and fails to take the steps necessary to ensure that discipline is restored for the future:

During his testimony [he] repeatedly stressed that, as a career military officer, he fully respected the laws of armed conflict. Several witnesses who

---

[64] *Ibid.* at paras. 733–4.

[65] *Ibid.* at paras. 780 and 792.

[66] *Prosecutor v. Krstić* IT-98–33-T, 2 August 2001 (Trial Chamber).

testified on his behalf confirmed his strict approach to ensuring compliance with the Geneva Conventions among his troops and the humanitarian manner in which he treated members of the civilian population during the course of the war in Bosnia."[67]

In fact, the tribunal was of opinion that

General Krstić appears as a reserved and serious career officer who is unlikely to have ever instigated a plan such as the one devised for the mass execution of Bosnian Muslim men, following the take-over of Srebrenica ... Left to his own devices, it seems doubtful that [he] would have been associated with such a plan at all ... Nonetheless ... [he] found himself squarely in the middle of one of the most heinous wartime acts committed in Europe since the Second World War. The plan to execute the Bosnian Muslim men may not have been of his own making, but it was carried out within the zone of responsibility of the Drina Corps [and] Drina Corps resources were utilised to assist with the executions ... By virtue of his position as Drina Corps Commander ... [he] must have known about this ... [Had he] intervened [when he first found out] thousands of prisoners ... might have been saved.[68]

Evidence of the need for a senior officer to supervise his troops properly in accordance with the behaviour expected of a disciplined officer may be seen when an accused questions or condemns the orders of his superior but continues, as a disciplined officer, to support his commander.[69] More usually, however, he will ignore the reports he receives concerning atrocities that have been committed within his area of command and will fail therefore to make the inquiries necessary to repress such activities for the future or to punish offenders.[70]

When considering the personal liability of General Krstić for the individual offences charged against him, in addition to referring to his personal involvement in some of the condemned activities, the tribunal constantly referred not only to his active participation or tolerance of some activities but also to the fact that he knew, or had been informed of, what was happening and did little or nothing to suppress or punish, thus failing to behave in a way that a disciplined officer, especially one of his rank, might be expected to

[67] *Ibid.* at paras. 301.
[68] *Ibid.* at paras. 420–3.
[69] *Ibid.* at paras. 416–17.
[70] See, for example, *ibid.* at paras. 434, 462–5, and 470–7.

conduct himself.[71] His failure to act was not only a breach of the international law of armed conflict but was also in direct conflict with the 1992 Order on the Application of the Rules of the International Law in the Army of the Serbian Republic of Bosnia and Herzegovina: "It is the duty of the competent superior officer to initiate proceedings for legal sanctions against individuals who violate the rules of the international law of war."[72] The combined effect of the Blaškić and Krstić judgments seems to be that, regardless of a commander's responsibility for any order he may have given or action in which he might personally have been involved, he will also be responsible for the acts of a criminal character carried out systematically throughout the region of his command, since such widespread activity must have come to his knowledge, while his failure to suppress or punish such acts must have led his subordinates to believe that he approved or was tolerant of such behaviour. Such failure would clearly amount to a breach of discipline by the superior concerned and is in line with the *Yamashita* decision.

As explained at the beginning of this comment, and as demonstrated by the early codes cited, discipline requires conformity with orders within the lines and not only during conflict. Extreme instances of a breakdown in discipline may result in mutiny or, as presaged in the early codes, conduct resulting in the punishment of an entire unit. Examples of such a breakdown may be seen in the British Navy mutiny at Spithead (the Nore) in 1797, the refusal to obey orders to go up the line by former members of the British Eighth Army at Salerno in 1943,[73] or the revolt by ships of the Royal Indian Navy at Bombay in 1946. Perhaps among the most glaring examples of the breakdown of discipline in recent years are the multiple charges of rape brought against British troops serving in Kenya and the failure of a senior officer to report and investigate these charges[74] and the charges against members of the Canadian Airborne Regiment for their actions in Somalia,[75] as well as the

---

[71] *Ibid.* at paras. 600 *et seq.*

[72] *Ibid.* at para. 2 — quoted at para. 649.

[73] See Saul David, *Mutiny at Salerno* (1995).

[74] Clayton, "Search for the Truth Hindered by British Rape Claim Forgery," *The Times (London)* (27 September 2003) at 22–3.

[75] See John A. English, *Lament for an Army — The Decline of Canadian Military Professionalism* (1998) at 2–5; Government of Canada, *Dishonoured Legacy — The Lessons of the Somalia Affair: Report of the Commission of Inquiry into the Deployment of Canadian Forces to Somalia* (1997); Peter Desbarats, *Somalia Cover-up — A Commissioner's Journal* (1997).

abuses of prisoners during the operations against Iraq, which were exposed in 2004.[76]

While engaged in peacekeeping operations in Somalia, members of the Canadian Airborne Regiment received orders relating to the treatment of local intruders in their encampments, and, pursuant to such orders, some members of the regiment abused detainees, which resulted in the murder of at least one of these. Non-commissioned officers who were aware of what was happening failed to take steps to stop the abuse and failed to report to their superiors, who themselves failed to take action or to maintain the discipline within the lines that was essential to proper military behaviour. Moreover, it transpired that unpunished major breaches of discipline had occurred prior to the regiment's departure from Canada, with such breaches sufficiently common that they must have been known to any superior concerned about the maintenance of discipline. As a result of the details becoming publicly known and of the inquiry that ensued, the regiment was disbanded — reminiscent of earlier punishments of an entire unit because of the breaches of discipline by some of its members.

In the course of its report, the Commission of Inquiry made comments that expressed most clearly what is meant by military discipline and the importance of ensuring its maintenance:

Discipline is fundamental to the military endeavour.

Discipline, for the military, has at least two important meanings. The first ... applies the same connotation to the term that the larger society would: namely, that discipline entails the enforcement of laws, standards and mores in a corrective and, at times, punitive way. The second, and arguably more important meaning from a military perspective, entails the application of control to harness energy and motivation to a collective end. Discipline, thus conceived, is more positive. It seeks actively to channel individual efforts into a collective enterprise. Where that enterprise is the waging of war or armed conflict, it permits the application of force in a controlled and focused manner. Controlling aggressivity so that the right amount of force is applied in exactly the right circumstances is of primary significance to the military. Discipline is the means of achieving such control.

Few professions are as dependent on discipline as the military. Since the chief purpose of military discipline is harnessing the capacity of the individual to the needs of the group, the possibility of success for a particular mission varies in proportion to the extent to which there is concert

---

[76] See accompanying text to notes 78–85.

or cohesion among soldiers. This cohesion occurs when soldiers are disciplined.

Discipline seeks to elicit from individuals their best and most altruistic qualities. It depends on the development of a sense of cooperation and teamwork in support of the group. While imposed initially through the rigours of training, the goal of discipline is to lead individuals gradually to the stage where, of their own volition, they control their own conduct and actions.

The task of ensuring the discipline of subordinates is a major priority of a commander. Good leadership begins with self-discipline, and, for the sake of those serving below, a commander must establish a standard of self-discipline that merits emulation. The capacity of the individual soldier for self-correction may originate in the fear of punishment but, over time, respect for authority and willing obedience must reflect the individual's own self-discipline.[77]

Should this standard of discipline be achieved, each individual soldier would, without further instruction, be aware of the "manifestly unlawful" character of an order or of an activity,[78] while superiors would be more aware of what is happening in their lines and of the propensity of those under their command to behave in a disciplined manner at all times. Equally, superiors would instinctively react properly to incidents affecting their subordinates, taking the action required to repress and punish when necessary.

Failure to exercise proper discipline frequently results in the ill-treatment of captives, even though most members of the armed forces know, or are presumed to know, that this is contrary to the law and is, in fact "manifestly unlawful."[79] Nevertheless, photographic evidence made available in April and May 2004 indicated how easily, in Iraq, discipline among those responsible for the welfare of captives had collapsed. Allegations against British personnel were noted by the International Committee of the Red Cross, and the processes that were implicated were terminated at an early date.[80]

[77] *Dishonoured Legacy, supra* note 75, vol. 1, 23–4.

[78] See definition of "manifest unlawfulness" in *Chief Military Prosecutor* v. *Melinke, supra* note 44.

[79] On joining the British Army in 1941, the writer was told that all he needed to know about the law of war was that if taken prisoner he was only obliged to give his name, rank, and number, and that he was not permitted to ill-treat or kill prisoners of war.

[80] Philip Webster and Roland Watson, "Red Cross Warned of Abuse Again and Again," *The Times (London)* (11 May 2004). See generally for the US position K.J.

In so far as American treatment of Iraqi prisoners was concerned, photographs and films indicated that that those responsible for the treatment of prisoners had assumed an attitude of cavalier-like superiority towards their captives, civilian and military alike, in which they treated them as sub-human[81] and the proper butt of any unreasonable or inhumane action in which the captors found it amusing to indulge. In addition, the conduct of the captors illustrated an attitude that completely ignored the requirements of the Geneva Conventions as well as the moral and religious prejudices and susceptibilities of the Muslim captives.[82] These actions appear to have been undertaken on a fairly extensive and regular basis[83] and were taken in the presence of, and often with the participation of, non-commissioned officers.

It was alleged by some of those individuals charged before courts martial with participation in these activities that they were in fact acting in accordance with orders, thus raising the whole issue of superior orders and command responsibility.[84] If senior personnel were in any way involved, there was clear evidence of a lack of discipline on their part. The same is true if they were aware of these activities and failed to terminate them and punish those responsible. The International Committee of the Red Cross drew attention to what was going on over a year ago and complained that "the abuse remained so persistent that 'it might be considered as a practice tolerated by the Coalition Forces.'"[85] However, disciplinary and judicial action was only taken after the scandal became publicly known. If senior personnel were unaware of what was taking place to such a large extent, it would mean that there was a disciplinary hiatus between the command and those under command. As to

---

Greenberg and J.L. Dratel, *The Torture Papers* (2005). A number of those accused were found guilty and sentenced to lengthy prison terms.

[81] One photograph showed a naked Muslim prisoner with a leash around his neck being dragged across the floor of his prison by a female American military guard.

[82] Thus, one person who had been released reported that he and his comrades had been made to strip naked and then ordered to masturbate in the presence of female guards. Those released stated that they had been fed pork and been made to praise Jesus.

[83] See report prepared by US Major General Antonio M. Taguba into alleged abuse of prisoners by members of the 800th Military Police Brigade at the Abu Ghraib Prison in Baghdad, text available at <http./www.agonist.org/annex/taguba.htm>.

[84] See, for example, Green, *supra* note 59.

[85] Tim Reid, "Repeated Warnings on Abuse Began Fourteen Months Ago," *The Times (London)* (11 May 2004).

those indulging in these practices, it is clear that they were not properly trained or supervised and were unconscious of any rules of discipline. The behaviour of those involved in these acts is indicative of perhaps the most extreme breakdown in military discipline, resulting from a lack of proper training and supervision by officers, since the end of the Second World War.

The situation has been well-described by retired Canadian colonel Michel Drapeau:

> Few professions are as dependent on discipline as the military. Discipline is fundamental to military efficiency, morale and esprit de corps. Discipline is what permits commanders to control the use of state-sanctioned violence so that the right amount and type of force can be applied in exactly the right time and place. Discipline ensures that in times of great danger, the individual can and will carry out orders, even if his natural instinct for self-preservation tells him otherwise. Discipline ensures adherence to laws, standards and values of civilian society during combat or operational deployments.
>
> The outrages that happened in Vietnam, Somalia and Iraq, therefore, are symptoms of the abdication of responsibility by field leaders to enforce and maintain discipline. In doing so, these officers have tarnished the honour of their institutions and countries. They have lost the moral ground. Shame.[86]

By way of contrast, as an example of a proper exercise of discipline we might cite the action of a senior viceroy's commissioned officer of a Muslim regiment in the Indian Army who, after the fall of Singapore and the creation of the rebel Indian National Army, took his men into the mosque, reminded them that they had sworn on the Koran to render allegiance to the King-Emperor and made them repeat that oath.[87] Even more significant is the order issued by von Rundstedt,[88] which is indicative of the conduct expected of a properly disciplined officer determined to maintain and enforce discipline among his subordinates.

At the beginning of this comment, reference was made to Ayala's emphasis on the importance of discipline in ancient Rome.[89] In

---

86 Michel Drapeau, "When One Is Tortured, Many Are Wounded," *Globe and Mail (Toronto)* (6 May 2004) at A17.

87 Personal knowledge based on the writer's military service in India during the Second World War. See Leslie C. Green, *Essays on the Modern Law of War* (1999), ch. XI, "The Azad Hind Fauj (The Indian National Army)."

88 See text accompanying note 53 in this text.

89 Ayala, *supra* note 18.

conclusion, and to reiterate that both superiors and subordinates alike must be disciplined, Ayala is again significant:

And, indeed, we read [in the classics] how numerous armies of slaves and unwarlike recruits have been made invincible and warlike merely by discipline and command and, on the other hand, how numerous armies of seasoned troops, hitherto unconquered, have been corrupted and sapped merely by license and by all their vices and by the neglect of discipline, and have been undone before they ever set eyes on the enemy ...

And, to be brief, we can not have a better instance of what the neglect or maintenance of military discipline means, than that of the Romans; for they who aforetime were superior to all people in their instinct for justice and their military glory, later on, when discipline decayed, were conquered by every one.[90]

L.C. GREEN
Professor Emeritus, Honorary Professor of Law, University of Alberta

Sommaire

Le rôle de la discipline militaire

L'auteur examine l'importance du rôle de la discipline militaire et en fait l'historique jusqu'à nos jours. L'article passe en revue les pratiques utilisées par différentes armées dans une diversité de conflits ainsi que les tentatives de codification des règles au moyen des conventions internationales et de la jurisprudence des tribunaux.

Summary

The Role of Discipline in the Military

The importance of the role of discipline in the military and the way in which it has been viewed from historical times to the present day are surveyed by the author. The practices of different armies in various conflicts are considered and attempts to codify rules through international conventions and decisions of tribunals are discussed.

---

[90] *Ibid.* at Bk. III, ch. I, paras. 2, 4 (English translation at 171 and 173).

Tribute to Ivan L. Head

—

Biography

Ivan Head was born in Calgary on 28 July 1930. He obtained BA and LL.B. degrees from the University of Alberta and practised law in Calgary before undertaking graduate studies at Harvard University. He obtained his LL.M. from Harvard in 1960, having written his thesis on Canadian claims to territorial sovereignty in the Arctic regions. That same year, he joined the foreign service, serving both in Ottawa and in southeast Asia. In 1963, he returned to the University of Alberta as a professor of law.

In 1967, he moved to Ottawa for what was supposed to be one year, working as associate counsel on the constitution to then minister of justice Pierre Elliot Trudeau. When Trudeau became prime minister in 1968, it marked the beginning of a ten-year period during which Ivan served first as legislative counsel and later as a foreign policy advisor. In this latter capacity, he worked closely with Trudeau on all aspects of international relations. Many years later, the two co-authored *The Canadian Way: Shaping Canada's Foreign Policy 1968–1984* (which was published in 1995).

In 1978, Ivan became president of the International Development Research Centre (IDRC), a position he was to occupy until 1991. Towards the end of his time at IDRC, Ivan published *On a Hinge of History: The Mutual Vulnerability of South and North*. The book encapsulated many of the most important themes in his approach to what he called "South-North" relations, which he saw as a more accurate reflection of the reality of the international system than the standard usage "North-South."

Ivan returned to academic life in 1991, when he was jointly appointed in the Faculty of Law and the Department of Political Science at the University of British Columbia (UBC). As a junior faculty member at the time, I clearly remember the sense of excitement that surrounded his appointment. He immediately launched a series of initiatives that were to have a profound influence on the way UBC approached international affairs. He started a new seminar on the law of South-North relations, became an active and dedicated graduate supervisor, and was extremely supportive of colleagues working on various aspects of international law and international relations. He became the founding director of the Liu Centre for the Study of Global Issues (which is now the Liu Institute).

Following his retirement from the university in 1999, Ivan remained actively involved in the Liu Institute and in a number of organizations dedicated to international development and humanitarian issues. He passed away on 1 November 2004 at seventy-four years of age. The sense of loss that his colleagues and friends experienced was captured by the statement that appeared on the Faculty of Law's website: "Much admired and loved around the world for his human decency, deep intellect, gracious manner, and humanitarian commitment, he was also one of the truly great Canadians and outstanding global citizens of the twentieth and twenty-first centuries. Ivan Head was an inspiration to several generations of Canadians, a major player in global affairs, and a much loved, highly admired colleague and friend. He will be sadly missed by all who knew him."

KARIN MICKELSON
Faculty of Law, University of British Columbia

Receiving the *Headian* Legacy: International Lawyers, South-to-North Resource Transfers, and the Challenge of International Development

OBIORA CHINEDU OKAFOR

> A new factor has recently reemerged: financial transfers from South to North. Reemerged, for it was also a common occurrence in earlier colonial periods.
>
> — Ivan Leigh Head[1]

INTRODUCTION

Written over fifteen years ago by Ivan Leigh Head, a highly distinguished Canadian international lawyer, foreign policy expert, and international development thinker, the words contained in the above quotation point firmly at this great man's analytic incisiveness and hint at the sheer depth of his fairness of mind. For although the net transfer of resources from the much poorer geopolitical "South" to a far richer "North" remains to this day one of the most important obstacles to international development, rarely have the dominant accounts of international development given this phenomenon the pride of place that it surely deserves. Ivan

Obiora Chinedu Okafor, Ph.D, LL.M (University of British Columbia), LL.M, LL.B (Hons.) (University of Nigeria, Enugu Campus), is an Associate Professor at Osgoode Hall Law School at York University in Toronto. This note is dedicated to the evergreen and loving memory of Ivan Leigh Head, my mentor, teacher, and international law colleague, whose death in late 2004 left a gaping hole in the fabric of humanist international legal thought. While it is sad that Ivan did pass away at all, it is heartbreaking that he did pass away just now, when the world needs, even more than ever before, his steady wisdom, his mild diplomatic tone, his deep appreciation of the South-North dangers that face us all, and his far-sighted developmental ecumenism. I should like to thank Tochi Uchendu for the many conversations and arguments that helped shape the thoughts contained in this note and Chinedu Idike for his research assistance.

1 See I.L. Head, "South North Dangers" (1989) 68 Foreign Affairs 71 at 78.

Head was therefore well ahead of his time in foregrounding, high-lighting, and criticizing this very disturbing, yet continuing, feature of South-North relations.

It is the insights that I have synthesized in whole or in part from Ivan Head's teaching and writing that frame and inform the brief intervention into international development and international legal thought that I want to offer in this note. These insights relate to, and concern, both the continuing need to foreground and reverse this worrisome trend in South-North relations and the important role that international lawyers can play in the execution of this challenging project.

The Phantom of the Foreign Aid Opera[2]

As favourable to the foreign aid-centred approach to international development as its overall conclusions were, the report on African development that was recently issued by the so-called Blair Commission[3] could not help but declare that

the system for allocating aid to African countries remains haphazard, un-coordinated and unfocused. Some donors continue to commit errors that, at best, reduce the effectiveness of aid. At worst, they undermine the long-term development of those they are supposed to be helping. Rich countries pursue their own fixations and fads, often ignoring the needs prioritized by African [and other developing country] governments ... They tie aid so that it can only be used to buy the donor's own products or services — effectively reducing the value of aid by as much as 30 per cent. Tied aid should be scrapped.[4]

The Blair Commission's assessment was thus that, although foreign aid can be well conceived and smartly delivered, foreign aid programs have all-too-often missed the mark. In the commission's view, "it is time ... to bring bad aid up to the standards of good aid."[5] This is a conclusion that Ivan Head would have himself reached were he still alive today. It is also a call to action with which he would have

2 I owe this expression to the title of the famous artistic production "The Phantom of the Opera."

3 See *Our Common Interest: Report of the Commission for Africa* (London: Commission for Africa, 2005), available at <http://news.bbc.co.uk/1/shared/bsp/hi/pdfs/11_03_05africa.pdf> (last visited on 16 April 2005) [Blair Commission Report].

4 *Ibid.* at 54.

5 *Ibid.*

agreed. Indeed, over fifteen years before the Blair Commission was empanelled, Head had pointedly declared that

[d]evelopment assistance [or foreign aid] programs that are designed primarily for the benefit of the Northern donors — to reduce agricultural surpluses, to create employment in sluggish sectors of the economy, or to spur the export of military hardware — must be recognized for their inherent cynicism and their eventual ineffectiveness.[6]

This similarity between Ivan Head's conclusions and the nature of the contemporary situation, as recognized and articulated in the Blair Commission's report, is most remarkable.

This similarity is also disturbing in its indication that, on the whole, not all that much has changed in international development praxis in the years that intervened between Head's visionary call to action in 1989 and the issuance of the Blair Commission report in 2005. While the Canadian International Development Agency (CIDA) is now widely recognized for its strenuous efforts to rethink its praxis in light of the kind of powerful insights that Head's writings have consistently offered,[7] and most other international development agencies have subscribed to the forward-looking Paris Principles on Aid Effectiveness,[8] to a highly significant extent, net transfers of resources from South to North still mar the development landscape; tied aid still frustrates the struggle to reduce poverty in the South while enriching many in the North; and too many rich countries still tend to pursue their own fixations and fads at the expense of the needs prioritized by developing countries.[9] It is no wonder then that almost nowhere in the geo-political South has foreign aid been isolated as the key factor in generating widespread and *sustainable* social development — certainly not in China, India, Singapore, Botswana, or Malaysia. While aid played some role in these relative development success stories, it did not play the central role.

---

[6] See Head, "South-North Dangers," *supra* note 1 at 85.

[7] See Canadian International Development Agency, Policy Statement, *Canada Making a Difference in the World: A Policy Statement on Strengthening and Effectiveness* (September 2005), available at <http://www.acdi-cida.gc.ca/aideffectiveness> (last visited on 21 March 2005).

[8] See Paris Principles on Aid Effectivenes (Declaration of the Paris High-Level Forum, 2 March 2005), available at <http://www1.worldbank.org/harmonization/ paris/finalparisdeclaration.pdf> (last visited on 21 March 2005).

[9] See Blair Commission Report, *supra* note 3 at 32.

Among the obstacles that have impeded the success of most foreign aid-centred international development efforts, the net transfer of wealth by other means from South to North ranks among the most important. The importance of this issue is underscored by the fact that international development efforts do not have a fighting chance of succeeding as long as there is a net loss of wealth from the much poorer South to the far richer North. It is on the nature of this worrisome trend, and on the means of reversing it, that the rest of this note will concentrate.

NET SOUTH-TO-NORTH RESOURCE TRANSFERS: A BRIEF ANATOMY OF THE PHENOMENON

While a range of factors contribute to the net flow of wealth from the South to the North (for example, debt servicing, diversion of public funds from developing countries to secure personal bank accounts in the North, and certain unfair trading and investment practices), only the "debt servicing" and "diversion of public funds" issues will be discussed in this section. The question of the relationship of fairer trade to strengthened development praxis will be dealt with in the following section. One of the most consequential avenues through which more and more of the South's resources are transferred to the North is through the payment by developing countries of the interest charged by Northern countries and Northern-controlled banks on the many loans that have been taken from these Northern sources by almost all governments in the South. Of some interest is the fact that many of these loans were in fact offered to these Southern countries as a form of "foreign aid." As is now widely recognized, the debt-servicing obligations of many developing countries has become so grand as to result in the diversion of huge resources from basic social developmental activities in these countries in favour of such debt repayments. Writing over a decade and a half ago, Ivan Head warned that this kind of debt servicing by the South had led most developing countries from "illiquidity" to "insolvency."[10] The Blair Commission has only recently issued a similar warning. It has noted that over the years developing countries in Africa (as elsewhere) have had serious difficulties paying down the interest on their debts, let alone the capital.[11] What is more, in most countries in the South, these debt obligations have

---

10 See Head, "South-North Dangers," *supra* note 1 at 79.

11 See Blair Commission Report, *supra* note 3 at 24.

become so relatively onerous that they cannot possibly be repaid.[12] This is so notwithstanding that the original sums borrowed have, in most cases, been paid back already and that the outstanding amounts are in reality the interest that is owed on the debt. As Ivan Head did point out, as of 1989, interest payments by the South accounted for over 50 per cent of its debt servicing payments to the North.[13] The Blair Commission's much more recent conclusions in this connection are very similar.[14] In both cases, Ivan Head's wise words serve to remind us, yet again, of our collective failure (in the time that has elapsed since his 1989 call to action) to act boldly, selflessly, and humanely to ameliorate this very serious threat to human security around the globe.

Another important reason for the net transfer of resources from South to North is the corrupt diversion of billions of dollars from the accounts of poor developing countries to personal bank accounts in the much richer North. While all too many (though certainly not all) politicians in the South have partaken of the vice of corrupt enrichment and looting of the national treasury in their respective countries, far too many Northern banks have profited from receiving, securing, and otherwise dealing in these illicit funds. For instance, it is estimated that the amount of such sums originating from Africa that are now held in Northern banks could suffice to repay over one-half of the total debt owed to the North by African countries.[15] By recommending that countries in the North should rapidly "track down money looted by corrupt African leaders, now sitting in foreign bank accounts, and send that money back to the states from whom it was stolen," the Blair Commission recognized the seriousness of this problem as an obstacle to social development in the South.[16] Yet, virtually all the relevant countries of the North have thus far been reluctant to take the kind of decisive action that is required to stem the tide of this type of illicit flow of resources from South to North. Although some limited action is now being taken in some of these countries, the overall picture is one of reluctance to repatriate these stolen funds. Were he still alive today, Ivan Head would have wisely warned the relevant

[12] *Ibid.* at 41.
[13] See Head, "South-North Dangers," *supra* note 1 at 79.
[14] See Blair Commission Report, *supra* note 3 at 24.
[15] See *ibid.* at 32.
[16] *Ibid.*

countries and their banks that "measured against the relentless momentum of current phenomena, indifference is not benign."[17]

BEYOND THE NET TRANSFER OF WEALTH FROM SOUTH TO NORTH

Among the key recommendations made by the Blair Commission are that for rapid social development to occur in most African countries (and by implication in many other developing countries), these countries will require a significant increase in the volume of their trade with each other and with the rest of the world as well as the enactment of fairer trading rules.[18] The implicit recognition in these two recommendations is that as long as the rules are fairer, a significant increase in the level of South-to-South and South-to-North trade will play a key role in stemming the tide of South-to-North resource transfers and in encouraging the achievement of higher levels of social development in the South. This conclusion is of course a commendable one. For example, although protectionism exists on both sides of the South-North divide, with regard to the specific issue of agriculture (on which a vast number of developing countries depend for much of their incomes and on which the fates of most Northern economies do not really rest), the heavy hand of Northern protectionism is one of the key factors that has marked and marred the possibility of greater and fairer South-North trade. Such unfair trade regimes also hinder the generation of the kind of enhanced earnings in the South that can sustain rapid social development in these countries.[19]

However, as commendable as its recommendations regarding the role of trade in development are, the Blair Commission report is unsatisfactory in at least one key structural respect. It fails to recognize *fully* the fact that "fairer trade" is much more likely than "better aid" to become the single most important driver of sustained social development in African and other Southern countries. The report's hopes for rapid social development within African countries rests much too heavily on the potential for the adoption by the North of an emergent "good aid" praxis. Yet, as has been argued already, over the last half-century or so, nowhere in the developing world has foreign aid functioned as the key factor producing sustained social development. The report's bias towards foreign aid is thus somewhat surprising. Given the Blair Commission's own

[17] See Head, "South-North Dangers," *supra* note 1 at 86.

[18] See Blair Commission Report, *supra* note 3 at 48–53.

[19] *Ibid.* at 50.

acknowledgment that all of the handful of countries in the South that have all but leapt into the developed world have done so largely because they have "used trade to break into new markets and change the face of their economies,"[20] this relative bias towards foreign aid (rather than fairer trade) as the central engine of social development in the South would, I dare say, be unconvincing to a mind as acute as Ivan Head's. Even the report's argument that, on the whole, Africa does not yet produce enough goods at the right quality and price to increase its share of global trade[21] does not really meet the challenge posed by an analysis of the available evidence of what has *in fact* worked in the developing world. It does not belie the underlying argument being made in this note that fairer trade is more likely than even the best foreign aid schemes to be sustainable as the central plank of a social development edifice. As the commission itself understands,[22] most of the appropriate goods/services for export to the North can, with the right effort, be manufactured in the South (perhaps with better-oriented foreign aid). Yet the key point is that if sustainable social development is to occur in most of the South, developing countries must make and sell goods in both Southern and Northern markets, and high-end services must be provided to the North by corporations and individuals in these countries.

The report is also significantly deficient in terms of its treatment of what I will refer to as the "remittance question." Although it acknowledges that remittances from the diasporic citizens of developing countries to their relatives in the developing world (totalling over US $100 billion in 2003) are a highly attractive source of social development finance in the South, and it does identify the barriers to increased remittances,[23] the report does not do a good job of analyzing and fathoming the true potential of this remarkable phenomenon. It does not also devote as much energy as it could to developing creative proposals for overcoming the obstacles in the path of the increased flow of such funds to key parts of the South. Furthermore, the report pays insufficient attention to the important economic implications of the inherent nature of the typical remittance of funds from a Northern country to a given African country as a culturally normative expression of a deep sense of

[20] *Ibid.* at 48.

[21] *Ibid.* at 50.

[22] *Ibid.* at 53.

[23] *Ibid.* at 295.

obligation (not simply charity). Typical foreign aid schemes allocate a significant percentage of aid funds to administrative costs (usually benefiting the citizens of the donor country); too often miss the mark in terms of accurately identifying and solving the priority development problems of the particular communities or persons in issue; and are hardly reliable or sustainable. By contrast, driven, sustained, and framed as they are by a deep sense of obligation (of the very kind that Ivan Head's writings and the Blair Commission report sought to imbue the world with), remittances to the South tend to be much more reliable. They are also far more accurate at reaching the intended beneficiaries and in solving the prioritized problem. What is more, remittances do not involve nearly as much administrative expense as the typical foreign aid project. In light of the great potential and important advantages of remittances, it is disappointing that the Blair Commission report did not spend more of its time brainstorming about ways of developing much larger flows of remittances to Africa and the rest of the developing world. This result may be because it instinctively leans towards foreign aid as the key driver of social development in Africa especially and in the third world in general. The argument that I am making is not, of course, that foreign aid ought to be abandoned in favour of a reliance on remittances. Good foreign aid schemes are much better than remittances at addressing the broad institutional needs of developing countries. By contrast, remittances tend to work best with individual and small group recipients. The argument that is being made is simply that since remittances tend to be significantly more efficient than foreign aid at ameliorating poverty in the South, much more attention ought to be paid to the task of designing systems and policies that are likely to encourage and increase such flows. The conditions within Northern polities that can encourage and lead to increases in remittances to the South (such as fairer migration rules, the facilitation of better jobs for qualified immigrant professionals, and the issuance of remittance tax credits for those diasporic individuals or families who sustain their parents or send young relatives to school in the South) ought to be enhanced or fostered.

Without the implementation of these kinds of measures, alongside the implementation of the other appropriate measures, the net transfers of resources from South to North that signal the relative failure, overall, of decades of Southern social development efforts and Northern-driven international development programming will most likely continue to pose a huge obstacle to sustained social development in the South. In my own estimation, unhappy as he was with the net transfer of wealth from the much poorer South to the far richer North, Ivan Head would have endorsed this argument.

ROLE OF THE INTERNATIONAL LAWYER

As Ivan Head's work has taught many of us, the discipline of international law and the virtual college of international lawyers that constitute it, have been traditionally insensitive to the cause of development. In his now classic contribution to the 1987 edition of this *Yearbook,* Head reminds us all that

[t]o assume ... that international law as now constituted is a prerequisite to development — or is even sympathetic to development — is at least subject to challenge. That international law can, indeed should, contribute to development, is not in question, but it must be remembered that some of the applications of legal principles, designed as they often were in the industrialized countries, are not always in the interest of developing countries.[24]

On any fair assessment of international legal history, Head's analysis was correct. Traditional international legal insensitivity to development has not only been reflected in our relative inattention as a discipline to this subject,[25] but it has also been revealed in the ways in which the content and silences of international law have too often worked to impede social development in the South. Some key areas where international law has functioned in this way are in its traditional reluctance (even refusal) to regulate effectively even the most rapacious multinational corporations;[26] the harmful effects that the strict application of international intellectual property rules have had on the access of poor people in the South to essential drugs for treating HIV/AIDS;[27] and the unfairness of some international trade (World Trade Organization-based) rules (such

---

[24] See I.L. Head, "The Contribution of International Law to Development" (1987) 25 Canadian Yearbook of International Law 29 at 30.

[25] *Ibid.* at 36–38.

[26] See S.C. Agbakwa, "A Line in the Sand: International Disorder and the Impugnity of Non-State Corporate Actors in the Developing World," in A. Anghie, et al., eds., *The Third World and International Order: Law, Politics and Globalization* (Leiden: Martinus Nijhoff, 2003) at 1.

[27] See J.T. Gathii, "The Legal Status of the Doha Declaration on TRIPS and Public Health under the Vienna Convention on the Law of Treaties" (2002) 15 Harvard Journal of Law and Technology 292 at 293–95.

as those related to agricultural subsidies) *vis-à-vis* most countries in the South.[28]

However, it must be said in favour of our discipline that it has improved significantly in its level of sensitivity to the cause of international development. Most serious scholars in the area now see development and international law as being linked. Under sustained pressure from a determined transnational coalition, the relevant intellectual property rules have changed somewhat in order to allow increased access in the South to cheaper AIDS drugs. And pressure has been applied to deploy legal reform towards the reduction (even abolishing) of the agricultural subsidies that have kept much produce from the South from reaching key markets in the North.

The underlying lessons are, thus, that international law can change and that it has in fact sometimes been changed in order to make it more sensitive to the cause of development. As such, it is not difficult to imagine an international legal regime that is much less tolerant of the global form of usury that has *helped* keep most Southern economies creaking and groaning under the weight of their debt obligations. It is also not that hard to think of ways in which existing or new international law norms can be deployed more smartly in order to increase the costs and dangers of looting public treasuries in the South or of accepting to launder such sums in the North. The fact that international trade rules can be modified to create the enabling environment for fairer agricultural trade is also well within the average person's imaginative capacity. All three measures can help greatly in stemming the tide of the net transfer of resources from South to North. And all of these measures are within our collective capacities to help foster (whether as citizens, international lawyers, foreign policy advisors, or even international decision-makers).

As such, as Ivan Head often reminded us, international lawyers do have an important role to play in the creation of the right normative environment for social development to flower. As Ivan Head saw it, ours ought to be a humanist vocation, not merely a rigorous discipline. While the vagaries of international politics will continue to frame and limit our reality and our capabilities, the power of ideas — indeed, the kinds of fresh, humanist, fair-minded international legal ideas that Ivan Head often dreamed up and argued in favour of — should not be lightly dismissed. And the more we think and act as if our collective purpose is not merely to capture and

---

28 See Blair Commission Report, *supra* note 3 at 51.

express the desires of international politicians but also to function, *à la* M. Koskenniemi, as the "gentle civilisers" of international politics,[29] the more fully we will have received Ivan Head's towering and worthy intellectual legacy.

RECEIVING THE *HEADIAN* LEGACY

One important theme that runs through this note is that Ivan Head was highly knowledgeable about international development, remarkably visionary in his conclusions regarding it, and deeply committed to its success. To many of those who worked with and knew him closely, it can only be gratifying that his knowledge of, and vision for, international development matches so closely the thinking of those who, nearly two decades after his first key writings on the area appeared, now seek to transform international development praxis. The tone of the Blair Commission report and the tenor of the new institutional discourses of the Canadian (and some other) international development agencies shows much promise and are remarkable in their conscious or unconscious reception and affirmation of the rich *Headian* legacy.

Yet, as has been argued in this note, far more needs to be done (mostly beyond the foreign aid praxis) if international development efforts are to achieve more success. For one, if most world leaders shared even half of Ivan's commitment to international development, the challenges facing international development praxis today would be far less daunting. After all, was this commitment deficit among world leaders not one of the important reasons for empanelling the Blair Commission?[30] The urgency of imbuing this kind of commitment in the relevant leaders cannot be overestimated. Second, a lot more thought and effort ought to be devoted to ways of ameliorating or even eliminating the debt crisis; ensuring fairer trade for the South; returning looted funds to their original sources in the South; enhancing remittances to the South; and fostering greater social development over all. It is then and only then that we can conclude that Ivan Leigh Head's towering and inspiring intellectual legacy has been as fully and truly received within international development praxis as it surely deserves.

[29] See M. Koskenniemi, "The Place of Law in Collective Security" (1996) 17 Michigan Journal of International Law 455.

[30] See Blair Commission Report, *supra* note 3 at 56.

Yet none of these recommended actions will likely be taken unless the basic current of Ivan Head's internationalist humanism and developmental ecumenism — that is, his much justified and evidence-based belief in "the mutual vulnerability of South and North" — is not itself more fully received and internalized across the South-North divide.[31] As Ivan Head himself did warn us: "[T]ime is not on the side of the North any more than it favors the South."[32]

[31] See I.L. Head, *On a Hinge of History: The Mutual Vulnerability of South and North* (Toronto: University of Toronto Press, 1991).

[32] See Head, "South-North Dangers," *supra* note 1 at 86.

"On a Hinge of History":
The Global Environmental and
Health Dimensions of Mutual Vulnerability
in the Twenty-First Century

OBIJIOFOR AGINAM

Humankind today, for the first time in five millennia of recorded activity, faces circumstances of global dimensions: possible nuclear cataclysm, environmental degradation, economic collapse. These are dangers of a quality that may not permit recovery. The circumstances contain margins of error so narrow as to be almost meaningless. Moreover, the combination of today's technologies and yesterday's politics has produced trends that, unless altered significantly, may well become irreversible.[1]

— Ivan Head

If the ever-decreasing open forests of developing countries are not to be destroyed in the ceaseless quest for firewood, thus broadening the deserts, sweeping away top soil, and silting up harbours and power dams; if social and political instability are not to lead increasingly to outside intervention and surrogate conflicts ... if economic uncertainty, unsupportable debt burdens, protectionist threats, and the ferment of widespread unemployment are to be contained before they combine to create a depression of global proportions — if these major factors are to be managed wisely, the co-operative involvement of developing countries is essential.[2]

— Ivan Head

Obijiofor Aginam, LL.B (Nigeria); LL.M (Queen's); Ph.D (British Columbia); Assistant Professor of Law, Carleton University, Ottawa. I am grateful for the opportunity to contribute this piece in honour of Ivan L. Head of blessed memory, a renowned international lawyer, humanist, and global champion in the fight against poverty. I studied under Ivan Head's supervision for my doctorate at the University of British Columbia (1998–2001), and, throughout my tenure as his doctoral student, I learned much from his vision of globalism, global governance, and international law as well as from his mentorship of many other graduate students in law and political science. Ivan Head passed away on 1 November 2004. I dedicate this short piece to his blessed memory.

[1] Ivan Head, "The Contribution of International Law to Development" (1987) 25 Canadian Yearbook of International Law 29.

[2] *Ibid.*

PROLOGUE: MUTUAL VULNERABILITIES IN THE GLOBAL VILLAGE

With the above words, Ivan L. Head, one of the most conspicuous faces in Canadian foreign policy circles in the 1970s, urges
international lawyers, foreign policy experts, and scholars interested
in North-South relations to reflect critically and deeply on the
emerging global issues of our time. These words, originally part of
Ivan Head's remarks at the annual meeting of the Canadian Council on International Law in 1986,[3] subsequently became the cen-
terpiece of his monumental contributions to the discourse of
international law and "South-North"[4] relations traversing approximately two decades.[5] Ivan Head's critical and illuminating contributions to the discourse of mutual vulnerability of nations and
peoples in a globalizing world are brilliantly articulated in his ma-
jestic seminal work *On a Hinge of History: The Mutual Vulnerability of
South and North,*[6] which is a *multum in parvo* on the complex and
multifarious web of South-North dangers confronting the world at
the end of the millennium and during the transition to the twenty-
first century — hunger, disease, and abject poverty in most of the
South, environmental degradation, civil conflict, biological and
chemical threats, and possible nuclear cataclysm. The interdepen-
dencies between the nations of the South and those of the North
are "a microcosm of the vulnerabilities that now beset all nations ...
as they face one another"[7] in the emerging "global neighbourhood."[8]

3   Ivan Head addressed the annual meeting of the Canadian Council on International Law (CCIL) in 1986 in his capacity then as the president of the International Development Research Centre (IDRC) in Ottawa. A revised version of Head's
remarks was subsequently published as "The Contribution of International Law
to Development" (1987) 25 Canadian Yearbook of International Law 29–45.

4   Head prefers the use of "South-North" as a more accurate reflection of the current state of the international system because the traditional usage of "North-
South" is misleading for "it lends weight to the impression that the South is the
diminutive." See I. Head, *On a Hinge of History: The Mutual Vulnerability of South
and North* (Toronto: University of Toronto Press, in conjunction with the International Development Research Centre, 1991) 14.

5   Some of Head's popular works on aspects of South-North relations include: *On a
Hinge of History, supra* note 4; *The Canadian Way: Shaping Canada's Foreign Policy
1968–1984* (with Pierre Elliot Trudeau) (Toronto: McCelland and Stewart, 1995);
"Contribution of International Law," *supra* note 1; and "South-North Dangers"
(1989) 68 Foreign Affairs 71.

6   *Ibid.*

7   Head, *On a Hinge of History, supra* note 4 at 1.

8   I borrowed the expression "global neighbourhood" from the Commission on
Global Governance. See *Our Global Neighbourhood: The Report of the Commission on
Global Governance* (New York: Oxford University Press, 1995).

Global disequilibria and the resulting mutuality of vulnerability of societies in both the industrialized and the developing regions of the world are starkly manifested in the multifarious and intricately inter-connected vicissitudes of South-North disparities: economics, demographics, disease, and environment. Of all of these, "the economics" has become the most visible, due largely to the activism of the Group-of-77 developing countries and their proposal and/or agitation for a new international economic order (NIEO) in the 1970s. As Mohammed Bedjaoui explored in his influential book *Towards a New International Economic Order*,[9] the great North-South divide exemplified by the crushing indebtedness and deteriorating terms of trade and poverty of Third World countries is inseparable from what he juxtaposes as the "international order of poverty" and the "poverty of the international order."[10] Well over a decade ago, Julius Nyerere of blessed memory (former president of Tanzania and then chair of the South Commission) aptly observed that, if all of humanity were to be a single nation-state, the present North-South divide would have made it an ungovernable, semi-feudal entity, split by internal conflicts. A small part of it (one-quarter) would be prosperous and industrialized, while its bigger portion (three-quarters) would be poor and underdeveloped.[11]

This note is a concise exploration of the global environmental and health vicissitudes of South-North vulnerabilities that have continued to implicate the poverty and indifference of the international legal order — a web of vulnerabilities that has continued to anchor our global neighborhood on a hinge of history.

---

9 Mohammed Bedjaoui, *Towards a New International Economic Order* (Paris: UNESCO, 1979).

10 Bedjaoui juxtaposes the two concepts to indict international law as a Eurocentric, oligarchic, and plutocratic discipline that has historically upheld a predatory economic order based on the economic exploitation of weak nations by the powerful, *ibid.* For a discussion of Bedjaoui's thesis in the context of contemporary Third World approaches to international law, see K. Mickelson, "Rhetoric and Rage: Third World Voices in International Legal Discourse" (1998) 16 Wisconsin Int'l L. J. 353. On the discourse of globalization and predatory economic order, see Richard Falk, *Predatory Globalization: A Critique* (Oxford: Blackwell, 1999); M. Chossudovsky, *The Globalization of Poverty: Impacts of IMF and World Bank Reforms* (Penang: Third World Network, 1997); J. Brecher and T. Castello, *Global Village or Global Pillage: Economic Reconstruction from the Bottom Up* (Boston: South End Press, 1994); and Walden Bello, *DeGlobalization: Ideas for a New World Economy* (London and New York: Zed Books, 2004).

11 See South Commission, *The Challenge of the South: The Report of the South Commission* (New York: Oxford University Press, 1990) at 1.

"ON A HINGE OF HISTORY": OUR GLOBAL NEIGHBOURHOOD AND
GLOBAL HEALTH GOVERNANCE

Today, in an interconnected world, bacteria and viruses travel almost as
fast as e-mail and financial flows. Globalization has connected Bujumbra
to Bombay and Bangkok to Boston. There are no health sanctuaries. No
impregnable walls exist between a world that is healthy, well-fed, and well-
off and another that is sick, malnourished, and impoverished. Globalization has shrunk distances, broken down old barriers, and linked people.
Problems halfway around the world become everyone's problems.

— Gro Harlem Brundtland[12]

Transcontinental networks of global interdependence, which have
propelled the complexities of the widely critiqued lopsided economic globalization, have globalized emerging and re-emerging
health risks and threats.[13] It is now generally accepted by scholars
of global health that the concept of state sovereignty is alien to the
microbial world as the geo-political boundaries of nation-states are
increasingly vulnerable to the dynamic processes of globalization.[14]
Kelly Lee has observed that contemporary globalism, premised on
the "death of physical and geographical distance," conceives the
world as a single place because of increased travel and other shared
experiences that lead to more localized, nationalized, and region-
alized feelings of spatial identity.[15]

---

[12] Gro Harlem Brundtland, "Global Health and International Security" (2003) 9 Global Governance 417.

[13] On the bourgeoning literature on globalization of public health, see D. Yach and D. Bettcher, "The Globalization of Public Health, I: Threats and Opportunities" (1998) 88 Am. J. of Pub. Health 735–38; D. Yach and D. Bettcher, "The Globalization of Public Health, II: The Convergence of Self-Interest and Altruism" (1998) 88 Am. J. of Pub. Health 738–41; David P. Fidler, "The Globalization of Public Health: Emerging Infectious Diseases and International Relations" (1997) 5 Ind. J. of Global Legal Stud. 1; G. Walt, "Globalization and International Health" (1998) The Lancet 434; Lincoln Chen, et al., eds., *Global Health Challenges for Human Security* (Cambridge: Harvard, 2003); and K. Lee and R. Dodgson, "Globalization and Cholera: Implications for Global Governance" (2000) 6 Global Governance 213–36.

[14] See Jan Art Scholte, *Globalization: A Critical Introduction* (New York: St. Martin's Press, 2000) at 16 (characterizing globalization as "the spread of supraterritoriality"). See also David Held et al., eds., *Global Transformations: Politics, Economics and Culture* (Cambridge: Polity Press, 1999).

[15] Kelly Lee, "Globalization, Communicable Disease and Equity: A Look Back and Forth" 42(4) (1999) Development (Special Issue on Responses to Globalization: Rethinking Health and Equity) 35.

In the twenty-first century, very few, if any, public health threats are "solely" within the jurisdiction of sovereign states. The spatial dimension of globalization means that a microbial superhighway now cuts across the entire global village. This, in turn, makes the distinction often drawn between national and international health threats obsolete and renders all of humanity mutually vulnerable to the potency of disease pathogens. The recent severe acute respiratory syndrome (SARS) outbreak, and its transcontinental spread from Asia to North America (Canada), like other infectious diseases before it, has challenged the orthodox Westphalian governance architecture as well as the embedded but flawed belief that there exists, in a globalizing world, a health sanctuary in the North, while the South remains a reservoir for disease.[16] The spatial dimension of globalization does not suggest that globalization, at least in the transnational health context, is a recent phenomenon. Seminal accounts of the transnational spread of infectious diseases suggest infallibly that the spatial dimension of globalization was a conspicuous feature of the earliest recorded epidemics in history. Thucydides, in his account of the plague of Athens during the Peloponnesian War in 430 BC, observed that the plague first originated in Ethiopia and then descended into Egypt and Libya and much of the Persian Empire before it was introduced into Athens by troops during the war.[17]

The cumulative effects of the erosion of geo-political boundaries as a result of the globalization of public health and the impact of the South-North divide on populations within such boundaries has traditionally placed global health within the agenda of multilateral institutions. Public health poses global challenges that require global governance approaches. Despite the enviable feat by the orthodox multilateral health institutions — the World Health Organization, the Food and Agriculture Organization, UNICEF,

---

[16] For a discussion of SARS and the Westphalian concept of sovereignty, see Obijiofor Aginam, "Between Isolationism and Mutual Vulnerability: A South-North Perspective on Global Governance of Epidemics in an Age of Globalization" (2004) 77 Temple Law Review 297; Obijiofor Aginam, "Globalization of Infectious Diseases, International Law and the World Health Organization: Opportunities for Synergy in Global Governance of Epidemics" (2004) 11 New Eng. J. of Int'l & Comp. L. 59.

[17] Thucydides, *History of the Peloponnesian War* (R. Warner, trans.) (Penguin Books, 1954). See also James Longrigg, "Epidemic, Ideas, and Classical Athenian Society," in T. Ranger and P. Slack, *Epidemics and Ideas* (Cambridge: Cambridge University Press, 1992) at 21.

and UNAIDS — new evidence that links health with pernicious poverty and underdevelopment in most of the South has emerged.[18] The mortality and morbidity burdens of leading killer diseases — HIV/AIDS, tuberculosis, and malaria, to mention a few — have rendered the South *de trop* in our global neighbourhood.

"On a Hinge of History": Our Global Neighbourhood and Global Environmental Governance

The life of all people, including the poor of the Third World, or the life of the planet, are not at the center of concern in international negotiations on global environmental issues ... Global environmental problems have been so constructed as to conceal the fact that globalization of the local is responsible for destroying the environment which supports the subjugated local peoples ... Multilateralism in a democratic set-up must mean a lateral expansion of decision-making based on the protection of local community rights where they exist, and the institutionalization of rights where they have been eroded.

— Vandana Shiva[19]

One of the policy lenses through which international lawyers explore global environmental issues that are within the parameters of South-North relations is the concept of sustainable development. Five years preceding the 1992 World Conference on Environment and Development in Rio de Janeiro, Brazil, the World Commission on Environment and Development (the Brundtland Commission)[20] had, in 1987, popularized the term "sustainable development" to strike a much-needed balance between environment and development. *Our Common Future,*[21] the widely cited report of the Brundtland Commission, defined sustainable development as "development that meets the needs of the present without compromising the ability

18 See World Health Organization, *Macroeconomics and Health: Investing in Health for Economic Development: Report of the WHO Commission on Macroeconomics and Health* (World Health Organization (WHO) with the Center for International Development, Harvard University), chaired by Jeffrey Sachs (Geneva: WHO, 2001).

19 Vandana Shiva, "The Greening of the Global Reach," in W. Sachs, ed., *Global Ecology: A New Era of Political Conflict* (Halifax: Fernwood, 1993) at 149, 151, 155.

20 Dr. Gro-Harlem Brundtland was former prime minster of Norway and the past director-general of the World Health Organization, Geneva, Switzerland.

21 Brundtland Commission, *Our Common Future* (Oxford: Oxford University Press, 1987).

of future generations to meet their own needs"[22] and asserted that environmental protection and developmental challenges are inexorably linked. The Rio Declaration on Environment and Development proclaimed in Principle 4 that, "in order to achieve sustainable development, environmental protection shall constitute an integral part of the development process and cannot be considered in isolation from it."[23] In the post-Rio years, sustainable development has emerged as the buzzword in local and global environmentalism. As the cornerstone of safeguarding the environment for present and unborn generations, the utility of sustainable development in the ecological struggles worldwide has become the centerpoint of a raging South-North debate. What then does sustainable development mean in the ecological struggles across societies South and North? Ten years after Rio, world leaders met in Johannesburg, South Africa, from 26 August to 4 September 2002 in search of concrete initiatives to move sustainable development forward in the multilateral ecological relations of states. The World Summit of Sustainable Development, according to the United Nations secretary-general Kofi Annan, would make a difference in five key areas: water and sanitation, energy, health, agricultural productivity, biodiversity, and ecosystem management, which were all identified by the acronym WEHAB.[24]

The road from Rio to Johannesburg in search of a holistic *corpus juris* on sustainable development has not only been long, it has also been traversed by normative deficits. An acrimonious South-North debate, socio-economic inequalities, and increasing ecological insecurity in most of the South have stained the balance sheet of sustainable development in the past twelve years since Rio. The pressures that global environmentalism exert on customary/indigenous approaches to conservation of floral and faunal resources in societies of the South are now aptly exemplified by the tensions between entrenched land and resource use by local communities as well as the pressure of global environmentalism catalyzed by the economic need of the South to attract powerful multinational corporations as foreign investors. Bedjaoui's "poverty of the international order" offers useful insights on the "timidity" and indifference of international law as an engine of ecological injustice

---

[22] *Ibid.* at 43.

[23] Rio Declaration on Environment and Development, 3 June 1992, UN Doc. A/CONF. 151/26/Rev. 1 (1992), reprinted in 31 I.L.M. 876 (1992).

[24] United Nations, Press Release DPI/2277, July 2002.

— for instance, in the interaction of local communities and multinational corporate giants in oil-producing regions of Nigeria, Ecuador, and other resource-rich societies of the South.[25] International law's indifference is not limited to the indiscriminate exploitation of natural resources in the South by influential multinational corporate actors. The phenomenon is a feature of international environmental law as a whole. Karin Mickelson has correctly observed that the discipline of international environmental law is ahistorical with the concomitant portrayal, by the discipline and its scholars, of the South as a grudging participant rather than an active partner in the formulation and generation of global environmental regimes.[26] One way to address the local-global environmental tensions is to "universalize" ecological concerns by genuinely placing humanity at the epicentre of sustainable development. To humanize this universalizing agenda, global environmental governance must tap the wealth of customary conservation practices across cultures. Judge Weeramantry's separate opinion in the International Court of Justice decision in *Case Concerning the Gabčíkovo-Nagymaros Project*[27] underscores the emerging *erga omnes* character of ecological disputes as well as the relevance and normative character of customary conservation practices across culturally divergent societies.

25 On the apparent "indifference" of international law to the ecological struggles in the exploitation of natural resources of the South by multinational corporations, see Obijiofor Aginam, "Saving the Tortoise, the Turtle, and the Terrapin: The Hegemony of Global Environmentalism and the Marginalization of Third World Approaches to Sustainable Development," in O. Okafor and O. Aginam, eds., *Humanizing Our Global Order: Essays in Honour of Ivan Head* (Toronto: University of Toronto Press, 2003) at 12; Scott Holwick, "Transnational Corporate Behavior and Its Disparate and Unjust Effects on the Indigenous Cultures and Environment of Developing Nations: *Jota v. Texaco,* a Case Study" (2000) 11 Colo. J. Int'l Envt'l. & Pol'y 183; Ike Okonta and Oronto Douglas, *When Vultures Feast: Shell, Human Rights, and Oil in the Niger Delta* (San Francisco: Sierra Club Books, 2001); R. Witzig and M. Ascencios, "The Road to Indigenous Extinction: Case Study of Resource Exploitation, Disease Importation, and Human Rights Violations against the Urarina in the Peruvian Amazon" 4(1) Health & Hum. Rts. 61; and Jennifer E. Brady, "The Huaorani Tribe of Ecuador: A Study of Self-Determination for Indigenous Peoples" (1997) 10 Harv. Hum. Rts. J. 291.

26 Karin Mickelson, "South, North, International Environmental Law and International Environmental Lawyers" (2000) 11 Y.B. Int'l Envt'l L. 52.

27 *Case Concerning the Gabčíkovo-Nagymaros Project (Hungary v. Slovakia),* [1997] I.C.J. Rep. The dispute involved the environmental sustainability of certain development projects on the Danube River.

EPILOGUE: MILLENIAL WAKE-UP CALL — NOT PROPHESY
OF DOOM

International scholars who explore the South-North dangers of
lopsided global health and environmental governance are often
accused of being doomsayers — they prophesy trivial environmental and transnational health problems in terrifying language. The
depletion of the ozone layer, destruction of biodiversity, extinction
of endangered species, and the return of the fourth horseman in
the apocalypse (with pestilence) would spell doom for all of humanity. What ought we to do to humanize our global order based
on a humane and cooperative South-North partnership? As Ivan
Head wrote in *On a Hinge of History,*

this volume contains no grand design for wondrous outcomes. Nor is it
intended to be a prophet of doom. Its purpose is to lay before the reader
the empirical results of sound research that illustrate the extent to which
Canada and the other countries of the North now are vulnerable to events
in the South, the enormity of the disequilibria now influencing our future, and the range of options open to us to ensure for ourselves and the
billions of human beings who live in the South a future of hope.[28]

In essence, *On a Hinge of History,* albeit replete with startling facts on
the vulnerabilities of South and North because of the prevailing
global predatory order, is never a doomsday message. It is about
ethics as an inherent human characteristic, ethics as a contributor
to the primacy of human dignity, and ethics as an inter-generational
obligation that we owe to unborn generations across geo-political
boundaries.[29] The fact that every human life is of value is the enriching legacy that Ivan Head, a man who was called "the Kissinger
of Canada"[30] on his death on 1 November 2004, bequeathed to
international lawyers and scholars of foreign policy in Canada
and the world over. This legacy, which was well articulated in *On a
Hinge of History* as an "end-of-millennium benediction,"[31] is acknowledged in *Humanizing Our Global Order*[32] as a "dawn-of-millennium

[28] Head, *On a Hinge of History, supra* note 4 at 8–9.

[29] *Ibid.*, preface at xii.

[30] See Ron Osillag, "Ivan Head: The Kissinger of Canada 1930–2004," *Globe and Mail,* 6 November 2004.

[31] Head, *On a Hinge of History, supra* note 4, preface at xii.

[32] Obiora Chinedu Okafor and Obijiofor Aginam, eds., *Humanizing Our Global Order: Essays in Honour of Ivan Head* (Toronto: University of Toronto Press, 2003).

wake-up call" by some international scholars — individuals who have been influenced in many ways by Ivan Head's vision of globalism and his legacy of international law and foreign policy disciplines.

Chronique de Droit international économique en 2003 / Digest of International Economic Law in 2003

I Commerce

préparé par

RICHARD OUELLET

I INTRODUCTION

L'année 2003 en fut généralement une de déception au plan du commerce multilatéral et régional. Les progrès dans les négociations de la ZLÉA se sont faits attendre. La Conférence ministérielle de l'OMC à Cancun fut un échec. Les différends commerciaux ont peu évolué. Sans être une année catastrophe, 2003 est à classer parmi les années de vache maigre.

Au plan national, il convient de signaler que le portefeuille du Commerce international est passé, en toute fin d'année 2003, de Pierre Pettigrew à Jim Peterson.

II LE COMMERCE CANADIEN AUX PLANS BILATÉRAL ET RÉGIONAL

A LES NÉGOCIATIONS COMMERCIALES AUX PLANS BILATÉRAL ET RÉGIONAL

1 Le projet de la ZLÉA

Le projet de création de la Zone de libre-échange des Amériques a continué de progresser avec lenteur en 2003. À la mi-février, des représentants des trente-quatre pays impliqués dans ce processus d'intégration ont échangé à Panama leurs offres initiales d'accès aux marchés en ce qui concerne les services, l'investissement et les marchés publics. Les offres canadiennes excluaient les secteurs de la santé, de l'éducation publique et des services sociaux, trois champs d'activités que le Canada considère non négociables. Le

---

Richard Ouellet est professeur à la Faculté de droit et à l'institut québécois des hautes études internationales, Université Laval.

Canada a aussi cherché à conserver un maximum de marge de manœuvre dans la poursuite de ses politiques culturelles.

Les 20 et 21 novembre, à Miami, en Floride, s'est tenue la Huitième Réunion ministérielle de la ZLÉA. Cette rencontre des trente-quatre ministres du Commerce des Amériques devait marquer la fin de la première moitié des négociations devant mener à la création de la ZLÉA. On pourra dire de la Déclaration ministérielle issue de la Réunion qu'elle contient essentiellement des énoncés de principe généraux.[1] Les principaux engagements figurant dans la Déclaration portent sur la coopération, sur la prise en compte des différences dans les niveaux de développement et la taille des économies, sur la transparence et sur la participation de la société civile. Pas de signe d'avancées importantes sur le fond des questions commerciales. Les trente-quatre Ministres responsables ont pourtant réaffirmé leur engagement à réussir les négociations de la ZLÉA pour janvier 2005.[2]

2   *Les autres développements aux plans bilatéral et régional*

La Réunion de la Commission du libre-échange de l'ALÉNA s'est tenue à Montréal le 7 octobre 2003. Le représentant américain au Commerce, M. Robert Zoellick, le secrétaire mexicain à l'Économie, M. Fernando Canales, et le ministre canadien du Commerce international, M. Pierre Pettigrew, ont alors convenu d'importantes mesures susceptibles de rendre le processus de règlement des différends du chapitre 11 plus transparent et d'amenuiser certaines barrières au commerce. Les trois ministres ont également profité de l'occasion pour célébrer, un peu à l'avance, les dix ans de l'ALÉNA, entré en vigueur le 1er janvier 1994.[3]

Les Ministres du commerce de l'ALÉNA ont donc adopté des directives qui permettront d'uniformiser les notifications d'intention à être déposées par les investisseurs qui souhaitent avoir recours à l'arbitrage en vertu de la section B du chapitre 11 de l'ALÉNA. Ils ont aussi approuvé des lignes directrices pour la pré-

---

1   Déclaration ministérielle, Zone de libre-échange des Amériques, Huitième Réunion Ministérielle, Miami, États-Unis, 20 novembre 2003, disponible à l'adresse <www.alca-ftaa.org/Ministerials/Miami/miami_f.asp>.

2   *Ibid.* au par. 5.

3   Déclaration conjointe, Commission du libre-échange de l'ALÉNA, Montréal, le 7 octobre 2003, disponible à l'adresse <www.dfait-maeci.gc.ca/trade/nafta-alena3statement-fr.asp>.

sentation de mémoires par des tierces parties aux mêmes arbitrages. Toujours dans l'optique d'améliorer la transparence du chapitre 11, les ministres du commerce ont réaffirmé leur engagement à tenir, quand cela est possible et accepté par la partie contestante, i.e. l'investisseur, des audiences publiques.

B   LES DIFFÉRENDS LIÉS À L'ALÉNA

Relativement peu d'événements intéressants au plan juridique sont à signaler en 2003 quant aux différends liés à l'ALÉNA. Quelques différends et tensions ont quand même assombri les liens commerciaux entre le Canada et les États-Unis en 2003. Bœuf, blé et bois d'œuvre ont été au cœur des débats entre Canadiens et Américains.

À la suite de la déclaration d'un cas d'encéphalopathie spongiforme bovine, les États-Unis ont fermé leur frontière au bœuf canadien. Des mesures d'aide du gouvernement canadien se sont avérées nécessaires pour assurer le maintien en activité des producteurs bovins.

Dans le secteur du blé, les autorités commerciales américaines ont imposé des droits anti-dumping sur le blé de force roux du printemps provenant du Canada. Cette décision américaine est à coup sûr le présage de longs débats entre le Canada et les États-Unis sur cette question.

Quant au bois d'œuvre, bien que des groupes spéciaux binationaux constitués en vertu du chapitre 19 de l'ALÉNA aient encore, en juillet, en août et en septembre,[4] donné raison au Canada, les États-Unis en fin d'année 2003 ont décidé une nouvelle fois d'imposer des droits sur le bois d'œuvre canadien.

III   LE COMMERCE CANADIEN ET L'OMC

A   LES NÉGOCIATIONS COMMERCIALES MULTILATÉRALES

Si l'année 2003 et la Conférence ministérielle de Cancun n'ont pas amené les résultats souhaités qui auraient relancé le processus de négociation commerciale multilatérale (sous-section 2), ce n'est pas faute par le Canada d'avoir été actif et d'avoir tenté de nourrir la dynamique des débats au sein de l'OMC (sous-section 1).

---

[4] On trouvera les textes complets de ces décisions sur le site de l'ALÉNA à <www.nafta-sec-alena.org>.

I   L'action canadienne au sein de l'OMC

L'année 2003 commençait sur les chapeaux de roue pour le ministre canadien du Commerce international, M. Pierre Pettigrew, qui confirmait, le 23 janvier, avoir proposé aux Membres de l'OMC une gamme d'améliorations au *Mémorandum d'accord sur le règlement des différends* en vue de le rendre plus efficace et plus transparent.[5] Cette proposition canadienne, qui s'inscrit dans le cours des négociations du cycle de Doha lancé en novembre 2001, a pour principal objet de permettre au public d'avoir accès aux audiences des Groupes spéciaux et de l'Organe d'appel. Elle vise aussi à ce que les exposés écrits déposés par les Membres de l'OMC auprès des Groupes spéciaux et de l'Organe d'appel soient rendus publics au moment de leur dépôt. Ces suggestions, on s'en doute, étaient assorties de modalités permettant d'assurer la protection des renseignements confidentiels émanant des entreprises impliquées dans les affaires portées devant les instances de l'Organe de règlement des différends. La proposition canadienne contenait enfin des recommandations ayant pour but d'améliorer l'efficacité du processus de sélection des membres des Groupes spéciaux.

En mars, le Canada recevait les félicitations de l'Organe d'examen des politiques commerciales de l'OMC pour le caractère libéral et transparent de sa politique commerciale.[6] Cet examen de la politique commerciale canadienne de 2003, septième exercice du genre pour le Canada depuis l'instauration en 1989 du *Mécanisme d'examen des politiques commerciales,* a amené l'Organe d'examen des politiques commerciales de l'OMC à reconnaître le Canada comme l'une des économies les plus ouvertes du monde et comme la cinquième plus grande nation commerçante.

---

5   On trouvera les termes complets de cette proposition canadienne sur le site WEB du Ministère canadien du Commerce international. Au moment de notre dernière visite, en avril 2005, l'adresse permettant d'avoir accès à cette proposition canadienne de janvier 2003 était toujours <www.dfait-maeci.gc.ca>. Le lecteur prudent voudra toutefois noter que la réorganisation du Ministère des Affaires étrangères et du Commerce international entraîne aussi une certaine réorganisation du site WEB du Ministère et qu'il nous a été permis de constater que de nombreuses pages WEB du Ministère changent d'adresse parce que modifiées, précisées et améliorées avec le temps.

6   Le texte de cet examen est disponible à <www.dfait-maeci.gc.ca/tna-nac/WTO-CTPR-fr.asp>. On aura aussi accès au texte de cet examen par le mécanisme de diffusion des documents du site de l'OMC à <www.wto.org>. Le Mécanisme d'examen des politiques commerciales peut quant à lui être consulté à <www.wto.org/french/tratop_f/tpr_f/tpr_f.htm> (dernière visite le 7 avril 2005).

Le 31 mars, le Canada rendait publics les engagements contenus dans son offre initiale en matière d'accès aux marchés pour le commerce des services.[7] Cette offre s'inscrit dans le cadre des négociations devant mener à l'élargissement de l'application de l'*Accord général sur le commerce des services*. Par son offre, le Canada s'est montré ouvert à améliorer l'accès aux marchés canadiens des services dans quelques secteurs où l'ouverture est particulièrement susceptible d'amener une baisse des prix pour les consommateurs canadiens: les services financiers, les affaires, les communications, les services de construction et de distribution, le tourisme et les services liés aux voyages, et les services de transport. Conformément aux engagements pris antérieurement par le gouvernement canadien, l'offre canadienne d'amélioration de l'accès aux marchés de services ne comprend aucun engagement concernant les secteurs de la santé, de l'enseignement public, des services sociaux et de la culture.

Du 28 au 30 juillet, le ministre canadien du commerce était l'hôte, à Montréal, d'une rencontre informelle réunissant vingt-cinq ministres du commerce provenant de pays Membres de l'OMC.[8] Cette rencontre voulait être l'occasion de faire le point sur l'état des négociations du *Programme de Doha pour le développement* et une ultime tentative d'ouverture des positions de négociation en matière d'agriculture, principale pierre d'achoppement des négociations, avant la Conférence ministérielle devant avoir lieu quelques semaines plus tard à Cancun. Ne permettant pas de rapprocher les parties, la Conférence aura surtout été l'occasion d'une prise de conscience du fossé séparant plusieurs Membres de l'OMC en matière de subventionnement agricole. Elle aura aussi été le présage de ce qui devait inévitablement arriver à Cancun.

2   *La Conférence ministérielle de Cancun*

Les représentants au niveau ministériel des 146 Membres de l'OMC se sont réunis du 10 au 14 septembre à Cancun, au Mexique, pour la Cinquième Conférence ministérielle de l'OMC.

---

[7] Le texte de cette offre est disponible par le site de l'OMC à <www.wto.org> ou par <http://strategis.ic.gc.ca>.

[8] Cette rencontre fut communément appelée la Mini-ministérielle informelle de Montréal. En plus du Directeur général de l'OMC, du Président du Conseil général de l'OMC et des représentants du Canada, elle regroupait des représentants au niveau ministériel provenant d'Afrique du Sud, d'Argentine, d'Australie, du Bangladesh, du Brésil, du Chili, de Chine, de Colombie, de Corée, du Costa Rica, des États-Unis, du Guyana, de Hong Kong, d'Inde, du Japon, du Kenya, du Lesotho, du Maroc, du Mexique, de Nouvelle-Zélande, de Singapour, de Suisse et de l'Union européenne.

Mises à part les accessions de deux nouveaux Membres, le Népal et le Cambodge, dont on peut se réjouir, il n'est pas exagéré de dire que cette Conférence ministérielle fut un échec. Alors qu'elle devait donner lieu à un examen à mi-parcours des négociations lancées à la Conférence ministérielle précédente à Doha et qu'elle devait permettre de convenir d'un nouvel agenda de négociation, elle n'a pas permis l'atteinte de consensus et n'a accouché que d'une courte et timide Déclaration ministérielle que l'on a, un temps, espéré beaucoup plus consistante. Ces piètres résultats ont amené le Directeur général de l'OMC, Supachai Panitchpakdi, à déclarer, à l'issue de la Conférence, que le blocage constaté à Cancun était un "contretemps." Il s'est dit "déçu mais pas déprimé." Pour comprendre la déception du Directeur général, il faut jeter un bref regard sur les événements qui ont précédé la Conférence de Cancun.

Le 26 juin 2003, soit quelques jours après la rencontre ministérielle informelle tenue à Montréal, l'Union européenne faisait connaître sa réforme de la Politique agricole commune (PAC).[9] Cette dernière mouture du mode général de gestion, de financement, de développement et de protection de la production agricole européenne constituait une avancée intéressante mais que le groupe de Cairns et les États-Unis s'empressaient de déclarer insuffisante pour les fins des négociations agricoles multilatérales. Pourtant, le 13 août, les États-Unis et l'Union européenne déposaient à l'OMC une proposition commune intitulée "Cadre pour une approche commune sur des questions agricoles."[10] Ce document, qui redonnait espoir à plusieurs, proposait quelques balises permettant de relancer les discussions relatives aux plus épineuses questions touchant le commerce agricole. Une semaine plus tard, le mal nommé Groupe des 21, une coalition de vingt-deux pays en développement parmi lesquels on comptait la Chine, l'Inde et le Brésil, déposait une position de négociation commune dans laquelle ils demandaient aux pays riches de réduire de façon substantielle leurs subventions agricoles et d'éliminer toute forme d'aide à l'exportation. Sur un tout autre thème, mais toujours dans l'esprit de faire progresser les négociations, les 146 Membres de l'OMC adoptaient le 30 août un accord facilitant l'importation de médicaments génériques pour les pays en développement démunis d'industrie

9 Voir le texte de cette réforme à l'adresse <http://europe.eu.int/comm/agriculture/mtr/index_fr.htm>.

10 Voir le texte de cette proposition à l'adresse <http://europe.eu.int/comm/trade/issues/sectoral/agri_fish/pr130803_en.htm>.

pharmaceutiques. Sur cette lancée, le président du Conseil général de l'OMC, M. Carlos Pérez del Castillo, et le Directeur général de l'OMC, M. Supachai, présentaient le 31 août un projet de Déclaration ministérielle qu'ils estimaient constituer une "base de discussion adéquate et gérable" utile dans la recherche d'un terrain d'entente à Cancun. Le texte de cette proposition, auquel devaient s'ajouter bon nombre de paragraphes et d'annexes qui auraient précisé les modalités de négociations, laissait clairement voir que les officiers de l'OMC espéraient pouvoir faire redémarrer les négociations dans tous les secteurs couverts par le Programme de Doha et sur d'autres questions plus pointues telles le subventionnement du coton amenées par certains Membres africains. Ainsi, à quelques jours de la Conférence ministérielle de Cancun, l'esprit général, sans être à la conciliation, permettait de croire que les Membres de l'OMC étaient disposés à débattre avec une certaine ouverture.

Les résultats de la Conférence ne furent donc pas à la hauteur des attentes qu'autorisaient les événements la précédant. Après cinq jours de négociations, au matin du 14 septembre, le président de la Conférence, le Ministre mexicain des relations extérieures, M. Luis Ernesto Delbez, constatant que l'atteinte d'un consensus était irréalisable à court terme, décidait de clore les négociations et la Conférence. Il s'est en effet avéré impossible de rapprocher les positions du Groupe des 21 d'une part et des États-Unis et de l'Union européenne d'autre part sur la question du subventionnement agricole. La question du coton africain a aussi été source d'importantes tensions. Le Bénin, le Burkina Faso, le Mali et le Tchad avaient présenté une initiative visant à obtenir l'élimination totale des subventions des pays du Nord, en particulier des États-Unis, et une indemnisation financière pour les pertes subies par les pays africains producteurs de coton. Le rejet de cette initiative a choqué bon nombre de PMA (pays les moins avancés) et de pays ACP (pays en voie de développement de l'Afrique, des Caraïbes et du Pacifique). L'échec des négociations sur ces préoccupations chères aux pays en voie de développement (PVD) eut un impact direct sur d'autres éléments inscrits à l'ordre du jour de la Conférence. Beaucoup de PVD, notamment africains, ont réagi à l'absence de compromis en matière agricole en s'opposant à l'ouverture des négociations sur ce qu'il est convenu d'appeler les questions de Singapour, c'est-à-dire les investissements, la concurrence, les marchés publics et la facilitation des échanges. Ce dernier blocage est frustrant pour le Canada parce qu'en plus de retarder des négociations très prometteuses pour l'économie canadienne, il faut noter que c'est le ministre canadien du commerce international, M. Pierre Pettigrew, qui était chargé de faciliter les échanges entre les Membres de l'OMC sur ces thèmes. Le Président de la Conférence, M. Delbez, a conclu en appelant les Membres de l'OMC à un examen de conscience et en les invitant à maintenir leur engagement à atteindre les objectifs fixés lors du lancement du Programme de Doha.[11] Il faut maintenant espérer que les positions de négociation des uns et des autres auront suffisamment évolué lorsque s'ouvrira la Sixième Conférence ministérielle de l'OMC, maintenant prévue pour décembre 2005 à Hong Kong.

B   LES DIFFÉRENDS DEVANT L'OMC IMPLIQUANT LE CANADA

Alors qu'il était en 2003 au cœur de tous les débats entourant l'avancement des négociations multilatérales, le Canada n'était pas particulièrement touché par des rebondissements spectaculaires dans les affaires litigieuses l'impliquant.

I   *Canada – Mesures concernant les exportations de blé et le traitement des grains importés*

Le 31 janvier 2003, les États-Unis et le Canada ont tenu les consultations que les États-Unis avaient requises en décembre 2002.[12] Ces consultations n'ayant pas permis de régler le différend, les États-Unis ont formellement demandé, le 6 mars 2003, l'établissement d'un groupe spécial.[13] En réaction à cette demande, le Canada a déposé une demande de décision préliminaire par laquelle il faisait valoir que certaines allégations formulées par les États-Unis dans leur demande d'établissement d'un groupe spécial ne satisfaisaient pas aux prescriptions de l'article 6:2 du Mémorandum d'accord sur le règlement des différends de l'OMC.[14] L'article 6:2

11 Voir le texte de la Déclaration ministérielle de Cancun et le résumé de la cinquième journée de la Conférence ministérielle de Cancun à l'adresse <www.wto.org/french/thewto_f/minist_f/min03_f/min03_14sept_f.htm>.

12 *Canada – Mesures concernant les exportations de blé et le traitement des grains importés,* Demande d'établissement d'un groupe spécial présentée par les États-Unis, OMC/WT/DS276/6, le 7 mars 2003. Pour une présentation des arguments des États-Unis à l'appui de leur demande de consultation, voir notre chronique «Commerce» dans le volume de l'an dernier de cet annuaire, à la p. 412.

13 *Ibid.*

14 *Canada – Mesures concernant les exportations de blé et le traitement des grains importés,* Demande d'établissement d'un groupe spécial présentée par les États-Unis, Décision préliminaire sur la compétence du groupe spécial au titre de l'article

prévoit que "La demande d'établissement d'un groupe spécial ... indiquera les mesures spécifiques en cause et contiendra un bref exposé du fondement juridique de la plainte, qui doit être suffisant pour énoncer clairement le problème." Le Canada s'est dit d'avis qu'en vertu de cet article, le groupe spécial chargé d'examiner la plainte américaine devrait se déclarer incompétent pour traiter de certaines allégations des États-Unis.[15] Ces derniers ont rétorqué que les prétentions canadiennes étaient dénuées de fondement et que les arguments canadiens à cet égard avaient de toute façon été présentés trop tard.[16] Le groupe spécial chargé de trancher cette question préliminaire a rejeté l'argument américain sur la tardiveté de la demande canadienne tout en indiquant que le système de règlement des différends de l'OMC était suffisamment flexible pour permettre aux États-Unis de déposer une nouvelle demande d'établissement de groupe spécial.[17] Les États-Unis ont suivi cette dernière suggestion dans les jours qui ont suivi la décision préliminaire.[18] Des suites plus concrètes dans cette affaire sont attendues en 2004.

2   *Canada – Mesures visant l'importation de lait et l'exportation de produits laitiers*

On se rappellera qu'à la fin de l'année 2002, les États-Unis, la Nouvelle-Zélande et le Canada étaient à la recherche d'un accord quant à l'application des décisions des groupes spéciaux et de l'Organe d'appel rendues dans cette affaire. Les négociations ont porté fruit. Le 17 janvier 2003, les parties ont demandé la suspension des arbitrages au titre de l'article 22:6 du Mémorandum d'accord sur le règlement des différends.[19] Le 9 mai, elles

---

6:2 du Mémorandum d'accord sur le règlement des différends, OMC/WT/DS276/12, le 21 juillet 2003. Dans les faits, cette décision fut transmise aux parties le 25 juin 2003.

[15] *Ibid.* au par. 2.

[16] *Ibid.* au par.3.

[17] *Ibid.* aux par. 64 et 65.

[18] *Canada – Mesures concernant les exportations de blé et le traitement des grains importés,* Demande d'établissement d'un groupe spécial présentée par les États-Unis, OMC/WT/DS276/9, le 1er juillet 2003.

[19] *Canada – Mesures visant l'importation de lait et l'exportation de produits laitiers,* Accord concernant la suspension de l'arbitrage au titre de l'article 22:6 du Mémorandum d'accord sur le règlement des différends, OMC/WT/DS103/31, le 22 janvier 2003; et Canada – Mesures visant l'importation de lait et l'exportation

confirmaient qu'un accord était intervenu entre toutes les parties à cette affaire.[20]

3   *Le bois d'œuvre résineux*

Quelques-unes des nombreuses procédures engagées par le Canada devant les instances de l'OMC relativement au commerce du
bois d'œuvre résineux avec les États-Unis ont connu des développements intéressants pendant l'année 2003.

Dans l'affaire *États-Unis – Détermination finale en matière de droits
compensateurs concernant certains bois d'œuvre résineux en provenance du
Canada*, le Groupe spécial chargé d'examiner la plainte canadienne
a rendu son rapport le 29 août.[21] Le Canada y a eu partiellement
gain de cause. Le Groupe spécial a conclu que la détermination
par le Département américain du commerce (DOC) de l'existence
d'un avantage conféré aux producteurs de bois d'œuvre résineux
et du montant de cet avantage était incompatible avec certaines
dispositions de l'*Accord sur les subventions et mesures compensatoires*.[22]
Le Groupe spécial a aussi décidé que le fait que le DOC n'a pas
effectué une analyse de la transmission en ce qui concerne les opérations en amont portant sur des grumes et du bois utilisés comme
matières premières entre des entités non apparentées était incompatible avec certaines dispositions de l'*Accord sur les subventions et
mesures compensatoires* et du GATT de 1994.[23]

Dans une affaire touchant des questions de dumping, *États-Unis
– Détermination finale de l'existence d'un dumping concernant certains bois
d'œuvre résineux en provenance du Canada*, la composition du Groupe
spécial dont le Canada avait demandé l'établissement fut connue

---

de produits laitiers, Accord concernant la suspension de l'arbitrage au titre de
l'article 22:6 du Mémorandum d'accord sur le règlement des différends, OMC/
WT/DS113/31, le 23 janvier 2003.

[20] On pourra prendre connaissance des termes de la solution convenue en consultant *Canada – Mesures visant l'importation de lait et l'exportation de produits laitiers*,
Notification de la solution convenue d'un commun accord, OMC/WT/DS113/
33, le 15 mai 2003.

[21] *États-Unis – Détermination finale en matière de droits compensateurs concernant certains
bois d'œuvre résineux en provenance du Canada*, Rapport du Groupe spécial, OMC/
WT/DS257/R, le 29 août 2003.

[22] *Ibid.* au par. 8.1b).

[23] *Ibid.* au par. 8.1c).

en août 2003.[24] Les travaux de ce groupe pouvaient donc commencer et des développements concrets sont attendus en 2004.

Une nouvelle affaire relative au bois d'œuvre a été portée devant les instances de l'OMC en 2003. Le Canada a en effet demandé l'ouverture de consultations dans une affaire intitulée *États-Unis – Enquête de la Commission du commerce international dans l'affaire concernant certains bois d'œuvre résineux en provenance du Canada.* Le Canada y attaque une décision rendue le 2 mai 2002 par la Commission internationale du Commerce des États-Unis et "selon laquelle une branche de production aux États-Unis est menacée de subir un dommage important en raison des importations de bois d'œuvre résineux en provenance du Canada dont le Département du Commerce a déterminé qu'elles sont subventionnées et vendues à un prix inférieur à leur juste valeur."[25] Le Canada prétend que cette décision est incompatible avec l'article VI:6a) du GATT de 1994 ainsi qu'avec de nombreuses dispositions de l'Accord antidumping et de l'Accord sur les subventions et mesures compensatoires. Le Groupe spécial chargé de cette affaire a été constitué en juillet. Il compte achever ses travaux et remettre son rapport en février 2004.

4   États-Unis – Loi de 2000 sur la compensation pour continuation du dumping et maintien de la subvention (CDSOA)

Dans cette affaire qui n'est pas sans lien avec le bois d'œuvre résineux,[26] les États-Unis avaient appelé de la décision rendue par le groupe spécial à la fin de l'année 2002. Le 16 janvier 2003, l'Organe d'appel faisait circuler son rapport dans lequel il confirmait en partie les constatations du Groupe spécial et déclarait que la Loi de 2000 des États-Unis sur la compensation pour continuation du dumping et maintien de la subvention (la CDSOA) était incompatible avec les articles 18.1 et 18.4 de l'Accord antidumping, 32.1 et 32.5 de l'Accord sur les subventions et mesures compensatoires

---

[24] *États-Unis – Détermination finale de l'existence d'un dumping concernant certains bois d'œuvre résineux en provenance du Canada,* Constitution du groupe spécial établi à la demande du Canada, OMC/WT/DS264/3, le 5 mars 2003.

[25] *États-Unis – Enquête de la Commission du commerce international dans l'affaire concernant certains bois d'œuvre résineux en provenance du Canada,* Demande de consultation présentée par le Canada, OMC/WT/DS277/1, le 7 janvier 2003.

[26] On trouvera un résumé de la décision du Groupe spécial rendue dans cette affaire en consultant notre chronique publiée dans le volume de l'an dernier de cet annuaire, à la p. 413.

et l'article XVI:4 de l'Accord sur l'OMC.[27] En juin, dans le cadre d'un arbitrage au titre de l'article 21:3c) du Mémorandum d'accord sur le règlement des différends, il était décidé que onze mois était le délai raisonnable à l'issue duquel les États-Unis devraient s'être conformés à la décision finale de l'Organe de règlement des différends (ORD).[28] Ce délai arrivait à expiration le 27 décembre 2003. Il sera intéressant, en observant les développements survenus en 2004, de vérifier si les États-Unis auront mis en œuvre la décision de l'ORD.

5 *Communautés européennes – Mesures affectant l'approbation et la commercialisation des produits biotechnologiques*

C'est peut-être un différend de l'ampleur de celui du bœuf aux hormones auquel le Canada a donné naissance au milieu de l'année 2003. Le Canada, comme les États-Unis, a en effet demandé l'ouverture de consultations[29] et, plus tard, l'établissement d'un groupe spécial,[30] en vue de déterminer la compatibilité avec les accords de l'OMC du moratoire appliqué *de facto* par sept pays européens sur l'approbation des produits génétiquement modifiés. Le Canada a vu ses ventes annuelles de canola en Europe passer de 185 millions de dollars à 1,5 million de dollars, depuis l'entrée en vigueur du moratoire européen en 1998. Le Canada prétend que ce moratoire n'est basé sur aucune évaluation scientifique du risque que posent les OGM et que le moratoire va à l'encontre de dispositions de l'Accord sur l'application des mesure sanitaires et phytosanitaires, de l'Accord sur les obstacles techniques au commerce, du GATT de 1994 et de l'Accord sur l'agriculture. L'affaire est à suivre. Elle risque de donner lieu à d'âpres débats.

---

27 États-Unis – *Loi de 2000 sur la compensation pour continuation du dumping et maintien de la subvention (CDSOA)*, Rapport de l'Organe d'appel, OMC/WT/DS217/AB/R et OMC/WT/DS234/AB/R, le 16 janvier 2003.

28 États-Unis – *Loi de 2000 sur la compensation pour continuation du dumping et maintien de la subvention (CDSOA)*, Arbitrage au titre de l'article 21:3c) du Mémorandum d'accord sur les règles et procédures régissant le règlement des différends, OMC/WT/DS217/AB/R et OMC/WT/DS234/AB/R, le 13 juin 2003.

29 *Communautés européennes – Mesures affectant l'approbation et la commercialisation des produits biotechnologiques*, Demande de consultation présentée par le Canada, OMC/WT/DS292/1, le 20 mai 2003.

30 *Communautés européennes – Mesures affectant l'approbation et la commercialisation des produits biotechnologiques*, Demande d'établissement d'un groupe spécial présentée par le Canada, OMC/WT/DS292/17, le 8 août 2003.

CONCLUSION

L'année 2003 en a été une de stagnation. Tant au plan régional qu'au plan multilatéral, les progrès en direction d'une économie plus ouverte ont été très modestes. Il est permis de s'inquiéter de cette situation, surtout au plan multilatéral. Des Membres importants de l'OMC, notamment les États-Unis, ne semblent pas s'émouvoir de cette situation. À défaut de pouvoir négocier au sein de grands forums, ils semblent pouvoir se contenter de bon gré de négociations commerciales bilatérales, quitte à multiplier les tables de discussion et les types d'accords qui en résulteront. Cette dynamique de l'intégration, si elle devait s'affirmer et se confirmer, serait une bien mauvaise nouvelle pour un État comme le Canada qui gagne à agir en contexte multilatéral.

II   Le Canada et le système financier international en 2003

préparé par

BERNARD COLAS

Depuis la perpétration des attentats terroristes du 11 septembre 2001 aux États-Unis, la communauté internationale a consacré une grande part de ses travaux à la lutte contre le terrorisme et le blanchiment d'argent ainsi qu'au renforcement de la transparence en matière d'informations financières. Ces travaux ont été menés de concert par le Groupe des vingt (I), les institutions financières internationales (II) et les organismes de contrôle des établissements financiers (III), le Groupe d'action financière (IV) et le Joint Forum (V) au sein desquels le Canada joue un rôle de premier plan.

I   LE GROUPE DES VINGT

À l'occasion de leur réunion annuelle tenue à Morelia au Mexique les 26 et 27 octobre 2003, le Groupe des vingt (G-20) a réaffirmé la nécessité de réduire la vulnérabilité extérieure des pays en développement et les déséquilibres entre ces derniers et les pays industrialisés.[1] À cet égard, il est essentiel selon le G-20 que d'une part les États accélèrent les réformes structurelles nécessaires à la croissance et à l'amélioration de la stabilité macro-économique et que d'autre part ces États se dotent d'un cadre politique propre à favoriser leur développement à moyen terme.[2]

Le G-20 a réaffirmé sa volonté d'accroître la prévention des crises financières et de réviser les mesures à prendre pour leur résolution.

Bernard Colas est Avocat associé de l'étude Gottlieb & Pearson (Montréal), Docteur en droit, et Vice-Président, Commission du droit du Canada. L'auteur remercie Xavier Mageau, LL.M., de la même étude pour son importante contribution à la préparation de cet article.

[1] *Communiqué, Fifth G-20 Finance Ministers' and Central Bank Governors' Meeting dated October 26–27, 2003*, au par. 1 (*Communiqué du G-20*).

[2] *Ibid.* au par. 1.

Le G-20 encourage le Fonds Monétaire International (FMI) à poursuivre ses travaux portant sur l'accroissement de sa capacité à identifier les différentes manifestations de la vulnérabilité telles que la monnaie et les autres incohérences dans les bilans. Le G-20 invite également le FMI à renforcer sa capacité de conseiller les membres quant aux réformes de leur politique économique. Le G-20 se félicite de l'utilisation croissante des clauses relatives aux actions collectives et encourage leur inclusion dans les obligations émises dans une juridiction étrangère. Le G-20 encourage également l'adoption des meilleurs pratiques composant les codes et standards internationaux, lesquels garantissent une bonne assistance, une croissance stable et une réduction des crises financières futures.[3]

Le G-20 prend également note de la diversité des moyens utilisés par les individus, les sociétés et les entités pour tirer profit du système financier international afin de se livrer à diverses activités illicites. Les membres du G-20 réitèrent leur engagement de coopérer dans la lutte à ces abus et lancent un appel à tous les États et particulièrement ceux de l'OCDE n'ayant pris aucune mesure à cette fin. Le G-20 s'engage également à assurer la surveillance des développements relatifs aux Centres Financiers Offshore basés sur les travaux du Fonds Monétaire International.[4]

Enfin, le G-20 réitère son engagement à lutter et à démanteler les réseaux de financement du terrorisme. Pour ce faire, le G-20 entend accroître ses efforts pour améliorer les systèmes financiers formels, pour étendre leur champ d'application et pour les protéger des abus. Le G-20 entend également se concentrer davantage sur les secteurs financiers informels pour assurer la surveillance appropriée et prendre les mesures d'applications appropriées.[5]

II   LES INSTITUTIONS INTERNATIONALES

A   FONDS MONÉTAIRE INTERNATIONAL (FMI)

La transparence du FMI et de ses opérations, la responsabilisation et l'ouverture du FMI sont l'objet d'une attention particulière du FMI des dernières années. Le FMI a notamment procédé à un examen de la politique de transparence du FMI. Suite à cet examen, le conseil d'administration du FMI a adopté une série de mesures afin d'accroître davantage la transparence. Le FMI a notamment

---

[3] *Ibid.* au par. 4.

[4] *Ibid.* au par. 5.

[5] *Ibid.* au par. 6.

convenu de passer de la publication volontaire à la présomption de publication des rapports relatifs à l'utilisation des ressources du FMI et de passer de la publication volontaire à la présomption de publication des rapports au titre de l'article IV à compter du 1er juillet 2004. Par ailleurs, la publication des rapports du personnel relatif à l'utilisation des ressources du FMI devient une condition préalable à toute recommandation de la direction du FMI d'autoriser un accord ou son examen par le conseil d'administration du FMI.[6]

La constitution du Bureau d'évaluation indépendant (BEI) en 2002 s'inscrit dans le souci du FMI d'accroître sa transparence. Suite à l'achèvement de l'évaluation relative à l'utilisation prolongée des ressources du FMI, le conseil d'administration du FMI a approuvé l'évaluation du BEI, qui a déposé son premier rapport annuel en 2003,[7] et la constitution d'un groupe de travail en charge du suivi. Le FMI a également vivement appuyé la mise en œuvre des recommandations de BEI affectant l'amélioration de la surveillance, la conditionnalité et la conception du programme.[8]

Par ailleurs, le FMI a continué à assumer un rôle de coordination en matière d'observation des normes et des codes au moyen de rapports sur l'observation des normes et des codes (RONC). Au cours de l'année 2003, le Canada a terminé un rapport sur les données. Outre le Canada, près de la moitié des 184 pays membres du FMI ont achevé au moins un module du RONC.[9]

Depuis les attentats terroristes du 11 septembre 2001, le FMI a œuvré au renforcement du secteur financier international. En 2003, le comité monétaire et financier international du FMI a souligné les mesures prises par la communauté internationale pour lutter contre le blanchiment de capitaux et le financement du terrorisme ainsi que les progrès du programme expérimental de douze mois sur les évaluations de la lutte contre le blanchiment de capitaux et le financement du terrorisme. Un rapport complet concernant ce programme expérimental devrait être remis au comité monétaire et financier international du FMI au cours de l'année 2004.[10]

---

[6] *Rapport sur les opérations effectuées en vertu de la Loi sur les accords de Bretton Woods et des accords connexes 2003* (ci-après *Bretton Woods 2003*) aux pp. 12 et 13.

[7] *Ibid.* à la p. 15.

[8] *Ibid.* à la p. 14.

[9] *Ibid.* à la p. 17.

[10] *Ibid.* aux pp. 17 et 18.

En ce qui concerne le réexamen du cadre juridique de la restructuration de la dette souveraine, le Canada a bien accueilli la proposition de la direction du FMI de mettre au point un mécanisme de restructuration de la dette souveraine qui soit semblable aux législations nationales sur les faillites. Toutefois, cette proposition n'a pu faire l'objet d'un consensus lors d'une réunion du comité monétaire et financier international du FMI en 2003.[11]

Au cours des dernières années, le FMI a adopté de nombreuses mesures en vue de prévenir les crises financières. L'une de ces mesures était la création d'une facilité de lignes de crédit préventives à la disposition des pays qui appliquent des politiques économiques saines contre les problèmes de balance de paiements découlant d'une contagion financière à l'échelle internationale. Comme cette facilité avait cependant été peu utilisée depuis sa création, le FMI a décidé, le 30 novembre 2003, de ne pas la renouveler.[12]

Les membres du FMI se sont également penchés sur la révision des quotes-parts. Cependant, comme aucun consensus ne s'est dégagé à propos de l'augmentation des quotes-parts, il a été convenu de vérifier au cours du treizième examen des quotes-parts si les ressources du FMI étaient suffisantes et d'envisager des mesures pour procéder à une répartition des quotes-parts tenant compte de l'évolution de l'économie mondiale et d'examiner des mesures pour renforcer la gouvernance du FMI.[13]

En septembre 2003, le Comité monétaire et financier international du FMI a rappelé l'importance de l'engagement à long terme du FMI envers les pays à faible revenu au moyen d'une aide technique ciblée, du renforcement de la capacité, de la surveillance et lorsque cela est justifié, d'une aide financière temporaire. Le Comité a également souligné l'importance de certaines initiatives concernant les cadres des politiques macro-économiques. Le FMI a notamment insisté sur le fait que ces initiatives doivent favoriser une croissance accrue, réduire la pauvreté et la vulnérabilité de ces pays aux chocs extérieurs, d'appuyer la croissance et le développement du secteur privé. Au cours de l'année 2004, le FMI procèdera à l'examen de son rôle à moyen terme auprès des pays à faible revenu et en particulier à l'examen de ses mécanismes et du financement de ces pays.[14]

---

11 *Ibid.* à la p. 22.

12 *Ibid.* aux pp. 23 et 24.

13 *Ibid.* à la p. 24.

14 *Ibid.* à la p. 27.

B   BANQUE MONDIALE

Au cours de l'année 2003, la Banque mondiale s'est engagée à accorder des prêts et des crédits totalisant 18,5 milliards de dollars américains à quatre-vingt-huit pays en développement ou en transition.[15]

En 2003, la Banque mondiale a poursuivi l'adaptation de son système de surveillance et d'évaluation des projets. Dans la cadre de cette adaptation, la Banque mondiale a, à la fin de l'année 2003, mis en place plusieurs projets pilotes axés sur les résultats obtenus dans le cadre des stratégies d'aide-pays. Les résultats obtenus dans ce cadre serviront à adapter les stratégies de la Banque mondiale.[16]

Au cours de cette même année, la Banque mondiale a poursuivi sa lutte en vue de réduire la pauvreté et de favoriser le développement humain. La Banque mondiale a notamment accru l'importance des enjeux du secteur social dans le cadre des programmes de stabilisation macro-économique et de réduction des objectifs de développment durable.[17]

La Banque mondiale a notamment approuvé un plan d'action concernant l'infrastructure dans le but de revitaliser les travaux de la Banque dans ce domaine. Cette revitalisation se fonde sur le constat que la croissance économique et le développement durable dépendent de façon importante des prestations de services rendus dans le domaine des infrastructures. Or, la diminution de l'investissement privé dans l'infrastructure des pays en développement a rendu nécessaire une adaptation importante du modèle administratif de la Banque mondiale. Grâce à un nouveau plan d'action, les services d'infrastructure seront fournis en mettant à contribution les fonds de toutes les sources publiques et privées appuyées par les produits de la BIRD, de l'IDA, de la SFI et de l'AMGI.[18]

En 2003, les engagements de la Banque mondiale en matière d'éducation ont augmenté de plus de 70 % par rapport à 2002 pour atteindre 2,3 milliards de dollars américains. Outre l'octroi de ces prêts, la Banque mondiale fournit un soutien important en matière d'éducation en effectuant des travaux consultatifs analytiques et stratégiques. La Banque mondiale continue d'offrir aux pays s'étant dotés de stratégies judicieuses en matière d'éducation une initiative d'aide accélérée. Cette initiative est complétée par

[15] *Ibid.* à la p. 34.
[16] *Ibid.* à la p. 41.
[17] *Ibid.* à la p. 47.
[18] *Ibid.* à la p. 47.

l'engagement de plusieurs donateurs bilatéraux de verser 200 millions de dollars américains pour appuyer l'éducation primaire de 2003 à 2005. Cette aide sera offerte à dix pays visés par l'initiative accélérée.[19] Le Canada s'est engagé à verser 135 millions de dollars canadiens de 2003 à 2008 pour des projets d'initiatives accélérées présentés par la Tanzanie, le Mozambique et le Honduras. Cette contribution canadienne vient s'ajouter aux engagements actuels pris par le Canada.[20]

Au cours des dernières années, la Banque mondiale a cherché à accroître son efficacité en réduisant les coûts. L'analyse de l'efficacité de la Banque mondiale est examinée par le Département de l'évaluation des opérations de la Banque mondiale (DEO). Au terme de l'examen mené en 2003, le DEO a conclu que 83 % des projets de la Banque mondiale obtenait une cote satisfaisante pour l'atteinte des objectifs visés.[21]

Sur le plan du développement du secteur privé, le Canada continue de travailler au développement d'un milieu propice à l'investissement et de cadres de saine réglementation permettant au secteur privé de croître de manière durable. En 2003, la Banque mondiale a publié un rapport intitulé *Doing Business in 2004* portant sur la réglementation dans les pays membres. Ce rapport, qui sera désormais publié annuellement, a pour objectif principal d'encourager les réformes en établissant des correspondances entre les pays.[22]

La lutte contre la corruption et la saine gouvernance est demeurée au fil des années l'une des priorités de la Banque mondiale. Dans le cadre de cette lutte, la Banque mondiale a, en 2003, rayé cinquante-six particuliers ou entreprises de la liste des personnes pouvant profiter des contrats adjugés dans le cadre des projets de financement de la Banque mondiale. La Banque mondiale a également émis cinq lettres de réprimandes à des personnes faisant affaires en 2003 avec elle en vertu de contrat qu'elle finançait.[23]

En ce qui concerne la gouvernance, la Banque mondiale a constaté que les problèmes de gouvernance demeurent endémiques dans un grand nombre de pays pauvres. Pour répondre à ce problème, la Banque mondiale a approuvé la création d'un fonds fi-

19 Ces pays sont le Burkina Faso, la Gambie, la Guinée, le Guyana, le Honduras, la Mauritanie, le Mozambique, le Nicaragua, le Niger et la République du Yemen.

20 *Bretton Woods 2003, op.cit.* note 6 à la p. 48.

21 *Ibid.* à la p. 49.

22 *Ibid.* aux pp. 50 et 51.

23 *Ibid.* aux pp. 52 et 53.

duciaire spécial de mise en œuvre de la stratégie des pays à faible revenus en difficulté. Ce fonds doit servir à financer de petits projets de démonstration ayant pour but d'améliorer la gouvernance et de raffermir la capacité des institutions.[24]

Dans le cadre du développement durable, la Banque mondiale a renforcé la mise en œuvre des politiques de protection permettant de déterminer les répercussions environnementales et sociales négatives d'un projet d'investissement financé par la Banque mondiale. Dans ce contexte, 83 % des nouveaux prêts à l'investissement sont maintenant assujettis à des niveaux variables d'évaluation environnementale. À cet égard, l'augmentation du nombre de projets assujettis à un examen environnemental et l'augmentation du nombre de documents divulgués s'expliquent par l'intégration accrue des préoccupations environnementales et sociales dans le portefeuille des prêts de la Banque mondiale.[25]

La Banque mondiale poursuit depuis plusieurs années ses efforts en vue d'accroître sa transparence. L'une des mesures adoptée à cette fin au cours des années précédentes est la création d'un panel indépendant chargé d'examiner les plaintes de l'extérieur concernant les projets soutenus par la Banque mondiale. Au cours de l'année 2003, le panel a reçu une nouvelle demande d'inspection se rapportant au deuxième projet touchant les égouts de Manille aux Philippines.[26]

Concernant l'allègement de la dette des pays pauvres très endettés (PPTE), des progrès encourageants ont été accomplis au cours de l'année 2003. En décembre 2003, 26 pays ont profité de l'allègement de la dette aux termes de l'initiative en faveur des PPTE, parmi lesquels dix ont bénéficié d'un allègement irrévocable de leur dette. Quatorze autres pays devraient achever le processus en 2004 et profiteront d'un allègement de la dette de 40 milliards de dollars américains dans le cadre de l'initiative en faveur des PPTE ainsi que de mesures additionnelles et le fardeau de la dette a été ou sera réduit en moyenne des deux tiers. Le Canada favorise également l'allègement de la dette des PPTE. Le Guyana a achevé les étapes de l'intiative à la fin de l'année 2003 alors que l'Éthiopie devrait l'avoir achevé au début de l'année 2004. Ces deux pays pourraient se prévaloir d'un effacement de leur dette en 2004.[27]

---

[24] *Ibid.* aux pp. 52 et 53.

[25] *Ibid.* à la p. 56.

[26] *Ibid.* aux pp. 58 et 59.

[27] *Ibid.* aux pp. 75 et 76.

III   ORGANISMES DE CONTRÔLE DES ÉTABLISSEMENTS FINANCIERS

A   COMITÉ DE BÂLE SUR LE CONTRÔLE BANCAIRE

En 2003, le Comité de Bâle sur le contrôle bancaire a poursuivi ses travaux portant sur la révision de l'Accord de Bâle sur les fonds propres qui sert maintenant de fondement à la réglementation d'une centaine de pays. Alors que la publication de l'Accord de Bâle II était prévue à la fin de l'année 2003, les changements de dernières minutes souhaités par les États-Unis ont retardé la promulgation au milieu de l'année 2004.[28]

Fin avril 2003, le Comité de Bâle a publié le troisième document soumis à consultation ainsi qu'une vue d'ensemble des principes de Bâle II. En octobre 2003, les autorités de surveillance américaine ont lancé une vaste consultation sur la proposition de mise en œuvre de Bâle II aux États-Unis d'Amérique qui ont conduit ces autorités à demander des modifications en réaction aux critiques émises par le secteur financier américain concernant le troisième document consultatif du Comité de Bâle.[29]

Suite à cette vaste consultation, les autorités de surveillance américaine ont conclu que l'application des méthodes les plus sophistiquées de Bâle II serait obligatoire pour les dix plus grandes banques américaines et facultatives pour dix autres alors que les méthodes de Bâle I demeureront applicables aux milliers d'établissements de petite et moyenne taille opérant au niveau local. Les autorités de surveillance américaine ont également affirmé que les filiales américaines de banques étrangères appliquant les méthodes simples de Bâle II bénéficieraient d'un traitement souple afin de simplifier le dispositif de contrôle consolidé selon le principe du pays d'origine.[30]

Le Comité de Bâle a convenu de modifier la base de calcul appliquée aux exigences de fonds propres pour les risques de crédit. De plus, suite à la demande des États-Unis, il a été décidé que seules les pertes non-anticipées doivent être couvertes par des fonds propres. Ces modifications ont été mises en consultation jusqu'au mois de décembre 2003. Le Nouvel Accord de Bâle devrait être publié au milieu de l'année 2004 alors que l'entrée en vigueur de Bâle II au Canada doit avoir lieu à la fin de l'année 2006.[31]

---

28   *Rapport de gestion de la Commission fédérale des Banques 2003* à la p. 110 (ci-après *Commission bancaire*).

29   *Ibid.* à la p. 111.

30   *Ibid.* à la p. 111.

31   *Ibid.* aux pp. 112 et 113.

Le groupe de travail sur les activités bancaires transfontalières a poursuivi ses travaux dans le domaine de la surveillance transfrontalière. Il a notamment concentré ses efforts sur le devoir de diligence en matière de prévention du blanchiment de capitaux et sur la surveillance mondiale ainsi que la limitation des risques juridiques et de réputation. Le groupe de travail a formulé diverses directives relatives à la procédure d'identification lors de l'ouverture de comptes. Ces travaux ont fait l'objet d'un document mis en consultation en août 2003. Ce document est notamment consacré à la surveillance consolidée des risques juridiques et de réputation. Les exigences posées à un système de gestion des risques destiné à identifier, limiter et surveiller les risques juridiques et de réputation sur une base consolidée y sont exposées.[32]

B ORGANISATION INTERNATIONALE DES COMMISSIONS DE VALEURS (OICV)

La conférence annuelle de l'OICV s'est tenue en octobre 2003 à Séoul en Corée du Sud. Cette conférence a été placée sous le thème «Les nouveaux défis pour les marchés des valeurs mobilières et les autorités de régulation». Les nombreuses débâcles financières d'entreprises ont clairement mis en évidence l'importance de la qualité des informations financières publiées. En effet, la probité des marchés de capitaux dépend fondamentalement de la qualité des informations financières publiées par les émetteurs et de la résolution adéquate des conflits d'intérêts auxquels sont confrontés les acteurs professionnels du marché.[33]

C'est dans ce contexte que l'OICV a publié en 2003 des principes concernant d'une part les conflits d'intérêts des analystes et d'autre part les conflits d'intérêts des agences de notation.

Les principes relatifs aux conflits d'intérêts des analystes prévoient principalement des mécanismes empêchant que les intérêts financiers des analyses ou des entreprises qui les emploient n'influencent pas les analystes et les recommandations. Les règles s'y rapportant doivent être conçues de façon à prévenir les conflits d'intérêts actuels et potentiels.

Les principes formulés par l'OICV à propos des agences de notation visent différents objectifs. Par leurs prises de position, les agences doivent égaliser le niveau de connaissance des emprunteurs, des bailleurs de fonds et des autres acteurs du marché. Leurs

[32] *Ibid.* à la p. 114.
[33] *Ibid.* à la p. 118.

évaluations doivent être formulées indépendamment de toute contrainte politique ou économique et sans dépendance financière. La divulgation des informations et la transparence doivent être considérées comme des objectifs majeurs de l'activité d'évaluation des agences qui doivent cependant traiter les informations de manière confidentielle lorsque le maintien du secret a été convenu.

IV GROUPE D'ACTION FINANCIÈRE SUR LE BLANCHIMENT
DE CAPITAUX (GAFI)

Le GAFI comptait trente-trois membres. Les pays membres du GAFI ont adopté en juin 2003 la nouvelle version des quarante recommandations. Cette révision apporte un certain nombre de changements importants dont la constitution d'une liste précise de crimes visant à étendre l'infraction de blanchiment de capitaux, l'instauration d'un devoir de vigilance relatif à la clientèle plus étendu pour les institutions bancaires, l'instauration de mesures renforcées pour les clients et les transactions présentant un degré de risque supérieur, notamment les relations de correspondant bancaire et les personnes politiquement exposées, une extension du champ d'application des mesures antiblanchiment aux entreprises et professions non financières désignées (casinos, agents immobiliers, avocats, comptables, notaires et professions juridiques) et l'introduction de mesures institutionnelles-clés, notamment en matière de coopération internationale.[34]

Par ailleurs, le GAFI avait publié dans la foulée des attentats du 11 septembre 2001 une série de mesures destinées à lutter contre le financement du terrorisme. Au cours de l'année 2003, le GAFI a publié des directives interprétatives sur trois des huit recommandations spéciales. Ces directives concernent la transparence des flux de paiement passant par les systèmes de transmission de fonds ou de valeurs quelque soit leur forme. D'autres directives portent sur la façon de s'assurer que les renseignements sur les donneurs d'ordre d'un virement électronique accompagnent le transfert et que ces renseignements soient immédiatement mis à la disposition des autorités de poursuite pénale, des cellules de renseignements financiers et des institutions bancaires bénéficiaires.[35]

Au cours de l'année 2003, les membres du GAFI ont poursuivi leurs efforts pour mettre en œuvre ces huit recommandations

[34] *Ibid.* à la p. 122 et *Rapport annuel du GAFI 2002–2003* aux pp. 4, 6–8 (ci-après *Rapport GAFI*).

[35] *Rapport GAFI, op.cit.* note 34 aux pp. 8–9.

spéciales. Plus des trois-quarts des membres du GAFI avait d'ailleurs en 2003 mis intégralement en œuvre la recommandation spéciale II sur la criminalisation du financement du terrorisme et du blanchiment de capitaux, la recommandation spéciale III sur le gel et la confiscation des avoirs des terroristes et la recommandation spéciale V sur la coopération internationale. Par ailleurs, plus de cent pays et territoires non membres du GAFI ont répondu au questionnaire d'auto-évaluation sur le financement du terrorisme.[36]

Au cours de l'année 2003, le GAFI a poursuivi sa coopération avec les organisations internationales. Cette coopération a débouché sur la mise au point d'une méthodologie commune pour évaluer le respect des normes de lutte contre le blanchiment de capitaux et le financement du terrorisme.

Le GAFI a également poursuivi ses travaux importants et permanents sur les pays et territoires non-coopératifs dans la lutte contre le blanchiment de capitaux en suivant de près les progrès que ces pays et territoires ont continué d'accomplir et en recommandant aux membres du GAFI d'appliquer des contre-mesures à ceux qui n'auraient pas fait de progrès suffisants dans ce domaine.

Les nouvelles recommandations définissent notamment les exigences minimales pour l'infraction sous-jacente au blanchiment de capitaux, l'identification du client et de l'ayant droit économique, l'attitude à l'égard des clients et les transactions présentant des risques particuliers, la conservation de documents, l'annonce des transactions et des clients suspects, l'extension des normes minimales en vigueur pour les établissements financiers à certaines professions n'appartenant pas au secteur financier (avocats, comptables, courtiers immobiliers) et le traitement réservé aux actions au porteur et aux trusts, de même que pour la surveillance et les autorités en charge de cette dernière, les attributions du bureau de communication ainsi que l'entraide judiciaire et administrative internationale.

V   LE JOINT FORUM

Le Joint Forum est un organisme de concertation créé en 1996. Il se penche sur des thèmes prudentiels transectoriels et s'attache à échanger des informations et à élaborer des normes de contrôle des conglomérats financiers. En août 2003, le Joint Forum a diffusé deux documents qui tiennent compte des constatations effectuées au cours des discussions informelles avec des groupes

---

[36] *Ibid.* aux pp. 8–9.

financiers opérant dans au moins deux ou trois secteurs tels les banques, les assurances et les valeurs mobilières.[37]

Le document intitulé *Trends in Risk Integration and Aggregation* constate que les groupes financiers diversifiés accordent une importance croissante à une maîtrise des risques intégrée et exhaustive qui s'applique à l'ensemble du groupe. Pour parvenir à la réaliser, ils font de plus en plus appel à des systèmes de mesures qui utilisent des modèles mathématiques visant à intégrer l'ensemble des risques, tous secteurs confondus.[38]

Le document intitulé *Operational Risk Transfer accross Financial Sectors* confirme que les groupes financiers sont bien convaincus de la nécessité de disposer d'une bonne gestion du risque opérationnel. Ce document analyse la manière dont ce risque peut être transféré d'un secteur à l'autre en particulier par le recours à l'assurance.

Le Joint Forum a par ailleurs décidé de poursuivre son examen du transfert du risque de crédit entre les secteurs financiers.

Ainsi, en 2003, les acteurs du système financier international ont concentré leurs efforts sur l'intensification de la lutte contre le blanchiment de capitaux et contre le financement du terrorisme et sur l'élaboration des mesures appropriées pour renforcer la transparence de leurs opérations, qu'il s'agisse du FMI et de la Banque mondiale ou du Comité de Bâle et de l'OICV. Dans le premier cas, le FMI et la Banque mondiale ont cherché à accroître la transparence de leur organisation alors que dans le second cas, le Comité de Bâle et l'OICV ont cherché à accroître la transparence dans les secteurs les concernant.

---

[37] *Commission bancaire, op.cit.* note 28 à la p. 124.

[38] *Ibid.* aux pp. 226–27.

III Investissement

préparé par
CÉLINE LÉVESQUE

INTRODUCTION

La chronique de l'année 2003 est l'occasion de faire un bilan des activités sous le régime du chapitre 11 de l'Accord de libre-échange nord-américain (ALÉNA) portant sur l'investissement. Les cinq années écoulées depuis le prononcé de la première sentence ont permis à certaines tendances de se profiler.[1] Selon les opinions, elles sont de bon ou de mauvais augure. D'une part, des remises en question directe et indirecte du système d'arbitrage font du chapitre 11 un régime mouvant (I). D'autre part, la situation est au beau fixe pour les États-Unis qui continuent, avec les sentences dans les affaires *Loewen* et *ADF*, d'échapper à une première condamnation (II).

Par ailleurs, des faits marquants de l'année 2003 méritent d'être soulignés. D'abord, sur la scène multilatérale, il faut prendre note de l'échec des négociations à la conférence ministérielle de l'Organisation mondiale du commerce (OMC) tenue à Cancun en septembre 2003. L'impossibilité de s'entendre sur le lancement de négociations sur l'investissement a contribué à cet échec. Les négociations de la Zone de libre-échange des Amériques (ZLÉA) ont

---

Céline Lévesque, professeure agrégée, Faculté de droit, Section de droit civil, Université d'Ottawa.

[1] La première sentence sur la compétence a été rendue dans l'affaire *Ethyl Corporation c. Canada*, Award on Jurisdiction (1999), 38 ILM 708 (le 24 juin 1998) (ci-après *Ethyl*). Par ailleurs, la première sur le fond a été rendue dans l'affaire *Azinian et al. c. Mexico*, ICSID Case No. ARB(AF)/97/2 (1999), 14 ICSID Rev. 535 et (2000), 39 ILM 537 (le 1er novembre 1999) (ci-après *Azinian*). Les sentences rendues sous le régime du c. 11 qui sont mentionnées dans cette chronique sont disponibles en ligne à partir de plusieurs sites internet, dont: T. Weiler à <http://www.naftaclaims.com/>; Commerce international Canada à <http://www.dfait-maeci.gc.ca/tna-nac/NAFTA-f.asp> et CIRDI à <http://www.worldbank.org/icsid/cases/awards.htm>.

473

également accusé un recul. À la réunion ministérielle de Miami, tenue en novembre 2003, les pays n'ont pu se mettre d'accord sur l'adoption de la formule de l'engagement unique. Or, on sait déjà que des pays comme le Brésil ne sont pas en faveur des procédures d'arbitrage investisseur–État prévues au chapitre de l'investissement. Aussi, la formule de négociations retenue est de nature à décevoir les partisans d'un accord global sur l'investissement dans le cadre de la ZLÉA.[2]

En revanche, les accords bilatéraux continuent de se multiplier. À la fin 2003, on en compte plus de 2200.[3] Cette augmentation marquée au cours des vingt dernières années s'est finalement répercutée dans le nombre de plaintes portées contre les États. Aussi, en 2003, le Centre international de règlement des différends relatifs aux investissements (CIRDI) a dépassé des records historiques d'activité. Fait notable, des trente nouvelles demandes d'arbitrage soumises au CIRDI durant l'année, vingt-neuf se fondaient sur un traité bilatéral portant sur l'investissement; l'autre était basée sur la Charte de l'Énergie.[4]

I   LE CHAPITRE 11: UN RÉGIME MOUVANT

Confrontées à des difficultés d'ordres divers, les Parties à l'ALÉNA ont réagi en s'attaquant au régime d'arbitrage prévu au chapitre 11. Le régime a fait l'objet d'un assaut direct quant à son manque de transparence et d'ouverture (A). Il a également été remis en question indirectement par des exceptions d'incompétence et des recours à l'encontre des sentences (B).

A   REMISE EN QUESTION DIRECTE

L'arbitrage commercial international est rarement associé à des concepts tels que la publicité, la participation de tierces parties ou

[2] Pour un traitement de ces négociations, voir la chronique du professeur Richard Ouellet portant sur le commerce dans cet Annuaire. Pour une description des enjeux des négociations sur l'investissement à l'OMC et dans le cadre de la ZLÉA, voir C. Lévesque, "Chronique de Droit international économique en 2001 — Investissement" (2002), 40 A.C.D.I. 453.

[3] CNUCED, Rapport sur l'investissement dans le monde 2004, Vue d'ensemble, Nations Unies, New York, 2004 à la p. 4. En ligne: <http://www.unctad.org/fr/docs/wir2004overview_fr.pdf>.

[4] Voir E. Gaillard, "Centre international de règlement des différends relatifs aux investissements (CIRDI) — Chronique des sentences arbitrales" (2004), 1 JDI 213 aux pp. 213-215 (ci-après Gaillard (2004)).

encore l'ouverture. Pourtant, sous le régime du chapitre 11, les Parties ont progressivement épousé ces concepts, en réaction aux décisions rendues par les Tribunaux arbitraux eux-mêmes ainsi qu'aux pressions de la critique.

La question de la confidentialité des procédures arbitrales a rapidement été l'objet de débats.[5] En juillet 2001, afin de clarifier la situation, la Commission du libre-échange a déclaré qu'aucune disposition de l'ALÉNA n'imposait de devoir général de confidentialité. Ainsi, sous réserve de certaines modalités et exceptions, les Parties peuvent rendre publics les documents soumis au tribunal ou produits par ce dernier.[6]

En 2003, les Parties ont fait un pas additionnel dans le sens de la transparence et d'une plus grande ouverture. D'une part, la Commission a confirmé le pouvoir des Tribunaux d'accepter les mémoires de tierce parties et recommandé des procédures applicables au traitement des demandes ainsi qu'à la procédure à suivre par les *amici curiae*.[7] D'autre part, le Canada et les États-Unis ont confirmé leur consentement à ce que les audiences d'arbitrage dans les affaires auxquelles ils sont parties soient publiques, sous réserve de l'acceptation des investisseurs contestants et des Tribunaux, et de la protection des renseignements confidentiels.[8]

---

[5] Certains ont tôt fait de souligner que l'arbitrage commercial international entre parties privées ne soulevait généralement pas les questions d'intérêt public qui étaient souvent au coeur des procédures investisseur–État. Voir par ex. H. Mann et K. von Moltke, *NAFTA's Chapter 11 and the Environment: Addressing the Impacts of the Investor-State Process on the Environment* (1999), International Institute for Sustainable Development aux pp. 50–59.

[6] Commission du libre-échange de l'ALÉNA, Notes d'interprétation de certaines dispositions du chapitre 11, 31 juillet 2001, en ligne: <http://www.dfait-maeci.gc.ca/tna-nac/NAFTA-Interpr-fr.asp> (ci-après Notes d'interprétation 2001).

[7] Voir Commission du libre-échange de l'ALÉNA, Déclarations sur le fonctionnement du chapitre 11, 7 octobre 2003. En ligne: <http://www.dfait-maeci.gc.ca/tna-nac/nafta_commission-fr.asp>.
Le Tribunal dans l'affaire *Methanex* a été le premier à accepter le principe de la participation de tierce parties. Voir *Methanex Corporation c. United States*, Decision of the Tribunal on Petitions from third persons to intervene as *"amici curiae"* (rendue le 15 janvier 2001). Voir aussi la décision dans l'affaire *United Parcel Service of America Inc. c. Canada*, Decision of the Tribunal on Petitions for intervention and participation as *amici curiae* (rendue le 17 octobre 2001). Par ailleurs, afin d'améliorer l'efficacité des procédures, la Commission a recommandé qu'un formulaire type de notification de plainte à l'arbitrage soit utilisé par les investisseurs.

[8] Voir Déclaration du Canada sur l'ouverture au public des audiences d'arbitrage au titre du chapitre 11 de l'ALÉNA, 7 octobre 2003. En ligne: <http://www.

Ces avancées, en commençant par l'accès aux documents qui ouvre la porte aux *amici* et informe le public qui peut assister à certaines audiences, ont l'avantage de combler le supposé déficit démocratique dont souffre le chapitre 11 de l'ALÉNA. En optant pour la transparence et l'ouverture, les Parties démontrent qu'elles non rien à cacher et espèrent que le public sera également de cet avis. Certains estiment plutôt que les nouvelles mesures nuisent à l'efficacité du processus et diminuent sa légitimité. Les *amici*, perçus comme représentants des intérêts particuliers, sont mal vus dans un monde où le gouvernement représente l'intérêt général. Aussi, certains pensent que la participation de tierce parties augmente non seulement les coûts directs de l'arbitrage mais nuit au règlement à l'amiable des différends.[9]

Somme toute, on peut penser que ces développements auront un effet bénéfique sur le chapitre 11. Il est douteux que l'on puisse en dire autant de certains comportements des Parties qui ont pour effet de remettre en question, cette fois de façon détournée, le régime d'arbitrage choisi par elles.

B   REMISE EN QUESTION INDIRECTE

Confrontées à un nombre croissant de différends, les Parties à l'ALÉNA ont adopté des comportements contrastants. Après avoir consenti à l'arbitrage à l'avance dans le Traité, les Parties s'opposent de façon quasi systématique à la compétence des arbitres. Après s'être dotées d'un système de règlement des différends où les sentences se veulent finales, les Parties démontrent une tendance marquée en faveur des contrôles judiciaires. On peut se demander s'il s'agit là d'un exercice légitime de droits conférés par les règles d'arbitrage ou plutôt d'efforts pour miner l'édifice créé par le chapitre 11.

I   Exceptions d'incompétence

En date de la fin 2003, les États avaient soulevé des exceptions à la compétence du Tribunal dans presque toutes les affaires portées

---

dfait-maeci.gc.ca/nafta-alena/open-hearing-fr.asp>. On entrevoit pour ce faire des arrangements tels l'utilisation de systèmes de télévision en circuit fermé et de diffusion sur le Web. De tels arrangements ont été utilisés par exemple dans les affaires *UPS* c. *Canada* et *Methanex Corporation* c. *United States*.

9   Voir A.K. Bjorklund, "La participation des *amici curiae* dans les poursuites engagées en vertu des dispositions du chapitre 11 de l'ALENA" 22 mars 2002. En ligne: <http://www.dfait-maeci.gc.ca/tna-nac/participate-fr.asp>.

contre eux. Le Tribunal arbitral a décliné sa compétence de façon préliminaire une seule fois,[10] et dans une autre affaire la plainte a été rejetée pour défaut de compétence après l'audience au fond de l'affaire.[11]

Il ne fait pas de doute que dans certains cas les exceptions sont légitimes. Aussi, pour brosser un tableau plus nuancé de la situation, il faudrait évaluer au cas par cas les instances où le Tribunal a admis certaines objections à sa compétence mais en a rejeté d'autres, ce qui a eu pour effet de permettre au Tribunal de procéder au fond. C'est le cas de la décision rendue en 2003 dans l'affaire *Fireman's Fund c. Mexico*.[12] Le danger, semble-t-il, existe toutefois que les États abusent de cette faculté en soulevant des exceptions d'incompétence qui n'en sont pas réellement ou qui sont sans mérite apparent. Trois décisions rendues en 2002 illustrent cette proposition: *Waste Management c. Mexico*,[13] *Methanex c. United States*[14] et *UPS c. Canada*.[15]

Dans l'affaire *Fireman's Fund*, la demanderesse est une compagnie d'assurance constituée aux États-Unis qui a investi dans une

[10] *Waste Management, Inc. c. Mexico*, ICSID Case No. ARB(AF)/98/2 (2000), 15 ICSID Rev. 214 et (2001), 40 ILM 56 (sentence rendue le 2 juin 2000) (ci-après: *Waste Management I*).

[11] *The Loewen Group, Inc. et al., c. United States* (2003), 42 ILM 811 (sentence rendue le 26 juin 2003). Voir l'analyse de la décision à la Partie II.A ci-dessous. La tendance chez les arbitres à se déclarer compétents de façon préliminaire ou, le plus souvent, à joindre cette analyse au fond prête à réflexion. Le rejet de la majorité des exceptions d'incompétence est peut-être simplement le reflet de l'attaque quasi systématique dont leur compétence fait l'objet. La décision de joindre au fond pourrait quant à elle refléter la complexité des affaires soumises. Un regard plus suspicieux y verrait peut-être un intérêt des arbitres, non pas monétaire en tant que tel, mais plutôt personnel ou professionnel, à décider des affaires au fond. En revanche, il s'agit peut-être là de la façon pour un tribunal en quelque sorte de donner sa chance au coureur en examinant la plainte au fond.

[12] *Fireman's Fund Insurance Company c. Mexico*, Decision on the Preliminary Question, ICSID Case No. ARB(AF)/02/01 (rendue le 17 juillet 2003) (ci-après *Fireman's Fund*).

[13] *Waste Management, Inc. c. Mexico*, ICSID Case No. ARB(AF)/00/3, Mexico's Preliminary Objection concerning the Previous Proceedings, Decision of the Tribunal (2004), 6 ICSID Rep. 549 et (2002), 41 ILM 1315 (rendue le 26 juin 2002) (ci-après *Waste Management II*).

[14] *Methanex Corporation c. United States*, Preliminary Award on Jurisdiction and Admissibility (rendue le 7 août 2002) (ci-après *Methanex*).

[15] *United Parcel Service of America Inc. c. Canada*, Award on Jurisdiction (rendue le 22 novembre 2002) (ci-après *UPS*).

société de holding financière mexicaine. À la suite de la crise financière au Mexique, des efforts sont faits pour venir en aide à la société de holding mais sans succès. La problématique soulevée dans cette décision est celle de l'articulation des chapitres 11 et 14 (services financiers) de l'ALÉNA.[16] Après avoir considéré certaines définitions, le contenu des annexes ainsi que la structure de l'ALÉNA, le Tribunal a estimé que le chapitre 14 était applicable aux faits de l'espèce. En conséquence, il avait uniquement compétence pour se prononcer sur la violation de l'article 1110 sur l'expropriation, car cet article avait été incorporé au chapitre 14 et était assujetti à la procédure d'arbitrage investisseur–État.[17]

Dans l'affaire *Waste Management II*, le Tribunal a rejeté tous les arguments de manque de compétence avancés par le Mexique: la décision dans l'affaire *Waste Management I* n'interdit pas à la demanderesse de présenter à nouveau sa plainte, elle n'a pas autorité de la chose jugée et la demanderesse n'a pas commis un abus de procédure en engageant plusieurs recours, nationaux et internationaux.[18] Le raisonnement du Tribunal démontre que les positions du Mexique ne trouvaient pas appui dans le texte de l'ALÉNA ni dans le droit international applicable.

L'affaire *Methanex* illustre la propension des gouvernements à soulever des exceptions d'incompétence visant des questions qui relèvent plutôt du fond.[19] L'approche préconisée par les États-Unis

16 Il est à noter que dans cette affaire le Mexique n'a pas soulevé d'exceptions d'incompétence liées à l'application de l'art. 1110. Voir l'art. 1110, applicable par le biais de l'art. 1401(2). Voir *ibid.* au par. 2.

17 Plusieurs dispositions du c. 11, dont l'art. 1110 (expropriation et indemnisation) ont été incorporées au c. 14, tandis que d'autres tels les art. 1102 (traitement national) et 1105 (norme minimale de traitement) ne l'ont pas été. Ainsi, le Tribunal devait déterminer si le c. 14 s'appliquait aux faits de l'espèce. Si oui, seule la plainte au sujet de l'art. 1110 tombait dans son champ de compétence. Au contraire, si le c. 14 n'était pas applicable, parce que les sociétés de holding n'étaient pas des "institutions financières" au sens de ce chapitre, le c. 11 était applicable. Il est à noter que le c. 14 contient une disposition sur le traitement national (art. 1405), mais l'arbitrage investisseur–État ne s'y applique pas. Voir *Fireman's Fund, supra* note 12.

18 *Waste Management II, supra* note 13. On se rappellera que le Tribunal dans *Waste Management I, supra* note 10, avait décliné sa compétence de façon préliminaire parce que la demanderesse ne s'était pas conformée aux conditions préalables de soumission d'une plainte à l'arbitrage prévues à l'art. 1121 de l'ALÉNA. Revenant à la charge, la demanderesse avait cette fois respecté les conditions.

19 Il faut admettre que l'affaire *Methanex, supra* note 14, est complexe et qu'il est difficile de traiter succinctement de la décision sur la compétence qui compte

peut se résumer ainsi: afin de se prononcer sur sa compétence, le Tribunal doit interpréter tous les articles pertinents et décider si les faits allégués peuvent constituer des violations de ces articles.[20] En ce qui concerne les obligations substantielles, le Tribunal a rejeté cette approche. L'interprétation définitive des articles 1102, 1105 et 1110 en l'espèce ne relevait pas de la compétence mais bien du fond.[21]

L'affaire *UPS* fournit une dernière illustration. Il y est question de l'articulation des chapitres 11 et 15 (Politique de concurrence, monopoles et entreprises d'État), en particulier de l'interprétation de l'article 1116 qui fait référence à deux articles tirés du chapitre 15. Certains arguments du Canada sont légitimement liés à la compétence du Tribunal et ce dernier en a admis plusieurs. En revanche, d'autres relèvent du fond. L'un de ces arguments est que l'article 1105 ne réglemente pas les comportements anticoncurrentiels. Le Mexique et les États-Unis ont soutenu comme le Canada qu'il n'existe pas de règles de droit international coutumier en matière de concurrence. Après analyse, le Tribunal a décliné pour ce motif sa compétence sur le fondement de l'article 1105.[22] Il est toutefois permis de croire que la norme minimale développée par le droit international coutumier, dont le contenu fait l'objet de vigoureux débats, ne porte pas sur une matière en particulier mais plutôt vise des comportements divers, qui se trouvent en deçà

---

94 pages et qui, par ailleurs, n'est pas sans ambiguïté. De surcroît, certains des arguments présentés par les États-Unis visaient à proprement parler la compétence du Tribunal. En revanche, plusieurs autres arguments ont été rejetés par le Tribunal, et c'est l'aspect qui retiendra notre attention.

[20] On doit se rappeler qu'à cette étape des procédures, le Tribunal n'a entendu aucune preuve, n'a évalué la véracité d'aucun fait. En conséquence, l'analyse de la compétence est uniquement basée sur la foi des faits présentés par la demanderesse. Voir *ibid.*, p.ex., aux par. 44–45.

[21] D'autres arguments, fondés notamment sur le lien de causalité, ont été rejetés pour des motifs similaires. En revanche, l'approche suggérée a été retenue pour ce qui est des articles attributifs de compétence qui comprennent selon le Tribunal les art. 1101 et 1116–21. Dans son analyse de ces questions, le Tribunal a étudié les distinctions entre "admissibility" et "jurisdiction" et conclu qu'il n'avait pas le pouvoir d'admettre les objections d'admissibilité. Voir *ibid.* aux par. 121–26.

[22] "The Tribunal accordingly concludes that those parts of the ASC [amended statement of claim], which are based on article 1105, and which challenge anticompetitive behavior and the failure to prohibit or control it are not within its jurisdiction." *UPS, supra* note 15 au par. 99.

d'un certain seuil de traitement des étrangers, dont l'État est responsable. En somme, l'interprétation de l'article 1105, dans un sens comme dans l'autre, est une question de fond qui ne relève pas de la compétence du Tribunal à juger de cette affaire.

Ces décisions récentes mettent en lumière une problématique inhérente au chapitre 11. Les investisseurs ont peu à perdre, sinon du temps et de la crédibilité, lorsqu'ils allèguent des violations diverses, fondés sur des motifs variés. Espérant qu'une d'elles au moins sera retenue, ils agissent de façon stratégique. Les États, par contre, ne peuvent se permettre ce luxe. Et s'ils le font malgré tout, ils agissent à leur dépens. Signataires du Traité, les États doivent l'interpréter de bonne foi. Leurs arguments devraient contribuer à la cohérence du régime, et non pas l'amoindrir.[23] Ils devraient éviter de nuire volontairement à l'efficacité du régime, notamment en adoptant des moyens dilatoires.

2   Contrôle judiciaire

À la fin 2003, on compte huit sentences rendues sur le fond.[24] L'État a été condamné à payer des dommages dans quatre des affaires: le Canada par deux fois[25] et le Mexique par deux fois.[26] Dans trois des quatre cas, l'État a eu recours à la procédure de contrôle judiciaire à l'encontre de la sentence.[27] Étant donné que le siège du Tribunal arbitral a été le Canada dans chaque cas, les tribunaux canadiens ont entendu ces trois demandes.

[23] J.C. Thomas, "Investor-State Arbitration under NAFTA Chapter 11" (1999), 37 A.C.D.I. 99 à la p. 115; et D.M. Price, "Chapter 11 — Private Party vs. Government, Investor-State Dispute Settlement: Frankenstein or Safety Valve?" (2000), 26 Can.-U.S. L.J. 107 aux pp. 113–14.

[24] Ce nombre exclut les affaires qui ont été réglées avant le prononcé d'une sentence sur le fond, par exemple l'affaire *Ethyl, supra* note 1.

[25] *S.D. Myers, Inc.* c. *Canada*, Second Partial Award (sentence rendue le 21 octobre 2002) (ci-après *S.D. Myers — dommages*) et *Pope & Talbot* c. *Canada*, Tribunal's Award in Respect of Damages (2002), 41 ILM 1347 (sentence rendue le 31 mai 2002) (ci-après *Pope & Talbot – dommages*).

[26] *Metalclad Corporation* c. *Mexico*, ICSID Case No. ARB/(AF)/97/1 (2001), 16 ICSID Rec. 168 et (2001), 40 ILM 36 (sentence rendue le 30 août 2000) (ci-après *Metalclad*); *Marvin Roy Feldman Karpa* c. *Mexico*, ICSID Case No. ARB(AF)/99/1 (2003), 18 ICSID Rev. 488 et (2003), 42 ILM 625 (sentence rendue le 16 décembre 2002) (ci-après *Feldman*).

[27] L'exception est l'affaire *Pope & Talbot*, où le Tribunal a accordé à l'investisseur des dommages au montant de 461566 de dollars américains, une somme minime comparativement à ce que Pope & Talbot avait réclamé, soit un montant de plus de 500 millions de dollars. Voir *Pope & Talbot — dommages, supra* note 25.

Le nombre de cas est trop peu élevé pour que ces chiffres soient réellement significatifs. Toutefois, ils indiquent une tendance lourde de conséquences. Aussi, la prise de position du Canada dans ces affaires est inquiétante. En effet, le Canada est intervenu dans les trois cas en faveur d'une interprétation qui mine l'autonomie et la finalité propres à l'arbitrage international.

Il sera question des décisions des tribunaux judiciaires au sujet des affaires *S.D. Myers c. Canada*[28] et *Feldman c. Mexico*,[29] rendues respectivement au début 2004 et à la fin 2003. La première décision en son genre dans le cadre de l'ALÉNA a été rendue en 2001 dans l'affaire *Metalclad* c. *Mexico*.[30]

Comme il se doit, le contrôle judiciaire a été exercé en vertu de la loi du siège de l'arbitrage. Dans chaque cas, les lois pertinentes étaient fondées sur la loi type sur l'arbitrage commercial international adoptée par la Commission des Nations Unies pour le droit commercial international (CNUDCI) en 1985. Cette loi type prévoit que le recours en annulation est le seul moyen admis de contrôle d'une sentence arbitrale. L'article 34 contient des motifs exhaustifs tels que l'impossibilité pour une partie de faire valoir ses droits et le fait que la sentence contient des décisions qui dépassent les termes de la convention d'arbitrage ou encore que la sentence est contraire à l'ordre public.[31] Ces motifs sont donc limités et reflètent les valeurs d'autonomie et de finalité de l'arbitrage commercial international.

Dans ces procédures, le Canada et le Mexique ont plaidé que si l'on doit traiter avec déférence les décisions rendues par les Tribunaux arbitraux de différends commerciaux entre parties privées, le même égard n'est pas approprié dans le contexte de l'ALÉNA. Selon eux, l'intérêt public commande l'application d'une norme

---

[28] *Canada (P.G.) c. S.D. Myers Inc.*, [2004] 3 C.F. 368 (ci-après: *S.D. Myers, CF*). En ligne: <http://decisions.fct-cf.gc.ca/cf/2004/2004cf38.shtml>.

[29] *The United Mexican States c. Marvin Roy Feldman Karpa* (3 décembre 2003), Ottawa 03-CV-23500 (Ont. Sup.Ct.) (ci-après *Feldman, CS Ont.*). En ligne: <http://www.economia-snci.gob.mx/sphp_pages/importa/sol_contro/consultoria/Casos_Mexico/Marvin/revision/031203_Decision_Chilcott.pdf>.

[30] *The United Mexican States c. Metalclad Corp.*, 2001 BCSC 664, [2001] B.C.J. No. 950 (QL) (ci-après *Metalclad, C.S.C.B.*). En ligne: <http://www.international-economic-law.org/Metalclad/metalclad_judrev.pdf>. Voir aussi Supplementary reasons for judgment, 2001 BCSC 1529, [2001] B.C.J. No. 2268 (S.C.).

[31] Voir Loi type de la CNUDCI sur l'arbitrage commercial international (1985). En ligne: <http://www.uncitral.org/french/texts/arbitration/ml-arb-f.htm>.

de contrôle plus exigeante de ces sentences.[32] La norme de révision proposée est celle de la "décision correcte" tirée de l'approche "pragmatique et fonctionnelle" développée par la Cour Suprême du Canada en matière de droit administratif.[33]

En réponse à ce type d'arguments, les tribunaux judiciaires ont adopté le discours de la retenue mais la mise en pratique a été inégale. On se souviendra d'abord de la décision judiciaire dans l'affaire *Metalclad*. Après avoir affirmé que la norme de révision ne pouvait être celle développée par la Cour Suprême dans le contexte du droit national, le juge a effectivement procédé à une révision au fond de la conclusion du Tribunal arbitral notamment sur l'article 1105.[34] Cette décision a été l'objet de nombreuses critiques surtout à cause du degré d'ingérence dans la sentence.[35]

Dans l'affaire *Feldman*, le juge de la Cour supérieure de l'Ontario a rejeté la demande d'annulation de la sentence.[36] Le Mexique a prétendu qu'il lui avait été impossible de faire valoir ses droits, que

[32] Voir p. ex. la décision de la Cour dans *S.D. Myers, CF, supra* note 28 au par. 33 et le mémoire du Canada soumis dans cette affaire aux par. 136–38 (ci-après *S.D. Myers, CF* — mémoire du Canada). En ligne: <http://www.dfait-maeci.gc.ca/tna-nac/documents/FactandLaw.pdf>. Voir aussi dans le contexte de la révision dans *Metalclad* "Outline of argument of Intervenor Attorney General of Canada" (ci-après *Metalclad, CSCB* — Intervention du Canada) en ligne: <http://www.economia-snci.gob.mx/sphp_pages/importa/sol_contro/consultoria/Casos_Mexico/Metalclad/BC-SCJ/escrito_canada.pdf>.

[33] Voir *S.D. Myers, CF* — mémoire du Canada, *ibid.* aux par. 121 et s. Voir aussi *Metalclad, CSCB* — Intervention du Canada, *ibid.* aux par. 17 et s.

[34] Il a en effet déterminé que le Tribunal avait pris une décision qui dépassait les termes de la convention d'arbitrage en outrepassant les limites du c. 11: "In the present case, however, the Tribunal did not simply interpret the wording of Article 1105. Rather, it misstated the law to include transparency obligations and it then made its decision on the basis of the concept of transparency." (*Metalclad, CSCB* au par. 70). La sentence a toutefois été maintenue pour un des motifs d'expropriation (voir *ibid.* aux par. 81 et s.). Ironiquement, malgré son opinion que l'interprétation du Tribunal était extrêmement large, le juge a déclaré ne pas avoir la compétence pour intervenir car la définition de l'expropriation était une question de fond.

[35] Voir E. Gaillard, "Centre international de règlement des différends relatifs aux investissements (CIRDI) — Chronique des sentences arbitrales" (2002), 1 JDI 189 aux pp. 191–93 (ci-après: Gaillard (2002)) et G. Sacerdoti, "Investment Arbitration Under ICSID and UNCITRAL Rules: Prerequisites, Applicable Law, Review of Awards (2004), 19 ICSID Rev. 1 aux pp. 40–41.

[36] Le Mexique avait été condamné à payer environ 1,6 million de dollars américains à l'investisseur pour avoir violé l'art. 1102 de l'ALÉNA, Voir *Feldman, supra* note 26.

la procédure arbitrale n'avait pas été conforme à la convention des parties et que la sentence était contraire à l'ordre public.[37] Ayant d'abord indiqué dans un court paragraphe que sa compétence était limitée, le juge procède à une évaluation des faits et de la sentence qui donne à penser qu'il se prononce sur le fond.[38] Ce n'est que dans les trois dernières pages que le juge traite de la norme de révision applicable: "In my view, a high level of deference should be accorded to the Tribunal, especially in cases where the Applicant Mexico is in reality challenging a finding of fact."[39] Par la suite, le juge semble appliquer principalement l'approche "pragmatique et fonctionnelle."[40]

Dans l'affaire *S.D. Myers*, la Cour fédérale a également rejeté la demande d'annulation présentée par le Procureur général du Canada.[41] Après avoir passé en revue la jurisprudence, la Cour s'est exprimée ainsi:

Il faut mentionner que l'article 34 du Code n'autorise pas le contrôle judiciaire d'une décision entrant dans la compétence du tribunal dans le cas où la décision repose sur une erreur de droit ou une conclusion de fait erronée. Le principe de la non-intervention judiciaire à l'égard des sentences arbitrales qui relèvent de la compétence du tribunal arbitral a été maintes fois répété.[42]

Par la suite, la Cour a décidé que les arguments du Canada, qui alléguaient que la sentence contient des décisions qui dépassent

---

[37] Voir *Feldman, CS Ont.*, *supra* note 29 au par. 3. Le Canada est intervenu pour faire valoir que le Tribunal n'avait pas respecté la loi applicable et ainsi avait excédé sa compétence en ne tenant pas compte de l'art. 2105 de l'ALÉNA. Voir *ibid.* aux par. 26–38 et 42–48.

[38] Par exemple, lorsqu'il écrit: "In my opinion, Mexico is not precluded by Mexican law from tendering evidence before the Tribunal as to whether the corporate domestic resellers in question were in the same circumstances as CEMSA or as to whether those resellers were receiving rebates in circumstances in which rebates were being denied to CEMSA" (*ibid.* au par. 68). Plus loin, en référence à la sentence, il affirme: "This Court can find no reason to disagree with that conclusion"(*ibid.* au par. 71).

[39] *Ibid.* au par. 77.

[40] Voir *ibid.* aux par. 82 et s. Le Mexique a porté appel de cette décision.

[41] Le Canada avait été condamné à payer environ 6 million de dollars canadiens plus intérêts pour avoir violé les art. 1102 et 1105 de l'ALÉNA; voir *SD Myers*, *supra* note 25.

[42] *S.D. Myers, CF*, *supra* note 28 au par. 42.

les termes de la convention d'arbitrage, touchent la compétence du Tribunal. En conséquence, ces arguments ne sont pas admissibles car ils n'avaient pas été régulièrement soulevés devant le Tribunal arbitral.[43] La Cour a également rejeté l'argument que la sentence est contraire à l'ordre public.[44] À titre subsidiaire, la Cour a évalué le mérite des arguments de compétence en appliquant la norme de la "décision correcte" aux questions de droit pures et de la "décision raisonnable" aux questions mixtes de droit et de fait.[45] Après avoir estimé que les conclusions du Tribunal étaient correctes et raisonnables, la Cour a finalement tranché que même si elle en avait le pouvoir elle n'aurait pas annulé la décision quant à l'interprétation de l'article 1102 de l'ALÉNA.[46]

Les décisions de contrôle judiciaire dans les affaires *Feldman* et *S.D. Myers* ont été accueillies plus favorablement que celle rendue dans *Metalclad*.[47] Il est vrai que le résultat dans ces affaires est davantage conforme à la retenue dont devraient faire preuve les tribunaux judiciaires. Il n'en demeure pas moins que le traitement de la norme de révision, fortement influencé par le droit administratif canadien, laisse à désirer.

Les difficultés posées par ces recours sont symptomatiques d'un mal plus grave: la tentation pour les Parties à l'ALÉNA d'utiliser les tribunaux judiciaires pour remédier à ce qu'ils considèrent être des "mauvaises décisions" arbitrales ou encore pour contrer toute condamnation à payer des dommages-intérêts.[48] Une telle utilisa-

---

43 *Ibid.* aux par. 47–53.

44 La Cour a souligné que "[l]'ordre public" ne s'entend pas de la position politique ou de la position internationale du Canada mais s'entend des "notions et principes fondamentaux de la justice" (*ibid.* au par. 55). La Cour a ensuite décidé que "[e]n l'espèce, les conclusions du tribunal sur les deux questions de compétence ainsi que sur l'article 1102 ne sont pas 'manifestement déraisonnables,' 'clairement irrationnelles,' ne manifestent pas un 'manque total de réalisme' ou ne sont pas 'un déni de justice flagrant.'" Par conséquent, la Cour conclut qu'aucun aspect des décisions du tribunal faisant l'objet du contrôle judiciaire n'"est contraire à l'ordre public du Canada" (*ibid.* au par. 56).

45 Voir *ibid.* aux par. 57–58.

46 Voir *ibid.* aux par. 72–74.

47 Voir Sacerdoti, *supra* note 35 aux pp. 40–41.

48 La Cour en révision dans *SD Myers* a qualifié les arguments du Canada, quant à la définition de "investisseur" et "investissement," de la façon suivante: "La position du procureur général est une interprétation étroite, légaliste et restrictive qui est contraire aux objectifs de l'ALÉNA et à l'interprétation téléologique prescrite par l'article 2.01 de l'ALÉNA et l'article 31 de la Convention de Vienne" (voir *SD Myers, CF, supra* note 28 au par. 69).

tion dénature le contrôle judiciaire des sentences. Qui plus est, cette attitude remet en question l'efficacité même du système établi par les Parties pour régler les différends qui les opposent à des investisseurs.

En conclusion, il faut ajouter que l'analyse des questions "de compétence" par la Cour Fédérale dans l'affaire *S.D. Myers* laisse présager des exceptions d'incompétence encore plus nombreuses. En effet, la Partie qui ne veut pas être empêchée de soulever ce motif pour demander le contrôle judiciaire aura avantage à soulever toutes les exceptions d'incompétence concevables devant le Tribunal arbitral.

II   "SAUVE QUI PEUT": LES ÉTATS-UNIS TOUJOURS INDEMNES

Le résultat des affaires décidées est éclatant: USA — 3, Investisseurs canadiens — 0. Évidemment, ce tableau pourrait être appelé à changer à tout moment, car au moins cinq autres plaintes contre les États-Unis ont été soumises à l'arbitrage en date de 2003.[49] Il reste que pour l'instant, les États-Unis échappent à une condamnation.

Ces victoires américaines ont une dimension politique considérable. On a cru à quelques reprises que l'assaut lui-même, entre autres du système judiciaire américain, allait causer des dommages irréparables au chapitre 11, ou du moins aux accords qui lui succéderaient. Aucune condamnation n'est venue dans l'affaire *Mondev* qui concerne des décisions des tribunaux du Massachussets et certaines immunités dont bénéficient les autorités locales.[50] On a attendu fébrilement la sentence dans l'affaire *Loewen* qui remet en cause le système permettant à un jury d'octroyer des sommes phénoménales à titre de dommages punitifs (A). Même la politique du "Buy America" a échappé à l'assaut des investisseurs canadiens dans l'affaire *ADF* (B). D'aucuns ont cru que le chapitre allait subir un test déterminant dans l'affaire *Methanex* qui concerne l'interdiction d'un additif pour l'essence pour des motifs environnementaux et de santé publique.[51] La décision dans cette affaire se fait toujours attendre.[52]

[49] Voir les sites internet de T. Weiler à <http://www.naftaclaims.com/> et du US Dept. of State à <http://www.state.gov/s/l/c3741.htm>.

[50] *Mondev International Ltd.* c. *United States* (2004), 6 ICSID Rep. 192 et (2003), 42 ILM 85 (sentence rendue le 11 octobre 2002) (ci-après *Mondev*).

[51] Voir *Methanex, supra* note 14.

[52] Durant ce temps, le danger grande à Washington. Le Congrès américain n'est pas d'humeur à octroyer à des investisseurs étrangers plus de droits que ceux

A   L'AFFAIRE *LOEWEN C. UNITED STATES*

Trois aspects de la sentence dans l'affaire *Loewen*,[53] rendue en juin 2003, retiennent notre attention: la compétence du Tribunal et la règle de la nationalité continue, l'interprétation de l'article 1105, et la règle de l'épuisement des recours internes.

Les faits suivants ont donné lieu à ce différend. Raymond Loewen, citoyen canadien, et la compagnie Loewen Group, Inc., constituée au Canada, opèrent dans le secteur des services et de l'assurance funèbres aux États-Unis par l'intentée d'autres compagnies (ci-après collectivement: Loewen). Jerry O'Keefe et ses compagnies opéraient dans le même secteur d'activités (ci-après collectivement: O'Keefe). Suite à une action en justice entreprise par O'Keefe contre Loewen, un tribunal avec jury du Mississipi a octroyé au demandeur des dommages au montant de 500 millions de dollars américains, dont 400 millions à titre de dommages punitifs. Il s'agissait là du montant le plus important jamais accordé dans cet État; montant, par ailleurs, qui n'avait aucune commune mesure avec les sommes en litige.[54]

Durant le procès, les avocats de O'Keefe ont insisté indûment sur la nationalité étrangère de Loewen, et sur des disparités de race et de classe sociale entre leur client et Loewen.[55] Le juge n'est pas intervenu pour faire cesser ces propos et a, par la suite, refusé de donner une directive claire au jury de ne pas tenir compte de considérations de nationalité, de race ou de classe sociale. Loewen a voulu faire appel de cette décision, mais a rapidement été confronté à l'exigence d'une caution équivalant à 125 % du montant du jugement afin d'en suspendre l'exécution. Incapable d'obtenir des

---

dont bénéficient les investisseurs américains aux États-Unis. Le "no greater rights mandate" a un effet direct sur les Accords de libre-échange négociés par l'administration américaine. Voir C. Lévesque, "Chronique de Droit international économique en 2002 — Investissement" (2003), 41 A.C.D.I. 433.

53 *Loewen, supra* note 11.

54 Voir *ibid.* aux par. 3–4. Le Tribunal décrit ainsi les montants en jeu: "The dispute concerned three contracts between O'Keefe and Loewen said to be valued by O'Keefe at $980,000 and an exchange of two O'Keefe funeral homes said to be worth $2.5 million for a Loewen insurance company worth $4 million approximately." (*Ibid.* au par. 3). Le litige mettait en cause le droit des contrats, la responsabilité extra-contractuelle et le droit de la concurrence.

55 Par exemple, le Tribunal indique que: "O'Keefe's case at trial was conducted from beginning to end on the basis that Jerry O'Keefe, a war hero and 'fighter for his country,' who epitomised local business interests, was the victim of a ruthless foreign (Canadian) corporate predator. There were many references

tribunaux une diminution de ce montant pour "juste cause," Loewen, en 1996, a réglé avec O'Keefe pour un montant de 175 millions de dollars.[56]

Dans la soumission à l'arbitrage de sa plainte en 1998, Loewen allègue que la responsabilité des États-Unis en vertu de l'ALÉNA a été engagée en raison des agissements de ses tribunaux, en l'espèce de l'État du Mississipi. En particulier, Loewen invoque que le verdict de 500 millions, ainsi que les décisions de ne pas réduire le montant de la caution, sont des "mesures adoptées ou maintenues par une Partie" qui sont en violation des articles 1102, 1105, et 1110 de l'ALÉNA.[57]

En 2001, le Tribunal arbitral a rendu une décision où il rejette certaines exceptions d'incompétence présentées par les États-Unis et joint les autres au fond. Le Tribunal confirme notamment la responsabilité des États pour les actes de leurs juridictions.[58] Suite à des procédures de faillite, et après l'audience au fond de l'affaire, Loewen a cédé ses droits dans l'arbitrage à une compagnie canadienne créée uniquement pour cette fin et détenue par une compagnie constituée aux États-Unis. Cette cession a donné lieu à une nouvelle exception d'incompétence de la part des États-Unis en janvier 2002.[59]

En définitive, le Tribunal a rejeté la plainte de Loewen pour motif d'incompétence en faisant application de la règle de la nationalité continue. Il a d'abord soutenu que l'ALÉNA ne pouvait offrir de recours à une "compagnie américaine" contre le gouvernement des États-Unis.[60] En réponse à l'argument de la demanderesse qui alléguait qu'elle avait la nationalité requise au moment où la plainte a été portée, le Tribunal a estimé que: "In international law parlance, there must be continuous national identity from the date of the events giving rise to the claim, which date is known as the *dies a quo*, through the date of the resolution of the claim, which date is known

---

on the part of O'Keefe's counsel and witnesses to the Canadian nationality of Loewen ('Ray Loewen and his group from Canada')." (*Ibid.* au par. 56).

[56] *Ibid.* aux par. 4–7.

[57] *Ibid.* aux par. 39–40.

[58] *Loewen* c. *United States,* Decision of the Arbitral Tribunal on Hearing of Respondent's Objection to Competence and Jurisdiction (rendue le 5 janvier 2001), notamment aux par. 45–49, 54–58 et 70.

[59] *Loewen, supra* note 11 au par. 29.

[60] *Ibid.* au par. 223.

as the *dies ad quem.*[61] En ce qui concerne Raymond Loewen, le citoyen canadien, qui prétendait que sa condition n'avait pas changé, le Tribunal a estimé qu'il n'avait pas été établi que Raymond Loewen possédait ou contrôlait directement ou indirectement Loewen Group Inc. lorsque la plainte avait été déposée ou depuis sa réorganisation.[62]

Le Tribunal a également choisi d'inclure dans sa sentence les motifs de fond de rejet de la plainte, étant donné que cette analyse était déjà avancée lorsque l'exception d'incompétence a été soulevée.[63] Après avoir revu en détail le déroulement des procédures judiciaires, le Tribunal a conclu que: "By any standard of measurement, the trial involving O'Keefe and Loewen was a disgrace. By any standard of review, the tactics of O'Keefe's lawyers, particularly Mr. Gary, were impermissible. By any standard of evaluation, the trial judge failed to afford Loewen the process that was due."[64] Le Tribunal a ensuite interprété l'article 1105 en soulignant que:

Neither State Practice, the decisions of international tribunals nor the opinion of commentators support the view that bad faith or malicious intention is an essential element of unfair and inequitable treatment or denial of justice amounting to a breach of international justice. Manifest injustice in the sense of a lack of due process leading to an outcome which offends a sense of juridical propriety is enough, even if one applies the Interpretation [de la Commission du libre-échange de 2001] according to its terms.[65]

Le Tribunal a aussi noté que le droit international accordait une importance particulière aux violations discriminatoires du droit

---

61 *Ibid.* au par. 225. L'ALÉNA ne traite pas de cette question et c'est pourquoi le Tribunal se réfère à la règle de droit international coutumier (*ibid.* au par. 226).

62 Voir *ibid.* au par. 239 et le dispositif aux pp. 69–70. Une demande de décision supplémentaire a été faite suite au prononcé de cette sentence. Voir aussi E. Gaillard (2004), *supra* note 4 à la p. 233.

63 En ce qui concerne l'art. 1102, le Tribunal a conclu sommairement qu'il ne possédait pas les éléments de preuve pour comparer le traitement reçu par Loewen au traitement "le plus favorable accordé en circonstances similaires." (*Ibid.* au par. 140). Quant à l'art. 1110, le Tribunal a décidé aussi sommairement qu'il ne pouvait conclure à la violation de cet article que si un déni de justice était établi en vertu de l'art. 1105 (*ibid.* au par. 141).

64 *Ibid.* au par. 119.

65 *Ibid.* au par. 132.

national.[66] En l'espèce, la Cour avait permis que le jury soit influencé par des appels répétés au favoritisme local au dépens du défendeur étranger.[67] En somme, le Tribunal a conclu que la procédure viciée ainsi que le verdict excessif étaient contraires à la norme minimale de traitement du droit international et au traitement juste et équitable.[68]

Le Tribunal n'a pas pour autant conclu à une violation de l'article 1105 et ce en raison de son interprétation de la règle de l'épuisement des voies de recours internes. Le Tribunal avait traité de cette règle de façon préliminaire dans sa décision sur la compétence de 2001 mais n'avait pas tranché. Les États-Unis prétendent que la règle de l'épuisement des voies de recours internes, de caractère procédural, doit être distinguée de celle du caractère définitif des décisions judiciaires, une règle de fond. Aussi, Loewen ne pouvait se plaindre d'un déni de justice tant que les tribunaux supérieurs n'avaient pas eu l'occasion de remédier à la situation, en d'autres mots de rendre une décision "finale." Loewen, au contraire, s'appuie sur le libellé de l'article 1121 pour affirmer que les parties à l'ALÉNA ont voulu déroger à cette règle.[69] Au demeurant, les règles de "procédure" et de "fond" dont traitent les États-Unis ne constituent en réalité qu'une et même règle.[70]

Dans son raisonnement, le Tribunal a dû revenir sur une affirmation faite dans sa décision de 2001 selon laquelle: "the rule of judicial finality is not different from the local remedies rule."[71] Il a cette fois affirmé que quoique similaires, elles servaient des objectifs différents. Ne pouvant imaginer que les Parties à l'ALÉNA aient voulu déroger au droit international de façon implicite, le Tribunal a conclu: "Article 1121 involves no waiver of the duty to pursue local remedies in its application to a breach of international law constituted by a judicial act."[72] Le Tribunal s'est ensuite penché

---

[66] *Ibid.* au par. 135.

[67] *Ibid.* au par. 136.

[68] *Ibid.* au par. 137.

[69] L'article 1121 de l'ALÉNA aux par. (1)(b) et (2)(b), prévoit comme condition préalable à la soumission d'une plainte à l'arbitrage que l'investisseur renonce à son droit "d'engager ou de poursuivre, devant un tribunal judiciaire ou administratif ... des procédures se rapportant à la mesure ..."

[70] Voir *Loewen, supra* note 11 aux par. 143–46.

[71] Voir l'analyse, *ibid.* au par. 158.

[72] *Ibid.* au par. 164. De façon prudente, le Tribunal a aussi remarqué que cet article: "may have consequences where a claimant complains of international law

sur la question de savoir si des voies de recours effectives, adéqua-
tes et raisonnablement disponibles étaient offertes à Loewen dans
les circonstances.[73] Après une analyse détaillée, le Tribunal a conclu de façon affirmative.[74] Le Tribunal a donc tranché que Loewen
n'avait pas épuisé les recours qui lui étaient offerts et, en conséquence, n'avait pas prouvé une violation du droit international
coutumier pour laquelle les États-Unis étaient responsables.[75]

Cette sentence, empreinte de conservatisme et de prudence, a
fait l'objet de plusieurs critiques.[76] En particulier, on a souligné le
caractère daté et incomplet de l'analyse en matière de nationalité
continue.[77] On a noté le manque de motifs justifiant la décision de
considérer la demanderesse comme américaine et que Raymond
Loewen n'avait plus d'intérêt à faire valoir dans ces procédures.[78]
On a reconnu que la décision "consiste bel et bien à maintenir,
sous couvert de règle de fond, l'exigence traditionnelle d'épuisement des voies de recours lorsque c'est la responsabilité de l'État
du fait de ses juridictions qui est en cause."[79]

Le sentiment de retenue que le lecteur peut percevoir à la lecture de cette décision est confirmé à la toute fin de la sentence où le
Tribunal tente, après son dispositif, d'expliquer en termes de politiques sa décision de ne pas compenser Loewen pour ses peines,
malgré le constat de violation de la norme minimale de traitement.

---

not constituted by a juridical act. That is not a matter which arises here." (*Ibid.*
au par. 163).

[73] *Ibid.*, en particulier aux par. 168 et 165–71.

[74] "Here we encounter the central difficulty in Loewen's case. Loewen failed to
present evidence disclosing its reasons for entering into the settlement agreement in preference to pursuing other options, in particular the Supreme Court
option that it had under active consideration and preparation until the settlement
agreement was reached. It is a matter on which the onus of proof rested with
Loewen. It is, however, not just a matter of onus of proof. If, in all the
circumstances, entry into the settlement agreement was the only course which
Loewen could reasonably be expected to take, that would be enough to justify
an inference or conclusion that Loewen had no reasonably available and adequate
remedies." (*Ibid.* au par. 215).

[75] *Ibid.* au par. 217.

[76] Voir p. ex. J. Paulsson "Continuous Nationality in Loewen" (2004), 20 Arb. Int'l
213 et E. Gaillard (2004), *supra* note 4 aux pp. 230–35.

[77] Gaillard (2004), *ibid.* aux pp. 231–33; Paulsson, *ibid.* aux pp. 214–15.

[78] Gaillard (2004), *ibid.* à la p. 233; Paulsson, *ibid.* à la p. 214, note 5.

[79] Voir Gaillard (2004), *ibid.* à la p. 235, qui remet en question le bien-fondé de
cette décision.

Il affirme que le rôle des Tribunaux arbitraux n'est pas de servir d'instance d'appel et poursuit avec un avertissement: "Too great a readiness to step from outside into the domestic arena, attributing the shape of an international wrong to what is really a local error (however serious) will damage both the integrity of the domestic judicial system and the viability of NAFTA itself."[80] En somme, les États-Unis sortent indemnes de cet épisode et la tempête qui aurait pu déferler suite à une décision de condamnation du système de justice américain est évitée de peu.

B   L'AFFAIRE *ADF C. UNITED STATES*

L'intérêt quant au fond de la sentence dans l'affaire *ADF*,[81] rendue en janvier 2003, réside dans son traitement de l'exception prévue à l'article 1108 visant les marchés publics, de l'article 1105 à la lumière de l'interprétation de la Commission du libre-échange, et de l'article 1103 dans le sillage de l'affaire *Maffezini*.[82]

La demanderesse, ADF Group Inc., est une compagnie constituée au Canada dont la filiale, ADF International Inc. (ci-après collectivement ADF), opère aux États-Unis. En mars 1999, ADF a obtenu un contrat à titre de sous-traitant pour la fourniture d'acier de charpente dans le cadre d'un projet de construction d'autoroute dans l'État de la Virginie. Le contrat principal, conclu entre l'entrepreneur et le Département des Transports de la Virginie (ci-après: VDOT) ainsi que le contrat de sous-traitance contenaient une clause "Buy America." Afin d'obtenir le financement du gouvernement fédéral pour ce projet, l'État devait agir en conformité avec différentes lois et règlements ayant pour objet de s'assurer que l'acier utilisé était produit aux États-Unis. ADF a donc proposé d'utiliser de l'acier "produit" aux États-Unis mais transformé au Canada. Le DVOT a rejeté cette proposition qui, selon lui, n'était pas conforme aux règles applicables, et a par la suite refusé de déroger à la clause "Buy America." ADF a quand même réussi à fournir l'acier requis à partir des États-Unis mais a encouru des dépenses importantes. En mars 2000, ADF a porté plainte contre les États-Unis en vertu du chapitre 11 de l'ALÉNA.[83]

---

[80] *Loewen, supra* note 11 au par. 242.

[81] *ADF Group Inc. c. United States*, ICSID Case No. ARB(AF)/00/1 (2003), 18 ICSID Rev. 195 (sentence rendue le 9 janvier 2003) (ci-après *ADF*).

[82] Quant à la procédure, cette sentence traite en détails du choix du lieu de l'arbitrage et de la question de la production de documents. Voir *Ibid.* aux par. 8–38.

[83] Voir *ibid.* aux para. 1 et 44–59.

Le Tribunal dans cette affaire a été le premier à faire application de l'exception visant les marchés publics prévue à l'article 1108 de l'ALÉNA. En bref, cette disposition prévoit que les articles 1102, 1103, 1107 et certains alinéas de l'article 1106 ne s'appliquent pas "aux achats effectués par une Partie ou par une entreprise d'État..." En l'espèce, l'investisseur a démontré *prima facie* que les mesures considérées étaient incompatibles avec l'article 1106.[84] Après analyse, le Tribunal a jugé que l'exception de l'article 1108 était applicable et qu'en conséquence la plainte de l'investisseur fondée sur l'article 1106 devait être rejetée.[85] La même conclusion aurait été applicable à l'article 1102, mais le Tribunal n'a pas eu à franchir cette étape car il a jugé que la preuve de discrimination, *de jure* ou *de facto*, n'avait pas été faite.[86]

Le Tribunal a également rejeté les allégations fondées sur l'article 1105. Le traitement des Notes de la Commission du libre-échange de juillet 2001 visant à clarifier l'interprétation de cet article mérite qu'on s'y arrête. On se souviendra que dans l'affaire *Pope & Talbot*, le Tribunal avait émis l'opinion que ces Notes constituaient un amendement à l'ALÉNA et non une interprétation.[87] Le Tribunal a rejeté l'argument en ce sens présenté par ADF de manière tranchante:

---

84 Les États-Unis n'ont pas contesté le fait que les mesures en question imposaient des exigences de contenu national (1106(1)(b)) et constituaient des prescriptions ayant pour effet de privilégier les biens et services produits ou fournis sur leur territoire (1106(1)(c)). Voir *ibid.* au par. 159.

85 Le Tribunal a interprété les expressions "achats effectués" et "par une Partie" (en anglais: "procurement" "by a Party") en faisant en particulier appel au c. 10 de l'ALÉNA qui porte sur les marchés publics. Il a conclu que l'obtention de l'acier requis pour le projet de construction constituait un achat effectué par l'État de la Virginie; un achat attribuable en vertu de l'ALÉNA aux États-Unis. Voir *ibid.* aux par. 160–70. En revanche, le Tribunal explique que le c. 10 de l'ALÉNA n'est pas applicable à l'État de la Virginie. Voir *ibid.* aux par. 167–70.

86 Voir *ibid.* au par. 157: "The Investor did not sustain its burden of proving that the U.S. measures imposed (*de jure* or *de facto*) upon ADF International, or the steel to be supplied by it in the U.S., less favorable treatment vis-à-vis similarly situated domestic (U.S.) fabricators or the steel to be supplied by them in the U.S."
La sentence traite de façon succincte de l'objection des États-Unis que la plainte est réellement liée au commerce des biens, ici l'acier, et non pas à l'investissement: "The correctness of this approach is not self-evident to us, in view of the many and comprehensive areas with respect to which the investment of a Canadian investor may claim national treatment under Article 1102." (*Ibid.* au par. 155).

87 *Pope & Talbot, dommages, supra* note 25 au par. 47. Le Tribunal a tout de même procédé comme si les Notes constituaient une interprétation de l'art. 1105.

But whether a document submitted to a Chapter 11 tribunal purports to be an amendatory agreement ... or an interpretation rendered by the FTC under Article 1131(2), we have the Parties themselves — all the Parties — speaking to the Tribunal. No more authentic and authoritative source of instruction on what the Parties intended to convey in a particular provision of NAFTA, is possible. Nothing in NAFTA suggests that a Chapter 11 tribunal may determine for itself whether a document submitted to it as an interpretation by the Parties acting through the FTC is in fact an "amendment."[88]

En réponse à l'argument de ADF qui prétendait que le pouvoir de déterminer la loi applicable dans chaque cas autorisait cette détermination, le Tribunal a ajouté ceci:

A principal difficulty with the Investor's submission is that such a theory of implied or incidental authority, fairly promptly, will tend to degrade and set at naught the binding and overriding character of the FTC interpretations. Such a theory also overlooks the systemic need not only for a mechanism for correcting what the Parties themselves become convinced are interpretative errors but also for consistency and continuity of interpretation, which multiple ad hoc arbitral tribunals are not well suited to achieve and maintain.[89]

Même en tenant compte de l'interprétation de la Commission, il revenait au Tribunal de définir la norme applicable de droit international coutumier. D'abord, le Tribunal a insisté sur le fait que la norme était en constante évolution et qu'on ne pouvait pour différentes raisons se fier, ou du moins se limiter, à l'affaire *Neer*.[90] Le Tribunal n'a pas tranché la question de savoir s'il existe une norme générale de traitement ou, au contraire, s'il existe une obligation de faire la preuve dans chaque cas de la violation d'une norme spécifique applicable à un contexte particulier.[91] Optant pour la prudence, le Tribunal a procédé à l'analyse des faits sur la base suivante: "Without expressing a view on the Investor's thesis, we ask: are the U.S. measures here involved inconsistent with a *general* customary international law standard of treatment."[92] Après avoir évalué les arguments de ADF un à un, le Tribunal a conclu que

[88] *ADF, supra* note 81 au par. 177.

[89] *Ibid.*

[90] Voir *ibid.* aux par. 179–81.

[91] *Ibid.* aux par. 182–85.

[92] *Ibid.* au par. 186.

l'investisseur n'avait pas démontré que les mesures américaines étaient contraires à l'article 1105.[93]

Le Tribunal a clos son analyse en abordant l'article 1103.[94] L'investisseur a allégué que les dispositions de deux traités bilatéraux conclus entre les États-Unis, d'une part, et l'Albanie et l'Estonie, respectivement, d'autre part, offrent un traitement plus favorable aux investisseurs de ces pays qu'aux investisseurs canadiens. En particulier, les mesures considérées constitueraient une violation des dispositions concernant le traitement "juste et équitable" et la "protection et sécurité intégrales" prévues dans ces traités. Aussi, il s'agissait d'une violation de l'article 1103, car l'article 1105 de l'ALÉNA, à la lumière de l'interprétation de la Commission du libre-échange, prévoit un traitement qui est moins favorable.[95] Qui plus est, en s'appuyant sur la sentence dans l'affaire *Maffezini*, l'investisseur a prétendu que l'article 1102 "covers not just the treatment of foreign investors in the territory of a NAFTA Party, but also the treatment demanded by that NAFTA Party for its own investors outside its own territory."[96]

En définitive, le Tribunal n'a pas eu à trancher, car l'exception de l'article 1108 portant sur les marchés publics s'appliquait également à l'article 1103. Il a quand même cru bon de traiter des arguments de ADF. Le Tribunal a d'abord noté que, malgré des différences dans les textes, il n'était pas clair que les Traités États-Unis–Albanie et États-Unis–Estonie contenaient une norme autonome, distincte du droit international coutumier. Et même en tenant pour acquis son existence, le Tribunal n'était pas convaincu que la norme aurait été violée en l'espèce. En ce qui concerne l'article 1102, et l'argument tiré de la sentence *Maffezini*, le Tribunal a souligné le peu de motifs présentés dans cette sentence ainsi que les différences entre les traités considérées. Toutefois, il a conclu, à nouveau, sur la base de l'exception de l'article 1108, applicable notamment aux articles 1102 et 1103.[97]

---

93 Voir *ibid.* aux par. 187–92.

94 Le Tribunal s'était déclaré compétent de façon préliminaire pour décider de cette question malgré le fait que l'investisseur n'avait pas allégué de violation de l'art. 1103 notamment dans la soumission de sa plainte à l'arbitrage. Voir *ibid.* aux par. 127–39. Par ailleurs, le Tribunal a déclaré que des allégations liées à d'autres projets n'étaient pas admissibles. Voir *ibid.* aux par. 140–46.

95 Voir *ibid.* aux par. 75–80, 193.

96 Voir *ibid.* au par. 80.

97 Voir *ibid.* aux par. 194–98.

Dans cette affaire, l'article 1108 a effectivement permis aux États-Unis d'échapper à une première condamnation, et au Tribunal de ne pas prendre position sur quelques questions épineuses. L'impact des clauses de traitement de la nation la plus favorisée, dont le libellé diffère selon les traités, est toujours incertain et controversé.[98] Quant à l'article 1105, le seul article impliqué qui ne tombait pas en définitive sous la coupe de l'article 1108, l'interprétation qui en a été faite par le Tribunal apparaît confirmer l'existence d'un "seuil" qui semble assez élevé, malgré la constatation de l'évolution continue de la norme en droit international coutumier et malgré le fait que le Tribunal n'ait pas tranché le débat de la norme "spécifique" per opposition à la norme "générale." Toutefois, c'est probablement la position tranchante du Tribunal sur le pouvoir d'interprétation de la Commission du libre-échange qui fera conserver la mémoire de l'affaire *ADF*.

CONCLUSION

Le bilan présenté fait état de certains mouvements qui sont les bienvenus, surtout en ce qui concerne la transparence et l'ouverture accrues des procédures arbitrales. Cependant, d'autres tendances, liées aux exceptions d'incompétence et à la révision judiciaire des sentences, sont à déplorer. On peut espérer que les Parties trouveront des solutions adaptées aux problèmes qu'ils perçoivent; solutions qui ne remettent pas en cause les fondements du régime de règlement des différends qu'ils ont choisi.

Quoi qu'il en soit, les États-Unis s'en sont sortis indemnes: sauvés par la cloche dans l'affaire *Loewen* et profitant d'une exception dans l'affaire *ADF*. On doit toutefois prendre garde de conclure hâtivement que ces résultats reflètent un certain particularisme américain ou encore la singularité des États-Unis au sein de l'ALÉNA. La réalité est manifestement plus complexe. Par exemple, si les mesures américaines avaient été de même nature que celles qui ont donné lieu aux condamnations du Canada et du Mexique, tout laisse à croire que les États-Unis auraient subi le même sort.

---

[98] Voir sur ce sujet R. Dolzer and T. Myers, "After Tecmed: Most-Favored-Nation Clauses in Investment Protection Agreements" (2004), 19 ICSID Rev. 49.

Canadian Practice in International Law / Pratique canadienne en matière de droit international

At the Department of Foreign Affairs and International Trade in 2003–4 / Au ministère des Affaires étrangères en 2003–4

compiled by / préparé par
COLLEEN SWORDS

INTERNATIONAL ECONOMIC LAW

Determination of "Like Product" under Article 2.6 of the Anti-Dumping Agreement

In a submission to a World Trade Organization panel dated 9 July 2003, the Legal Bureau wrote:

An investigating authority cannot satisfy its obligation to define a like product in accordance with the requirements of Article 2.6 by determining only whether some of the characteristics of a proposed like product closely resemble isolated characteristics of a product under consideration. It certainly cannot meet its obligation by examining the characteristics of only a subset of the product under consideration.

The requirement of Article 2.6 is that the like product must be identical to, or, in the absence of an identical product, have characteristics closely resembling the product under consideration ...

Colleen Swords, Legal Advisor, Department of Foreign Affairs and International Trade, Ottawa. The extracts from official correspondence contained in this survey have been made available by courtesy of the Department of Foreign Affairs and International Trade. Some of the correspondence from which the extracts are given was provided for the general guidance of the enquirer in relation to specific facts that are often not described in full in the extracts within this compilation. The statements of law and practice should not necessarily by regarded as definitive.

Article 31 of the *Vienna Convention on the Law of Treaties* provides that international agreements "shall be interpreted in good faith in accordance with the ordinary meaning to be given to the terms of the treaty in their context and in light of its object and purpose."

In order to determine the ordinary meaning of "characteristics closely resembling those of the product under consideration" in Article 2.6, one must compare the characteristics of the putative like product to those of the product under consideration. The *New Shorter Oxford English Dictionary* (1993) defines "characteristic" as "[a] distinctive mark; a distinguishing trait, peculiarity or quality." It defines "close" as "[v]ery near in position, relation or connection," and "resemble" as "[b]e like, have a likeness or similarity to, have a feature or property in common with." When these three words are taken together, as they are in Article 2.6, they must mean that the essential, distinctive traits of one product must be very nearly identical to the essential, distinctive traits of the other product.

Article 2.6 does not permit the investigating authority to pick isolated characteristics of a subset of the product under consideration, compare them to the characteristics of an item for which separate product status is claimed, and then to start the process anew, using a different subset of the product under consideration and different characteristics for each challenged product. The characteristics, defined as essential or distinctive traits, must be those of the "like product," and must be "very nearly identical" to the characteristics of the "product under consideration."

This understanding is consistent with that expressed in the panel decision in *Indonesia – Autos*. There, the European Communities argued that all passenger cars at issue should be considered the same "like product" as the term is used in the *Agreement on Subsidies and Countervailing Measures ("SCM Agreement")*. While agreeing that the range of automobiles shared "the same basic physical characteristics and identical end-use," the panel rejected "such a broad approach" to like product determinations. Instead, the Panel relied on the like product definition in the *SCM Agreement* (identical to Article 2.6), and, in particular, on the terms "characteristics closely resembling":

> On its face, this term is quite narrow. It is not enough that the products have characteristics which resemble the Timor [the domestic product]; rather they must have characteristics which "closely" resemble the Timor.

Notably, in distinguishing "closely resembling" from "resembling," the Panel ruled that the "quite narrow" definition of "like product" does not automatically embrace even a range of products with the "same basic characteristics" or "identical end use."

Relationship between Article 1(E) of the Agriculture Agreement and Article 3.1(A) of the Agreement on Subsidies and Countervailing Measures (SCM Agreement)

In a submission to a World Trade Organization panel dated 15 July 2003, the Legal Bureau wrote:

> The determination of a "benefit" in transactions involving agricultural commodities is necessarily factual. However, any assessment of the facts in this dispute must be undertaken within an appropriate legal framework. The applicable framework in this dispute is based on well-established WTO case law.

In a finding later upheld by the Appellate Body in *Canada – Aircraft*, the panel ruled that:

> ... a financial contribution will only confer a "benefit," i.e., an advantage, if it is provided on terms that are more advantageous than those that would have been available to the recipient on the market ...

Based on this reasoning, the question is whether there is a difference between the amount that the firm receiving the guarantee pays on credit guaranteed under the U.S. programs and the amount that the firm would pay on a comparable commercial loan absent that guarantee. The benefit is the difference between these two amounts adjusted for any differences in fees. The useful context provided by Article 14(c) of the *SCM Agreement* supports such a standard ...

The panel in *Canada - Aircraft II* established a similar standard in respect of equity guarantees provided through a Canadian provincial government financing institution called Investissement Québec (IQ).
...
The panel found that:

> ... a "benefit" could arise if there is a difference between the cost of equity with and without an IQ equity guarantee, to the extent that such difference is not covered by the fees charged by IQ for providing the equity guarantee. In our opinion, it is safe to assume that such cost difference would not be covered by IQ's fees if it is established that IQ's fees are not market-based.

Regarding IQ loan guarantees, the panel applied the same reasoning and concluded that ...

> an IQ loan guarantee will confer a "benefit" when "there is a difference between the amount that the firm receiving the guarantee pays

on a loan guaranteed by [IQ] and the amount that the firm would pay on a comparable commercial loan absent the [IQ] guarantee. In this case the benefit shall be the difference between these two amounts adjusted for any differences in fees."

The same standard applies in the current dispute ...

Article 10.2 refers to "disciplines to govern the provision of export credits, export credit guarantees or insurance programmes" and not to "disciplines to govern the provision of export subsidies in the form of export credits, export credit guarantees or insurance programmes." This provision sets out an intention on the part of Members to undertake further work regarding these measures — the simple fact of agreeing to do so, however, does not amount to a permission to use those measures to confer export subsidies without consequence and without limit.

Standard of Review under Article 17.6 of the Anti-Dumping Agreement and Article 11 of the Dispute Settlement Understanding

In a submission to a World Trade Organization panel dated 28 July 2003, the Legal Bureau wrote:

As this dispute involves both the *Anti-dumping Agreement* and the *Agreement on Subsidies and Countervailing Measures* (*"SCM Agreement"*), both Article 11 of the *Dispute Settlement Understanding* ("DSU") and Article 17.6 of the *Anti-dumping Agreement* apply. Article 11 of the DSU sets out the appropriate standard of review for panels established under all the covered agreements, subject to the special provisions that apply in the case of the *Anti-dumping Agreement*. Given the Appellate Body's and panel's interpretations of Article 11 in past cases, this Panel should consider whether the Commission: evaluated all the relevant factors that it was required under the Agreements to investigate; examined all the facts in the record before it and all of the relevant facts it could have obtained (including those facts which might have supported a negative determination); and provided a reasoned and adequate explanation of how the facts as a whole supported the findings made on each legal issue. According to the Appellate Body in *US – Lamb Safeguards*, if there is a plausible alternative explanation of the facts as a whole, in the light of which the Commission's explanation does not seem adequate, the Panel should find that the Commission has not provided a reasoned and adequate explanation of how the facts support its determination.

In *US – Hot-Rolled Steel*, the Appellate Body determined that certain elements of Article 17.6 of the *Anti-dumping Agreement* complement or supplement the standard of review contained in Article 11 of the DSU. With respect to the obligation of panels to make an objective assessment of the facts of the matter before them, the Appellate Body found that both provisions require panels to "assess" the facts and that this "clearly necessitates an active review or examination of the pertinent facts." Noting the duty of panels under Article 11 to make an objective assessment of the facts, the Appellate Body stated that it is "inconceivable that Article 17.6(i) should require anything other than that panels make an objective 'assessment of the facts of the matter.'"

Interpretation of the Schedule of a Member under the General Agreement on Trade in Services with the Vienna Convention on the Law of Treaties

In a submission to a World Trade Organization panel dated 14 November 2003, the Legal Bureau wrote:

Pursuant to Article XX:3 of the *General Agreement on Trade in Services* ("GATS"), the Schedule of a Member forms an integral part of the GATS. The rules of interpretation that apply with respect to a GATS Schedule thus are the same as those applicable with respect to the rest of the Agreement. This means that the Schedule of a Member, and the specific commitments contained therein, must be interpreted in accordance with Articles 31 and 32 of the *Vienna Convention on the Law of Treaties* ["*Vienna Convention*"].

Although this position has not been specifically stated in the context of the GATS, it is supported by findings of the Appellate Body in the context of the *General Agreement on Tariffs and Trade 1994*. In *EC – Computer Equipment*, the Appellate Body stated that:

A Schedule is [...] an integral part of the GATT 1994 [...]. Therefore, the concessions provided for in that Schedule are part of the terms of the treaty. As such, the only rules which may be applied in interpreting the meaning of a concession are the general rules of treaty interpretation set out in the *Vienna Convention*.

This position was later affirmed by the Appellate Body in *EC – Poultry, Canada – Dairy* and *Korea – Beef*. While there are differences between tariffs and specific commitments, the Appellate Body's reasoning is equally applicable with respect to the interpretation of a GATS Schedule.

This accords with Article 3(2) of the *Dispute Settlement Understanding* and the Appellate Body's view that "the rules of treaty interpretation in Articles 31 and 32 of the *Vienna Convention* apply to *any* treaty, in *any* field of public international law."

The specific commitments of a Member — in this case the United States — must therefore be interpreted in good faith in accordance with the ordinary meaning to be given to the terms of the Schedule in their context and in the light of the object and purpose of the GATS (and the *Marrakesh Agreement Establishing the World Trade Organization* more generally). To the extent appropriate, recourse may also be had to supplementary means of interpretation.

The W/120 Classification List, including the CPC numbers referred therein, is a relevant source for the purpose of interpreting the specific commitments in the United States' Schedule. This conclusion is legally justified under Article 31 or, alternatively, Article 32 of the *Vienna Convention*.

Submissions by a Non-Disputing Party to an Investment Arbitration

In Canada's 2003 *Model Foreign Investment Protection Agreement* (*FIPA*), the Legal Bureau drafted the following provisions:

ARTICLE 39
Submissions by a Non-Disputing Party

1. Any non-disputing party that is a person of a Party, or has a significant presence in the territory of a Party, that wishes to file a written submission with a Tribunal (the "applicant") shall apply for leave from the Tribunal to file such a submission, in accordance with Annex C.39. The applicant shall attach the submission to the application.

2. The applicant shall serve the application for leave to file a non-disputing party submission and the submission on all disputing parties and the Tribunal.

3. The Tribunal shall set an appropriate date for the disputing parties to comment on the application for leave to file a non-disputing party submission.

4. In determining whether to grant leave to file a non-disputing party submission, the Tribunal shall consider, among other things, the extent to which:

(a) the non-disputing party submission would assist the Tribunal in the determination of a factual or legal issue related to the arbitration by bringing a perspective, particular knowledge or insight that is different from that of the disputing parties;

(b) the non-disputing party submission would address a matter within the scope of the dispute;

(c) the non-disputing party has a significant interest in the arbitration; and

(d) there is a public interest in the subject-matter of the arbitration.

5. The Tribunal shall ensure that:

(a) any non-disputing party submission does not disrupt the proceedings; and
(b) neither disputing party is unduly burdened or unfairly prejudiced by such submissions.

6. The Tribunal shall decide whether to grant leave to file a non-disputing party submission. If leave to file a non-disputing party submission is granted, the Tribunal shall set an appropriate date for the disputing parties to respond in writing to the non-disputing party submission. By that date, the non-disputing Party may, pursuant to Article 34 (Participation by the Non-Disputing Party), address any issues of interpretation of this Agreement presented in the non-disputing party submission.

7. The Tribunal that grants leave to file a non-disputing party submission is not required to address the submission at any point in the arbitration, nor is the non-disputing party that files the submission entitled to make further submissions in the arbitration.

8. Access to hearings and documents by non-disputing parties that file applications under these procedures shall be governed by the provisions pertaining to public access to hearings and documents under Article 38 (Public Access to Hearings and Documents).

ANNEX C.39
Submissions by Non-Disputing Parties

1. The application for leave to file a non-disputing party submission shall:

(a) be made in writing, dated and signed by the person filing the application, and include the address and other contact details of the applicant;
(b) be no longer than 5 typed pages;
(c) describe the applicant, including, where relevant, its membership and legal status (*e.g.*, company, trade association or other non-governmental organization), its general objectives, the nature of its activities, and any parent organization (including any organization that directly or indirectly controls the applicant);
(d) disclose whether the applicant has any affiliation, direct or indirect, with any disputing party;
(e) identify any government, person or organization that has provided any financial or other assistance in preparing the submission;
(f) specify the nature of the interest that the applicant has in the arbitration;

(g) identify the specific issues of fact or law in the arbitration that the applicant has addressed in its written submission;
(h) explain, by reference to the factors specified in Article 39(4), why the Tribunal should accept the submission; and
(i) be made in a language of the arbitration.

2. The submission filed by a non-disputing party shall:

(a) be dated and signed by the person filing the submission;
(b) be concise, and in no case longer than 20 typed pages, including any appendices;
(c) set out a precise statement supporting the applicant's position on the issues; and
(d) only address matters within the scope of the dispute.

Scope of a Measure under the Agreement on the Application of Sanitary and Phytosanitary Measures (SPS Agreement)

In a submission to a World Trade Organization panel dated 21 April 2004, the Trade Law Bureau wrote:

Annex A of the *SPS Agreement* defines sanitary or phytosanitary measure to mean any measure applied:

(a) to protect animal or plant life or health within the territory of the Member from risks arising from the entry, establishment or spread of pests, diseases, disease-carrying organisms or disease-causing organisms;
(b) to protect human or animal life or health within the territory of the Member from risks arising from additives, contaminants, toxins or disease-causing organisms in foods, beverages or feedstuffs;
(c) to protect human life or health within the territory of the Member from risks arising from diseases carried by animals, plants or products thereof, or from the entry, establishment or spread of pests; or
(d) to prevent or limit other damage within the territory of the Member from the entry, establishment or spread of pests.

Two elements are necessary to meet the definition of a SPS measure. The first relates to form: it must be a "measure." The second relates to purpose: it must be applied to protect against one or more of the risks identified in Annex A ...

Paragraph 1 of Annex A of the *SPS Agreement* provides a non-exhaustive list of the types of instruments that constitute measures for the purposes of the *SPS Agreement:*

Sanitary or phytosanitary measures *include* all relevant laws, decrees, regulations, requirements and procedures, *including inter alia* … approval procedures [emphasis added].

It is clear that the definition of measure set out above is not exhaustive in nature given the use of the words "include," "including," and the phrase "*inter alia*." Accordingly, the *SPS Agreement* provides an illustrative list of the types of instruments that fall within the definition, but does not provide an exhaustive definition of "measure."

In principle, under the WTO Agreements, a measure may be any act or omission of a WTO Member attributable to that Member. As observed by the Appellate Body in *Guatemala – Cement I:*

In the practice established under the GATT 1947, a "measure" may be any act of a Member, whether or not legally binding, and it can include even non-binding administrative guidance by a government. [citation omitted]

It is now well established in WTO jurisprudence that an act or omission of a non-binding or non-mandatory administrative nature may also constitute a measure for the purposes of the WTO Agreement.

Accordingly, a measure need not be a formal, mandatory or legally binding act in order to be considered a measure under the *SPS Agreement*. The context of paragraph 1 of Annex A supports this conclusion. That context includes similar terms — such as "regulation" and "measure" contained in other parts of the *SPS Agreement* and in other WTO Agreements, and the interpretation of those terms by panels and the Appellate Body. For example, the panel in *Japan – Agricultural Products II* found that the definition of "sanitary and phytosanitary regulations" in paragraph 1 of Annex B to the *SPS Agreement* was broad enough to include non-mandatory requirements. In reaching its conclusion, the panel specifically noted that paragraph 1 of Annex A "does not … require that such measures be mandatory or legally enforceable." Thus, in the words of the panel in *Japan – Agriculture Products II:*

This context indicates that a non-mandatory government measure is also subject to WTO provisions in the event compliance with this measure is necessary to obtain an advantage from the government or, in other words, if sufficient incentives or disincentives exist for that measure to be abided by.

Moreover, in the context of the *SPS Agreement*, an act or omission similar in character to the instruments explicitly referred to in the illustrative list can constitute a measure for the purposes of the *SPS Agreement*. Where pre-marketing approval is a pre-condition to placing a product on the market, a suspension of an indefinite duration in the approval procedures has the effect of converting that pre-marketing approval requirement into an across-the-board marketing ban.

Further, the object and purpose of the *SPS Agreement* supports a broad interpretation of what constitutes a "measure." A primary objective of the *SPS Agreement* is to minimize the negative effects of SPS measures on international trade. A narrow interpretation of the term "measure" would serve to exclude some acts or omissions applied for the purposes listed in Annex A and that affect international trade. This would enable WTO Members to circumvent the obligations of the *SPS Agreement* by adopting administrative practices that undermine or run counter to formal laws and regulations.

Burden of Proof Required by Article 1102 of NAFTA (Thunderbird 1128)

In a submission to a North American Free Trade Agreement (NAFTA) tribunal dated 21 May 2004, the Trade Law Bureau wrote:

The text of Article 1102 makes it clear that its interpretation requires no shifting burden of proof. The Article is a statement of the obligation the NAFTA Parties owe to each other. The obligation has a certain content; to demonstrate that a Party has violated the obligation, a claimant must show that the Party has failed to meet that content. It is well-established in international law that the burden of proving a fact rests with the party asserting it — indeed, this is one of the rules applying to the proceedings in this arbitration. The claimant therefore necessarily bears the responsibility of demonstrating all the elements of an Article 1102 claim.

The only question, then, is the identification of these elements. Again applying the interpretive principles of the *Vienna Convention on the Law of Treaties*, the first place to turn in this task is the text of Article 1102. In Canada's submission, all the elements are clearly expressed in this text. While Canada does not purport to set out here the exact order of analysis for the interpretation of Article 1102, a violation of the obligation clearly requires that the foreign investor or investment be accorded less favourable treatment (within the meaning of the Article) than that accorded, in like circumstances, to domestic investors or investments.

There is nothing in the text of Article 1102 to justify concluding that the question of "in like circumstances" is a defence that the NAFTA Party must assert. It is plain on the face of the text that the existence of treatment "in like circumstances" is a constituent element of the obligation, not an exception to its application. It must follow that it is the investor's burden to demonstrate it.

The investor must therefore demonstrate that a NAFTA Party has accorded it (or its investment) and a domestic investor (or its investment) treatment "in like circumstances." Again, "in like circumstances" means that all the relevant circumstances of according the treatment are "like," except that the investor or investment is domestic. Absent this demonstration, there can be no violation of Article 1102.

The investor must further demonstrate that the treatment accorded "in like circumstances" is less favourable to it or its investment than to domestic investors or investments. Just as with "in like circumstances," absent this demonstration there can be no violation of Article 1102.

INTERNATIONAL OCEANS LAW

Whether Canadian Coast Guard Marine Navigation Service Fees (MNSF) Are Subject to and Consistent with the Provisions of Article I of the 1909 Boundary Waters Treaty

In October 2004, the Legal Bureau wrote:

The focus of our opinion is on the consistency of the fee structure with the 1909 Boundary Waters Treaty (BWT) to the extent that the latter is implemented into Canadian law ...

Boundary Waters Treaty Act Implementation: Before considering the text of Article I, it is first necessary to determine its status in Canadian law, that is to say, is this an obligation owed by Canada at international law, or has it also been implemented into Canadian law. If the former, it may only be useful as a form of statutory interpretation in reading the *Oceans Act* and regulations made under it (including the MNSF); if the latter, it is equivalent in force and status and different tests may be applied to it.

Section 3 of the BWTA purports to implement much of the BWT in Canadian domestic law as follows:

The laws of Canada and of the provinces are hereby amended and altered so as to *permit, authorize and sanction* the performance of the obligations undertaken by His Majesty and in and under the treaty, as so as to *sanction, confer and impose* the various rights, duties and disabilities intended by the treaty to be conferred or imposed or to exist within Canada [emphasis added].

Section 3 sets out two levels of "implementation," the first to "permit, authorize and sanction the performance of the obligations undertaken by His Majesty" and separately to "sanction, confer and impose the various rights, duties and disabilities intended by the treaty to be conferred or imposed or to exist within Canada." A preliminary question is whether Article One of the BWT is implemented by the first or second arm of Section 3 of the BWTA.

In our view, the answer to that question is driven by the purposes served by the BWT and to the extent that they are administrative or legal in character. The BWT established, for example, the International Joint Commission, consisting of three commissioners on each side and making it responsible to the respective governments for a variety of tasks. In our view, it is these activities that Section 3 implements in a way to "permit, authorize and sanction." However, the substantive rights created for private individuals, e.g. the "inhabitants, vessels and boats of both countries" in Article I, or access to Canadian courts for USA residents in Article II, are meaningless if not fully implemented and made enforceable in Canadian law. As such, they require the fuller implementation provided in the second arm of Section 3, that is that rights created such as these are implemented by the "laws of Canada ... [being] amended ... so as to sanction, confer and impose the various rights, duties and disabilities intended by the treaty ..." This conclusion not only makes practical sense, it is also consistent with Canadian constitutional practice and statutory interpretation that presumes any implementation of international law obligations into domestic law should be read, if possible, to achieve that result.

As Mr. Justice Gonthier declared in *National Corn Growers Assn.* v. *Canada (Canadian Import Tribunal)*, 2 S.C.R. 1324:

> In interpreting legislation which has been enacted with a view towards *implementing international obligations*, [Gonthier's emphasis] as is the case here, it is reasonable for a tribunal to examine the domestic law in the context of the relevant agreement to clarify any uncertainty. Indeed where the text of the domestic law lends itself to it, one should also strive to expound an interpretation which is consonant with the relevant international obligations.

In our view, as the Article I BWT obligations require domestic implementation and Section 3 of the BWTA can be read to achieve that result, as a matter of statutory interpretation and Canadian constitutional practice, we should assume that the implementation is sufficient to meet Canadian international obligations ...

Object and Purpose: The object and purpose of the BWT is manifold but can be summarized as follows. The BWT at its heart is a bargain to allocate and prioritize the use of both boundary waters and transboundary waters shared between Canada and the United States. The principal focus was on use rather than transit of waters. In the former context, the bargain was comprehensive, that is applying to all shared water resources. It was traditional, by effectively negotiating a common understanding that would replace the vagaries and uncertainties of applying private common law riparian rights in a transboundary context (e.g. the irrigation allocation in Article VI for the St. Mary and Milk rivers). It was forward looking by allocating water flow for newly discovered hydro-electric generation (Article V) and especially novel in its obligation not to pollute waters flowing into the other country (Article IV). In terms of the transit of waters, it was at once both conservative, creating a treaty obligation of access to both sides of the Great Lakes by both countries for purposes of commerce, yet also progressive by anticipating challenges to access that might arise from regulation and imposing obligations intended to ensure that the flow of water-borne commerce between the countries not be obstructed.

Context: The phrase "Free and open ... equally" utilized at the beginning of Article I is a concept that is well-established in a number of treaties between Great Britain (on behalf of or respecting Canada) and the United States but it is important to note that as both the British Empire and the United States moved from mercantile monopoly to free trade and the need of open and free access lessened, the formulations in successive treaties became more elaborate and, in our view, took on issues beyond mere physical access.

The phrase occurs first in our treaty history in the 1783 *Treaty of Peace* where Great Britain and the United States agreed to free and open navigation but only along the Mississippi River (Article VIII). This access was broadened greatly in the 1794 *Jay Treaty* to allow USA ships to participate in trade with the British colonies in the West Indies.

Thereafter, successive treaties in the 19th century opened up more of Canada and the United States to free and open trade by waterways as the previous regime of mercantile monopolies gradually evaporated. Each treaty utilized the phrase "free and open," though this basic formulation was itself changed to grant access "forever" later in the century.

As between Canada and the United States, several treaties provided for free and open access of waters to the ships of both countries, notably the 1918 *Convention of Commerce* (waters of the North West coast), the 1842 *Webster-Ashburton Treaty* (waters from Lake Superior to Lake of the Woods, the Saint John and Saint Lawrence Rivers), the 1846 *Oregon Treaty* (waters of the Columbia River) and the 1871 *Treaty Of Washington* (waters of the Saint Lawrence, Yukon, Porcupine and Stikine rivers).

The basic formulation, "free and open" alone has not been judicially considered to impose any obligations on the two Parties beyond that to allow physical access of one's waters to ships from the other. Instead, courts have paid attention to the tendency late in the 19th century for more elaborate formulations and from them to derive obligations beyond mere physical access.

These additional formulations are comparable to Article I (ii) of the BWT. Most are simpler than that provided in the BWT, e.g. *Webster-Ashburton* is the simplest, providing only for free and open navigation *subject to laws and regulations* while others, notably the *Treaty of Washington*, also has the additional element of being "subject to laws and regulations *not inconsistent with free navigation*." It must be kept in mind, however, that no other treaty has the benefit of the full formulation or the legislative enactment as has Article I of the BWT.

The phrase "free and open *subject to laws and regulations*" as appearing in the *Webster-Ashburton Treaty* has been subject to interpretation in both Canadian and USA courts, both of which agreed that the imposition of tolls for improvements in navigation, for example, was not inconsistent with free and open navigation (see *Arrow River & Tributaries Slide and Boom Co. v. Pigeon Timber Co.* [1932] SCR 495 and *Pigeon River Improvement, Slide and Boom Co. v. Charles W. Fox, Ltd.* S. Ct 361, 78.)

Considering now the ordinary meaning of this clause of the BWT, we would make the following further points:

(i)   "Laws and regulations" can certainly include the imposition of fees for services rendered by the Canadian Coast Guard.

(ii) Either country may impose its own laws and regulations on navigation. There is no requirement on reciprocity or to agree on identical forms of regulation.

(iii) Equal treatment, while a close kin to "identical" treatment, is not inevitably the same; it is possible, at least hypothetically, for a regime to be applied to USA ships that is different from that of Canadian, yet not violating the obligation, so long as the different treatment imposed is not otherwise objectively unequal or without discrimination.

Beyond these reasonable conclusions, a real question remains in terms of what the BWT means when it creates a capacity to create regulations so long as they are applied "equally and without discrimination." For it to challenge the MNSF, it must include a concept of "objective" versus "subjective" discrimination and an ability to "pierce" the basic structure of the fees regime to examine underlying inequality and discrimination.

For the first, we are able to conclude that the BWT would set an objective rather than subjective standard of non-discrimination and equal treatment. Looking beyond this Article, the BWT provides a range of obligations, including the very forward-looking obligation not to pollute one's waters to the injury of health or property on the other (Article IV). That provision has been given critical consideration in a range of References to the International Joint Commission, whose Article IX recommendations have always applied an objective standard for pollution and have never considered any *male fides* or intention to pollute as relevant or necessary (see the 1977 *Garrison Diversion Unit Reference,* the 1981 *Poplar River Basin Reference* and the 1988 *Flathead River Basin Reference*). By the BWT itself, these Article IX References are not binding to the parties but that has not prevented them becoming an influential and respected commentary on the meaning of the BWT.

This can be allied with an ability in Article I to pierce a collective standard to find underlying inequality. This is so because a rough collective equality in treatment is not sufficient to meeting the BWT obligation. The BWT requires equality of treatment "to the inhabitants, ships, vessels and boats" of both countries. As such, any individual, on behalf of any vessel, should be able to assert discrimination or inequality of treatment in his case. That he may have been so treated, but that the overall balance between countries is one of rough equality, is insufficient to meet the BWT standard.

Parliamentary Declarations in 2003–4 / Déclarations parlementaires en 2003–4

compiled by / *préparé par*
ALIAKSANDRA LOGVIN

A STATEMENTS MADE ON THE INTRODUCTION OF LEGISLATION /
DÉCLARATIONS SUR L'INTRODUCTION DE LA LÉGISLATION

1 *Bill C-56 (Bill C-9): An Act to Amend the Patent Act and the Food and Drugs Act*[1] / *Loi C-56 (Loi C-9): Loi modifiant la Loi sur les brevets et la Loi sur les aliments et drogues*

Hon. Allan Rock (Minister of Industry):

I ... [am] very proud today to table ... legislation which will lead the developed world in dealing with the urgent health needs of least developed countries. What Canada has done today is global leadership for the health interests of the developing world. We ... are anxious to see this bill become law and to see the regulations enacted so that those drugs can be provided where they are most needed.

(House of Commons Debates, 6 November 2003, pp. 9231–32, 9268)
(Débats de la Chambre des Communes, le 6 novembre 2003, pp. 9231–32, 9268)

M. Serge Marcil (secrétaire parlementaire du ministre de l'Industrie):

Depuis des années, les intervenants dans les milieux des organisations non gouvernementales et les pays en voie de développement ont demandé l'aide des gouvernements occidentaux afin de les appuyer dans la lutte contre les différentes maladies graves, les épidémies et les autres maladies que l'on retrouve dans ces endroits ... [L]e Canada joue un rôle de leader

---

Aliaksandra Logvin is currently on contract with the government of Canada.

[1] Editor's note: Bill C-56 was reintroduced in the House of Commons as Bill C-9 on 12 February 2004. *House of Commons Debates*, 12 February 2004, p. 469.

dans le domaine de l'aide aux pays en voie de développement ... Le Canada devient le premier pays du G-7 à rendre accessibles ses connaissances, ses recherches et tous ses produits médicaux à des pays en voie de développement ...

[L]oi [C-56] ... est très bien structuré et qu'il reflète réellement la pensée du gouvernement du Canada, qui est orientée vers l'aide humanitaire ...

Aujourd'hui, le gouvernement du Canada adopte une position de leadership dans le mouvement mondial visant à promouvoir l'accès aux produits pharmaceutiques dont ont besoin les pays en voie de développement pour répondre aux problèmes de santé publique tels que le sida, la tuberculose, le paludisme et d'autres épidémies ... On parle du sida. Une des causes mortelles les plus grandes parmi les enfants est le paludisme et la diarrhée. Ce sont deux causes mortelles, et beaucoup de recherches s'effectuent sur ces maladies. Nous, en tant que Canadiens faisant partie de cette planète, nous nous devons de participer à ces recherches et également à l'amélioration de la qualité de vie des gens dans les pays en développement ...

Aujourd'hui, nous donnons l'exemple, mais nous faisons également appel à d'autres pays occidentaux afin qu'ils suivent le geste du Canada, le geste que nous posons aujourd'hui. J'espère que ce soit autant les Américains que les Français, les Allemands ou les Britanniques et ainsi de suite, soit ceux qui font partie de l'Organisation mondiale du commerce, du G-7 et qui se promènent tous les ans pour démontrer leur puissance économique. J'aimerais qu'à partir d'aujourd'hui, ces pays commencent à réfléchir au fait que la planète n'appartient pas seulement à une minorité, mais qu'elle appartient à tout le monde. Chaque individu sur notre planète a sa place. Ceux et celles qui ont le privilège de vivre dans un environnement leur permettant d'évoluer sainement doivent prendre en charge et se retourner vers ceux et celles qui ont des besoins. Ceux-ci ont droit au même respect humain, ils ont besoin de notre aide et ils ont besoin de vivre.

(House of Commons Debates, 7 November 2003, pp. 9321–23)
(Débats de la Chambre des Communes, le 7 novembre 2003, pp. 9321–23)

Hon. Aileen Carroll (Minister for International Cooperation):

The bill is the Government of Canada's response to the agreement reached at the WTO called the TRIPS agreement. It was an acknowledgement on the part of all the members of the WTO that drugs are desperately needed in Africa and other developing countries to assist them in dealing with the pandemic of HIV-AIDS, malaria, TB, and all of the diseases that are rampant there, and to make those drugs available at a price that people in developing countries could afford.

As one of the members of the WTO, Canada joined with our colleagues in signing the TRIPS agreement. That agreement puts an onus on all members within their own countries to bring forward domestic legislation that will have as its objective the distribution, production and availability of drugs for the diseases that I have just described. In order to meet that onus, our legislation will meet changes requisite in the Food and Drugs Act, Intellectual Property Law Improvement Act, and the Patent Act.

I am proud of this bill ... I am proud of my government that we are the very first member of the WTO to bring this legislation forward. ... Until one country comes forward and does exactly that, these kinds of agreements can sometimes linger in a hiatus situation that would be beneficial to no one. Canada has come forward and has received accolades from our NGO communities worldwide, as well as the domestic community ...

We have broadened, right at the beginning with our legislation, the number of countries who will benefit from this [action], and who will now be able to access drugs at a price that they are able to afford ... [These are] not just the countries that are members of the WTO but countries who meet the criteria as established by the DAC committee.[2] [The legislation] ... would include all countries that are officially recognized recipients of ODA, official development assistance ... We have included two lists in the regulations, lists of countries that will be able to benefit from this legislation and lists of the drugs that will be available as a result.

(House of Commons Debates, 28 April 2004, pp. 2516–18)
(Débats de la Chambre des Communes, le 28 avril 2004, pp. 2516–18)

2 *Bill C-15: International Transfer of Offenders Act (An Act to Implement Treaties and Administrative Arrangements on the International Transfer of Persons Found Guilty of Criminal Offences) / Loi C-15: Loi sur le transfèrement international des délinquents (Loi de mise en oeuvre des traités ou des ententes administratives sur le transfèrement international des personnes reconnues coupables d'infractions criminelles)*[3]

[2] Editor's note: The Development Assistance Committee (DAC) is the principal body of the Organisation for Economic Co-operation and Development (OECD). Through DAC, the OECD deals with issues related to cooperation with developing countries.

[3] Editor's note: Bill C-15 (formerly Bill C-33) was introduced in the House of Commons on 12 February 2004 by Hon. Jacques Saada (for the Deputy Prime

L'hon. Yvon Charbonneau (secrétaire parlementaire de la vice-première ministre et ministre de la Sécurité publique et de la Protection civile (protection civile)):

[L]'actuelle Loi sur le transfèrement des délinquants remonte à 1978, suite à une réunion des Nations Unies. Au cours de cette réunion, les pays membres avaient convenu que le transfèrement international des délinquants était le corollaire approprié à la mobilité accrue des personnes et permettrait aux États de mieux coopérer dans les affaires de justice pénale.

Depuis 1978, seules des modifications techniques ont été apportées à la suite de la promulgation de cette loi. L'expérience accrue du Canada en matière de traités et les modifications aux lois contenues dans la Loi sur le système correctionnel et la mise en liberté sous condition, en 1992, le projet de loi C-41 sur la détermination de la peine, en 1995, et le projet de loi C-45 sur la réforme du calcul des peines, en 1996, ont cependant permis de faire ressortir des questions plus substantielles.

Le projet de loi C-15 ... moderniserait le cadre législatif autorisant la mise en oeuvre des traités, y compris les conventions multilatérales concernant le transfèrement international des délinquants. Je suis particulièrement fier de parrainer ce projet de loi à cause des objectifs qu'il comporte sur le plan de la sécurité publique et des objectifs humanitaires qu'il fera avancer.

L'objectif de ce projet de loi sur le transfèrement des délinquants et des traités est essentiellement humanitaire. Souvent, les citoyens canadiens sont incarcérés dans des pays dont ils ne connaissent ni la langue ni la culture. Il n'est pas rare non plus que le lieu où ils sont détenus ne réponde pas aux normes canadiennes les plus élémentaires en matières de santé, d'hygiène et de sécurité. L'isolement qu'éprouvent les Canadiens, dans des conditions de détention souvent difficiles, s'ajoute aux épreuves qu'ils connaissent, particulièrement en l'absence de contacts réguliers avec leur famille et leurs amis. La connaissance de ces conditions cause aussi des souffrances aux familles des délinquants, qui elles sont au Canada ... Voilà pourquoi il est si important de pouvoir rapatrier les Canadiens chez eux.

La Loi sur le transfèrement des délinquants contribue aussi à l'administration de la justice. Les délinquants canadiens qui sont renvoyés au Canada doivent purger leur peine étrangère jusqu'à la fin. À l'arrivée au Canada, ils tombent sous l'autorité du Service correctionnel du Canada ou des responsables des services correctionnels provinciaux qui sont chargés de leur réinsertion graduelle et contrôlée dans la société. Cette solution est préférable à l'expulsion des délinquants au Canada au terme de leur peine. En effet, en cas d'expulsion, ils arrivent ici sans aucun contrôle correctionnel et sans aucune aide pour se réinsérer dans la société.

La plupart des États reconnaissent l'importance de la coopération en matière de justice pénale. Les lois pénales et les peines sont appliquées par les États dans le but de dissuader la population d'adopter une conduite interdite. Or, le délinquant n'échappe pas à la justice si l'on fait en sorte qu'il purge le reste de sa peine étrangère chez lui. C'est ce que le régime de transfèrement international des délinquants permet aux pays de faire ...

Le consentement volontaire du délinquant à son transfèrement est ... un principe clé qui est en réalité le point d'ancrage du régime de transfèrement international des délinquants adopté par le Canada. Cette notion repose sur les objectifs humanitaires traditionnels des traités. Il s'agit d'une notion cruciale, car le transfèrement d'un délinquant contre son gré aurait pour effet de réduire considérablement la probabilité de succès de sa réadaptation et de sa réinsertion dans la société. En outre, des pays pourraient être moins disposés à consentir à un transfèrement pour des raisons humanitaires si le délinquant n'y donnait pas manifestement son consentement éclairé. Voilà la raison pour laquelle cet important principe se reflète dans le projet de loi C-15 ...

L'actuelle Loi sur le transfèrement des délinquants ne prévoit pas le transfèrement de jeunes délinquants en probation dans le régime de transfèrement. Cette omission est incompatible avec les dispositions de la loi. Celle-ci autorise en effet le transfèrement des délinquants adultes qui sont en probation ou qui purgent une peine de prison. Le projet de loi C-15 corrigerait cette incohérence en rendant les jeunes délinquants en probation admissibles à un transfèrement.

L'actuelle Loi sur le transfèrement des délinquants ne prévoit pas le transfèrement au Canada d'enfants qui pourraient être en train de purger une peine à l'étranger. Le projet de loi C-15 corrigerait cela en autorisant le transfèrement au Canada d'enfants de moins de 12 ans d'origine canadienne qui sont détenus à l'étranger. Le projet de loi préciserait aussi que, par la suite de leur transfèrement au Canada, les enfants ne seraient pas détenus en vertu de leur peine étrangère; ils seraient plutôt assujettis aux mesures législatives concernant le bien-être des enfants de la province ou du territoire d'accueil. Voilà une illustration du caractère humanitaire de ce projet de loi.

À l'heure actuelle, le Canada ne peut conclure de traité pour le transfèrement des délinquants qu'avec des pays reconnus. Toutefois, les événements internationaux récents, comme en témoignent par exemple la dissolution de l'URSS et celle de la Yougoslavie, soulignent la nécessité d'un mécanisme de transfèrement qui tienne compte des Canadiens qui purgent une peine dans des territoires ou des États non reconnus par le Canada comme États étrangers ... [L]e projet de loi C-15, à son article 31 ... prévoit la négociation d'ententes administratives avec un État étranger ou avec une entité non étatique afin de rendre le régime de transfèrement plus sensible à la conjoncture internationale. Il permettrait au Canada de transférer ses citoyens chez lui ...

J'aimerais souligner la nécessité manifeste d'une plus grande souplesse de la loi, afin de faire avancer l'objectif humanitaire que nourrit le Canada par ce projet de loi sur le transfèrement international des délinquants. La nécessité d'une coopération accrue entre des pays dans les affaires de la justice pénale saute aux yeux, tout comme celle de mieux protéger le public par la réinsertion sûre, graduelle et contrôlée des délinquants dans la société.

Le projet de loi C-15 répondrait à tous ces besoins en reflétant les principes traditionnels des traités internationaux, en comblant les lacunes qui ont été décelées et en assurant la conformité aux autres mesures législatives. Ce projet de loi contribuerait en outre à des objectifs importants en étendant le régime à un plus large éventail de délinquants et en élargissant la catégorie d'entités avec lesquelles le Canada pourrait conclure des ententes de transfèrement.

(House of Commons Debates, 23 April 2004, pp. 2348–50)
(Débats de la Chambre des Communes, le 23 avril 2004, pp. 2348–50)

3   *Bill C-19: An Act to Amend the Corrections and Conditional Release Act and the Criminal Code / Loi C-19: Loi modifiant la Loi sur le système correctionnel et la mise en liberté sous condition et le Code criminel* [4]

Hon. Anne McLellan (Deputy Prime Minister and Minister of Public Safety and Emergency Preparedness):

[T]he success of our system depends on collaboration, on dialogue and on research based knowledge. It is founded on Canadian values, on the rule of law and on respect for human dignity. It is a system that reflects these values.

Respect for human rights as reflected in the Canadian Charter of Rights and Freedoms, in the international covenants that Canadians have supported

4 Editor's note: Bill C-19 was introduced in the House of Commons on 13 February 2004 by Hon. Mauril Bélanger (for the Minister of Public Safety and Emergency Preparedness). *House of Commons Debates*, 13 February 2004, p. 558.

over the years, such as the universal declaration of human rights, and in our adherence to United Nations norms and standards for the treatment of prisoners, represent the fundamental building blocks of our corrections system. In fact, these principles and values have been enshrined in Canada's Corrections and Conditional Release Act ... By moving forward with Bill C-19, the government is signalling its commitment to the protection of public safety.

(House of Commons Debates, 20 February 2004, p. 857)
(Débats de la Chambre des Communes, le 20 février 2004, p. 857)

4   Bill C-21: An Act to Amend the Customs Tariff / Loi C-21: Loi modifiant le Tarif des douanes[5]

Hon. Denis Paradis (for the Minister of Finance):

[C]e projet de loi prévoit le maintien d'une politique de longue date consistant à accorder un traitement tarifaire préférentiel aux pays en développement et aux pays les moins développés. Les deux programmes tarifaires en question, le tarif de préférence général et le tarif des pays les moins développés, sont mis en oeuvre dans le Tarif des douanes et doivent prendre fin le 30 juin 2004. Ce projet de loi propose que les programmes soient prolongés pour 10 autres années, du 1er juillet 2004 au 30 juin 2014, conformément à la pratique antérieure ...

During the mid-1960s there was a growing recognition that preferential trade treatment for developing countries was a means of fostering growth and the well-being of poorer nations. Following a recommendation by a United Nations conference on trade and development, developed countries implemented unilateral tariff preferences for goods originating from developing countries in order to help them increase their export earnings and stimulate their economic growth.

Canada's general preferential tariffs program, the GPT, was implemented on July 1, 1974, for a 10 year period and has been renewed twice since then, in 1984 and 1994. As indicated, it is now set to expire on June 30, 2004. Under the GPT, more than 180 countries and territories are entitled to zero or low tariffs on a range of products that are covered under the customs tariff, with the exception of some agricultural products, refined sugar and most textiles, apparel and footwear. In 2003, Canadian imports under the GPT were valued at $9.3 billion and accounted for 2.8% of total Canadian imports.

[5] Editor's note: Bill C-21 was introduced in the House of Commons on 24 February 2004 by Hon. Reg Alcock (for the Minister of Finance). *House of Commons Debates,* 24 February 2004, p. 958.

En 1983, le Canada a instauré le tarif des pays les moins développés, ou le TPMD, afin d'appliquer un traitement tarifaire préférentiel encore plus généreux pour les marchandises des pays les plus pauvres désignés par les Nations Unies d'après un certain nombre de critères, comme la santé, l'éducation et le revenu au niveau national. Ce programme arrive également à échéance le 30 juin 2004, comme je l'ai déjà indiqué. Depuis janvier 2003, conformément à un engagement pris au sommet du G-8, tenu en 2002 à Kananaskis, on s'en rappellera, le gouvernement applique, dans le cadre de ce programme, un accès entièrement libre de droits à toutes les importations des 48 pays les moins développés, sauf pour certains produits agricoles, comme les produits laitiers, la volaille et les oeufs. En 2003, les importations canadiennes aux termes du TPMD ont été évaluées à 408 millions de dollars, soit 0,12 p. 100 du total des importations canadiennes ...

[L]e fait de prolonger pour dix autres années le TPG et le TPMD réaffirme l'engagement du gouvernement en faveur de la capacité d'exportation et de la croissance économique des pays en développement et des pays les moins développés, soit la principale raison pour laquelle ces programmes ont initialement été mis sur pied. Il établit aussi, pour les commerçants qui utilisent ces programmes, un milieu prévisible, tant dans les pays en développement qu'ici même, au Canada. De même, la prolongation serait conforme à la pratique observée dans les autres pays industrialisés, comme les États-Unis, les membres de l'Union européenne et le Japon, qui maintiennent également des programmes semblables. De plus, le fait de poursuivre ces deux programmes de tarifs préférentiels unilatéraux de longue date sera bien accueilli par les pays bénéficiaires, qui considèrent ces programmes comme un important facteur favorisant leur développement.

The decision on whether to extend the GPT and the LDCT affects a number of stakeholders. First, it affects the exporters in developing and least developed countries that benefit from the preferential access provided by the two programs. The premise that originally led to the establishment of preferential tariff programs — that they would encourage and increase exports from developing and least developed countries and hence stimulate economic growth — still holds today. Various studies by international organizations such as the International Monetary Fund and the World Bank support the principle that export expansion contributes to economic growth. While these programs clearly benefit developing and least developed countries, Canadians also benefit from them. As a result of lower tariffs on goods from the developing world, Canadian consumers enjoy access to imported goods at competitive prices and will continue to do so if these programs are extended. In addition, Canadian producers will continue to benefit from the reduced tariffs on inputs they import from the developing world and use in production of goods in Canada, which ultimately increases the competitiveness of Canadian industry. If these programs were not extended, the increased duty costs incurred by Canadian importers and consumers would be approximately $272.8 million. Not continuing these programs would also raise questions about Canada's commitments to international development.

(House of Commons Debates, 25 February 2004, pp. 1051–52)
(Débats de la Chambre des Communes, le 25 février 2004, pp. 1051–52)

5   *Bill C-34: An Act to Amend the Migratory Birds Convention Act,*
    1994 and the Canadian Environmental Protection Act, 1999 /
    Loi C-34: Loi modifiant la Loi de 1994 sur la convention concernant
    les oiseaux migrateurs et la Loi canadienne sur la protection de
    l'environnement (1999)[6]

Hon. David Anderson (Minister of the Environment):

I rise today to discuss one of the ways in which human activity is affecting the future of nature, a problem that the bill before us is designed to address ... There are probably none among us here who do not remember the *Exxon Valdez* disaster in the northeast Pacific and the horrifying pictures of dead fish, birds, seals and other marine life that had no chance against this thick oil on top of the water ... [M]arine birds are killed every year ... by the chronic oil pollution in the ocean that comes from the discharge of oily waste from the bilges or ballast tanks of ships ... [T]hese ships are not supposed to dump this waste into the oceans. It is already against the law. But they do it and the impact is huge ... One reason we have this problem is that the level of penalties does not act as a sufficient deterrent for this kind of activity by shipowners and ship captains ... Fines have been quite inadequate in Canada in past years, even when the shipowner or ship captain is brought to justice. I draw members' attention to the United States, where there have been some recent high profile prosecutions ... In March, a Norwegian shipping company was fined $3.5 million after one of its ships discharged oil off the United States west coast. It is the largest fine ever levelled for this type of environmental violation. Not only will the company pay the fine, it will also launch a comprehensive anti-pollution program on board all its ships. We need to be consistent with the United States. We share these coastlines and we share these oceans,

[6]   Editor's note: Bill C-34 was introduced in the House of Commons on 6 May 2004 by Hon. David Anderson (Minister of the Environment). *House of Commons Debates,* 6 May 2004, p. 2829.

and we certainly do not want to be viewed as an area where it is somehow easier to dump oil. We have an opportunity now with this bill to make amendments to two key environmental laws that will address the tragedy that is birds oiled at sea.

(House of Commons Debates, 7 May 2004, pp. 2901–2)
(Débats de la Chambre des Communes, le 7 mai 2004, pp. 2901–2)

L'hon. Serge Marcil (secrétaire parlementaire du ministre de l'Environnement):

Le projet de loi devant nous enverra un message très clair. Il dira aux personnes qui oeuvrent dans l'industrie du transport maritime et qui ne se préoccupent aucunement des espèces avec lesquelles ils partagent l'océan, que leurs gestes nous sont répugnants et que nous allons les poursuivre, conformément à toutes les dispositions de la loi ...

Ce ne sont pas toutes les compagnies maritimes, tous les armateurs, ni tous les navires qui défient la loi. La plupart des ports sont équipés d'équipements permettant, justement, la vidange de ces navires. La majorité des compagnies maritimes sérieuses utilisent ces équipements. Ceux qui ne le font pas sont souvent ceux qu'on peut appeler "des vaga-bonds de mer," des gens qui profitent justement de l'obscurité et qui attendent d'avoir quitté le pays. Évidemment, lorsque cela se produit à l'intérieur de nos terres, que ce soit dans les Grands-Lacs, le fleuve Saint-Laurent, ou la voie maritime, il est plus facile d'intervenir car ils ne sont pas sortis des eaux territoriales. Donc, on peut toujours les contraindre en arraisonnant les navires. C'est souvent lorsqu'ils quittent la Voie maritime du Saint-Laurent, lorsqu'ils quittent nos côtes, dans les 200 miles prévus comme zone économique, que ces vagabonds des mers profitent de l'occasion pour faire la vidange de leurs hydrocarbures, et c'est toute la nature qui en subit les conséquences ... [I]l y avait eu des causes assez importantes, soit le cas du *Tecam Sea* et du *Olga*. Ces deux causes nous ont justement permis de découvrir les trous qui existaient dans notre loi. Nous nous sommes aperçu que même avec les preuves que nous avions pour les poursuivre, nous n'avions pas la certitude d'être capables d'aller jusqu'au bout et de les punir soit par des amendes, soit par la réquisition des bâtiments et ainsi de suite ... La Loi [C-34] ... fourniront ... une clarté pour les agents de l'application de la loi ainsi que pour les propriétaires et exploitants de navires dans les eaux relevant de la compétence canadienne, y compris la zone économique exclusive de 200 milles.

(House of Commons Debates, 14 May 2004, pp. 3177–79)
(Débats de la Chambre des Communes, le 14 mai 2004, pp. 3177–79)

6   *Bill C-36: An Act to Prevent the Introduction and Spread of
Communicable Diseases (Quarantine Act) / Loi C-36: Loi visant à
prévenir l'introduction et la propagation de maladies transmissibles
(La Loi sur la quarantaine)*[7]

Hon. Carolyn Bennett (Minister of State (Public Health)):

The legislation before the House today delivers on our pledge to court
many of the problems brought to our attention by recent events such as
SARS, which underscored how fast and how hard disease can hit our health
care system.

With Bill C-36 we will replace the outdated quarantine legislation with
an improved and modern Quarantine Act so we can better protect Canadians from the importation of dangerous communicable diseases and ensure Canada can meet its international obligations to help prevent the
spread of these diseases beyond our borders.

Where there are incidents of risk to public health, the act continues to
allow for public health measures at Canadian points of entry such as:
screening travellers entering and leaving Canada, whether by customs
officials or detection devices; referring travellers to a quarantine officer
who may conduct a health assessment, order a medical examination, vac-
cination or other measures, order the traveller to report to a public health
authority, or detain anyone refusing to comply with measures to prevent
the spread of the disease; requiring owners of public transport conveyances, such as jets or ships, to report an illness or death of a passenger
before arrival in or departure from Canada; detaining either passengers
or conveyances until there is no longer a risk to public health; and in-
specting such conveyances and ordering their decontamination or destruction, if required.

As well, the modernized act ... would provide the Minister of Health
with additional powers. For example he could appoint screening officers,
environmental health officers and analysts as well as quarantine officers;
establish quarantine facilities at any location in Canada; take temporary
possession of premises to use as a detention facility if necessary; and divert
airplanes and ships to alternate landing sites. While these powers would
only be used in rare instances where circumstances warrant, these changes
are essential if we are to keep pace with emerging infectious diseases and
protect the health of Canadians ... The updated Quarantine Act will give us
an additional layer of protection by providing strong, flexible up to date

[7] Editor's note: Bill C-36 was introduced in the House of Commons on 12 May
2004 by Hon. Joseph Volpe (for the Minister of Health). *House of Commons Debates,* 12 May 2004, p. 3081.

regulations that will allow us to respond more effectively to ongoing and future health risks while ensuring adequate protection for human rights.

(House of Commons Debates, 14 May 2004, pp. 3203–4) (Débats de la Chambre des Communes, le 14 mai 2004, pp. 3203–4)

B   STATEMENTS IN RESPONSE TO QUESTIONS / DÉCLARATIONS EN RÉPONSE AUX QUESTIONS

1   Environment / Environnement

(a) Aquatic ecosystem / Écosystème aquatique

Mr. Pat Martin (Winnipeg Centre):

[A] U.S. plan to divert water from Devils Lake, North Dakota, will result in the inter-basin transfer of water into the Red River and on into Lake Winnipeg. It is a serious threat to Manitoba's aquatic ecosystem and is in direct violation of the Boundary Waters Treaty act. Will the government agree today to immediately refer this issue to the International Joint Commission?

Hon. Bill Graham (Minister of Foreign Affairs):

[The Government] totally agree[s] ... that this is a serious matter ... The last time I met with the secretary of state of the United States I raised this matter with him. He has assured me that under his responsibilities in respect of the Boundary Waters Treaty act he is referring this to his authorities to ascertain whether it is in conformity with the Boundary Waters Treaty. From there, there are other remedies. We will pursue them. We will protect Canadians ... We are ensuring that the United States respects its obligations under the Boundary Waters Treaty act.

(House of Commons Debates, 22 October 2003, p. 8604) (Débats de la Chambre des Communes, le 22 octobre 2003, p. 8604)

(b) St. Lawrence Seaway / Voie maritime du Saint-Laurent

M. Bernard Bigras (Rosemont — Petite-Patrie):

[D]ans le dossier du dragage et de l'élargissement de la Voie maritime du Saint-Laurent afin de permettre aux bateaux géants de transiter directement des Grands Lacs à l'océan Atlantique, le gouvernement fédéral, en juin, refusait même l'idée de faire une étude du projet. Or, quelques mois plus tard, on apprend que le gouvernement endosse maintenant le projet. Que s'est-il passé, depuis quatre mois, pour que le gouvernement fédéral change ainsi totalement sa position au sujet de la Voie maritime du Saint-Laurent?

L'hon. David Collenette (ministre des Transports):

[L]e gouvernement des États-Unis a décidé d'examiner la possibilité d'une expansion de la Voie maritime du Saint-Laurent. De notre côté, nous sommes intéressés par cela, mais nous avons besoin d'études avant de compléter une expansion.

M. Bernard Bigras (Rosemont — Petite-Patrie):

[L]e ministre des Transports ... a donné son appui de principe au projet ... [E]st-ce que le ministre de l'Environnement peut nous dire s'il a donné son aval au projet de dragage et d'élargissement de la Voie maritime du Saint-Laurent, lorsqu'on sait l'impact environnemental négatif du projet sur le fleuve Saint-Laurent?

L'hon. David Collenette (ministre des Transports):

[C]'est la raison pour laquelle nous étudions la situation. Il faut déterminer s'il y aura un problème avec l'environnement.

(House of Commons Debates, 20 October 2003, p. 8485)
(Débats de la Chambre des Communes, le 20 octobre 2003, p. 8485)

Mr. Christian Jobin (Lévis-et-Chutes-de-la-Chaudière):

Est-ce que le gouvernement canadien est pour l'élargissement de la Voie maritime et est-ce qu'il y a un impact majeur sur le Saint-Laurent?

Hon. Tony Valeri (Minister of Transport):

The Government of Canada recognizes that the St. Lawrence Seaway is a vital part of our economy and we will continue to ensure its viability. The study is looking at the ongoing maintenance and long term capital requirements to sustain the existing seaway infrastructure. The study is not looking at expanding the seaway.

(House of Commons Debates, 23 March 2004, p. 1605)
(Débats de la Chambre des Communes, le 23 mars 2004, p. 1605)

(c) Cartagena Protocol / Protocole de Carthagène[8]

Hon. Charles Caccia (Davenport):

Given that 57 nations have ratified the [Cartagena] biosafety protocol, given the fact that it has entered into force and given that Canada is host to the UN Secretariat on Biodiversity, when will ... the government ... ratify this important protocol?

M. Claude Duplain (secrétaire parlementaire du ministre de l'Agriculture et de l'Agroalimentaire):

[L]e gouvernement du Canada a vraiment à coeur la conservation et l'utilisation durable de la biodiversité et appuie les objectifs environnementaux du Protocole sur la biosécurité.

Le Canada a signé le protocole en 2001 et s'engage à aborder les préoccupations des intervenants de l'industrie agroalimentaire et de la biotechnologie. Les secteurs agroalimentaires appuient les objectifs du protocole et s'engagent à travailler avec nous selon le protocole établi et à réduire au minimum les incertitudes liées au commerce.

(House of Commons Debates, 16 September 2003, p. 7415)
(Débats de la Chambre des Communes, le 16 septembre 2003, p. 7415)

M. Bernard Bigras (Rosemont — Petite-Patrie):

[L]e Protocole de Cartagena sur la biosécurité est entré en vigueur sans le Canada, plaçant ce dernier hors du consensus international sur le contrôle des OGM. Le Canada doit ratifier le protocole avant le 22 novembre prochain s'il veut participer à la première rencontre sur la mise en vigueur de l'accord prévue à Kuala Lumpur du 23 au 27 février 2004. Est-ce que le [gouvernement] ... se rend compte qu'en ne ratifiant pas le Protocole de Cartagena, le Canada ne pourra défendre ses intérêts sur la scène internationale et qu'il lance le message que le commerce est plus important que la protection de la santé publique?

Hon. David Anderson (Minister of the Environment):

[N]o decision has been taken on ratification because we are still engaged in consultation with stakeholders, particularly stakeholders in the agricultural

---

8 Cartagena Protocol on Biosafety to the Convention on Biological Diversity (Montreal, Canada, 29 January 2000; entered into force 11 September 2003), reprinted in (2000) 39 I.L.M. 1027. Canada has been a party to the Convention on Biological Diversity since 4 December 1992 by ratification; it has been a signatory (non-party) to the Cartagena Protocol since 19 April 2001.

sector. That said, the Government of Canada and certainly most of the stakeholders support the objectives of the protocol and we hope a decision can be taken in short order.

(House of Commons Debates, 17 September 2003, p. 7459)
(Débats de la Chambre des Communes, le 17 septembre 2003, p. 7459)

M. Bernard Bigras (Rosemont — Petite-Patrie):

La première rencontre des parties sur la mise en vigueur du Protocole de Cartagena aura lieu à Kuala Lumpur, en février prochain. Est-ce que ... le gouvernement a l'intention de se présenter à cette importante rencontre?

L'hon. David Anderson (ministre de l'Environnement):

Nous ... serons à Kuala Lumpur.

(House of Commons Debates, 7 November 2003, p. 9317)
(Débats de la Chambre des Communes, le 7 novembre 2003, p. 9317)

(d) Kyoto Protocol / Protocole de Kyoto[9]

Hon. Charles Caccia (Davenport):

With great foresight, the British government has adopted a reduction target for carbon dioxide emissions of 60% by the year 2050.[10] Could the minister inform the House as to whether a similar and needed target will be set by the Canadian government so as to repair the climate and reduce the increasing damage to Canada's economy caused by climate change?

Hon. David Anderson (Minister of the Environment):

[T]o date discussions have been almost exclusively about the first Kyoto period, which is 2008–12. We will begin discussions on the second Kyoto period, which is the five years that follow, in 2005. That said, I would like to point out that the Prime Minister has asked the National Round Table on the Environment and the Economy to study and inform Canadians on

[9] Kyoto Protocol to the United Nations Framework Convention on Climate Change (Kyoto, Japan, 11 December 1997; entered into force 16 February 2005), UN Doc. FCCC/CP/1997/L.7/Ad.1, reprinted in (1998) 37 I.L.M. 32. Canada ratified the Kyoto Protocol on 17 December 2002.

[10] Editor's note: The British government made the relevant announcement on 24 February 2003. See, for example, S. Bird, "Blair Plans 60% Cut in Greenhouse Gas Output," *The Times*, 24 February 2003, available at <http://www.timesonline.co.uk>.

the potential for future emissions reductions and, similarly, the Canadian Foundation for Climate and Atmospheric Sciences to report to Canadians on the science of climate change. We welcome the statement by Prime Minister Blair. We believe it is important to consider the long term issues related to climate change.

(House of Commons Debates, 19 September 2003, p. 7575)
(Débats de la Chambre des Communes, le 19 septembre 2003, p. 7575)

Mr. John Herron (Fundy — Royal):

[L]ast December many Canadians and the international community expected the Canadian government to be genuine in its intent to not only ratify but implement the Kyoto accord ... Today the commissioner of the environment confirmed that the Government of Canada is behind in all its Kyoto initiatives ... Is the ... [Government] content ... [with] its promises on environmental public policy?

Mr. Alan Tonks (Parliamentary Secretary to the Minister of the Environment):

[T]he government has not only been actively implementing and working toward the objectives of the Kyoto accord since the last budget, but back two budgets: $1.7 billion under the action plan at that time was implemented toward new technologies, $2 billion, $1 billion of which has been on retrofitting, new technologies and looking at new forms of fuels and so on. This is a record of accomplishment.

(House of Commons Debates, 7 October 2003, p. 8273)
(Débats de la Chambre des Communes, le 7 octobre 2003, p. 8273)

Mme Yolande Thibeault (Saint-Lambert):

Le Défi d'une tonne a été lancé le 26 mars 2004. [Pour quelles] ... raisons ... les Canadiens et les Canadiennes devraient[-ils] participer à ce défi?

Hon. Serge Marcil (Parliamentary Secretary to the Minister of the Environment):

Effectivement, dans le processus de mise en oeuvre du Protocole de Kyoto, on s'aperçoit que les Canadiens produisent annuellement en moyenne cinq tonnes de gaz à effet de serre. Si on veut absolument atteindre les objectifs canadiens en termes de réduction de gaz à effet de serre, nous invitons les Canadiens, individuellement, à participer à une campagne pour essayer de réduire d'au moins 20 p. 100 leur production de gaz à effet de serre, ce qui fait à peu près une tonne par personne.

(House of Commons Debates, 2 April 2004, p. 2033)
(Débats de la Chambre des Communes, le 2 avril 2004, p. 2033)

2   *Foreign Affairs / Affaires étrangères*

(a) Burma / Birmanie

Mr. Bryon Wilfert (Oak Ridges):

[O]n May 17, the military junta in Burma will hold talks concerning the establishment of a new constitution in which some members of the National League for Democracy, headed by Aung San Suu Kyi, most likely will participate. Since annulling her election in 1990, the military has abused human rights, political detentions have occurred, and torture has been rampant. Since Canada maintains diplomatic relations with Burma ... [w]hat useful messages we are sending to indicate our support for the process that must lead to fair and transparent elections?

Hon. Bill Graham (Minister of Foreign Affairs):

We use our representation in Burma, together with our international presence in the Human Rights Commission, in the United Nations General Assembly and in meetings like the ASEAN Regional Forum, to put pressure on Burma and to bring democracy to Burma.

(House of Commons Debates, 10 May 2004, p. 2967)
(Débats de la Chambre des Communes, le 10 mai 2004, p. 2967)

(b) Canadian representation abroad / Représentation canadienne à l'étranger

Hon. Charles Caccia (Davenport):

Strasbourg is the seat of the Council of Europe, the European Parliament, the European Court of Human Rights, the International Human Rights Institute and the Assembly of European Regions ... [G]iven the fact that the Department of Foreign Affairs has just announced the opening of seven consulates in the United States, could the Minister of Foreign Affairs inform the House as to when a consulate is likely to be opened in Strasbourg, France [?]

Hon. Bill Graham (Minister of Foreign Affairs):

[O]ur opening of seven consulates in the United States ... is very important. We have also opened an embassy recently in Kabul, which is equally important for Canada ... I recognize the importance of Strasbourg but we must look at the way in which we are represented abroad to make sure that Canada and its interests are fully and properly represented in a global sense.

(House of Commons Debates, 18 September 2003, p. 7533)
(Débats de la Chambre des Communes, le 18 septembre 2003, p. 7533)

(c) Caribbean Islands / Îles antillaises

Ms. Alexa McDonough (Halifax):

Yesterday the Nova Scotia legislature adopted a motion unanimously to invite the Turks and Caicos to join the Canadian federation[11] ... Now that the Prime Minister's Office has been considering this proposition, is the government ready to support the Turks and Caicos as part of the Canadian family?

Hon. Bill Graham (Minister of Foreign Affairs):

[I]t is very important in matters like this that we should get an indication from the people of Turks and Caicos as to whether they wish to join Canada. This matter was studied by a parliamentary committee some years ago ... The Prime Minister has had a telephone conversation with the leader of the Turks and Caicos. We are more than happy to consider this issue and discuss with the people of the Turks and Caicos, as Canadians, how we can work with them, whether it is by way of an association or by working with all of our Caribbean partners to make the Caribbean a better place for all of us.

(House of Commons Debates, 23 April 2004, p. 2342)
(Débats de la Chambre des Communes, le 23 avril 2004, p. 2342)

---

11 Editor's note: On 21 April 2004, the Parliament of Nova Scotia affirmatively voted for Resolution 1001, which proclaimed that "the Government of Nova Scotia initiate discussions with the Turks and Caicos to become part of the Province of Nova Scotia and encourage the Government of Canada to welcome the Turks and Caicos as part of our country." (*Debates of the House of Assembly of Nova Scotia*, 21 April 2004, pp. 2378–79, available at <http://www.gov.ns.ca>).

(d) Denmark / Danemark

Mr. Stockwell Day (Okanagan — Coquihalla):

[T]he nation of Denmark ... is challenging our sovereignty ... Its military, from its warship, hoisted its flag on our arctic territory without permission, without warning, and without any fear of being stopped ... [T]he scandal has led to the recall of our ambassador to Denmark ... [How the Government of Canada is dealing with the situation?]

Hon. Aileen Carroll (Minister for International Cooperation):

Canada has consistently defended its interests in the past and it will continue to do so. Hans Island constitutes part of the national territory of Canada. No assertion by the Danish ambassador or other Danish officials detracts from the absolute sovereignty that Canada enjoys over Hans Island.

(House of Commons Debates, 26 March 2004, pp. 1755–56) (Débats de la Chambre des Communes, le 26 mars 2004, pp. 1755–56)

Hon. Bill Graham (Minister of Foreign Affairs):

In the meantime, I can assure ... [Canadians] that we are telling Denmark clearly Hans Island is Canada's, and we will continue to do that.

(House of Commons Debates, 30 March 2004, p. 1874) (Débats de la Chambre des Communes, le 30 mars 2004, p. 1874)

(e) Francophonie / Francophonie

M. Christian Jobin (Lévis-et-Chutes-de-la-Chaudière):

[L]e secrétaire d'État pour l'Amérique latine, l'Afrique et la Francophonie a participé à la conférence ministérielle de la Francophonie sur la Société de l'information les 4 et 5 septembre derniers au Maroc. Le secrétaire d'État peut-il faire rapport à la Chambre sur les conclusions de cette conférence?

L'hon. Denis Paradis (secrétaire d'État (Amérique latine et Afrique) (Francophonie)):

Le but de la conférence ministérielle était de préparer le terrain pour le Sommet mondial sur la société de l'information qui aura lieu à Genève en décembre prochain. J'en ai profité, bien sûr, pour promouvoir les initiatives canadiennes en matière de technologies de l'information et pour démontrer le leadership du Canada dans ce domaine. J'en ai aussi profité pour annoncer que nous allons faciliter la participation de jeunes Canadiens et Africains francophones à ce sommet.

(House of Commons Debates, 17 September 2003, p. 7459) (Débats de la Chambre des Communes, le 17 septembre 2003, p. 7459)

M. Raymond Simard (Saint-Boniface):

[L]e Canada reçoit cette semaine la visite de l'administrateur général de l'Agence internationale de la francophonie. Le secrétaire d'État à l'Amérique latine, à l'Afrique et à la Francophonie peut-il expliquer à cette Chambre quel est le rôle du Canada au sein de la Francophonie?

L'hon. Denis Paradis (secrétaire d'État (Francophonie)):

[L]e Canada est fier d'être un partenaire majeur au sein de la Francophonie internationale. L'Organisation internationale de la Francophonie comprend 54 pays et deux gouvernements participants, soit le gouvernement du Québec et le gouvernement du Nouveau-Brunswick. Elle s'occupe de divers dossiers, notamment la langue, la culture et des dossiers concernant les valeurs propres aux Canadiens, soit la démocratie, les droits de la personne et la bonne gouvernance. Il s'agit d'une occasion exceptionnelle pour le Canada de se faire valoir sur la scène internationale.

(House of Commons Debates, 6 October 2003, p. 8213) (Débats de la Chambre des Communes, le 6 octobre 2003, p. 8213)

(f) Haiti / Haïti

L'hon. Don Boudria (Glengarry — Prescott — Russell):

La crise à Haïti sévit, voire grandit de jour en jour. Il y a une quarantaine de morts depuis quelques jours et une douzaine de villes touchées par une violence épouvantable. Qu'est-ce que le gouvernement du Canada entend faire, de concert avec les autres pays tels, par exemple, la France et les États-Unis, pour redonner une stabilité ou même donner une lueur d'espoir au peuple haïtien?

L'hon. Bill Graham (ministre des Affaires étrangères):

[L]a situation à Haïti est évidemment très préoccupante. J'ai parlé ce matin au secrétaire d'État Powell à ce sujet. Nous travaillons avec les États-Unis. Le premier ministre est en contact avec les leaders du CARICOM au sujet de Haïti. Nous mettons en place des mesures suivies par CARICOM. Nous travaillons avec la Francophonie, avec les États-Unis, avec l'OEA et avec

CARICOM pour qu'on puisse mettre fin à la violence à Haïti et avoir un dialogue politique. C'est la seule façon de résoudre les problèmes à Haïti. Nous sommes très actifs et nous continuons nos actions.

(House of Commons Debates, 10 February 2004, p. 384)
(Débats de la Chambre des Communes, le 10 février 2004, p. 384)

(g) International Civil Aviation Organization / Organisation de l'aviation civile internationale

Mrs. Diane Ablonczy (Calgary — Nose Hill):

[T]here are serious problems with the government's plan to spend $10 million to add a facial recognition biometric to Canadian passports. Why ... [is the Government doing this]?

L'hon. Yvon Charbonneau (secrétaire parlementaire de la vice-première ministre et ministre de la Sécurité publique et de la Protection civile (protection civile)):

[C]ette orientation de la part du gouvernement a été annoncée parce que c'est la norme la plus récente à avoir été établie par l'Organisation de l'aviation civile internationale ... Si nous nous orientons vers la biométrie, c'est parce que c'est ce qu'on a trouvé de plus à jour et de plus fonctionnel sur le plan international.

(House of Commons Debates, 29 April 2004, p. 2584)
(Débats de la Chambre des Communes, le 29 avril 2004, p. 2584)

(h) International Court of Justice / Cour internationale de Justice

Hon. Elinor Caplan (Thornhill):

The Palestinian authority is currently challenging the legality of Israel's security fence in the International Court.[12] Israel does not recognize the jurisdiction of the International Court to rule on matters of its internal security ... [W]hat is Canada's position regarding these proceedings?

---

[12] Editor's note: See International Court of Justice (ICJ), *Legal Consequences of the Construction of a Wall in the Occupied Palestinian Territory* (2003–4). On 9 July 2004, the ICJ issued the Advisory Opinion (reprinted in (2004) 43 I.L.M. 1009), dismissing the arguments of Israel. The court recognized that Israel violated international law in the routing of the security fence and called on Israel to dismantle sections built in the West Bank and East Jerusalem.

Hon. Bill Graham (Minister of Foreign Affairs):

Canada has made its vote known in the United Nations with respect to the security fence. It is clear that Israel must take actions to protect itself and its citizens. However we have serious reservations about the placing of the fence, where it is going, and we have raised those with Israel and internationally. That said, we strongly believe that this matter can only be resolved by negotiation between the parties as authorized by the Security Council. We encourage the parties to do that. We do not believe that legal proceedings are correct at this time. We have raised those convictions in our submissions.[13]

(House of Commons Debates, 26 February 2004, p. 1118)
(Débats de la Chambre des Communes, le 26 février 2004, p. 1118)

(i) Israel/ Israël

Mme Francine Lalonde (Mercier):

[L]e vice-premier ministre israélien a reconnu que l'assassinat faisait partie des options qu'envisageait Israël pour se débarrasser du président de l'Autorité palestinienne, Yasser Arafat. Est-ce que le [gouvernement du Canada] entend convoquer l'ambassadeur d'Israël au Canada pour lui signifier sa profonde désapprobation à l'endroit des propos tenus par le vice-président du gouvernement israélien, qui préconise notamment l'assassinat comme méthode de résolution des conflits politiques?

L'hon. Bill Graham (ministre des Affaires étrangères):

[L]a position du gouvernement canadien [est], qui est la même que celle du gouvernement américain et de beaucoup d'autres gouvernements dans le monde, à l'effet qu'il n'est pas sage pour le gouvernement israélien, à ce moment-ci, dans l'intérêt de sa sécurité, de prendre des mesures qui pourraient nuire à ses intérêts à long terme, c'est-à-dire la réalisation de la feuille de route.

(House of Commons Debates, 15 September 2003, p. 7338)
(Débats de la Chambre des Communes, le 15 septembre 2003, p. 7338)

---

13 Editor's note: Canada argued against the ICJ issuing an advisory opinion, emphasizing the importance of a politically negotiated solution (rather than a decision reached at the judicial hearing) to resolve the conflict in question. See *Written Statement of the Government of Canada*, 29 January 2004, available at <http://www.icj-cij.org>.

Mr. Pat O'Brien (London — Fanshawe):

Canada has strongly criticized the illegal and inflammatory wall built by Israel in the West Bank and Gaza. This provocative incursion beyond the 1967 borders makes the Palestinian people prisoners in their own towns ... What specific action is Canada prepared to take to persuade Israel to tear down this illegal and inflammatory wall?

Hon. Bill Graham (Minister of Foreign Affairs):

Canada has clearly indicated in our vote in the United Nations that in our view this wall is not contributing to the ultimate security and peace of Israel. We strongly support Israel in its security measures, but we believe that the construction of the wall and where it is going is such that it is inhibiting the peace discussions. That said, Canada has continually urged the parties to work with the Security Council, to work with all the partners, to dialogue between them. It is a dialogue that will ultimately solve this ... Canada's balanced position in urging the parties to this political solution makes a contribution to that process.

(House of Commons Debates, 4 February 2004, pp. 103–4)
(Débats de la Chambre des Communes, le 4 février 2004, pp. 103–4)

Right Hon. Joe Clark (Calgary Centre):

The European Union has condemned the killing of Sheikh Ahmed Yassin as an extra-judicial killing. It said that in this case, the condemnation has to be even stronger than usual. Is that also the position of the Government of Canada and if so, what action is Canada intending beyond condemnation?

Hon. Bill Graham (Minister of Foreign Affairs):

[W]e recognize entirely the right of Israel to take steps to protect itself and its citizens against acts of terrorism. But we have condemned the death of Sheikh Yassin because, in our view, this is a matter that is contrary to international legal obligations on behalf of the state of Israel and will contribute to instability in the area and will make peace, which we all work for so hard, more difficult to achieve. We call upon all parties to return to the road map. We call upon a return to a concept of peace in the area. We ask for restraint on behalf of all parties in this difficult time.

(House of Commons Debates, 22 March 2004, p. 1511)
(Débats de la Chambre des Communes, le 22 mars 2004, p. 1511)

(j) Sudan / Soudan

Mr. Stockwell Day (Okanagan — Coquihalla):

[T]he ongoing documented atrocities in Sudan include the mass execution of civilians, the killing of children, the systematic rape of women, destruction of villages, and the forced displacement of thousands of civilians. In referring to Sudan's election yesterday to the United Nations Commission on Human Rights, Joanna Weschler, who is the UN Human Rights Watch representative, said: "A government that engages in wholesale abuses of its citizens should not be eligible for a seat at the table." Does the Prime Minister agree with that statement?

Hon. Bill Graham (Minister of Foreign Affairs):   .

African delegates are put up by African countries, and that Canada, Europe and other countries do not control those elections. We have made it very clear when we voted against Libya to be the chair the last time that we take a strong stand. We believe strongly that we are working toward the reform of the UN Commission on Human Rights. This is a very important institution of the United Nations. It does need improvement. We will be working toward that and at this time I am proud to say that CIDA is making significant contributions to the helping of refugees in the region ... I met today with Senator Jaffer, who is ... our special envoy to the Sudan peace process ... She has been actively pursuing the peace process on behalf of the government and Canadian people.

(House of Commons Debates, 5 May 2004, pp. 2800–1)
(Débats de la Chambre des Communes, le 5 mai 2004, pp.2800–1)

(k) United States / États-Units

Mrs. Carol Skelton (Saskatoon — Rosetown — Biggar):

[L]ast week the international panel came out with their findings and recommendations for the U.S. cattle industry. One of those recommendations is to ban the feeding of animal protein to ruminants ... How have the USDA and Secretary Veneman responded to this proposal about blood products?

Hon. Bob Speller (Minister of Agriculture and Agri-Food):

[T]he international peer review panel reported in the United States last week, and it had reported to us. It has not told us the same things as it has told the Americans because there are different situations depending upon the country ... [F]irst and foremost what is important is that Canada and the United States co-ordinate these measures. That is why next week officials will be sitting down with our American counterparts to do exactly that.

(House of Commons Debates, 9 February 2004, pp. 318–19)
(Débats de la Chambre des Communes, le 9 février 2004, pp. 318–19)

(1) Zimbabwe / Zimbabwe

Mr. Keith Martin (Esquimalt — Juan de Fuca):

A recent report by the South African Council of Churches clearly shows that Zimbabwe's president, Robert Mugabe, is forcing children as young as 10 to carry out brutal atrocities such as murder and torture against innocent civilians. Will the [Canadian Government] ... indict Robert Mugabe for crimes against humanity?

Hon. Bill Graham (Minister of Foreign Affairs):

[T]he government is ... pursuing effectively through the Commonwealth, through the United Nations and through every other forum to put pressure on the government of Robert Mugabe to change, to allow democracy to develop in Africa. The Prime Minister will be attending the Commonwealth conference at the end of this year. This will be a primary subject of conversation, as it has been with myself and other foreign ministers when we met in New York last week. The problems in Zimbabwe and the people of Zimbabwe are a great preoccupation of ours. We will take concrete actions to protect them, not just threats, but concrete actions ...

[W]e will continue to do the right thing for the people of Zimbabwe by taking actions through every multilateral and bilateral forum to enable us to bring pressure on the government of Zimbabwe to change its conduct for the betterment of the people of Zimbabwe. Indicting the president of Zimbabwe might be one option, but there are many other options. This government has been pursuing them for years and will continue to do so with our African partners in a positive way to obtain positive results.

(House of Commons Debates, 1 October 2003, p. 8037)
(Débats de la Chambre des Communes, le 1 octobre 2003, p. 8037)

3   *Health / Santé*

(a) Framework Convention on Tobacco Control /
Convention-cadre de l'OMS pour la lutte antitabac [14]

---

[14] World Health Organization Framework Convention on Tobacco Control (Geneva, Switzerland, 21 May 2003; entered into force 27 February 2005). Canada has been a party to the convention since 26 November 2004 by ratification.

Hon. Don Boudria (Glengarry — Prescott — Russell):

In May 2003 the World Health Assembly, with the support of the Canadian government, approved the tobacco convention framework to control tobacco use ... Will ... the Government of Canada ... ratify this important convention?

Hon. Bill Graham (Minister of Foreign Affairs):

Canada played an important role in the negotiations of this important convention. We are committed to ratifying it as soon as possible ... Canada does not ratify conventions until such time as provincial, regulatory and stakeholder engagement has been done. This is what we are doing ... [T]he convention has important provisions in it for farmers. We will be working with all stakeholders to ensure that the convention applies in Canada, for the good of our health and for the good of our farming community.

(House of Commons Debates, 8 March 2004, p. 1215)
(Débats de la Chambre des Communes, le 8 mars 2004, p. 1215)

(b) Human cloning / Clonage humain

Mr. Rob Merrifield (Yellowhead):

[A]n international convention on human cloning is being debated at the United Nations. Many countries want to see a comprehensive ban on human cloning, both therapeutic and reproductive ... [T]he government's Bill C-13 calls for prohibitions on both reproductive and therapeutic cloning,[15] but our negotiators at the United Nations are seeking prohibitions on reproductive cloning alone. Why the double standard?

Hon. Anne McLellan (Minister of Health):

In fact ... there is no double standard. Let me be absolutely clear ... that in Bill C-13 ... we ban all forms of human cloning. However, achieving a broad international consensus to ban all forms of cloning may not be possible at this time. But it is clear that the international community is ready to pass a ban on human reproductive cloning. I would suggest that Canada is supporting this effort. We should all support this effort because not taking that step at this time may mean having no convention at all.

---

15 Editor's note: Bill C-13, *An Act Respecting Assisted Human Reproduction and Related Research*, originally introduced in the first session of the thirty-seventh Parliament as Bill C-56, was introduced in the House of Commons on 9 October 2002. See *House of Commons Debates*, 9 October 2002, p. 519.

(House of Commons Debates, 6 October, 2003, p. 8212)
(Débats de la Chambre des Communes, le 6 octobre 2003, p. 8212)

Mr. Rob Merrifield (Yellowhead):

[T]oday at the United Nations Canada abstained from a crucial vote on human cloning. A resolution to delay a decision on human cloning for two years was passed by just one vote, 80 to 79 ... [T]he Minister of Health promised ... that Canada would support a comprehensive ban ... [W]ould the minister [comment on that]?

Hon. Anne McLellan (Minister of Health):

[T]he resolution that the government indicated we would support, the Costa Rican resolution, unfortunately never made it to a vote yesterday at the United Nations. It did not make it to a vote because the Organization of Islamic States decided to put forward a motion that called for a hoisting or deferral of the issue for two years because the Organization of Islamic States believed that there was no consensus and therefore no agreement could be reached. Unfortunately, because of that motion, we were unable to reach the vote on the substance of the Costa Rican motion.

(House of Commons Debates, 6 November 2003, p. 9270)
(Débats de la Chambre des Communes, le 6 novembre 2003, p. 9270)

(c) HIV-AIDS/ VIH-SIDA

Ms. Libby Davies (Vancouver East):

[T]oday we hear yet again about the pandemic of AIDS in Africa. We hear again how literally millions of people are dying tragically because they cannot afford the drugs to keep them alive ... Stephen Lewis says that Africa needs just one G-7 country to step forward and help the cheap drugs flow.[16] Will Canada be that country?

Hon. Susan Whelan (Minister for International Cooperation):

Canada has already pledged $150 million to the global fund for fighting HIV-AIDS, tuberculosis and malaria. On top of that, we have contributed $50 million to the Canada fund for Africa for the vaccine initiative for

---

[16] Editor's note: Mr. Stephen Lewis is a special envoy of the secretary-general of the United Nations on HIV/AIDS in Africa. As for his speech, see, for example, "UN AIDS Envoy Wants Looser Drug Laws: Report," *CTV News Online* (25 September 2003), available at <http://www.ctv.ca>.

HIV and AIDS. Canada has stepped forward and Canada will continue to step up to the plate to help fight HIV-AIDS, particularly in Africa.

(House of Commons Debates, 25 September 2003, p. 7816)
(Débats de la Chambre des Communes, le 25 septembre 2003, p. 7816)

Ms. Libby Davies (Vancouver East):

Africa needs [drugs] ... to fight AIDS. Will Canada ... let cheap drugs fight AIDS in Africa?

Hon. Pierre Pettigrew (Minister for International Trade):

[L]et me tell the House how proud I was, like all Canadians, when we made the TRIPS agreement and when the whole WTO membership agreed to give privileged access to Africans so they could fight these pandemics of AIDS, malaria and tuberculosis. Of course, we will want Canadian companies to be part of the effort and to contribute to alleviating the suffering and the difficulties they are having in Africa while respecting of course the intellectual property, as the TRIPS agreement requires us to do.

(House of Commons Debates, 29 September 2003, pp. 7913–14)
(Débats de la Chambre des Communes, le 29 septembre 2003, pp. 7913–14)

(d) Pharmaceutical industry / Industrie pharmaceutique

M. Paul Crête (Kamouraska — Rivière-du-Loup — Témiscouata — Les Basques):

[L]ors de l'achat de BioChem Pharma, fleuron de l'industrie pharmaceutique québécoise, par la britannique Shire, cette dernière avait promis d'investir 27 millions de dollars pendant quatre à six ans pour la recherche et le développement en matière de leucémie et du cancer du pancréas.

   Suite à cette entente entre Shire et Industrie Canada en 2001, le ministre approuvait la transaction. Le ministre peut-il nous confirmer que cette approbation dépendait de telles conditions ... maintenant que Shire a fermé le laboratoire de BioChem Pharma à Laval?

L'hon. Allan Rock (ministre de l'Industrie):

[L]e gouvernement a la ferme intention de s'assurer que les engagements seront respectés ... [J]'ai l'intention de respecter la loi. J'ai également

l'intention de faire en sorte que la compagnie respecte tous les engagements qui ont été pris à l'occasion de l'acquisition de BioChem Pharma.

(House of Commons Debates, 15 September 2003, p. 7337)
(Débats de la Chambre des Communes, le 15 septembre 2003, p. 7337)

(e) World Health Organization / Organisation mondiale de la santé

Mr. John Duncan (Vancouver Island North):

Due to objections from China, democratic Taiwan has been denied World
Health Organization status. Last spring Parliament passed a ... motion
that called for Canada to support the admission of Taiwan as an observer
at the World Health Organization.[17] Why is the government refusing to
support Taiwan at the World Health Organization?

Hon. Bill Graham (Minister of Foreign Affairs):

[P]articipation in the World Health Organization requires the support of
all members of the World Health Organization. We have ... offered [the
Taiwanese government] ... complete help for World Health Organization
issues through other means. We inform and participate with the government of Taiwan. We recognize their legitimate interest in these issues ...
To suggest that we are anti-Taiwan is completely erroneous.

(House of Commons Debates, 12 March 2004, p. 1454)
(Débats de la Chambre des Communes, le 12 mars 2004, p. 1454)

4 Human Rights / Droits de la personne

(a) Freedom of Speech, Association and Religious Belief /
Liberté d'expression, d'association et de croyance religieuse

Mr. Pat O'Brien (London — Fanshawe):

[T]here are serious allegations that anti-Christian persecutions are being
carried out by police and soldiers in the Lai Chau province of Vietnam.
These reported persecutions are apparently aimed at having Vietnamese
Christians recant their faith and abandon their Christian religious practices. Could the Minister of Foreign Affairs comment on the accuracy of

[17] Editor's note: On 27 May 2003, a majority of 163 members of all parties in the
House of Commons voted in favour of the motion supporting Taiwan's observer
status with the World Health Organization. (*House of Commons Debates*, 27 May
2003, pp. 6540–41).

these allegations and outline what actions Canada has taken or will take to protest these persecutions?

Hon. Dan McTeague (Parliamentary Secretary to the Minister of Foreign Affairs):

The government is ... aware of the reports of religious persecution in Vietnam, including those in the province of Lai Chau. Indeed, our embassy in Hanoi has been extremely involved with this. The government raised this issue with the Vietnamese foreign affairs minister last year ... [L]ast week on March 25 we said [at the meeting of the UN commission on human rights] in our country's statement that we encourage Vietnam to stop the detention of citizens for their political and religious views and to allow greater freedom of speech and association.

(House of Commons Debates, 31 March 2004, p. 1913)
(Débats de la Chambre des Communes, le 31 mars 2004, p. 1913)

(b) Immigration versus border security / Immigration et sécurité aux frontières

Mrs. Diane Ablonczy (Calgary — Nose Hill):

An independent commission found evidence of widespread fraud at a Canadian embassy. It says Triad members have likely been allowed to immigrate, with criminal backgrounds scrubbed from our government computers ... [Is] the ... [government] ... hiding the truth about the criminals getting into Canada?

Hon. Denis Coderre (Minister of Citizenship and Immigration):

[W]e do not perceive immigrants as potential terrorists or criminals. We take every allegation very seriously ... I can assure members that security is ... a priority for the government.

(House of Commons Debates, 18 September 2003, p. 7532)
(Débats de la Chambre des Communes, le 18 septembre 2003, p. 7532)

M. Richard Marceau (Charlesbourg — Jacques-Cartier):

Ahmad Cheriam, un individu recherché par le corps policier de Québec dans le cadre du réseau de prostitution juvénile, a passé la frontière canadienne sans être inquiété d'aucune façon par la sécurité, malgré deux mandats d'arrestation et un avis de recherche national. Comment le gouvernement peut-il expliquer que les frontières, malgré les investissements qui ont été faits au chapitre de la sécurité, soient toujours des passoires?

Hon. Elinor Caplan (Minister of National Revenue):

[T]here was no lookout in our system at the time that this individual entered Canada ... [S]ince July 2000 customs officers have apprehended and arrested 2,136 individuals, criminals who were in our system. If they are in our system, we stop them and arrest them.

(House of Commons Debates, 20 October 2003, p. 8490)
(Débats de la Chambre des Communes, le 20 octobre 2003, p. 8490)

(c) Protecting Canadians abroad / Protection des Canadiens à l'étranger

Mr. Stockwell Day (Okanagan — Coquihalla):

[T]his summer a female Canadian photographer, Zahra Kazemi, was wrongly arrested by the Iranian regime, tortured and beaten to death ... Another Canadian, William Sampson, was wrongly arrested by the Saudi regime and for nearly three years was tortured and beaten, almost to the point of death ... [W]hy will the government not send ... [the Saudi ambassador] home to Saudi Arabia until he gets restitution for Mr. Sampson and an apology to all Canadians?

Hon. Bill Graham (Minister of Foreign Affairs):

[T]he responsibility of the government is to protect Canadians abroad [and] ... to rest in communications with governments where Canadians are in problems. We are making statements. We are working with the Iranian government. We have taken strong positions with the Iranian government to deal with the Kazemi case. We are taking strong steps with the Saudi government to deal with the treatment of Mr. Sampson ... I will not put Canadians at risk abroad by breaking off public relations.

(House of Commons Debates, 15 September 2003, p. 7331)
(Débats de la Chambre des Communes, le 15 septembre 2003, p. 7331)

Ms. Alexa McDonough (Halifax):

[I]ndications are that Syria is about to subject Maher Arar to a trial ... [T]here is no Canadian ambassador in Syria at the moment ... [H]ow are the rights of this Canadian citizen to be protected?

Hon. Bill Graham (Minister of Foreign Affairs):

[W]e have been in regular contact with the government of Syria. In fact when our ambassador last visited Mr. Arar, he specifically said that our representations had aided his position, had helped him. He was very grateful for the fact that his position had improved there. Obviously this is a matter of Mr. Arar being a Syrian national as well as a Canadian national. The Syrian authorities are saying they are going to press charges against him. We have taken the position that they must release him to Canada. We seek to get his release but obviously we must deal with the Syrian authorities in dealing with a Syrian national under Syrian law. We are using all efforts we can to make sure Mr. Arar is well

(House of Commons Debates, 17 September 2003, p. 7457)
(Débats de la Chambre des Communes, le 17 septembre 2003, p. 7457)

Mme Diane Bourgeois (Terrebonne — Blainville):

[L]e 10 juillet dernier, la photo-reporter montréalaise d'origine iranienne, Zahra Kazemi, mourait en prison après un interrogatoire mené sous la direction du procureur général de Téhéran. Les proches du président Khatami ont qualifié cette mort d'assassinat. Est-ce que le premier ministre entend donner suite aux demandes du fils de Mme Kazemi et de la coalition des 19 organisations qui l'appuient et qui exigent un plan d'action immédiat?

L'hon. Bill Graham (ministre des Affaires étrangères):

Nous regrettons énormément la mort de Mme Kazemi. C'était tragique. C'était une journaliste qui accomplissait ses fonctions. J'ai fait des promesses à la famille et à la population canadienne. Je travaille avec tous nos partenaires dans le monde pour faire en sorte que l'Iran protège les journalistes sur son territoire. Nous avons un plan d'action qui est multilatéral et bilatéral, et nous le suivrons.

(House of Commons Debates, 18 September 2003, p. 7534)
(Débats de la Chambre des Communes, le 18 septembre 2003, p. 7534)

Right Hon. Joe Clark (Calgary Centre):

[Could] ... the Minister of Foreign Affairs [inform Canadians on his meeting with Secretary of State Colin Powell on the matter of] ... the deportation to Syria of Mr. Arar?

Hon. Bill Graham (Minister of Foreign Affairs):

I protested strongly to the United States that when Canadians are in the United States they should be treated as Canadians and returned to Canada. In the course of that discussion, he said to me that advice from his officials was that this was appropriate in terms of international law by the United States and it was covered by arrangements ... Secretary Powell ... said that the American authorities had acted within their jurisdiction.

(House of Commons Debates, 8 October 2003, p. 8321)
(Débats de la Chambre des Communes, le 8 octobre 2003, p. 8321)

Mme Francine Lalonde (Mercier):

Guy-André Kieffer, ce journaliste franco-canadien de 54 ans qui a travaillé ici sur la Colline pendant plusieurs années, a disparu dans des circonstances nébuleuses à Abidjan en Côte-d'Ivoire, le vendredi 16 avril dernier ... [Est-que le gouvernement du Canada trace le plan de] intervenir ... et faire pression sur la Côte-d'Ivoire pour que celle-ci fasse progresser l'enquête?

L'hon. Dan McTeague (secrétaire parlementaire du ministre des Affaires étrangères):

[L]e gouvernement du Canada prend au sérieux la situation de la disparition de M. Kieffer ... [L]e gouvernement et ... notre ambassade se sont impliqués dans les recherches pour le retrouver dès l'instant où il est disparu.

(House of Commons Debates, 28 April 2004, p. 2512)
(Débats de la Chambre des Communes, le 28 avril 2004, p. 2512)

(d) Racial discrimination / Discrimination raciale

Mr. Svend Robinson (Burnaby — Douglas):

Last week, two respected Canadian Muslim religious leaders and Islamic scholars, Ahmed Kutty and Abdool Hamid, travelled to Florida to lead prayer services. Instead, they were handcuffed, thrown in jail, interrogated and kicked out of the United States. Why has the ... [Canadian] government not called for a full independent inquiry and apology and ... not protested this shameful racist treatment?

Hon. Bill Graham (Minister of Foreign Affairs):

[C]learly we recognize that the United States of America determines who goes across its borders and who does not, as every sovereign country does.

What we do is we tell our American friends on every occasion that those of us living in Canada are not involved in terrorism and we wish to work with Americans to establish moderate voices. I understand the people who went there were moderate people trying to establish links with moderate voices in the United States of America. We will continue to make sure the American government understands that from Canada we come as friends. That is the voice we have with the United States and we will continue to keep that tone.

(House of Commons Debates, 15 September 2003, p. 7336)
(Débats de la Chambre des Communes, le 15 septembre 2003, p. 7336)

Ms. Sophia Leung (Vancouver Kingsway):

Why is it important to celebrate March 21 as the International Day for the Elimination of Racial Discrimination? What is the multiculturalism program doing to highlight the importance of this day?

Hon. Jean Augustine (Minister of State (Multiculturalism and Status of Women)):

March 21 is indeed the International Day for the Elimination of Racial Discrimination. We will continue the annual March 21 campaign which is entitled "Racism. Stop It!" We know, and we must acknowledge, that racism exists in our society. The ethnic diversity survey tells us that 35% of visible minorities experience some form of discrimination or unfair treatment. Racism affects everyone. All Canadians must be encouraged to take action.

(House of Commons Debates, 11 March 2004, p. 1406)
(Débats de la Chambre des Communes, le 11 mars 2004, p. 1406)

Ms. Paddy Torsney (Burlington):

[T]his morning, Mr. Doudou Diène, the United Nations special rapporteur on contemporary forms of racism, racial discrimination, xenophobia and related intolerance, reported on his visits over the past two years to Canada, Colombia, Côte d'Ivoire, Guyana, and Trinidad and Tobago ... How is this government addressing the issues on Canada that were raised by the special rapporteur?

Hon. Jean Augustine (Minister of State (Multiculturalism and Status of Women)):

Canada welcomes the report of the special rapporteur and we will give special consideration to its recommendations and its conclusions. Many of the issues that the special rapporteur raised are not unknown to us and are no surprise to us, because we know that we have work to do in Canadian society through the multiculturalism program, which is designed to address those issues. Combatting racism remains a priority of the government and of all Canadians. Therefore, my top priority is an action plan against racism.

(House of Commons Debates, 22 March 2004, p. 1510)
(Débats de la Chambre des Communes, le 22 mars 2004, p. 1510)

Ms. Sophia Leung (Vancouver Kingsway):

Over the past few years racial profiling has emerged as one of the primary issues facing African, Asian, Arabian and Muslim Canadians and the aboriginal communities, in cities across the country. How does the Government of Canada address this concern surrounding racial profiling?

Hon. Jean Augustine (Minister of State (Multiculturalism and Status of Women)):

[T]he Government of Canada considers the selective treatment of individuals solely on the basis of ethnic or racial characteristics as unacceptable ... Just last week I spoke to about 100 leaders at a consensus conference on racial profiling in Toronto. I will have the chance this weekend ... to speak with the Atlantic Region Association of Immigrant Serving Agencies to discuss this important matter.

(House of Commons Debates, 26 March 2004, p. 1759)
(Débats de la Chambre des Communes, le 26 mars 2004, p. 1759)

Mr. Bryon Wilfert (Oak Ridges):

[P]rosecutions by authorities in ... Cambodia of ethnic minorities ... are increasing. Religious persecution, confiscations of land, and arrests have occurred recently ... Given Canada's stand on human rights, what steps has the government taken, either with the United Nations commissioner for refugees or through diplomatic channels, to convey our concerns and opposition to these actions?

Hon. Bill Graham (Minister of Foreign Affairs):

[T]he government regularly expresses Canadians' concerns about human rights violations against minority groups, both in Vietnam and in Cambodia

548 The Canadian Yearbook of International Law 2004

... For several years now, Canada has co-sponsored a commission on human rights resolution on Cambodia, and Canada has called on Cambodia to improve its cooperation with the UNHCR.

(House of Commons Debates, 4 May 2004, p. 2756)
(Débats de la Chambre des Communes, le 4 mai 2004, p. 2756)

(e) Right to water / Droit à l'eau

M. Serge Cardin (Sherbrooke):

[L]e Canada est le seul des 53 pays membres de la Commission des droits de l'homme à s'être prononcé contre la reconnaissance de l'eau comme un droit humain essentiel. Comment le Canada peut-il maintenir son attitude alors qu'aujourd'hui, à l'occasion de la Journée mondiale de l'eau, quatre organisations, dont Développement et Paix, ont déposé une pétition en vertu de laquelle 177 000 personnes au Québec et au Canada dénoncent le refus du gouvernement de reconnaître l'accès à l'eau comme un droit humain essentiel?

L'hon. Bill Graham (ministre des Affaires étrangères):

[N]ous examinons toutes les propositions de la Commission des droits de l'homme. Il est très important de connaître quels sont les droits sociaux et économiques. Mais pour dire que tout le monde a droit à l'eau, il faut reconnaître que nous sommes voisins d'un pays qui a ses perceptions relatives à l'accès à l'eau. C'est le rôle du Canada d'examiner avec d'autres États quelle est la mesure de ce très important concept en droit international. Il faut travailler avec les communautés internationales pour que cela ait une conséquence réelle.

(House of Commons Debates, 22 March 2004, pp. 1510–11)
(Débats de la Chambre des Communes, le 22 mars 2004, pp. 1510–11)

(f) Rights of women / Droits des femmes

Mrs. Judi Longfield (Whitby — Ajax):

[W]hat ... is [the Government] doing to help protect women who are innocent victims in such dreadful things as international sex trade transgressions and trafficking?

Hon. Irwin Cotler (Minister of Justice and Attorney General of Canada):

[T]rafficking women in particular is one of the most heinous of crimes. It is the new global slave trade and it violates all the rights of the Universal Declaration of Human Rights, in particular the rights of women. Accordingly, today on International Women's Day I am hosting a two day international seminar, releasing a 10 point proposal in order to prevent trafficking, in order to protect victims and in order to bring the perpetrators to justice.

(House of Commons Debates, 8 March 2004, p. 1215)
(Débats de la Chambre des Communes, le 8 mars 2004, p. 1215)

Ms. Sarmite Bulte (Parkdale — High Park):

The United Nations Commission on the Status of Women is holding its 48th session at its New York headquarters from March 1 to 12 of this year ... [Is] Canada ... participating in these sessions?

Hon. Jean Augustine (Minister of State (Multiculturalism and Status of Women)):

I was pleased and honoured to represent Canada and be there with the Canadian delegation to address the 48th session of the Commission on the Status of Women. The session focused on the participation of women in conflict prevention, conflict management and resolution, as well as an emphasis on the role of men and boys as partners in achieving gender equality. This government is committed to gender equality and we work in the interests of and in participation with all Canadians.

(House of Commons Debates, 10 March 2004, p. 1309)
(Débats de la Chambre des Communes, le 10 mars 2004, p. 1309)

(g) Self-Determination / Autodétermination

Mr. Bryon Wilfert (Oak Ridges):

The Chinese national people's congress standing committee has stated universal suffrage will not apply for 2007 for the Hong Kong special administrative region. In 1997 Beijing promised autonomy: one country, two systems. This decision goes against that pledge. Since Canada has championed and supported this approach, what representations will Canada make to ensure that China fulfills its obligations?

Hon. Bill Graham (Minister of Foreign Affairs):

We have always made it very clear that we believe that the people of Hong Kong should determine the political structure which is most suited to their needs in accordance with the democratic objectives which are laid down in the basic law. We urge the Chinese authorities to ensure that the power to interpret the basic law will not be used to prevent political evolution in Hong Kong in accordance with the wishes and democratic aspirations of the people of Hong Kong. We will convey that message to all Chinese authorities at the appropriate meetings.

(House of Commons Debates, 27 April 2004, p. 2467)
(Débats de la Chambre des Communes, le 27 avril 2004, p. 2467)

5   *International Criminal Law / Droit pénal international*

(a)   UN Convention against Corruption / Convention de l'ONU contre la corruption[18]

Mr. Deepak Obhrai (Calgary East):

Next week the Prime Minister is planning to visit Secretary General Kofi Annan at the United Nations Headquarters. Canada has refused to sign the UN convention against corruption, which was adopted on October 31, 2003, at the United Nations General Assembly. Why is Canada refusing to sign this convention?

Hon. Bill Graham (Minister of Foreign Affairs):

Canada is not refusing to sign the convention. Canada has been a leader in trying to eliminate global corruption around the world. Every convention raises complicated domestic legal issues as well as international legal issues. We will continue to pursue ... to bring the American states together around anti-corruption ... We are taking measures in the Americas ... [,] in Africa [and] ... in Asia. We take measures globally. We will examine that convention ... We are extremely active on this file ... When the legal problems around it are resolved, we will of course adhere to it.

(House of Commons Debates, 26 February 2004, pp. 1116–17)
(Débats de la Chambre des Communes, le 26 février 2004, pp. 1116–17)

(b)   War crimes and crimes against humanity / Crimes de guerre et crimes contre l'humanité

Mr. David Pratt (Nepean — Carleton):

[T]he special court in Sierra Leone faces the prospect of closure within two months if donor nations do not step up to the plate and provide more

18 Doc. A/58/422; New York, United States, 31 October 2003; not yet in force. Canada became a signatory to the convention on 21 May 2004.

resources. [T]he ... [Canadian Government] is ... very supportive of the work of the court and has made strong representations to existing and prospective donor nations ... Canada has already made, as the chair of the management committee of the court, a sizable contribution. Will the [Government] renew ... [its] efforts on an urgent basis to ensure the court has the funding it needs to continue its critical work [?]

Ms. Aileen Carroll (Parliamentary Secretary to the Minister of Foreign Affairs):

[T]he position of the government is that Mr. Taylor should stand trial before the special court for Sierra Leone for the war crimes and the crimes against humanity with which he has been charged. With regard to funding, the foreign minister of Canada has personally engaged his counterparts in other countries to honour their pledges or to make new commitments to ensure that the court is able to continue its very important legal processes.

(House of Commons Debates, 25 September 2003, p. 7818)
(Débats de la Chambre des Communes, le 25 septembre 2003, p. 7818)

L'hon. Don Boudria (Glengarry — Prescott — Russell):

Plus tôt cette semaine, la Chambre a adopté unanimement une motion ... déclarant le 7 avril de chaque année Journée commémorative du génocide rwandais ... [Q]uels gestes tangibles le gouvernement a-t-il l'intention de prendre pour que les Canadiens et les Canadiennes se souviennent de ce jour si tristement célèbre et important dans l'histoire du Rwanda et même de l'humanité?

L'hon. Hélène Scherrer (ministre du Patrimoine canadien):

[Le gouvernement] ... travaille ... pour trouver la meilleure stratégie pour souligner cette tragédie, au Canada. J'invite tous les Canadiens à se joindre à nous afin de souligner cet événement triste de l'histoire de l'humanité, le 7 avril prochain.

(House of Commons Debates, 27 February 2004, p. 1162)
(Débats de la Chambre des Communes, le 27 février 2004, p. 1162)

6   *International Humanitarian Law / Droit international humanitaire*

(a) Humanitarian intervention and aid / Aide et intervention humanitaire

(i)   Afghanistan / Afghanistan

Mr. Jay Hill (Prince George — Peace River):

[Canadian] armed forces ... face chronic underfunding for troops and equipment. Why do[es this happen?]

Hon. John McCallum (Minister of National Defence):

[T]he government, in the last budget, had a 7% increase in its baseline budget at a time when many NATO countries have experienced cuts in their defence budgets. The government has maintained a very strong commitment to the military. We are embarked on a crucially important mission in Afghanistan where we represent 40% of the ISAF [International Security Assistance Force] ... and I am very proud of that contribution ... The Afghanistan mission is important and it is right, and at the same time we are taking great care of the Canadian Forces and their families.

(House of Commons Debates, 15 September 2003, p. 7334)
(Débats de la Chambre des Communes, le 15 septembre 2003, p. 7334)

M. Christian Jobin (Lévis-et-Chutes-de-la-Chaudière):

[L]a ministre de la Coopération internationale assiste présentement aux assemblées annuelles de la Banque mondiale et du Fonds monétaire international à Dubaï, aux Émirats arabes unis. Elle participe également au Forum sur le développement de l'Afghanistan, où l'on discute de l'appui international fourni à ce pays. Est-ce que le [gouvernement] ... pourrait informer cette Chambre sur ce que fait l'ACDI pour construire un avenir meilleur au peuple afghan?

M. André Harvey (secrétaire parlementaire de la ministre de la Coopération internationale):

[L]e peuple afghan ... constitue l'une des grandes préoccupations du gouvernement canadien. Je peux l'assurer qu'en 2003–2004, 250 millions de dollars seront investis dans des priorités qui ont été définies par le gouvernement afghan lui-même, soit dans des secteurs comme l'aide à l'agriculture, l'aide humanitaire et la sécurité. Permettez-moi ... de rendre hommage aux ONG, aux organismes non gouvernementaux afghans et aux organismes non gouvernementaux multilatéraux qui aident le peuple afghan à avoir un avenir meilleur.

(House of Commons Debates, 22 September, 2003, p. 7629)
(Débats de la Chambre des Communes, le 22 septembre 2003, p. 7629)

Mr. David Pratt (Nepean — Carleton):

We are all aware of the superb job the Canadian Forces are doing in Afghanistan to provide security assistance to the provisional government of Hamid Karzai, but Canadians are less aware of the significant reconstruction efforts that are being conducted by Canadian Forces. [Could] ... the parliamentary secretary ... provide us with some details [on this ?]

Mr. Dominic LeBlanc (Parliamentary Secretary to the Minister of National Defence):

The Canadian Forces as part of their efforts in Afghanistan work with local people to rebuild schools, provide safe drinking water, rebuild health facilities ... [W]e are very proud of the remarkable contribution that the men and women of the Canadian Forces are making to make Afghanistan a stable and safe country.

(House of Commons Debates, 26 September 2003, p. 7874)
(Débats de la Chambre des Communes, le 26 septembre 2003, p. 7874)

Mr. Jay Hill (Prince George — Peace River):

[D]espite the Prime Minister now admitting that our armed forces are, and I quote, "stretched very thin," last night on CBC television he announced he intends to leave 500 of our Canadian troops behind in Afghanistan after the current mission ends in August. Why do our soldiers ... have to stay ... overseas?

Right Hon. Paul Martin (Prime Minister):

[T]here is no doubt that our troops ... have to come back. At the same time, there are other jobs and other vocations which certain of our troops can fill that would not interfere with their rotation and would not in fact lead to stretching them even more thinly. Under those circumstances, the Government of Canada has said that up to 500, not more, could remain or could be rotated [in Afghanistan].

Hon. David Price (Parliamentary Secretary to the Minister of National Defence):

We are very proud of the work that our troops have been doing ... They will continue to do that, and we must not forget that we are in command of that NATO operation until the end of the year.

(House of Commons Debates, 5 February 2004, p. 210)
(Débats de la Chambre des Communes, le 5 février 2004, p. 210)

(ii) Balkans / Balkans

Ms. Alexa McDonough (Halifax):

[T]omorrow marks the fifth anniversary of NATO's bombing of Yugoslavia. Just last week another 1,000 Serbs fled their homes, joining the 200,000 forced to flee since NATO entered Kosovo in 1999 ... What has the government done to halt the violence and contribute to lasting peace in this troubled region?

Hon. Bill Graham (Minister of Foreign Affairs):

The [Government] ... met with Javier Solana, the representative of Europe and the European representatives ... last week. We discussed this very important issue. Canada remains committed to bringing peace in the Balkans. We have made a tremendous contribution there in terms of our troops and our stability forces in that region. The Europeans are presently under NATO command responsible for security in that region. However, we will continue to work with them and other countries to bring peace in the Balkans and to ensure that human rights are respected there.

(House of Commons Debates, 23 March 2004, pp. 1608–9)
(Débats de la Chambre des Communes, le 23 mars 2004, pp. 1608–9)

(iii) China / Chine

Mr. Deepak Obhrai (Calgary East):

CIDA gave $50 million in bilateral aid to the government of China. The government of China ranked number two on CIDA's list of countries receiving bilateral aid. At the same time, the Chinese government is spending billions of dollars on its space program. Will the minister call on the Chinese government to do its part to reduce its own people's poverty?

M. André Harvey (secrétaire parlementaire de la ministre de la Coopération internationale):

[I]l n'y a pas de versements de fonds faits directement au gouvernement chinois ni au gouvernement indien. Nous intervenons pour combattre la pauvreté. Il y a des organismes internationaux qui sont sous la responsabilité des Nations Unies, comme le Programme alimentaire mondial et le Comité international de la Croix-Rouge. Nous sommes très fiers du travail que nous faisons pour les 250 millions de Chinois qui sont dans la misère ... [L]es Nations Unies considèrent comme urgent, au sein de leur programme, le combat contre la pauvreté. Des poches de pauvreté touchent des centaines de millions de personnes, et par l'entremise des organismes internationaux nous sommes assurés de ne pas commettre d'erreurs dans nos interventions.

(House of Commons Debates, 10 October 2003, pp. 8440–41) (Débats de la Chambre des Communes, le 10 octobre 2003, pp. 8440–41)

(iv) Haiti / Haïti

Hon. David Kilgour (Edmonton Southeast):

Canada, since Rwanda, has spoken much about humanitarian interventions. Is ... [Canada] prepared to consider asking the UN to stage a humanitarian intervention in the case of the terrible situation happening in Haiti?

Hon. Bill Graham (Minister of Foreign Affairs):

[O]bviously there is a great deal of concern ... Any intervention in Haiti has to be seen in a way which can be effective, but it has to be the international community working together. Canada is working with our international community to ensure that we can intervene in Haiti in a way that will be effective. It depends upon a political solution.

(House of Commons Debates, 23 February 2004, p. 928) (Débats de la Chambre des Communes, le 23 février 2004, p. 928)

Mme Francine Lalonde (Mercier):

Le ministre peut-il nous dire ... sous quelles conditions politiques il est prêt à participer à une intervention pour empêcher un bain de sang à Port-au-Prince[, Haïti]?

L'hon. Bill Graham (ministre des Affaires étrangères):

[N]ous sommes prêts à intervenir. Nous avons travaillé avec tous nos collègues des Amériques ainsi qu'avec nos partenaires européens, comme la France, pour qu'il y ait une condition politique qui est à la fois légitime en vertu du droit international et en vertu de la Constitution d'Haïti. Il est évident qu'il faut un accord en Haïti pour qu'il y ait un gouvernement ou une union pour qu'on puisse faire en sorte que le peuple haïtien sorte de cette crise.

(House of Commons Debates, 26 February 2004, p. 1119)
(Débats de la Chambre des Communes, le 26 février 2004, p. 1119)

M. Claude Duplain (Portneuf):

Est-ce que le ministre de la Défense nationale pourrait nous dire ce que le gouvernement canadien entend faire pour assurer la paix et la stabilité en Haïti?

Hon. David Pratt (Minister of National Defence):

[O]n Friday ... [the Government announced] Canada's contribution to Haiti, which consists of approximately 425 personnel, some of whom are going to be coming from the second battalion of the Royal Canadian Regiment, a company group, as well as a helicopter detachment from the 430 squadron based in Valcartier.

(House of Commons Debates, 8 March 2004, pp. 1212–13)
(Débats de la Chambre des Communes, le 8 mars 2004, pp. 1212–13)

(v) Iraq / Irak

Ms. Alexa McDonough (Halifax):

Canadians seek assurances that the government will not support any resolution at the UN that puts multinational forces in Iraq under U.S. command ... Could the [government] ... assure us that Canada ... will ... not allow the UN to be subjugated to [U.S.] unilateral dictates?

Ms. Aileen Carroll (Parliamentary Secretary to the Minister of Foreign Affairs):

[T]he [Canadian] Prime Minister ... is at the United Nations. His speech while he is there ... reinforces this country's very strong belief in the processes at the United Nations. We continue to support a multilateral approach in the reconstruction of Iraq and we have contributed $300 million to do that.

(House of Commons Debates, 23 September 2003, p. 7702)
(Débats de la Chambre des Communes, le 23 septembre 2003, p. 7702)

Mme Yolande Thibeault (Saint-Lambert):

[L]a ministre de la Coopération internationale dirige une délégation canadienne à la Conférence internationale de Madrid sur la reconstruction en Irak, qui réunit les donateurs qui contribuent à cette cause. Est-ce que le secrétaire parlementaire de la ministre pourrait informer cette Chambre sur la contribution de l'Agence canadienne de développement international pour faire de l'Irak un pays stable et prospère?

M. André Harvey (secrétaire parlementaire de la ministre de la Coopération internationale):

[L]e Canada a été l'un des premiers pays au monde à s'engager formellement pour la reconstruction de l'Irak. Un montant de 300 millions de dollars a été affecté à la fois pour des raisons humanitaires et pour le volet de la reconstruction. Ce matin, la ministre, qui nous représente à Madrid, a annoncé un montant de 100 millions de dollars dans un fonds multilatéral pour la reconstruction et 10 millions de dollars pour la formation des policiers irakiens ... [L]e Canada est de plus en plus engagé dans les interventions multilatérales dans le monde.

(House of Commons Debates, 24 October 2003, p. 8724)
(Débats de la Chambre des Communes, le 24 octobre 2003, p. 8724)

(vi) Palestine / Palestine

Hon. Elinor Caplan (Thornhill):

Could the ... [Government] assure ... all Canadians that the federal government's humanitarian and developmental funding directed to assist and improve the lives of Palestinians and the funding for the United Nations refugee relief association, the aid programs of UNRRA, which is intended for humanitarian assistance, is not being diverted to the Palestinian authority for unauthorized uses that do not support peace?

Hon. Aileen Carroll (Minister for International Cooperation):

[T]he main priority of the Government of Canada is to achieve peace and security in the Middle East. As such, the Canadian aid to the Palestinian people is channelled through Canadian agencies and international organizations which have reputable accounting processes, or we also administer them directly through our missions in the region.

(House of Commons Debates, 10 March 2004, p. 1309)
(Débats de la Chambre des Communes, le 10 mars 2004, p. 1309)

(b) Landmines / Mines terrestres

Ms. Paddy Torsney (Burlington):

Canada led the way internationally to ban landmines. The Ottawa convention is binding international law and this year it celebrates its fifth anniversary[19] ... Could the Minister of Foreign Affairs please update the House on progress on the convention?

Hon. Bill Graham (Minister of Foreign Affairs):

[T]he banning of landmines around the world is an extremely important measure that this country has undertaken for years. Throughout the country during the week of March 1, we will be celebrating Canadian Landmines Awareness Week. I know that many church groups, many schools and others will be having dinners to raise money to help people in countries that are affected by this scourge. As a government, we are committed to ridding the world of landmines. As a people, we are committed to helping other people who suffer under this scourge.

(House of Commons Debates, 25 February 2004, p. 1046)
(Débats de la Chambre des Communes, le 25 fevrier 2004, p. 1046)

(c) Prisoners of war / Prisonniers de guerre

Mr. Sarkis Assadourian (Brampton Centre):

[What is the Government] reaction to the abuse and torture of Iraqi prisoners by the U.S. forces in Iraq?

Hon. Bill Graham (Minister of Foreign Affairs):

Canadians, the House and the government condemn, absolutely, the treatment of those prisoners in Iraq. We welcome the fact that the United States

19 Editor's note: Convention on the Prohibition of the Use, Stockpiling, Production and Transfer or Anti-Personnel Mines and on Their Destruction (Ottawa, Canada, 18 September 1997; entered into force 1 March 1999), reprinted in (1997)36 I.L.M. 1507. Canada both signed and ratified the Ottawa Convention on 3 December 1997.

government, the Senate, the House of Representatives and other American authorities are doing their best to rectify a terrible situation and one that has had an impact on the difficult situation in Iraq. We ... in the government urge all of us to look at the fact that what we need are clear international norms and international rules with enforceability so that all people can be protected at all times, which is why this government has the international policy that it has.[20]

(House of Commons Debates, 11 May 2004, p. 3041)
(Débats de la Chambre des Communes, le 11 mai 2004, p. 3041)

Mme Francine Lalonde (Mercier):

[O]n sait que les militaires canadiens basés en Afghanistan remettent leurs prisonniers aux autorités américaines. À la suite des terribles sévices subis par les prisonniers irakiens aux mains des Américains dans une prison de Bagdad, il y a de quoi être très inquiet. Le ministre des Affaires étrangères peut-il nous donner l'assurance que les prisonniers capturés en Afghanistan et remis par les soldats canadiens aux autorités américaines n'ont pas subi le même traitement que ceux de Bagdad?

Hon. David Pratt (Minister of National Defence):

[T]he Government of Canada and the Canadian Forces take our obligations under international covenants, especially the Geneva convention,[21] very seriously. In fact we do a significant amount of pre-deployment training in that regard and we have legal counsel as well in theatre to ensure that the rules of engagement and all of our responsibilities and obligations are fulfilled. I can say without hesitation as well that there have been absolutely no instances, no reports of any abuses of prisoners that have gone through Canadian hands.

(House of Commons Debates, 13 May 2004, p. 3154)
(Débats de la Chambre des Communes, le 13 mai 2004, p. 3154)

---

[20] Editor's note: Canada has been a party since 14 May 1965 (by ratification) to the Geneva Convention Relative to the Treatment of Prisoners of War (Geneva Convention III; Geneva, Switzerland, 12 August 1949; entered into force 21 October 1950). In addition, it has been a party since 20 November 1990 (by ratification) to the Protocol Additional to the Geneva Conventions of 12 August 1949, and relating to the Protection of Victims of International Armed Conflicts (Protocol I, 8 June 1977; entered into force 7 December 1978). Both the convention and the protocol provide for the treatment of prisoners of war.

[21] Editor's note: See note 20 in this section.

(d) Refugees / Réfugiés

Mme Madeleine Dalphond-Guiral (Laval-Centre):

[U]ne centaine de demandeurs d'asile palestiniens déboutés seront déportés sous peu vers les camps de réfugiés au Liban ... Comme ces demandeurs n'ont pour ainsi dire aucun pays d'accueil et que leur retour dans les camps de réfugiés peut, à l'évidence, mettre leur vie en danger, le ... [gouvernement] peut-il nous dire s'il compte intervenir dans ce dossier en suspendant immédiatement le processus de déportation en cours?

L'hon. Allan Rock (ministre de l'Industrie):

[L]e ... [gouvernement] est pleinement conscient de la situation. Naturellement ... [nous allons] réagir de façon humanitaire. [Nous sommes] ... toujours prêt à agir selon les principes de la loi canadienne.

(House of Commons Debates, 7 November 2003, pp. 9314–15)
(Débats de la Chambre des Communes, le 7 novembre 2003, pp. 9314–15)

Hon. Elinor Caplan (Thornhill):

The Canada-U.S. 30-point smart border plan included a provision for a safe third country agreement. As the minister knows, up to 60% of refugee claimants arriving in Canada come from the United States, which is a Geneva signatory country[22] and offers safety to refugees in need. [H]as the safe third country agreement ... been implemented [?]

Hon. Anne McLellan (Deputy Prime Minister and Minister of Public Safety and Emergency Preparedness):

[I]t is very important for us, with the United States, to ensure that we are able to deal with refugee claimants along our common land border in an efficient and fair way ... [N]ot only has Canada issued its draft regulations under the safe third agreement, but yesterday the United States of America issued its draft regulations for comment. We are very hopeful that this agreement will be implemented in the very near future.

(House of Commons Debates, 9 March 2004, p. 1257)
(Débats de la Chambre des Communes, le 9 mars 2004, p. 1257)

22 Editor's note: The United States is a party to the Fourth Geneva Convention (Convention Relative to the Protection of Civilian Persons in Time of War, Geneva, 12 August 1949; entered into force 21 October 1950) since 2 August 1955. Under the Fourth Convention, refugees receive international humanitarian law protection.

(e) Militarization of space / Militarisation de l'espace

Ms. Alexa McDonough (Halifax):

[A] few months ago, U.S. Air Force Secretary James Roche declared that war in space had begun.[23] The U.S. acknowledges its ballistic missile defence system is an evolving project that will include weapons in space ... [W]ill the government ... reject any Canadian participation in weaponizing space?

Hon. Bill Graham (Minister of Foreign Affairs):

[W]e are interested in protecting Canadians and ensuring the security of North America in partnership with the United States, with whom we have always acted in the interests of security of North America. We will do that in discussions with the Americans in respect to missile defence ... However, in the course of those discussion, we make it plain that we have strong policy considerations. One of them is the non-weaponization of space. We have made that clear to our American friends and they understand that ... Congress does not allow weaponization of space.

(House of Commons Debates, 6 November 2003, p. 9269)
(Débats de la Chambre des Communes, le 6 novembre 2003, p. 9269)

7   Trade and Economy / Commerce et économie

(a) Canadian economy / Economie canadienne

Mr. Loyola Hearn (St. John's West):

[A]ccording to the World Economic Forum, Canada has dropped off the world's top ten in growth competitiveness, with countries like Singapore, Iceland, Norway and the Netherlands all surpassing us. In 1994, Canada was ranked third. In 2000, Canada was ranked sixth. Today Canada is ranked sixteenth. How can the Prime Minister explain this dramatic drop?

Right Hon. Jean Chrétien (Prime Minister):

[T]hat was a survey that was taken during the time that we had some problems with SARS, with mad cow disease, and so on. There are many surveys. For example, a month ago, the Economist Intelligence Unit report said that Canada will be the best place to invest for the next five years. The

---

[23] Editor's note: "War in Space Has Begun," US Air Force Secretary James Roche declared to the officers and defence industry representatives at the April 2003 conference. See David Pugliese, "Weapons in Space: It's Only a Matter of Time," *Ottawa Citizen*, 20 October 2003.

2003 World Competitiveness Yearbook ranked Canada number three. In 2002, KPMG said Canada has the lowest business costs among advanced industrial countries. There are other very good statements made by everybody about Canada ... [I]s it a failure that ... [Canada] is the only country that has balanced its books for six years? Is it a failure to have created three million jobs in the last 10 years? Is it a failure that we took interest rates down from 11.5% to 6%?

(House of Commons Debates, 30 October 2003, p. 8968)
(Débats de la Chambre des Communes, le 30 octobre 2003, p. 8968)

(f) Canadian exports / Exports canadiens

M. Guy St-Julien (Abitibi — Baie-James — Nunavik):

Quelles seront les mesures qui seront mises en place pour que les manufacturiers indépendants québécois exportent en franchise de droit la grande majorité de leurs produits?

Mr. Murray Calder (Parliamentary Secretary to the Minister for International Trade):

NAFTA and WTO rulings ruled that U.S. duties are unjustifiable and Canadian industry should not be subject to these measures. U.S. and Canadian negotiators worked out a draft agreement that provided free access for most exports, including the independent remanufacturers. The U.S. industry's response is unreasonable demands. We have won an important WTO ruling that the U.S. did not treat remanufacturers appropriately in its investigations,[24] and we are also pursuing remanufacturers' interests in the U.S. administrative review of the duties.

(House of Commons Debates, 15 September 2003, p. 7335)
(Débats de la Chambre des Communes, le 15 septembre 2003, p. 7335)

Mr. Peter MacKay (Pictou — Antigonish — Guysborough):

[Canadian] farmers ... are concerned over the ongoing ban of beef that is keeping their product from the market. The border is still not open ... The Prime Minister is scheduled to be in New York for a meeting at the

[24] Editor's note: See, for example, *United States – Preliminary Determinations with Respect to Certain Softwood Lumber from Canada,* Report of the Panel Doc. WT/DS236/R, 27 September 2002 (the WTO Panel ruled that US duties on Canadian softwood lumber exports violate international trade rules).

UN ... [W]ill he ... intensely make the case on behalf of Canadian farmers to open the border to Canadian cattle?

Right Hon. Jean Chrétien (Prime Minister):

I have always done that with the President [of the U.S.A.] and other people at the White House with whom I have had the occasion to meet ... [The U.S. President] had always said and agreed with me that this had to be based on a scientific basis. I wish to report that the only country that has managed to go back into the American market after having a case of mad cow is Canada. The beef has started to move but not fast enough and we are keeping the pressure on the American government.

(House of Commons Debates, 16 September 2003, p. 7412)
(Débats de la Chambre des Communes, le 16 septembre 2003, p. 7412)

Mrs. Karen Redman (Kitchener Centre):

Canada has a very reputable wine and spirits industry. In fact, some international award winning vintages have been produced from some of our over 170 wineries from all provinces of Canada. Yet the industry faces obstacles to access its product in the European Union ... [W]hat developments have happened regarding our increased access to the European Union?

Mr. Murray Calder (Parliamentary Secretary to the Minister for International Trade):

I am very pleased to announce today that the Minister for International Trade, along with his colleague, the Minister of Agriculture and Agri-Food, in Niagara-on-the-Lake signed the Canada-EU wines and spirits agreement ... This agreement will benefit both Canadian and EU wine and spirits industries. It will enhance trade opportunities for both regions while providing a larger variety for consumers.

(House of Commons Debates, 16 September 2003, p. 7418)
(Débats de la Chambre des Communes, le 16 septembre 2003, p. 7418)

Mr. Bill Blaikie (Winnipeg — Transcona):

[T]he U.S. International Trade Commission came out with its decision today.[25] Unfortunately, it seems that the harassment of Canadian farmers

[25] Editor's note: The US International Trade Commission, in its final ruling on 3 October 2003, found that imports of Canadian hard red spring wheat (HRSW)

will continue ... What does the Minister of Agriculture and Agri-Food intend to do now to protect Canadian farmers from this ... harassment of Canadian exports to the United States?

Hon. Lyle Vanclief (Minister of Agriculture and Agri-Food):

[W]e would take every step that we possibly could, including launching panels in both NAFTA and WTO if that is seen necessary. We have very successfully demonstrated in the past that the Canadian Wheat Board works and acts within WTO compliance. We have proven that in the past and I am confident we can prove it in the future.

(House of Commons Debates, 3 October 2003, p. 8156)
(Débats de la Chambre des Communes, le 3 octobre 2003, p. 8156)

Mr. Peter Adams (Peterborough):

Mexico has reopened its border to Canadian beef products. Will the minister bring us up to date on this? When will shipments start and are there similar opportunities in other countries?

Hon. Lyle Vanclief (Minister of Agriculture and Agri-Food):

[W]e are very pleased that the country of Mexico has opened its borders to boneless beef. This will now allow certificates to be granted and shipments started to Mexico. It is our second largest trading country. That will add to what we have already shipped to the United States, this month's certificates, 35 million pounds. We are looking forward in the near future to making similar announcements for countries such as the Philippines, Russia and others.

(House of Commons Debates, 3 October 2003, p. 8158)
(Débats de la Chambre des Communes, le 3 octobre 2003, p. 8158)

Mr. Gerry Ritz (Battlefords — Lloydminster):

[F]or years now the Canadian elk industry has been fighting issues concerning closed borders all by itself. Its producers have been denied

---

have materially injured American wheat farmers. In this decision, the Commission approved countervailing and anti-dumping duties on Canadian HRSW of 14.15 per cent. The commission found the duties imposed on durum wheat imports from Canada to be illegal though. For a follow-up information, see, for example, International Trade Canada website, which is available at <http://www.dfait-maeci.gc.ca>.

access to the U.S. and Korean markets ... Why does the government continue to deny elk producers a stand-alone chronic wasting disease compensation package?

Hon. Pierre Pettigrew (Minister for International Trade):

This morning I raised the issue of chronic wasting disease with the minister of trade of Korea who happens to be in Ottawa today. We have agreed to work on it. Our experts will sit down and based on technical evaluations that we will make, we will work very hard at finding a resolution to the issue.

(House of Commons Debates, 30 October 2003, p. 8973)
(Débats de la Chambre des Communes, le 30 octobre 2003, p. 8973)

Mr. Gurmant Grewal (Surrey Central):

Canada is losing its ability to compete in Asia. The Asia Pacific Foundation in its latest report reveals that our share of the top Asian markets has plummeted by nearly one-third since 1996 and by 13% in the last year alone. We need to diversify our trade ... to revitalize our trading relationship in Asia. When will the government ... open Asian markets to Canadian companies?

Hon. David Kilgour (Secretary of State (Asia-Pacific)):

[T]he only region of the world where our trade is up is southeast Asia. Therefore we are doing better in southeast Asia ... [The] point about our market share being down in most Asian markets, unfortunately, is true and ... [we] have do more trading with Asia generally.

(House of Commons Debates, 31 October 2003, p. 9030)
(Débats de la Chambre des Communes, le 31 octobre 2003, p. 9030)

L'hon. Charles Caccia (Davenport):

Compte tenu de la déclaration du président de la Commission canadienne du blé selon laquelle le blé Roundup Ready de Monsanto aura un effet économique dévastateur pour les céréaliculteurs de l'Ouest, notamment, et je cite: "la perte de certains marchés à prime," et compte tenu de l'importance du marché européen pour le blé canadien non modifié génétiquement, le ministre du Commerce international peut-il dire ce qu'il compte faire pour prévenir la perte éventuelle des marchés européens?

Hon. Jim Peterson (Minister of International Trade):

Last week in Europe I stressed that EU treatment of Canadian products must be based on science, not on politics. Since then, Commissioner Lamy has returned to me and said that the commission has approved GM sweet maize BT.

(House of Commons Debates, 4 February 2004, p. 100–1)
(Débats de la Chambre des Communes, le 4 février 2004, p. 100–1)

Mr. Peter Adams (Peterborough):

[T]he ... [Government] is working hard on the BSE[26] file ... [T]he Prime Minister made that issue a priority for his meeting with President Bush ... Can the minister give us some hope that there will be an end to the BSE crisis and give us an update on the U.S. investigation into BSE?

Hon. Bob Speller (Minister of Agriculture and Agri-Food):

[T]he Government of Canada takes this issue very seriously ... [W]e will continue to work hard internationally to get the borders open to Canadian beef.

(House of Commons Debates, 4 February 2004, p. 103)
(Débats de la Chambre des Communes, le 4 février 2004, p. 103)

Hon. Charles Caccia (Davenport):

[G]iven that Canadian farmers' groups, including the National Farmers Union and the Canadian Wheat Board, oppose the release of Monsanto's genetically modified wheat variety because of a potential loss of premium markets, does the Minister of Agriculture and Agri-food intend to turn down Monsanto's application?

Hon. Bob Speller (Minister of Agriculture and Agri-Food):

[T]he Government of Canada has a science based regulatory system which assures Canadian consumers and world markets that in fact the food they eat is not only some of the highest quality but some of the safest food in the world. An environmental assessment is a key component of this ...

---

[26] Editor's note: Bovine spongiform encephalopathy (BSE). The first case of BSE in Canada was reported on 21 May 2003. For a follow-up on BSE (including the government measures to combat BSE), see speech by Hon. Bob Speller (Minister of Agriculture and Agri-Food), delivered at the House of Commons on 4 February 2004. *House of Commons Debates,* 4 February 2004, pp.137*ff.*

[N]othing will go on the market until it is first studied in terms of its environmental impact [as well as] its impact on animal feed.

(House of Commons Debates, 5 February 2004, p. 212)
(Débats de la Chambre des Communes, le 5 février 2004, p. 212)

(g) Imports into Canada / Importations au Canada

M. Stéphane Bergeron (Verchères — Les-Patriotes):

[O]n apprend que plusieurs bateaux contenant environ 80 000 tonnes d'acier d'armature seraient en voie de prendre le large ... en partance de la Turquie vers le Québec et l'est du Canada. Une décision rendue en août 2002 par le Tribunal canadien du commerce extérieur sur une enquête de sauvegarde concernant l'importation au Canada de certaines marchandises d'acier recommandait au gouvernement fédéral l'imposition d'une surtaxe sur les barres d'armature.[27] Puisque cette décision exclut les États-Unis, le ministre des Finances compte-t-il finalement la mettre en application, afin d'empêcher le dumping de cet acier sur les marchés québécois et canadien?

Hon. Maurizio Bevilacqua (Secretary of State (International Financial Institutions)):

The government is very much aware of the problems of the international steel market caused by overcapacity and cheap imports. The overcapacity is a global problem that we are attacking on several fronts, particularly in the context of discussions and negotiations with the OECD.

(House of Commons Debates, 3 October 2003, p. 8161)
(Débats de la Chambre des Communes, le 3 octobre 2003, p. 8161)

Mrs. Rose-Marie Ur (Lambton — Kent — Middlesex):

[T]he Canadian Food Inspection Agency is currently reviewing comments it received on a proposed rule that could allow live honeybee imports into Canada from the United States. Could the [Government] ... assure ... all bee producers in Canada that foreign bee diseases and pests ... will not be permitted to enter Canada under this proposed rule?

---

[27] Editor's note: See Canadian International Trade Tribunal, *Safeguard Inquiry into the Importation of Certain Steel Goods* (GC-2001–001), 19 August 2002, available at <http://www.citt-tcce.gc.ca>.

Hon. Bob Speller (Minister of Agriculture and Agri-Food):

[I]t will not be happening. Based on a risk assessment, the Canadian Food Inspection Agency has indicated that it is willing to have queen bees imported from the United States ... [T]he provinces, if they wish, may be able to ban these bees coming into the country.

(House of Commons Debates, 13 May 2004, p. 3156)
(Débats de la Chambre des Communes, le 13 mai 2004, p. 3156)

(h) Free trade agreements / Accords de libre-échange

Mr. Bryon Wilfert (Oak Ridges):

Japan and Mexico have recently concluded a free trade agreement. Companies such as Nissan and Sony are able to compete on a level playing field in Mexico against rivals such as the U.S. and Europe. Japan has realized that FTAs are important for its national security interests. Given that Japan is Canada's second largest trading partner, with an economy greater than that of all of Asia combined, and given that the United States is also aggressively seeking FTAs in Asia ... what steps ... [the Government] is taking to secure Canada's economic and trade interests with Japan, since members of the Japanese Diet are interested in an FTA with Canada?

Hon. Jim Peterson (Minister of International Trade):

[T]he area of northeast Asia is truly a driving force in global trade, and yes, Japan is indeed Canada's second largest trading partner. We will continue to explore with Japan ways in which we can enhance our investment and our trading relationship, but as a start we would ask that Japan open its markets to Canadian beef. That is our priority.

(House of Commons Debates, 5 May 2004, p. 2802)
(Débats de la Chambre des Communes, le 5 mai 2004, p. 2802)

(i) FTAA / ZLÉA

Hon. Charles Caccia (Davenport):

[T]he text of the free trade area of the Americas agreement incorporates investor-state rules, similar to NAFTA's chapter 11. To ensure that private sector abuse at the expense of the public interest ... is avoided, can the [Government] ... assure the House that the chapter 11 experience is not repeated in the final text of the free trade area of the Americas agreement?

Hon. Pierre Pettigrew (Minister for International Trade):

Canada does not advocate the replication of a chapter 11 in the free trade area of the Americas agreement. We do, however, believe that investors need clear rules on the treatment and protection of investment in a free trade environment; however, these rules must not enable investors to circumvent domestic laws, or things such as labour standards, environmental protection or consumer protection ... [O]ur experience with NAFTA's chapter 11 would be fully taken into account in the negotiations.

(House of Commons Debates, 23 October 2003, p. 8673)
(Débats de la Chambre des Communes, le 23 octobre 2003, p. 8673)

Mr. Svend Robinson (Burnaby — Douglas):

At the upcoming FTAA meeting in Miami, will ... [the Government] ... take health care off the table entirely [?]

Hon. Pierre Pettigrew (Minister for International Trade):

Canada will not negotiate health care in any of our trade agreements and negotiations. We have preserved full policy flexibility for health care in all of our trade agreements, including NAFTA. We are continuing with this approach in our current trade negotiations, including the GATS and the free trade agreement of the Americas.

(House of Commons Debates, 4 November 2003, pp. 9148–49)
(Débats de la Chambre des Communes, le 4 novembre 2003, pp. 9148–49)

(j) NAFTA / ALÉNA

Mr. Walt Lastewka (St. Catharines):

January 1, 2004, represents an important milestone in the trade and economic relationship between Canada, the United States and Mexico. This date marks the 10th anniversary of the North American Free Trade Agreement, making North America the largest free trade area, with about one-third of the world's GDP ... [W]hat is being done to ensure that the North American region remains the most dynamic in the world?

Hon. Pierre Pettigrew (Minister for International Trade):

[Y]esterday in Montreal I had a very interesting and productive meeting with my colleagues, Ambassador Zoellick of the United States and Secretary

Canales of Mexico. We agreed on a number of practical steps to enhance trade and investment in North America that will increase the transparency and efficiency of NAFTA's chapter 11, establish a North American steel trade committee that will promote more openness and integration in the North American steel market and reduce exports related transaction costs in the NAFTA region. It is a work in progress, and we will continue.

(House of Commons Debates, 8 October 2003, p. 8321)
(Débats de la Chambre des Communes, le 8 octobre 2003, p. 8321)

(k) Softwood lumber / Bois d'œuvre

Mr. Charlie Penson (Peace River):

[T]here are reports today that a deal with the U.S. on softwood lumber could be reached within weeks. The last softwood lumber agreement with the United States included quotas and other market restrictions to Canadian softwood lumber. Could the trade minister [update] us on his efforts on free trade in softwood lumber?

Hon. Pierre Pettigrew (Minister for International Trade):

[T]he negotiators of Canada and of the United States met recently and compared notes to see the progress of the file since the July proposal, the best effort they had put on the table. We are looking to the WTO and NAFTA decisions that have come our way to strengthen our hand. We will take into consideration, when continuing this dialogue with the United States, our progress before the courts. ... We will continue to push these cases. We have six of them at the WTO and at NAFTA. However we continue to explore with the United States other possibilities that could advance this file in the best interest of our industry. We always do it in close communication and close contact with the industry, but we will get the best possible outcome for the Canadian softwood lumber industry.

(House of Commons Debates, 23 October 2003, p. 8675)
(Débats de la Chambre des Communes, le 23 octobre 2003, p. 8675)

Hon. Bill Blaikie (Winnipeg — Transcona)

[Y]esterday, the WTO [ruled] ... on the softwood lumber case ... in Canada's favour.[28] Will the Prime Minister now pick up the phone and tell George Bush to call off the dogs?

28 Editor's note: See WTO, *United States – Investigation of the International Trade Commission in Softwood Lumber from Canada*, Panel Report (Doc. WT/DS277/R), 22

Hon. Jim Peterson (Minister of International Trade):

The softwood lumber industry affects almost 300,000 jobs in this country. This is why ... it my first priority to follow our two track policy. This means that we are litigating before the WTO and NAFTA. We are continuing to seek a prevailing view to see if a counter-offer can be made.

(House of Commons Debates, 23 March 2004, p. 1602)
(Débats de la Chambre des Communes, le 23 mars 2004, p. 1602)

M. Stéphane Bergeron (Verchères — Les-Patriotes):

[U]ne des questions importantes qui seront abordées par le premier ministre canadien avec le président Bush est celle du conflit du bois d'oeuvre, pour laquelle un jugement de l'ALÉNA vient tout juste d'être rendu public.[29] Les États-Unis ont trois semaines pour lever les droits compensateurs et les droits antidumping imposés sur le bois d'oeuvre québécois et canadien. Le premier ministre entend-il réclamer du président Bush qu'il mette fin aux tactiques dilatoires, afin de revenir sans délai au libre-échange intégral dans ce domaine?

Hon. John Harvard (Parliamentary Secretary to the Minister of International Trade):

The NAFTA panel, on the alleged threat of injury to the U.S. softwood lumber industry, released its decision today. It is good news for Canada and it is a total victory for Canada. We said all along that the U.S. was wrong. Our industry does not threaten injury to the U.S. industry ... The decision today supports our position. We hope the U.S. respects the decision.

(House of Commons Debates, 29 April 2004, pp. 2583–84)
(Débats de la Chambre des Communes, le 29 avril 2004, pp. 2583–84)

March 2004. The panel found that the US International Trade Commission (ITC) "threat of injury" determination of 22 May 2002 that the US softwood lumber industry was "threatened" with material injury by reason of alleged subsidized and dumped imports of softwood lumber from Canada was inconsistent with the United States's WTO obligations.

29 Editor's note: The NAFTA panel found, as did the WTO panel (see note 28 earlier in this section), that the US International Trade Commission's (ITC) second "threat of injury" determination of 15 December 2003 (which in fact reaffirmed the original determination of 22 May 2002 (see note 28)) was "not in accordance with the [U.S.] law" and was "not supported by substantial evidence" (pp. 51–52 of the decision). See NAFTA, *Certain Softwood Lumber Products from Canada: Final Affirmative Threat of Injury Determination,* Remand Decision of the Panel, 19 April 2004, available at <http://www.dfait-maeci.gc.ca>.

(l) WTO / OMC

Mr. Rick Casson (Lethbridge):

[W]ith the collapse of the trade talks in Cancun,[30] Canadian agriculture producers have been dealt yet another blow ... The Minister for International Trade stated that WTO members must redouble their efforts to build bridges and find consensus ... When will the ... government rebuild damaged relationships with our farmers and our international trading partners?

Mr. Murray Calder (Parliamentary Secretary to the Minister for International Trade):

[A]dditional insights have been gained, and that will lead to further discussions which will be taking place on December 15 in Geneva when the WTO group meets again.

(House of Commons Debates, 15 September 2003, pp. 7337–38) (Débats de la Chambre des Communes, le 15 septembre 2003, pp. 7337–38)

Mr. Charlie Penson (Peace River):

The European Union has signalled it is willing to eliminate its export agricultural subsidies. The U.S. has responded by showing flexibility in its export programs ... [W]hat is the ... [G]overnment doing to get the Doha round back on track?

Hon. Bob Speller (Minister of Agriculture and Agri-Food):

[P]resently the Minister of International Trade is over in Paris meeting with his counterparts to talk about the importance of the Canadian position. There are a number of issues within this trade round that are of concern to Canadian farmers, for instance, supply management ... The Government of Canada plays a very important role in these talks. We can join together countries in the G-8 with some of the developing countries.

(House of Commons Debates, 13 May 2004, pp. 3154–55) (Débats de la Chambre des Communes, le 13 mai 2004, pp. 3154–55)

---

[30] Editor's note: The fifth WTO Ministerial Conference in Cancún, Mexico (10–14 September 2003) ended without conclusion, when conference chairman and Mexican foreign minister, Luis Ernesto Derbez, determined that it would not be possible to reach consensus across the agenda and closed the meeting. See International Trade Canada, the fifth WTO Conference in Cancún, available at <http://www.dfait-maeci.gc.ca>.

(m) Law of the sea / Droit de la mer

(i) UN Convention on the Law of the Sea / Convention de l'ONU sur le droit de la mer [31]

Hon. Charles Caccia (Davenport):

When can Canadians finally expect the ratification of the United Nations law of the sea to take place?

Right Hon. Jean Chrétien (Prime Minister):

I am pleased to inform ... the House that this afternoon the Minister of Foreign Affairs will sign Canada's instrument of ratification for the UN convention on the law of the sea. The instrument will be deposited with the secretary general of the United Nations soon after. This is great news for all Canadians. By ratifying, Canada gains a voice in an international institution set up by the convention and will be able to advance our commitment to improving the conservation of fisheries on the high seas.

(House of Commons Debates, 6 November 2003, p. 9270)
(Débats de la Chambre des Communes, le 6 novembre 2003, p. 9270)

(ii) Fisheries / Pêches

Mr. Joe McGuire (Egmont):

[L]ast week the Minister of Fisheries and Oceans attended the annual meeting of the Northwest Atlantic Fisheries Organization, NAFO, where they came to a long term agreement for conservation for turbot ... Could the Minister of Fisheries and Oceans tell us what action Canada has taken recently to combat overfishing outside the 200 mile limit?

Hon. Robert Thibault (Minister of Fisheries and Oceans):

[O]ver the past few days Canadian inspectors working with national defence boarded two Portuguese vessels fishing outside the 200 mile limit. Both vessels were issued citations for misreporting an illegal bycatch. The first vessel, the *Santa Mafalda*, has been ordered back to Portugal for an inspection that will include two Canadian inspectors. The second vessel, the *Joanna Princesa*, has been ordered to Halifax for inspection. Both of

---

[31] United Nations Convention on the Law of the Sea (Montego Bay, Jamaica, 10 December 1982; entered into force 16 November 1994), 1833 U.N.T.S. 397, reprinted in (1982) 21 I.L.M. 1261. Canada has been a party to the convention since 7 November 2003 by ratification.

these responses represent positive steps taken by the Portuguese government. They also demonstrate Canada's commitment to work with its NAFO partners to combat illegal fishing in international waters.

(House of Commons Debates, 22 September 2003, pp. 7626–27)
(Débats de la Chambre des Communes, le 22 septembre 2003, pp. 7626–27)

Mr. Loyola Hearn (St. John's West):

[O]ver a year ago a Russian flag boat with an Icelandic crew, the *Olga*, was caught in the NAFO zone with an excessive amount of cod. The boat was sent back ... Recently a reporter in St. John's ... asked what happened to the *Olga*. The minister's department replied that it did not know. The Standing Committee on Fisheries and Oceans found the *Olga* in Iceland ...[Could the Government comment on that]?

Hon. Robert Thibault (Minister of Fisheries and Oceans):

We continue to take any infraction very seriously and work with our partners internationally to reduce those amounts. We have in the past and we will in the future.

(House of Commons Debates, 10 October 2003, p. 8438)
(Débats de la Chambre des Communes, le 10 octobre 2003, p. 8438)

Mr. Norman Doyle (St. John's East):

[There is a list prepared by] the Minister of Fisheries and Oceans [, containing] ... 319 foreign vessels that have been issued citations over the last decade for breaking NAFO rules in the east coast fishery ... Can the Minister of Fisheries and Oceans explain why only 21 of these offenders, 7%, were actually convicted of their crimes?

Hon. Geoff Regan (Minister of Fisheries and Oceans):

[F]oreign overfishing is a serious concern ... of the government. In fact, the Prime Minister discussed the issue of foreign overfishing recently in meetings with the EU president. The president of the EU indicated that they are open to addressing this problem ... [W]e are increasing at-sea patrols and aerial surveillance on the Grand Banks and we will follow up with the EU to make sure we can enforce the rules. ... We are taking effective, strong action.

(House of Commons Debates, 4 May 2004, p. 2755)
(Débats de la Chambre des Communes, le 4 mai 2004, p. 2755)

Treaty Action Taken by Canada in 2003 / Mesures prises par le Canada en matière de traités en 2003

compiled by/préparé par

ANDRÉ BERGERON

I   BILATERAL

Australia

Agreement on Social Security between the Government of Canada and the Government of Australia. Ottawa, 26 July 2001. *Entered into force* 1 January 2003. CTS 2003/4

Barbados

Agreement between the Government of Canada and the Government of Barbados on the Transfer of Offenders. Bridgetown, 20 May 2003. *Entered into force* 1 August 2003.

Belgium

Treaty between the Government of Canada and the Government of the Kingdom of Belgium on Mutual Legal Assistance in Criminal Matters. Brussels, 11 January 1996. *Entered into force* 1 April 2003.

Czech Republic

Agreement on Social Security between Canada and the Czech Republic. Prague, 24 May 2001. *Entered into force* 1 January 2003. CTS 2003/3

European Space Agency

Arrangement between the Government of Canada and the European Space Agency concerning participation by the Government of Canada in the Info-Terra/TerraSAR Element of the European Earth Watch Programme. Paris, 22 September 2003. *Entered into force* 22 September 2003.

Arrangement between the Government of Canada and the European Space Agency concerning participation by the Government of Canada in the development and validation activities of the GalileoSat program. Paris, 6 October 2003. *Entered into force* 6 October 2003.

Germany (Federal Republic of)

Supplementary Agreement to the Agreement on Social Security of 14 November 1985 between Canada and the Federal Republic of Germany. Toronto, 27 August 2002. *Entered into force* 1 December 2003.

Hungary

Agreement on Social Security between Canada and the Republic of Hungary. Budapest, 4 March 2002. *Entered into force* 1 October 2003.

Iceland

Agreement amending the Audiovisual Co-production Agreement between the Government of Canada and the Government of the Republic of Iceland signed on October 15, 1997. Ottawa, 28 March

André Bergeron is Treaty Registrar in the Legal Advisory Division at the Department of Foreign Affairs / Greffier des Traités, Direction des consultations juridiques, Ministère des Affaires étrangères.

2003. *Entered into force* 11 December 2003.

Israel
Exchange of Notes constituting an Agreement between the Government of Canada and the Government of the State of Israel amending Annexes 2.1.2 A and 2.1.2 B of the Canada-Israel Free Trade Agreement. Jerusalem, Ottawa, 15 September 2003. *Entered into force* 1 November 2003.

Interim Agreement on Social Security between the Government of Canada and the Government of Israel. Jerusalem, 9 April 2000. *Entered into force* 1 September 2003.

Japan
Exchange of Notes between the Government of Canada and the Government of Japan constituting an agreement allowing the Government of Japan to contribute logistic support, supplies, and services to the armed forces of Canada. Tokyo, 28 March 2003. *Entered into force* 28 March 2003.

Kuwait
Agreement between the Government of Canada and the Government of the State of Kuwait for the Avoidance of Double Taxation and the Prevention of Fiscal Evasion with respect to Taxes on Income and on Capital. Ottawa, 28 January 2002. *Entered into force* 26 August 2003.

Latvia
Audio-visual Co-production Agreement between the Government of Canada and the Government of the Republic of Latvia. Riga, 15 October 2003. *Entered into force* 19 November 2003.

Mexico
Agreement between the Government of Canada and the Government of the United Mexican States regarding the Application of their Competition Laws. Veracruz, 15 November 2001. *Entered into force* 20 March 2003.

Peru
Convention between the Government of Canada and the Government of the Republic of Peru for the Avoidance of Double Taxation and the Prevention of Fiscal Evasion with respect to Taxes on Income and on Capital. Lima, 20 July 2001. *Entered into force* 17 February 2003.

Senegal
Agreement between the Government of Canada and the Government of the Republic of Senegal on Audio-visual Co-production. Santorini Island, 27 September 2000. *Entered into force* 7 October 2003.

Convention between the Government of Canada and the Government of the Republic of Senegal for the Avoidance of Double Taxation and the Prevention of Fiscal Evasion with respect to Taxes on Income. Dakar, 2 August 2001. *Entered into force* 7 October 2003.

Slovak Republic
Agreement on Social Security between Canada and the Slovak Republic. Bratislava, 21 May 2001. *Entered into force* 1 January 2003. CTS 2003/2

Sweden
Agreement on Social Security between the Government of Canada and the Government of Sweden. Ottawa, 30 January 2002. *Entered into force* 1 April 2003.

Trinidad and Tobago
Treaty between the Government of Canada and the Government of the Republic of Trinidad and Tobago on Mutual Legal Assistance in Criminal Matters. Ottawa, 4 September 1997. *Entered into force* 11 October 2003.

United Kingdom of Great Britain and Northern Ireland
Exchange of Notes (January 22 and February 27, 2003) between the Government of Canada and the Government of the United Kingdom of Great Britain and Northern Ireland extending the

application of the Agreement between the Government of Canada and the Government of the United Kingdom of Great Britain and Northern Ireland regarding the Sharing of Forfeited Assets or their Equivalent Funds, done at London on February 21, 2001, to the United Kingdom's Overseas Territories of Anguilla, the British Virgin Islands, the Cayman Islands, Gibraltar, Montserrat and the Turks and Caicos Islands. Ottawa, 27 February 2003. *Entered into force* 27 February 2003.

United Nations High Commissioner for Refugees
Agreement between the Government of Canada and the Office of the United Nations High Commissioner for Refugees for the purpose of deploying two Royal Canadian Mounted Police officers to the Republic of Guinea. Geneva, 7 January 2003. *Entered into force* 7 January 2003.

United States
Agreement on Air Transport Preclearance between the Government of Canada and the Government of the United States of America. Toronto, 18 January 2001. *Entered into force* 2 May 2003.

Exchange of Notes amending the Agreement between the Government of Canada and the Government of the United States of America for the Establishment of a Binational Educational Exchange Foundation. Ottawa, 29 July 2003. *Entered into force* 29 July 2003.

Second Protocol amending the Treaty on Extradition between the Government of Canada and the Government of the United States of America. Ottawa, 12 January 2001. *Entered into force* 30 April 2003.

Exchange of Notes (22 and 29 April 2003) between the Government of Canada and the Government of the United States of America relating to the Application and Interpretation of the Rush-Bagot Agreement of 1817 concerning the Naval Forces on the Great Lakes. Ottawa, Washington, 29 April 2003. *Entered into force* 29 April 2003.

Exchange of Notes (31 July and 4 August 2003) constituting an Agreement between the Government of Canada and the Government of the United States of America concerning the SciSat-1 Atmospheric Chemistry Experiment Mission. Washington, 4 August 2003. *Entered into force* 4 August 2003.

II   MULTILATERAL

Aviation
Convention for the Unification of Certain Rules for International Carriage by Air. Montréal, 28 May 1999. *Signed* by Canada 1 October 2001. *Ratified* by Canada 19 November 2002. *Entered into force* for Canada 4 November 2003.

Conservation
Protocol on Environmental Protection to the Antarctic Treaty. Madrid, 4 October 1991. *Signed* by Canada, 4 October 1991. *Ratified* by Canada 13 November 2003. *Entered into force* for *Canada* 13 December 2003.

Fisheries
Agreement to Promote Compliance with International Conservation and Management Measures by Fishing Vessels on the High Seas. Rome, 24 November 1993. *Accession* by Canada 20 May 1994. *Entered into force* for Canada 24 April 2003.

Human Rights
Optional Protocol to the Convention on the Elimination of All Forms of Discrimination against Women. New York, 6 October 1999. *Accession* by Canada 18 October 2002. *Entered into force* for Canada 18 January 2003.

Law of the Sea
United Nations Convention on the Law of the Sea. Montego Bay, 10 December 1982. *Signed* by Canada 10 December 1982. *Ratified* by Canada 7 November 2003. *Entered into force* for Canada 7 December 2003.

Agreement relating to the Implementation of Part XI of the United Nations Convention on the Law of the Sea of 10 December 1982. New York, 28 July 1994. *Signed* by Canada 29 July 1994. Provisionally in force 16 November 1994. *Ratified* by Canada 07 November 2003. *Entered into force* for Canada 7 December 2003.

Pollution
Protocol to the 1979 Convention on Long Range Transboundary Air Pollution Heavy Metals. Aarhus, 24 June 1998. *Signed* by Canada 24 June 1998. *Ratified* by Canada 18 December 1998. *Entered into force* for Canada 29 December 2003.

Protocol to the 1979 Convention on Long-Range Transboundary Air Pollution on Persistent Organic Pollutants. Aarhus, 24 June 1998. *Signed* by Canada 24 June 1998. *Ratified* by Canada 18 December 1998. *Entered into force* for Canada 23 October 2003.

Terrorism
Inter-American Convention against Terrorism. Bridgetown, 3 June 2002. *Signed* by Canada 2 December 2002. *Ratified* by Canada 2 December 2002. *Entered into force* for Canada 10 July 2003.

Transnational Crime
United Nations Convention against Transnational Organized Crime. New York, 15 November 2000. *Signed* by Canada 14 December 2000. *Ratified* by Canada 13 May 2002. *Entered into force* for Canada 29 September 2003.

Protocol to Prevent, Suppress and Punish Trafficking in Persons, Especially Women and Children, Supplementing the United Nations Convention against Transnational Organized Crime. New York, 15 November 2000. *Signed* by Canada 14 December 2000. *Ratified* by Canada 13 May 2002. *Entered into force* for Canada 25 December 2003.

I   BILATÉRAUX

Agence spatiale européenne
Arrangement entre le gouvernement du Canada et l'Agence spatiale européenne relatif à la participation du gouvernement du Canada à l'élément InfoTerra/TerraSAR du Programme européen de surveillance de la Terre. Paris, le 22 septembre 2003. *En vigueur* le 22 septembre 2003.

Arrangement entre le gouvernement du Canada et l'Agence spatiale européenne concernant la participation du gouvernement du Canada aux activités de développement et de validation du programme GalileoSat. Paris, le 6 octobre 2003. *En vigueur* le 6 octobre 2003.

Allemagne (République fédérale d')
Accord supplémentaire à l'Accord sur la sécurité sociale du 14 novembre 1985 entre le Canada et la République fédérale d'Allemagne. Toronto, le 27 août 2002. *En vigueur* le 1er décembre 2003.

Australie
Accord de sécurité sociale entre le gouvernement du Canada et le gouvernement de l'Australie. Ottawa, le 26 juillet 2001. *En vigueur* le 1er janvier 2003. RTC 2003/4.

Barbade
Accord entre le gouvernement du Canada et le gouvernement de la Barbade sur le transfèrement des condamnés. Bridgetown, le 20 mai 2003. *En vigueur* le 1er août 2003.

Belgique
Traité d'entraide judiciaire en matière pénale entre le gouvernement du Canada et le gouvernement du Royaume de Belgique. Bruxelles, le 11 janvier 1996. *En vigueur* le 1er avril 2003.

États-Unis d'Amérique
Accord entre le gouvernement du Canada et le gouvernement des États-Unis d'Amérique relatif au précontrôle dans

le domaine du transport aérien. Toronto, le 18 janvier 2001. *En vigueur* le
2 mai 2003.

Échange de notes modifiant l'Accord
entre le gouvernement du Canada et
le gouvernement des États-Unis d'Amérique portant création d'une fondation
binationale pour les échanges dans le
domaine de l'éducation. Ottawa, le 29
juillet 2003. *En vigueur* le 29 juillet
2003.

Deuxième protocole modifiant le Traité
d'extradition entre le gouvernement du
Canada et le gouvernement des États-
Unis d'Amérique. Ottawa, le 12 janvier
2001. *En vigueur* le 30 avril 2003.

Échange de notes (22 et 29 avril 2003)
entre le gouvernement du Canada et le
gouvernement des États-Unis d'Amérique concernant l'application et l'interprétation de l'Accord Rush-Bagot de
1817 relatif aux forces navales sur les
Grands Lacs. Ottawa, Washington, le 29
avril 2003. *En vigueur* le 29 avril 2003.

Échange de notes (31 juillet et 4 août
2003) constituant un Accord entre le
gouvernement du Canada et le gouvernement des États-Unis d'Amérique concernant la mission sur l'Expérience de
chimie atmosphérique SciSat-1.
Washington, le 4 août 2003. *En vigueur*
le 4 août 2003.

*Haut Commissariat des Nations Unies pour
les Réfugiés*
Accord entre le gouvernement du Canada et le Haut Commissariat des Nations Unies pour les Réfugiés ayant pour
but de déployer deux agents de la Gen-
darmerie royale du Canada en République de Guinée. Genève, le 7 janvier
2003. *En vigueur* le 7 janvier 2003.

Hongrie
Accord sur la sécurité sociale entre le
Canada et la République de Hongrie.
Budapest, le 4 mars 2002. *En vigueur* le
1ᵉʳ octobre 2003.

Islande
Accord modifiant l'Accord de coproduction audiovisuelle entre le gouvernement du Canada et le gouvernement de
la République d'Islande signé le 15 octobre 1997. Ottawa, le 28 mars 2003. *En
vigueur* le 11 décembre 2003.

Israël
Accord sous forme d'échange de notes
entre le gouvernement du Canada et le
gouvernement de l'État d'Israël modifiant les annexes 2.1.2 A et 2.1.2 B de
l'Accord de libre-échange Canada-Israël.
Jérusalem, Ottawa, le 15 septembre
2003. *En vigueur* le 1ᵉʳ novembre 2003.

Accord intérimaire sur la sécurité sociale
entre le gouvernement du Canada et le
gouvernement d'Israël. Jérusalem, le 9
avril 2000. *En vigueur* le 1ᵉʳ septembre
2003.

Japon
Échange de notes entre le gouvernement du Canada et le gouvernement du
Japon constituant un accord permettant
au gouvernement du Japon de mettre à
la disposition des forces armées du Canada un soutien logistique, des fourni-
tures et des services. Tokyo, le 28 mars
2003. *En vigueur* le 28 mars 2003.

Koweït
Accord entre le gouvernement du Canada et le gouvernement de l'État du
Koweït en vue d'éviter les doubles impositions et de prévenir l'évasion fiscale
en matière d'impôts sur le revenu et sur
la fortune. Ottawa, le 28 janvier 2002.
En vigueur le 26 août 2003.

Lettonie
Accord de coproduction audiovisuelle
entre le gouvernement du Canada et le
gouvernement de la République de Lettonie. Riga, le 15 octobre 2003. *En vigueur* le 19 novembre 2003.

Mexique
Accord entre le gouvernement du Canada et le gouvernement des États-Unis

du Mexique concernant l'application de leurs lois sur la concurrence. Veracruz, le 15 novembre 2001. *En vigueur* le 20 mars 2003.

Pérou
Convention entre le gouvernement du Canada et le gouvernement de la République du Pérou en vue d'éviter les doubles impositions et de prévenir l'évasion fiscale en matière d'impôts sur le revenu et sur la fortune. Lima, le 20 juillet 2001. *En vigueur* le 17 février 2003.

République slovaque
Accord sur la sécurité sociale entre le Canada et la République slovaque. Bratislava, le 21 mai 2001. *En vigueur* le 1ᵉʳ janvier 2003. RTC 2003/2.

République tchèque
Accord sur la sécurité sociale entre le Canada et la République tchèque. Prague, le 24 mai 2001. *En vigueur* le 1ᵉʳ janvier 2003. RTC 2003/3.

Royaume-Uni de Grande-Bretagne et d'Irlande du Nord
Échange de notes (22 janvier et 27 février 2003) entre le gouvernement du Canada et le gouvernement du Royaume-Uni de Grande-Bretagne et d'Irlande du Nord visant à étendre l'application de l'Accord entre le gouvernement du Canada et le Royaume-Uni de Grande-Bretagne et d'Irlande du Nord concernant le partage des biens confisqués ou des sommes d'argent équivalentes, fait à Londres le 21 février 2001, aux territoires d'outre-mer du Royaume-Uni, soit Anguilla, les îles Vierges britanniques, les îles Caïmans, Gibraltar, Montserrat et les îles turques et caïques. Ottawa, le 27 février 2003. *En vigueur* le 27 février 2003.

Sénégal
Accord entre le gouvernement du Canada et le gouvernement de la République du Sénégal sur la coproduction audiovisuelle. Île Santorin, le 27 septembre 2000. *En vigueur* le 7 octobre 2003.

Convention entre le gouvernement du Canada et le gouvernement de la République du Sénégal en vue d'éviter les doubles impositions et de prévenir l'évasion fiscale en matière d'impôts sur le revenu. Dakar, le 2 août 2001. *En vigueur* le 7 octobre 2003.

Suède
Accord sur la sécurité sociale entre le gouvernement du Canada et le gouvernement de la Suède. Ottawa, le 30 janvier 2002. *En vigueur* le 1ᵉʳ avril 2003.

Trinité-et-Tobago
Traité d'entraide judiciaire en matière pénale entre le gouvernement du Canada et le gouvernement de la République de Trinité-et-Tobago. Ottawa, le 4 septembre 1997. *En vigueur* le 11 octobre 2003.

II   MULTILATÉRAUX

Aviation
Convention pour l'unification de certaines règles relatives au transport aérien international. Montréal, le 28 mai 1999. *Signée* par le Canada le 1ᵉʳ octobre 2001. *Ratifiée* par le Canada le 19 novembre 2002. *En vigueur* pour le Canada le 4 novembre 2003.

Conservation
Protocole au Traité sur l'Antarctique relatif à la protection de l'environnement. Madrid, le 4 octobre 1991. *Signé* par le Canada le 4 octobre 1991. *Ratifié* par le Canada le 13 novembre 2003. *En vigueur* pour le Canada le 13 décembre 2003.

Criminalité transnationale
Convention des Nations Unies contre la criminalité transnationale organisée. New York, le 15 novembre 2000. *Signée* par le Canada le 14 décembre 2000. *Ratifiée* par le Canada le 13 mai 2002. *En vigueur* pour le Canada le 29 septembre 2003.

Protocole additionnel à la Convention des Nations Unies contre la criminalité transnationale organisée visant à prévenir, réprimer et punir la traite des personnes, en particulier des femmes et des enfants. New York, le 15 novembre 2000. *Signé* par le Canada le 14 décembre 2000. *Ratifié* par le Canada le 13 mai 2002. *En vigueur* pour le Canada le 25 décembre 2003.

Droit de la mer
Convention des Nations Unies sur le droit de la mer. Montego Bay, le 10 décembre 1982. *Signée* par le Canada le 10 décembre 1982. *Ratifiée* par le Canada le 7 novembre 2003. *En vigueur* pour le Canada le 7 décembre 2003.

Accord relatif à la mise en oeuvre de la partie XI de la Convention des Nations Unies sur le droit de la mer de 1982. New York, le 28 juillet 1994. *Signé* par le Canada le 29 juillet 1994. *Ratifié* par le Canada le 7 novembre 2003. *En vigueur* pour le Canada le 7 décembre 2003.

Droits de la personne
Protocole facultatif à la Convention sur l'élimination de toutes les formes de discrimination à l'égard des femmes. New York, le 6 octobre 1999. *Adhésion* par le Canada le 18 octobre 2002. *En vigueur* pour le Canada le 18 janvier 2003.

Pêches
Accord visant à favoriser le respect par les navires de pêche en haute mer des mesures internationales de conservation et de gestion. Rome, le 24 novembre 1993. *Adhésion* par le Canada le 20 mai 1994. *En vigueur* pour le Canada le 24 avril 2003.

Pollution
Protocole à la Convention sur la pollution atmosphérique transfrontière à longue distance, de 1979, relatif aux métaux lourds. Aarhus, le 24 juin 1998. *Signé* par le Canada le 24 juin 1998. *Ratifié* par le Canada le 18 décembre 1998. *En vigueur* pour le Canada le 29 décembre 2003.

Protocole à la Convention sur la pollution atmosphérique transfrontière à longue distance, de 1979, relatif aux polluants organiques persistants. Aarhus, 24 juin 1998. *Signé* par le Canada le 24 juin 1998. *Ratifié* par le Canada le 18 décembre 1998. *En vigueur* pour le Canada le 23 octobre 2003.

Terrorisme
Convention interaméricaine contre le terrorisme. Bridgetown, le 3 juin 2002. *Signé* par le Canada le 2 décembre 2002. *Ratifié* par le Canada le 2 décembre 2002. *En vigueur* pour le Canada le 10 juillet 2003.

Cases / Jurisprudence

Canadian Cases in
Public International Law in 2003–4 /
Jurisprudence canadienne en matière de
droit international public en 2003–4

compiled by / préparé par
GIBRAN VAN ERT

Trade treaties — implementation

UL Canada Inc. v. Quebec (Attorney General), [2003] JQ no. 13505
(1 October 2003). Court of Appeal for Quebec.[1]

The appellant UL appealed the dismissal of its application for declaratory relief and mandamus concerning section 40(1)(c) of the Regulation Respecting Dairy Products Substitutes,[2] which excludes pale yellow as a permissible colour of margarine for sale in Québec. The Regulation derives from section 42 of the Dairy Products and Dairy Products Substitutes Act,[3] by which the government of Québec may regulate the colour of dairy substitutes (among other

---

Gibran van Ert is an associate with Hunter Voith Litigation Counsel, Vancouver.

[1] Leave to appeal to the Supreme Court of Canada was granted on 6 May 2004. The appeal was dismissed from the bench: 2005 SCC 10 (18 March 2005). The English version of the reasons of LeBel J. for the court was as follows:

> The appellant has not shown that this Court should intervene to reverse the judgments of the courts below. Based on the constitutional principles governing the division of legislative powers, the impugned regulatory provision is within the limits of the provinces' legislative authority over local trade. Also, the provision respecting the colour of margarine was authorized by the enabling legislation, the words of which are clear. Furthermore, the statutory interpretation arguments drawn by the appellant from provincial and international trade agreements have no effect on the validity of this provision. Finally, the appellant's freedom of expression is not compromised in light of the scope this Court has previously attributed to that fundamental freedom. For these reasons, the appeal is dismissed without costs.

[2] R.R.Q. 1981, c. P-30 r 15.

[3] R.S.Q. c. P-30.

584   The Canadian Yearbook of International Law 2004

things). UL is a UK-based manufacturer of margarine and other food products. In late 1997, it imported from its US operations some 480 containers of non-conforming yellow margarine into Québec, apparently to provoke a legal challenge to the regulation.

Before the Court of Appeal and the court below, UL contended that section 40(1)(c) of the Regulation was invalid on several grounds including federalism, administrative law, and freedom of expression as guaranteed by the Canadian Charter of Rights and Freedoms and the Quebec Charter of Human Rights and Freedoms. All of these submissions were rejected by the Court of Appeal and are not considered here.

UL also argued for the section's invalidity on the basis of two international trade treaties to which Canada is a party, namely the North American Free Trade Agreement (NAFTA)[4] and the Agreement Establishing the World Trade Organization (WTO),[5] and a third, federal-provincial agreement, namely the Agreement on Internal Trade (AIT).[6] UL submitted that all three of these agreements are implemented in Québec law, citing the Act respecting the Implementation of International Trade Agreements (Treaties Act)[7] and the Act respecting the Implementation of the Agreement on Internal Trade (AIT Act).[8] UL argued that the yellow margarine requirement of section 40(1)(c) must therefore be examined in light of Quebec's obligations, under all three agreements, not to obstruct trade. To the extent that section 40(1)(c) conflicts with the agreements and their implementing legislation, UL argued, it is invalid.

Nuss J.A. (for the court) began his consideration of this argument by affirming that, as a matter of international law, a country is bound by a treaty from the moment it ratifies it,[9] yet as a matter of municipal law the treaty does not have force or effect unless implemented by the legislative body having jurisdiction to do so, in accordance with the division of powers established by the Constitution

---

4 [1994] Can. T.S. no. 2.

5 (1994) 33 I.L.M. 114.

6 At the time of writing, the agreement was available at: <http://strategis.ic.gc.ca/epic/internet/inait-aci.nsf/en/il00021e.html>.

7 R.S.Q. c. M-35.2.

8 R.S.Q. c. –M-35.1.1.

9 UL Canada Inc. v. Quebec at para. 76. This is only true, of course, if that treaty in question is in force when the state ratifies it.

Act 1867.[10] Whether or not an agreement (whether international
or internal) has been implemented is a question of statutory interpretation. The question to be considered is: Did the legislature
intend to incorporate the agreement into internal law?[11]

Nuss J.A. began by considering the preamble to the Treaties Act:

Attendu que le Québec souscrit aux principes et aux règles établis par
l'Accord de libre-échange nord-américain, l'Accord nord-américain de
coopération dans le domaine de l'environnement, l'Accord nord-américain
de coopération dans le domaine du travail et l'Accord instituant
l'Organisation mondiale du commerce;

Attendu qu'il est loisible au Québec de souscrire aux principes et règles
établis dans d'autres accords de commerce international qui comportent
des dispositions ressortissant à sa compétence constitutionnelle;

Attendu que le Québec est seul compétent pour assurer la mise en oeuvre
de ces accords dans chacun des domaines de sa compétence;

Whereas Québec subscribes to the principles and rules established by the
North American Free Trade Agreement, the North American Agreement
on Environmental Cooperation, the North American Agreement on Labor Cooperation and the Agreement Establishing the World Trade Organization;

Whereas Québec is at liberty to subscribe to the principles and rules established in other international trade agreements containing provisions falling within its constitutional jurisdiction; and

Whereas Québec alone is competent to implement those agreements in
each field coming under its jurisdiction.

Nuss J.A. described these passages as setting out a statement of fact
and then enunciating a truism with respect to legislative competence. The preamble "is not the expression of an intention to make
the Agreements part of internal Quebec Law, nor can such an intention be inferred from the text."[12]

Nuss J.A. then considered section 2 of the Act which, at the time,
read as follows:

---

[10] *Ibid.* at para. 76.

[11] *Ibid.* at para. 77, citing *Re Vancouver Island Railway,* [1994] 2 S.C.R. 41 and *Cree
Regional Authority v. Canada,* [1991] 3 F.C. 533 (CA).

[12] *UL Canada Inc. v. Quebec* at para. 80.

2. Sont approuvés les accords suivants :
— l'Accord de libre-échange nord-américain;
— l'Accord de coopération sur l'environnement;
— l'Accord coopération sur le travail;
— l'Accord instituant l'Organisation mondiale du commerce.

2. The following agreements are hereby approved:
— the North American Free Trade Agreement;
— the Environmental Cooperation Agreement;
— the Labour Cooperation Agreement;
— the Agreement Establishing the World Trade Organization.

Nuss J.A. observed that this section "merely states that the Agreements are approved without any statement that they are to be part of Quebec internal law."[13] He added that there is nothing in the rest of the Treaties Act "from which one could determine that it was the intention of the legislator to incorporate these two international Agreements into internal Quebec law"[14] and that the same conclusions applied to the legislation purporting to implement the AIT. Nuss J.A. therefore found the three agreements unimplemented in Québec law and held that they could not be invoked to invalidate section 40(1)(c) of the Regulation. Having reached this conclusion, Nuss J.A. saw no need to consider UL's trade-agreement submissions any further.

It is hard to fault Nuss J.A.'s findings. He was, with respect, quite right to conclude that he could not find the preamble to the Treaties Act sufficient to implement the treaty. It is a well-known rule of legal interpretation that preambles are to be distinguished from the legally effective portions of statutes and contracts. More importantly, the preamble in question simply does not reveal much implementing intent on the part of the legislature, apart from an ambiguous declaration concerning Québec's exclusive competence (as a matter of constitutional law) to implement these treaties to the extent that they fall within provincial jurisdiction. Nuss J.A. was also right to conclude that a mere declaration that a treaty is "approved" by the legislature does not give them domestic legal effect.[15]

It is nevertheless unsatisfactory that the Québec legislature should enact two laws bearing the word "implementation" in the title and

---

[13] *Ibid.* at para. 81

[14] *Ibid.* at para. 82.

[15] See *Re Vancouver Island Railway*, [1994] 2 S.C.R. 41 at 109.

yet those laws be found not to have such effect. It is not just the titles that cause this unease. The explanatory note attached to Bill 51 (as the Treaties Act then was) read:

Ce projet de loi prévoit l'approbation de certains accords de commerce international. Il harmonise également le droit interne québécois avec les obligations internationales auxquelles le Québec souscrit afin d'assurer la mise en oeuvre de ces accords.

This bill provides for the approval of certain international trade agreements. It also brings Québec internal law into harmony with international obligations to which Québec subscribes, and thus ensures the implementation of those agreements.

Whatever the interpretive weight to be given to such notes,[16] it seems clear that somebody — whether the legislative drafters, the ministry that introduced the bill, the government of Québec, the members of the National Assembly who voted for it, or some or all of the above — thought this bill would implement the NAFTA and the WTO Agreements in Québec law. (There is no similar note in the AIT Act.)

It is hard to know what to make of all this. I hesitate to venture an explanation for the drafting of the Treaties Act (which has since been amended),[17] or to elaborate on Nuss J.A.'s reasons (which were perhaps too brief on this point), or to speculate about what UL hoped to achieve in its arguments before the motions judge and the Court of Appeal. Instead, I propose to describe some of the uncertainties that continue to plague legislatures, courts, and litigants on the meaning and requirements of treaty implementation — without specifically ascribing any of them to the actors in this case.

The first point is about the meaning of implementation. To implement a treaty is to make whatever changes are required to give legal effect to its provisions in domestic law. There are numerous

---

[16] See R. Sullivan, *Driedger on the Construction of Statutes*, 3rd ed. (Markham, ON: Butterworths, 1994) at 273-5.

[17] Section 2 of the Treaties Act, as amended by S.Q. 2002, c. 8, s. 13, now provides: "The object of this Act is to implement the following agreements," namely the NAFTA, the WTO Agreement, and two others. Nevertheless, it is very hard to see how the remaining ten sections of this act, even as amended, implement these trade treaties in any significant way in Québec law. By contrast, the AIT Act (which has not been amended) clearly does amend Québec legislation in implementation of the Agreement on Internal Trade.

ways of doing this. There is no doubt that an act which reads simply: "This treaty has the force of law in Quebec [or wherever] and prior laws inconsistent with this treaty are repealed to the extent of their inconsistency" would suffice to implement a treaty. Yet, in most cases, this kind of implementation would be messy, so Canadian legislatures implement treaties by more elaborate, specific amendments or additions to existing law. One way to determine whether a treaty is implemented is simply to ask: "Is there any law in place that does what this treaty requires?" Note that it does not matter whether the implementing legislation expressly refers to the treaty or not. If Canada promises Mexico by treaty that it will enact a law making the Cinco de Mayo a national holiday, and Parliament duly amends the Holidays Act[18] accordingly, the treaty is implemented — whether the Holidays Act refers to the treaty or not.

The second point is that treaty implementation is not all or nothing. A given treaty may be entirely implemented in domestic law or wholly unimplemented in domestic law. But it may also be only partially implemented in domestic law. Of course, if Canada or its provinces fail to implement parts of a treaty that require implementation, Canada will be answerable to its treaty partner at international law.

The third point (which is related to the second) is that treaties, or treaty provisions, that do not purport to affect domestic law do not need implementation. The point of implementation is to give domestic effect to the treaty. But the treaty may not need domestic effect. Indeed, most treaties Canada concludes every year are in the nature of government-to-government agreements that do not purport to affect the domestic law of either party. Similarly, some treaties will require implementation of a few of their provisions but not of the rest. It would be wrong to say that such a treaty is not implemented. If the treaty contains five promises, only one of which concerns domestic law, and the legislature implements that one but not the others, the treaty is fully implemented: every promise in it that required domestic legal change has received it.

The fourth point is implicit in the previous three. The fact that a treaty is implemented does not necessarily mean that the treaty's provisions take precedence over domestic law or may found judicial review of existing laws. Those treaty provisions that do not purport to affect domestic law clearly cannot be relied on to invalidate existing laws, though they may, in proper cases, be looked to as

18 R.S.C. 1985, c. H-5.

guides to interpretation. As for treaty provisions that do address domestic law, it is the character and terms of their implementing provisions that determine their relationship to other domestic laws. So if Parliament amends the Holidays Act to make the Cinco de Mayo a national holiday, but a provincial law makes 5 May a different holiday, the problem is resolved according to the rules of federalism. Alternatively, if Parliament amends the Holidays Act to grant cabinet the power to create new holidays by regulation as required by international law, and cabinet instead makes 5 May a different holiday, the problem is resolved by recourse to administrative law. If Parliament creates Cinco de Mayo by legislation and someone objects on equality grounds, the problem is governed by the Charter and other applicable human rights laws. In all of these cases, the underlying treaty will be at least a relevant and persuasive factor, and the disputed provisions may even be interpreted as presumably consistent with international law. But the treaty itself does not trump, or even directly act upon, domestic law.

Immunité des états — Taiwan

Parent c. Singapore Airlines Ltd. (2003) JE 2003–2160 (22 octobre 2003). Cour supérieure du Québec.

Parent est blessé à la suite de l'écrasement du vol SQoo6 de la Singapore Airlines Limited (SAL) entre Singapore et Montréal avec escales à Taipei, Los Angeles et Toronto. L'accident s'est produit au moment du décollage de Taipei à destination de Los Angeles. Parent et autres ont alors intenté un recours en dommages contre SAL. SAL ce dernier a plaidé que la responsabilité de l'accident reposait sur le gestionnaire et exploitant de l'aéroport, l'administration de l'aviation civile du ministère des Transports de la république de Chine (Taiwan), d'où son recours en garantie contre la Civil Aeronautics Administration (CAA) de Taiwan.

CAA, de son côté, invoquait l'immunité de juridiction devant tout tribunal au Canada dont bénéficie l'État étranger. SAL contestait cette réclamation en soutenant que Taiwan n'est pas un État étranger au sens de la Loi sur l'immunité des États[19] (la Loi) puisque le ministre canadien des Affaires étrangères et du Commerce international a refusé d'émettre le certificat prévu à l'article 14 de cette loi. La question en litige était donc: CAA bénéficie-t-elle de l'immunité des États? Deux sous-questions découlaient de celle-ci: (1)

[19] L.R.C. 1985, c. S-18.

Quel est l'effet de l'absence de certificat émis aux termes de l'article 14? et (2) Taiwan est-il un État étranger au sens de la Loi?

CAA a produit nombreux éléments de preuve pour appuyer sa position que Taiwan constitue un État étranger, y compris plusieurs déclarations publiques du Gouvernement du Canada à l'égard de Taiwan et quelques accords bilateraux entre les gouvernements du Canada et de Taiwan. La juge St-Pierre a par ailleurs conclu que, "quel que soient les effets susceptibles d'en résulter sur les plans politique, diplomatique ou juridique," l'île de Taiwan constitue un territoire défini occupé par une population permanente dotée d'un gouvernement effectif qui entre en relation avec d'autres États.[20] La juge a aussi accepté (ce qui n'a pas été disputé) que CAA est un organisme de Taiwan qui sera assimilé à Taiwan pour les fins de l'art. 2 de la Loi si Taiwan constitue un "État étranger" dans le sens de la Loi.[21]

Quant au certificat prévu par l'art. 14, CAA n'en a pas produit. Par contre, SAL a communiqué avec le ministère des Affaires étrangères à ce sujet. La réponse du ministère lisait comme suit:

This is in response to your letter of March 19, 2003, in which you requested that a certificate be issued by the Minister or his authorized person under section 14 of the State Immunity Act to establish whether "Taiwan" is a foreign state for the purposes of that Act.

I wish to inform you that the Department cannot respond positively to your request and no such certificate will be issued at this time.

Canada has a one-China policy which recognizes the People's Republic of China, with its government located in Beijing, and it has full diplomatic relations with that government. Canada does not have diplomatic relations with "Taiwan" or the "Republic of China."[22]

SAL soutenait que l'absence de certificat et le refus du ministère d'en émettre un avait comme résultat que CAA ne saurait bénéficier de l'immunité alléguée. CAA répliquait que le certificat constitue tout au plus un moyen de preuve et non pas le seul moyen de preuve recevable. Il appartenait encore au Tribunal d'appliquer la Loi en vu de la preuve administrée et, ceci étant, de déterminer si Taiwan était un "État étranger" au sens de cette loi.

---

20 *Parent* au para. 20.

21 Voir *ibid.* aux paras. 8 et 14.

22 *Ibid.* au para. 25.

La juge St-Pierre en est arrivé à la même conclusion que CAA. Les termes utilisés dans l'art. 14(1) sont les suivants:

> A certificate issued by the Minister of Foreign Affairs ... with respect to any of the following questions ... is admissible in evidence as conclusive proof of any matter stated in the certificate with respect to that question ... Le certificat délivré par le ministre des Affaires étrangères ... est admissible en preuve et fait foi pour toute question touchant ... [etc.].

Selon la juge, ces mots indiquent que tout ce qui est mentionné dans un certificat prévu par l'art. 14 est prouvé par son simple dépôt en preuve. Toutefois, les termes ne requièrent pas cette preuve.[23] La juge a de plus signalé son désaccord avec la conclusion d'un tribunal de Singapour (dans une affaire basée sur une loi semblable à celle du Canada) que la qualification "d'État étranger" relevait exclusivement de l'exécutif par le biais du certificat:

> La situation n'est pas la même au Canada: absence de certificat émis aux termes de l'article 14 de la Loi ne veut pas nécessairement dire absence de droit à l'immunité. En effet, le législateur ne dit pas "la qualité d'État étranger aux termes de la présente loi s'établit par le dépôt en preuve d'un certificat émis par le ministère"; le législateur dit "un certificat est admissible" pour établir cette qualité ... Les mots utilisés par le législateur canadien ... permettent l'introduction d'une preuve councluante (les faits mentionnés au certificat) sans formalité autre que le dépôt du certificat et sans déplacement de témoins.[24]

La juge a ajouté que la situation politique ou diplomatique pourra éxiger au gouvernement canadien de ne pas octroyer la reconnaissance pleine, inconditionnelle ou permanente. "La Loi oblige d'ailleurs le Tribunal à faire le nécessaire pour assurer, même d'office, l'application de l'immunité."[25] Elle a conclu:

> Ainsi interprétée, la Loi atteint sa finalité (intégrer au droit canadien le principe de l'immunité de juridiction, avec exceptions, découlant du droit coutumier international) dans le respect des principes de droit international public sur lesquels reposent cette immunité (souveraineté, indépendance, dignité et égalité des États).[26]

---

[23] *Ibid.* aux paras. 36–37.

[24] Voir *Ibid.* aux paras. 38–40; *Woo v. Singapore Airlines Limited and Civil Aeronautics Administration*, [2003] S.G.H.C. 190.

[25] Voir *Parent* aux paras. 42–46.

[26] *Ibid.* au para. 51.

Il restait alors de déterminer si Taiwan était un "État étranger" pour les fins de la Loi. Cette expression n'est pas défini dans la Loi. Mais vu que la Loi cherche à intégrer au droit canadien le principe de l'immunité de juridiction découlant du droit coutumier international, la juge a invoqué la présomption de conformité du droit domestique avec le droit international et a eu recours à ce dernier pour définir "État."[27] Se fiant aux quatres critères énoncés dans l'article premier de la Convention de Montevideo sur les droits et devoirs des États 1933,[28] et du concept de la reconnaissance d'États,[29] la juge a conclu que CAA bénéficiait de l'immunité. Comme elle l'avait déjà indiqué, la preuve était concluante que CAA faisait partie de Taiwan et que Taiwan satisfaisait aux quatres éléments Montevideo. Quant à la reconnaissance, la juge soutenait que la reconnaissance d'un État par les autres ne crée pas l'État: la naissance et l'existence d'un État est une question de fait.[30] L'existence de l'État de Taiwan et sa reconnaissance (si limitée soit-elle) étaient confirmées, selon la juge, par les déclarations gouvernementales du Canada et par la doctrine.[31] La requête de CAA en rejet de la demande en garantie a été accueillie, et la demande en garantie de SAL contre CAA a été rejetté.

Certaines conclusions de la juge St-Pierre semblent peut-être trop peu équivoque. Prenons par exemple sa courte discussion de la théorie déclarative de la reconnaissance d'États, à laquelle elle donne son aval sur la base d'un seul texte (celui du Professeur Emanuelli) et sans même mentionner son rival (la théorie consti-tutive). Pourtant, cette approche est autant une force du jugement qu'une faiblesse. L'interprétation de la Loi adoptée par la cour, et sa conclusion sur le droit de Taiwan à l'immunité, démontrent un esprit pratique louable. Le jugement est en accord avec la réalité de la situation que vit Taiwan, sans dériver aux nombreux bourbiers que presentait cette cause. Pour cela, le jugement mérite un accueil chaleureux.

[27] *Ibid.* au para. 53.
[28] (1936) 165 L.N.T.S. 19. Les critères sont: (a) une population permanente; (b) un territoire défini; (c) un gouvernement; et (d) la capacité d'entrer en rela-tion avec les autres États. La juge ignore que le Canada n'a pas adhéré à cette convention. Pourtant, ces critères font parti du droit coutumier.
[29] *Parent* aux paras. 54–55.
[30] *Ibid.* au para. 55.
[31] *Ibid.* aux paras. 56–59.

Arbitral awards — NAFTA — judicial review

Mexico v. Karpa, [2003] OTC 1070 (3 December 2003). Ontario Superior Court of Justice.[32]

This case, better known as *Feldman,* was an application by Mexico to set aside an arbitral award against it under Chapter 11 of the 1992 North American Free Trade Agreement (NAFTA).[33] The application was made pursuant to Article 34 of the 1985 UNCITRAL Model Law on International Commercial Arbitration as implemented in Ontario by section 2 of the International Commercial Arbitration Act.[34] The majority of the arbitral tribunal found that Mexico discriminated against an American investor, Feldman, contrary to NAFTA Article 1102 (national treatment). Against the award, Mexico relied on Articles 34(2)(a)(ii) (applicant unable to present his case), 34(2)(a)(iv) (arbitral procedure not in accordance with agreement of parties), and 34(2)(b)(ii) (award conflicts with public policy). The attorney-general of Canada intervened in support of Mexico.

Feldman was in the business of exporting cigarettes out of Mexico through his company, CEMSA. His main allegation was that Mexico discriminated against CEMSA by failing to extend to it a rebate on export taxes enjoyed by domestic cigarette exporters. To prove this allegation, Feldman sought production by Mexico of the taxpayer records of his competitors. Mexico objected that Article 69 of its Fiscal Code prevented the production of such evidence. Instead, Mexico filed a statement by one of its taxation officials. On the basis of this and other evidence, the tribunal concluded that Feldman had made out a *prima facie* case of discrimination and that Mexico had failed to meet its burden of adducing evidence to show otherwise.[35]

---

[32] An appeal from this judgment was dismissed by the Court of Appeal for Ontario on 11 January 2005 (Docket: C41169). The court of appeal's reasons will be considered in the next edition of the *Canadian Yearbook of International Law.*

[33] [1994] Can. T.S. no 2.

[34] R.S.O. 1990, c. I-9. The first paragraph of Chilcott J.'s reasons, describing the application by quoting from Mexico's pleadings, must be disregarded. Mexico claimed to rely on section 34 of the International Commercial Arbitration Act (which does not exist) and described the award as having been made "in Ottawa, Ontario at the International Centre for Settlement of Investment Disputes (Additional Facilities)" (which also does not exist; the ICSID is located in Washington, DC; the Additional Facilities are not facilities in the physical sense but a set of rules administered by the ICSID).

[35] See para. 187 of the tribunal's award, quoted in *Mexico v. Karpa* at para. 70.

Annuaire canadien de Droit international 2004

Chilcott J. made several observations concerning the applicable standard of review. He noted that Article 5 of the Model Law provides that "no court shall intervene except where so provided in this Law" and that the grounds upon which arbitral awards may be set aside under the Model Law are established by Article 34.[36] He affirmed that "the jurisdiction of this court to review the award is strictly limited to those instances provided for in Article 34 of the Model Law which allows for a very limited opportunity for the courts to provide any recourse against an award."[37] He later observed that "a high level of deference should be accorded to the Tribunal," particularly in respect of findings of fact, and quoted Canadian authorities to this effect.[38] He described Article 34 of the Model Law, together with Article 53(4) of the ICSID Additional Facility Rules, as forming a privative clause[39] of the kind discussed by the Supreme Court of Canada in *Pushpanathan v. Canada (Minister of Citizenship and Immigration)*.[40] These and other observations made throughout the reasons rightly establish a highly deferential standard of review. But they do not do so as clearly as one would like. In particular, reference to *Pushpanathan* and Canadian standards of review jurisprudence is at odds with Model Law Article 5, which, as Chilcott J. rightly observed, establishes Article 34 as the only grounds for judicial review of arbitral awards. The rococo and increasingly unstable edifice of Canadian standards of review jurisprudence is of no relevance. References to it serve only to parochialize what is intended to be an international standard. In proceedings under the Model Law, the "pragmatic and functional approach" should simply be ignored.

Mexico argued that the majority's award drew an impermissible adverse inference against it due to its restricted production of documents. This restriction was imposed by Mexico's Fiscal Code and served, according to Mexico, to protect taxpayer privacy. This provision of Mexico's domestic law, combined with the adverse inference it allegedly provoked from the majority, made Mexico unable to present its case — a ground for setting aside the award under Article 34(2)(a)(ii) of the Model Law.[41] Chilcott J. rejected this

36 *Ibid.* at paras. 9–10, 52.

37 *Ibid.* at para. 53; see also para. 43.

38 *Ibid.* at paras. 77–80.

39 *Ibid.* at paras. 84–5.

40 [1998] 1 S.C.R. 982.

41 *Mexico v. Karpa* at para. 13.

argument, observing that there was no evidence before him that Article 69 of Mexico's Fiscal Code really did prevent it from leading evidence[42] and that a high level of deference should be accorded to the tribunal on this point, especially given that "Mexico is in reality challenging a finding of fact."[43]

Mexico's second argument was that that award be set aside on the ground that the arbitral procedure was not in accordance with the agreement of the parties (Article 34(2)(a)(iv)). Mexico relied on NAFTA Article 2105:

> Nothing in this Agreement shall be construed to require a Party to furnish or allow access to information the disclosure of which would impede law enforcement or would be contrary to the Party's law protecting personal privacy or the financial affairs and accounts of individual customers of financial institutions.

Mexico argued that, by drawing an adverse inference against it for complying with its Fiscal Code, the majority award is contrary to Article 2105.[44] Similarly, the attorney-general for Canada argued that the majority's failure to consider Article 2105 resulted in an excess of jurisdiction.[45] Chilcott J. rejected these submissions, noting that Mexico had not raised Article 2105 before the tribunal and that it was improper to raise it now, given the restrictions on judicial review of arbitral awards imposed by Model Law Article 34.[46]

Finally, Mexico submitted that the majority's award was contrary to Ontario public policy (Article 34(2)(b)(ii)) because it required Mexico to pay Feldman, as damages, tax rebates to which the tribunal had previously held that he had no right. Chilcott J. found no breach of public policy here. Citing a previous decision, he said that for an arbitral award to be against public policy it "must fundamentally offend the most basic and explicit principles of justice and fairness in Ontario, or evidence intolerable ignorance or corruption on the part of the arbitral tribunal." In Chilcott J.'s words, the award must be "contrary to the essential morality of Ontario."[47]

---

[42] *Ibid.* at paras. 68–9; see also para. 45.

[43] *Ibid.* at para. 77.

[44] *Ibid.* at paras. 14–16.

[45] *Ibid.* at paras. 26–38.

[46] *Ibid.* at paras. 42–43.

[47] *Ibid.* at para. 87, quoting *Corporacion Transnacional de Inversiones SA de CV v. STET International SpA* (1999) 45 O.R. (3d) 183, aff'd 49 O.R. (3d) 414 (CA).

He added that the measure used by the majority to assess damages was "fair and proper."[48]

Mexico's strained attempts to convert the largely procedural grounds for review of Article 34 into substantive grounds for appeal were rightly rejected by Chilcott J. But problems remain concerning the relationship between Article 34 and Canadian standards of review jurisprudence. Indeed, one senses from this judgment that international commercial arbitration in general continues to be unfamiliar territory for Canadian courts.

Canada (Attorney General) v. S.D. Myers, Inc. 2004 FC 38 (13 January 2004). Federal Court of Canada.

This was an application by the government of Canada to set aside three awards made against it by an arbitral tribunal established under Chapter 11 of the 1992 NAFTA.[49] The application was made in Federal Court pursuant to Article 34 of the Commercial Arbitration Code, which grants domestic courts a limited jurisdiction to review and set aside the awards of arbitral tribunals. The Code is based on the UNCITRAL Model Law on International Commercial Arbitration 1985[50] and is enacted as a schedule to the federal Commercial Arbitration Act.[51]

The impugned arbitral awards found Canada in breach of its obligations under NAFTA Articles 1102 and 1105 (national treatment and minimum standard of treatment, respectively) and awarded damages and costs to the claimant, SDMI. The dispute arose out of Canada's 1995 decision to prevent the export of Canadian-held PCB wastes to the United States by closing the border to such materials. SDMI was an Ohio-based waste remediation firm that hoped to do cross-border business with Canadian waste-holders. SDMI brought a claim under NAFTA Chapter 11, arguing, in essence, that Canada's border closure protected Canadian waste remediation firms from the cheaper competition of SDMI and its Canadian affiliate, Myers Canada, contrary to the NAFTA. The tribunal agreed and awarded SDMI $6.05 million plus interest and costs.

---

48 *Mexico v. Karpa* at para. 95.

49 [1994] Can. T.S. no 2.

50 Adopted by the United Nations Commission on International Trade Law (UNCITRAL) on 21 June 1985.

51 R.S.C. 1985, c 17 (2nd Supp) as amended.

There being no appeal mechanism under the NAFTA, Canada sought to set aside the tribunal's awards in the Federal Court. Article 34 of the Code provides in part as follows:

(2) An arbitral award may be set aside by the court specified in article 6 only if:

    (a) the party making the application furnishes proof that: ...

        (iii) the award deals with a dispute not contemplated by or not falling within the terms of the submission to arbitration, or contains decisions on matters beyond the scope of the submission to arbitration, provided that, if the decisions on matters submitted to arbitration can be separated from those not so submitted, only that part of the award which contains decisions on matters not submitted to arbitration may be set aside; or ...

    (b) the court finds that: ...

        (ii) the award is in conflict with the public policy of Canada.

(2) La sentence arbitrale ne peut être annulée par le tribunal visé à l'article 6 que si, selon le cas :

    (a) la partie en faisant la demande apporte la preuve : ...

        (iii) soit que la sentence porte sur un différend non visé dans le compromis ou n'entrant pas dans les prévisions de la clause compromissoire, ou qu'elle contient des décisions qui dépassent les termes du compromis ou de la clause compromissoire, étant entendu toutefois que, si les dispositions de la sentence qui ont trait à des questions soumises à l'arbitrage peuvent être dissociées de celles qui ont trait à des questions non soumises à l'arbitrage, seule la partie de la sentence contenant des décisions sur les questions non soumises à l'arbitrage pourra être annulée;

    (b) le tribunal constate : ...

        (ii) soit que la sentence est contraire à l'ordre public du Canada.[52]

Canada argued that the tribunal's awards exceeded the scope of the arbitration agreement and contravened Canadian public policy. In particular, Canada argued that the tribunal:

(a) erred in concluding that SDMI was an "investor" and Myers Canada its "investment" for the purposes of NAFTA chapter 11;

(b) misconstrued the meaning and application of NAFTA art. 1102;

(c) erred in its interpretation of NAFTA art. 1105; and

[52] [Emphasis removed]. (The text uses italics to indicate deviations from the text of the UNCITRAL Model Law.)

(d) exceeded the scope of the arbitration by applying NAFTA chapter 11 obligations to what, in Canada's submission, was a dispute concerning the cross-border trade in services (a matter governed by NAFTA chapter 12).[53]

Canada's challenge was to turn these submissions — many if not all of which seemed to go to the merits of the tribunal's awards — into grounds for the court to exercise its limited powers under Article 34.

Kelen J. began the substantive portion of his reasons by considering the proper standard of review. Canada argued for a correctness standard, but Kelen J. inclined to greater deference, noting:

> Courts restrain themselves from exercising judicial review with respect to international arbitration tribunals so as to be sensitive to the need of a system for predictability in the resolution of disputes and to preserve the autonomy of the arbitration forum selected by the parties.[54]

Kelen J. also observed that the grounds of review established by the Code do not allow for review on the basis of errors of law or erroneous findings of fact[55] and that the so-called pragmatic and functional approach to determining the applicable standard of review (as enunciated in the administrative law jurisprudence of the Supreme Court of Canada) has no application to the Code, for the Code's standards of review are expressly provided for by Article 34.[56]

The first of those express grounds of review at issue in this case was that the impugned award dealt with "a dispute not contemplated by or not falling within the terms of the submission to arbitration" (Article 34(2)(a)(iii)). Without elaborating, Kelen J. declared himself satisfied that the tribunal's awards could not be set aside on this ground.[57] Article 34(2)(a)(iii) establishes a second ground for setting aside an arbitral award, namely that it "contains decisions on matters beyond the scope of the submission to arbitration." Canada submitted that the tribunal's decision that SDMI was an "investor" or that Myers Canada was an "investment of the investor" for the purposes of NAFTA Chapter 11 were matters beyond the scope of the submission to arbitration. Kelen J. viewed this submission as a challenge to the tribunal's jurisdiction to entertain SDMI's claim in the first place. Yet he noted that Canada failed to raise any objection to the tribunal's jurisdiction at the outset

---

53 *SD Myers* at paras. 25–26.

54 *Ibid.* at para. 39; see generally paras. 35–42.

55 *Ibid.* at para. 42.

56 *Ibid.* at para. 39.

57 *Ibid.* at para. 45.

of the arbitration. Having failed to do so then, Kelen J. held that Canada could not do so now.[58]

Kelen J. also rejected Canada's public policy submissions under Code Article 34(2)(b)(ii). He described public policy as referring to "fundamental notions and principles of justice." He continued:

Such a principle includes that a tribunal not exceed its jurisdiction in the course of an inquiry, and that such a "jurisdictional error" can be a decision which is "patently unreasonable," such as a complete disregard of the law so that the decision constitutes an abuse of authority amounting to a flagrant injustice.

In the case at bar, the Tribunal's finding with respect to the two jurisdictional questions, and with respect to Article 1102, are not "patently unreasonable," "clearly irrational," "totally lacking in reality" or "a flagrant denial of justice." Accordingly, the Court concludes that there is not aspect of the Tribunal decisions under review which "conflicts with the public policy of Canada."[59]

The meaning of much of this is unclear. The judge appears to assimilate "the public policy of Canada" with the ill-defined "patently unreasonable" standard of review of Canadian administrative law — in spite of finding that body of jurisprudence inapplicable earlier in his reasons. What does clearly emerge from this passage is that an arbitral award would have to be very bad indeed for Kelen J. to set it aside on the ground that it conflicted with Canadian public policy.

These findings sufficed to dismiss Canada's judicial review application. But Kelen J. went on, in brief *obiter dicta*, to address Canada's other submissions. Kelen J. concluded that the tribunal had correctly defined the terms "investor" and "investment of an investor" (as found in NAFTA Article 1139) and that it had reasonably applied these definitions to the facts before it.[60] Kelen J. found the tribunal correct in entertaining SDMI's NAFTA Chapter 11 claim in spite of the alleged overlap with NAFTA Chapter 12.[61] He deemed the tribunal's interpretation of NAFTA Article 1102 (more particularly, the phrase "in like circumstances"), to be "reasonably open to it."[62] Finally, Kelen J. declined to express any view on the tribunal's interpretation and application of NAFTA Article 1105.

[58] *Ibid.* at paras. 47–54.
[59] *Ibid.* at paras. 55–6.
[60] *Ibid.* at paras. 62–70.
[61] *Ibid.* at para. 71.
[62] *Ibid.* at paras. 72–4.

S.D. Myers was the first application to set aside a NAFTA Chapter 11 award to be heard by the Federal Court. The novelty of the case may account for the uncertainty it displays about the applicable standard of review. At points, Kelen J. is very clear that domestic courts must be wary of disturbing international arbitral awards and that Canadian jurisprudence on standards of review has no place in the court's analysis. These comments (which occur in *ratio* not *obiter*) are most welcome. So, too, is the court's result. Kelen J. resisted Canada's dubious attacks on the tribunal and upheld its award. And yet Kelen J.'s reasons are marked by uncertainties and inconsistencies. His account of public policy as a ground for reviewing arbitral awards is difficult to follow. His approval of the tribunal's conclusions as "correct" or even "reasonable" in *obiter* passages is at odds with his earlier affirmations of the court's limited review power under Article 34; it is not a mark of deference to an arbitral tribunal to express agreement with its conclusions. These difficulties might have been avoided had Kelen J. considered precedents and commentary from other Model Law jurisdictions on the meaning and interpretation of Article 34. Such sources may not have been drawn to his attention by counsel. It is a regrettable omission, for the UNCITRAL Model Law has been the subject of significant judicial and academic scrutiny around the world.[63] The words of Lord Macmillan in a similar context are apt:

It is important to remember that the Act of 1924 was the outcome of an International Conference and that the rules in the Schedule have an international currency. As these rules must come under the consideration of foreign Courts it is desirable in the interests of uniformity that their interpretation should not be rigidly controlled by domestic precedents of antecedent date, but rather that the language of the rules should be construed on broad principles of general acceptation.[64]

---

[63] Legislation based on the UNCITRAL Model Law has been enacted in Australia, Azerbaijan, Bahrain, Bangladesh, Belarus, Bermuda, Bulgaria, China (Hong Kong Special Administrative Region and Macau Special Administrative Region), Croatia, Cyprus, Egypt, Germany, Greece, Guatemala, Hungary, India, Iran, Ireland, Japan, Jordan, Kenya, Lithuania, Madagascar, Malta, Mexico, New Zealand, Nigeria, Oman, Paraguay, Peru, Russia, Singapore, South Korea, Spain, Sri Lanka, Thailand, Tunisia, Ukraine, the United Kingdom (Scotland), the United States (California, Connecticut, Illinois, Oregon, and Texas), Zambia, and Zimbabwe. Furthermore, Article 34 of the Model Law closely resembles Article V of the 1958 New York Convention on the Recognition and Enforcement of Foreign Arbitral Awards [1986] Can. T.S. no 43, a treaty with over 100 states parties.

[64] *Stag Line Ltd. v. Foscolo, Mango & Co. Ltd.* [1932] A.C. 328 at 350.

In judgments under the Commercial Arbitration Act and other Canadian laws enacting the UNCITRAL Model Law, our courts should strive not only to conform to, but to contribute to, the international law of commercial arbitration. *S.D. Myers* is rightly decided, but it makes little contribution.

Treaties — application in domestic law — presumption of conformity

Canadian Foundation for Children, Youth and the Law v. Attorney General in Right of Canada, [2004] 1 SCR 76 (30 January 2004). Supreme Court of Canada.

Section 43 of the Criminal Code provides:

Every schoolteacher, parent or person standing in the place of a parent is justified in using force by way of correction toward a pupil or child, as the case may be, who is under his care, if the force does not exceed what is reasonable under the circumstances.

Tout instituteur, père ou mère, ou toute personne qui remplace le père ou la mère, est fondé à employer la force pour corriger un élève ou un enfant, selon le cas, confié à ses soins, pourvu que la force ne dépasse pas la mesure raisonnable dans les circonstances.[65]

The effect of this provision is to exempt from criminal sanction what would otherwise constitute a criminal assault. The Canadian Foundation for Children, Youth and the Law challenged the constitutionality of section 43 on the grounds of sections 7, 12 and 15(1) of the Charter. McLachlin C.J. for the majority of the Supreme Court of Canada dismissed the appeal, finding no infringement of the Charter. Arbour and Deschamps JJ. dissented in separate reasons. Binnie J. dissented in part. International human rights law played a significant role in the chief justice's finding that section 43 did not infringe Charter section 7. International law and the opinions of treaty bodies also figured in Arbour J.'s dissent. This note focuses on these aspects of the judgment.

The attorney-general for Canada (respondent) conceded that section 43 adversely affects children's security of the person, as guaranteed by Charter section 7, but denied that it does so contrary to the principles of fundamental justice. The Foundation identified three such principles with which, in their submission, section 43 did not accord.

[65] R.S.C. 1985, c. C-46.

First, the Foundation sought to draw an analogy to the right of accused persons to adequate procedural safeguards in the criminal process. This supposed principle of fundamental justice was rejected by McLachlin C.J. and was not picked up in the opinions of the other justices.[66]

More significantly, the Foundation argued that the best interests of the child is a principle of fundamental justice with which section 43 fails to accord. McLachlin C.J. identified three criteria of principles of fundamental justice (PFJs) for the purpose of Charter section 7: (1) the supposed PFJ must be a legal principle; (2) there must be consensus that the supposed PFJ is vital or fundamental to our societal notion of justice; (3) the supposed PFJ must be capable of being identified with some precision.[67] The chief justice considered these criteria in turn. She acknowledged that the best interests of the child is "an established legal principle in international and domestic law." She noted Canada's adherence to the 1989 Convention on the Rights of the Child (CRC)[68] and the 1980 Convention on the Elimination of All Forms of Discrimination against Women,[69] both of which enunciate the best interests principle. She also cited several federal and provincial statutes that explicitly identify the principle as a legal consideration. Yet McLachlin C.J. concluded that the best interests of the child is not a PFJ. It fails to meet the second criterion. While the principle is widely supported in legislation and social policy, it is not a foundational requirement for the dispensation of justice. The chief justice noted that CRC Article 3(1) identifies the best interests of the child as "'a primary consideration' rather than 'the primary consideration.'" McLachlin C.J. was also of the view that the principle did not meet the third criterion of being identifiable with sufficient precision, for the requirements of the best interests of the child principle are "inevitably highly contextual and subject to dispute."[70]

The Foundation's third section 7 argument was founded on the established rule that vague or overbroad laws that deprive persons of life, liberty or security of the person do not accord with the principles of fundamental justice and therefore infringe section 7. The

---

[66] *Canadian Foundation* at paras. 5–6.

[67] See *R. v. Malmo-Levine*, [2003] 3 S.C.R. 571 at para. 113.

[68] [1992] Can. T.S. no. 3 art. 3(1).

[69] [1982] Can. T.S. no. 31 arts 5(b) and 16(1)(d).

[70] *Canadian Foundation* at paras. 8–11.

Foundation attacked section 43's exemption from criminal sanction of force that is "reasonable under the circumstances" as unconstitutionally vague. McLachlin C.J. described an unconstitutionally vague law as one that fails sufficiently to delineate a risk zone for criminal sanction. She proceeded closely to examine the meaning of section 43's operative terms. The terms "schoolteacher," "parent," and "person standing in the place of a parent" were clear on their face or in light of decided cases. The phrase "by way of correction" yielded two limitations. First, the person applying the force must intend it to be for educative or corrective purposes. Section 43 does not protect outbursts of violence against children prompted by anger or frustration. Second, the child must be capable of benefiting from the correction. The evidence at trial was that children under two years of age are incapable of understanding the corrective intent of force. Disability or other contextual factors may also prevent such understanding. The use of force against children in these cases is therefore not within the sphere of immunity provided by section 43.[71]

McLachlin C.J. turned next to consider the requirement that section 43 force be "reasonable under the circumstances." She noted that while these terms are broad "on their face," they are subject to "a number of implicit limitations." First, section 43 does not exempt from criminal sanction conduct that causes harm or raises a reasonable prospect of harm. Its operation is limited to "the mildest forms of assault."[72] More significantly for our purposes,

further precision on what is reasonable under the circumstances may be derived from international treaty obligations. Statutes should be construed to comply with Canada's international obligations: *Ordon Estate v. Grail*, [1998] 3 S.C.R. 437, at para. 137. Canada's international commitments confirm that physical correction that either harms or degrades a child is unreasonable.

Elaborating on this statement, McLachlin C.J. reviewed CRC Articles 5, 19(1), and 37(a), emphasizing states parties' obligations to protect children from all forms of physical or mental violence and to ensure that no child be subjected to torture or other cruel, inhuman, or degrading treatment or punishment. She also cited Canada's obligation to prevent such treatment or punishment under Article 7 of the 1966 International Covenant on Civil and

[71] *Ibid.* at paras. 21–5.
[72] *Ibid.* at para. 30.

Political Rights (ICCPR),[73] observing that the ICCPR's preamble "makes it clear that its provisions apply to 'all members of the human family.'" The chief justice found that neither the CRC nor the ICCPR require states parties to ban corporal punishment of children. Yet she noted that the UN Human Rights Committee has expressed the view that corporal punishment of children in schools engages ICCPR Article 7's prohibition of degrading treatment or punishment. The chief justice also briefly considered the jurisprudence of the European Court of Human Rights on what constitutes inhuman and degrading treatment.[74]

Apart from these treaty considerations, McLachlin C.J. also looked to social consensus, expert evidence and judicial interpretation as guides to the meaning of "reasonable under the circumstances."[75] She concluded:

> When these considerations are taken together, a solid core of meaning emerges for "reasonable under the circumstances," sufficient to establish a zone in which discipline risks criminal sanction. Generally, s. 43 exempts from criminal sanction only minor corrective force of a transitory and trifling nature. On the basis of current expert consensus, it does not apply to corporal punishment of children under two or teenagers. Degrading, inhuman or harmful conduct is not protected. Discipline by the use of objects or blows or slaps to the head is unreasonable. Teachers may reasonably apply force to remove a child from a classroom or secure compliance with instructions, but not merely as corporal punishment. Coupled with the requirement that the conduct be corrective, which rules out conduct stemming from the caregiver's frustration, loss of temper or abusive personality, a consistent picture emerges of the area covered by s. 43. It is wrong for law enforcement officers or judges to apply their own subjective views of what is "reasonable under the circumstances"; the test is objective. The question must be considered in context and in light of all the circumstances of the case. The gravity of the precipitating event is not relevant.[76]

Having thus interpreted section 43, the chief justice held that it succeeds in delineating a risk zone for criminal sanction and therefore does not violate the principle of fundamental justice that laws must not be vague or arbitrary.

---

[73] [1976] Can. T.S. no. 47.

[74] *Canadian Foundation* at paras. 26–34.

[75] *Ibid.* at paras. 36–9.

[76] *Ibid.* at para. 40.

McLachlin C.J. also rejected the Foundation's contention that section 43 is overbroad because it fails to exclude from its ambit children against whom corrective force is ineffective, namely teenagers and children under two. This concern is addressed by Parliament's decision to confine section 43 to reasonable corrective force: force applied to children under two is not corrective, and therefore does not come within the provision; likewise, expert consensus indicates that force applied to teenagers creates a serious risk of psychological harm, and is therefore excluded from section 43 as unreasonable.[77]

Having dispensed with the section 7 challenge, McLachlin C.J. turned to sections 12 and 15(1). She held that section 12 (protection from cruel and unusual treatment or punishment) was not in issue here — force rising to the level of "cruel and unusual" is not permitted by section 43.[78] Section 15(1) (the Charter's equality guarantee) was engaged by section 43, but McLachlin C.J. found no infringement. Applying the equality analysis established in *Law v. Canada (Minister of Employment and Immigration)*,[79] she held that a reasonable person acting on behalf of a child, apprised of the harms of criminalization that section 43 avoids, the presence of other governmental initiatives to reduce the use of corporal punishment, and the fact that abusive and harmful conduct is still prohibited by the criminal law, would not conclude that the child's dignity has been offended in the manner contemplated by section 15(1). The chief justice noted that, without section 43 in place, Canada's broad assault law would criminalize force falling far short of what we think of as corporal punishment. Criminalizing such conduct would bring the blunt instrument of the criminal law into family and educational relationships in a potentially destructive way — a burden that in large part would be borne by children and outweigh any benefit derived from applying the criminal process.[80]

McLachlin C.J.'s reasons attracted the support of five other justices. Of the remaining three justices, only Arbour J. considered international law in her reasons at any length. Arbour J. held section 43 to be an infringement of Charter section 7 not justified by section 1. More specifically, she found section 43 to be unconstitutionally vague and, therefore, a deprivation of children's right to

[77] *Ibid.* at paras. 45–6.
[78] *Ibid.* at paras. 47–9.
[79] [1999] 1 S.C.R. 497.
[80] See *Canadian Foundation* at paras. 50–68.

security of the person not in accordance with the principles of fundamental justice. She criticized the majority for effectively rewriting section 43 in the guise of interpreting it. Rather than invoking the presumption of conformity with international law and other considerations as a basis for giving section 43 a constitutionally compliant interpretation, Arbour J. reviewed at length the conflicting (and sometimes shocking) case law surrounding the section and concluded that it speaks for itself: section 43 has failed to provide an adequate basis for legal debate. Arbour J. invoked observations of the UN Committee on the Rights of the Child to support this conclusion. After explaining the origins of the committee in the CRC, Arbour J. quoted its complaints that the UK's equivalent of section 43 (which speaks of "reasonable chastisement") lacked precision and was open to subjective and arbitrary interpretations. Arbour J. also noted that the committee has called on Canada to repeal section 43 and to prohibit all forms of violence against children, however light.[81]

In separate reasons, Binnie and Deschamps JJ. found section 43 to infringe the equality guarantees of Charter section 15(1). Binnie J. criticized the majority for allowing justificatory considerations, properly part of the section 1 analysis, to inform its interpretation of section 15(1). In his view, section 43 infringes Charter section 7 but is justifiable under section 1 in relation to parents, though not in relation to teachers. He agreed with the majority's conclusion on section 7. Deschamps J. found section 43's infringement of Charter section 15(1) unjustifiable under section 1. She also expressed broad agreement with Arbour J.'s analysis of the section 7 question.

Canadian Foundation is a remarkable case both as a matter of international human rights law and Canadian reception law. On the international level, the case is a considered opinion by the Supreme Court of Canada that states parties to the CRC (and indeed the ICCPR) are not obliged to prohibit all corporal punishment of children within their jurisdictions. As Arbour J. noted in dissent, this conclusion is in tension with repeated statements by the Committee on the Rights of the Child. This tension is unfortunate but does not necessarily indicate a violation by Canada of its CRC obligations. Though entitled to careful attention, the committee's views of the legal obligations of states parties under the CRC are not binding on the states parties. In spite of the committee's admonitions, McLachlin C.J.'s conclusion that the CRC does not require

---

[81] *Ibid.* at paras. 175–92, especially paras. 186–8.

Canada to prohibit all corporal punishment is certainly defensible and seemingly right.

On the domestic level, the majority's use of the presumption of conformity with international law reveals how powerful this interpretive tool — and the international law behind it — can be, in spite of our legal system's dualistic requirement that treaties be implemented by legislation before taking direct effect in Canadian law. International law — specifically, the prohibitions of child violence and cruel, inhuman, or degrading treatment or punishment in the CRC and the ICCPR — served to give section 43 part of its content and help save it from the allegation of unconstitutional vagueness. Indeed, if one agrees with Arbour J.'s critique, McLachlin C.J. invoked international law — along with the all-important findings of fact at trial — to read down and, therefore, spare a fundamentally unconstitutional provision. Constitutional lawyers may debate the proper interpretive approach to allegedly unconstitutional laws in such cases. That debate aside, McLachlin C.J.'s application of the presumption of conformity to section 43 should not be controversial. Indeed, it should be applauded. For the court not to read section 43 in light of the CRC and other relevant human rights treaties would be legal parochialism of a kind displayed so often in US courts but generally eschewed in the Canadian and Commonwealth traditions. Our courts are rightly concerned to avoid internationally unlawful interpretations of domestic laws whenever possible. In *Canadian Foundation,* the Supreme Court of Canada has seemingly done so. It has also displayed a heartening familiarity with UN human rights treaties and the work of their reporting bodies.

State immunity — torture claims — customary international law

Bouzari v. Islamic Republic of Iran (2004), 71 OR (3d) 675 (30 June 2004). Court of Appeal for Ontario. Leave to appeal to Supreme Court of Canada dismissed 27 January 2005.

Bouzari was abducted, imprisoned, and tortured by agents of the Islamic Republic of Iran between June 1993 and January 1994. He was an Iranian national at the time. He became a landed immigrant of Canada in 1998 and has since become a citizen. He brought an action against Iran in the Ontario Superior Court of Justice in 2000. Iran did not defend and was noted in default. It was therefore deemed under Ontario procedure to have admitted the truth of Bouzari's allegations. On a motion to determine whether the court had jurisdiction and could proceed to assess damages,[82] Swinton J. held the action to be barred by the State Immunity Act (SIA).[83] She found no exception in the SIA itself, nor any rule of the Charter or public international law, preserving the court's jurisdiction over the action.

Goudge J.A. for the court began by considering the matter from the conflict of laws perspective. Acknowledging that Iran was not an available forum for the case, and finding that no forum other than Ontario might entertain the action, Goudge J.A. found the *forum conveniens* test to be met. The question was whether Ontario had jurisdiction *simpliciter*. Bouzari argued that the status of torture as a international crime recognized as a peremptory norm of customary international law rendered his claim one of universal civil jurisdiction, limited only by the required presence of the plaintiff in the jurisdiction and continuing torture-related harm. The attorney-general for Canada (intervening) argued against this position, raising comity concerns. Goudge J.A. agreed with the attorney-general, finding

nothing in the SIA nor in any treaty by which Canada is bound that would require Ontario to apply a rule of universal jurisdiction, even modified as the appellant suggests, to a civil action for torture abroad by a foreign state. Nor does there appear to be any norm of customary international law to that effect. There is no general practice nor widespread legal acknowledgement by states that civil jurisdiction is to be accorded on this basis for an action based on foreign torture.[84]

Having rejected universal jurisdiction, Goudge J.A. went on to apply the real and substantial connection test. He noted that Bouzari had "absolutely no connection with Ontario" at the time of the torture, nor did Iran have any connection to the jurisdiction beyond the diplomatic.[85] Yet he was troubled by the prospect of Iran benefiting from its own failure to offer a forum for the case, leaving Bouzari with nowhere to sue if Ontario failed to assume jurisdiction.[86] Having made these observations, Goudge J.A. found it

---

[82] *Bouzari v. Islamic Republic of Iran,* [2002] O.T.C. 297. SIA section 3(2) requires courts to give effect to any immunity a foreign state enjoys under the act notwithstanding that the state has failed to take any step in the proceedings.

[83] R.S.C. 1985, c S-18.

[84] *Bouzari* at para. 28.

[85] *Ibid.* at para. 33.

[86] *Ibid.* at paras. 36–7.

unnecessary to determine how the real and substantial connection test would apply here, given the conclusion he had reached on the issue of state immunity.

Section 3(1) of the SIA provides that foreign states are immune from the jurisdiction of Canadian courts except as provided for in the act. Goudge J.A. quickly dispensed with the exceptions created by section 18 (criminal proceedings) and section 6 (torts occurring in Canada). This action was civil not criminal in nature and concerned torts inflicted on Bouzari in Iran. The learned judge then turned to the commercial activity exception recognized in customary international law and declared in SIA section 5: "A foreign state is not immune from the jurisdiction of a court in any proceedings that relate to any commercial activity of the foreign state." Bouzari claimed to fall within this exception because Iran's motives for mistreating him were commercial: the Iranian president's son was attempting to extort US $50 million from him in connection with a rich oil and gas field Bouzari was developing in southern Iran. Affirming Swinton J.'s finding, Goudge J.A. held that it was not enough that the mistreatment of Bouzari be related to commercial activity; the mistreatment must itself be commercial activity. Applying La Forest J.'s observations on the commercial activity exception in *Re Canada Labour Code*,[87] Goudge J.A. held that, even if the purpose of torturing Bouzari was to affect the commercial activity of Iran, this purpose was not enough to turns the acts of torture into commercial activity. Goudge J.A. added that the proceedings before the court were not related to the alleged purpose of the torture, but to the torture itself.[88] Goudge J.A. concluded by briefly rejecting an argument raised by the intervenor Canadian Lawyers for International Human Rights (CLAIHR) that the SIA has not displaced the common law of state immunity and that, under the common law, torture is not a government act and cannot therefore attract immunity. He found SIA section 3(1) to be a complete answer: "Except as provided by this Act, a foreign state is immune from the jurisdiction of any court in Canada / Sauf exceptions prévues dans la présente loi, l'État étranger bénéficie de l'immunité de juridiction devant tout tribunal au Canada."

Bouzari also sought to rely on public international law and, more particularly, international human rights law. He argued that the SIA must be read in conformity with treaties binding on Canada

[87] [1992] 2 S.C.R. 50.

[88] *Bouzari* at paras. 48-54.

and customary international law. He argued that Canada's international obligations require an exception to state immunity in torture cases.

In response, Goudge J.A. began with a brief review of "the interplay between Canada's obligations at public international law and its domestic legislation."[89] He affirmed that courts should, "so far as possible," interpret domestic legislation consistently with Canadian treaty obligations.[90] He observed that the same presumption applies in respect of rules of customary international law, and "even more so where the obligation is a peremptory norm of customary international law, or jus cogens." He noted that the attorney-general acknowledged that customary international law is directly incorporated into Canadian domestic law unless explicitly ousted by contrary legislation.[91] Finally, he noted that it is "open to Canada to legislate contrary to" its international obligations, saying, "[s]uch legislation would determine Canada's domestic law although it would put Canada in breach of its international obligations."[92] This latter rule meant that, even if Canada were required by international law to permit a civil remedy for torture abroad by a foreign state, it has declined to do so by according states complete immunity except as provided by the SIA: "Canada has clearly legislated so as not to create this exception to state immunity whether it has an international law obligation to do so or not."

In spite of this finding, Goudge J.A. went on to consider whether Canada has any such obligation at international law. Swinton J. had done the same in the court below, relying in part on the evidence of two professors of international law, Ed Morgan and Christopher Greenwood. Swinton J. had preferred the evidence of Greenwood. Goudge J.A. agreed, saying:

> While the motion judge's acceptance of Professor Greenwood's opinion over that of Professor Morgan is not a finding of fact by a trial judge, it is a finding based on the evidence she heard and is therefore owed a certain deference in this court. I would depart from it only if there were good reason to do so and, having examined the transcript, I can find none.

Goudge J.A. then turned to Canada's obligations under human rights treaties and customary international law. Reviewing the 1984

---

[89] *Ibid.* at para. 63.

[90] *Ibid.* at para. 64.

[91] *Ibid.* at para. 65.

[92] *Ibid.* at para. 66.

Convention against Torture (CAT),[93] he found no obligation on Canada to provide a civil right of redress for torture committed by foreign states outside Canada. He noted that Swinton J. had "properly accepted expert evidence" from Greenwood on the meaning of the treaty.[94] Swinton J. also looked to state practice concerning the CAT (particularly Article 14), as provided for in Article 31(3)(b) of the 1969 Vienna Convention of the Law of Treaties.[95] Goudge J.A. found "ample evidence to sustain" Swinton J.'s conclusion that no state interprets CAT Article 14 to require it to take civil jurisdiction over a foreign state for acts committed outside the forum state.[96] Goudge J.A. also briefly considered Article 14(1) of the 1966 International Covenant on Civil and Political Rights[97] (entitlement to a fair hearing). Again he affirmed Swinton J.'s reliance on the evidence of Greenwood that this provision "has not been interpreted to require a state to provide access to its courts for sovereign acts committed outside its jurisdiction" and his opinion that "this provision carries no such obligation." Goudge J.A. said Swinton J.'s finding on this point "is due deference" but added his view that "it is the right conclusion."[98]

Having found no treaty-based obligation on Canada to provide a forum for Bouzari's claim, Goudge J.A. looked to customary international law. Bouzari argued that this obligation was not only customary but had attained *jus cogens* status. Goudge J.A. defined *jus cogens* norms as "a higher form of customary law ... from which no derogation is permitted."[99] He noted that Swinton J. held the prohibition of torture to be *jus cogens*, and that no one, including the attorney-general of Canada, disputed that finding before the court of appeal.[100] The question, however, was whether this prohibition extended to requiring states to make exceptions to state immunity

---

[93] [1987] Can. T.S. no. 36.

[94] *Bouzari* at paras. 69–75.

[95] [1980] Can. T.S. no. 37.

[96] *Bouzari* at paras. 77–9.

[97] [1976] Can. T.S. no. 47.

[98] *Bouzari* at para. 83.

[99] *Ibid.* at para. 86.

[100] It is remarkable (and heartening) that the Court of Appeal, the court below, and all participants in the appeal seem to disregard the Supreme Court of Canada's bewildering conclusion in *Suresh v. Canada (Minister of Citizenship and Immigration)*, [2002] 1 SCR 3 at para. 65, that the prohibition on torture is only an "emerging" peremptory norm that "cannot easily be derogated from."

for torture claims. Goudge J.A. found that it did not, saying "the extent of the prohibition against torture as a rule of jus cogens is determined not by any particular view of what is required if it is to be meaningful, but rather by the widespread and consistent practice of states."[101] State practice did not support the existence of any customary international obligation to provide a civil remedy for victims of foreign state torture. Goudge J.A. allowed that international law may, in future, develop in the direction Bouzari argued for, but declared that such a change is "not ... to be effected by a domestic court adding an exception to the SIA that is not there, or seeing a widespread state practice that does not exist today."[102]

Finally, Goudge J.A. rejected Bouzari's claim that the grant of state immunity in SIA section 3 violates section 7 of the Charter by denying Bouzari his right to security of the person. There was no sufficient causal connection between the harm suffered by Bouzari and any act of Canada. Nor could it be said, on the record before the court, that the SIA itself caused the kind of harm necessary to trigger section 7.[103]

The court of appeal's judgment reveals an admirable fluency in public international law and its reception in Canada. Goudge J.A.'s analysis of customary international law is especially welcome for he takes care to explain the elements of custom, its relationship to *jus cogens*, and its direct incorporation into Canadian common law. While these points will seem elementary to the international lawyer, they have so frequently been misstated in Canadian judgments, from the Supreme Court of Canada downwards, that their correct enunciation in *Bouzari* is something of a landmark.

The judgment is not beyond criticism, however. The court's treatment of the evidence of Greenwood and Morgan is confusing. In fairness to the court of appeal, the difficulties began with the motions judge, who admitted expert testimony not only on state practice (a question of fact to which expert evidence ought to be admissible) but also on the meaning of treaties (a question of law that ought to be decided by the judge alone). Goudge J.A. compounded the problem by failing to enunciate a clear approach to such evidence: did he defer to it as a finding of fact or agree with its substance as a finding of law? In principle, the opinions of experts on questions of law — including public international law — ought

101 *Bouzari* at para. 90.

102 *Ibid.* at para. 95.

103 *Ibid.* at paras. 99–101.

to be inadmissible or, if admitted, given no deference.[104] One might also question Goudge J.A.'s rather summary rejection of CLAIHR's argument. Though the reasons do not reveal CLAIHR's full submission, the gist of it appears to have been that the SIA is no obstacle to the continuing incorporation of new developments in customary international law by Canadian common law. The SIA is a sort of legislative snapshot of the customary/common law position as it stood at the time.[105] The act was intended to assure Canadian conformity with recent (at the time) developments in the customary law of state immunity. It was not intended to inhibit the incorporation of further customary developments into Canadian common law, and should therefore not be interpreted to exclude such developments, if they can be proved. This argument has greater merit than Goudge J.A. acknowledged, though his ultimate finding that no such customary development had occurred renders this point, for the time being at least, academic.

Copyright — Internet — unratified treaties

- *Society of Composers, Authors and Music Publishers of Canada v. Canadian Association of Internet Providers* 2004 SCC 45, [2004] 2 SCR 427 (30 June 2004). Supreme Court of Canada.

The Society of Composers, Authors and Music Publishers of Canada (SOCAN) is a collective society recognized under the Copyright Act[106] as the administrator of copyright for its Canadian members and foreign affiliates. In 1995, SOCAN applied to the Copyright Board for approval of Tariff 22, which would allow it to collect royalties from Internet service providers located in Canada (ISPs) on the ground that such ISPs infringe copyright owners' exclusive rights to communicate and authorize the communication of their works to the public by telecommunication. The Copyright Board declined to approve Tariff 22, finding that the normal activities of ISPs do not attract liability under the Copyright Act because section 2.4(1)(b) protects intermediaries from copyright liability. The board also found that Internet communications occur in Canada only if they originate from a server in Canada.

---

[104] See *Lord Advocate's Reference No. 1 of 2000* 2001 S.L.T. 507; and G. van Ert, "The Admissibility of International Legal Evidence" (2005) 84 Can. Bar Rev. 31.

[105] See *Re Canada Labour Code*, [1992] 2 S.C.R. 50 at 73–4 per La Forest J.

[106] R.S.C. 1985, c. C-42 as amended.

The majority of the Federal Court of Appeal allowed SOCAN's application for judicial review on this point. They found that a communication (and therefore a royalty) may arise in respect of any telecommunication that has a real and substantial connection with Canada. The majority also found that ISPs who employ caches to enhance the speed of Internet transmissions may not claim the protection of section 2.4(1)(b).

The Canadian Association of Internet Providers and other ISPs appealed to the Supreme Court of Canada. Binnie J. for the majority of the court allowed the appeal in part. In doing so, the court made significant remarks on extraterritoriality and the interpretation of the Copyright Act in light of international copyright law. These aspects of the judgment are the focus of this note.

Binnie J. agreed with the Court of Appeal that the applicable standard of review of the Board's decision was correctness. He also observed that the board's view of the underlying facts was not in dispute.[107] The controversy centred on the purely legal questions of the proper application and scope of the Copyright Act.

Copyright has long been a field of international cooperation and treaty-making. Canada's Copyright Act serves to implement multilateral treaties dating from as early as 1886.[108] The advent of the Internet has raised new copyright challenges to which the World Intellectual Property Organization (WIPO) has responded (with debatable success) with the 1996 WIPO Copyright Treaty[109] and the 1996 WIPO Performances and Phonograms Treaty.[110] Canada signed both of these treaties in 1997 but has yet to ratify them or to implement them in Canadian law. While some states have now legislated to address Internet-specific copyright issues (in implementation of the WIPO treaties or otherwise), Canada is still considering the needed legislation.[111] "In the meantime," Binnie J. observed, "the

---

107   See *SOCAN v. CAIP* at paras. 48–50.

108   *Ibid.* at para. 43.

109   WIPO Doc. CRNR/DC/94.

110   WIPO Doc. CRNR/DC/95.

111   See, for example, Industry Canada, *Supporting Culture and Innovation: Report on the Provisions and Operation of the Copyright Act*, October 2002, available at <http://strategis.ic.gc.ca/epic/internet/incrp-prda.nsf/en/rp00863e.html> at ch. 3B:

> Canada signed both WIPO treaties in 1997 but has yet to ratify them. The Government of Canada is committed to bringing the Copyright Act in conformity with the WCT and WPPT once the issues involved are thoroughly analyzed and appropriately consulted upon. Ultimately, the purpose of ratification is to ensure that Canadian rights holders will benefit from copyright protection recognized in all treaty countries. Canada's obligations under these treaties could not be met without amending the Copyright Act.

courts must struggle to transpose a *Copyright Act* designed to implement the *Berne Convention* ... to the information age, and to technologies undreamt of by those early legislators."[112]

Faced with this difficult task, Binnie J. began from first principles. He noted that while Parliament enjoys legislative competence to enact extraterritorial laws, the courts presume that it does not intend to do so. In the words of La Forest J., "chaotic situations would often result if the principle of territorial jurisdiction were not, at least, generally, respected."[113] Binnie J. added that copyright law itself "respects the territorial principle, reflecting the implementation of a 'web of interlinking international treaties' based on the principle of national treatment."[114] This much is uncontroversial. The difficulty lies in applying these principles to Internet communications.

To do so, Binnie J. (like the Court of Appeal) resorted to the "real and substantial connection" test:

The applicability of our Copyright Act to communications that have international participants will depend on whether there is a sufficient connection between this country and the communication in question for Canada to apply its law consistent with the "principles of order and fairness ... that ensure security of [cross-border] transactions with justice."[115]

From the outset, the real and substantial connection test has been viewed as an appropriate way to "prevent overreaching ... and [to restrict] the exercise of jurisdiction over extraterritorial and transnational transactions." The test reflects the underlying reality of "the territorial limits of law under the international legal order" and respect for the legitimate actions of other states inherent in the principle of international comity ... A real and substantial connection to Canada is sufficient to support the application of our Copyright Act to international Internet transmissions in a way that will accord with international comity and be consistent with the objectives of order and fairness.

In terms of the Internet, relevant connecting factors would include the situs of the content provider, the host server, the intermediaries and the end user. The weight to be given to any particular factor will vary with the circumstances and the nature of the dispute.[116]

---

[112] *SOCAN v. CAIP* at para. 43.

[113] *Ibid.* at para. 54, quoting *Tolofson v. Jensen*, [1994] 3 S.C.R. 1022 at 1051. See also para. 55.

[114] *SOCAN v. CAIP* at para. 56.

[115] *Ibid.* at para. 57.

[116] *Ibid.* at paras. 60–1.

In these passages, Binnie J. depicted the real and substantial connection test as the means of assuring the application of Canadian
law in ways consistent with international comity and the territoriality principle.

Binnie J. went on to describe the acceptance of jurisdiction in
situations where Canada is either the country of transmission or
the country of reception as "consistent with international copyright
practice."[117] He began by citing and quoting from European Commission decisions and directives on electronic commerce. He also
quoted Article 8 of the 1996 WIPO Copyright Treaty, noting first
that Canada is a signatory but not yet a party to it.[118] Next, Binnie J.
surveyed American, Australian, and French laws and jurisprudence,
which he described as confirming that *"either* the country of transmission *or* the country of reception may take jurisdiction over a
'communication' linked to its territory, although whether it chooses
to do so is a matter of legislative or judicial policy."[119] Accordingly,
Binnie J. held that Canada may exercise copyright jurisdiction in
respect of transmissions originating either in Canada or abroad, as
determined by the application of the real and substantial connection test to the circumstances of individual cases. The difficulty with
this conclusion, Binnie J. admitted, is that it "raises the spectre of
imposition of copyright duties on a single telecommunication in
both the state of transmission and the state of reception." But, "as
with other fields of overlapping liability (taxation for example),
the answer lies in the making of international or bilateral agreements, not in national courts straining to find some jurisdictional
infirmity in either State."[120]

Having established this framework for deciding the question,
Binnie J. turned to the facts of the appeal. The ISPs contended
that any liability they might otherwise have to SOCAN was barred
by section 2.4(1)(b) of the Copyright Act. They also denied
SOCAN's allegation that they had authorized communications
contrary to section 3(1). Binnie J. agreed with the ISPs on both

---

117 *Ibid.* at para. 63.

118 Article 8 reads in part:

> [A]uthors of literary and artistic works shall enjoy the exclusive right of authoriz-
> ing any communication to the public of their works, by wire or wireless means,
> including the making available to the public of their works in such a way that
> members of the public may access these works from a place and at a time individu-
> ally chosen by them.

119 *SOCAN v. CAIP* at para. 68.

120 *Ibid.* at para. 78.

points. By section 2.4(1)(b), Parliament has deemed intermediaries to telecommunications not to communicate copyrighted works to the public at all.[121] He described this provision as "not a loophole but an important element in the balance struck by the statutory copyright scheme."[122] So long as an Internet intermediary does not itself engage in acts that relate to the content of the communication but confines itself to providing a conduit for information communicated by others, it will enjoy the protection of section 2.4(1)(b).[123] Binnie J. observed that this interpretation of the provision is consistent with Article 8 of the 1996 WIPO Copyright Treaty and quoted from the agreed statements that accompany that treaty.[124] He did not, however, invoke the presumption of conformity with international law, perhaps because Canada is not yet a party to the treaty. Binnie J. also held that a content provider may not immunize itself from copyright liability simply by employing a host server located outside of the country[125] and that the use of caches by ISPs does not, without more, exclude them from the protection of section 2.4(1)(b).[126] Finally, Binnie J. rejected SOCAN's argument that the ISPs were guilty of authorizing copyright infringements, contrary to section 3(1) of the Copyright Act, simply because they knew that copyright material was placed on their facilities and would be accessed by end users. An intermediary must sanction, approve, or countenance more than the mere use of its equipment to attract liability under section 3(1).[127]

LeBel J. dissented in part. He would have affirmed the board's approach whereby an Internet communication occurs in Canada when it originates from a server located in Canada. Like Binnie J., LeBel J. recognized Parliament's competence to legislate extraterritorially. But he emphasized the "common law presumption" against such legislation, saying that it "flows from the principle of territoriality, a tenet of international law." He observed,

Neither s. 3(1)(f), nor any related provision of the Act expressly states that it applies beyond Canada's territorial limits. Moreover, nothing in the

---

[121] *Ibid.* at para. 87.
[122] *Ibid.* at para. 89.
[123] *Ibid.* at para. 92.
[124] *Ibid.* at para. 97.
[125] *Ibid.* at paras. 104–12.
[126] *Ibid.* at para. 113–19.
[127] *Ibid.* at paras. 120–8.

Act impliedly gives s. 3(1)(f) extraterritorial effect, particularly given the principle of territoriality of copyright law.[128]

Given that Parliament did not intend the act to have effect outside Canada, LeBel J. would have affirmed the board's view that a communication occurs within Canada where it originates from a host server located in Canada. He would not have applied the real and substantial connection test, which he described as applicable only to the courts and "not a principle of legislative jurisdiction."[129] LeBel J. emphasized the territorial nature of copyright law, citing the Berne Convention, the 1994 Agreement on Trade-Related Aspects of Intellectual Property Rights,[130] and the two WIPO treaties. He disagreed with the board's view that it should not interpret the Copyright Act in light of the WIPO Copyright Treaty 1996:

> Although Canada has not ratified the treaty, this does not mean that it should not be considered as an aid in interpreting the Act ... The purpose of art. 8 of the WCT is to harmonize domestic copyright laws in the party States with respect to the right of communication of copyrighted works. We should not ignore that fact.[131]

> As L'Heureux-Dubé, Gonthier, and Bastarache JJ. recently held, even though international norms are generally not binding without domestic implementation, they are relevant in interpreting domestic legislation: see *R. v. Sharpe*, [2001] 1 S.C.R. 45, 2001 SCC 2, at para. 175. Parliament is presumed not to legislate in breach of a treaty, the comity of nations and the principles of international law. This rule of construction is well established: see *Daniels v. White*, [1968] S.C.R. 517, at p. 541. Although the Copyright Act has not yet been amended to reflect the signing of the WCT, I believe this cannon of interpretation is equally applicable to the case at bar.

In LeBel J.'s view, the more internationally compliant interpretation of the act was the board's host server test, for the real and substantial connection test "may reach out and grasp content providers located in Bangalore who post content on a server in Hong Kong based only on the fact that the copyrighted work is retrieved by end users in Canada." He added that Binnie J.'s assertion that his approach "accords with national and international copyright

---

[128] *Ibid.* at para. 144.

[129] *Ibid.* at para. 147.

[130] 1869 U.N.T.S. 299.

[131] *SOCAN v. CAIP* at para. 149.

practice overstates the case. A review of various national laws demonstrates precious little harmonization in law or practice."[132]

This appeal placed the Supreme Court of Canada in a difficult position. The court was asked to resolve, as a question of statutory interpretation, an issue that the federal government considers to be a matter for amending legislation.[133] The court's predicament is highlighted by Binnie J.'s unusual (but entirely appropriate) reference to the need for an international, treaty-based solution to the problem of overlapping copyright liability. In the absence of such international agreement, one can hardly criticize the differing solutions proposed by Binnie and LeBel JJ. With the support of the international community, it seems that either approach could be made to work.

One matter that deserved more consideration from the court is the propriety of resorting to a signed but unratified treaty for the purposes of statutory interpretation. The interpretive presumption that statutes conform with international law is well established, but to what extent does it apply to a treaty Canada has signed but not yet ratified? The board felt it could have no regard to the 1996 WIPO Copyright Treaty while it remained non-binding on Canada as a matter of international law. LeBel J. disagreed, saying the court could nevertheless consider it "as an aid in interpreting the Act" and even as presumptively conformed to by the Copyright Act. Binnie J. also had regard to the treaty, but it is unclear what weight he gave to it as a tool of statutory interpretation. Though this problem does not arise often, it is an interesting one and was squarely before the court. It is regrettable that Binnie J. did not give his view on LeBel J.'s opinion that a signed but unratified — and therefore non-binding — treaty should be the subject of the presumption of conformity. At first glance, it is questionable that the presumption should ever apply in respect of a non-binding instrument. I have suggested elsewhere, however, that this result may be warranted in cases where failure to apply the presumption would defeat the object and purpose of the treaty contrary to the state's obligations under Article 18(b) of the Vienna Convention on the Law of Treaties 1969.[134] Whether that view is

---

[132] *Ibid.* at para. 152.

[133] It is regrettable that the attorney-general for Canada did not intervene to present the government's views on the questions before the court, particularly that of the proper interpretive weight to be given to a signed but unratified treaty.

[134] [1980] Can. T.S. no. 37. See M. Freeman and G. van Ert, *International Human Rights Law* (Toronto: Irwin Law, 2004) at 157.

right or wrong, a closer examination of the question from the court would have been welcome.

Finally, a stylistic point. In this judgment as in many others,[135] the court's legal editors list the treaties referred to in the reasons under the heading "Statutes and Regulations Cited." This is awkward. A treaty is neither a statute nor a regulation. The editors should adopt a new heading under which to list treaties as well as those non-binding international instruments occasionally referred to by the court. The heading "Treaties and Other International Instruments" would suffice.

135 For example, *Singh v. Minister of Immigration and Employment*, [1985] 1 S.C.R. 177; *Re Ng Extradition*, [1991] 2 S.C.R. 858; *Re Secession of Quebec*, [1998] 2 S.C.R. 217; *Baker v. Canada (Minister of Citizenship and Immigration)*, [1999] 2 S.C.R. 817; *USA v. Burns*, [2001] S.C.R. 283; and *Canadian Foundation for Children, Youth and the Law v. Canada (Attorney General)*, [2004] 1 S.C.R. 76, and so on.

Canadian Cases in Private International Law in 2003–4 / Jurisprudence canadienne en matière de droit international privé en 2003–4

compiled by / préparé par

JOOST BLOM

M.J. Jones Inc. v. Kingsway General Ins. Co. (2004), 242 D.L.R. (4th) 139, 72 O.R. (3d) 68 (Ontario Court of Appeal)

Jones, a company resident in Ontario, said it faced bankruptcy as the result of the enforcement against it in Ontario of a judgment from Michigan. The judgment creditor had obtained summary judgment in Ontario on its foreign judgment, and Jones's application for a stay of execution of the summary judgment had failed both at first instance and on appeal, although execution had not yet taken place. While the litigation about the foreign judgment was under way, Jones brought an action in Ontario against its insurer and its insurance broker, both resident in Ontario, and its Michigan lawyer and his law firm. The Michigan defendants did not attorn to the court's jurisdiction and sought to have the action against them dismissed on the ground of lack of jurisdiction *simpliciter* — the minimum connection with the province that is constitutionally required in order for the province's courts to exercise jurisdiction — as well as *forum non conveniens*. Their challenges to the court's jurisdiction were dismissed by the motions judge and the Court of Appeal, and they were now seeking leave to appeal to the Supreme Court of Canada on the jurisdiction *simpliciter* question. In the present proceeding, they applied to the Court of Appeal for a stay

Joost Blom is in the Faculty of Law at the University of British Columbia.

of the Ontario action against them, pending the outcome of their application for leave to the Supreme Court of Canada.

In granting the stay, the court noted first that the issue on which leave to appeal was being sought was a serious one because the test for jurisdiction *simpliciter* applied by the Ontario courts, including in this case, was different from that used by the courts in British Columbia. Second, the Michigan defendants might suffer irreparable harm if the stay were denied, because they would then be forced to defend the action, which would arguably be an attornment to the Ontario court's jurisdiction so as to preclude any further argument on the jurisdictional issues. Their application for leave to appeal on the jurisdictional issues would then be moot. The third aspect was the balance of convenience. Jones argued that it would be prejudiced by the delay in pursuing its action, because that would worsen its financial prospects and increase the chances of execution on the summary judgment enforcing the Michigan judgment. The court held that this argument was not entitled to great weight, given that Jones had already tried to get a stay of execution of the summary judgment based on its dire financial condition, and the courts had not been persuaded. The present proceeding should not operate as an indirect appeal of that decision, and in any event it was unclear that refusal of a stay would have the desired result of staying the hand of the judgment creditor. The balance of convenience therefore favoured staying Jones's action against all parties. There was a risk of irreparable harm to the Michigan defendants, and the claims against them were inextricably connected to those against the Ontario defendants.

Note. The above decision was given on 10 August 2004. The Michigan defendants obtained leave to appeal but discontinued the appeal on 7 December 2004, [2004] 3 S.C.R. viii. The British Columbia and Ontario approaches to jurisdiction *simpliciter* are not clearly inconsistent, but to this point they certainly have differed in emphasis. In Ontario, the courts are directed by *Muscutt v. Courcelles* (2002), 213 D.L.R. (4th) 577 (Ont. C.A.) (noted in "Canadian Cases in Private International Law 2001–2" (2002) 40 Can. Y.B. Int'l L. 583), to decide on jurisdiction *simpliciter* according to eight criteria, most of which are evaluative rather than factual. Unfairness to the defendant if jurisdiction is assumed, unfairness to the plaintiff if jurisdiction is not assumed, and avoiding a multiplicity of proceedings are three of the evaluative ones. (For an elaborate example of the *Muscutt* factors in operation, see *Grammercy Ltd. v.*

Dynamic Tire Corp., noted immediately below.) In British Columbia, the Court of Appeal has tended simply to ask whether there is a minimum factual connection, with evaluative factors being given much less of a role: see *Cook v. Parcel, Mauro, Hultin & Spaanstra, P.C.* (1997), 143 D.L.R. (4th) 213, *Marren v. Echo Bay Mines Ltd.* (2003), 226 D.L.R. (4th) 622, 2003 BCCA 398 (noted in "Canadian Cases in Private International Law 2002–3" (2003) 41 Can. Y.B. Int'l L. 570), and *Roth v. Interlock Services Inc.* (see below in this note). The two lines of authority draw on, respectively, the "order and fairness" and "real and substantial connection" sides of the concept of jurisdiction *simpliciter* as developed by the Supreme Court of Canada in *Morguard Investments Ltd. v. De Savoye*, [1990] 3 S.C.R. 1077, 76 D.L.R. (4th) 256, and *Spar Aerospace Ltd. v. American Mobile Satellite Corp.*, [2002] 4 S.C.R. 205, 220 D.L.R. (4th) 54, 2002 SCC 78 (noted in "Canadian Cases in Private International Law 2002–3" (2003) 41 Can. Y.B. Int'l L. 592).

In *Roth v. Interlock Services Inc.* (2004), 33 B.C.L.R. (4th) 60, 2004 BCCA 407, litigation in British Columbia involved a resident of the province suing an American corporation in connection with the latter's acquisition of the plaintiff's Nevada company, which did business over the Internet. The court, reversing the chambers judge, found that jurisdiction *simpliciter* was established by various connections to the province, including the plaintiff's residence and the facts that the Internet company did business in the province and certain agreements had been drawn up and signed there. The chambers judge had, however, rightly declined jurisdiction on the ground that either Nevada or New York was a more appropriate forum.

Challenges to jurisdiction *simpliciter* seldom succeed, given the extremely flexible nature of the test. One situation in which they have succeeded is where the plaintiff suffered in the province the after-effects of a physical injury that took place elsewhere. That fact alone has been held an insufficient connection with the province. *Markandu (Litigation Guardian of) v. Benaroch* (2004), 242 D.L.R. (4th) 101 (Ont. C.A.), found there was no jurisdiction *simpliciter* in a medical malpractice action where the infant plaintiff had moved to Ontario after the injury. *Hirsi v. Swift Transportation Co.* (2004), 1 C.P.C. (6th) 135 (Ont. S.C.J.), reached the same conclusion where an Ontario-resident trucker sued his Arizona-based employer and its Connecticut insurer for injuries he suffered in a road accident in Missouri.

Grammercy Ltd. v. Dynamic Tire Corp. (2004), 69 O.R. (3d) 210, 45
C.P.C. (5th) 268, additional reasons (2004), 71 O.R. (3d) 191
(Ontario Superior Court of Justice)

Grammercy, a United Kingdom corporation, entered into a joint
venture agreement (JVA) with Fei Chi, incorporated in the People's
Republic of China (PRC), to manufacture tires in China. A joint
venture company (JV Co.) was incorporated in the PRC for that
purpose. The JVA provided "[t]he making of this contract, its validation, interpretation, execution, amendments and termination,
and any disputes or arbitration arising out of this contract and its
appendices, shall be bound by the jurisdiction of Chinese law." The
relationship between the two joint venturers broke down.
Grammercy brought an action in Ontario against Fei Chi, which
did no business and had no presence in Ontario, as well as Dynamic, an Ontario corporation; its president, Sherkin, an Ontario
resident; and Fendley, an Ontario businessman resident in the PRC
but also often in Ontario. Fei Chi and Fendley were served *ex juris.*
Fei Chi was said to have broken the JVA. Dynamic, Sherkin, and
Fendley were sued for intentional interference with Grammercy's
economic interests under the JVA and conspiracy to deprive it of
its rights under that contract. A claim for breach of fiduciary duty
was made against Fendley, he being a former member of
Grammercy's senior management. Sherkin, Dynamic, and Fendley
were said to have agreed in Ontario, and begun there to implement their agreement, to work with Fei Chi to distribute JV Co.'s
tire products through Dynamic, depriving Grammercy of its rights
under the JVA. All the defendants made motions for orders setting
aside service or staying the proceedings on the ground that the
court had no jurisdiction over the claim against them or should
decline it on the ground of *forum non conveniens.* Each of them also
sought a stay of the action pursuant to section 8 of the International Commercial Arbitration Act, R.S.O. 1990, c. I.9, based on
the arbitration clause in the JVA.

Before these motions were argued, Fei Chi commenced an action for breach of the JVA against Grammercy in the PRC and the
Ontario judge reserved judgment on the motions until the PRC
court's decision came down. Grammercy did not defend the PRC
action. The PRC court held that Fei Chi had fulfilled its investment
obligations under the JVA but Grammercy had broken the contract by failing to make its technical capital contribution, preventing JV Co. from going into normal operation. Fei Chi was awarded

damages against Grammercy in the limited amount provided by the JVA.

The Ontario court held that it had jurisdiction and that the action should proceed against all the defendants. In respect of each of them the court canvassed the eight factors laid down for determining jurisdiction *simpliciter* in *Muscutt v. Courcelles* (2002), 213 D.L.R. (4th) 577 (Ont. C.A.) (noted in "Canadian Cases in Private International Law 2001–2" (2002) 40 Can. Y.B. Int'l L. 583). Fendley had a real and substantial personal connection to Ontario and the claims against him were based in part on torts he allegedly committed in the province. The court clearly had jurisdiction over the claims against Dynamic and Sherkin because they were served in Ontario and some of their impugned acts took place there. Ontario was also *forum conveniens* for the claims against those three defendants. Key witnesses and evidence were in both Ontario and the PRC, and, depending on the facts, the law of Ontario might apply to the claims. Declining jurisdiction in favour of the PRC would mean a signficant loss of a legitimate juridical advantage to Grammercy, in that its causes of action against those three parties were not known in PRC law but did exist in Ontario.

As for Fei Chi, the judgment it obtained in the PRC was entitled to recognition in Ontario. The PRC was a natural forum for the breach of contract action against Grammercy. The PRC court had conclusively found that Grammercy breached the JVA but it had not determined whether Fei Chi breached the JVA, the claim now being advanced by Grammercy. Nothing in the Chinese judgment therefore precluded Grammercy from asserting the claims it made in the Ontario action. As for the arbitration agreement, based upon expert testimony on Chinese law the clause in the JVA, being optional, was void and the PRC court had implicitly so held. Fei Chi could therefore not take the position now that the clause was binding. The clause did not, in any event, bind the other defendants because they were not parties to the JVA.

The court had jurisdiction *simpliciter* over the claims against Fei Chi. If the Ontario action were solely between Grammercy and Fei Chi, there would be no rational basis for Ontario assuming jurisdiction over those claims. There was no real and substantial connection between Ontario and Fei Chi as such, but a real and substantial connection did exist with the claims made against Fei Chi. The allegations were that the other three defendants had, by agreement with Fei Chi, engaged in conspiracy and intentional interference with economic interests and done so by means of acts partly carried out in Ontario. Based on the alleged facts, the acts done in Ontario could be considered as done on behalf of Fei Chi. Jurisdiction *simpliciter* was also supported by two further *Muscutt* factors, namely, the desirability of avoiding multiplicity of proceedings, and the likelihood that an Ontario court would recognize a foreign judgment granted on the same jurisdictional basis. It was admittedly unlikely that an Ontario judgment against Fei Chi would be rcognized in the PRC (another *Muscutt* factor), but on balance jurisdiction *simpliciter* was established. On the *forum conveniens* question relating to Fei Chi, looking at all claims in the case, geographical factors suggested that a PRC court had a somewhat stronger claim to being the natural forum. However, the scales were tipped in favour of Ontario by the very substantial loss of legitimate juridical advantage that Grammercy would suffer if jurisdiction were declined. Except for breach of contract, the causes of action advanced by it against Fei Chi were unknown to PRC law, and if it could not sue in Ontario it would lose the right to have those claims heard on their merits.

Note. This was a case in which jurisdiction *simpliciter* over the claims against party A, which by themselves were not strongly connected with the province, was found on the basis of their connection with claims against party B, over which the court more clearly had jurisdiction. Another such case was *JLA & Associates Inc. v. Kenny* (2003), 41 C.P.C. (5th) 151, 2003 BCSC 1670, in which a British Columbia solicitor, who was sued by a Texas corporation for the return of funds, joined as third parties the individual shareholders of the plaintiff company, who were resident in the United States, claiming that they had tortiously concealed from him the illegal scheme for which the funds were to be used. Jurisdiction *simpliciter* in respect of the third party claims was based on their connection to the main action.

Bouzari v. Islamic Republic of Iran (2004), 243 D.L.R. (4th) 406, 71 O.R. 675 (Ontario Court of Appeal), leave to appeal to S.C.C. refused, 27 January 2005

The plaintiff immigrated to Canada from Iran in 1998 and subsequently became a Canadian citizen. He brought the present action against the government of Iran, claiming damages for torture that he had allegedly suffered at the hands of agents of the Iranian government in 1993–94. The state of Iran obtained summary judgment from the motions judge. The Ontario Court of Appeal affirmed the dismissal of the plaintiff's claim on the basis that Iran was entitled to immunity under the State Immunity Act, R.S.C. 1985, c. S-18. One of the other issues that was argued was whether the Ontario court had a "real and substantial connection" with the case so as to have jurisdiction *simpliciter.* The defendant pointed to the lack of any connection between the facts of the case and the province, other than the current residence there of the plaintiff. The plaintiff contended that since an Iranian forum was closed to him, the "real and substantial connection" with the province should not be interpreted so as to deprive him of an Ontario forum as well. The Court of Appeal considered the problem at some length. It noted that *Muscutt v. Courcelles* (2002), 213 D.L.R. (4th) 577 (Ont. C.A.) (noted in "Canadian Cases in Private International Law 2001– 2" (2002) 40 Can. Y.B. Int'l L. 583), held that the concept of the "real and substantial connection" was extremely flexible in order to be adaptable to widely different factual situations. It was meant to be guided ultimately by the requirements of order and fairness, not a mechanical counting of connections with the proposed forum. If this were the usual case of a foreign defendant sued here for a foreign tort, the application of the eight factors outlined in *Muscutt* would probably yield the conclusion that there was no real and substantial connection with Ontario. It was true that the connection of the case with Ontario was very tenuous, but militating in favour of jurisdiction was the fact that it was an action based on an alleged violation of both international human rights and peremptory norms of public international law, and the state where it happened, otherwise the logical forum, had excluded itself by being the perpetrator. If Ontario refused jurisdiction, the plaintiff would be left with no other place to sue. Given that he was now connected to Ontario by his citizenship, the requirement of fairness that underpins the real and substantial connection test would seem to be of elevated importance if the alternative was that he could not bring the action anywhere. Thus, the application of the "real and substantial connection" test in these circumstances was not easy, but given its conclusion on the state immunity issue the court did not need to determine the question finally.

Note. A similar situation arose in *Samson v. Hooks Industrial Inc.* (2003), 42 C.P.C. (5th) 299 (Ont. S.C.J.), in which an export-import broker resident in Ontario sued a Texas-based client in Ontario, claiming payment of commissions on equipment sales that the American firm had made, via a Québec company, to Iraq as a result of his efforts. He argued that he could not bring the action in the United States because, in the aftermath of the World Trade Center attacks on 11 September 2001, he might well be arrested at the border on account of his Iraqi birth. The Ontario court gave considerable weight to this factor in finding that jurisdiction *simpliciter* was established and the court was *forum conveniens*.

Parties outside the territory of the province or Canada — rules for taking jurisdiction

Note. In the common law provinces, the rules for taking jurisdiction over persons outside the province are usually found in the rules of court dealing with service *ex juris*. Occasionally, they may also be found in special statutes. *Denys v. Chatur* (2004), 252 Sask. R 249, 2004 SKPC 89, applied a rule in the Consumer Protection Act, S.S. 1996, c. C-30, s. 69, that deems manufacturers who market consumer products in Saskatchewan to be carrying on business in the province and so to be subject to the jurisdiction of Saskatchewan courts.

Under the Federal Court Rules, jurisdiction over parties outside Canada is not defined, as it is in most Canadian rules of court, in terms of certain classes of cases that are connected with the territory of Canada. The court's jurisdiction is restricted to a list of matters that are subject to federal law, and if a claim falls within the list there is a blanket right to serve foreign parties *ex juris*. For an example, see *DSL Corp. v. Bulk Atlantic Inc.* (2003), 241 F.T.R. 153, 2003 FC 1061 (Prothonotary).

Presence in the territory

Note. The advent of the "real and substantial connection" test for jurisdiction has thrown into doubt whether the common law jurisdictional grounds are still automatically valid. In *Beals v. Saldanha*, [2003] 3 S.C.R. 416, 234 D.L.R. (4th) 1, 2003 SCC 72 (noted below under 3. Foreign Judgments, (a) Common law and federal, (i) Defences to recognition and enforcement — fraud), a foreign judgment case, Major J. for the majority said at para. 37, "The presence of more of the traditional indicia of jurisdiction (attornment, agreement to submit, residence and presence in the foreign jurisdiction) will serve to *bolster* the real and substantial connection to the action or parties" [emphasis added]. Although this was said in relation to the jurisdiction of a foreign court, it also applies to the domestic rules for jurisdiction *simpliciter*, which the court has previously indicated are subject to the same principles. The passage has been interpreted as meaning that the real and substantial connection is the *sine qua non* of jurisdiction and that mere presence in the jurisdiction is not always going to be enough: *Newton v. Larco Hospitality Management Inc.* (2004), 70 O.R. (3d) 427, 3 C.P.C. (6th) 172 at paras. 10–11 (S.C.J.), aff'd (14 February 2005), C41753 (Ont. C.A.); see also *Toronto-Dominion Bank v. Switlo* (2004), 49 C.P.C. (5th) 335, 2004 ABQB 207 at paras. 16–17, aff'd 2005 ABCA 170. In both cases, however, the real and substantial connection test was met because the defendant's presence was more than merely transitory. (Consent will always be enough, as Major J. indicated in the next sentence in para. 37: "Although [a real and substantial] connection is an important factor, parties to an action continue to be free to select or accept the jurisdiction in which their dispute is to be resolved by attorning or agreeing to the jurisdiction of a foreign court.")

Attornment to the court's jurisdiction

Note. Rules of court may deprive a party of the right to dispute the court's jurisdiction once a certain step is taken in the proceeding. This occurred in *Lashburn AG Ventures Ltd. v. Western Grain Cleaning & Processing* (2003), 241 Sask. R. 97, 2003 SKCA 60, where the defendant waived its right to arbitration by filing a statement of defence without objecting to jurisdiction (Saskatchewan Queen's Bench Rules, R. 99(1)). Even if the rules do not make it an automatic submission, a delay in making the application for a stay may be grounds for exercising the court's discretion against the stay, as in *Mobile Mini Inc. v. Centreline Equipment Rentals Ltd.* (2004), 190 O.A.C. 149 (C.A.).

In *Coldmatic Refrigeration of Canada Ltd. v. Leveltek Processing LLC* (2004), 70 O.R. (3d) 758, 47 C.P.C. (5th) 139, aff'd (2005), 5 C.P.C. (6th) 258 (Ont. C.A.), the defendant, a company based in West Virginia, was held not to have attorned to the Ontario court's jurisdiction merely by the filing on its behalf of a notice of intent to defend. Lawyers instructed by the defendant's insurer had filed the notice without consultation with the defendant.

Declining jurisdiction — exclusive choice of forum clause

Note. In *BC Rail Partnership v. Standard Car Truck Co.* (2003), 20 B.C.L.R. (4th) 1, 2003 BCCA 597, a clause in an agreement to lease rail cars provided that the lessee "irrevocably and unconditionally submits to the jurisdiction of and venue in, federal and provincial courts located in Nova Scotia." This was interpreted by the British Columbia court as an exclusive jurisdiction clause, not just an attornment clause. The defendant had not shown "strong cause" for overriding the clause, the test that was affirmed in *Z.I. Pompey Industrie v. Ecu-Line N.V.*, [2003] 1 S.C.R. 450, 224 D.L.R. (4th) 577, 2003 SCC 27 (noted in "Canadian Cases in Private International Law 2002–3" (2003) 41 Can. Y.B. Int'l L. 573). A clause in a distributorship contract giving exclusive jurisdiction to the courts of Kansas, where the supplier was based, was enforced in *Navair Inc. v. IFR Americas Inc.* (2003), 38 B.L.R. (3d) 306 (Ont. S.C.J.). An exclusive jurisdiction clause in favour of Colorado, contained in a contract for the transfer of a franchising business from franchisor A to franchisor B, was not enforced in *Clayton Systems 2001 Ltd. v. Quizno's Canada Corp.* (2003), 27 B.C.L.R. (4th) 247, 2003 BCSC 1573. Franchisor A was being sued by a franchisee in British Columbia, and it would be a costly duplication of proceedings if A's claim over B, which had assumed A's obligations to its franchisees, had to be separately litigated in Colorado.

Declining jurisdiction — forum non conveniens — *defendant in the jurisdiction*

Note. In two wrongful dismissal cases, the employee had worked in Ontario for the Canadian arm of a multinational employer and then been transferred to a position with the American arm in the United States, after which the dismissal took place. In both cases, the Canadian arm was a defendant along with the American arm and the employee argued that Ontario law continued to apply notwithstanding the transfer. The court in both cases refused to stay the proceeding on the ground of *forum non conveniens,* and in both cases the court was swayed by the employee's argument that he would be at a disadvantage in the alternative forum in the United States when seeking to have the more favourable rules of Ontario employment law applied to his case: *Newton v. Larco Hospitality Management Inc.* (2004), 70 O.R. (3d) 427, 3 C.P.C. (6th) 172 (S.C.J.), aff'd (14 February 2005), C41753 (Ont. C.A.); *McCrea v. Philips Electronics Ltd.* (2004), 43 C.P.C. (5th) 388 (Ont. S.C.J.). Ontario was also held to be *forum conveniens* in a wrongful dismissal action where the employee worked in Ontario for an employer based in Québec: *Kuhlkamp v. Apera Technologies Inc.* (2004), 188 O.A.C. 361 (C.A.).

Jurisdiction was declined in an Ontario action by an insured against his insurer, because the insurance policy had been entered into in Québec to cover risks in Québec and the insured had moved to Ontario only after the loss took place: *Maddaloni v. ING Groupe Commerce* (2003), 43 C.P.C. (5th) 377 (Ont. S.C.J.), aff'd (2004), 3 C.P.C. (6th) 22 (Ont. C.A.). Jurisdiction was not declined in a Saskatchewan action between residents of the province in respect of the proceeds of the sale of land in Pakistan. The defendants had moved back to Pakistan after the action was commenced but still had assets in the province, namely, $137,000 that was paid into court by their bank pursuant to a garnishing order obtained by the plaintiff: *Jafferey v. Hydrie* (2004), 246 Sask. R. 98, 2004 SKQB 111.

Declining jurisdiction — forum non conveniens — *defendant outside the jurisdiction*

Note. A *forum non conveniens* argument succeeded in *Royal & Sun Alliance Ins. Co. v. Wainoco Oil & Gas Co.* (2004), 364 A.R. 151, 2004 ABQB 643, aff'd 2005 ABCA 198, involving coverage issues in policies of liability insurance. The fact that the policies were issued in Alberta was of less weight than the fact that the claims against the insured were being made in the courts of California. Ontario was found to be *forum non conveniens* in *Danks v. Ioli Management Consulting* (2003), 43 C.P.C. (5th) 242, 29 C.C.E.L. (3d) 258 (Ont. S.C.J. (Master)), aff'd (2 May 2005), 699/03 (Ont. Div. Ct.), a wrongful dismissal action by an Ontario resident against his Virginia-based employer; the job had involved servicing clients throughout the United States, Europe, and Canada. See also the cases involving *lis alibi pendens* noted immediately below.

Declining jurisdiction — lis alibi pendens

Shell Canada Ltd. v. CIBC Mellon Trust Co. (2003), [2004] 4 W.W.R. 393, 24 Alta. L.R. (4th) 259, 2003 ABQB 1058 (Alberta Queen's Bench)

Shell Canada (Shell), a federally incorporated company, agreed to issue a share certificate for a large number of shares to Cede and Co. as nominee for Depository Trust Co. (DTC). Both Cede and DTC were American corporations based in New York. Shell instructed CIBC Mellon Trust (Mellon), as transfer agent, to prepare and send the certificate. The certificate was not received. Six years later, after extensive discussion with Shell and Mellon, Cede and

DTC brought an action in federal court in New York against them, claiming declaratory relief and damages. Shell then commenced a proceeding by originating notice in Alberta against Mellon, Cede, and DTC, for declaratory relief and an order that Mellon deliver a new share certificate to Cede as nominee for DTC, subject to certain conditions. Those conditions included undertakings by Cede and DTC not to deal with and to return the original certificate to Mellon, should it turn up; to pursue all available rights of recovery against a purported purchaser for value of the original certificate, if the purchaser claimed it under a purported endorsement; and to provide Shell with an indemnity bond for any losses and legal expenses arising from a failure to observe those undertakings. Shell claimed to be entitled to these assurances and the bond under section 80 of the Canada Business Corporations Act, R.S.C. 1985, c. C-44 (CBCA). Shell had served Cede and DTC with process *ex juris*, pursuant to an order of the Alberta court, and those two parties now sought to have service on them set aside or to have the action stayed on the ground of *forum non conveniens*.

The court upheld service and refused a stay. The court considered a range of factors relevant to the issue of *forum conveniens*. The fact that harm was suffered in New York was of little weight in deciding on the appropriate forum, because harm alone, without any conduct by Shell personally subjecting itself to New York law, was not a real and substantial connection. The need for the American parties to provide evidence in Alberta could presumably be met with affidavits, since the facts were not disputed. It was true that Cede and DTC were at a disadvantage in the Alberta proceeding in that, the proceeding having been brought by originating notice, a claim for damages against Shell could only be made if the court gave leave to amend the procedure to provide for use of a statement of claim. The fact that proceedings were also underway in New York was of very little weight, given the short time between the commencement of the two proceedings, and the fact that the New York ones were still in the very preliminary stages. The paramount factor was that the issue concerned the interpretation of the CBCA provisions, which reflected a public policy to use indemnity bonds to protect the other public shareholders of Shell Canada, who were unrepresented in these proceedings. A decision would set a precedent for the future on where the risks lay in situations such as the present. The fact that Canadian public policy was at stake favoured a decision by a Canadian court.

Note. The common law knows no doctrine of *lis alibi pendens;* the existence of a parallel proceeding in another jurisdiction is not preclusive but is a factor in assessing whether the local court is *forum non conveniens.* The existence of the foreign proceeding was treated as a virtually negligible element in *Shell Canada Ltd. v. CIBC Mellon Trust.* Although the court probably gave too much importance to the need for Canadian "public policy" — which was really just legislative policy — to be interpreted by Canadian courts, the decision is consistent with a strong tendency to see disputes between corporations and shareholders as being presumptively a matter for the courts of the incorporating jurisdiction.

By contrast with the *Shell* case, in *Blinds To Go Inc. v. Harvard Private Capital Holdings Inc.* (2003), 232 D.L.R. (4th) 340, 2003 NBCA 57, a company's action in the jurisdiction of incorporation, New Brunswick was stayed in favour of proceedings the shareholder had already brought in Massachusetts. In both actions, the core issue was the price at which the corporation was obliged to repurchase certain preferred shares. An important distinction from the *Shell* case is that the company originally sold the shares to the shareholder under an agreement that was expressly governed by Massachusetts law, and the right to have the company repurchase them arose out of that agreement.

In *Saskatchwan Wildlife Federation v. Vantage Financial Services Inc.* (2003), 239 Sask. R. 1, 2003 SKQB 353, aff'd (2004), 249 Sask. R. 237, 2004 SKCA 90, a contract action in Saskatchewan by the Federation against Vantage was not stayed although Vantage had already sued the Federation in Massachusetts and obtained default judgment. No proceedings had yet been taken to enforce the default judgment in Saskatchewan. On the other hand, in *Multiactive Software Inc. v. Advanced Service Solutions Inc.* (2003), 48 C.P.C. (5th) 125, 2003 BCSC 643, a British Columbia seller's action for goods supplied to its Florida purchaser was stayed in favour of proceedings the purchaser brought against the seller in Florida, even though the Florida action was begun after the British Columbia action. In *Design Recovery Inc. v. Schneider* (2003), 238 Sask. R. 212, 2003 SKCA 94, the same party had brought actions on the same cause of action in both Ontario and Saskatchewan. The Saskatchewan action was not set aside because one of the claims in it was for an interest in a parcel of real property in Saskatchewan. That claim, being *in rem* in nature, could only be brought where the property was situated. The action was stayed, however, pending a decision in the main action in Ontario. See also *Dent Wizard International Corp.* c. *Mariano,* noted below under (c) Foreign judgments, (ii) Québec — Compétence internationale du tribunal étranger — Contrat de travail), in which American proceedings brought by an employer, which had already resulted in a judgment, were held to be superseded by parallel Québec proceedings brought by the employee because the Civil Code of Quebec guarantees employees and consumers who are domiciled or resident in Québec access to the Québec courts.

(b) Infants and children

Custody — jurisdiction

   Note. In some provinces, jurisdiction in custody is defined by statute, using the child's habitual residence as the primary criterion. *Ok v. Ok* (2004), 3 R.F.L. (6th) 154, 2004 NLSCUFC 12 (*sub nom. O.(S.) v. O.(I.)*), decided that the children's habitual residence had not been changed when their mother took them from British Columbia to Newfoundland without notice to the father; the mother could therefore not seek a custody order in Newfoundland.

Custody — extraprovincial order

Rasaiah v. Rose (2004), 30 B.C.L.R. (4th) 352, 2004 BCCA 250 (British Columbia Court of Appeal)

   The mother and father were divorced in 1999 in Maryland, where they both lived. The court gave a consent order that it would continue to have jurisdiction over issues of custody and access. In August 2000, the mother moved with the children to British Columbia, precipitating a further round of litigation in Maryland. Eventually, in April 2001, the parties entered into a new consent order that contemplated that the children would reside in British Columbia, the mother would have custody, and the father would have access including four weeks' summer vacation with the children. In the summer, the mother refused to allow the children to go on the vacation with their father. The father obtained a contempt order from the Maryland court, and an interim order from the British Columbia court that the April 2001 Maryland order be recognized under section 48 of the Family Relations Act, R.S.B.C. 1996, c. 128, and so deemed to be an order of the British Columbia court. The mother applied to vary the British Columbia order and obtained a new order that, *inter alia,* jurisdiction in the matter rested with the

British Columbia court instead of the Maryland court because the children were now habitually resident in the province.

On the father's appeal, the Court of Appeal reversed the variation. It had been made under section 49 of the act, which requires a material change in circumstances that justifies superseding an extraprovincial order for custody or access. No material change in circumstances had been shown. The mother's move with the children to British Columbia was contemplated by the original Maryland order. The fact that she had since had two more children in British Columbia did not affect the issue of jurisdiction. Nor did the father's obtaining a contempt order against her in Maryland. All of these were within the experience of the parties prior to the making of the consent order and were contemplated by the very fact that the order was made. Even if the British Columbia court had had jurisdiction to supersede the Maryland order, this was not an appropriate case to do so. The April 2001 order was made with the assistance of counsel for both parties and a guardian *ad litem* acting for the children, as well as with the assistance of the court. There was no basis for concluding that the Maryland order was inadequate or failed in a material respect to deal with the best interests of the children. In these circumstances, it was more appropriate for jurisdiction to be exercised in Maryland in these child-related matters.

Note. In *Spurgeon v. Spurgeon* (2003), 48 R.F.L. (5th) 219 (Ont. S.C.J.), a father obtained an order for $10,000 costs in respect of the enforcement of a British Columbia order awarding him custody. The order for costs was made jointly against the mother and the Ontario Provincial Police, which at the mother's behest had refused to act to enforce the custody order and so prolonged the proceedings.

Custody orders, whether interim or final, that are made corollary to Canadian divorce proceedings are made under the federal Divorce Act, R.S.C. 1985, c. 3 (2nd Supp.), and so have automatic nation-wide operation; see *Bedard v. Bedard* (2004), 242 D.L.R. (4th) 626, 2004 SKCA 101.

Child abduction — Hague Convention on the Civil Aspects of International Child Abduction

Korutowska-Wooff v. Wooff (2004), 242 D.L.R. (4th) 385, 5 R.F.L. (6th) 104 (Ontario Court of Appeal), leave to appeal to S.C.C. refused, 14 July 2005

The father, a Canadian diplomat, and the mother, a national and resident of Poland, had married in Canada and had two children there. In 1996, the father was posted to Poland, where the family lived for the next seven years. The father was transferred back to Ottawa, Ontario, in 2003. He unsuccessfully tried to obtain other employment that would permit the family to stay in Europe. He instructed Foreign Affairs that his wife and children would be remaining in Warsaw, where the mother had a good job. The wife bought a new home there for herself and the children. In August 2003, the children came to Ottawa with the father for their annual visit with their grandparents. They had return tickets to Warsaw, where they were registered to return to school in September. At the beginning of September, the father sent the mother an e-mail that he wished to separate and would be keeping the children in Canada. The mother applied in Ontario for an order for the return of the children to Poland under the Hague Convention on the Civil Aspects of International Child Abduction, implemented by section 46 of the Children's Law Reform Act, R.S.O. 1990, c. C.12. The application judge made the order, finding that the children were habitually resident in Poland and were wrongfully detained in Canada by their father because he acted in violation of the mother's joint custody rights under Polish law.

The Ontario Court of Appeal affirmed the order. The children's habitual residence depended on that of their custodial parents, and until September 2003 both parents had a settled intention to continue the family residence in Poland despite the father's relocation to Ottawa. The father's later intention to separate from his wife and stay in Ottawa did not affect the children's habitual residence because under Polish law he could not alter their habitual residence without the mother's consent. The court also rejected the father's argument that the judge should have ordered a trial rather than proceed summarily. While there might be a need for a trial in some cases, the normal practice was to determine a convention application through a summary procedure. In this case, the judge was able to make the necessary findings based on the record before her.

Note. A similar fact situation arose in *C.(J.R.) v. M.(L.C.)* (2003), 46 R.F.L. (5th) 306, 233 Nfld. & P.E.I. R. 1, 2003 NLSCTD 173, and the children were ordered returned to the United States. In *deHaan v. Gracia* (2004), 351 A.R. 358, 1 R.F.L. (6th) 140, 2004 ABQB 74, the mother was found not to have detained the children wrongfully in Canada because the father had agreed to the family's move there from France; it was only after he arrived in Canada that he announced he wanted to take the children back to France.

(c) Antisuit injunctions

Note. An injunction against an Italian equipment supplier, enjoining it from suing a New Brunswick purchaser in Italy, was refused in *PCI Chemicals Canada Co. v. ABB Transmissione & Distribuzione S.p.A.* (2005), 229 N.S.R. (2d) 341, 2005 NSSC 18. The New Brunswick company had not applied to the Italian court for a stay, which was usually a prerequisite for seeking an antisuit injunction, and anyway the Italian court could not be said to be an inappropriate forum.

2 *Québec*

(a) Famille

Garde d'enfant — retour d'enfant en vertu de la Loi sur les aspects civils de l'enlèvement international et interprovincial d'enfants

E.(S.) c. R.(T.), [2004] R.J.Q. 2568 (Cour supérieure du Québec)

Les parties, mariées en 1985, ont deux enfants, nées respectivement en 1991 et 1995. Celles-ci ont vécu au Québec jusqu'à leur départ en France, en 2001. Leurs parents projetaient en effet depuis longtemps d'aller vivre en Europe. Selon la lettre d'embauche fournie par l'employeur du père, la durée de l'affectation était de deux ans. Une fois cette période écoulée, le contrat de travail avait une durée indéterminée. Selon l'épouse, la famille devait revenir au Québec après l'expiration des deux ans, tandis que, pour le mari, son affectation en France revêtait un caractère plus permanent. Pendant le séjour, la relation entre les époux s'est détériorée et ils ont cessé de faire vie commune. À l'été 2003, le mari a obtenu des billets d'avion pour que son épouse et ses enfants viennent passer les vacances au Québec. À l'insu de son mari, l'épouse a cependant planifié son déménagement permanent et a intenté une action en séparation de corps devant la Cour supérieure du Québec. Le mari a alors demandé le retour des enfants en France, se fondant sur les dispositions de la Loi sur les aspects civils de l'enlèvement international et interprovincial d'enfants, L.R.Q., c. A-23.01. L'épouse prétend que cette loi ne s'applique pas en l'espèce puisqu'il n'y a pas eu déplacement illicite des enfants. Elle soutient par ailleurs qu'elle a quitté la France à l'expiration du délai de deux ans prévu au contrat d'embauche de son mari et que, après cette période, la résidence habituelle des enfants était de nouveau au Québec. Elle ajoute qu'il ne peut y avoir eu violation d'un droit de garde puisque les enfants habitaient avec elle et que le père n'exerçait que des droits de visite. Subsidiairement, elle fait valoir que, en raison du comportement violent du père et de son alcoolisme, il existe un risque grave que les enfants soient exposées à un danger physique ou psychique ou soient placées dans une situation intolérable si elles devaient retourner en France. Les deux filles, qui sont actuellement de 7 ans et 11 ans, s'opposent également à leur retour en France.

M. le juge Emery a rejeté toute les prétentions de l'épouse, sauf celle fondée sur l'article 22, paragraphe 1 de la Loi, qui se lise:

> 22. La Cour supérieure peut aussi refuser d'ordonner le retour de l'enfant: 1o si elle constate que celui-ci s'oppose à son retour et qu'il a atteint un âge et une maturité où il se révèle approprié de tenir compte de cette opinion.

La résidence habituelle des enfants était située en France immédiatement avant leur déplacement. L'intention des parents importe peu dans la détermination de la résidence habituelle, car il s'agit d'une notion purement factuelle. D'ailleurs, même si l'on examinait la situation plus globalement en allant au-delà de la situation factuelle, la conclusion serait la même. La mère a déplacé illicitement les enfants en violation d'un droit de garde. Le droit de décider du lieu de résidence des enfants appartenait aux deux parents et en aucun cas l'un ou l'autre ne pouvait se l'arroger sans violer le droit de garde de l'autre parent. En effet, comme aucun jugement n'a modifié l'exercice de l'autorité parentale après la séparation des parties, celle-ci continuait à être exercée conjointement par les parents au moment du déplacement, suivant le Code civil français. Le fait que les enfants se soient trouvées plus souvent dans l'appartement de leur mère ne change rien. Quant aux exceptions prévues par la loi et invoquées par la mère pour empêcher le retour des enfants en France, on constate d'abord que le père n'a pas acquiescé au déplacement définitif des enfants. Par ailleurs, le fait de vivre à Paris avec un père stressé par son travail mais affectueux ne constitue nullement un risque grave de danger physique ou psychique pour les enfants. Il n'existe aucune preuve que le père ait déjà été violent ni qu'il ait un problème de consommation d'alcool. Il y a cependant lieu de refuser d'ordonner le retour des enfants, car celles-ci souhaitent rester au Québec, lieu où elles sont nées et ont passé la plus grande partie de leur vie. Les entretiens qu'a eus le juge avec les enfants ont révélé qu'elles avaient atteint une maturité certaine et que leur opposition à un retour en France ne résultait d'aucun ressentiment à l'égard de leur père. Elles ont le sentiment de vivre une vie d'étranger à Paris, alors qu'elle sont bien enracinées au Québec, où elles ont grandi. Leur intérêt commande de ne pas ordonner leur retour en France.

B PROCEDURE / PROCÉDURE

1   Common Law and Federal

(a) Remedies

Damages — foreign currency — conversion

Note. Some provinces have enacted statutory rules to determine the date as of which damages quantified in foreign currency are to be converted into Canadian dollars. *Society of Lloyd's v. McNeill* (2003), 233 Nfld. & P.E.I. R. 37, 45 C.P.C. (5th) 354, 2003 PESCTD 76, applied such a rule in section 46(1) of the Supreme Court Act, R.S.P.E.I. 1988, c. S-10. The applicable date was the date of payment of the judgment. *Brown & Root Services Corp. v. Aerotech Herman Nelson Inc.* (2004), 238 D.L.R. (4th) 594, 2004 MBCA 63, leave to appeal to S.C.C. refused, 13 June 2005, applied the common law rule, which it held to be the date that gives the fairest result in the circumstances. That date was found in the case in question to be the date of the trial judgment. The dissenting judge thought the Canadian authorities dictated that the conversion be calculated as of the date of breach of the original obligation.

Injunction — extraterritorial scope

Barrick Gold Corp. v. Lopehandia (2004), 239 D.L.R. (4th) 577, 71 O.R. (3d) 416 (Ontario Court of Appeal)

The defendant, a resident of British Columbia, was found at trial to have posted on various websites a mass of defamatory matter about the plaintiff company, against which he held a grievance about a mining property in Chile. One of the issues on appeal was whether the trial judge had been right to refuse the plaintiff an injunction against the defendant's making further publications on the Internet or elsewhere. The trial judge held that she ought not to make such an order because, *inter alia*, there was no evidence that the defendant had any assets or presence in Ontario, and the claim for injunctive relief should have been pursued in British Columbia, where the courts would be able to supervise the injunction.

The Court of Appeal held the injunction could be granted. Civil Procedure Rule 17.02(i) authorized service *ex juris* if the claim was for an injunction "ordering a party to do, or refrain from doing, any thing in Ontario or affecting real or personal property in Ontario." Even if it was unclear that the defendant was doing anything in Ontario, his campaign of libel certainly meant he was doing something affecting personal property in Ontario. And there was evidence he was doing something in Ontario because one of the websites to which he posted his material was operated by an Internet service provider in Ontario. It was true that courts are traditionally reluctant to grant injunctive relief against defendants who are outside the jurisdiction. However, in some circumstances courts do permit service of claims outside the jurisdiction seeking to prevent publication in the jurisdiction of libelous material originating outside the jurisdiction. This was such a case. Moreover, there was a real and substantial connection between the plaintiff and Ontario as well as between the publication of the libel and Ontario.

There was no way to determine from where the defendant's postings originated. They could as easily be initiated in an Internet café in downtown Toronto as anywhere else in the world. The highly transmissible nature of the tortious misconduct here was a factor to be addressed in considering whether a permanent injunction should be granted. Even if an injunction might only be enforced in Ontario against the defendant if he entered the province personally, there were two reasons why it could nevertheless be effective. One is that it would operate to prevent the Toronto-based Internet service provider from continuing to post the defamatory messages. Second, the injunction might be enforceable in British Columbia. *Morguard Investments Ltd. v. de Savoye*, [1990] 3 S.C.R. 1077, 76 D.L.R. (4th) 256, found an implicit constitutional "full faith and credit" obligation owed by each province to recognize judicial measures taken in another, and it was not yet settled whether this obligation extended to non-monetary judgments.

Note. The enforceability of a non-monetary judgment from outside Canada was at issue in *Pro Swing Inc. v. ELTA Golf Inc.* (2004), 71 O.R. (3d) 566 (C.A.), leave to appeal to S.C.C. granted, 17 March 2005. An American manufacturer of customized golf clubs sought to enforce in Ontario an order granted by a United States Federal

Court against an Ontario company, holding that company in contempt of an earlier consent order not to sell golf clubs or other golf
components bearing a certain trade mark. The Ontario company
had been ordered by the American court to make an accounting of
all the infringing items it had sold. The Ontario Court of Appeal
held that even if private international law had now evolved to the
point where non-monetary judgments from outside Canada could
be enforced, the orders in question were too uncertain to be given
effect by a Canadian court.

(b) Obtaining evidence locally for foreign proceedings

Letters rogatory — enforcement

   Note. The applicant in *Prima Tek II v. Sonneman Packaging Inc.*
(2003), 68 O.R. (3d) 451, 32 C.P.R. (4th) 151 (S.C.J.), presented
letters rogatory from a United States court, requiring that the respondents, two Ontario businesses, produce full customer lists for
the purpose of proving that a Canadian licensee of the applicant
was in contempt of an order of the United States court not to sell
certain goods into the United States; the licensee was said to have
clandestinely made such sales through the respondents. The
Ontario court ordered the documents produced, acting under section 60 of the Evidence Act, R.S.O. 1990, c. E.23, because they
were the very evidence required by the American court to adjudicate the fraudulent infringement of the patent at issue.

C   FOREIGN JUDGMENTS / JUGEMENTS ÉTRANGERS

1   Common Law and Federal

(a) Conditions for recognition or enforcement

Finality of the judgment

   Note. Collier sued Hartford in Ontario on a judgment of an Irish
court, which was under appeal. On the basis of the rule that a judgment under appeal is still to be considered final, judgment was
given, but execution of it was stayed pending the outcome of the
Irish appeal. The appeal was dismissed in 2002. Eighteen months
later, Collier applied to have the stay lifted. Hartford had started a
new proceeding in Ontario arising out of the same relationship
but had not moved it along. Hartford argued the stay should continue until the new proceeding was resolved. On 17 March 2004,

the court ordered that the stay would come to an end as of 1 June 2004, unless Hartford fulfilled two conditions: (1) by 15 April 2004 pay $400,000 into court or provide a letter of credit guaranteeing payment of the Collier judgment and costs; (2) by 31 May 2004 take all steps necessary to set down his action for trial: *Collier v. Hartford* (2001), 46 C.P.C. (5th) 366, further proceedings (17 March 2004), 98-BN-07841 (Ont. S.C.J.).

Jurisdiction of the original court — no consent — real and substantial connection with the foreign jurisdiction

Parsons v. McDonald's Restaurants of Canada Ltd. (2004), 45 C.P.C. (5th) 304 (Ontario Superior Court of Justice)

A class action was brought in Illinois state court against McDonald's for consumer fraud in promotional contests that McDonald's had run at its restaurants in Canada and the United States. Under the Illinois class action rules, Canadian residents were members of the class unless they opted out. Notice of their right to do so had been published in *Macleans,* a Canadian weekly magazine, and in three French-language newspapers in Québec. Evidence in American criminal proceedings against McDonald's employees suggested that Canadian participants in the contests had been deliberately excluded from the larger prizes. Partly on the basis of this evidence, Parsons, a Canadian resident, began a class action in Ontario against McDonald's and its Canadian subsidiary. A month later, a second class action was begun by another Canadian resident, Currie. Parsons and several other Canadian residents, but not Currie, subsequently obtained leave to make representations at the Illinois court hearing on the fairness of a proposed settlement. The Illinois class action was settled without giving effect to the objections of Parsons and the other Canadians. The consent judgment of the Illinois court included very broad releases from further claims against McDonald's or its subsidiaries. McDonald's and McDonald's Canada now moved to dismiss the Parsons and Currie class actions on the ground that the Illinois judgment made the claims *res judicata.*

The court held that Parsons and the other claimants who had participated in the Illinois hearing had attorned to the Illinois court's jurisdiction and so were bound by the settlement approved by that court and could not be plaintiffs in a class action in Ontario. The Parsons action was therefore struck out. As for the remaining claimants, the Ontario court held that the Illinois court had jurisdiction to decide on the claims of all the Canadian resident plaintiffs in the class because their claims had a real and substantial connection with the Illinois forum. However, the Canadian-resident claimants, other than Parsons and the others who attorned, were not bound by the Illinois judgment because the notice given to Canadian claimants had been wholly inadequate and the proceedings had therefore been contrary to natural justice as far as they were concerned. They were not bound by the attornment of Parsons and the others because, although their claims were identical to those who attorned, they were not in privity with them.

Note. This is the first case to consider the recognition of a foreign class-action judgment in Canada. Statutes that govern class actions typically allow residents of other jurisdictions to be included in the class of claimants, either on the basis that the non-residents must opt in (as under the Class Proceedings Act, R.S.B.C. 1996, c. 50, s. 16(2)) or on the basis that they are in unless they opt out (as under the Ontario legislation as interpreted by the courts: see *Boulanger v. Johnson & Johnson Corp.* (2003), 226 D.L.R. (4th) 747, 64 O.R. (3d) 248 (Div. Ct.)). In the domestic setting, it has been held that the court in a class proceeding has jurisdiction *simpliciter* over the claims of non-resident plaintiffs if their claims are sufficiently connected with the residents' claims to justify taking jurisdiction over the former as well as the latter: *Harrington v. Dow Corning Corp.* (2000), 193 D.L.R. (4th) 67 (B.C.C.A.). The *Parsons* case applies the same reasoning to foreign class proceedings, but with the important proviso that non-residents are only bound if they receive adequate notice of their right to opt out. The judge thought this could be viewed equally well as a requirement of jurisdiction or a requirement of natural justice. The notice here was inadequate because, outside Québec, the only publication in which it appeared was a magazine having a fairly restricted circulation (half a million subscribers nationally).

On the application of the real and substantial connection test to foreign judgments generally, see the note of *Beals v. Saldanha,* below under (b) Defences to recognition or enforcement — Fraud.

Jurisdiction of the original court — no consent — real and substantial connection with the foreign jurisdiction — arbitration clause

Note. The debtor under an Illinois default judgment sought to be enforced in Ontario argued without success that the Illinois court had taken jurisdiction contrary to an arbitration agreement between the parties. The Ontario Court of Appeal held that a defendant who wants to rely on an arbitration clause must raise the argument before the foreign court unless, possibly, there are circumstances that justify relieving the defendant of this requirement: *United Laboratories Inc. v. Abraham* (2004), 50 C.P.C. (5th) 68, 188 O.A.C. 326 (Ont. C.A.), leave to appeal to S.C.C. refused, 3 March 2005.

Jurisdiction of the original court — consent — submission by the defendant

   Note. See *1302926 Ontario Inc. v. 2334425 Nova Scotia Ltd.*, noted below under (d) Registration under uniform reciprocal enforcement of judgments legislation — Defences to registration.

(b) Defences to recognition or enforcement

Fraud

Beals v. Saldanha, [2003] 3 S.C.R. 416, 234 D.L.R. (4th) 1, 2003 SCC 72 (Supreme Court of Canada)

   The defendants, a couple resident in Ontario, together with the Thivys, friends who were also Ontario residents, bought a lot in Florida for US $4,000, intending eventually to build a cottage on it. Three years later the Thivys were contacted by a Florida real estate agent who asked about purchasing the lot. Rose Thivy, on behalf of all four owners, said that they would sell for $8,000. When they received a written offer for that amount from the plaintiffs, Florida residents, it referred to "lot 1," which they corrected to "lot 2" and returned. The counter-offer was accepted by the plaintiffs. After closing, the plaintiffs began to build a model home for their construction business, but after some months they discovered that they were building on lot 1 rather than on lot 2, the one they had bought. The plaintiffs sued the defendants in state court in Charlotte County, Florida, claiming that the defendants had misled them as to which lot was which. The defendants received notice of the action and, without consulting a lawyer, filed a defence that Rose Thivy sent. Seven months later the defendants were notified that this action was dismissed because it had been brought in the wrong county. Soon afterwards the defendants were served in Ontario with process in a new action in Sarasota County. American defendants were also named. The claim was to rescind the contract of purchase and sale, and for damages in excess of $5,000, treble damages, and other relief authorized by statute. The complaint was identical to the earlier one except for the addition of an allegation of fraud. An amended complaint was received, dropping one of the other defendants. Rose Thivy filed a statement of defence identical to the one she had sent in the Charlotte County action. This time, the defendants (it was found) did not sign the statement of defence or authorize Ms. Thivy to file it on their behalf, so they were not bound by it.

Neither the defendants nor the Thivys took any further steps to defend the Florida action. They received a second and a third amended complaint, each of which changed only allegations against other defendants but repeated the allegations against them. Under Florida law, a failure by a defendant to reply to an amended complaint was deemed to be an admission of the allegations in the complaint, even if the defendant had replied to identical allegations made in an earlier complaint. So, in July 1990, the Florida court entered default judgment against the defendants and the Thivys on the basis that they had admitted the allegations in the third amended complaint. A date was set to have damages assessed by a jury and the defendants were notified of the date; they did not respond. At the hearing, the jury heard from the plaintiffs, former business associates who had been involved with the purchase of the land, and an expert on business losses. The jury awarded $210,000 in compensatory damages, $50,000 punitive damages, plus post-judgment interest at 12% per annum. The defendants received notice of this judgment in December 1991. At this point, for the first time, the defendants sought legal advice. Their lawyer advised them that if they applied in Florida to have the judgment set aside they would be deemed to have submitted to the Florida court's jurisdiction, but that if they did nothing the judgment against them would not be enforceable in Ontario because the Florida court had had no jurisdiction over them. Florida law would have permitted the defendants to apply within ten days to appeal, and within a year to have the default judgment set aside if they could show "excusable neglect," "fraud," or "other misconduct of an adverse party." The defendants, relying on their lawyer's advice, did nothing.

In 1993, the plaintiffs brought an action in Ontario on the judgment, which by then amounted to some CAN $800,000, including interest. The trial judge dismissed the action on the ground that the Florida judgment had been obtained on the basis of fraudulent evidence given by the plaintiffs. The Ontario Court of Appeal reversed, holding that the evidence did not support a finding of fraud and that no other defence had been made out. On further appeal, the Supreme Court of Canada held by a majority of six to three that the judgment was enforceable against the defendants.

The defendants conceded that the Florida court had jurisdiction that Canadian law would recognize, based upon the real and substantial connection of the case with Florida. Nevertheless, the court considered whether truly foreign judgments ought to be subject to the "real and substantial connection" test, which it had mandated for Canadian judgments in *Morguard Investments Ltd. v. De Savoye,* [1990] 3 S.C.R. 1077, 76 D.L.R. (4th) 256. The judges were unanimous that, although international cases did not give rise to the constitutional "full faith and credit" obligation recognized in *Morguard,* the "real and substantial connection" test properly extended to judgments from outside Canada. In international as well as interprovincial cases, both comity and the need to facilitate cross-border transactions and movement called for a modernization of the concept of jurisdiction. The common law formerly recognized only two grounds, the defendant's submission to the court's jurisdiction and the defendant's presence in the foreign country when the action commenced. As a result of *Morguard,* the law had recognized that a real and substantial connection was necessary to support the taking of jurisdiction, and this had been applied both to the recognition of judgments from elsewhere in Canada and to the validity of the courts' own assumption of jurisdiction. Given that Canadian courts now judged their own jurisdiction by this standard, it was appropriate that they recognize the jurisdiction of courts from outside Canada on the same basis. Only LeBel J., dissenting on other grounds, drew a distinction between the way the "real and substantial connection" test applied to international and interprovincial cases. He emphasized that, in international cases, courts should explicitly factor into their decisions the potential hardship to a Canadian defendant from being forced to litigate abroad. None of the judges, however, doubted that a real and substantial connection was present, where Florida-resident purchasers sued Ontario vendors in respect of a contract for the sale of an immovable that was situated in Florida.

As for defences, the judgment debtors made a general argument that the increased readiness, since *Morguard,* of Canadian courts to enforce foreign default judgments ought to bring with it some expansion of the defences to enforcement. The majority judgment, given by Major J., conceded that unusual situations might call for the creation of a new defence, but said this was not such a case. In any event, new defences, like the old ones, should be narrow in scope, address specific facts, and raise issues not covered by the existing defences. The majority, as will be outlined below, rejected fraud, natural justice, and public policy as defences against enforcement in this case. Binnie J., dissenting, with whom Iacobucci J. concurred, agreed that a new defence was not needed, but thought that this was a case in which natural justice had been violated. LeBel J., dissenting, would have broadened the defence of natural justice and applied it here, and indicated that other defences, too, ought to be reconsidered to meet the exigencies of enforcing default judgments from outside Canada.

On fraud as a defence, the majority resolved uncertainties in the case law as to what kind of fraud will preclude enforcement of a foreign judgment. Canadian cases were ambiguous on whether the fraud had to be "extrinsic," in the sense of going to jurisdiction only (*Woodruff v. McLennan* (1887), 14 O.A.R. 242 (C.A.)), or could go to the merits of the decision so long as proof of the fraud rested upon new and material facts that the defendant could not have discovered and brought to the attention of the foreign court through the exercise of reasonable diligence (*Jacobs v. Beaver* (1908), 17 O.L.R. 496 (C.A.)). The latter approach was the correct one. The distinction between extrinsic and intrinsic fraud was of no apparent value. At the other end of the spectrum, the English rule that fraud can be raised against the enforcement of a foreign judgment even if it could have raised before the foreign court, was too great an inroad into the principle that the merits of the foreign decision should not be retried. The rule in *Jacobs v. Beaver* steered an appropriate middle course.

The facts here did not support a defence of fraud, because, the defendants having made a conscious decision not to defend, the plaintiffs' pleadings became the basis for the Florida judgment and the defendants could not now attack the evidence presented to the Florida judge and jury as being fraudulent. The defendants did not claim that there was fraud that they could not have discovered if they had defended. There was, moreover, no indication that any of the evidence put before the Florida court had been fraudulent. Binnie J. did not comment on fraud. LeBel J. agreed both with the test for fraud and with its not being established in this case, but would not rule out the possibility that a broader test should apply to default judgments in cases where the defendant's decision not to participate was a demonstrably reasonable one and the plaintiff, for instance, took advantage of the defendant's absence to perpetrate a deliberate deception on the foreign court.

Natural justice, in the view of the majority, was not violated by the Florida decision. The procedure was not unfair. The defendants received notice of all the steps taken. The terms of the third amended complaint made it clear that the damages being sought were potentially significant. The plaintiffs were alleging fraud and claiming punitive damages as well as treble damages. Given that the types of damages claimed were known, the fact that the defendants were not provided with a specific dollar value of the amount of damages was not a denial of natural justice. The defendants were mistaken when they assumed the damages could not be much more than the price they had received for the property. Nor could they complain that they were not told about the witnesses who would testify as to the damages; the identity of the witnesses was not usually included in notice of a hearing. Nor — contrary to LeBel J.'s suggestion (para. 239) — was there an obligation on the plaintiffs to inform the defendants as to the legal steps they should take if they wished to avoid a default judgment. Defendants are presumed to know the law of the jurisdiction seized with an action against them when that jurisdiction is in Canada, and the same applied in international litigation. To find otherwise would unduly complicate cross-border transactions and hamper trade with Canadian parties. The defendants were advised of the case to meet and were granted a fair opportunity to do so. Once they received notice of the amount of the judgment, they had precise notice of the extent of their financial risk. They failed to act, not because of a lack of notice, but because they received incorrect legal advice.

Binnie J. disagreed with the decision on natural justice. Scrutinizing the notices the defendants had received from the Florida court, he concluded that the defendants were not sufficiently informed of the case against them, both with respect to liability and the potential financial consequences, to allow them to determine in a reasonable way whether or not to participate in the action or let it go by default. The way the case had evolved through successive stages had transformed it, in his view, from the one of which the defendants had been informed in the complaint. In particular, the defendants were not informed that failing to refile their defence after each amended complaint would amount to conceding the plaintiff's case. Nor were they apprised of the fact that settlements with the American defendants had left them alone as targets of the lawsuit. Their failure to appeal, once they had notice of the judgment, was not fatal. This was a foreign default judgment obtained without compliance with the rules of natural justice. Even if they had appealed, no transcript of the Florida proceeding had been made on which the appeal could be based. And it was unclear whether an application to set aside the judgment for "excusable neglect" to defend, as Florida law permitted, would have succeeded. LeBel J. emphasized the same factors in concluding that natural justice had not been observed, although as already noted he thought that the standard by which to measure natural justice was more exacting, in respect of default judgments from abroad, than the traditional test. The claimant, he thought, bore a certain responsibility for ensuring that a defendant who was not reasonably in a position to understand the particular workings of the foreign process did not inadvertently give up defences or waive rights as a result.

Public policy, the majority held, should not be expanded to include perceived injustices that did not offend the Canadian sense of morality. Public policy condemned the foreign law on which the judgment was based and was not a defence to be used lightly. The Florida jury's award of damages did not violate Canadian principles of morality. It was not a public policy issue that the claim in the foreign jurisdiction would not have yielded comparable damages in Canada. LeBel J., while agreeing that the present case did not support the defence of public policy, suggested that a foreign default judgment should not be enforced if to do so would "shock the conscience of Canadians and cast a negative light on our justice system" (para. 265). This, he thought, was such a case. The defendants had acted in good faith throughout and had diligently taken all the steps that appeared to be required of them, based on the information and advice they had. An Ontario court should not have to set its seal of approval on the judgment without regard for the dubious nature of the claim, the fact that the parties did not compete on a level playing field, and the lack of transparency in the Florida proceedings.

Note. This is the most sweeping private international law decision from the Supreme Court of Canada since *Morguard* itself, reviewing as it does virtually all the ground rules for the enforcement of foreign judgments. It lays to rest any lingering doubt that truly foreign default judgments can be recognized and enforced in Canada if the litigation had a real and substantial connection with the foreign country. Unfortunately, since the connection in this case was so obvious, the court did not have to examine how far the actual application of the real and substantial connection test in the international setting may have to differ from that in the interprovincial setting. Only LeBel J. examined this problem, and highlighted in particular the problems that international cases might pose for the "order and fairness" side of the equation, such as hardship on particular defendants from having to defend a case in a legal system or a language they do not know.

Despite — or maybe because of — the elasticity of the jurisdictional principle, the majority saw no reason to liberalize any of the existing defences to recognition and enforcement. The clarification of the rule with respect to fraud is welcome, as is the refusal to broaden public policy beyond its present, reasonably well-defined limits. Both the majority and Binnie J. applied what they saw as the traditional meaning of natural justice, but reached opposite conclusions. The way the majority saw it, the defendants knew they were being sued in Florida and knew what the lawsuit was about, but they chose not to defend. They knowingly gambled and they lost. Binnie J. saw a denial of natural justice in the fact that the information from Florida left the defendants in the dark about important aspects of the case, so that they were gambling in ignorance of how high the stakes were and how, as things progressed, the odds were increasingly stacked against them.

The problem with Binnie J.'s view and that of LeBel J., who reasoned along the same lines, is that it makes natural justice a concept subjective to the defendant. Even if the foreign court's procedure was fair in the abstract, natural justice can still be offended if the procedure worked unfairly in relation to the particular person sued. To test this point, one can ask whether the natural justice argument would have got as far as it did with Binnie and LeBel JJ. if the Saldanhas had been business people rather than just ordinary folks who liked to vacation in Florida.

However correct the law laid down by *Beals v. Saldanha,* the result is undeniably harsh. The dissenting judges characterized the problem as one of process, because natural justice was the defence that came most readily to hand, but the core problem is actually not process but substance. The Saldanhas' co-owners, the Thivys, presumably could not complain about process because they submitted to the court's jurisdiction, but the result is just as harsh for them. To Canadian legal eyes, it is startling that a litigant should be able to get such enormous damages, even as against an absent opponent, out of so small and everyday a transaction. The hard reality is, however, that litigation in the United States is fought on different rules and with different weapons and tactics than it is in Canada. No suggestion is made in the case that the outcome of the Florida lawsuit was in any way extraordinary by American standards.

If Canadians who choose to do business in the United States are to be shielded from the full force of the American (or some other) legal system, it ought to be done directly rather than indirectly by loading a concept like natural justice. Yet the only way of doing it directly is to make an inroad into the rule that foreign judgments cannot be impeached on their merits in enforcement proceedings. Such an inroad would have to be carefully circumscribed, and if it were to be done it would probably be better done by legislation than by judicial fiat. Judges must frame the common law on the basis of principle, whereas the issue here has less to do with principle than with an intuitively felt disproportion between acts and their legal consequences. It is hard to see how one could express the necessary criterion here other than as LeBel J. would have done, namely, a very broad discretion to refuse enforcement if the foreign judgment offends the Canadian sense of justice. Such a discretion would invite litigation and seriously impair the predictability of the enforcement of foreign judgments. More manageable than a common law rule — though still of very debatable wisdom — would be to give judges a statutory discretion, which could be restricted to certain classes of case, to vary or refuse to enforce a judgment if enforcing it in full would be egregiously unfair. Compare the Foreign Extraterritorial Measures Act, R.S.C. 1985, c. F-29, s. 8, which enables the attorney-general of Canada to order, in the name of averting injury to Canadian interests in international trade or commerce, that a foreign antitrust judgment not be enforced or be enforceable only for a reduced amount.

Public policy

Note. Beals v. Saldanha, noted immediately above, confirmed the narrow scope of the public policy defence. Because it is narrow, the public policy defence rarely succeeds, but it did so in *K.(E.) v. K.(D.)* (2003), 233 D.L.R. (4th) 101, 43 R.F.L. (5th) 403, 2003 BCSC 1296. The order of a New Jersey court, made in divorce proceedings, incorporated the parties' agreement as to support and also an agreement that a domestic violence complaint made by the wife against the husband would be dismissed upon execution of the agreement. The British Columbia judge refused to enforce the support order under the Interjurisdictional Support Orders Act, S.B.C. 2002, c. 29, which incorporates the public policy defence in section 19(3)(b)(ii). Domestic violence was a public offence in New Jersey, and it was against British Columbia public policy to agree to compromise the prosecution of such an offence. As the legislation directed it to do, the court went on to make its own support order against the husband. The public policy defence failed in *Great America Leasing Corp. v. Yates* (2003), 68 O.R. (3d) 225 (C.A.). A defendant contended that a Michigan judgment on a guarantee included interest and other charges that amounted to a criminal rate of interest under Canadian law and so violated essential moral principles in Ontario. The court rejected the argument because the proceedings in Michigan were entirely fair, the defendant had been represented, and the facts were centred in Michigan. Moreoever, a criminal rate of interest had not been shown on the evidence.

Natural justice

See *Beals v. Saldanha,* noted above under Fraud, and *Parsons v. McDonald's Restaurants of Canada Ltd.*, noted above under (a) Conditions for recognition or enforcement — Jurisdiction of the original court — no consent — real and substantial connection with the foreign jurisdiction.

Limitations

Note. Lax v. Lax (2004), 239 D.L.R. (4th) 683, 70 O.R. (3d) 520, application for rehearing dismissed (2004), 4 C.P.C. (6th) 194 (Ont. C.A.), held that because a foreign money judgment is sued upon as a simple contract debt, the applicable limitation period under the Limitations Act, R.S.O. 1990, c. L.15 (now replaced by the Limitations Act, 2002, S.O. 2002, c. 24, Sch. B), was that for contract (six years), not judgments (twenty years). The judgment creditor argued that running of the limitation period was postponed by lack of knowledge that the judgment debtors had come to Ontario. This argument was based on combining the rule, found in case law (and expressly in the new act), that a cause of action does not arise until it is reasonably discoverable, with the rule in section 48 of the act (not found in the new act) that if the debtor is absent from Ontario when the cause of action arises the period starts to run only when the debtor comes to Ontario. That argument could not be disposed of in the summary proceedings.

(c) Effect of recognition or enforcement

Recognition — issue estoppel

Note. In *Cook Nook Hazelton Lanes Ltd. v. Trudeau Corp. 1889 Inc.* (2003), 48 C.P.C. (5th) 330 (Ont. S.C.J.), issues in Ontario litigation were said to have been decided by foreign courts, but the Ontario judge held that the foreign decision did not cover the issues. The same occurred in *Grammercy Ltd. v. Dynamic Tire Corp.*, noted above under A. Jurisdiction, 1. Common Law and Federal, (a) Jurisdiction *in personam* — Constitutionally based territorial limits on jurisdiction.

(d) Registration under uniform reciprocal enforcement of judgments legislation

Defences to registration — defendant did not voluntarily appear or otherwise submit to the jurisdiction

Note. The old uniform reciprocal enforcement legislation, still in force in many provinces, does not allow for the registration of default judgments under the *Morguard* "real and substantial connection" principle. See *1302926 Ontario Inc. v. 2334425 Nova Scotia Ltd.* (2004), 221 N.S.R. (2d) 285, 2004 NSSC 55, where, although the dispute certainly had strong connections with Ontario, a default judgment from that province was held not registrable under the Reciprocal Enforcement of Judgments Act, R.S.N.S. 1989, c. 388. The judgment debtor had a defence under section 3(5)(g), because it neither carried on business nor was ordinarily resident in Ontario, and had not submitted to the jurisdiction merely by having its Ontario lawyer serve the judgment creditor with a demand for particulars in the dispute.

(e) Registration under uniform reciprocal enforcement of maintenance orders legislation

Variation of registered order — obligation on party paying support to disclose finances

Note. See *Trylinski-Branson v. Branson* (2003), 346 A.R. 133, 48 R.F.L. (5th) 446, 2003 ABCA 296, leave to appeal to S.C.C. refused, [2004] 1 S.C.R. vi. An Alberta-resident father, liable to pay child support under an Australian order registered under the Reciprocal Enforcement of Maintenance Orders Act, R.S.A. 1980, c. R-7.1, resisted having to disclose details of his financial situation at the instance of the Australian-resident mother, who wished to apply for variation. The father argued the statute did not oblige him to disclose, but the court held that the court had authority under other laws of the province to make the disclosure order.

2 *Québec*

(a) Compétence internationale du tribunal étranger

Contrat de travail — clause d'élection de for — travailleur domicilié au Québec — art. 3149 C.C.Q. — litispendance internationale — identité de parties

Dent Wizard International Corp. c. Mariano, [2004] R.J.Q. 1921 (Cour supérieure du Québec) (inscription en appel, 25 juin 2004 (Qué. C.A.))

Dent Wizard International (DWI) est une société américaine qui a embauché les deux défendeurs par l'intermédiaire d'une société liée ontarienne, Dent Wizard Canada (DWC). Ils signent tous deux un contrat d'emploi auquel est jointe une entente de confidentialité, lesquelles ententes contiennent, entre autres, des clauses restrictives de non-concurrence, de non-sollicitation et de non-divulgation. Après la signature des ententes, les défendeurs se rendent à Saint-Louis, dans l'état de Missouri, pur recevoir des cours de formation professionnelle. DWI exige alors qu'ils signent une deuxième entente de confidentialité, identique à celle qu'ils ont déjà signée avec DWC. La période d'emploi des défendeurs débute respectivement en 1996 et 1997 pour se terminer en 2000. En novembre 2001, DWC a intenté des procédures au Québec contre les défendeurs, alléguant qu'ils avaient violé les restrictions de non-concurrence de leur contrat de travail. Subséquemment, en juillet 2002, DWI a intenté des procédures aux États-Unis contre les défendeurs, invoquant une violation de la deuxième entente de confidentialité. En octobre 2002, un jugement a été prononcé par le tribunal américain condamnant les défendeurs. DWI demande la reconnaissance et l'exécution de ce jugement au Québec. Les défendeurs contestent cette demande aux motifs que le tribunal américain n'était pas compétent pour rendre les ordonnances et qu'il y a litispendance avec l'action introduite au Québec par DWC. DWI réplique que le tribunal américain était compétent en raison de la clause d'élection de for comprise dans les ententes de confidentialité et qu'il ne peut y avoir litispendance puisqu'il n'y a identité ni de parties ni d'objet.

Mme la juge Grenier a rejeté la requête en reconnaissance et en exécution des jugements américains. Les défendeurs étaient des employés de DWI et de DWC. Les ententes de confidentialité étaient des accessoires de leur contrats d'emploi. Le jugement américain fait référence au contrat d'emploi intervenu entre DWI et les défendeurs. Il y a substitution de rôles entre DWC et DWI. L'article 3168 paragraphe 5 C.C.Q. se lise:

Art. 3168. Dans les actions personnelles à caractère patrimonial, la compétence des autorités étrangères n'est reconnue que dans les cas suivants:
...
50. Les parties leur ont soumis les litiges nés ou à naître entre elles à l'occasion d'un rapport de droit déterminé; cependant, la renonciation du consommateur ou du travailleur à la compétence de l'autorité de son domicile ne peut lui être opposée ...

Cette paragraphe reprend à son compte le principe établi par l'effet combiné du deuxième alinéa de l'article 3148 ainsi que de l'article 3149 C.C.Q. qui se lisent comme suit:

Art. 3148. Dans les actions personnelles à caractère patrimonial, les autorités québécoises sont compétents dans les cas suivants:
...
Cependant, les autorités québécoises ne sont pas compétentes lorsque les parties ont choisi, par convention, de soumettre les litiges nés ou à naître entre elles, à propos d'un rapport juridique déterminé, à une autorité étrangère ou à un arbitre, à moins que le défendeur n'ait reconnu la compétence des autorités québécoises.

Art. 3149. Les autorités québécoises sont, en outre, compétentes pour connaître d'une action fondée sur un contrat de consommation ou sur un contrat de travail si le consommateur ou le travailleur a son domicile ou sa résidence au Québec; la renonciation du consommateur ou du travailleur à cette compétence ne peut lui être opposée.

L'article 3149 ajoute le domicile ou la résidence du *demandeur,* consommateur ou travailleur à la liste des facteurs de rattachement prévue à l'article 3148. Il s'agit d'une mesure de protection d'ordre public. L'article 3149 ne trouve pas uniquement application à l'égard d'actions fondées sur un contrat d'emploi intentées par le travailleur lui-même en tant que demandeur mais il peut, à l'occasion, être invoqué en défense pour s'opposer à ce qu'un litige fondé sur un contrat d'emploi soit décidé dans un for étranger. La renonciation des deux défendeurs à la compétence de l'autorité de leur domicile ne peut leur être opposée pour soutenir que l'autorité étrangère était compétente en raison justement de la présence dans le contrat d'emploi d'une clause d'élection de for qui, bien que valide, est présumée par le législateur québécois être défavorable au travailleur ou au consommateur qui y consent. Sans la présence dans le contrat d'emploi de cette clause d'élection de for en faveur des tribunaux de Missouri, le jugement ne pourrait faire l'objet d'une reconnaissance puisqu'il ne rencontre pas les autres exigences de l'article 3168.

En ce qui concerne la litispendance, la réparation intégrale du préjudice évalué à partir des mêmes données constitue l'objet essentiel des deux actions, et les conclusions injonctives incluses dans l'action américaine de même que celles en dommages exemplaires sont secondaires. L'identité d'objet existe donc entre les deux actions. De plus, la communauté d'intérêts entre DWI et DWC est à ce point complète et étroite qu'elle laisse supposer une certaine forme de représentation mutuelle, un mandat tacite qui permet à l'une de gérer les affaires de l'autre. Même si la structure corporative de DWI et DWC diffère en apparence, la communauté d'intérêts entre ces deux entreprises fait en sorte qu'elles ne peuvent véritablement prétendre posséder une identité juridique distincte. Épousant les intérêts matériel et moral de DWC, DWI ne peut prétendre s'en distinguer en occultant les faits réels et rationnels qui sont à l'origine des actions identiques intentées au Missouri et au Québec. Il y a, en fait, identité de sujets dans un même rapport de droit.

Article 3155 alinéa 1 C.C.Q. — absence de compétence du tribunal étranger quand les tribunaux québécois ont compétence exclusive — article 3129 C.C.Q. — exposition à une matière première provenant du Québec

Worthington Corp. c. Atlas Turner Inc., [2004] R.J.Q. 2376 (Cour d'appel du Québec), autorisation de pourvoi à la C.S.C. refusée 14 mars 2005

Une décision rendue par les tribunaux américains a condamné l'appelante Worthington solidairement avec l'intimée Atlas Turner à indemniser la victime d'une maladie causée par une exposition à l'amiante. Worthington a acquitté toute l'indemnité et, subrogée, elle veut réclamer à Atlas Turner, une compagnie dont le siège social est au Québec, ce qu'elle a payé pour elle aux États-Unis. Elle a demandé que le jugement américain soit reconnu au Québec et devienne exécutoire. Atlas Turner s'est opposée à cette demande, alléguant que l'État américain n'avait pas compétence pour rendre jugement puisqu'il s'agit d'un produit dont la matière première vient du Québec et que, en vertu des articles 3129 et 3151 C.C.Q., seuls les tribunaux québécois ont compétence. Worthington a alors invoqué l'inconstitutionnalité de ces articles et le procureur général du Québec a été mis en cause. Le premier juge a refusé de reconnaître le jugement américain en raison de l'incompétence du tribunal étranger. Il a aussi estimé que la demande d'exécution était prématurée, Worthington devant d'abord intenter un recours récursoire. (Veuillez voir "La jurisprudence canadienne en matière de droit international privé en 2002–3" (2003) 41 A.C.D.I. 604.)

La Cour d'appel a rejeté l'appel. Après avoir conféré, dans l'article 3151 C.C.Q., une compétence exclusive aux tribunaux québécois pour connaître en première instance de toute action fondée sur la responsabilité civile pour préjudice résultant de l'exposition à une matière première provenant du Québec ou de son utilisation, le législateur a exclu l'application possible de la recherche du lien réel et substantiel, qui est au cœur même de la théorie du miroir, en ajoutant que la compétence des autorités étrangères ne serait pas reconnue par les autorités québécoises dans un tel cas (art. 3155 paragr. 1 et 3165 paragr. 1 C.C.Q.). Ces dispositions impératives ne sont pas inéquitables puisque, si elles font obstacle aux procédures à l'extérieur du Québec, elles n'empêchent pas les plaignants de poursuivre avec succès au Québec. Elles paraissent toutefois contraires au principe de la courtoisie internationale. Bien que ce principe puisse constituer un impératif constituionnel au sein de la fédération candienne, la courtoisie au sens juridique n'est une question ni d'obligatîon absolue ni de simple politesse et de bonne volonté. Dans le contexte international, il faut rechercher un compromis qui permet de donner à la protection des défendeurs canadiens toute l'importance qu'elle mérite, sans pour autant négliger les intérêts légitimes des demandeurs étrangers. Par ailleurs, pour déterminer la constitutionnalité des lois provinciales ayant virtuellement une portée extraterritoriale, il faut rechercher le caractère véritable de la loi afin de voir si cette portée extraterritoriale est le but visé ou si elle n'est qu'un effet accessoire. Les effets extraprovinciaux accessoires ou incidents que produit une loi provinciale peuvent ne pas altérer sa validité si cette loi porte sur une matière qui présente un lien suffisant avec la province. Les dispositions législatives contestées en l'espèce ont certes un lien avec la province de Québec. Elles visent l'exploitation et la gestion des ressources naturelles non renouvelables, la propriété et les droits civils ainsi que l'administration de la justice. L'objectif fondamental des articles contestés est de protéger les biens à l'intérieur du Québec même s'ils peuvent accessoirement avoir une portée extraterritoriale. Ces mesures législatives font partie de la souveraineté du Québec et doivent être jugées constitutionnellement valides. Le premier juge a donc eu raison de refuser la reconnaissance du jugement américain.

D   CHOICE OF LAW (INCLUDING STATUS OF PERSONS) / CONFLITS
      DE LOIS (Y COMPRIS STATUT PERSONNEL)

1   Common Law and Federal

(a) Characterization

Procedure and substance — limitation statute

Note. The Limitations Act, R.S.A. 2000, c. L-12, s. 12, says: "The limitations law of the Province shall be applied whenever a remedial order is sought in this Province, notwithstanding that, in accordance with conflict of law rules, the claim will be adjudicated under the substantive law of another jurisdiction." *Castillo v. Castillo* (2004), 244 D.L.R. (4th) 603, [2004] 9 W.W.R. 609, 2004 ABCA 158, affirmed the trial decision (noted in "Canadian Cases in Private International Law 2001–2" (2002) 40 Can. Y.B. Int'l L. 612) that this section did not authorize an Alberta court to give effect to a tort claim governed by foreign law when that claim was statute-barred under the law of the place of the accident. The decision in *Tolofson v. Jensen,* [1994] 3 S.C.R. 1022, 120 D.L.R. (4th) 289, which declared rules of limitation to be substantive, meant that upon expiry of the limitation period there was no claim that an Alberta court could adjudicate. The Supreme Court of Canada granted leave to appeal on 20 Jaunary 2005. On 17 March 2005, it granted the respondent's motion to state the constitutional question whether the section was *ultra vires* of the Alberta legislature to the extent that it purported to apply the law of Alberta to an accident that occurred outside the province, contrary to the territorial limits on provincial jurisdiction.

(b) Contracts

Proper law — implied agreement as to choice of law

Note. An implied agreement on the law governing the contract occurs when the the terms of the contract, properly construed, show the parties' common intention that a particular system of law apply to their contract. This is a genuine, albeit implicit, choice of law by the parties as distinct from the judicial determination of the system of law that has the closest and most real connection with the contract. An implied choice of Québec law was found in *Re Ivaco Inc.* (2003), 1 C.B.R. (5th) 204 (Ont. S.C.J.). An insurance financing contract included provisions that were required by the Quebec Charter of the French Language and the Quebec Consumer Protection Act, as well as references to a "mandatory" and a "hypothecary creditor," terms distinctive of Québec law. Alternatively, the contract had its closest and most real connection with Québec law, based upon the content and form of the agreement as well as the location in Québec of the offer, the acceptance, and the place of performance.

(c) Torts

Applicable law

Note. Bezan v. Vander Hooft (2004), 26 Alta. L.R. (2d) 23, 45 C.P.C. (5th) 203, 2004 ABCA 44, affirmed the trial decision (noted in "Canadian Cases in Private International Law 2002–3" (2003) 41 Can. Y.B. Int'l L. 613) that Alberta-resident plaintiffs could not escape from the *lex loci delicti* rule according to which any claim arising out of an automobile accident in Saskatchewan was governed by Saskatchewan law. They were therefore confined to the no-fault insurance benefits provided by that law.

(d) Property

Transfer inter vivos — tangible movables — personal property security

GMAC Commercial Credit Corp. v. TCT Logistics Inc. (2004), 238 D.L.R. (4th) 487, 45 B.L.R. (3d) 68 (Ontario Court of Appeal), leave to appeal to S.C.C. refused, (*sub nom. Xtra Canada, a Division of Extra Inc. v. KPMG*) [2004] 3 S.C.R. xiv

The plaintiff had leased a number of truck trailers to a company based in Alberta that subsequently went into bankruptcy. The plaintiff brought proceedings in Ontario to determine priorities as between itself, the company's trustee in bankruptcy, and a lender that had taken a security interest over all the company's assets. The plaintiff had registered a financing statement under the Personal Property Security Act, R.S.A. 2000, c. P-7, but this registration was found in these proceedings to be invalid because it was not against the correct party. The plaintiff's position was that the failure to register in Alberta did not impair its rights to the trailers because the lease was a true lease. Although true leases are security interests under the Alberta statute, they are not considered security interests under the registration provision in section 2 of the Personal Property Security Act, R.S.O. 1990, c. P.10. The plaintiff contended that, by the same token, a true lease must also fall outside the choice of law provision in section 7(1) of the Ontario Act, according to which the validity, perfection and effect of perfection or non-perfection of a security interest in property like the trailers is governed by the law of the jurisdiction where the debtor is located at the time the security interest attaches, in this case Alberta.

The Ontario Court of Appeal, affirming the trial judge, held that section 7(1) did apply, that Alberta law therefore governed, and that the plaintiff lost its priority on account of its failure to register its security interest validly in Alberta. In applying section 7(1), the first consideration was not to determine whether the transaction created a security interest as defined in the Ontario statute, but to determine whether the dispute gives rise to a question regarding the validity, perfection, or the effect of perfection or non-perfection of a security interest in the relevant type of property. If it does, the choice of law provisions must be applied to determine the proper law governing the resolution of that dispute. "Security interest" in section 7(1) was therefore not confined to security interest as defined in the Ontario Act. Giving section 7(1) an effect independent of section 2 and broader in its scope was consistent with the purposes and objects of the act. Applying it in circumstances such as this made it clear, in conformity with the similar choice of law provisions of other provincial statutes, that multi-jurisdictional disputes concerning movable equipment such as the trailers would be resolved on the basis of a standard premise across the country, that is, based upon the law of the province where the debtor has its principal place of business. Predicability is enhanced and forum shopping is avoided.

Transfer inter vivos — *tangible movables* — *maritime lien*

Royal Bank of Scotland v. Ship Golden Trinity (2004), 254 F.T.R. 1, 2004 FC 795 (Federal Court Trial Division (Prothonotary))

This case concerned priorities among various claimants to the proceeds of the court-ordered sale of four ships managed by Pronoia. Tramp had long arranged the bunkering of Pronoia's fleet under a contract with Pronoia that was governed by English law. It claimed a maritime lien against one of the ships on the basis that it had arranged and paid for the bunkering of the ship by a third party in Long Beach, California. Suppliers of necessaries receive maritime liens according to United States law but not according to Canadian or English law. Hargrave, Prothonotary, applied United States law as the law most closely connected with the supply of the necessaries. The lien was therefore created. This conclusion was reinforced by the fact that the Long Beach agent had demanded that the ship grant a maritime lien as a term of delivery, even though a maritime lien would automatically arise as a matter of American law. Tramp became subrogated to the American supplier's lien rights by operation of United States law when it paid the supplier's invoice.

Transfer inter vivos — *bankruptcy and insolvency*

Note. *Financial Asset Management Services Ltd. v. Panther* (2003), 44 C.B.R. (4th) 213, 2003 BCCA 346, features a "Cross Border Insolvency Stipulation" (CBIS) among the parties to bankruptcy proceedings that certain issues would be determined by a United States court according to California law, and others by a Canadian court applying Canadian law. The first instance judge ordered that the Canadian proceedings would apply only Canadian internal law, not conflict of laws principles, because this was the proper construction of the CBIS, as well as corresponding with the approach the United States had already taken. The Court of Appeal refused leave to appeal from the order.

2   *Québec*

(a) Obligations

Responsabilité contractuelle — assurance responsabilité — droit du tiers lésé de pursuivre à la fois l'assuré et l'assureur — règle d'application nécessaire

Ferme avicole Héva inc. c. Boréal Assurances agricoles inc., [2003] R.J.Q. 1857 (Cour supérieure du Québec)

Grenville Mutual Insurance Co., la défenderesse en garantie et en arrière garantie, est poursuite par la Coopérative fédérée de Québec à titre d'assureur-responsabilité de Hutchinson, le défendeur en garantie. Hutchinson était domicilié en Ontario et y exploitait son entreprise. L'objet de la vente intervenue entre Hutchinson et la Coopérative, la demanderesse en garantie, était des œufs fécondés, dont la Coopérative a pris livraison en Ontario.

Le prix d'achat des œufs a été payé à Hutchinson à son établissement en Ontario. La police d'assurance a été consentie en Ontario par l'intermédiaire d'un agent y faisant affaire. La compétence des tribunaux québécois n'est pas contestée. Grenville demande le rejet de l'action, alléguant que c'est le droit ontarien qui s'applique à sa poursuite et qu'en vertu des lois ontariennes le tiers lésé ne peut poursuivre à la fois l'assureur et l'assuré comme le permet l'article 2501 C.C.Q.

M. le juge Viens a accueilli la requête pour rejet d'action. D'une part, l'article 2501 C.C.Q. ne contient pas une règle québécoise d'application nécessaire au sens de l'article 3076 C.C.Q.:

3076. Les règles du présent livre s'appliquent sous réserve des règles de droit en vigueur au Québec dont l'application s'impose en raison de leur but particulier.

Les dispositions de l'article 2414 C.C.Q., qui empêchent de déroger au droit du tiers lésé de faire valoir son droit d'action à la fois contre l'assuré et l'assureur, n'ont pas pour effet d'élever l'article 2501 C.C.Q. au rang de règle de droit en vigueur au Québec dont l'application s'impose en raison de son but particulier ni d'en faire l'une des règles d'application nécessaire qui se rapportent à un authentique intérêt vital étatique et non privé. D'ailleurs, il paraît difficile de retenir que l'article 3076 C.C.Q. a pour effet de consacrer toutes les règles ou les lois auxquelles on ne peut déroger comme étant des règles d'application nécessaire. D'autre part, l'article 3126 C.C.Q., qui prévoit que, si le préjudice est apparu dans un autre état, la loi de cet état s'applique si l'auteur devait prévoir que le préjudice s'y manifesterait, ne s'applique pas en l'espèce. Il n'y a rien dans le dossier qui permette de croire que l'assuré devait prévoir qu'un préjudice se manifesterait au Québec à la suite de la vente des œufs fécondés à la Coopérative. De plus, en vertu de l'article 3127 C.C.Q., les prétentions fondées sur l'inexécution d'une obligation contractuelle sont régies par la loi applicable au contrat, en l'occurrence la loi ontarienne. Par conséquent, c'est à bon droit que Grenville demande le rejet de l'action en garantie et en arrière-garantie dirigée contre elle.

Book Reviews / Vecensions de livres

Sustainable Development Law: Principles, Practices, and Prospects. Edited by M.-C. Cordonier Segger and A. Khalfan. Oxford: Oxford University Press, 2004. 490 pages. ISBN: 0–19–927671–4, US $54.95.

It almost does not need saying, but one cannot now discuss the goals of the international community in virtually any arena without mentioning sustainable development. It has been universally accepted as an integral aspect of the international community's stated vision for the twenty-first century. Sustainable development has thus been embraced domestically and globally as an *ideal* that is — rhetorically at least — worth striving towards. Developed and developing states have both endorsed sustainable development as apparently the *mot juste* that they were looking for to describe the necessary answer to the myriad of unprecedented and inter-locking social, economic, and environmental concerns that the world is currently facing. The World Summit on Sustainable Development (WSSD), which took place in Johannesburg in 2002, captured something of this spirit. World leaders, corporate chief executive officers, international organizations, influential think tanks, international non-governmental organizations, and grass-roots community groupings all sought to have an input into framing the international sustainable development agenda. At the same time, the WSSD also revealed the tensions and challenges of implementation and — arguably, as important — underlying conceptual paradoxes that sustainable development inevitably continues to raise.

Much has been written about the policy and political implications of sustainable development. Yet what is equally interesting is the role of the law (and the lawyer) in the promotion of sustainable development. The relationship between law and global change

663

is always interesting; however, what is equally important is that the relationship between international law and sustainable development is also absolutely crucial. Law is not only a passive reflector of developments elsewhere, but law itself has a fundamental part to play in the shaping of the wider political debate. Though it certainly should not be said without qualification and much clarification, it is now quite clear that sustainable development will not be achieved without the elaboration and refinement of a much more sympathetic legal system than currently exists.

This book admirably and with much merit seeks to highlight what changes may be necessary within the current international legal paradigm to bring about *on-the-ground* sustainable development, which will then begin to impact positively on the lives, in particular, of the poorest communities in the international community. The fact that this book never loses sight of the reality of the present global situation and that the authors never make the fatal error of placing law in a social vacuum also ensures a solid grounding to the book's legal analysis.

The book is the product of the work of the Centre for International Sustainable Development Law (CISDL), a research centre based in Montreal. Though the text is primarily the responsibility of the two lead authors, Cordonier Segger and Khalfan, the book also relies on the work of numerous other contributors, particularly in the final part, which focuses more specifically on the relationship between sustainable development and other substantive areas of the law.

The book is divided into five parts. Part 1 sets out, what it terms, the "foundations" of the topic. In particular, it analyzes the outcomes of the WSSD, with particular reference to the entailing legal consequences. Part 1 also outlines its perspective on what it terms "international sustainable development law." This aspect is key and one that is worthy of further comment. As the book itself states, "[i]nternational sustainable development law is found at the intersection of three principal fields of international law, each of which contribute to sustainable development,"[1] namely international economic law, international social law, and international environmental law. These "fields of law" may themselves require further clarification. In particular, international social law is taken to include human rights law, international labour law, international

---

[1] M.-C. Cordonier Segger and A. Khalfan, eds., *Sustainable Development Law: Principles, Practices, and Prospects* (Oxford: Oxford University Press, 2004) at 51.

humanitarian law, and what the book refers to as "international social development agreements" — primarily declarations and plans of action adopted by various UN global conferences over the past decade or so.

While there may be those that dislike the reference to "international sustainable development law" as implying anything as coherent as a sub-discipline of law,[2] the authors themselves perceive a distinctiveness in the law that deserves recognition. As they note, "while there is doubt that a legally binding 'principle of sustainable development' exists as such, a growing body of 'international law in the field of sustainable development' or 'sustainable development law' can be identified, analysed and implemented. This is not just a change in semantics. It is a conceptual shift."[3]

Part 2 then seeks to move the legal analysis forward with a discussion of certain relevant principles of international law relevant to the implementation of sustainable development. In many ways, this section is the heart of the book. The book bases this discussion primarily on the seven principles as formulated by the International Law Association (ILA) Committee on Legal Aspects of Sustainable Development, chaired by Kamal Hossain, with Nico Schrijver as rapporteur. The 2002 New Delhi Declaration on Principles of International Law Relating to Sustainable Development[4] provides the book with the springboard by which the authors consider many further legal issues surrounding the practical operationalization of sustainable development. Much of the text of the New Delhi Declaration is usefully set out within the body of the book.

The third part focuses upon what it terms "practices," which includes case studies of the utility of sustainability impact assessments, regional integration agreements, and, more generally, the role of economic, social, and cultural rights in the promotion of sustainable development. There is also an interesting discussion of the implementation challenges that sustainable development

---

[2] "Sub-discipline" seems to me much more appropriate than "sub-system" (another term that one might be tempted to use) as the integrationist nature of sustainable development militates against the creation of simply another strata in the law.

[3] Cordonier Segger and Khalfan, *supra* note 1 at 50.

[4] New Delhi Declaration on Principles of International Law Relating to Sustainable Development, ILA Resolution 3/2002, annex as published as UN Doc. A/57/329.

faces, with particular emphasis on governance and compliance issues.

Part 4, which is entitled "prospects," provides, in the words of the book, "proposals for a future legal research agenda."[5] Importantly, if somewhat of an under-statement, the authors note that the aim of this part is "not to attempt to draw broad conclusions, but seeks to define future sustainable development law issues and agendas in key areas, and discusses the international regimes that seek to address them."[6] Though these chapters may not be comprehensive in content, they are nevertheless important contributions in their own right to the literature, and most range beyond merely prospective in nature. The topics covered by Part 4 are trade, investment and competition law, international natural resources law, human rights and poverty law, international health law, biodiversity law, and climate change law. There is also a brief discussion of certain cross-cutting issues. While purists might object to some of these classifications (such as poverty law), these terms nevertheless represent important areas that are certainly in need of further legal elucidation. The final part contains an interesting and thought-provoking conclusion.

If one accepts that sustainable development touches the very heart of the nature and purpose of the international community, this book therefore becomes an essential read for anyone interested in the state of the global society. It is thoroughly researched and very well written. Not only is it academically rigorous in its analysis of the problem and the potential way forward but it also possesses a certain missionary zeal in the urgency in which it wishes to see progress fostered. The authors conclude by noting that the principal challenge is not the application of formal and technical rules but rather the "contextual reconciling and balancing" of legal norms. In their own words, "[t]his may be the path less travelled, but it is all the more interesting, as new discoveries await."[7] If this is true — and I think it may well be — this is an excellent roadmap for the journey.

DUNCAN FRENCH
Department of Law, University of Sheffield

---

5 Cordonier Segger and Khalfan, *supra* note 1 at 278.

6 *Ibid.*

7 *Ibid.* at 372.

The European Community, The European Union and the International Law of Treaties. By Delano Rubin Verwey. The Hague: T.M.C. Asser Press, 2004, ix + 308 pages including index. Paperback ISBN 90–6704–182–3, US $90.00

This book, according to its preface, aims to provide a comparative analysis of the treaty-making practices and rules of the European Community (EC) and European Union (EU), with those of the Vienna Conventions of 1969 and 1986. Central to this analysis is the constitutional problem of the separation of powers between the international organization (the author indeed accepts that the EC and EU are *sui generis* international organizations) and its member states and the determination of the institutions attributed with the treaty-making powers. The author begins by addressing the dichotomy between the EC, which has been representing its member states in the international trade arena for decades, and the EU, which since the 1993 Treaty of Maastricht (TEU) has been emerging as the driving force of the Common Foreign and Security Policy or what is usually referred to as the EU diplomacy. Yet another examination of such a unique development of the external relations is highly topical in the aftermath of the recent referenda results. Indeed, the French and Dutch rejection of the EU constitution halted the proposal to resolve the duality between the Community and the Union by granting explicitly legal personality to the Union and extending the treaty-making practice beyond the area of common commercial policy towards the subjects of external security issues and police and judicial cooperation in criminal matters.

The book is divided into five substantive chapters focusing on the EC and EU's external treaty-making competences, the applicability of the basic rules of the international law of treaties on the treaty-making practices of the EC and the EU, in particular, on the applicability of those rules on mixed agreements, as a unique instrument of the EC's treaty-making practice, and on dispute settlement. In his final remarks, the author proposes some amendments to the law of the treaties in order to facilitate the functioning of the EC and the EU as very unique international organizations within the existing regime of international law. In fact, these five chapters gravitate around two main topics or controversies that are central to this book — first, what are the limits of the external competence of the EC and the EU and, second, what is the relationship between the treaty-making practice of the EC and the EU and the international rules on treaty-making established in the 1969 Vienna Convention on the Law of Treaties and the 1986 Vienna Convention on the Law of Treaties between states and international organizations or between international organizations.

Part 1 of the book primarily re-confirms the competence of the EC to conclude international treaties with third states and international organizations and summarizes numerous academic discussions on the EU legal personality paradox. The initial analysis focuses on the treaties establishing the EC and the EU in order to determine which of the two is granted legal personality in accordance with the theory of international law. The first three chapters illustrate that external treaty-making powers clearly exist in the case of the EC and that its nature has been defined by the 1958 Treaty of Rome (EC Treaty). From this point, the author proceeds to a more intriguing area, identifying the treaty-making practices of the EU. First, he reiterates the arguments already given by other scholars that the lack of explicitly recognized international legal personality in the TEU does not necessarily prevent the EU from undertaking certain international obligations. Second, he enumerates all doctrines put forward by EU legal scholars and the European Court of Justice in order to explain the functional competences and capacities of the EU to act externally. In a nutshell, he concludes that, despite its intergovernmental nature, the EU has an implied legal personality and that Article 24 of the TEU is the legal basis for the conclusion of international agreements by the EU.

The third chapter turns its focus to an examination of the EC and the EU treaty practices in the context of the rules of the two Vienna Conventions and the comparison of their practices with the practice of other international organizations in general. The author simply progresses through the numerous provisions of the conventions to assess the existing practice of the EC and the EU against international rules (such as those on negotiation, signature, conclusion, ratification, reservations, and the application of the treaties), only to conclude that, despite the internal and external controversies caused by the lack of explicit legal personality of the EU and the occasional lack of necessary competence of the EC to conclude international agreements, very few cases appear to be challenging the validity of the concluded agreements.

The final two chapters, which are the core of the book's second part, are arguably the most interesting sections as they point to a truly unique treaty-making practice of the EC and the EU — that is, the mixed agreements. These agreements mandate the participation of both member states and EU institutions in the process of the conclusion of international agreements between the EC/EU and the third states. While the author admits that this practice of the Community has been internally and externally recognized and accepted (by the European Court of Justice and by the international community respectively) and that it has become the primary type of international agreement concluded by the Community, he questions its compatibility with the general rules of international law and suggests in the final remarks of the book several amendments to both the Vienna Conventions. The amendments would not only regulate mixed agreements more effectively but would also take into account possible diversity among international organizations and/or recognize explicitly the uniqueness of the EU. Finally, the author proposes the merger of the existing Vienna Conventions into one convention on the law of the treaties.

The book does not provide easily accessible material for students or anyone who does not already possess significant familiarity with the EU law and fundamental principles and doctrines of international law. It is extremely technical and assumes a pre-existing knowledge of the history of European integration, institutional structure, constitutional controversies, and EU case law. That said, considering its far reaching index, reference to case law and academic publications in the area, and, in particular, its proposal for the amendments of the Vienna Conventions, it could be a useful starting point for further research of the international treaty law.

LJILJANA BIUKOVIC
Faculty of Law, University of British Columbia

Mezhdunarodnoe pravo. Elementarnyy kurs. By I.I. Lukashuk and G.G. Shinkaretskaya. Moscow: Yurist, 2003. 216 pages. ISBN: 5-7975-0354-9, US $12.00.

The present work represents a *tour d'horizon* of contemporary public international law by two Russian international jurists of long standing. I.I. Lukashuk, one of the Russian Federation's most eminent international jurists and a former member of the International Law Commission, requires little introduction — his scholarly works

The views advanced in the foregoing review are solely the author's views and should not be taken as expressing any view of the Department of Justice Canada.

on international legal issues have appeared since the Khrushchev era.[1] G.G. Shinkaretskaya also began publishing important scholarly works on international law under the Soviets.[2] These jurists' present work evokes foremost the question of its significance for readers in the Russian Federation and abroad seeking information about contemporary public international law.

One preliminary response to this question arises from the sheer breadth of the topics treated. Lukashuk and Shinkaretskaya begin by introducing public international law: the various understandings of international law that have surfaced since the Middle Ages; the sources, fundamental principles, and subjects of international law; international law as a collection of norms; the interrelationship between international and domestic law; international legal responsibility; and sanctions for subjects of international law that fail to fulfil their responsibilities. Then they explore the international legal role of states: states as the primary subjects of international law; the recognition of states and governments; state succession; the territorial sovereignty of states; and the sovereignty of states over their populations. Finally, they examine various

---

[1] A sampling of Lukashuk's works includes: I.I. Lukashuk, *Struktura i forma mezhdunarodnykh dogovorov* (Saratov: Izdatel'stvo Saratovskogo Yuridicheskogo Instituta imeni D. Kurskogo, 1960); I.I. Lukashuk, *Storony v mezhdunarodnykh dogovorakh* (Moscow: Yuridicheskaya literatura, 1966); I.I. Lukashuk, *Otnosheniya mirnogo sosushchestvovaniya i mezhdunarodnogo prava: problemy mezhdunarodno-pravovogo regulirovaniya* (Kiev: Vishch shkola, Izdatel'stvo pri Kievskom universitete, 1974); N.B. Krylov, *Pravotvorcheskaya deyatel'nost' mezhdunarodnykh organizatsiy*, ed. by I.I. Lukashuk (Moscow: "Nauka," 1988); I.A. Ledyakh and I.I. Lukashuk, *Nyurnbergskiy protsess: pravo protiv voyny i fashizma* (Moscow: Institut gosudarstva i prava Rossiyskoy Akademii Nauk, 1995); L.B. Alekseeva, V.M. Zhuykov, and I.I. Lukashuk, *Mezhdunarodnye normy o pravakh cheloveka v primenenie sudami Rossiyskoy Federatsii: prakticheskoe posobie* (Moscow: Izdatel'stvo "Prava cheloveka," 1996); I.I. Lukashuk, *Globalizatsiya, gosudarstvo, pravo, XXI vek* (Moscow: Spark, 2000); I.I. Lukashuk, *Iskusstvo delovykh peregovorov: uchebno-prakticheskoe posobie* (Moscow: BEK, 2002); I.I. Lukashuk, *Pravo mezhdunarodnoy otvetstvennosti* (Moscow: Volters Kluwer, 2004). This sampling alone suggests how widely Lukashuk's international legal interests have ranged.

[2] Shinkaretskaya's publications include: G.G. Shinkaretskaya, *Gosudarstva na arkhipelagakh: mezhdunarodno-pravovoy rezhim* (Moscow: "Mezhdunarodnye otnosheniya," 1977); V.I. Menzhinsky, S.V. Vinogradov, and G.G. Shinkaretskaya (eds), *Sotrudnichestvo gosudarstv v issledovanii i ispol'zovanii Mirovogo okeana* (Moscow: Akademiya nauk SSSR, Institut gosudarstva i prava, 1986); G.G. Shinkaretskaya, *Mezhdunarodnaya sudebnaya protsedura* (Moscow: "Nauka," 1992); D.D. Caron and G. Shinkaretskaya, "Peaceful Settlement of Disputes through the Rule of Law," in L.F. Damrosch, ed., *Beyond Confrontation: International Law for the Post-Cold War Era* (Boulder, CO: Westview Press, 1995), 309.

specialized topics in international law: the law of international organizations; the law of international relations; and, especially, the law of treaties; the law governing attempts to maintain international peace and security; the pacific resolution of international disputes; territories with special international legal regimes — the Arctic, Antarctica, and Spitzbergen; international human rights, humanitarian and criminal law; the law of the sea; aviation and space law; and international economic and environmental law. Thus, the topics that Lukashuk and Shinkaretskaya treat in the present work — while conventional — are broad enough to mark it as a potentially helpful reference text for a wide readership. However, a concluding chapter situating the observations about the individual topics within a broader interpretative framework would have been a desideratum.

A second preliminary response to the question relates to the depth in which Lukashuk and Shinkaretskaya treat the foregoing topics. Their treatment eschews an exhaustive analysis of the issues that the topics raise in favour of a more descriptive approach. They have provided a minimal scholarly apparatus — footnote references to international instruments are few and indices are lacking. At the same time, their treatment of the topics shows them as familiar with the pertinent treaties, conventions, judgments of the International Court of Justice, and so forth. On balance, they have distilled the essential elements of a sizeable corpus of materials on public international law. Most likely their distillation will be accessible to non-specialists, although aficionados of public international law may find that other overviews, Russian[3] and western[4] alike, conform more closely to the requirements of meticulous scholarship.

A third preliminary response to the question concerns the substantive content of the treatment that Lukashuk and Shinkaretskaya accord the topics. Most importantly, their treatment shows the extent to which Russian international legal scholarship has repudiated the ideological constraints that shackled jurists before the Soviet Union collapsed in December 1991. The

[3] For example, Yu. M. Kolosov and E.S. Krivchikova, *Mezhdunarodnoe pravo* (Moscow: "Mezhdunarodnye otnosheniya," 2000).

[4] For example, Sir R. Jennings and Sir A. Watts, eds., *Oppenheim's International Law*, 9th edition, 2 volumes (London: Longman Group, 1992); C. Rousseau, *Droit international public*, 5 volumes (Paris: Sirey, 1971–83).

latest edition of Professor G.I. Tunkin's *Theory of International Law*[5] suggests what these constraints entailed in the later Soviet era. To take a few examples, they included homage to the role of V.I. Lenin and the Communist party in shaping Soviet ideas of international law; acknowledgment of the chasm between the understandings of international law held by socialist and capitalist countries; and recognition that socialist and capitalist countries could coexist peacefully under general international legal norms arising through agreement between states. Not only have Lukashuk and Shinkaretskaya avoided these canons of later Soviet international legal scholarship but their treatment of the topics also shows significant convergence with the corresponding treatment by western jurists.[6] However, their treatment retains a distinctively Russian flavour for they refer repeatedly to the practices of the Russian Federation and the Commonwealth of Independent States even as they expound familiar propositions of international law.

The foregoing preliminary observations furnish a basis for appraising generally the significance of Lukashuk and Shinkaretskaya's work. Arguably, this work is not significant — its topics are standard in overviews of public international law and the exposition of the topics is distinguished in neither its analytical rigour nor the novelty of its insights. Paradoxically, the work is still a significant publication precisely because it is pedestrian: it implies that the Russians' early exposure to public international law today resembles that of their counterparts in the West. After generations in which Russian international jurists consciously renounced mainstream Western public international law, the shift to which Lukashuk and Shinkaretskaya's work testifies is welcome — and significant.[7] Equally significantly, their work suggests that

---

5 G.I. Tunkin, *Theory of International Law*, foreword by L.N. Shestakov, translated, introduced, and edited by W.E. Butler, 2nd edition (London: Wildy, Simmonds and Hill Publishers, 2003). Tunkin's work is reviewed by E. Myles (2003) 41 Can. Yb. Intl. L. 619.

6 The treatment that Lukashuk and Shinkaretskaya accord the sources of international law represents a case in point. Whereas Tunkin saw international legal norms as stemming primarily from treaties (Tunkin, *supra* note 5 at 147), Lukashuk and Shinkaretskaya recognize treaties and custom alike as sources of international law, *inter alia* (I.I. Lukashuk and G.G. Shinkaretskaya, *Mezhdunarodnoe pravo. Elementarnyy kurs* (Moscow: Yurist, 2003) at 22–29 *passim*).

7 The shift accords with Macdonald's view that Soviet international legal scholarship has bequeathed few valuable directions to post-Soviet jurists, particularly on "the organizational framework of an evolving international legal community."

Canadian and other Western international jurists can now debate public international legal issues more easily with their Russian colleagues.

ERIC MYLES
Department of Justice Canada, Ottawa

R. St. J. Macdonald, "Rummaging in the Ruins: Soviet International Law and Policy in the Early Years: Is Anything Left?" in K. Wellens, ed., *International Law: Theory and Practice. Essays in Honour of Eric Suy* (The Hague: Martinus Nijhoff, 1998), 61.

Analytical Index / Index analytique

THE CANADIAN YEARBOOK OF INTERNATIONAL LAW

2004

ANNUAIRE CANADIEN DE DROIT INTERNATIONAL

(A) Article; (NC) Notes and Comments; (Ch) Chronique;
(P) Practice; (C) Cases; (BR) Book Review
(A) Article; (NC) Notes et commentaires; (Ch) Chronique;
(P) Pratique; (C) Jurisprudence; (BR) Recension de livre

Aarhus Convention, multilateral environmental agreements and, 94, 98, 110

Adsett, Hugh et al., "Compliance Committees and Recent Multilateral Environmental Agreements: The Canadian Experience with Their Negotiation and Operation" (A), 91–142

Afghanistan, parliamentary declarations, 552–54

Africa, Blair Commission report, 426–32, 435

Aginam, Obijiofor, "On a Hinge of History: The Global Environmental and Health Dimensions of Mutual Vulnerability in the Twenty-First Century" *(Tribute to Ivan Head),* 437–46

Agriculture Agreement, Department of Foreign Affairs practice, 499–501

ALÉNA. *Voir aussi* NAFTA; ZLÉA
commerce, 448–49
investissement, 473–95

Anti-Dumping Agreement, Department of Foreign Affairs practice, 497–98, 500

aquatic ecosystem, parliamentary declarations, 524

Arar, Maher, parliamentary declarations, 543–45

arbitral awards cases, 593–601

armed intervention. *See* unilateral armed intervention

L'Australie, ANZCERTA, 389–97

Balkans, parliamentary declarations, 554

Banque Mondiale (BM), et le Canada, 465–67

Basel Convention, multilateral environmental agreements and, 94–95, 97, 102, 111–12, 130–32

Bergeron, André, "Canadian Practice in International Law: Treaty Action Taken by Canada in 2003," (P), 575–81

"Biography," by Karin Mickelson *(Tribute to Ivan Head),* 423–24

Biukovic, Ljiljana, review of, *The European Community, The European Union and the International Law of Treaties,* by Delano Rubin Verwey (BR), 667–69

Blair Commission report, 426–32, 435

Blom, Joost, "Canadian Cases in Private International Law in 2003–4," (C), 621–62

Index of Cases /
Index de la jurisprudence

———

1302926 Ontario Inc. v. 2334425 Nova Scotia Ltd., 644, 653

A.-G. Ont. v. A.-G. Can. (Local Prohibition) (1896), 64 n. 142
A.-G. Ont. v. A.-G. Can. (Reference Appeal) (1912), 61 n. 123
Activités militaires et paramilitaires au Nicaragua et contre celui-ci (Nicaragua c. États-Unis d'Amérique), 68 n. 164
ADF Group Inc. c. United States, 473, 485, 491–95
Affaire des plates-formes pétrolières (Iran c. États-Unis d'Amérique), 81 n. 210, 87
Anglo-Iranian Oil Co., 360 n. 26
Applicabilité de l'obligation d'arbitrage en vertu de la section 21 de l'accord du 26 juin 1947 relatif au siège de l'Organisation des Nations Unies, 57 n. 104, 70 n. 169
Applicabilité de la section 22 de l'article VI de la convention sur les privilèges et immunités des Nations Unies, 70 n. 168, 78 n. 195, 78 n. 197
Argentina – Measures Affecting the Export of Bovine Hides and the Import of Finished Leather, 301–3, 327 n. 269
Arrow River & Tributaries Slide and Boom Co. v. Pigeon Timber Co., 510
Australia – Measures Affecting Importation of Salmon, 296 n. 178, 336 n. 287, 337 n. 289, 337 n. 290, 337 n. 291
Azinian et al. c. Mexico, 473 n. 1

Baker v. Canada (Minister of Citizenship and Immigration), 620 n. 135
Barcelona Traction, Light and Power Co. (Second Phase) (Belgium v. Spain), 7 n. 13
Barrick Gold Corp. v. Lopehandia, 639–40

BC Rail Partnership v. Standard Car Truck Co., 629–30
Beals v. Saldanha, 628–29, 643, 644–51, 652
Bedard v. Bedard, 635
Beer and Regan v. Germany, 242 n. 152
Belgian Family Allowances, 284 n. 130
Bezan v. Vander Hooft, 659
Blinds To Go Inc. v. Harvard Private Capital Holdings Inc., 633
Border Tax Adjustments, 284 n. 130, 306 n. 205, 310, 318, 319, 320, 323
Boulanger v. Johnson & Johnson Corp., 643
Bouzari v. Islamic Republic of Iran, 607–13, 626–27
Brazilian Internal Taxes, 310 n. 216
Brown & Root Services Corp. v. Aerotech Herman Nelson Inc., 639

C.(J.R.) v. M.(L.C.), 636
Canada – Certain Measures Concerning Periodicals, 307 n. 205, 313 n. 224, 320 n. 247
Canada – Import, Distribution and Sale of Certain Alcoholic Drinks by Provincial Marketing Agencies, 317 n. 234, 325–26
Canada – Import Restrictions on Ice Cream and Yogurt, 302 n. 196, 329 n. 273
Canada – Measures Affecting Exports of Unprocessed Herring and Salmon, 280 n. 119, 293 n. 163
Canada – Measures Affecting the Importation of Milk and the Exportation of Dairy Products (Canada – Dairy), 501. See also *Canada – Mesures visant l'importation de lait et l'exportation de produits laitiers*
Canada – Measures Relating to Exports of Wheat and Treatment of Imported Grain, 301 n. 193, 326 n. 265, 327